CW00347154

CONTEMPORARY RESEARCH ON TERRORISM

AUP Titles of Related Interest

US AND THEM
A Study in Group Consciousness
W A Elliott

PRODUCT ADULTERATION AND EXTORTION
Edited by Paul Wilkinson

CONTEMPORARY RESEARCH ON TERRORISM

edited by
Paul Wilkinson and Alasdair M Stewart

in association with
George D Smith, Andre YaDeau and Thomas Schiller

ABERDEEN UNIVERSITY PRESS

First Published 1987
Aberdeen University Press
A member of the Pergamon Group

© The Contributors 1987

All rights reserved. No part of this publication may be reproduced, stored in a retrieval system or transmitted in any form or by any means, electronic, mechanical, photocopying, recording or otherwise without prior permission in writing of the publishers.

British Library Cataloguing in Publication Data

Contemporary research on terrorism.
1. Terrorism
I. Wilkinson, Paul II. Stewart, A M
322.4′2 HV6431

ISBN 0-08-035068-2

PRINTED IN GREAT BRITAIN
THE UNIVERSITY PRESS
ABERDEEN

Contents

Preface

This book originated from the international academic research conference on research on terrorism, held at Aberdeen University under the auspices of the Department of Politics and International Relations, 15–17 April 1986. It is not a complete version of the conference proceedings. The editors have selected papers for publication on the grounds of their intrinsic interest and originality and their relevance to the development of future research on terrorism. In most cases the papers have not been published elsewhere. In many cases the papers presented at the conference have been modified or abridged for the purposes of this publication.

The editors would like to express their gratitude to the contributors for their cooperation in preparing their articles for inclusion, and to the eminent scholars who served as chairmen of the specialist panels: Professor Raymond Corrado, Professor J Dautricourt, Professor WF Gutteridge, Dr Robert Kupperman, Dr David Rapoport, Dr Edna Reid, Professor Todd Sandler, Professor Marco Sassoli, Dr Robert W Taylor, and Dr Maurice Tugwell. Their work in inviting and advising those who contributed conference papers, and in guiding the debate was outstanding, and was deeply appreciated.

I wish to pay a personal tribute to Dr G D 'Tim' Smith, for his dedicated and expert work in supervising the conference administration, to Mrs Audrey Macfarlane for her patient secretarial support, and to Dr André YaDeau and Mr Thomas Schiller for their hard work as Treasurer and Panel Coordinator respectively.

My co-editor wishes to add his thanks to Mrs A M Robertson and most especially to Miss Marjorie Leith, AUP.

Last, but not least, thanks are due to Mr Colin McLean of AUP for his encouragement and help.

Paul Wilkinson

March 1987

Foreword
Terrorism: An International Research Agenda?

Paul Wilkinson

PROBLEMS OF DEFINITION AND TYPOLOGY

One major complexity, which has bedevilled debate and scholarly analysis concerning terrorism, has been the problem of definition. In recent years, however, a surprisingly broad consensus has emerged in the academic usage of the term in liberal democratic societies.[1] There is general recognition that terrorism is a specific method of struggle rather than a synonym for political violence or insurgency. Brian Jenkins has aptly described it as a kind of weapons-system. It can and has been employed by an infinite variety of actors in the international system, including governments, political factions, criminal gangs and even religious movements and cults. It is by no means the monopoly or exclusive weapon of any particular ideology, political philosophy or religion. It is also generally accepted in the specialist literature that what distinguishes terrorism from other forms of violence is the deliberate and systematic use of coercive intimidation. The terrorist is one who tries to terrify people into doing what he or she wants. For the politically motivated terrorist the object is generally to create a climate of fear among a wider target group than the immediate victims of the violence. Campaigns of terror violence can be used to publicise the terrorists' cause, as a kind of propaganda of the deed, as well as to coerce the wider target group to accede to the terrorists' aims. Thus there are at least five major participants in the process of terror; the *perpetrators of the violence*, the *immediate victims*, the *wider target group* or society which the terrorists seek to intimidate, the *'neutral' bystanders* within the society experiencing the terrorism, and *international opinion*, in so far as it is aware of these events.

One obvious additional complication in operationalising this broad definition is that in many conflicts the use of terror violence is interwoven with a wider repertoire of unconventional warfare. In Central America, for example, terrorism is typically used in conjunction with rural guerrilla and economic and political warfare in all-out bids to topple governments. But in Western Europe and North America terrorism is usually seen in its 'pure' form, i.e. it is unaccompanied by any wider insurgency. Terrorism is most easily identifiable precisely when it is being used in isolation by a weak and desperate minority surrounded by a 'peaceful' society rather than the fog of war. A common feature of such terror campaigns is that innocent civilians, including foreign citizens who know nothing of the terrorists' political quarrel, are either killed or injured or held hostage. Typical tactics of the modern terrorist are explosive and incendiary bombings, shooting attacks and assassinations, hostage taking and kidnapping, and hijackings. Terrorism as we have defined it is clearly a very broad concept. The role of taxonomies and typologies of terrorism is to sub-divide the field into categories which are more manageable for research and analysis.[2] One basic distinction is between *state* and *factional* terror. There is of course a very considerable historical and social scientific literature on aspects of state terror.[3] In view of the sheer scale of crimes against humanity and mass terror that have been and are being committed by modern tyrannies there should be no doubt that this is a far more severe and intractable problem for humanity than the containment and reduction of factional terror. However, the present essay and the other contributions to this symposium will not be dealing with the problems of internal terror by states. We shall, in addition to looking at the activities of terrorist movements, take into account the activities of certain states in sponsoring acts of international terrorism abroad, and the particularly complex and dangerous problems this poses for the democratic states' response. Nevertheless historically state terror has often been an antecedent and to varying degrees a contributory cause, of campaigns of factional terrorism. Once regimes assume that their ends justify any means, they tend to get locked into a spiral of terror and counter-terror against their adversaries.

It is also very important to distinguish between *international* and *internal* terrorism. Internal terrorism is systematic violence which is largely confined to a single nation-state, or specific localities within a state. International terrorism in its most obvious manifestation is a terrorist attack carried out across international frontiers, or against a foreign target in the terrorist's state of origin. Yet in reality international dimensions often take a more indirect form: a terrorist group may seek foreign cash, weapons, political support or other resources. Or its members and leaders may occasionally find safe havens abroad or establish ad hoc cooperation with friendly foreign states and terrorist groups. Historically it is very hard to find a pure case of internal terrorism. Even the obsessively regionalised campaigns of the Provisional IRA in Northern Ireland and ETA-militar in the Basque region of Spain constantly spill over their respective international frontiers and raise international problems of bilateral security cooperation and extradition. For the purposes of the present essay we will only be considering the phenomena and implications of *international terrorism*, including reference to internal terror violence when it clearly impinges upon or spills over into the international system.

It is useful to employ a basic typology of international terror perpetrators, based on their main declared aims and motives:

(i) *Nationalist terrorists.* These are groups seeking political self-determination. They may wage a combined struggle in the territory they seek to liberate and from bases abroad. Or, as in the cases of the Armenians and Croatians, for example, they may be forced by police action to campaign entirely in exile.

(ii) *Ideological terrorists.* These groups profess to want to change the whole nature of the existing political, social and economic system, either to an extreme Left or extreme Right model. These groups have proved less durable than the well-established nationalist groups, and they are very prone to internal splits. Until comparatively recently they have been almost exclusively internal in character. However, since late 1984 a loose alliance of extreme leftist terror groups has emerged with the declared aim of striking at NATO and defence-related targets Europe-wide, which is more co-ordinated than the occasional bilateral cooperation between such groups in the 1970s.

(iii) *Religious fanatics.* Certain religious groups employ international terrorism to undermine and ultimately overthrow what they regard as a corrupt and evil prevailing religious order. The best-known and perhaps most feared contemporary example is the Islamic Jihad group of fundamentalist Shiites who have been inspired by the Iranian revolution, and now challenge many of the moderate Arab regimes.

(iv) *Single issue fanatics.* These groups are obsessed with the desire to change a specific policy or practice within the target society, rather than with the aim of political revolution. Examples would be anti-nuclear, anti-abortion and 'animal rights' extremists. There are some indications of international cooperation between the extreme anti-nuclear and 'ecological' campaigners in Europe.

(v) *State-sponsored international terrorism.* This is used as a tool of domestic policy (e.g. Gadaffi's hit-squads sent abroad to murder dissidents) and as a tool of foreign policy (e.g. Soviet assistance to Palestinian extremists in the late 1970s and early 1980s in order to disrupt the Soviet Union's adversaries in the Middle East and generally to help serve Soviet policy goals). State sponsors may use their own directly recruited and controlled terror squads, or may choose to work through proxies and client movements. They almost invariably work covertly in such support, so that they are able to plausibly deny any involvement.[4]

Before leaving the subject of definition and typology, it is important to dispose of two surprisingly widespread misconceptions about the use of the concept of terrorism. First, it is sometimes objected that the word terrorism should be abandoned because it has an evaluative aspect. Of course it is true that in deciding to apply the word 'terrorism' to describe a particular campaign or act of violence the historian or social scientist is making a judgement solely about the means used, but it is a designation that nevertheless most terrorists seek to resist. Few wish to see themselves as terrorists. But this does not mean we can happily jettison the term terrorism from our discourse. Those who believe one can devise a totally value-free language for the study of politics and society are philosophically naive or disingenuous. Does any serious scholar suggest we abandon terms such as 'dictatorship', 'imperialism', and 'democracy'?

A second widespread misunderstanding arises from the confusion of means and ends. It is true that whatever criteria we may choose for assessing the legitimacy of a terrorist group to speak for the minority it claims to represent, the claim of the terrorists to speak for even a bare majority of their 'own people' are generally spurious. It is only in democratic societies that terrorist groups have the alternative of forming political parties and fighting elections. Even when given the chance, few take it, and if they do their election results are often derisory. (The ideological and religious fanatics do not even care about such tests of legitimacy because they already believe that their belief-systems are superior to all others and that these beliefs give them a transcendental justification for imposing their will by violence.) But even in those few clear cases where we may be persuaded that a terrorist group is motivated by a legitimate grievance or sense of injustice and can claim a degree of popular legitimacy among its professed constituency, does this mean we must refrain from designating any of their acts as terroristic in nature? Surely not, because terrorism is not a philosophy or a movement: it is a method of struggle. There have been a number of historical cases where terrorism has been used on behalf of causes most western liberals would regard as just.

In any worthwhile analysis of a specific terrorist campaign it is, of course, essential to take account of the unique political, historical, and cultural context, and the ideology and aims of the groups involved. Context is all in the analysis of any form of political violence. One needs to interpret the role and effectiveness of terrorism in the overall development of each conflict in which it appears. Is it being used as an auxiliary weapon in a wider strategy of revolutionary warfare? Or is it being used in isolation in a pre-insurgency mode? What degree of popular support, if any, do the perpetrators of terrorism enjoy? How severe and prolonged is the violence? Is it merely spasmodic and small in scale and destruction caused? Or is it growing in intensity, frequency, and lethality to the point where it threatens to trigger a full-scale civil or international war?

UNDERLYING CAUSES OF THE BURGEONING OF MODERN INTERNATIONAL TERRORISM IN THE LATE 1960s

One can identify certain conducive conditions which explain the considerable growth in international terrorism statistics. First, there is the general strategic situation, which favours unconventional war as a whole. The balance of terror and the fact that all major states wish to avoid an escalation of violence that could lead to a possible nuclear conflict are important factors. Most states today are even afraid of becoming involved in protracted and vastly expensive conventional conflicts which might escalate. Unconventional war thus becomes relatively more attractive. In terms of cost-effectiveness, it is the best means of achieving political-diplomatic objectives by coercion.

The balance of terror is also an important factor in the creation of a climate of thought about use of violence. The balance of terror provides a paradigm of a mode of deterrence, and it is possible that revolutionary movements see terror and the holding of hostages as the most appropriate weapons to use in microconflicts. There is also the fact that since the end of the colonial independence struggles, national borders have become firmly established. It is now very difficult for any minority movement to achieve a renegotiation of frontiers in its favour through some general diplomatic conference. Hence the desperation, the argument from weakness mentioned earlier. Another factor is relative deprivation psychology—the feelings of political injustice felt by particular groups. Research has shown that feelings of political injustice—deprivation of political rights or exclusion from power or influence within a community—are especially likely to lead to violent rebellion.

Weaknesses within the international community in general, and particular nation states in responding to terrorism also contributed to the rise in terrorism. This was particularly true up until 1972. Since then, certain Western European states have begun to take a firmer line; and there has been a widespread growth of elite units of special forces designed for hostage rescue, a development inspired by the success of the Entebbe and Mogadishu rescues. But since the TWA hijack to Beirut in 1985 and the disastrous loss of life in a hijack to Malta in the same year it has become clear that such rescue forces are not a panacea and do not necessarily restrain potential hijackers of the more fanatical type. The shift of revolutionary theory in the Third World away from the rural guerrilla concept toward the idea of urban struggle is an important feature of contemporary terrorism. European revolutionaries in the nineteenth and early twentieth centuries have been through a similar process. The hunger for publicity tends to drive the revolutionary to the cities. As one Front de Liberation National (FLN) leader put it, 'It was more effective propaganda to shoot a couple of French businessmen in the middle of Algiers than to shoot a hundred or so soldiers in a lonely gully'. Other factors precipitating the move to cities are technological opportunity and the vulnerability of industrial societies and cities to terrorist techniques. One should also stress the contagion. Information flow effects of terrorism over a long span of time can cause a kind of bandwagon reaction. There is also the growth of proterrorist ideologies and subcultures in Western cities right in the hearts of the countries that had the highest numbers of terrorist attacks in the last decade. Maverick states have also been active in funding and giving sanctuary to terrorists.

But of course all the factors mentioned so far are of a general nature. They characterise the international system of the late 1950s and 1960s. How does one explain the significance of 1968 as the starting-point for the upsurge in modern international terrorism? All specialists in the study of terrorism would agree that there were two international developments which had a key role in triggering this outbreak.

First and foremost there was the overwhelming defeat of the military forces of the Arab states in their June 1967 war with Israel. Terrorism was by no means new to the Middle East, but there is no doubt that as a result of this setback and the Israeli occupation of the West Bank, Gaza and the Sinai peninsula, and the Israeli takeover of the whole of Jerusalem, Palestinian militants concluded that the routes of defeating Israel by conventional military force, or regaining their homeland by diplomatic negotiation were blocked to them. The Arab states were too divided and Israel was too militarily powerful. They concluded that they would gain more by a campaign of ruthless political violence striking at Israel and its supporters internationally in a war of terrorist attrition. Hence from 1968–1972 there follows a tremendous upsurge of hijack attempts, bombings, shootings, and other terrorist attacks against Israeli targets both in Israel and abroad, and against airline facilities, and personnel of the United States and other western powers seen in Palestinian eyes to be guilty of supporting and collaborating with Israel. This shift to terrorism was intensified after the further disastrous defeat of the Fedayeen at the hands of Hussein's forces in Jordan in Autumn 1970. Between 1967 and 1974, about fifteen per cent of all international terrorist incidents were carried out by Palestinian groups, many of them spilling over into Western Europe.

The impact of Palestinian terrorism should not be assessed purely in quantitative terms. Reports of their actions and the huge international publicity they achieved, undoubtedly had the effect of interesting other militant groups in other parts of the world in exploiting the techniques of international terror. And we should not neglect the direct influence of the PFLP and Fatah and the other Palestinian organisations through their work of training foreign terrorists in various camps in the Middle East and in the constant Palestinian contacts with other terrorist groups around the world.

The second historical development was the resurgence of the extreme neo-Marxist and Trotskyist left among the student populations of all the industrial countries. Their common rallying points were bitter opposition to US policy in the Vietnam War, and to American policy in the Third World generally, which they designated neo-imperialism. Although the majority of the student left abandoned political violence following the street demonstrations and battles with the police in 1968–1969, there was in each case a small hardcore of ideological extremists who decided that what was really needed was a more professional and long-term campaign of urban violence against the 'system'. These groups decided to form an 'underground' which engaged in a sustained campaign of terrorism. The main groups that sprang from this movement included the Baader–Meinhof Gang in the Federal Republic of Germany, the Red Brigades in Italy, and the Japanese Red Army. With their shared neo-Marxist ideology and self perceptions as part of a broader international revolutionary movement, they maintained international links with movements abroad, including the Palestinians. There is considerable evidence that they learned from each other.

THE ABERDEEN ACADEMIC CONFERENCE

The international research conference on terrorism at Aberdeen University, 15–17 April 1986, exceeded the expectations of its organisers. It attracted over 150 participants from over twenty countries, including the People's Republic of China. It exposed a number of widespread myths about research on terrorism:

1 The fact that terrorism is a fashionable concern of governments and the media does not mean that it has attracted comparable attention and effort in academia. We found that terrorism studies are very small-scale, and even peripheral, in most universities and research institutes. Apart from the research groups working in a few well-known major centres such as Rand Corporation, Santa Monica, and the Department of International Relations at Aberdeen University, most scholars working in this field are working alone, or at most with one or two colleagues in a larger academic institution.

2 An inevitable corollary of this relatively marginal role in the universities is the conspicuous lack of funding for major research projects. Some of the most valuable and pioneering work in the field is being financed on a shoestring basis, and is only completed successfully because of the total dedication of individual scholars, and their ability to fund their terrorism research on the back of other projects and industrial contract work. One obvious consequence of this pattern is that terrorism scholarship is strong on individual scholarly theses and monographs and weak on team-based high-cost projects. This helps to explain the lag in developing high quality open-source computerised databanks, statistical analysis, and operational research applications, in the field of terrorism studies.

3 It is false to assume that terrorism studies are exclusively or even primarily a West European and North American concern. Conference sessions on areas such as the Middle East, Latin America, and Southern Africa were well attended and showed a clear awareness that terror violence constitutes not only a growing threat to human rights in such regions, but also an increasing danger to internal and international peace and security.

4 Finally, the conference exploded the myth that terrorism research is biased in favour of Western governments and their policies, and, by the same token, incapable of rigorous critical examination of government policies and measures. The Conference commenced, by

> an extraordinary coincidence, the morning after the US air strikes on Libya. Although there was no paper or panel devoted to Libya as such, inevitably much of the informal discussion between sessions focused on the US raid. It is interesting to note that although there were many leading American scholars in attendance, few of them were convinced supporters of their government's action. Many conference delegates were outspoken in their criticism of their own and other governments for their alleged failings and errors in policy.

It should be emphasised that the Aberdeen conference was multi-disciplinary. There were papers on definitional problems, data bases, ethical issues, underlying causes of terrorism, terrorist ideology, sociological and psychological aspects, legal measures against terrorism, terrorism and the media, Latin America, South Africa, future trends, and possible pathways out of terrorism. Disciplines represented included history, political science, international relations, psychology, sociology, psychiatry, criminology, criminal and international law, religious studies, information science, computing science, and area studies. The mixture was rich and enormously rewarding and confirmed my conviction that we should be seeking to promote more multi-disciplinary projects as well as far more international cooperation in terrorism research.

As conference chairman I would like to take this opportunity to identify some of the themes and topics which suggested themselves as major priorities for the international research agenda on terrorism over the next ten to fifteen years.

A clear need is for major in-depth case studies and comparative studies of terrorist movements and campaigns in particular countries. Context is all in the study of political violence. Unless we can begin to understand the specific political, social, economic and cultural background to a terrorist conflict and the personalities and ideas of its leading figures, we will simply not have sufficient knowledge to begin to discern and understand the underlying causes and etiology of a particular conflict. Nor will we be able to grasp its wider implications for society and government and, where relevant, for international relations.

In particular there is a dearth of studies on terrorist campaigns and movements in the recent history of contemporary Asia, the Middle East and Latin America. Groups with nationalist and religious motivations should be given particularly high priority for research. For example, we have a grave shortage of good published research on terrorist movements in modern India, Sri Lanka, and the Far East.

Detailed case studies of state sponsored terrorism and single issue fanatic groups are also badly needed. It is of course true that access to data on state sponsorship is extremely difficult, but this is not a reason for abandoning the effort. The international implications and problems stemming from state involvement in international terrorism are such that we should be making major attempts to mount studies of the phenomena of state sponsorship.

Comparative studies could usefully focus on investigating the reasons for the dramatic growth of international terrorism since the late 1960s. Just how important was the effect of the extreme Palestinian factions' terrorism as a stimulus and model for other groups? To what extent did the doctrines, theories and political ideas of foreign-based revolutionary writers and leaders influence movements in West Europe, Japan, and Latin America? Was some of the apparent convergence and 'linkage' between terrorist movements in various countries coincidental rather than the result of systematic planning? Which state sponsors, if any, were important in aiding the development of specific foreign-based client movements? What factors appear to lead to a client being 'adopted' and which lead to one being 'dropped'? What are the crucial determinants on 'success' or 'failure' in the terrorists' campaign? In view of the historical rarity of terrorists achieving their strategic aims, what sustains their commitment and activity over long periods of time? How important are particular short-term objectives, such as the attainment of media coverage, in the eyes of the terrorists themselves? To what extent, and by what means, do terrorist states and groups and their leaders learn by their mistakes and succeed in adapting to new challenges and changes in their political environment and general situation? And to what extent do the requirements of sustaining the organisation take over from the longer-term political objectives of the movement as the primary concern? What is the relative importance, in specific groups, of racketeering and other forms of crime in terrorist fund raising, as compared with raising cash from friendly states and supporters?

In studying the important field of response to terrorism, a major priority should be to investigate the relationship betwen progress and setbacks in political reform and diplomatic negotiations in conflict situations and the levels of political violence. How far do terrorists deliberately seek to exploit the political opportunities afforded by such developments? Under what circumstances are terrorist efforts to sabotage or block political change ultimately counter-productive or ineffective? Under what circumstances are they successful?

It is a sign of my own bias to political science and international relations that I have concentrated mainly on those possibilities in the international research agenda. But there was plenty of evidence presented at Aberdeen, much of it presented in this volume, suggesting further projects in other disciplines that would greatly enrich our knowledge of terrorism. In the study of legal measures, for example, how can the inadequacies of extradition as a method for recovering fugitive terrorists to justice be reduced or overcome? How can the *enforcement* of international legal measures on terrorism be strengthened? How can emergency laws be adequately scrutinised and controlled by democratic legislatures? How can individual civil liberties be protected adequately in terrorist emergency situations? Are the special courts set up to try terrorist offences sufficiently equipped to maintain proper standards of procedure and evidence? In the fields of psychology, criminology, and psychiatry, much work needs to be done on the impact of current sentencing of terrorist offenders, and on the long-term effectiveness of different penal regimes on imprisoned terrorists. Are there valuable lessons to be learnt from the experience of certain penal systems in using techniques of rehabilitation and re-education of terrorist offenders? What proportion of terrorists released from gaol return to terrorist crime? What are the long-term results of the policy of capital punishment of terrorists in countries where this is part of the criminal code?

There are a myriad other topics and themes one could suggest. I have simply identified some aspects which I believe deserve the very highest priority on the international agenda for terrorism research. It is the editor's hope that the wide range of interesting papers in the present volume helps to stimulate new research efforts in these directions and to encourage research foundations and sponsors to provide more generous long-term support for serious academic research on terrorism. Terrorism research is far too important to be left to our political masters. Scholars of many disciplines must now take up the challenge of seeking greater knowledge of the characteristic mode of political violence of the late twentieth century, and how it might be curbed, or at least alleviated.

NOTES

1 There is an impressive array of evidence for the 'common ground' among scholars in Alex P Schmid, *Political Terrorism: A Research Guide to Concepts, Theories, Data Bases and Literature*, North Holland Publishing Company, Amsterdam, 1983, pp. 5–159. For early discussions of the definitional problem see Paul Wilkinson 'Three Questions on Terrorism', *Government and Opposition*, Vol. 8, No. 3, Summer 1973, pp. 290–312, and at greater length the same author's *Political Terrorism*, Macmillan 1974.

2 For fuller discussions of typology see Alex P Schmid, *op. cit.*, Paul Wilkinson, *Terrorism and the Liberal State* (second edn.) Macmillan 1986, pp. 23–33 and Eugene V Walter, *Terror and Resistance, A Study of Political Violence*, OUP, 1969, pp. 3–27.

3 For example, Hannah Arendt, *The Origins of Totalitarianism* (3rd edn.) Allen & Unwin, 1967, Leo Strauss, *On Tyranny*, Free Press, Glencoe, Illinois, 1963: Barrington Moore, Jr, *Terror and Progress—USSR*, Harvard University Press, Cambridge, Massachusetts, 1966; and Robert Conquest, *The Great Terror: Stalin's Purge of the Thirties*, Macmillan 1968.

4 The nature and *modus operandi* of state sponsored international terrorism is discussed in the writer's *Terrorism and the Liberal State* (2nd edn.) 1986, Chapter 16. For a historical study of the Soviet role see Galia Golan, *The Soviet Union and the PLO*, Adelphi Paper No. 131, International Institute for Strategic Studies, 1976.

I

Definitional and Conceptual Aspects

Terrorism as Political Communication: The Relationship between the Controller and the Controlled

R D Crelinsten

In this chapter, I intend to demonstrate what I consider to be a fruitful approach to the study of terrorism which avoids some of the major pitfalls which plague contemporary research of this complex phenomenon. First, I shall outline the nature of these pitfalls and why I think they are so prevalent. Then I shall point to various conceptual and methodological approaches which offer more promise for developing an adequate research framework for analysing terrorism. Finally, I shall develop this framework by means of a schematic model.

WEAKNESSES IN THE STUDY OF TERRORISM

The major weaknesses in current approaches to the study of terrorism are: (a) *a truncated object of study*, which reflects (b) *a skewed focus of the researcher*, which stems from (c) *a narrow policy orientation on prevention and control*, which yields (d) *narrow conceptual frameworks* which ignore the political dimension of terrorism and (e) *ahistorical, linear, causal models* which ignore the historical and comparative aspects of terrorism and focus selectively on individual actors, their characteristics, their tactics, and their stated ideologies.

(a) *A truncated object of study*. While many researchers recognise and some even acknowledge that terrorism can be perpetrated by those with power or those without power,[1] most contemporary researchers focus exclusively on terrorism perpetrated by small groups of non-state actors, i.e., non-state or anti-state terrorism.[2] Many writers mention the two forms in their introductory remarks, only to confine their analysis to insurgent forms and non-state actors.[3] Some explicitly exclude from their definitions of terrorism the terror tactics of sovereign states.[4]

The main problem that a truncated object of study creates for research is that it precludes the possibility of comparative analysis. It blinds the researcher to possible similarities across contexts, as well as to significant factors which differentiate the use of terrorism in one context from its use in another. Perhaps most importantly, by limiting the object of study to one specific form of terrorism, we lose sight of the fact that terrorism is a specific tool of persuasion in a wide variety of power relationships, not just that of the insurgent who contests the power of the State. By relating the use of terrorism to the exercise of power, we can avoid some of the pitfalls identified below.

(b) *Skewed research focus.* Scientific research is a form of social activity. As such, it is subject to social and political influences which shape and direct the organisational and individual behaviour of the scientific community and its members. A skewed interest in insurgent forms of terrorism reflects the selective concerns of policy makers and government agencies who solicit and fund research. Governments which exercise terrorism are not really interested in funding evaluative research or basic research into causes of state terrorism.[5] The skewing of research interests towards insurgent forms of terrorism can also be a function of the selective focus of public opinion makers, most notably the mass media. Moral repugnance at random murder and destruction by insurgent groups is heightened by sensational coverage which focuses on the violence to the exclusion of political and social analysis of the context of the incident. This creates a sense of urgency for governments and policy makers to solve the serious social problem—the 'scourge of terrorism'. Like-minded researchers then tailor their projects to suit the perspectives of the funding agencies.

The situation is compounded by the skewed nature of the data sources. Researchers interested in a broader focus or a larger object of study are faced with a plethora of data on insurgent groups, their methods and their organisation, but precious little on state actors. However, a skewed focus on the use of terrorism by those without power can lead us to equate terrorism, per se, with insurgency. This obscures the fact that terrorism is used in a wide variety of contexts and that its form varies according to where in the power structure it is exercised.

(c) *Policy-oriented research.* Most research on terrorism is what one researcher calls 'narrowly policy prescriptive'.[6] The real agenda of much research on terrorism is to advise policy makers on how best to prevent or control the kinds of terrorism with which they are most concerned, i.e., insurgent forms. This concern with prevention and control can lead to a narrowing of conceptual and methodological frameworks. An urgent concern with what to do about a specific problem needing to be solved can lead to a narrow conception of what is really a very complex phenomenon. The research then becomes prescriptive in that it seeks specific solutions to narrowly perceived problems. The researcher's understanding of the phenomenon is selectively shaped by the solutions he or she envisages to the problem.[7] As Abraham Maslow used to say, if we have a hammer at our disposal, we will tend to treat everything as if it were a nail. Similarly, there is an intimate connection between how terrorism is conceived and what social institution is charged with its control. Forms of terrorism which are not defined as problems needing to be controlled remain invisible to the researcher who restricts his or her research to policy-oriented problems.

(d) *Narrow conceptual frameworks.* A narrow focus on insurgent forms of terrorism separates the non-state actor from the larger context within which he acts and, in particular, from the behaviour of state actors. Moral condemnation of outrageous acts of violence can blind the researcher and the policy maker to the place of terrorism in the wider range of options available to the non-state actor. Because other options exist, the choice of terrorism is viewed as an irrational choice, a symptom of pathology. What then passes as scientific discourse is really polemics, where conceptual typologies become catalogues of pejorative labels. The muddled state of definitions in the field of terrorism stems directly from this narrowing of conceptual frameworks to just those actors whose goals we find unacceptable. By defining terrorism by the context in which it occurs rather than as a tool of political communication which can be used in a wide variety of contexts, we preclude the possibility of anything more than a superficial understanding of a narrow aspect of the phenomenon.

What is more, because our narrow focus stems from specific policy concerns, it is easy to define out of our purview official forms of terrorism that are legitimised and institutionalised. In a similar vein, TR Gurr limits his definition of 'civil strife' to 'collective manifestations of substantial discontent that typically occur outside institutional frameworks for action'. On the other hand, 'regime coercion and violence' represent 'both a cause of and a response to civil strife…, not…an integral part of strife.'[8] Such a narrow conception of strife precludes the possibility of comparing institutionalised and non-institutionalised forms of action, or legalised and criminalised forms.[9]

(e) *Linear, causal models.* The prescriptive nature of much scientific research leads the researcher to seek out the Holy Grail of root causes. If a cause or set of causes can be isolated, then a policy recommendation can be made. Because the insurgent actor is studied in isolation from other actors in the polity, and particularly state actors, all theory is directed towards identifying parameters of the insurgent actor and his environment. The causal model is basically a linear one, even if many causes are identified. There is little room for feedback and interaction, over either space or time. Such models tend to be ahistorical, static, actor oriented or incident oriented. The causal model assumes that insurgent terrorism has unique causes which, if addressed, would lead to the elimination of the phenomenon. Because insurgent terrorism is isolated from other forms of terrorism, its explanatory models are also divorced from comparable social and political phenomenon, such as reigns of terror, protection rackets, deterrent models of punishment, or the use of terrorism[10] in child rearing and education (operant uses of negative reinforcement). Because such models are focused exclusively on forms which are currently illegitimate, they tend to accommodate poorly to historical analysis where processes of legitimation and delegitimation become visible.

WHAT IS NEEDED

In view of the problems outlined above, what is needed to advance theory in the area of terrorism research is

(a) to broaden the object of study to include all forms of terrorism and all contexts in which terror tactics are employed. This would facilitate comparative analysis and would enable theory to address the question of why terrorism is likely to be viewed as a viable tool for political action;
(b) to avoid or at least to render explicit any skewed focus or research bias. This would facilitate a more coherent analysis of what is at present a highly fragmented literature;
(c) to avoid purely prescriptive research which inevitably narrows the focus. While difficult to achieve in practice due to the perceived urgency of the terrorist problem as narrowly defined, plus the reality of research funding priorities, basic non-applied research on terrorism is the best means of advancing theory, if not practice;
(d) to seek a conceptual framework which permits analysis of the socio-political context of individual incidents and events. To do so, such a framework must address the issue of legitimation and power;
(e) to abandon the search for causes (as clues for policy recommendations) and focus on the use of terrorism as a tool of social and political action. This would permit the development of theory which could accommodate the historical dimension.

TERRORISM AS POLITICAL COMMUNICATION

For the purpose of this chapter, terrorism is conceived as a form of political communication. More specifically, it is the deliberate use of violence and threat of violence to evoke a state of fear (or terror) in a particular victim or audience. The terror evoked is the vehicle by which allegiance or compliance is maintained or weakened. Usually, the use and threat of violence are directed at one group of targets (victims), while the demands for compliance are directed towards a separate group of targets. Hence, we tend to speak of a triangular relationship between the terrorist and two distinct target groups. As for allegiances, the allegiance to be established or maintained is that between the terrorist and one group of targets, while the allegiance to be weakened is that between that same group of targets from whom allegiance is sought and other groups perceived by the terrorist to be enemies to his cause. No matter what the specific end, all terrorism is designed to affect, in some way or another, relationships among people, individuals or groups.[11] In sum, then, terrorism is a tactic involving the use and threat of violence for communicative purposes. How and why it is used varies according to the particular context.

AN UNSKEWED FRAMEWORK FOR THE STUDY OF TERRORISM

The conception of terrorism as a specialised tactic of communication designed to strengthen certain allegiances and to weaken others leads to a broad framework in which the actions of the terrorist must always be analysed in terms of their impact on other people, i.e., the various targets or audiences involved in a particular incident. To study, for example, the actions of insurgent terrorists in isolation from the reactions of intended and unintended audiences is to ignore a key element of the terrorist phenomenon—its communicative nature. Furthermore, to treat official uses of terrorism as merely the cause or the result of insurgent terrorism is to obscure the functional similarity between official and unofficial forms.

What these forms of terrorism share is a communication function, and the conceptual framework proposed here includes the behaviour of both state actors and non-state actors within the unit of analysis.[12] The object of study becomes the interactive dialogue—over space and over time—between those seeking change within a specific polity and those resisting it. This interactive process includes the formation and maintenance of allegiances, the institutionalisation of means of collective action and advocacy, the legitimation of such means, the attempts to marshall support for one's side and to discredit the other side. The changes can be in the power structure (who governs and decides the implements policy) or in the social structure (policy content, distribution of resources, etc, without a change in who makes these decisions). The term 'controller' will be used for the state actor, while the term 'controlled' will be used for the non-state actor.

Within this framework, terrorism is viewed from two different levels of analysis. First, as a tactic of communication to manipulate certain target audiences by the use and threat of violence. Second, as a concept whose meaning can vary according to the legitimacy of the actor. It is only by combining both these levels—the descriptive and the semantic—that we can understand why the word 'terrorism' is generally used only for some forms of terrorist communication and not others. Two theoretical traditions lend themselves most readily to this kind of approach. They are symbolic interactionism and conflict theory.[13] In the interactionist paradigm, the meaning of a particular action derives from the social reaction which it evokes. This in turn defines that action in a particular way, labelling it and thereby confining its meaning to a particular interpretation. The conflict approach recognises that groups compete for resources and power and that institutions of social control serve as instruments in such conflicts.

In the framework proposed here, I suggest that one domain in which power struggles are carried on is that of the meaning we attach to certain political behaviour. This is why one man's terrorist is another man's freedom fighter. The two labels represent different interpretations of the same form of political activity. This is also why state torturers are rarely called terrorists.[14] One manifestation of a power struggle is that different meanings are attached to the same action, depending upon the particular allegiances held by the definer. Terrorism has become a pejorative term meaning the 'extranormal' use of violence.[15] Whoever has the power defines the meaning; those labels that prevail are those promulgated by groups with the power to make them stick.

To summarise: terrorism is a tactic of communication which combines the use and threat of violence to compel allegiance and compliance in a variety of target groups. The meaning attached to this communicative strategy can vary according to the legitimacy of the actor and his place in the social structure. State actors who use terrorism are better able to resist the terrorism label, while non-state actors who use terrorism are more likely to be labelled in ways which counter their claims to legitimacy. A non-truncated, unskewed, comprehensive study of political terrorism must analyse its use by both the controller and the controlled, even if it does not always go by the name of 'terrorism'. The terrorisms of controller and controlled—and the labels attached to them—are related aspects of a larger unit, the political life of a society. To isolate any one form of terrorism from the behaviour of its targets and audiences is to ignore the communicative nature of the phenomenon, its role in the broader context of political communication.

THE RELATIONSHIP BETWEEN CONTROLLER AND CONTROLLED

The model I wish to present here took its initial form during the course of previous work on the prevention and control of insurgent terrorism and hostage taking[16] and was developed and tested in a detailed case study of one incident—the FLQ Crisis of 1970 in Canada.[17] It was observed that there are basically two control models, each of which reflect a different conception of terrorism itself. First, there is the *criminal justice model*, which treats individual acts of insurgent terrorism as crime and makes use of criminal codes, traditional policing, criminal prosecutions and penal procedures and sentencing, to deal with those who commit these acts. Second, there is the *war model*, which treats individual acts of insurgent terrorism as tactics in a guerrilla or revolutionary war, and makes use of military personnel and weaponry to deal with the perpetrators. In the first case, the 'rule of law' prevails, and the agents of social control follow specific procedures of due process in the control of the terrorist. The official use of violence and deterrence/terror is confined to the 'guilty'. In the second case, the 'rules of combat' prevail, and the distinction between combattant and non-combattant, usually defined by the use of distinctive uniforms, POW status and specified combat zones, becomes important. Insurgent and state actors alike target specific personnel, who are identified as combattants. Each model has its distinct set of rules and procedures. Both controllers and controlled know these rules and the controlled must be prepared to accept the consequences (apprehension and punishment in the criminal justice model; capture and elimination in the war model) if he is caught by the controller, just as the controller must play by certain rules if he catches the controlled. To retain legitimacy in its use and threat of violence, the State must convince the general public that the target of official violence is guilty according to law or is an enemy of the State, constituting a threat to national security.

Separating these two clearly defined models is what I call a grey zone of ambiguity. The insurgent terrorist works within this zone (hence the concept of extranormality). On the one hand, he claims political ends for his criminalised actions, thus breaking down the distinction between crime and politics. On the other hand, he targets civilians and non-military institutions, claiming that there are no innocents, and thereby breaks down the distinction between crime and war. In doing so, he draws the controller into a symmetrical grey zone which mirrors the one in which he operates. From one end, the police bend the rules of due process, arrest and search warrants are obtained illegally or not obtained at all, charges are laid without sufficient evidence and what Otto Kirchheimer calls 'political justice' becomes more prevalent as use of the criminal justice system becomes politicised.[18] From the other end, the military starts to target civilians, to use torture to gain information, death squads are formed. As the sharp distinction between the police and the military breaks down and the imperatives of due process and the rules of combat are replaced by the demands of national security, the controller slides into the grey zone of terrorism 'from above' to match the terrorism 'from below'. Of course, the latter is usually no match for the former, in terms of personnel, resources and power. Furthermore, in the accompanying battle of words, the word 'terrorist' is usually applied selectively to the latter.

Figure 1 depicts this mirror relationship between the controller and the controlled in the form of an equation. As in any equation, the *relationship* between the elements above and below each line is the same for each dyad ('fraction'), when compared across the equal signs.

The virtue of this model is that the terrorism of either the state actor or the non-state actor is placed along a spectrum of other forms of protest or control (horizontal comparisons) and that the tactics of the two sides are

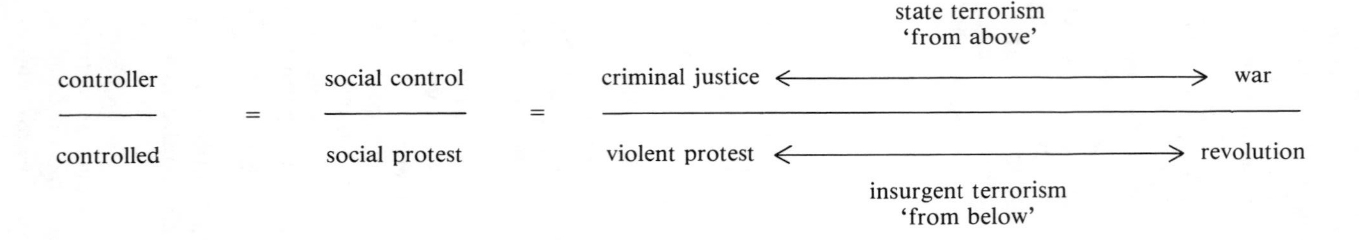

Figure 1. The mirror relationship between controller and controlled including the symmetrical relationship between grey zones. Terrorism 'from below' falls within the grey zone between the radical fringe of political protest and full-blown revolution. It aims to draw the political authorities away from legitimised control activities to illegitimate, illegal ones and, eventually, to institutionalised terrorism 'from above', or state terrorism. This, in turn, is meant to alienate the population from the government, to gain widespread sympathy for the terrorist cause and to lead ultimately to revolution via a popular uprising against the repression of the State. This mass uprising gives the terrorist a chance to win the war which he previously dared not fight because he lacked a sufficient power base. State terrorism falls within the grey zone between judicial and military control. It aims to suppress legitimate dissent and reform by forcing critics and reformers underground and treating all regime opponents as terrorists. This is meant to alienate the population from any reform movements and to win public support for a control strategy emphasising national security over civil liberties. Public desire for peace and security from random violence can allow a State to claim a degree of legitimacy from less-than-free elections where electoral choice is severely limited in the name of national security. The State can then claim to truly represent the will of the people without risking truly free elections.

placed in relationship to each other (vertical comparisons). To introduce the model, I began with the insurgent form of terrorism, that of the controlled. But I could just as easily begin with the state form. A reign of terror, such as in a post-revolutionary society like eighteenth-century France or twentieth-century Iran, or in a military regime like pre-Alfonsin Argentina, can draw violent protest by isolated (and therefore easily criminalised) individuals towards collective action (towards revolution and the right-hand part of the equation). State terrorism can also draw military action of revolutionaries towards clandestine insurgent terrorism (towards crime and the left-hand part of the equation), to mirror the dirty tactics of the secret police or the death squads.

Another virtue of the model is that the communicative nature of terrorism is made explicit. It is a tactic in a power struggle which, in turn, is represented by the dialectic relationship between protest and control, between actions in support of political or social change and actions in support of maintenance of the status quo. The model also highlights the labelling process whereby the word 'terrorism' itself becomes a tool by which the controller stigmatises the controlled, who resorts to the use and threat of violence in his struggle for political power, and justifies the official use of terrorism in the name of national security and 'counterterrorism'. By using the word 'terrorism' for both controller and controlled, the model accentuates the functional similarity of terrorist communication regardless of who uses it.

POLITICAL COMMUNICATION AND THE VIOLENCE THRESHOLD

The astute reader will note that the model as presented in Figure 1 confines itself to violent forms of action which escalate through low-level violence to full scale conflict. As one proceeds from left to right across the grey zones in the equation, the level of violence increases, as does the number of actors. In addition, as we move from left to right, the breadth of target selection widens in the grey zones and narrows again in the war model. For the controller, the *overtness* of official violence increases from left to right, as does its level and its scope. In the criminal justice model, the violence of the State is masked by the legitimacy bestowed by labels such as 'arrest', 'preventive detention', 'trial', 'conviction' and 'punishment'. It is limited and contained by the imperatives of due process, which restrict the exercise of violence to those found guilty of crimes previously encoded in law. In war, the violence is overt, unmasked. It can also be argued that the legitimacy of official violence decreases in the grey zone of state terrorism in that states which resort to the use and threat of torture and murder, to control those who oppose the regime or who fight for change, have abandoned the legitimising mantle of criminal justice. Whether it rises again as internal war develops depends on the relative strength of the two sides. As for the controlled, the degree of support for the insurgent cause increases from left to right. In the case of successful revolution (as in Nicaragua in the years leading up to 1979), the legitimacy of state and insurgent violence is inversely related as one moves from left to right. As the legitimacy of the insurgent cause increases, the legitimacy of the State decreases.

But what about non-violent forms of protest and control? Can the model be extended to include these as well? Figure 2 attempts to do this by extending the equation leftwards towards peaceful forms of protest and control. The term 'government' has been adopted for the most general form of control or maintenance activity. This would include all the apparatus of government—legislative, executive, administrative and judicial.[19] The term 'politics' has been adopted for the most general form of protest or dissent activity. This would include opposition political parties, interest groups, labour unions, the media—in short, all forms and avenues of legal, legitimised dissent. As such, the word 'politics' includes those forms of social protest which do not necessarily call for a change of government, but restrict themselves to some change in social policy (e.g., the peace movement, pro- and anti-abortion movements, single-issue politics).

As soon as we identify this third pole of peaceful activity, a second grey zone appears. For the controlled, this grey zone marks an area of ambiguity which separates legal dissent from illegal dissent. What usually separates these two is what I call the 'violence threshold'. As soon as dissent takes on a violent form, the institution of social control becomes the criminal justice system and the activity of the controlled is labelled 'crime'. The problem arises when the controller tries to predict where and when violence will erupt. This leads to the grey area of 'subversion' or the *advocacy* of violent action. Violent rhetoric and the advocacy of violent revolution are usually considered as *sedition*. But sedition and conspiracy laws are difficult to apply and notoriously prone to abuse. Certain countries at certain times have even repealed them, only to re-enact them in times of crisis or political uncertainty.[20]

The symmetrical grey zone on the controller's side is that of security intelligence (specifically *domestic* intelligence services). Just as police can be drawn into the grey zone of state terrorism (rightwards along the equation), so they can be drawn into the grey zone of security intelligence (leftwards along the equation). What often happens is that the vocal, but legal, dissenter (as in a mass demonstration or a political tract of violent rhetoric) becomes the target of security intelligence, while those actually engaged in planning violence and terrorism escape detection because of their clandestineness.

Here we have the vexing problem of distinguishing between terrorists and fellow travellers, between subversives and sympathisers.[21] This is one of the most pernicious problems for both theory and practice, as both police and security personnel and so-called terrorism experts tend to overestimate the size of insurgent terrorist movements by counting among their members those who merely express publicly their support for the same political ends. By clearly identifying this intelligence model and its mirror counterpart, subversion, the extended model of Figure 2 addresses this problem area of differentiating between dissent and subversion. At the same time, the extended

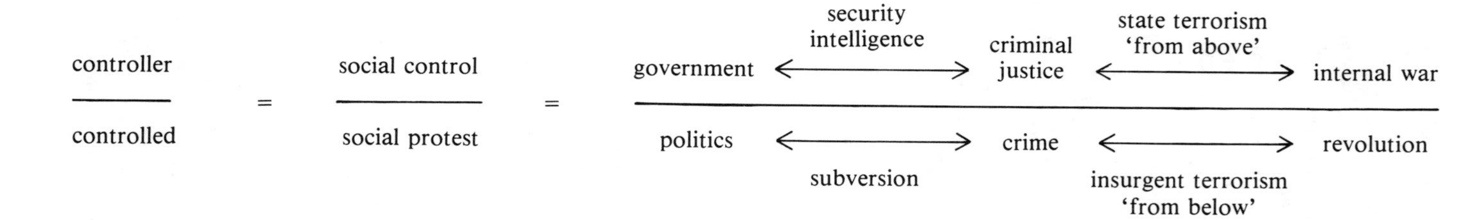

Figure 2. The mirror relationship between controller and controlled, including non-violent forms of control and protest and the symmetrical grey zones which separate them from violent forms.

model highlights the importance of the labelling phenomenon in the demarcation of grey zones, since it is usually the perceptions of security intelligence agents which determine whether a particular political statement or action will be treated as subversive or as a threat to national security.

The grey zone for the controller can also involve the use of covert tactics of 'countersubversion'—recruitment, penetration, facilitation, entrapment—which mirror the activities they are presumed to control. It is a moot point whether some of what passes as subversion and terrorism by insurgent radicals is really the work of underground state agents.[22]

SOCIALISATION, EDUCATION AND THE POLITICS THRESHOLD

To complete the process of embedding the phenomenon of terrorism within its broader sociopolitical context and the spectrum of strategies and tactics of protest and control which are available to state and non-state actors, we must extend the model leftwards one more step towards non-political forms of social control. At this point, the terms 'social protest' and 'dissent' are no longer appropriate for the controlled. Instead, the term 'deviance' is most useful. Social control is a strategy of maintaining a social consensus and the institutions are not political, but social. They include the big three: family, school and church. But they also include the job, the profession, the community and all the complex array of social roles which we humans are trained for, adopt and adapt to in the course of growing up.

I lump all these forms of social control under the broad rubric of 'socialisation', while the experience of the controlled is called 'education'. These complementary processes are *pre-political.* One cannot dissent or protest without knowledge of what society is, how one fits into it or what divisions of resources and power exist. Nor can one govern or rule effectively without such knowledge. One cannot participate in political and social life without the proper social tools and knowledge of the social roles within which it is deemed appropriate to function.

Figure 3 presents the complete model, showing the entire spectrum of social and political life, which ranges from 'peace' and an ideal 'consensual' society to 'war' and an ideal 'conflictual' society. The term 'internal war' is used[23] to highlight the fact that the model is designed for the domestic, intra-state context.[24] At the consensual end of the equation, the forms of social deviance (in the denominator) mirror the forms (and institutions) of social control (in the numerator) by which socialisation is exercised and the 'upright citizen' is educated. As such, they also reflect the different 'social problems' which have traditionally been identified by social scientists as 'causing' crime and revolution: broken homes (divorce, alcoholism), lack of schooling, low IQs, lack of moral training, unemployment, low socioeconomic status, lack of economic opportunity, social disintegration, anomie.[25] Such social deviants

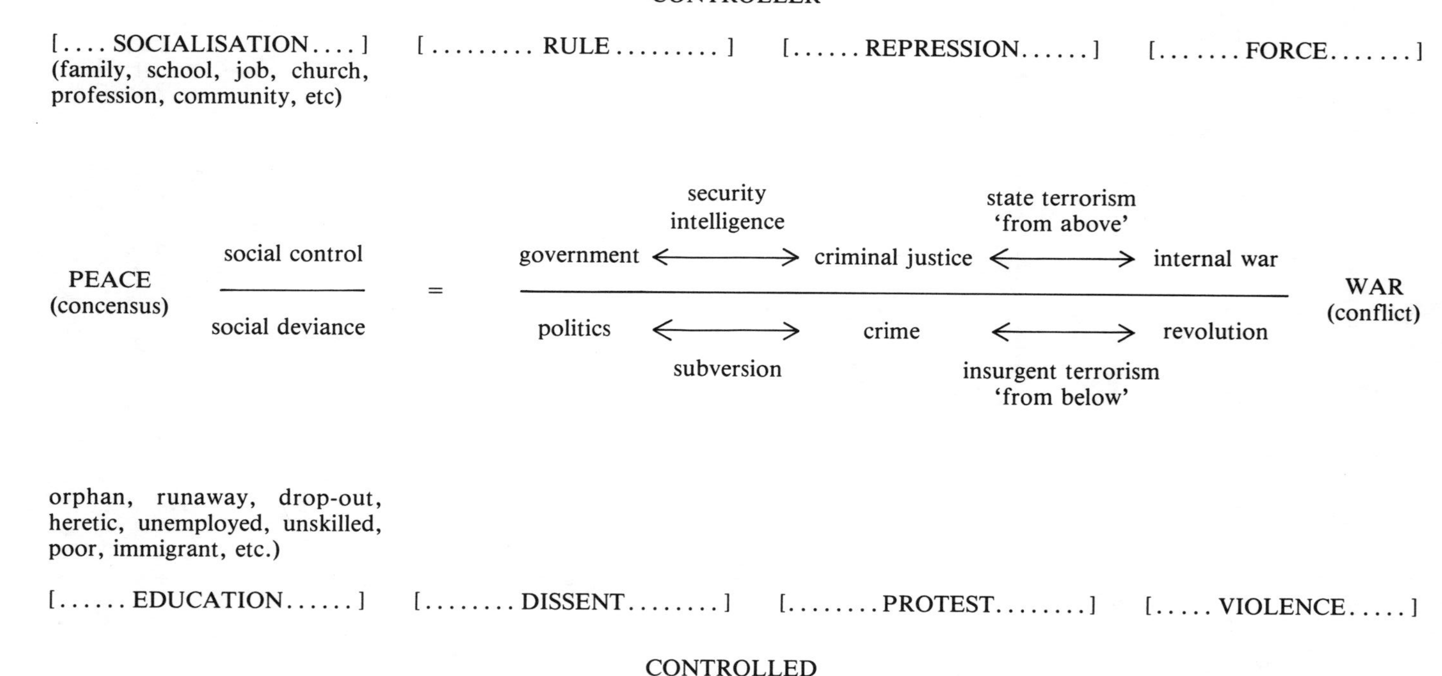

Figure 3. The mirror relationship between controller and controlled, including non-political forms of control and deviance. The series of words in brackets depict commonly used labels for the different spheres of activity of controller and controlled.

have also traditionally been perceived by revolutionaries as ideal targets for politicisation and radicalisation. Similarly, intelligence services consider them to be ideal targets for recruitment as operatives or informers.

The socialisation processes identified in Figure 3 can serve as tools of oppression and indoctrination in totalitarian regimes and can reinforce structural inequalities in democratic societies. The corresponding forms of social deviance can sometimes serve as pathways to liberation in oppressive regimes and avenues to innovation in liberal democracies. What the model makes clear is that the same dialectic relationship that connects political and violent forms of social control and social protest also connects these non-political and non-violent forms of social control and social deviance.

THE QUESTION OF LEGITIMACY AND LABELS

Figure 3 includes a series of words in capital letters for the controller and the controlled. These represent an attempt to characterise the most common labels which are used in the social science literature to describe the activities of state actors and non-state actors.[26] Moving from left to right, we see that social control begins right at the beginning, with child rearing, schooling, religion, and moves on to professional training, employment, marriage, community service and so on. While this is generally called 'socialisation' by the controller and by most social scientists, the terms 'oppression' or 'structural violence' are frequently used by social critics and revolutionaries.[27] As we cross the politics threshold, we can speak of the ruling class, which governs the State via the maintenance of peace, order and good government. Through the legislative process, rules are set and the threat of punishment deters the socialised citizenry from breaking them. When rule breaking does occur, the State exercises its right to punish the offender. Typically, we speak of 'repression', specifically 'legal representation', instead of 'violence', although the legal concepts of 'arrest', 'bail', 'imprisonment' and 'capital punishment' have their mirror counterparts in 'abduction', 'extortion', 'forcible confinement' and 'murder'. When the level of state violence escalates, we then tend to use the word 'force' instead of 'violence'.

As for the controlled, all individuals who do not adapt to the various institutional settings employed to socialise the individual are called 'deviants', while the process of inculcating conformity to pre-established social structures is generally called 'education'. It can also be called 'indoctrination' or 'brainwashing' by social critics. If an educated/socialised person begs to differ with the status quo, we can speak of 'dissent'. If he takes action, we speak of 'protest' and if his action causes damage to property or person, and sometimes merely to rules, we call it 'violence', 'crime' or 'violent crime'.[28] As the violence escalates and collective action develops, we speak of other categories, such as 'terrorism', 'guerrilla', 'insurgency' and, ultimately, 'revolution'. All these labels are generally subsumed under the rubric of 'political violence'. Rarely is this term used for the political violence of state actors.

The different labels applied to the actions of controller and controlled reflect differences in the legitimacy of the actor and his place in the social structure. In short, the violent actions of deviants tend to be labelled 'violence' or 'terrorism', while the violent actions of the powerful tend to be labelled 'repression' or 'force'. By focusing on the communicative nature of the use of violence and terrorism, and the intimate relationship between its use and non-use by both controller and controlled, the model proposed here helps us to understand how the phenomenon of terrorism fits into the broader framework of social and political life and how its *description* varies according to who uses it and why.

CONCLUSION

In this chapter, I have set out to develop a model which places the phenomenon of terrorism within a larger framework designed to facilitate research which avoids the definitional and ideological problems which currently plague the field. The heuristic value of the model is twofold. First, it demonstrates the intimate relationship between state and insurgent forms of terrorism, which share a grey zone of ambiguity separating two clearly defined poles (the crime model and the war model). This mirror relationship is captured by the vertical dimension of the model, which shows the similar forms which social control and social protest take at any point in the model.

Second, the model demonstrates the relationship between terrorism and other forms of political action by both controller and controlled. This relationship is captured by the horizontal dimension of the model, which identifies various thresholds which separate the different categories of action.[29] A violence threshold separates crime from politics and criminal justice from government, and is situated in a grey zone separating legal and criminal dissent. Similarly, a legitimacy threshold seems to lie within the grey zone of terrorism itself. In this zone, the legitimacy of the controller and the controlled come into direct conflict in a kind of zero-sum game of winner take all. If the conflict moves into the war model, the winner gains all the legitimacy and the loser is relegated to the crime model (war criminal, traitor).

A politics threshold separates these reciprocal forms of action from the sphere of more purely social activity embodied in socialisation and education.[30] What is most interesting about this threshold is its potential for linking aetiological research (the question of root causes) with an unskewed analysis of terrorism prevention and control. The intimate relationship between institutions of social control and forms of education, which is identified in the model, should alert us to the dangers of a selective focus on education and opportunity as long-term solutions to insurgent terrorism. Political radicals and social critics tend to view reform efforts as a form of cooptation.[31] As such, social reform can lead to increased polarisation as radicals view the State's reform efforts as oppressive. Furthermore, if reform leads to lost privileges for previously favoured groups, new sources of discontent can be created. By drawing attention to the relationship between controller and controlled at all points along the continuum separating 'peace' and 'war', the model forces us to include the impact of all control efforts, even social reform, in our analysis.

Some might argue that the model presented here defines terrorism out of existence by drowning it in a continuum of concepts which rightly belong to separate and distinct areas of inquiry. However, I believe that to advance theory, it is necessary to analyse the phenomenon of terrorism within the broader context of political behaviour and the struggle for power and legitimacy. To do so, we must cross disciplinary boundaries and combine different levels of analysis. Definitional ambiguities exist because terrorism is an ambiguous phenomenon, lying in a grey zone separating two distinct phenomena. By broadening our framework of analysis, such ambiguities can be fruitfully addressed.

Others might argue that, by highlighting the functional similarity between actions of the State and actions of the insurgent, the model falls into moral relativism. On the contrary, the model allows an unequivocal condemnation of terrorism, but ensures that such a condemnation is not hypocritical. If one condemns the terrorism of the insurgent, the model forces one to condemn the terrorism of the State as well. More to the point, however, the model precludes the possibility that moral condemnation disguises itself as scientific discourse. By identifying the communicative nature of terrorism and its place in a continuum of communication strategies, the model allows us to move beyond ideological and moral posturing and to include the process of labelling in the analysis itself. The very confusion about whether terrorism is really a form of crime or a form of war, an instrument of protest or an instrument of control, is thereby confronted. What terrorism is and what is called terrorism depends on who is acting and in what context. As such, the model presented here provides an heuristic framework within which the complexities of the terrorist problem can be meaningfully addressed.

NOTES

1 Thornton's classic distinction is between enforcement terror and agitational terror, cf. TP Thornton, 'Terror as a Weapon of Political Agitation', *in* H Eckstein (ed.), *Internal War: Problems and Approaches*, New York: Free Press, 1964, p. 72. A more common distinction is that between state terrorism and insurgent terrorism, although Schmid suggests 'regime terrorism' as a more general category than state terrorism. Cf. AP Schmid, *Political Terrorism: A Research Guide to Concepts, Theories, Data Bases and Literature*, New Brunswick, US: Transaction Books, 1983, p. 105.

2 Schmid (1983, p. 104) estimates that 90% of the literature falls in this category.

Cf. also M Stohl, 'Introduction: Myths and Realities of Political Terrorism', *in* M Stohl (ed.), *The Politics of Terrorism*, 2nd edn., New York: Marcel Dekker, 1983, pp. 6–7. Thornton (1964, p. 73) refers to 'an extensive literature on enforcement terror, called forth especially by the Soviet and German experiences'. These references cluster in the 1930s and 1940s for Nazi terror and the 1950s for Stalinist terror. For a collection of articles which focuses on a wider spectrum of more recent cases, including Latin America, the Philippines and South Africa, cf. M Stohl and GA Lopez (eds.), *The State as Terrorist: The Dynamics of Governmental Violence and Repression*, Westport, Connecticut Greenwood Press, 1984. Even this literature on state terrorism tends to remain isolated from the literature on insurgent terrorism, often standing in opposition to the mainstream literature rather than attempting a more general synthesis.

3 Cf., for example, Thornton (1964, p. 73), G Wardlaw, *Political Terrorism: Theory, Tactics, and Counter-measures*, Cambridge: Cambridge University Press, 1982, p. 8. In my earliest work, I, too, have resorted to this approach: cf. RD Crelinsten, D Laberge-Altmejd and D Szabo, *Terrorism and Criminal Justice*, Lexington, Massachusetts: Lexington Book, 1978, pp. 5–6.

4 Schmid (1983, p. 103) found that 26% of a sample of 109 definitions did this.

5 Cf. A Liazos, 'The Poverty of the Sociology of Deviance: Nuts, Sluts, and Perverts', *Social Problems*, 1972, **20**, p. 113, note 6, for a similar remark concerning research on deviance and its silence on institutional deviance.

6 TM Mitchell, 'Politically-motivated Terrorism in North America: The Threat and the Response'. Unpublished Doctoral Dissertation, Carleton University, Ottawa, Canada, 1985, p. 15.

7 Cf. RD Crelinsten, 'International Political Terrorism: A Challenge for Comparative Research', *International Journal of Comparative and Applied Criminal Justice*, 1978, **2**, pp. 110–112, for a more detailed discussion of this phenomenon.

8 TR Gurr, 'A Comparative Study of Civil Strife', *in* HD Graham and TR Gurr (eds.), *Violence in America: Historical and Comparative Perspectives*, New York: Signet Books, 1969, p. 545.

9 For discussions of how legitimised forms of violence come to be excluded from the conceptual frameworks of those who study political and collective violence, cf. E Currie and JH Skolnick, 'A Critical Note on Conceptions of Collective Behavior', *in* JF Short, Jr. and ME Wolfgang (eds.), *Collective Violence*, Chicago: Aldine-Atherton, 1972, pp. 60–71; SJ Ball-Rokeach, 'The Legitimation of Violence', *in* Short and Wolfgang (1972, pp. 100–111).

10 I might have said 'terror' or 'terror tactics' instead of 'terrorism' here, but I wish to imply that 'terrorism' as a concept, word or label should apply to all forms of communication in which the use and threat of violence are combined in order to compel allegiance or compliance of some kind. I realise that this use of the word flies in the face of a tradition which restricts the word 'terrorism' to systematic use of terror tactics by political insurgents and the word 'terror' to reigns of terror by governments. Schmid (1983: 64–72) discusses the relationship between terrorism and terror at some length. My purpose in enumerating this list is to highlight the functional similarity which exists when we compare the use of terror tactics across a diverse array of contexts. I am currently preparing a separate article which explores this issue in greater depth (RD Crelinsten, 'Terrorism, Violence and the Question of Root Causes', in preparation).

11 For various descriptions of the diversity of victims, targets and audiences involved in terrorism, cf. RD Crelinsten and D Szabo, *Hostage-Taking*, Part I. Lexington, Massachusetts: Lexington Books, 1979, pp. 3–12; RD Crelinsten,

'Terrorist Victimization: The Interface between Research and Policy', in RD Crelinsten and D Szabo (eds.), *Hostage-Taking*, Part III, 1979, pp. 127–134; A Kaplan, 'The Psychodynamics of Terrorism', *Terrorism*, 1978, **1**, pp. 234–254; Schmid (1983, pp. 87–96; 110–112). While most of these typologies were developed for insurgent forms of terrorism, they can be applied as well to state forms. The demands for compliance or allegiance are often implicit in state terrorism, however.

12 One of the rare examples of an analysis which approaches this framework, in that it studies the relationship between insurgent violence and its control, is a recent series of case studies which analyses the impact of anti-terrorist policies on five urban terrorist campaigns, over an extended period of time. Cf. C Hewitt, *The Effectiveness of Anti-Terrorist Policies*, Lanham, Maryland: University Press of America, 1984. However, while the author explicitly states that 'one kind of terrorism, that carried out by groups seeking to defend the *status quo*, is not examined in this study' (p. xii), he fails to consider that some of the anti-terrorist policies studied, such as the use of collective punishment in Cyprus or the use of torture and in-depth interrogation in Uruguay and Northern Ireland, could be considered as forms of state terrorism within the definition presented in this chapter.

13 For symbolic interactionism, it is generally recognised that the social psychology of George Herbert Mead served as the basis for this tradition. Cf. GH Mead, *Mind, Self and Society: From the Standpoint of a Social Behaviorist*, Chicago: University of Chicago Press, 1934. This approach was later incorporated, along with other sociological traditions, into what is now known as 'labelling theory' or the 'societal reaction school'. Cf. M Petrunik, 'The Rise and Fall of Labelling Theory: The Construction and Destruction of a Sociological Strawman', *Canadian Journal of Sociology*, 1980, **5**, pp. 213–233. This tradition has been criticised for ignoring the rationality of the actor and the political dimension of 'human agency'. Cf. FF Piven, 'Deviant Behavior and the Remaking of the World', *Social Problems*, 1981, **5**, pp. 489–508. For conflict theory, two of the early formulations are L Coser, *The Functions of Social Conflict*, London: Routledge & Kegan Paul, 1956; R Dahrendorf, 'Out of Utopia: Toward a Reconstruction of Sociological Analysis', *American Journal of Sociology*, 1958, **67**, pp. 115–127. Cf. also R Dahrendorf, *Class and Class Conflict in an Industrial Society*, London: Routledge & Kegan Paul, 1959.

14 Cf., however, 'Confessions of a State Terrorist', *Harper's*, June 1985, pp. 15–17. The term 'state terrorist' is used to describe an ex-member of the Chilean secret service under Pinochet.

15 Thornton (1964, pp. 75–77); Schmid (1983, pp. 106–110). It is interesting to note, however, that such a normative definition is rarely used for the state actor. If the use and threat of torture cannot be considered terrorism, is this because it is a normal tool of social control in authoritarian regimes?

16 Crelinsten *et al.*, *Terrorism and Criminal Justice*, 1978; Crelinsten and Szabo, *Hostage-Taking*, 1979. (Cf. n. 11 above.)

17 RD Crelinsten, 'Limits to Criminal Justice in the Control of Insurgent Political Violence: A Case Study of the October Crisis of 1970', Unpublished Doctoral Dissertation, Université de Montréal, Montreal, Canada, 1985. 'FLQ' stands for *Le Front de libération du Québec*, which served as a rubric for diverse groups using terror tactics—bombing and kidnapping—in the name of Quebec independence between 1963 and 1971. Cf. L Fournier, *FLQ: Histoire d'un mouvement clandestin*, Montréal: Quebec-Amérique, 1982. In translation: L Fournier, *FLQ: The*

Anatomy of an Underground Movement, Transl. by E Baxter. Toronto: NC Press, 1984.

18 O Kirchheimer, *Political Justice*, Princeton, New Jersey: Princeton University Press, 1961.

19 The creation of laws can be distinguished from their enforcement, the latter belonging to the criminal justice model.

20 B Ingraham, *Political Crime in Europe: A Comparative Study of France, Germany and England*, Berkeley: University of California Press, 1979.

21 For an excellent discussion of this problem in the Canadian context, see Canada, *Freedom and Security under the Law*, Second Report, Volume I of the Commission of Inquiry Concerning Certain Activities of the Royal Canadian Mounted Police (The McDonald Report). Ottawa: Minister of Supplies and Services, 1981, pp. 427–511.

22 Much of the FLQ terrorism in the years following the 1970 October Crisis in Canada was carried on under close police surveillance and was sometimes even facilitated or encouraged. Cf. J-P Brodeur, 'Legitimizing Police Deviance', *in* C Shearing (ed.), *Organizational Police Deviance*, Toronto: Butterworth, 1981, pp. 149–151. Only recently, in the Federal Republic of Germany, it was revealed that a 1978 bomb explosion attributed to the Red Army Faction was really the work of the anti-terrorist elite corps, GSG-9, and was aimed at facilitating the infiltration of an undercover agent into the terrorist group (Toronto *Globe and Mail*, May 3, 1986, p. A9). For an excellent discussion of the problems surrounding police undercover work in a wide variety of areas, cf. G Marx, 'The New Police Undercover Work', *Journal of Urban Life and Culture*, 1980, **8**, pp. 400–446; G Marx, 'Ironies of Social Control: Authorities as Contributors to Deviance through Escalation, Nonenforcement, and Covert Facilitation', *Social Problems*, 1981, **28**, pp. 221–246.

23 Cf. H Eckstein, *Internal War: Problems and Approaches*, New York: Free Press, 1964.

24 The model can be applied to the international context as well, particularly as it relates to post-revolutionary conditions and the role of other states in what has been variously called 'state-sponsored terrorism', 'aid to freedom fighters', and 'surrogate warfare'. The concepts of 'diplomacy', 'international law' and 'war' would replace those of 'government', 'criminal justice' and 'internal war'. 'Espionage' and 'international' or 'transnational' terrorism would constitute the grey zones. The distinction between controller and controlled would be clearest in the colonial context and in the spheres of influence of the superpowers.

25 Stanley Cohen, in his discussion of definitions of 'social control', distinguishes between 'planned and programmed responses to expected and realized deviance' and 'general institutions of society which produce conformity'. Cf. Cohen, *Visions of Social Control: Crime, Punishment and Classification*, Cambridge: Polity Press, 1985, p. 2. Clearly, when I use the term 'socialization', I am referring to the latter, more general conception of social control. However, I also include the more organised responses to deviance which interest Cohen, such as social work, psychiatry, and even penal responses to delinquency and 'common' crime, all of which are more concerned with the prevention and control of 'serious' or 'persistent' deviance than with the broader socialisation process.

26 The terms 'state terrorism' and 'insurgent terrorism' in Figure 3 are not labels in this sense (the second level of analysis), but descriptive terms for a particular communication strategy, using threat and violence (hence the first level of analysis). One could add the *label* 'TERRORISM', but then it would appear only on

the bottom line of the figure. Most commonly, the label is used as a synonym for violence. A similar ambiguity surrounds the word 'crime'. In Figure 3 (and, for that matter, Figure 2), the word 'crime' is a descriptive term for behaviour that is proscribed by law (the first level of analysis). However, the word 'crime' can also be a pejorative label used to characterise behaviour of which one does not approve. As with the labels 'VIOLENCE' and 'TERRORISM', the label 'CRIME' is most often used to describe activities of the controlled and rarely is it used to describe behaviour of state actors.

27 The term 'structural violence', in particular, represents an attempt by critics of a regime to justify insurgent violence as a response to state violence. The concept of structural violence, just as that of corporate crime or of environmental crime (e.g., pollution or hazardous working conditions), is rendered highly problematic by the common assumption that violence is an act committed by someone, with intent to harm another or to damage property. It thereby stretches the very notion of 'violence'. Yet to the degree that it goes beyond specific acts to focus on broader societal relationships, the concept of structural violence mirrors that of deviance, which also goes beyond the specific acts of the individual actor to focus on the very nature of the person in relationship to others. Both concepts move away from intentional actions of individuals to structural factors. The difference is that, for the 'oppressor', the primary focus is on societal structure, with personality factors remaining implicit, while, for the 'deviant', the primary focus is the 'deviant personality', with societal factors remaining implicit.

28 The distinction between deviance and dissent sidesteps the controversy within the sociology of deviance and radical criminology concerning the tendency of deviance theory to ignore the rationality of the deviant actor or what Piven (1981, p. 491) calls 'human agency'. Cf. also I Taylor, P Walton and J Young, *The New Criminology: For a Social Theory of Deviance*, London: Routledge & Kegan Paul, 1973, chapters 5 and 6. Such critics suggest that deviance can be a form of dissent. By placing the two concepts on opposite sides of the politics threshold, I mean to suggest that 'dissent', as I use the term, refers to political, fully conscious disagreement with current governmental policies or power elites. I do not mean to imply that certain forms of social deviance cannot be rationally elected or that they cannot have an impact on the political life of a society.

As for the distinction between 'dissent' and 'protest', this too is not as clear-cut as implied in the model. One can dissent by joining an opposition party or by founding a newspaper with divergent views from the mainstream opinions of the day. Both can be seen as forms of protest. By 'protest', I mean to suggest a moving away from mainstream, legitimised avenues of dissent to forms of protest that are more radical, innovative and, usually as a consequence of this, more obtrusive, abrasive, disruptive (in escalating order?) to the status quo. 'Sometimes merely to rules' refers to the fact that protest that is too obtrusive, abrasive or disruptive can be illegal without necessarily being violent, such as a demonstration or a strike. Such actions are often labelled as 'violent'—and treated violently—by controllers, simply because they have been declared illegal.

29 I am currently working on an extension of the model which further subdivides the grey zones. This will facilitate a more fine-grained analysis of the transition points along the continuum and refine those distinctions which called out for qualification in these endnotes.

30 It can even be argued that a third grey zone is therefore identified, namely that which separates the social from the political. Further development of this idea would probably help to define the distinction between deviance and dissent.

31 Cf., for example, M Raboy, *Movements and Messages: Media and Radical Politics in Quebec*, Toronto: Between the Lines, 1984, pp. 28–29. Cohen (1985, p. 240) calls this intellectual position 'adversarial nihilism'—the idea 'that most radical and oppositional attacks on the system will end up being absorbed, coopted and even strengthening it'.

Terrorism: A Definitional Problem

R Thackrah

The emotive nature of the subject matter, the term's derogatory thrust and the political discourse are major contributory factors to the complexity of the concept of terrorism.[1] Rather than being considered as a technique of applying violence, which in principle can be used by anyone in all sorts of conflict situations, the concept is linked to certain actors only for certain types of conflicts.

The result has been what to many is a trite and hackneyed phrase, namely that 'one man's terrorist is another man's patriot'. The concept has thereby often been subjected to a double standard based on the power of definition, and an in-group, out-group distinction.[2]

The concept of terror when discussed in the domain of international policy escapes definition. It is not that terror is intrinsically more difficult to define than any other political concept, but it does escape definition when it becomes embellished with value under political meaning.[3] In historical terms, terrorism can't be a universal phenomenon and is a historical one emerging only at particular times and associated with particular developments in people's consciousness.[4]

Based partly on historical grounds and currently on political ones, the confusion over aims and definitions is very great. Thus the United States sees terrorism atrocities as 'senseless acts', a view supported by democratic countries; and the West go it alone as a community of free states and act as a group against terrorism.[5]

In spite of the spread of terrorist incidents throughout the world, the term has neither a precise definition, nor one which is widely acceptable. Like many political terms it is pejorative. Some governments are prone to label as terrorism all violent acts committed by their political opponents, while anti-government extremists claim to be the victims of government terror. It can have a moral judgement and the attaching of the label 'terrorist' to one's opponent can have a knock-on effect. The media can exploit the term and they see the word as attention-getting to heighten drama. The imprecise nature of the term means that with some accuracy it can refer to a specific set of fear-producing actions which can serve a variety of purposes. More generally it can apply to similar acts of violence—kidnappings and hijackings—which are not intended by the perpetrators to be terror-producing.

Many researchers and authors on this subject, including Walter Laqueur, and in certain instances the author of this chapter, believe there is no defining agency, but a Babylonic confusion of meanings. The term is carelessly used—even by academic students of the subject—as a synonym for rebellion, street battles, civil strife, insurrection, rural guerrilla war and coup d'état. The indiscriminate use of the term not only inflates the statistics but makes understanding the specific character of terrorism and how to cope with it more difficult:[6]

Yet to some extent this is exaggerated because all the synonyms utilised by Laqueur denominate anti-governmental forms of violence.

Political sociologists argue that no definition can in principle be reached because the very process of definition is in itself part of the wider conflict between ideologies or political objectives. This cumulative research on an empiricist scientific model is not possible. The problem is not one of comprehensiveness or degree of detail of definition, but is one of the framework of the definition. Yet, lexicographically, to define is to explain something new by something old, adding the distinctive feature. In this way, the new object or phenomenon becomes embedded into a known framework of reference.

The definition problem has become far more than an exercise in semantics. The problem of ascertaining characteristics is vital if guidelines are to be established by which social scientists collect and evaluate data on strife incidents. The minimum consensus is now leading to some effective framework.

What definitions do support is the argument that the perspectives change with the change in the position on the place/time matrix. The question of the definition of terrorism is central to an understanding of the phenomenon and to the success of any rational measures directed against it. I am inclined to agree with the Wardlaw thesis, that to many almost any act of violence may be included under the rubric of terrorism. Others, however, would not label as terrorism violent acts carried out within a revolutionary context which a number of people would recognise as terroristic. Confusion can arise over a seeming similarity of behaviour when a violent act is carried out by a politically motivated individual, a criminal or the mentally unbalanced. For example, is a member of Al Fatah to be equated with someone who explodes bombs in a commercial location or a deranged murderer? No one would deny that they all contain elements of terror, but does it contribute to an understanding or design of countermeasures to treat them all as instances of something called 'terrorism'?[7] Linking together all violent acts under the label terrorism could provoke repression which is unnecessary and fatal to the type of society it is intended to maintain.

It is against this background that vague generalisations set in, born out of frustration at not being able to be more specific. Thus the phrase 'one man's terrorist is another man's freedom fighter' helps to delimit the boundaries of terrorism for purposes of academic research. Terrorism is also a moral problem and definitional attempts are predicted on the assumption that some classes of political violence are justifiable whereas others are not. For instance, many academic students of terrorism find little difficulty in labelling an event as 'terrorist' without making a moral judgement about the act.[8] Governments and lawyers and politicians find themselves unable to take such a detached view. It is hardly surprising that vacilations in policy characterise the responses of most individual states to terrorism, and there is complete failure of the international community to launch any effective multilateral initiatives to combat the problem. Even looking at the more general definition of violence (in relation to terror) it has been hard to encounter any pair of researchers in the field using the same definitions. There is not even any single tradition that has crystallised as the dominant one, with others competing for recognition.[9] Hence violence has been defined in terms of force, coercive power, authority and legitimacy.

One of the problems of implementing criminal sanctions concerns acts of terrorism that produce a terror outcome by threats of violence, without actual physical injury to any human or non-human target. Legislative efforts to create a crime of terrorism at the international or state level have to include a definition that realistically mirrors the terror process. An effort to punish terroristic conduct by using an overly broad definitional or jurisdictional focus (as simply murder, attempted murder, threats or assault) is unwise and unworkable in the long run. At the national level, an attempt to prosecute as 'terrorism' many types of conduct that produce no actual terror outcome would seem politically and functionally unwise and constitutionally unsound. It goes without saying that a generally accepted definition of terrorism requires an element of 'terror' and a coercive purpose.[10]

There is no consensus, nor even in many cases a recognition, that the discussion is carried out at cross purposes about subjects few have ever seen at the point of a gun. A paucity of data has never deterred the academic mind, rather, one suspects, the contrary. Thus attracted by the recent spurt of spectacular acts of violence, scholars have rushed into print almost as fast as the journalists, fashioning typologies, defining, explaining and usually prescribing. The definitional problem remains: who is a terrorist, and what is terrorism? The term is now pejorative, the label of the threatened. However, the world is full of situations where one group is pitted against another.

The Rand Corporation, which has kept an inventory of terrorist incidents for a number of years, believes that an objective definition of terrorism can be formulated. It it were not possible to formulate such a definition, there could be no chronology of terrorist acts and their analysis would be extremely difficult.

Terrorism is defined by the nature of the act, not by the identity of the perpetrators or the nature of their cause. All terrorist acts involve violence or the threat of violence, often coupled with specific demands. The violence is directed mainly against civilian targets. The motives are political. The actions are carried out in a way that will achieve maximum publicity. The perpetrators are usually members of an organised group, and unlike other criminals, they often claim credit for the act. And finally, the act is intended to produce effects beyond the immediate physical damage.[11]

The problem created is clear from the qualifying terms it uses—'often', 'mainly', 'generally' and 'usually'. These qualifiers allow for the injection of personal views in deciding whether a particular act is or is not 'terrorist'. On the other hand, defining terrorism by focusing on the nature of the act rather than on the identity of the perpetrators or the nature of their cause makes a substantial degree of objectivity possible. The Rand definition of terrorism implies that governments as well as individuals and groups may be terrorist. A survey of Rand chronologies indicates that very few examples of the use of terror by goverments against their own nationals are included. Furthermore, incidents generally are not listed in which terrorists operate within their own nation against their own countrymen.[12] For example, when Irishmen in Northern Ireland kill or otherwise terrorise each other the incidents are not included in the chronologies; when members of the Irish Republican Army kill Englishmen, the incidents are included.

The Central Intelligence Agency distinguishes between 'transnational terrorism' or 'terrorism' carried out by basically autonomous non-state actors, whether or not they enjoy some degree of support from 'sympathetic states', and 'international terrorism', which is terrorism carried out by individuals or groups controlled by a sovereign state.[13] Whether or not a particular terrorist act was financed by a 'sympathetic' state or commissioned by a foreign government is usually so difficult to determine that the distinction would seem to be meaningless in the real world. Did Gaddafi 'control' or merely 'support' Carlos the Jackal? If the answer to that question is known it is so only through using the most sensitive and classified sources and methods and is probably not available to any ordinary scholar. However, attempts by Congress to develop a viable definition of international terrorism have not, so far, yielded tangible results. Many definitions do not distinguish between common crimes and acts normally regarded as within the realm of international terrorism. For example, Section 202 of HR 1179, 'A Bill to amend the Internal Security Act of 1950 to control and penalise terrorists and for other purposes', defines 'crimes of terrorism' as:

> espionage, sabotage, kidnapping, extortion, skyjacking, robbery, bombing, holding a person prisoner or hostage or any threat or attempt to kidnap, extort, skyjack, bomb, or hold prisoners or hostages, or any threat to do any injury to a human being, animal or personal or real property or any conspiracy to do any of the above in order to compel an act or omission by any person, or any governmental entity.[14]

The United Nations has held discussions on terrorism for several years, and to this body the definition of a threat becomes feasible only when a particular activity, like skyjacking, becomes sufficiently onerous to a majority of the members of the three major blocs in the Organisation. In the case of terrorism, that stage has not yet been reached, judging by the failure of the UN General Assembly to agree on a definition of international terrorism. If the time ever comes when there is general agreement that international terrorism must be curbed, any definition adopted will have to be couched in universal, and not in pro-Western, terms. How to define the national security interests of the United States is a partially subjective question. However, it appears to focus attention where it is needed, on those terrorist acts which affect adversely American power, stability and security.

The UN argues that the imprecision of definition should not be allowed to render complete confusion desirable,[15] and that a definition can be useful in leading decision makers to a comprehensive consideration of varying claims to authority in varying contexts of the terroristic process with greater insight into content, greater rationality in choice, greater overall policy realisation and greater efficacy during the process of authoritative response.[16] Thus in the 1970s, the Secretary General's report on international terrorism reflected the need for a definitional approach by attempting to articulate certain basic definitional components.[17] These included terror outcome, instrumental or 'immediate' victims, primary targets, violence and political purpose. Divisions, political differences and sectional interests have prevented agreement on this topic. One of the central problems bedevilling international cooperation is the definition of terrorism. Because treaties are couched in legal terms they rely heavily on definitions acceptable to all parties. Debates on the subject have been acrimonious; in the 35-member UN General Assembly *Ad Hoc* Committee on Terrorism in its three prolonged sessions of 1973, 1977 and 1979, quarrels over the nature of innocence, acts of national liberation, modalities of state terrorism and motivation of actors have resulted in innocuous debates. Yet many member states of the UN believe terrorism to be an attack on the prevailing legal order, but are unsure how to respond. International terrorism can be distinguished from purely domestic terror/violence by the presence of an international jurisdictional element. Transnational terrorism, a term that is often used erroneously—as a synonym for international terrorism—can be considered a subclassification with specific reference to non-state, non-political actors. It is the confusion and misuse of terminology that has complicated, at least from the legal perspective, an already badly misunderstood phenomenon.

Although specially constituted UN committees have continually condemned acts of international terrorism in principle, they have exempted from the definition of such acts those activities that derive from 'the inalienable right to self-determination and independence of all peoples under colonial and racist regimes and other forms of alien domination and the legitimacy of their struggle, in particular the struggle of national liberation movements in accordance with the purposes and principles of the Charter and the relevant resolutions of the organs of the United Nations'. This exemption from the 1973 *Ad Hoc* Committee report on International Terrorism is corroborated by Article 7 of the UN General Assembly's 1974 Definition of Aggression. According to Article 7:

> Nothing in this definition and in particular Article 3 (inventory of acts that qualify as aggression) could in any way prejudice the right to self-determination, freedom and independence as derived from the Charter of peoples forcibly deprived of that right and ... particularly peoples under colonial and racist regimes or other forms of alien domination.[18]

The text of the US Draft Convention for the Prevention and Punishment of Certain Acts of International Terrorism clearly gives the impression that terrorism relates to any act performed by an individual or group of individuals that is designed to undermine the authority of a legitimate government or state. The Draft Proposal submitted by the Non-aligned Group of the *Ad Hoc* Committee on International Terrorism concerning the definition of international terrorism gives the equally clear impression that terrorism is related to the suppression of personal liberties of individuals by a ruling authority or military regime.[19]

Such opposing views of terrorism rely on the political context of the country providing the definition. In general, well-established, developed Western democracies are concerned with disruption of societal functioning by persons engaged in terrorist activity against the State, while relatively new 'under-developed' countries, often founded on the basis of revolution or protracted guerrilla activity, are concerned with oppression of indigenous populations and suppression or restriction of the freedom of dissent by repressive governments.

From the point of view of the United States, that country needs a capacity for coping with a wide variety of terrorist individuals and groups. Definitionally, terrorists, from their point of view, can be classified by type of perpetrator, motive and kind of action taken. How, for example, to define the national security interests of the United States is a partially subjective question. It appears to focus attention where it is needed, on those terrorist acts which affect adversely American power, stability and security. If the time ever comes when there is general agreement that international terrorism must be curbed, any definition adopted will have to be couched in universal, and not in pro-Western, terms. The Americans particularly would find this state of affairs hard to take. In law enforcement circles in the United States terrorism has come to be identified with the criminal mode of operation rather than with specific intent or motivation of the actors.[20] The United States see terror atrocities as senseless acts.[21]

Perhaps, in the absence of an international definition, the West will go it alone as a community and act as a group against terrorism. The Gordian Knot can be cut only by an independent framing or norms by democracies—terror is the deliberate intentional killing and maiming of innocent civilians, so as to inspire fear to gain political ends. Under the Northern Ireland (Emergency Provisions) Act 1973, for the first time in UK Statute Law, terror was defined as the use of violence for political ends, including any use of violence for the purpose of putting the public in fear.[22] This view was also held by Merlyn Rees, the then Ulster Secretary. Senator Henry Jackson and the Jerusalem Conference on International Terror defined terror as the deliberate, systematic murder, maiming and menacing of the innocent to inspire fear in order to gain political ends. Recently, consideration has again been given to whether democracies should convene a conference of all states which respect the principles of democracy and the rule of law. Especially useful would be the enforcement of an international convention against terrorism for which the European Convention on Terrorism would serve as a working model and which would cover the definition of terrorism as an international crime, the denial of political status for criminals so defined, common procedures for extradition, appropriate penalties and the exchange of evidence.

Governments often use the word 'terrorist' to describe their opponents, even when these opponents have not used violence. Guerrilla groups refuse to let themselves be seen by governments as terrorists and will prefer to call themselves guerrillas. The original use of the word as meaning someone who uses violence indiscriminately to achieve his ends can easily be forgotten.

While it is easier for governments than for terrorists to legitimate their activities, terrorists often strive for legitimacy. Governments are portrayed as having substantial resources, and as rational beings whose actions serve a longer goal, while individuals have little social claim and are typified by mearge resources and frugal modes of violence, coupled with an irrational drive and a deranged mind. The powerful in the Western world can label all sorts of violence against the State 'terroristic'. Despite the ambiguity and subjectivity that may surround an act of terrorism, there are certain characteristics that differentiate terrorism from other violent criminal acts. While the indiscriminate murders, maimings and mayhem associated with terrorism often appear to result from irrational behaviour by the terrorist, it is important to assume that violence, however barbaric, has its own rationality. This point may perhaps be difficult to accept but unless the responding forces and concerned officials do so, they will not be able to differentiate between terroristic violence and other forms of strife and will fail to understand the patterns that take place when the hostage-taker initiates an incident. Acts of terrorism are not to be treated as just another form of criminal violence.[23] Terrorism, by definition, is an act that seeks to influence a population significantly larger than the immediate target. Thus the quality of the public's understanding and its response to terrorism of all varieties is highly significant. One of the prime purposes of terrorist activity is to put a grievance on the public agenda. Ultimately, it is public opinion in a democracy that will help shape the political environment within which government officials must act.[24]

Thornton believes terrorism is the use of terror as 'a symbolic act' designed to influence political behaviour by extranormal means, entailing the use or threat of violence.[25] In this view an insurgent group has to disrupt the internal relationship between incumbents and citizenry. Here, there is concentration on its extranormal quality, which can be placed above political violence such as riots. It is the extranormal nature of the use of terror that distinguishes it from other forms of political violence. The problem with this situation is in defining extranormal. Thornton then characterises its highly symbolic content which contributes to its high efficacy. Both Thornton and May divide terror types into two: the enforcement and regime of terror which is the service of established order to suppress challenges to their authority, and the siege of terror or agitational terror in the hands of revolutionary movements who wish to disrupt existing order and ascend to political power themselves.[26] Both authors admit it is much easier to focus on a specific perpetrator than on an amorphous system. Groom is partly supportive in that he believes it is far easier to conceptualise the use of terror as a weapon to achieve a specific goal rather than as a form of regular and normal government.[27]

The terrorist seeks instant gratification from his abominable act and takes pleasure in the attention occasioned by the consequences of violence. According to Fromm, political terrorists are more interested in destruction than they are in creation. Not only do they hate their enemies, 'but their destructiveness is protection against life itself'.[28]

What distinguishes terrorism from pure criminality in the statutes of afflicted countries is the focus upon particular consequences rather than upon mere criminal intent—whether it be in Israel, West Germany, Italy or Spain. A concomitant view—and as the Rand Corporation reiterate regularly—is that once a group carries out a terrorist act it acquires the label 'terrorist', a label that tends to stick. Thus terrorism is a strategy whereby violence is used to produce certain effects upon a group of people. With special reference to substate terrorism this strategy is one of four 'ideal type' strategies, whereby a group out of power can effect violent social change, the other three being coup d'état, insurrection and guerrilla warfare.

To the terrorist the ends invariably justify the means. International conventions proscribing interference with air transport have had the effect of making aerial hijacking, for example, per se an act of terrorism.[29] Likewise, by international and regional conventions, as well as domestic statutes, attacks upon heads of state, certain specified government officials and diplomats are categorised as forms of terrorism.[30] The reasons for this derive from history, custom and tradition, but the end result has been to obscure the real nature of terrorist activity. The structural duality of terror/violence has also been a complicating factor. State or governmental terror has become far more pervasive and barbaric than individual or group terrorism. Only for the past two decades have social scientists been interested in terroristic violence. Some believed that it was a relatively rare phenomenon and others neglected it for different reasons.[31] In studying and comparing violence in many countries, a broad generalisation can be concluded—that a little repression increases instability whereas a great deal has the opposite effect. Nevertheless, in saying this, although a good case can be made for a comparative study of terrorism, it has to be apparent that not everything can be compared with everything else.

In considering the link between terrorism and violence, it becomes clearer that many of the definitional problems plaguing analysts of terrorism can be found back in the scientific and ideological discourse on violence. It has been defined in terms of force, coercive power, authority, legitimacy, behaviour, motives, intentions, antecedents and consequences. It has been defined in terms of violation, violation of corporal integrity, violation of territorial or special integrity, of moral and legal decency, of rules and expectations and even violations of self-esteem, dignity and autonomy.[32] The distance between the defining social scientist and the political defining agency or the common language definitions can be a source of frictions and misunderstandings. While an author might use a narrow definition of violence to start with, the reader belonging to either the political defining elite or to the common language users group is likely to forget about the 'given' definition in the course of reading and introduce his own meaning, in consonance with his interests and experience.

Looked at on a wider political scale, terrorism has been defined as violent criminal behaviour designed primarily to generate fear in a large part of the community for political purposes. When such behaviour hinges on the consciousness and concerns of the entire nation, then the nation becomes the community in the definition. The definition is deliberately 'innocentric', in that it labels as terrorists all those who use violent, criminal behaviour to attack the vital interests of Western countries. In the international forum neither the Soviet bloc nor most Third World countries would be likely to vote in favour of a definition geared to Western interests. The Soviet Union has an interest in trying to label all individuals and groups working against Western interests in a violent manner as 'freedom fighters' participating in 'wars of national liberation', not in terrorist acts. Many Third World countries achieved independence as the result of an armed struggle which typically began with terrorist acts, and as we have seen graphically in recent years, they are hardly likely to condemn many of the terrorists operating in the world today. Bearing in mind that not all violence is terrorism, but all terrorism is violence (psychologically as well as physically), there is a framework for defining terrorism as the use of force or the threat of force directed against innocent third parties for primarily ideological, financial or psychological purposes.[33] Innocence is the quintessential condition of terrorist victimology, for the terrorist victim is not the ultimate target. When political terrorists strike out at innocent third parties, their real intent is the destabilisation of governments and a demoralisation or even panic among the public-at-large. Anyone can be a potential victim, for to the idealist and the radical liberationist, no one is truly innocent. Thus one stands with the terrorists or against them; there is no middle ground.

While the term 'terrorism' is often indiscriminately used and it is difficult to use accurately in a strictly legal context, it raises little doubt in the mind of the man in the street. Though definitional precision is difficult, terrorism is not hard to describe and for those who have experienced it, easy to comprehend. Terrorism is thus an easily recognised activity of a bad character, subjectively determined and shaped by social and political considerations. The term is somewhat 'Humpty Dumpty'—anything we choose it to be.[34] An aspect which makes defining terrorism difficult, other than the involvement of varying nationalities and cultures, is that it may be committed for several purposes. Individual acts of terrorism may aim at wringing specific concessions such as the payment of a ransom or release of prisoners. Terrorism may also attempt to gain publicity; it may aim at causing widespread disorder, demoralising society and breaking down social order. Terrorism may target the deliberate provocation of repression, hoping to induce the government to self-destruct. It may be used to enforce obedience and cooperation; and, as we have seen in the Irish troubles, it is frequently meant to punish. Terrorists often declare the victim of their attack is somehow guilty.

No one desires to have the appellation terrorist applied to his activity. Terms such as 'freedom fighter' or 'liberator' are attempts to mitigate what is in fact an ugly profession. A fine line can be encountered between terror and terrorism with attempts to legalise or justify the former being made while proscribing the latter. Terror practised by a government in office appears as law enforcement and is directed against the opposition, while terrorism on the other hand implies open defiance of law and is the means whereby an opposition aims to demoralise government authority. While the terrorist group makes no pretence at legality, legitimate government must at least formally adhere to the law. In the absence of directly supporting legislation, governmental terror is made to appear justified by declaring a state of emergency and the issuing of decrees.[35] From a legal point of view there is nothing strange or incongruous about the dualism with which the phenomenon of terrorism is viewed. The true definitional struggle is between those who claim an exception at law for certain manifestly harmful acts and those who will not admit it. In this context, terrorism is more the why of an act than the what.[36]

International terrorism should be applied to groups or individuals controlled by a sovereign state if one takes into account the views expressed above. The term should not imply the existence of a 'terrorist international' in the sense of a body coordinating the activities of terrorists in different countries. No evidence of such a body has been discovered.[37] Transnational terrorism is carried out by basically autonomous non-state actors whether or not they enjoy some degree of support from sympathetic states.[38] The difficulty that surrounds accurate definitions of terrorism presents itself again in dealing with typologies. It can be viewed in three ways: committed or taking effect outside the territory of a state which the alleged offender is a national of; intended to damage the interests of a state or an international intergovernmental organisation; and committed neither by nor against a member of the armed forces of a state in the course of military hostilities.[39]

The term 'non-territorial' was coined when researchers found other terminology is lacking a precision needed to provide effective analysis. Non-territorial terrorism is defined as a form of terror not confined to a clearly delineated geographical area.[40] Today's terrorist is seen as having the potential of striking virtually anywhere at will since, due to modern technology, he is not limited by space or geographical area. While this definition removes barriers encountered in trying to squeeze a group into either the international or transnational definition, it removes in a sense all barriers encompassing any group and can be deemed by many critics as too broad.

The International Chiefs of Police see terrorism as a purposeful human activity primarily directed towards the creation of a general climate of fear designed to influence, in ways desired by the protagonist, other human beings and, through them, some course of events.[41] If the word 'political' is inserted between the words 'human' and 'activity' one avoids mixing terrorism with gangland intimidation or similar acts. Terrorism is directly concerned with the exercise or the attempt to exercise public powers or influence the allocation of values by a ruling body.

Definitional approaches which relate merely to 'acts of violence', the 'threat or use of violence', 'repressive acts' and similar categorisations are incomplete and unhelpful in terms of meaning and effective guidance for decision. Such approaches ignore the critical need for a focus upon the use of intense fear or anxiety for coercion of a primary target into behaviour or attitudinal patterns sought in connection with a demanded power outcome. In regard to a 'threat versus attempt' problem, each foreign definitional approach includes prohibitions of threat or is sufficiently broad to include any act, i.e., threat or attempt which produces prohibited outcomes. The only exception could be the Soviet Union. Efforts made to exclude forms of terrorism from community review by definitional exercise may be seen as attempts by claimants or sympathisers to place their preferred types of terrorism in a class of 'non-terrorism' which would remain permissible for all time and in all forms, regardless of consequences. Definitional exclusion does not seem likely to contribute to efforts to exclude entire contexts of social violence from legal regulation as in unsuccessful attempts to exclude situations of violence against 'aggressors', struggles of self-determination, violence and oppressors and 'guerrilla wars'. State guerrillas, belligerent guerrillas and insurgent guerrillas should not be used simplistically to exclude from consideration various types of terrorist strategy that can occur within or with such forms of social interaction. One should distinguish situations but not exclude them at the start of an enquiry by definitional exercise. This applies particularly in investigating the intertwined aspects of a variety of labels and events, e.g., guerrilla, state terrorism, self-determination, aircraft hijackings, 'oppression', diplomatic assassination, or kidnapping in connection with terrorism and the conflict in the Middle East, or the development of Euroterrorism.

In describing an act of terrorism, there must be a terror outcome, or else the process could hardly be labelled as terrorism. The judicial dividing line between fear and intense fear is very small. In many cases the type of strategy could well be prohibited under different normative provisions of the law of war. An attack upon or hijacking of a civil aircraft in the zone of armed conflict which produces no terror outcome among the crew, passengers or others may nevertheless violate prohibitions against attacks upon non-combatants or the taking of hostages as well as new international treaty norms governing hijacking. These kinds of attacks cannot properly be referred to as terrorism (perhaps attempted terrorism in some cases). Terrorism can also be precipitated by governments, groups or individuals. Consequently any exclusion of one or more sets of precipitators from the definitional framework are unrealistic. Definitional criteria which are also not respected refer to 'systematic' uses of violence. Terrorism can occur at an instant and by one act. Laws of war make no distinction between singular or systematic terroristic processes, governmental or non-governmental precipitations or governmental and no-governmental targets.

Those definitional approaches[42] which relate merely to 'acts of violence', the 'threat or use of violence', 'repressive acts' and similar categorisations are incomplete and unhelpful in terms of meaning and effective guidance for decision. These types of approach ignore the critical need for a focus upon the use of intense fear or anxiety for coercion of a primary target into behaviour or attitudinal patterns sought in connection with a demanded power outcome. Bluntly, they cannot help to guide us to effective and realistic responses to terrorism.

This response must be effective and foolproof, for terrorism's success is measured not only by the ability to topple social order but also to loosen that order in symbolic terms; by weakening the legitimating capacities of elected officials and casting doubt on the concept of rights in society and the obligations of the state.

There is a popular belief which perhaps terrorists wish to hold of their actions, that violent or lawless acts from skyjacking through indiscriminate bombing to ritualistic murder and politically inspired kidnappings, assassinations and the destruction of property, are simple manifestations of man's basic aggressive and destructive nature. Although the belief that man is by nature evil is an ancient idea, terrorists today perhaps see in this phrase an excuse for their actions. Terrorism appears to include practically any type of violence involving some interference with the general functioning of society, but does not seem to include gang fights, muggings and other such violent personal actions.

To the anarchist as terrorist the action itself was to bring society down by actions which destroyed symbols of the oppressive state. This belief in propaganda by the deed not only provided for the removal of an oppressive individual or institution, but would, it was hoped in these extremist circles, begin the unravelling of society.

Terrorism is not simply the act of a demented few, but represents a deeper academic impulse against repression in its most fundamental sense. Terrorism increases among political activists as well as among psychopaths in direct ratio to control and rationalisation to modern technological society and the seeming failure of other paths of revolutionary activity, that is, the failure of 'socialism' in the Soviet Union. To the New Left of recent memory the hero was the urban guerrilla with such violence-glorifying slogans as 'in order to get rid of the gun it is necessary to take up the gun'. Such slogans were reflected in their definitional language of violence. To many, the only viable morality was that which came from the muzzle of a gun—especially when working, say for example, in a police state. There is nothing specifically right wing or left wing about the repressive terror of police states. They come about when government rules by repressive terror rather than popular consent and when the security forces are allowed too much autonomy. But it is noteworthy that ideological regimes and in particular postrevolutionary regimes have been responsible for some of the worst repression. Terrorism in many communist-held areas of the Third World (where there has been an undeclared war against what is perceived as right-wing repression) has ranged from oral intimidation and 'home surveillance' to 'thought reform' in special camps, and execution.

The terrorists of today see no essential difference between the local authority they fight against and the diplomatic and commercial representatives of foreign powers. Many Third World governments see the anti-terrorist efforts of the West as part of a broader campaign aimed at outlawing irregular methods of warfare, and some current and recent Third World leaders were once called terrorists themselves and were used to leading insurgents. It is in Third World countries where one notices the process of terror as a compound of three elements: the act or threat of violence, the emotional reactions and the social effects.

Discussion about the Third World brings to the fore further problems in definitions as in this context, for example, terrorism cannot be a universal phenomenon and is a historical one emerging only at particular times and associated with particular developments in people's consciousness. Terror can be seen as a counter value campaign in terms of what is attacked, and a guerrilla campaign in terms of what is being defended. Conversely, Stohl believes that interpretive problems can be sidestepped by using an empirical definition of 'political terrorism' that makes no prior assumptions about what effects the users hope to accomplish by their actions or about how their would-be victims react.[43]

From a rational viewpoint an important question that has to be asked is—is this form of terrorism illegal? Moreover, one cannot try to define away certain types of terrorism as if they did not exist—this could be most unhelpful.[44] Nevertheless having made this statement, one has also to say that the introduction of the term 'transnational terrorism' has confused the definitional debate. Martha Crenshaw has argued that terrorism 'becomes transnational when it involves individuals of different nationalities'.[45] Some analysts believe this definition to be unnecessary because the term 'international' has never been restricted exclusively to intergovernmental relations as such and is generally used to apply to cultural, economic and other activities and transactions involving citizens from different countries. Other writers, including the author of this chapter, suggest a more specialised use of 'transnational', applying the designation to those terrorists who operate internationally with the express long-term aim of global revolution or establishing a revolutionary supranational world order.

To a large number of observers terror is by definition political. Changes sought by terrorists, short of total revolution, have to be achieved within a given political context, i.e., the government institutes reforms, the government falls or alternatively the government represses the terrorists. Although terror is in part political violence, not all political violence is in fact terrorism. No expert during the past two decades has been able to come forward effectively with a successful explanation of why terrorists terrorise, although several attempts have been made to do so. Many people are accustomed to definitions of terror that restrict activity to political violence,[46] and it is generally recognised in both law enforcement and media circles that the motivations behind an act are less important than the nature of the act itself.

As people have conflicting interests, the best hope is for a definition acceptable to social science analysts, leaving the political definition to parties involved in terror and counter terror. Terrorists rarely use the word terror at all (Carlos Marighela was exceptional in this regard) when referring to their own activities. There has to be, contrary to some views, a general definition of terrorism in order for legal powers to be effective. Confusions can be dissipated by categorising terrorism by factions, or state-sponsored terrorism.[47]

The definition problem is far more than an exercise in semantics.[48] Definition is being increasingly seen as a question of life or death, not a semantic exercise. While it is generally recognised that political terrorists know how to achieve their goals by dramatic acts, the responding forces often do not know that their own actions may define the roles of those whom they are facing. The subjective dimension of terroristic violence must be recognised. To define the response simply in terms of the police versus the criminals is to ignore the different motivations and training of criminals and political terrorists. Difficult decisions must be made that call for concerted action. Those who act must recognise that there is an ambiguity that cannot be eliminated by simple tactical solutions. Only common agreement can lead to the development of systematic research and analysis of particular types of violence. Vague, generalised definitions can mean that the scope of the analysis is too broad and so the findings may be meaningless. Too narrow a definition means there is little opportunity for comparative analysis which can show patterns common to a variety of acts of terrorism. Thus the force used can be deliberate and the goals, although limited, are nevertheless specific. Fear can be the chief weapon and the aims, political.

For the most part, each definition has yielded a limited understanding of the actual phenomenon. This is especially true when analysing the current wave of international incidents. To clarify meanings, many authors[49] have used case study approaches to analyse voluntary incidents, the hidden agendas and the critical issues that characterise terrorism as an activity defined in regard to the perspectives of different political groups. They feel the need for case studies as definitions of terrorism vary tremendously, both among governments and among researchers. Terrorism is seen as the apex of violence and once violence is defined in many researchers' views, an attempt can be made on the task of defining terrorism, when they are faced with the terms 'terrorist', 'freedom fighter', 'Partisan', 'commando', 'guerrilla fighter', which are often used interchangeably, although they all mean something different and each carries with it a value judgement.

Terrorism, if nothing else, is violence or threats of violence, but it is not mindless violence as some observers have charged. A terrorist campaign that causes a significant threshold of fear among the target population may achieve its aims. In some instances, terrorism is potentially more effective, especially from a cost–benefit perspective, than conventional or guerrilla warfare.[50] Unlike other forms of warfare, however, the goal of terrorism is not to destroy the opposing side but instead to break its will and force it to capitulate. Terrorism has changed the way most of us live, whether it be in Israel, Ulster or Sri Lanka. While indiscriminate violence may produce greater fear and alarm among the general population, selective but unpredictable attacks may cause greater alarm within the selected group. Put bluntly, terrorism is bit-by-bit genocide and we need no more to define genocide, but we have to substantiate the range and content of 'bit-by-bit' with all its penological and inter-state organisational implications. There also is clearly no consensus among the authors as to the specific differentiation between guerrilla and terrorist. The response to an act of terror or guerrilla activity can vary greatly depending on the danger of repetition and the degree of identification with the victim. If the observer identification is not with the victim but with the target of terroristic coercion it is unlikely to be terror or guerrilla activity, and if the identification of the observer is with the terrorist himself it might even be euphoria.

At the end of this chapter, I cannot offer a true or correct definition of terrorism. Terrorism is an abstract phenomenon of which there can be no real essence which can be discovered and described. Definitions serve as agreements on the way concepts should be used. The correct definition would be one consistently used by all users. Scholarly treatments of terrorism do not suggest that terrorism as a tactic is irrational or psychopathic. Terrorism is not mindless, but is a deliberate means to an end. It has objectives, a point often obscured by the fact that to the observer, terrorist acts are random and directed at killing those whose deaths can be of no value to the terrorist cause. The serious student has to decide how to treat the term—ignore it, or acknowledge that some useful distinction is possible between the types of violence if the concept is retained. The author of this chapter faced with the accusation of self-destruction on this topic, is fully aware that the study of terrorism has to find its way between vagueness and confusion, and the sterile, purist fixation on definitions *in isolation*, to make any progress at all. Definitions of terrorism have to be studied within the overall subject matter of terrorism and related to its history, philosophy, psychology, sociology, politics, statistics, language and law. It has become a pejorative term for both positive and negative reasons, but it can never be dismissed as a fad word. To treat it lightheartedly is to court disaster in a world of increasing uncertainty.

In the field of terrorism there is no agreement about any single definition, but there is considerable agreement about the main elements which definitions should contain. Based on the discussion in this chapter, the author has tentatively come to the following definition:

> Terrorism is an organised system of extreme and violent intimidation to create instability within democracies. International terrorists seek to launch indiscriminate and unpredictable attacks on groups (police, army, multinational, business etc.) or nations to change the politicoeconomic balance of the world.

Whether the view helps or is an improvement on other authors' definitions it is up to the reader to judge. On such a complex and controversial issue one can only hope to try and stimulate further thinking and research. In this humble way, authors of definitions of terrorism have tried to contribute towards the understanding of a complicated and urgent subject. An open mind and objectivity can be the best lessons learnt, and act as a guide for the future.

NOTES

1 AP Schmid, *Political Terrorism*, New Brunswick, USA: Transaction Books, 1983, p. 113.
2 *Ibid.* p. 113.
3 Abraham H Miller, *Terror and Hostage Negotiations*, p. 10.
4 DC Rapaport and Yonah Alexander (eds.), *The Morality of Terrorism—Religious and Secular Justification*, Oxford: Pergamon Press, 1982, p. xiii.
5 Benjamin Netanyahu (ed.), *International Terrorism.*
6 W Laqueur, 'Terrorism—A Balance Sheet', *Harper's Magazine*, March and November 1976, reprinted in W Laqueur, *The Terrorism Reader*, 1978, p. 262.
7 Grant Wardlaw, *Political Terrorism*, Cambridge: Cambridge University Press, 1982, pp. 1–17, for excellent discussion of the problems of defining terror.
8 *Ibid.*
9 This comment has been raised by J Galtung, *The Specific Contribution of Peace Research for Study of Causes of Violence*, Paris: UNESCO, 1975, p. 1.
10 AE Evans and JF Murphy, *Legal Aspects of International Terror*, Massachusetts; Lexington Books, 1978, p. 318.
11 Brian M Jenkins, *The Study of Terrorism: Definitional Problems*, Santa Monica, California: Rand Corporation, December 1980, pp. 2–3.
12 Alvin Hugh Buckelew, 'Terrorism and the American Response', PhD, California: Golden Gate University, 1982, p. 26.
13 David L Milbank, *International and Transnational Terrorism: Diagnosis and Prognosis*, Washington, DC: CIA, April 1976, pp. iii, 9.
14 Cited in E Nobles Lowe and Harry D Shargel (eds.), *Legal and Other Aspects of Terrorism*, New York: Practising Law Institute, 1979, p. 357.
15 F Cohen, 'Transcendental Nonsense and Functional Approach', *Columbia Law Review*, Vol. 89, 34, 1935.
16 J Paust, 'Responses to Terrorism: A Prologue to Decision Concerning Measures of Sanction', *Stanford Journal International Studies*, Vol. 12, 1977.
17 1972 US Doc. A/C6/418 pp. 6–7.
18 Rene Beres, *Terrorism and Global Security: The Nuclear Threat*, Westview: Special Studies on International Terrorism, 1979, p. 5.
19 Ronald D Crelinsten, Danielle Laberge-Altmejd and Denis Szabo, *Terrorism and Criminal Justice: An International Perspective*, Massachusetts: Lexington Books, 1978, p. 5.
20 Abraham H Miller, *Terrorism and Hostage Negotiations*, p. 11.
21 Benjamin Netanyahu (ed.), *International Terrorism*, p. 5.
22 *Ibid.* p. 277.
23 Stephen Sloan, *Simulating Terrorism.* Oklahoma: University of Oklahoma Press, 1981, pp. 14–15.

24 Miller, *op. cit.*, p. 57.
25 TP Thornton, 'Terror as a Weapon of Political Agitation', *in* H Eckstein (ed.), *Internal War*, London: Collier-Macmillan, 1964, p. 73.
26 WF May, 'Terrorism as Strategy and Ecstasy', *in Social Research*, 1974, Vol. 41, pp. 277–298.
27 AJR Groom, 'Coming to Terms with Terrorism', *British Journal of International Studies*, 1978, Vol. 4, p. 62.
28 Erick Fromm, *The Anatomy of Destructiveness*, New York: Holt, Rinehart and Winston, 1973, p. 201.
29 Robert A Friedlander, 'Banishing Fear from the Skies: A Statutory Proposal', *Duquesne Law Review*, Vol. 16, No. 3 (1977–78), pp. 283–286.
30 *Ibid. Terrorism: Documents of International and Local Control*, Vol. II, New York: Oceana Publications, 1979, pp. 521–525.
31 For an interesting discussion on these approaches, including one of the earliest definitions of terrorism by Hardman published in 1930, namely the method (or theory behind the method) whereby an organised group or party sought to achieve its avowed aims chiefly through the systematic use of violence, *see* Walter Laqueur, 'Interpretations of Terrorism', *in Journal of Contemporary History*, Vol. 12, No. 1, January 1977.
32 Schmid, *op. cit.*, p. 11.
33 RA Friedlander, *Terror-Violence Aspects of Social Control*, New York: Oceana Publications, 1983, p. 159.
34 WR Farrell, *The US Government Response to Terrorism: In Search of an Effective Strategy*, Boulder, Colorado: Westview Press, 1982, p. 6.
35 JBS Hardman, 'Terrorism', *The Encyclopaedia of the Social Sciences*, v. XIV, New York: Macmillan, 1964, p. 576.
36 One of the dangers embodied in the European Convention of 1978 is its potential for not concerning itself with the 'why' of a particular act. Blanket prohibition may be an over-reaction and exemplify deterrence through overkill. The several attached reservations tend to endorse this view.
37 While a central authority may be missing, there are many indications of cooperation between groups and open support from governments who support their objectives. A good example of this is the case of the Japanese terrorists who carried out the Lod Airport attack (1972). They had received training in Syria and Lebanon, received money passing through Germany, received their arms in Italy and carried out their act for the Popular Front for the Liberation of Palestine.
38 Given the element of governmental patronage that is common to both, the boundary between transnational and international terrorism is often difficult to draw. To the degree that it can be determined, the key distinction lies in who is calling the tune with respect to a given action or campaign. Hence groups can and do drift back and forth across the line. For example, even a one-time 'contract' job undertaken on behalf of a governmental actor by a group that normally acts according to its own rights qualifies as international terrorism.
39 The basis of this definition was taken from Article 1 of the Draft Convention for Prevention and Punishment of Certain Acts of International Terrorism, submitted by the USA to the UN General Assembly, 26 September 1972. If we were to concern ourselves with the particular groups we would seek to examine not only the site of the act but also such relevant aspects as the nationalities or foreign ties (i.e., training, funding, arms) of the group, sanctuaries, declared ideology and mechanics of the act's resolution.

40 Stephen Sloan and Richard Kearney, 'Non-territorial Terrorism: An Empirical Approach to Policy Formulation', *Conflict*, Vol. I, Nos. 1 & 2, 1978, p. 132. See also Sloan, *The Anatomy of Non-territorial Terrorism: An Analytical Essay*, Gaithersbury, Maryland: International Association of Chiefs of Police (IACP) Inc., 1978. Brian Jenkins makes reference to this same phenomenon when he describes terrorism as 'a warfare without territory, waged without armies as we know them. It is warfare that is not limited territorially; sporadic 'battles' may take place worldwide. It is warfare without neutrals, and with few or no civilian bystanders'. *International Terrorism: A New Kind of Warfare*, Report p. 5216. Santa Monica, California: Rand Corporation, June 1974, p. 1.

41 Farrell, *op. cit.*, p. 12.

42 Y Alexander and SM Finger (eds.), *Terrorism: Interdisciplinary Perspectives*, New York: McGraw Hill, 1977, pp. 18–25 provide analyses of the varied approaches to terroristic violence.

43 M Stohl (ed.), *The Politics of Terrorism*, New York: Marcel Dekker, 1979, pp. 24–25.

44 Alexander and Finger (eds.), *op. cit.*, p. 20.

45 Martha Crenshaw Hutchinson, 'Transnational Terrorism and World Politics', *The Jerusalem Journal of International Relations*, Vol. 1, No. 2 Winter 1975, p. 10.

46 Patrick J Montana and GS Roukis, *Managing Terrorism: Strategies for the Corporate Executive*, Quorum Books, 1983, p. 92.

47 For a general appraisal of this issue see Professor Paul Wilkinson's report on the Ditchley Park Conference in December, 1984. Ditchley Conference Report No. 5, 1984/85. 'How do Democratic States Cope with Terrorism'.

48 For one of the strongest arguments in favour of a definition, see Stephen Sloan, *Simulating Terrorism*, pp. 11–15.

49 For instance, Robert W Taylor and Harry E Vanden, 'Defining Terrorism in El Salvador: La Matanga', *Annals*, *AAPSS*, 463, September 1982, pp. 106–109.

50 Neil C Livingstone, *The War Against Terrorism*, Massachusetts: Lexington Books, D C Heath & Co., 1982, p. 4.

II

Moral and Religious Aspects

Liberation Theology, Politics and Violence in Latin America

R W Taylor

INTRODUCTION

It is impossible to avoid the conclusion that the serious economic, political and social problems confronting Latin America will continue to exist far into the next century. Massive poverty and blight will continue to characterise the area as exploitive and oppressive governments rule a peasant population. This is especially true in Central America where little if any industrialised complex exists. Poor public health and illiteracy still remain widespread and brutality in the form of state terrorism appears to be a condition of the political history of most nations. To make matters even worse, open conflict between factions within nations such as El Salvador, Nicaragua, Chile and Argentina threatens the involvement of the East–West superpowers.

Amidst this rather gloomy scenario grows a remarkably strong social movement embedded in the historical, religious and cultural roots of the area. This emerging force, known as the theology of liberation, provides the people with both a spiritual and physical uplifting, calling for action and serious social reflection.

It is the purpose of this chapter to examine the intertwinings of liberation theology, politics and violence in Latin America and to suggest a philosophical justification for the liberation movement.

POLITICS AND THEOLOGY

The theology of liberation has received little attention as a force for political and social reform in Latin America. Although religion and politics have been relatively inseparable in Latin American history, most scholars still fail to address the dynamic and dialectical relationship existing between these two cultural entities. Daniel H Levine writes that the relationship between theology and politics is 'both mutual and multifaceted'; mutual because religion and politics have evolved together taking material and symbolic support from one another, and multifaceted because they both embrace interinstitutional conflict and accommodation (such as 'church–state' relations) as well as more subtle exchanges whereby religious and political orders give legitimacy and moral authority to one another.[1] Excellent examples of this can be found throughout the colonisation period of Latin America where the zeal to 'convert' the native population of the area gave rise to political legitimacy, tyranny and imperialism.

In the past, 'religion' has referred to those activities which centred on belief and faith within church institutions. Traditionally, religion was viewed as an individual choice, a personal experience concerned with spirituality, cult, ritual and/or salvation. Politics, on the other hand, was left to describe the actions of government. Levine argues that these conventional usages are no longer sufficient to characterise the terms; that an important part of the dynamic relation between theology and politics in contemporary Latin America rests on the expanded and altered meaning of the terms themselves.[2]

Reflecting on the dimensions of the word 'politics' proves to be a conflicting and complicated exercise. In Latin America, nations began to achieve formal political independence from colonial rule (from Spain) more than a century and a half ago; yet today some are still engaged in defining 'independence'. The illustrative cases here have been El Salvador, Nicaragua, Chile, Bolivia and Argentina where the people were involved in rebellion against political bodies that maintained authority and legitimacy by force. Politics here did not describe the actions of government, for as the great political theorists and philosophers (such as Emerson, Thoreau, Hobbs, Locke, Rousseau, Marx and Sinclair) indicated, government only exists when people enter into an agreement to make one order, one society or one body politic for the good of the public. By reason then, those nations in conflict and revolution fail to meet the definition of 'politic' since no unified government actually exists.

There has been an over-riding interest on the part of writers to dwell on the empirical description and explanation of how Latin American political systems 'functioned or failed to function' throughout history.[3] Little attention has been paid either to Latin American politics as a tradition, or to the development crisis in Latin America from the vantage point of critical reflection on basic human values and rights.[4]

Theology too, has undergone a similar metamorphosis from individual to collective perspectives. This is especially true in Latin America where the economic and political contradictions of imperialism have had time to mature. The oppression of the people within a state by selected governmental bodies (state terrorism) has given rise to a relatively new type of religious–political motivation. Starting with Paulo Friere's classic work in 1968, the poor and oppressed have been called to action.[5] Friere virtually revolutionises the concept of education: since culture is a creation of man, then education should be the subversive process by which people create their own culture and their own government.

Friere's analysis links historical exploitation with what he labels 'conscientizacao' or a move towards destiny and power on the part of oppressed people. His work is one of the first to place theology in the light of praxis and away from the classical or traditional perspective of the tasks of religion.

Yves Congar points out that early concepts of religion and theology were closely linked to the spiritual aspects of life, above all being monastic and removed from worldly concerns; the ultimate goal of theology being to attain a life of spiritual perfection ending in an everlasting sanctity approaching divinity.[6] Some break from this perspective arose during the twelfth century with the writings of St Thomas Aquinas. His essential contribution viewed theology as an intellectual discipline, born of the meeting of faith and reason whose main function was to develop a rational knowledge on which to understand life.[7]

Today, Latin America is embroiled in a controversial movement stemming from the writings of Paulo Friere, Camillo Torres and Gustavo Gutierrez and involving the refinement or re-definition of Christian belief. Gutierrez' treatise on the theology of liberation integrates several Marxian thrusts. First, Christian life is viewed as a 'praxis' or involvement in the transformation of this world.[8] Communion with the Christ inescapably means a life centred around commitment of service to others, and necessarily the uplifting (economic and socioculturally) of individuals oppressed throughout the world.[9] Secondly, theology is reflection, a critical attitude focusing on praxis. This reflection calls for a 'liberating theology, a theology of the liberating transformation of the history of mankind'.[10] Regarding Latin America, Gutierrez states that the root causes of oppression exist because of the economic, social, political and cultural dependence of some countries upon others—an expression of the domination of some classes over others. The only hope for renewal is liberation:

> Only a radical break from the status quo, that is, a profound transformation of the private property system, access to power of the exploited class, and a social revolution that would break this dependence would allow for the change to a new society.[11]

The Western world looks upon this philosophy as provoking violence and terrorism. Further, the United States government links such a philosophy with involvement from the Soviet Union and Cuba.[12] Religion, therefore, and politics are once again inseparable entities in Latin American history as the theology of liberation is maligned as an ideology to foment revolution, aided and abetted by the Societ Union.

LIBERATION THEOLOGY AND SOCIAL REFORM

In 1968, the Council of Latin American Bishops met in Medellin, Columbia. The conference had a significant influence not only within the Catholic

Church, but also on the formation of socioeconomic and political issues surrounding Latin America. In particular, the episcopate addressed the subject of change in Latin America and the role of the Church in social reform. Medellin deeply and thoroughly analysed the reality of Latin America and, from the standpoint of faith, legitimised the current process of socioeconomic change and the promotion of justice and peace throughout the area.[13] This was a critical juncture from the past, as the Church took a more radical position on social issues and their demand for change. This attitude had been, previous to that date, only the emanations from 'Marxist groups' or Catholic orders espousing a liberation of theology doctrine.

However, as important as Medellin's official stance was in 1968. Dodson suggests that the real value came in the stimulation of critical reflection and radical activism following the conference; the greatest single source of religious innovation was the direct experience of clergy involved pastorally and socially with the poorest sectors of Latin American society.[14] Dodson contends that the theology of liberation essentially grew out of the Church's involvement with the working-class poor, both urban and rural, in Latin America. He writes:

> This involvement began quietly and modestly in the early 1960's as a result of worker-priest programs in such countries as Argentina, Chile, and Uruguay. As the Church seemed to be losing contact with the masses, particularly in the cities, bishops in many dioceses supported a plan for parish priests to take employment in factories and workshops in order to get closer to working people, gain a better understanding of their needs, and develop an appropriate pastoral ministry. The case of Argentina is a good illustration of the results of the project. For most worker-priests direct involvement was a profoundly unsettling experience. They soon realised that the Church was alienated from the poor, and they began to see both religion and the social order through a Marxian lens. Their church appeared as an agent of pacification and cooptation in the absence of any effort to change or draw attention to the real-life situation of the poor and the structural causes responsible for their plight. The clergy, in short, became radicalised by their experience; and those who wished to bring about changes from within the Church had to reassess the priestly vocation, the mission of the Church, and the very meaning of faith itself.[15]

Thus, according to the Medellin Conference, the liberation of man must be total: God sent his Son 'so that He might come to liberate all men from ... hunger, oppression and ignorance ... from the injustice and hatred which have their origins in human selfishness'.[16] The word 'liberation' is often found in Medellin documents to indicate the process of helping man free himself from the oppressiveness often found in Latin American countries. The documents have strong words aimed at the laity in Latin America with the challenge to 'liberate men from cultural, social, economic, and political slavery, all of which oppose development'.[17]

The theology of the liberation movement finds support in Vatican II and the writings of Pope John XXIII. The 'revolutionary' character of the Second Vatican Council expressed, for the first time in history, a social conscience. In one of its central documents, *The Pastorial Constitution on the Church in the Modern World*, the Council indicated that the Church has a role of being a 'servant . . . to read carefully the signs of the times and to discern in worldly action what God is asking it to do'.[18] Certainly, the call to praxis is evident in this document. Then too, the impact of the *Pastorial Constitution* was amplified by John XXIII's second encyclical, *Pacem in Terris*.[19] A detailed defence of human rights appears in its opening sections, including a defence of the dignity and rights of women, of minorities and of the right to live in a free and unoppressed world. McNamara states that subsequent social teachings within the Church by John's successor, Paul VI, reaffirm these themes and become even more appropriate to Latin America.[20] Specifically, Paul VI's encyclical letter entitled *Populorum Progressio* hails the Church's 'conscience' in the Third World; reaffirming the social character of private property and the expropriation of the 'manifest wrong' this inflicts on specific countries.[21] Further, the letter strongly rejects 'private ownership as the means of production as an absolute right that has no limit and carries no corresponding social obligations'.[22] The major principle expressed within the document focuses on the idea that economic growth is not synonymous with social development but requires efforts to establish conditions promoting the total growth of individuals as persons and assuring a wider distribution of income among all strata of society, especially in Latin America.[23]

From the Western eye, these statements contradict the historical non-involvement in secular politics which the Church has traditionally followed. Not until the 1960s did the Catholic Church ever call for direct action or even passive resistance in political movements attempting to achieve social reform or social justice. The Church has now defined social justice as the fair distribution of material and non-material wealth (to include land) and rewards among all peoples within a society.[24] An interesting point here is that some scholars believe that these recent changes in the Church are part of a 'new church' in a modernisation role. Turner points out for example, that the Church in Latin America has been at the forefront of the struggle for social justice and that most recently there has been a breakdown of the centralised authority leading to a development of pluralism.[25] Certainly, some 'radical' priests or groups of priests, such as Camillo Torres and Archbishop Arturo Romero, have proven to be salient leaders or even martyrs which gives legitimisation for the new social teachings of the Church in Latin America. According to Turner, these developments and teachings are authentically Latin American and not so much the result of impositions from Rome.[26] I seriously question the saliency of Turner's hypothesis, especially after reviewing the political actions and statements of the current Pope, John Paul II, regarding the social unrest in Poland, Afghanistan and India. There can be no doubt in John Paul II's attention to the conditions of humankind under oppressive regimes throughout the world, notwithstanding Latin America.

LIBERATION THEOLOGY, VIOLENCE AND TERRORISM

While the theology of liberation has been mostly a Catholic movement in Latin America, there are indeed a significant number of Protestant clergy emerging as leaders in this arena. One such spokesman is Jose Miquez Bonino who has attempted to parallel the new Christian ideology with Marxist-oriented movements. He describes this linkage as follows:

> It rejects the 'developmentalist' attempt to solve Latin American problems with the capitalist international system ... instead, it envisages a breaking away from the domination of the 'empires' though not necessarily an isolation from them.
>
> Elimination of dependence (on major capitalist nations) is impossible without a parallel revolution in the social structure of Latin American societies.
>
> Development is not seen as merely economic or structural change; rather, there is a strong emphasis on the human dimension. A Marxist revolutionary like Guevara and Christians like Dom Helder Camara or Camilo Torres are at one on this point: liberation is the process through which and in which a 'new man' must emerge, a man shaped by solidarity and creativity over against the individualistic distorted humanity of the present system.[27]

Although most leaders of the liberation movement espouse a moderate and non-violent strategy for reform, there is considerable support for the use of violence. In Medellin in August 1968, over 900 priests and bishops endorsed the following statement:

> We cannot condemn an oppressed people when it finds itself obliged to use force to liberate itself ... under no circumstance should the unjust violence of the oppressors, who maintain this odious system, be compared with the just violence of the oppressed.[28]

Then too, Camillo Torres' total conviction to the liberation movement and subsequent guerrilla resistance in Columbia led to widespread acceptance of violent revolution as a means to achieve social justice. Fabio Vasquez said of Torres:

> He united the scientific conception of revolutionary warfare, considering it the only effective way to develop the fight for freedom, with a profound Christianity which he extended and practiced as a limitless love for the poor, the exploited and oppressed and as a complete dedication to the battle for their liberation.[29]

This same perspective on the unity of Christian and Marxist liberation has been vocalised within the Sandinista Revolution in Nicaragua. Documented examples of participating Christians—both lay and clergy—can be found as integral parts of the Sandinista National Liberation Front (FSLN) and the Government of National Reconstruction in Nicaragua. This appears to be a logical outgrowth of the theological movement as dedicated Christians participated in the struggle against the Somoza dictatorship.

What appears to be most distressing is the over-riding insistence on the part of some Western nations, that the move to armed struggle against oppression is some type of 'terrorism'. Theoretically, terrorism encompasses the threat and/or use of violence for the purpose of achieving a specific set of political objectives or goals.[30] Is then, the movement of liberation theology a motivator towards revolution, and subsequently a strategy for terrorism? Where does revolution end and terrorism begin? Or better yet, when is revolution justified?

In an earlier work, I argue that 'terrorism' is a label placed on individuals or groups of individuals to cloud factual issues surrounding social reform in Latin America; that hidden agendas (from East–West involvement) focusing on national security concerns, political economic motivations and media exploitation tend to distort the sovereign interests of people. Indeed, associated names like 'terrorist', 'communist-supported revolutionaries' and 'Marxist guerrillas' are labels which tend only to heighten ideological sentiment and play to emotion rather than intellect.[31] In Latin America, these labels often represent those striving for social justice from the liberation perspective.

LIBERATION THEOLOGY, FREEDOM AND DEMOCRACY

The critically important linkage here is that the very qualities embodied in a democracy are represented in the theology of the liberation movement. The concept of freedom as a social state in which all men are free from alienation, servitude and oppression is a genuine characteristic prescribed by the ideals of democracy. In the liberation movement, freedom is inseparably connected with history, and some political theorists give support to this concept. For Hegel, 'world history is the progression of the awareness of freedom'.[32] In Latin America, we see a history replete with violence and revolution gradually evolving to a society wherein the people of each nation are only now starting to grasp the reins of their own destiny—freedom. In almost every case in history, freedom has been the result of revolution or violent social reform.

To some Western philosophers, such as Hobbs and Locke, violence is treated as the antithesis of freedom and political choice; a form of archaic realm of the state of nature. Hobbs and Locke saw politics as an attempt to create a tool to avoid violence and revolution, and thereby make freedom and civilisation possible. But what if 'civilisation' as expressed by Hobbs and Locke does not exist? At best, the history of Latin America expresses a decline in the growth of civilisation—from the annihilation of the great Inca, Mayan and Aztec culture to the most recent genocide of the Mestizo Indians. I argue that civilisation and hence freedom, by the standards of Hobbs and Locke, has never flourished for Latin American people since the imposition of colonial rule in the New World.

Further, some of the post-war philosophy of violence derived from Nietzsche through Heidegger, and widely populated by Sartre, finds some credence in Latin America.[33] It is Sartre who identifies certain types of political framework, such as dictatorships and suppressive regimes, as the equivalent of 'violence', thus justifying violent correctives, terrorism from the left and revolution. Sartre further expresses violence as a liberation process for the oppressed. Unfortunately his writings, along with those of Frantz Fanon, tend to breach the realm of justification for rational men. Fanon inaccurately expresses violence as a 'cleansing force' that frees the oppressed from their inferiority complex, their despair and inaction.[34] This type of ideology symbolises radicalism and justifies violence and terrorism as positive and almost creative expressions in social reform—a justification not expressed in the liberation of theology movement as founded in Latin America.

The profound basis of liberation theology is rooted in the democratic ideal. Man is a child of God, and as such demands the freedoms of expression and equality so universal to his creation and existence. In some countries in Latin America, this human destiny is thwarted by repressive governments and imperialistic nations.

CONCLUSION

If one reads the texts of the theology of liberation one might get the impression that there is no room for the existential, personal dimensions of life. With all of the talk about social, economic and political change, about global structures, there seems to be an overlooking of individual anxiety and reflection.[35] Alves argues that we are 'born into a world that is alienated from our true desires, a repressive world that imposes itself on us with inflexible cruelty . . . a world characterized by man's selfishness and materialism; that we are the function of a material, profit-oriented social game'.[36] Liberation theology offers a philosophical base and justification for man's freedom amidst such a world. Its aim is to transform this world. The concept of 'reflection' is both a moral obligation on the part of those in power as well as a deep-seated reassessment of one's own personal faith and testimony as a Christian.

In Latin America, the theology of liberation movement is aligned with the weak and oppressed, the exploited and the poor. It gives direction for the building of a better world, and as we have seen throughout history, this rebuilding may involve violent social reform and revolution.

However, what is most unfortunate, is the insistence on the part of some scholars to group indiscriminately the liberation theology movement with radical terrorism and to dismiss totally the legitimate grievances of a sovereign people. There is a careless linking of the movement with a moral justification for murder and terror—a position denied by the theology of liberation. There seems to be a juxtaposition of arguments: on one hand the yearnings for freedom and democracy within a repressive state and on the other, a naivety that such a condition will evolve simply over time and without action. It is ridiculous to assume the latter.

Further complication is added by those who inaccurately state that the liberation of theology movement is an outgrowth of the urban insurgency movements during the 1960s (in Latin America). Careful investigation reveals that the urban variation of guerrilla warfare proposed by Che Guevara is quite different to the proposition set forth in the liberation movement. Unlike Guevara's strategy to use terrorist tactics such as bombings, robberies, kidnappings and assassinations to strike at the heart of the enemy, the liberation movement strives to develop a political infrastructure and mobilisation of the masses through a historical, cultural and religious ideology. Some Western nations use this linkage in an effort to discredit the entire movement. However, the theology of liberation does not reject politics as a means to resolve community conflict and it does not attempt to use indiscriminate violence as a political weapon.

The final important point to be re-emphasised here is that terrorism is often incorrectly associated with the left wing and is supposedly always revolutionary in character. This is simply not true. State terrorism consists of actions conducted by a nation–state within its own borders.[37] The unusually high number of missing persons, the formation of 'death squads' and the imposition of military rule in some Latin American countries point to this type of terror. Scholars and government officials alike need to reassess their definition and perception of terrorism in Latin America and focus on the philosophical justification of the liberation movement.

NOTES

1 Daniel H Levine, 'Religion and Politics, Politics and Religion', *Journal of Inter-American Studies and World Affairs*, Vol. 21, No. 1, February 1979, p. 5.
2 *Ibid.*, p. 7.
3 Michael Dodson, 'Prophetic Politics and Political Theory', *Polity*, Vol. 12, No. 3, Spring 1980, p. 390.
4 *Ibid.*
5 Paulo Friere, *Pedagogy of the Oppressed*, New York: Seaburg Press, 1968.
6 Yves Congar, 'Theologie', Foie et Theologie, *Situation et Taches*, Tournai: Desclee, 1962.
7 See C Dumont, SJ, 'La reflexion sur la methode theologique', *Nouvelle Revue Theologique*, Vol. 83, December 1961, pp. 1034–1050 and Gustavo Gutierrez, *A Theology of Liberation*, Maryknoll, New York: Orbis Books, 1973, p. 5.
8 Gustavo Gutierrez, *A Theology of Liberation*, p. 9.
9 *Ibid.*, p. 11.
10 *Ibid.*, p. 15.
11 *Ibid.*, pp. 26–27.

12 President Ronald Reagan, 'US Interests in Central America', Department of State Current Policy No. 576. Washington, DC: USGPO, 9 May 1984.
13 Renato Poblete, 'From Medellin to Puebla: Notes for Reflection', *Journal of InterAmerican Studies and World Affairs*, Vol. 21, No. 1, February 1979, p. 35.
14 M Dodson, 'Prophetic Politics and Political Theory', p. 394.
15 *Ibid.*, p. 395.
16 G Gutierrez, *A Theology of Liberation*, p. 110.
17 Synod of Bishops (CELAM), Second General Assembly, *Justice in the World*, 30 November 1971, par. 1,4,7.
18 John Coleman, 'Political Theology—Its Roots, Branches, and Growth, *National Catholic Review*, February 3, 1963.
19 Pope John XXIII, 'Pacem in Terris', *in* Joseph Gremillion (ed.), *The Gospel of Peace and Justice: Catholic Social Teaching Since Pope John*, Maryknoll, New York: Orbis Books, 1976, par. 112.
20 Much of this section has been adapted from Patrick H McNamara, 'Conscience, Catholicism and Social Change in Latin America, *Social Research*, Vol. 46, Summer 1979, p. 335.
21 Pope Paul VI, 'Populorum Progressio', *in* Joseph Gremillion, *The Gospel of Peace and Justice*, par. 26.
22 *Ibid.*
23 H McNamara, 'Conscience, Catholicism and Social Change in Latin America', p. 336.
24 Hubert Schwan and Antonio Ugalde, 'Orientations of the Bishops of Columbia toward Social Development, 1930–1970', *Journal of Church and State*, Vol. 16, Autumn 1974, p. 473.
25 Federick C Turner, *Catholicism and Political Development in Latin America*, Chapel Hill, North Carolina: University of North Carolina Press, 1971, pp. 4, 216–217.
26 *Ibid.*, p. 195.
27 Jose (Bonino) Miguez, *Doing Theology in a Revolutionary Situation*, Philadelphia, Pennsylvania: Fortress Press, 1976, p. 40.
28 Synod of Bishops (CELAM), *Justice in the World*, par. 10.
29 Fabio Vasquez, noted in John Gerassi, *Revolutionary Priest: Camillo Torres*, New York: Vantage Books, 1971, p. 31.
30 Richard Schultz, 'Conceptualizing Political Terrorism: A Typology', *Journal of International Affairs*, Vol. 4, Spring/Summer 1978, p. 8.
31 Robert W Taylor and Harry E Vanden, 'Defining Terrorism in El Salvador: "La Matanza", *The ANNALS*, American Academy of Political and Social Science, Vol. 463, September 1982, pp. 108–109.
32 Alexandre Kojeve, *Introduction to the Readings of Hegel*, New York: Basic Books, 1969, p. 48.
33 Paul Johnson, 'The Seven Deadly Sins of Terrorism', *in* Herbet M Levine, *World Politics Debated*, New York: McGraw-Hill Books, 1983, p. 249.
34 Frantz Fanon, *The Wretched of the Earth*, New York: Grove Press, 1963, p. 10.
35 Rubem Alves, 'Personal Wholeness and Political Creativity: The Theology of Liberation and Pastoral Care', *Pastoral Psychology*, Vol. 26(2), Winter 1977, pp. 134–135.
36 *Ibid.*
37 Richard H Schultz, Jr, and Stephen Sloan, *Responding to the Terrorist Threat*, New York: Pergamon Press, 1980, p. 2.

Religious Violence in Islam: Towards an Understanding of the Discourse on *Jihad* in Modern Egypt

R C Martin

The problem of violence and religion has been largely ignored by historians of religions and religious studies specialists. Most of the literature on the association of religious groups with violent acts has been written by social scientists and public policy experts. This chapter contends that the near silence of historians of religions on this problem is lamentable and argues that it is unjustified. Although 'violence and religion' is a current topic in the marketplace of ideas, much of the analysis to date provides little understanding of religion as such, the importance of ritual, symbol and myth for human religious behaviour. Historians of religions tend to describe something they regard as true or essential religion and consequently to dismiss manifestations of violence as aberrant behaviour and thus not 'essentially' religious. History overwhelmingly confutes such idealism.

Violence in the Middle East is often associated with the Muslim doctrine of *jihad*, which is usually translated 'holy war'. Like many religious terms which connote violence (e.g., sacrifice, victim, retribution, divine wrath etc.), jihad can be understood in the broader semiotic context of the religious discourse and world views from which it derives its specific cultural meanings. The historical contexts in which the call for jihad has been efficacious provide case studies for the analysis of religious attitudes towards and justifications of violence in some quarters of Islamic society. This chapter seeks to explain fundamental aspects of religious world views in Islamic texts and cultural symbolism, which are the necessary framework for specific discourses on violence in Islamic social history.[1]

A well-known case of religious and political violence—one in which specific interpretations of jihad formed a discourse of power leading up to the event—was the assassination of Anwar al-Sadat, President of Egypt, in October 1981. Viewed widely during the aftermath and explained since as the work of militant Muslim extremists, Sadat's murder has been assessed primarily in terms of its impact upon Western political interests and the implications for further violence. Attempts to understand its significance within the context of Muslim world views in Egypt have received less attention.[2] A recent study of the background to the Sadat assassination and other acts of violence between Muslims and Coptic Christians in Egypt at the same time has been published by Gilles Kepel.[3] Kepel traces the development of a discourse on power, including the role of jihad, within the Muslim Brotherhood, principally by Sayyid Qutb, with later variations among ideologues and activists in different sociocultural contexts in Cairo and in Middle Egypt, principally the city of Asyut. The life and thought of Sayyid Qutb forms a key ingredient of the analysis in the latter part of this chapter. In order to understand better the senses in which the violent action against the Egyptian government and the Copts was justified by Sayyid Qutb and his followers but abhorred by others (ironically on similar religious grounds), it is necessary to first explore the general doctrine of jihad in terms of the semiotics of Muslim world views.

THE QURANIC BACKGROUND TO MUSLIM NOTIONS OF JIHAD

The Muslim term *jihad* invokes a large semantic field which connotes *inter alia* 'holy war'[4] but is more broadly understood by the notion of 'striving in the path of God'. The Qur'an contains this and related phrases concerning the path or way of God (*sabil allah*) in about 180 verses, clearly a major theme. Striving in the path of God, in turn, is a particular instance of a basic principle implicit in the Quranic cosmology. Therefore, understanding jihad must begin with a brief assessment of the cosmography of the Qur'an, by which I mean the textual expressions of the structure of the cosmos, the main actors within it and their dynamic interaction and communication, which are presented in the Qur'an, the canonical scripture of Muslims.

The Qur'an is a text, meant to be recited aloud following carefully learned and practised rules. For many Muslims with little or no literacy, the oral text has been the only form available for reference in world view formation. The text is replete with noticeable patterns, formulae and cadences at many levels. At the surface level of the text, even the untrained ear hears some of the richly textured repetion of phrases, similarly inflected, and words following the same morphology, which trained reciters are able to enunciate to dramatic affect and effect. Indeed, the text provides a vast arsenal of phrases which come quickly to mind for traditional Muslims in the face of common social–psychological experiences, such as fearing, anxiety, entreating, warning, condoling, congratulating, cursing and so on.[5] Although the majority of Muslims in the world are not native speakers of Arabic, and Arabs generally do not discourse in the archaic language of the sacred text, nonetheless, through socialisation children learn to quote appropriate Arabic religious phrases—most of them Quranic—inserted into vernacular rhetoric and discourse. The socially reproduced world views[6] which characterise Muslim ways of thinking in turn evince the formulaic elements of the Quranic cosmology.

In the Qur'an, two realms of being animate the cosmos. They are referred to in various spatial and temporal categories such as the seen and the unseen, the phenomenal or here-and-now and the hereafter. The beings who dramatise the Quranic cosmography correspond to the realms of being and are fundamentally divided between God (*Allah*) and humankind (*insan*), the latter of whom are helped or hindered by other agents and actors, such as angels, satans and the jinn. The inherent conflict between angels and satans in the heavenly unseen sphere(s), reflecting those who obey God and those who disobey, gets worked out in the phenomenal sphere of humankind, which also is divided between those who submit and do the will of God, including the performance of divinely prescribed religious duties (literal meaning of *muslim*) and who believe (*mu'min*), and those who disbelieve and act ungratefully (*kuffar*, sing. *kafir*). Believers, for example, are 'those who expend their wealth in the path of God'[7] while unbelievers go about giving the lie to God's signs and messengers and leading believers astray.[8] An ambiguous but frequently mentioned class of human beings in the Qur'an pretends to believe but actually consorts with satans and works against divine purposes.[9]

Into this cosmologically framed drama of the *muslim/mu'min* striving in the path of God, constantly against humanly and satanically inspired attempts to thwart and lead astray, God has sent prophets (of whom Muhammad was the last and seal), to warn their peoples to fear God and obey the teachings and guidance of the prophets. The Quranic theme of past communities rejecting their prophets and of divine retribution against such communities establishes the context of Muhammad's mission to the seventh-century Arabs, which is referred to throughout the Qur'an but not developed in continuous narrative form. The privilege of Islam and hence of the Muslim *umma* 'community' is the finality of the Qur'an, 'sent down' to the Arabs in a miraculously inimitable form of their native Arabic tongue through the Angel Gabriel, with Muhammad serving as the historical mouthpiece. The narrative of Muhammad's 'historical' role as prophet in Mecca and Medina is represented primarily in biographies of the Prophet,[10] and in a genre of Quranic commentary known as the 'occasions of sending down' (the revelations).[11]

Another aspect of religious studies analysis of such concepts as 'jihad' is that the events of the Qur'an, framed largely by the mission of the Prophet Muhammad to Mecca and Medina between AD 610 and 632, must be seen as paradigmatic for Islamic history generally. In the Muslim world view, in some crucial sense one must see and understand 'that' history in order to understand 'this' history: what happened to the Prophet and his followers places important perspective on what is happening here and now in the context of one's own striving in the path of God. The generic character of Quranic speech and the indefiniteness of referents easily allows the primal reference to the *umma* or community established by Muhammad to refer also to one's own contemporary experience. The Quranic *jahiliyya* or time of religious ignorance prior to Islam can also refer to contemporary non-Muslim cultures which, like the ancient communities mentioned in the Qur'an, reject

Allah and His prophets, or to secular governments ruling over Muslims; the *shirk* or polytheism of Arabia proscribed by the Qur'an can also refer to contemporary forms of Islamic secularism, modernism or other deviations from a putative purer interpretation of Islam. A more specific application of this thesis will be made regarding the Muslim Brotherhood ideologue of reform in Egypt, Sayyid Qutb, in the latter part of this chapter.

If it is possible to say that one can't, as a Muslim, properly understand this (that is, one's own) history unless one understands the determinative history of the prophet, one can also say that one can't understand that history except by reference to one's own horizon of understanding, say, in Tripoli, or South Beirut or Tehran in the 1980s. This is what Martin Heidegger referred as the 'preunderstanding' which readers bring to a text; interpretation involves the dialectic or 'hermeneutical circle' which archs from reader/hearer to a text produced by a writer/speaker and back, generating the interpretive process.[12]

Finally, the analysis of the Quranic cosmology for what it might say about violence in Muslim world views provides at this level a set of verbal symbols—what semioticians, such as Thomas Sebeok, call textual constituents[13]—which do not in and of themselves generate violent or any other form of human behaviour. The historian of religions is conducting his or her analysis below the surface of the text at this stage. Although what has been said thus far might lead one to suspect that expressions of violence in Islamic societies could be traced to the Quranic cosmological dynamics between the forces of the seen and unseen worlds, Islamic historical examples of love, dignity and peace-making acts have the same cosmological basis, as will be shown in the next section on jihad in the discourse of Islamic mysticism and piety. Hayden White has argued that the processes by which, say, sex becomes transformed into sexuality and then mythologised into rituals of love in a human society, or how aggression becomes transformed into violence and mythologised into rituals of sacrifice, require us to analyse the discourses of mastery and control.[14] Violence does, of course, exist among Muslim peoples as it does in all human societies. To the extent that historians of religion have something to contribute towards understanding violence, the task is to analyse it within the framework of religious world views as evidenced by religious texts and their worldly contexts.

Having constructed an interpretive backdrop, the problem now is to explore semantics of jihad and related notions, around which violent behaviour may form its discourse. The argument moves, then, from the cosmographical structure of the Quranic text to its semantics, as employed by Muslims in discourse about jihad. Social, historical contexts now come more directly into play.

SEMANTIC ASPECTS OF JIHAD FI SABIL ALLAH

In Quranic cosmology, as we have seen, that basic group of humans who submit to the will of Allah and believe in His religion (*din*) and obey His messengers must strive in the Path of Allah. To understand the enormous importance of this demand in Muslim world views we need only turn to the first surah (chapter) of the Qur'an, known as the Opener (*al-fatiha*), which is frequently recited during personal prayers and in social contract situations, such as when two families seal a marriage arrangement, and on countless other private and public occasions.[15] Following a brief invocation, the popular opening surah contains this supplication:

> Praise be to God, Lord of the worlds; most gracious, most merciful; master of the Day of Judgment; Thee do we worship, and Thine assistance de we seek; lead us in the Upright Path (*sirat al-mustaqim*), the Path of those on whom Thou hast bestowed Thy grace, not wrath, and (who do) not go astray.[16]

The Arabic verb for this 'striving in the path of God' is *jahada* and its verbal noun is *jihad*. As the third form of the root *juhd*, it connotes a transitive relationship to some 'other'. One who strives in the path of God is known as a *mujahid*, a term which has contemporary coinage, as for example its use by numerous counterrevolutionary groups, such as Afghani freedom fighters. As mentioned previously, the Qur'an refers to the 'path' of God in over one hundred and eighty passages, and the term *jahada* and cognates such as *mujahid* and *jihad* occur about thirty-five times. Some passages associate *jihad* with bearing patiently;[17] others identify the strivers with those who believe.[18] In some cases the Prophet's or the believers' *jihad* is pitted against the unbelievers and hypocrites.[19] In other cases the focus of personal striving is against oneself.[20] It is frequently pointed out that God knows those who strive in His path,[21] that such behaviour receives divine guidance[22] and has eschatological consequences.[23] Islamic literature and public discourse abound with references to these several connotations of jihad. At the level of semantics, then, the observation by Western observers that jihad is a major preoccupation of Muslims is entirely correct, although it says very little about a presumed Muslim penchant for violence and holy war.[24]

Islamic literature identifies a variety of senses of jihad by peaceful means and for peaceful purposes.[25] There is the *jihad al-lisan*—'striving of the tongue', and the *jihad al-qalam*—'striving with the pen': both are ways to conduct the *jihad al-tarbiya*—'striving through education' or *jihad al-da'wa*—'striving by propagating' (the faith). Other non-aggressive psychological connotations of jihad are found in such concepts as *jihad al-nafs*—'struggle against oneself' and *jihad al-shaytan*—'struggle against satan'. In general, the jihad by peaceful means is referred to in Islamic law as *al-jihad al-kabir*, the greater jihad, and is distinguished from *al-jihad al-saghir*, the lesser jihad, that is, legitimate forms of strife with other human beings through war, violence and so on. In support of this distinction between striving peacefully and striving in war is a *hadith* 'saying' attributed to the Prophet Muhammad, in which he is reported to have said after returning from battle one day: 'we have now returned from the smaller jihad to the greater jihad.'[26]

In so far as violent behaviour towards others is rationalised within Islamic world views, it is done primarily in discourse which rests on the semantics of the lesser jihad. Moreover, the term jihad as such, when left unqualified, almost always refers to the jihad of armed struggle and justified violence.[27] In the broadest conceptual sense, the lesser jihad is a perdurable state of affairs existing between Muslim society (*dar al-islam*, the domain of Islam) and non-Muslim societies (*dar al-harb*, the domain of war). Khadduri makes the distinction as follows:

> the jihad was the just war of Islam. God commanded the believer to spread His word and establish His Law and Justice over the world [Qur'an 9:5]. The dar al-Islam was the house of the believer where Law and Justice were given practical expression, and the dar al-Harb was the house of the unbeliever and an aspect of the jihad. Religion, however, was and still is to be carried out by peaceful means, as there should be no compulsion in the spread of the word of God [Qur'an 2:257]. The expansion of the state carried out by jihad, was an entirely different matter. Thus the jihad, a duty prescribed by Religion and Law, was surely as pious and just as *pium* and *justum* in the way described by St Augustine and St Thomas and later Hugo Grotius.[28]

The Islamic discourse on jihad in the sense of striving against other human beings was established in the classical works on Islamic law. In this body of literature, the discussion is closely tied to Quranic and early Islamic legal distinctions among categories of human beings against whom jihad may be directed, and under what circumstances.[29] These include *kuffar*—'unbelievers', *mushrikun*—'polytheists', *irtadda*—'apostacy', *baghi*—'(political) dissent', criminals, *ahl al-kitab*—'non-Muslim scriptuaries' and enemies at the *ribat*—'frontier(s)' of Muslim-held territories, i.e., *dar al-islam*. The greatest body of literature on the lesser jihad of striving against one's enemies, however, has been that which has been written since the beginning of the colonial period. In an important study of the discourses of jihad in national liberation contexts and reform movements, Rudolph Peters has examined many of the contextual variables which modulated the classical doctrine of jihad in modern times, introducing new conceptual categories, or newer interpretations of older categories.[30]

A major distinction between the broader religious sense of striving in God's Path and the duty of war is that the former has usually been defined as an obligation on each individual (*fard al-cayn*) while the latter is regarded as a duty to be fulfilled by society as a whole (*fard al-kifaya*), in which case it is sufficient to raise an army for battle and for the rest of Muslim society to be represented by those who go to battle, lending material and moral support as may be needed. The practicalities of diplomacy and statecraft led many jurists to avoid the conclusion that the duty of jihad should be 'waged against non-Muslims solely on the grounds of disbelief'. A genuine threat or attack against Muslims became the practical grounds for war, indeed, a defensive war.[31] In the next section we will examine a recent discourse on jihad in which the disbelief of both Muslims and non-Muslims became grounds for a call to jihad.

THE RADICAL DISCOURSE ON JIHAD IN MODERN EGYPT

On 6 October 1981 a military vehicle suddenly stopped in front of a reviewing stand in Cairo, where President Sadat and other officials were watching a parade commemorating the eighth anniversary of the Sinai war with Israel. Four men leaped from the halted truck and began firing automatic weapons, killing Sadat and some of his bodyguards, and wounding several others. The grenades which were hurled into the crowd did not explode, thus averting a more general massacre. The leader of the assassin squad, Lieutenant Khalid Istambuli, was associated with a Muslim extremist group known as 'al-Jihad'. Gilles Kepel[32] has shown that Istambuli was not an ideologue for the group known as al-Jihad, nor did he contribute to the discourse on Islamic revitalisation directed against the State and/or the West. Despite the enormity of this act, Khalid Istambuli was a minor figure. He can be seen as having responded to the more radical speech acts of others who defined Islam against the perceived otherness and alien character of the Egyptian government and the non-Muslim West. Istambuli also did what he did, of course, in light of his own personal circumstances. In the background lay various spokesmen and movements, tolerated and untolerated by the Egyptian regime. While most scholarship on Islamic extremism has focused on the Muslim Brotherhood, especially its founder, Hasan al-Banna',[33] Kepel initiates his study of Muslim extremism in Egypt with an analysis of the writings of Sayyid Qutb and the social world from which they emerged.

Although Sayyid Qutb has had very little name recognition in the West, either in life or since his political execution in 1966, he has nonetheless been an important voice in Egyptian religious thought, and his writings continue to influence revival movements in Egypt and elsewhere in the Islamic world. Far better known in relation to the Muslim Brotherhood (*ikhwan al-muslimin*), for whom Qutb wrote from prison in the 1950s and 1960s in Cairo, was Hasan al-Banna', its founder. More widely read, translated and discussed by Western scholars was the ideologue of the Iranian revolution, Ali Shariati. Better known for his impact upon political events was the Pakistani reformer and publicist, Mawlana Mawdudi.[34] Indeed, it was not until the late Egyptian President Anwar al-Sadat lifted a political ban on the publication of the religious, revivalist writings of the Brotherhood in the early 1970s, some six years after Sayyid Qutb's death, that the latter was to be widely read beyond membership circles of the Brotherhood.

For all that, Sayyid Qutb was what poststructuralist critics would call a 'strong reader' of Islamic religious texts. His re-readings of the Qur'an and other textual resources within the conservative Hanbali tradition of Islamic piety and reform[35] have become an inspiration to thousands of contemporary Muslims. For Qutb as well as for most Islamic visionaries of reform, the rationale for using violence is framed by the doctrine of jihad and related notions of justified conflict with one's enemies. The historical context for such discussions was the colonial and postcolonial period, the rise of nationalism and the general Muslim ethos of weakness caused by the perceived and real domination of Western power and culture.[36]

Sayyid Qutb was born the son of a mildly prosperous landowner in Asyut province, Egypt, in 1906, a year after the demise of Muhammad Abduh, the famous al-Azhar rector, judge and Islamic modernist reformer who influenced the direction of Islamic thought on reform during the preceding generation.[37] Qutb acquired a more or less traditional education, learning the Qur'an by heart on his own, a firm basis for much of his later education and intellectual activity. His father sent him to Cairo to study at Dar al-'Ulum, a religious academy meant to train Muslim scholars more broadly than the more traditional al-Azhar University. At Dar al-'Ulum he learned to appreciate Western literature and was introduced to the ideas of Muslim intellectuals who sought to Westernise and modernise Islamic society. After his education he took a post in the Ministry of Education, inspecting government schools, which brought him into contact with other parts of Egypt. As a result of his appointment to the Ministry, in 1949 he was sent to the United States for two years to study educational administration in Washington, DC and in California.

Yvonne Haddad has singled out two aspects of Sayyid Qutb's experiences in the United States which were to influence his later writing. First was the wide support he correctly perceived that Americans gave to Israel and, at the same time, the growing anti-Arab feelings in America. The creation of the state of Israel and the first Arab–Israeli war, with disastrous results for Arabs materially and mentally, had an enormous effect on Qutb, especially as he sought to understand and endure them in the American cultural context, which was so alien to him. Second, he has been described as a slight, dark, sickly man, said to be reticent, intense and humourless. As a result, he complained of having experienced social estrangement and even racial prejudice, as well he might have, especially in the late 1940s and early 1950s in the US. Soon he returned to Cairo, disenchanted with the culture (Western) whose literature he had once eagerly sought and read.[38]

From his return to Egypt in about 1951 to his execution in 1966, Sayyid Qutb became progressively more radical. This can be seen in the growing urgency of his interpretation of Islamic responses appropriate to outside political, economic and cultural forces which he believed threatened an authentic Muslim existence in the world. If American racial conflict and support for Israel helped shape his experiences and thoughts abroad, the 1952 Egyptian revolution provided a different sort of context when he returned to Cairo. He joined the activist and reform-oriented Muslim Brotherhood, which was most of the time regarded and treated as subversive by the Nasser government which the revolution had brought into power. He read more widely the writings of other Muslim reformers and fundamentalist figures, such as Pakistan's al-Mawdudi. It took only until 1954 for Qutb to be imprisoned with a fifteen-year sentence for his views. There he remained but for a brief respite in the early 1960s. In 1965 he was re-imprisoned, largely owing to the more outspoken radicalism of his writings, and executed a year later.

What contributed to Qutb's demise were the more radical implications of his interpretations of Islam, which he drew out in his writings done in prison. As Haddad observers, 'the ideology he proposed in the early fifties as a guideline, a "tentative blueprint," by 1965 acquired a dogmatic nature, an absolute given'.[39] Kepel's analysis of Qutb also stresses the brutality and violence of prison life for members of the Brotherhood (a theme which is currently popular in social–psychological analyses of violence fomented by Palestinians from the ghettos of South Beirut).[40] Under these conditions for Qutb in prison, where his poor health was constantly exacerbated, proposals for reform gave way to radical solutions for restoring an authentic Islamic government and society against those forces in the world which opposed it.[41] And those forces which opposed it were the secular ideologies which dominated humankind in the twentieth century, primarily capitalism and communism. The colonial experience had divided and made the world of Islam (*dar al-islam*) dependent upon Western economic, political and cultural systems which were clearly in trouble and in conflict with one another on their own terms. Muslims were being tempted by non-Islamic ideologies, to which they were turning for political survival in the modern world. Islam, in Qutb's view, however, was the most perfect, divinely established resource for establishing a good and just society; Muslims have no need, he argued, for turning to communism, socialism or capitalism, all of which are palpably in trouble in today's world, when a better 'way' is at hand.

The solution for Muslims with respect to politics, economics, culture and morality, but especially religion (all of which are inextricably bound up together in a single 'Way' in any strict understanding of Islam), was to return to the Islam established by the Prophet Muhammad. Qutb's prose tacks back and forth between the Qur'an and the paradigmatic events of the Prophet's *umma* in Arabia on the one side and the situation of Muslims at mid-twentieth century on the other as he attempts to set the course of Islam back to the moorings from which he believes it has drifted.[42] Indeed, for Qutb and most radical Muslim visionaries, the view of Islam presented in their discourse is ahistorical.The tendency has been to view the 'history' of Islam from the golden age of the past to the critical juncture of the present as much less important in shaping the present than the more cosmic forces of the Quranic cosmography and the paradigmatic time of the nascent *umma*.[43] On the other side, his critiques of Western civilisation are serious and informed by his earlier reading in English literature as well as his personal experiences in America.

Qutb held that ultimately humankind as created by God is a single community whose divinely intended unity had been seriously fractured by the time Islam came to seventh-century Arabia. Islam arose to restore human unity and bring peace to the world. In this most widely read and translated book in the West, *This Religion of Islam* (1967), he argued, using ample Quranic references, that 'God distinguishes between people on the basis of belief, irrespective of ties of ancestry, race or homeland between them'.[44] This generally held view among Muslims, that ethnic, economic and political human differences are artificial and unimportant *sub specie aeternitatis* but that the distinction between belief and unbelief is all important, provides the linkage to Sayyid Qutb's interpretation of the doctrine of Jihad. In his own words:

> [God] has established only one cause for killing—when there is no other recourse—and that is striving for the sake of God (*jihad*). He has defined the aim of the believer and the aim of the disbeliever in a clear and decisive manner:
>
> 'Those who believe fight for the sake of God. And those who disbelieve fight for the sake of idols. Fight then the followers of Satan, surely the guild [sic, guile] of Satan is but feeble.'[45]

In a work written in 1951 titled 'International Peace and Islam',[46] Sayyid Qutb sought to revise what Majid Khadduri suggests is the Islamic equivalent of the doctrine of the just war, an interpretation of jihad found articulated already in the classical texts on jurisprudence.[47] In this view, war for religious purposes, that is, to defend Islam against its enemies, is the only allowable or 'justified' war in the Quranic world view and early legal definitions. War for other political or economic purposes is not condoned.

Sayyid Qutb's discourse about violence, then, parallels the structure of the Quranic cosmological polarity between the believer and the unbelieving 'other', the bearers of truth and falsehood, respectively, in the world. For Qutb and for those who have read him and continued his agenda in Egypt for the past two decades since his hanging, the 'other' was primarily the Egyptian government, although the Christian Copts of Egypt and the non-Muslim West have also been occasional targets of polemic and even violence. Qutb argued that only divine purposes justified war, but he did not restrict war to defensive ends. He reasoned that non-Muslim societies destroyed world peace by fighting over economic, racial and political (that is, not divinely sanctioned) issues and thus posed a threat to peaceful existence of Muslim societies, a very plausible reading of the situation for the Third World in the period of neocolonialism and the Cold War. Thus, the traditional consensus that jihad against non-Muslims should be fought only in defence of Islamic society was not sufficient for Qutb and his followers. They were driven from passive to active interpretations of the fundamental texts.

In a chapter on jihad in 'International Peace and Islam'[48] Qutb states explicitly that contemporary Muslims should return to the original policy of the era of conquests and empire of inviting (*da'wa*) non-Muslims to become Muslim. Those who wish to remain within their own confessional communities, a status called *dhimma*, should then be required to pay the poll tax (*jizya*) in exchange for the license to propagate their own religion. If non-Muslims reject Islam or *dhimma* status, then 'fighting (*qital*) is the only remaining response under the circumstances', for by their refusal they deny the word of God and thus oppose the means He has provided for a comprehensive peace among humankind (*bashariya*).[49] Clearly, Qutb had reduced Islamic perceptions of 'otherness' in the twentieth century to the categories discussed above from Quranic cosmology—People of the Book and client converts to Islam: all others must be forcibly brought to Islam.

The most radical agenda for the actions which Qutb felt would have to be taken in the Path of God if Islam was to fulfil its divine mandate was worked out in 'Signposts Along the Way', which Qutb wrote in prison.[50] In a chapter on 'Jihad in the Path of God', Qutb refutes the traditional Muslim interpretation of the lesser jihad as war taken only in defence of Islam.[51] He explores other meanings more appropriate to his own belief that the Nasser government represented a *jahiliyya*, a time of religious boorishness hostile to the practice of Islam. Jihad is the proper Muslim response, the divinely enjoined responsibility of Muslims to combat those who would lead humankind astray from the Path of God. A movement (*haraka*) must be formed to implement the teachings of the discourse (*bayan*)[52] on how to confront one's enemies in order to live in the Path. Kepel notes that in the growing official discourse against radical Islam there was an attempt to establish a (pejorative) link between Qutb's radical programme and the early Muslim separatist group, the Kharijites, who had called for the expulsion of those who failed to live up to the teachings of Islam, including the Caliph (Egyptian President Nasser, in Qutb's schema).[53] In 'Signposts', then, Qutb had brought the doctrine of jihad to bear upon secular powers, like the Nasser government, which ruled over Muslims. Again, a concept was borrowed from Islamic beginnings, one which was a certain term of opprobrium, namely, *jahiliyya*. The semi-official response of the Nasser regime, by levelling the charge of 'kharijite' against Qutb, countered one term of opprobrium with another. 'Religious ignorance' versus 'secessionist' were the charges, couched ostensibly in references to history, but such terms in modern Islamic discourse must be understood within the semiotics of texts about sacred beginnings.

The significance of the writings of Sayyid Qutb goes beyond what the texts he left behind say in themselves—what they might tell us about the man and how he might have come to have held such views over and against more moderate and traditional Muslim conceptions of, say, jihad. From 1966 to 1981, others beyond the confines of prison, yet in different ways constrained by the same dynamic environment in Egypt, thought, wrote and in some cases acted on their conceptions of jihad in the Path of God. A discourse on Islamic action, or counteraction, in a world gone astray from its ideal beginnings in seventh-century Arabia had come into being.

The most striking case was that of Lieutenant Khalid Istambuli, an errant member of the movement called al-Jihad, who took it upon himself to assassinate President Sadat. More broadly a part of the general discourse of radical Islamic alternatives as the cautiously permitted continuance of the Muslim Brotherhood, student groups under the influence of Qutb's writings and of the earlier ethos of the Muslim Brotherhood, the popular preaching of Shaykh Kishk, the movement known as *al-takfir wal-hijra* [excommunication and (Islamic) emigration], and more radical ideologues such as Abd al-Salam Faraj, leader of al-Jihad and author of its manifesto, a pamphlet called *al-farida al-ghayba*—'Hidden Imperative'.

Kepel has done the best job to date in deconstructing our vague conceptions of Muslim extremism in Egypt by examining each of these movements, the common aspects of their world views as well as their differences, and the particular circumstances of their activities.[54] If his work suffers any defect it is that shared by all attempts to analyse radical groups which foment violence, namely, the lack of effective participant observation in order to understand better the contextual determinants of the texts of Islamic resurgence in Egypt, as speech acts. This does not as such render Kepel's interpretations wrong; it simply signals another dimension of interpreting meaning—the social experiences of the group which produced the texts—a dimension to which no non-Muslim and few Muslim scholars have had sustained, direct access.

SOME FINAL REFLECTIONS

What Sayyid Qutb had wanted, a return to power of the idealised model of the Prophet's *umma* of the seventh century, he structured around a discourse on peace. He organised 'International Peace and Islam'[55] concentrically around internal or personal tranquility, *salam l-damir*, then domestic or household peace, *salam al-bayt*, then social quietude, *salam al-mujtamac* and finally international peace, *salam al-calam*. Personal, internal peace was basic, he felt, and without it there could be no world peace.[56]

The need to define Islam and Muslim society in pursuit of a sanctioned course of action 'in the Path of God' over and against the enemies of that Path were also given by Sayyid Qutb's own experience of power—the economic and political power of America, the influence of Western culture and morality upon Muslims subject to decades of colonial rule and postcolonial imperialism, the power of the Free Officers' movement and the Nasser government to restrict and control Muslim political pursuits. His radical understanding of jihad was more in response to his social circumstances than a mystical striving within himself; though the latter was not entirely absent from his thought, it simply was a stage in the development of his thought which finally came to ask how Muslims should act in and upon the world in the 1960s. The successive development of a discourse on jihad—by the Muslim Brotherhood, student groups, Shaykh Kishk, Excommunication and Emigration and al-Jihad—provided further instances of speech acts, doing things with words to effect change in society.

The importance of Sayyid Qutb's concept of jihad is that he employed socially shared symbols, the texts of Islamic religion, and used them, primarily in literary speech acts, to try to produce social results. He is important also because others joined him and created a discourse about jihad that went beyond the traditional, legal understanding of the term. That is why their texts are worth reading and understanding within the several contexts in which they operate.

It is acceptable and even desirable, however, as Kepel advises the reader in his conclusion,[57] to admit that one is surprised, even shocked, by the otherness of non-Western cultures, such as Islam. That admission is the first step towards demythologising one's conceptions of the 'other', so that 'we' can deconstruct 'their' discourses about a world they are trying to change, by examining their texts and the contexts in which they use them. For Kepel, as for J Smith, who has analysed the Jonestown massacre, pointing to the shock of some forms of otherness—assassination of heads of state and massive communal suicides—must be attended by framing modes of interpretation so that we may understand.[58] The form of understanding argued for here is the historian of religions' examination of religious texts and their human contexts of use. This line of scholarship needs to be part of the research on violence and terrorism, to which other scholars and public officials have turned their attention so sharply in recent years.

APPENDIX

ANNOTATED BIBLIOGRAPHY ON JIHAD AND RELATED TOPICS

Although the study of religion and violence has received little attention from historians of religions, an important recent attempt is by Jonathan Z Smith, 'The Devil in Mr Jones', *Imagining Religion: From Babylon to Jonestown*, Chicago: University of Chicago Press, 1982, pp. 102–134; Smith analyses the Jonestown White Night of Terror in relation to Euripides' 'Bacchae' and Cargo Cult parallels and speculates why religious studies scholars in the American Academy of Religion have not formed panels or published on religion and violence in recent times. Smith's study and the work of several other historians of religions now underway on religion and violence have been influenced by Rene Girard, *Violence and the Sacred*, transl. Patrick Gregory, Baltimore and London: Johns Hopkins University Press, 1977. Based on literary-critical re-readings of the classic Greek dramatists, ethnographic studies of tribal rituals and the sociocultural theories of Nietzsche and Freud, Girard sets forth a revisionist theory of the sacred as generative violence which religious ritual contains through the symbolisation of victims.

In Islamic studies, the most general resource on religious concepts, historical movements and personalities, and institutions is *The Encyclopaedia of Islam*, 2d edn., HAR Gibb *et al.* (eds.), Leiden: EJ Brill and London: Luzac & Co., 1960. The article on 'Djihad' (jihad) is by E Tyan. A comprehensive international bibliographical database on scholarly books and articles on Islamic topics is *Index Islamicus*, edited by JD Pearson *et al.*

Majid Khadduri is the author of two works on the history of Islamic understandings of war and religiously justified violence; *War and Peace in the Law of Islam*, Baltimore: Johns Hopkins University Press, 1955, and *The Islamic Conception of Justice*, Baltimore and London: Johns Hopkins University Press, 1984. Texts and commentary on important documents on jihad by Averroes (d. 1198) and the late Rector of al-Azhar University in Egypt, Mahmud Shaltut is *Jihad in Mediaeval and Modern Islam*, transl. Rudolph Peters, Leiden: EJ Brill, 1977. Rudolph Peters, *Islam and Col-*

onialism: The Doctrine of Jihad in Modern History, Religion and Society 20, The Hague: Mouton Publishers, 1979, focuses on the interpretations of jihad by Muslims in modern times in response to European colonial rule and postcolonial influence. Peters also provides a good overview of the history of Muslim legal and theological discussions of the justification of jihad as well as an extended bibliography and analysis of important literature which is inaccessible to non-Arabists.

Still the most important work on religious revival in modern Egypt because it combines comprehensive textual and social research is Richard P Mitchell, *The Society of Muslim Brothers*, London: Oxford University Press, 1969. Sa'd al-Din Ibrahim, 'Anatomy of Egypt's Militant Islamic Groups', *International Journal of Middle East Studies*, 12, 1982, is a brief but useful analysis of interviews Ibrahim conducted with the indicted assassins of President Anwar Sadat. Yvonne Y Haddad, 'Sayyid Qutb: Ideologue of Islamic Revival', in John L Esposito (ed.) *Voices of Resurgent Islam*, New York and Oxford: Oxford University Press, 1983, along with several other contributions to the volume, is useful for general information and instruction on resurgent Islam in the contemporary world. To date, the most important work, upon which the present chapter is primarily based, is Gilles Kepel, *Muslim Extremism in Egypt: The Prophet and Pharaoh*, transl. Jon Rothschild, Berkeley and Los Angeles: University of California Press, 1986.

NOTES

1 At the end of the chapter an annoted bibliography of works in Western languages on jihad and related topics is provided.

2 See Sa'd al-Din Ibrahim, 'Anatomy of Egypt's Militant Islamic Groups', *International Journal of Middle Eastern Studies*, 12, 1980, pp. 423–453.

3 Gilles Kepel, *Muslim Extremism in Egypt: The Prophet and Pharaoh*, Berkeley and Los Angeles, California: University of California Press, 1986.

4 Rudolph Peters, *Islam and Colonialism: The Doctrine of Jihad in Modern History*, The Hague: Mouton, 1979, p. 4 notes that in modern Islamic writing, terms such as *al-jihad al-muqaddas*—'holy war' are 'probably a *calque*, coined under the influence of Western languages. At the same time it seems to reflect a growing awareness among some Muslims that much of Military conflict today is not religious and that hence the religious character of some wars needs to be emphasized'.

5 An excellent semantic analysis of Muslim religious speech acts is Moshe Piamenta, *Islam in Everyday Arabic Speech*, Leiden: EJ Brill, 1979.

6 Dale F Eickelman, *The Middle East: An Anthropological Approach*, Englewood Cliffs, New Jersey: Prentice-Hall, Inc., 1981, p. 175 defines world view as 'shared cultural assumptions about the nature of the social world'. The social process of transmitting and adapting world views from one generation to the next has been studied by Eickelman in relation to a traditional mosque university in Morocco, in Dale F Eickelman, 'The Art of Memory: Islamic Education and Its Social Reproduction', *Comparative Studies in Society and History*, 20(4), 1978, pp.

485–516. An interesting study of Quranic education in Moroccan schools is Daniel A Wagner and Abdelhamid Lotfi, 'Traditional Islamic Education in Morocco: Sociohistorical and Psychological Perspectives', *Comparative Education Review*, 1980, pp. 238–251.

7 Qur'an 2:262, *inter alia.*

8 Qur'an 2:39, 3:184, *inter alia.*

9 A good treatment of the semantic fields of the Quranic cosmography is Toshihiko Izutsu, *God and Man in the Koran: Semantics of the Koranic Weltanschauung*, Tokyo: Keio Institute of Cultural and Linguistic Studies, 1964. Michel Allard *et al.*, *Analyse conceptuelle du Coran sur cartes perforees*, 2 volumes, Paris: Mouton & Co., 1963, vol. 2, 27–42 mapped out the dynamics of the cosmographical actors and the kinds of 'communication' that go on between and within the two realms of being. I have attempted to re-deploy the findings of Izutsu and Allard *et al.* in a 'constituent analysis' of the Quranic text. See Richard C Martin, 'Understanding the Qur'an in Text and Context', *History of Religions*, 21(4), 1982, pp. 361–384 and *idem*, 'Symbol, Ritual Community: An Approach to Islam', *Islam in the Modern World* (1983 Payne Lectures in Religion), Jill Raitt (ed.), Columbia, Missouri: University of Missouri, Department of Religious Studies, 1983. 'Constituents' are redundant semantic units into which texts may be divided for analytical purposes, e.g., God sending prophets, humankind heeding prophets, satans leading astray, etc. On constituent analysis, see Thomas A Sebeok, *Structure and Texture: Selected Essays in Chemeris Verbal Art*, The Hague: Mouton & Co., 1974 and Sam D Gill, *Sacred Words: A Study of Navajo Religion and Prayer*, Westport, Connecticut: Greenwood Press, 1981.

10 The most important biographical text is that of Ibn Ishaq, an eighth-century Muslim scholar whose collection of pericopes about the life and doings of Muhammad and his companions is far more comprehensive and written closer to the time of the prophet than is the case in most other world religions. A usable translation is Alfred Guillaume, *The Life of Muhammad: A Translation of Ishaq's Sirat Rasul Allah*, London: Oxford University Press, 1955.

11 On the analysis of *asbab al-nuzul* genre, see Andrew L Rippin, 'The Quranic *asbab al-nuzul* Material: An Analysis of Its Use and Development in Exegesis'. PhD Dissertation, McGill University, Montreal, Canada, 1981.

12 For a discussion of the implications of Heidegger's hermeneutical theory for contemporary criticism and historiography, see David Cousins Hoy, *The Critical Circle: Literature, History, and Philosophical Hermeneutics*, Berkeley, California: University of California Press, 1978.

13 See note 9 above on constituent analysis.

14 Hayden White, 'The Redemption of Myth', Religious Studies Faculty Seminar, Arizona State University, 19 March 1986. White's analysis is a reaction to but nonetheless structurally similar to Rene Girard, *Violence and the Sacred*, transl. Patrick Gregory, Baltimore, Maryland and London: Johns Hopkins University Press, 1984.

15 A good study of Muslim prayers and the Quranic component in them is Constance E Padwick, *Muslim Devotions: A Study of Prayer Manuals in Common Use*, London: SPCK, 1961.

16 Qur'an 1:2–7.

17 Qur'an 3:142.

18 8:74, 75; 61:11.

19 66:9; 25:52.

20 8:72; 9:41; 49:15.

21 47:31; but see 9:16.
22 29:6; 60:1.
23 29:6; 60:1.
24 This point is made by Peters, *Islam and Colonialism*, p. 3 and confirmed by my own experience. The ubiquitousness of literature on jihad may well be what has led writers such as Raphael Patai, *The Arab Mind*, New York: Charles Scribner's Sons, 1979, p. 215 to write about jihad as evidence of a putative quarrelsome quality of 'the Arab mind'.
25 Good summaries of the various semantic qualifications of jihad are found in Peters, pp. 117–121 and Majid Khadduri, *War and Peace in the Law of Islam*, New York: Johns Hopkins University Press, 1955, pp. 55–82.
26 Quoted by Peters, p. 118.
27 Quoted by Peters, p. 10 (citing numerous sources).
28 Majid Khadduri, *The Islamic Conception of Justice*, Baltimore and London: Johns Hopkins University Press, 1984, p. 165.
29 See Khadduri, *War and Peace*, pp. 74–-82.
30 Peters, *op. cit.*
31 Khadduri, *Justice*, p. 165.
32 Peters, *op. cit.*
33 On the Muslim Brotherhood and its founder, see the article 'al-Ikhwan al-Muslimun' *in The Encyclopaedia of Islam*, 2nd edn, HAR Gibb (ed.) *et al.*, Leiden: EJ Brill and London: Luzac & Company, 1960 and Richard P Mitchell, *The Society of Muslim Brothers*, London: Oxford University Press, 1969 and Kepel, *op. cit.*
34 Brief treatments of these and other modern Muslim reformers are found in John L Esposito (ed.), *Voices of Resurgent Islam*, New York and Oxford: Oxford University Press, 1983.
35 See Mitchell, *Muslim Brothers* and *The Encyclopaedia of Islam*, articles on Ahmad ibn Hanbal and Ibn Taymiyya.
36 Wilfred Cantwell Smith's well-known characterisation is that 'the fundamental *malaise* of modern Islam is that something has gone wrong with Islamic history'. (Wilfred Cantwell Smith, *Islam in Modern History*, Princeton, New Jersey: Princeton University Press, 1957, p. 47). Smith and Gustav E von Grunebaum, *Modern Islam: The Search for Cultural Identity*, Berkeley and Los Angeles, California: University of California Press, 1962 laboured at mid-century to measure the impact of modernity upon traditional Islam and to diagnose structural characteristics of Islam which impeded, in their views and in the views of many of their Islamicist contemporaries, an effective Islamic response to modernity and the West.
37 Sayyid Qutb's Arabic biography is Mahdi Fadlallah, *Ma'a Sayyid Qutb fi fikrihi al-siyasi wa-l-dini*, Beirut: Mu'assasat al-Risala, 1978, which is summarised by Yvonne Y Haddad,'Sayyid Qutb: Ideologue of Islamic Revival', *in* Esposito (ed.), *Voices*, *op. cit.* Kepel, *Muslim Extremism*, is the current most readily available source of information about his intellectual and religious *vitae*. Without access to Fadlallah's work, I have relied on Haddad and Kepel in preparing this chapter.
38 Haddad, 'Sayyid Qutb', p. 69.
39 Haddad, p. 78.
40 Kepel, *Muslim Extremism*, pp. 26–35. At the meeting of the American Psychological Association, a number of papers were presented on the association of Palestinians and others suspected of terrorism with violent and politically unstable

conditions in childhood. See Daniel Goleman, 'The Roots of Terrorism Are Found in Brutality of Shattered Childhood', *The New York Times*, 9 February 1986, pp. 19, 23.

41 Haddad, p. 78.
42 See Sayyid Qutb, *This Religion of Islam* (*Hadha 'd-Din*), transl. Islamdust, Palo Alto, California: Al-Manar Press, 1967.
43 See Kepel, pp. 227–228.
44 Qutb, *This Religion of Islam*, p. 87.
45 *Ibid.*, citing Qur'an 4:76.
46 Sayyid Qutb, *Al-Salam al-'alami wa-l-islam* [International Peace and Islam], Beirut: Dar al-Shuruq, 1974.
47 Khadduri, *Justice*, pp. 164–167.
48 Qutb, 'International Peace', pp. 169–177.
49 Qutb, *Al-Salam*, p. 174; see Haddad, p. 83.
50 Sayyid Qutb, *Ma'alim fi l-tariq* [Signposts Along the Way], Beirut: Dar al-Shuruq, 1985.
51 See Kepel, p. 54.
52 The term *bayan* normally is translated as 'announcement, explanation'. Kepel captures its rhetorical force in polemical literature by translating it as 'discourse', which should be understood as Michel Foucau has used the term.
53 Kepel, pp. 58–60.
54 Kepel, especially his conclusion, pp. 223–240.
55 Qutb, *Al-Salam*, *op. cit.*
56 *Ibid.*, p. 38.
57 Kepel, p. 223.
58 Jonathan Z Smith, 'The Devil in Mr Jones', *Imagining Religion from Babylon to Jonestown*, Chicago and London: University of Chicago Press, 1982, pp. 102–134.

Why Does Religious Messianism Produce Terror?

D C Rapoport

A most striking development in recent years has been the use of theological concepts to justify terrorist activity, a phenomenon which I have called 'holy terror'.[1] The most notorious instance has occurred among the Shia where the revival of jihad (holy war) doctrines has produced some remarkable incidents in Lebanon and elsewhere. A major feature of the Shia episodes has been a striking willingness, even eagerness, to die, a disposition created by the belief that one who is killed while fighting in a jihad is guaranteed a place in paradise. This promise of personal benefit for assailants who die gives Shia terror an awesome dimension in the eyes of potential victims.[2] In the United States abortion clinic bombers cite Scripture to justify their deeds. A third case came to light in Israel last in 1984 when the government convicted Jewish terrorists who had organised 'The Temple Mount Plot', a conspiracy to destroy Muslim sacred shrines built on Judaism's holiest site, that of the Second Temple. If they were obliterated, the construction of a Third Temple would be possible at last, a circumstance which some visualise to be a pre-condition of the coming of the Messiah.[3] It has been alleged, too, that American Christian messianic groups (who may be interested in creating conditions for Armageddon) have furnished funds for Third Temple enterprises—a project certainly which has been very dear to them for more than a century.[4] I do not know whether the Messiah will come if the Third Temple is rebuilt; but I do know that if the Muslim holy sites are blown up, catastrophic result could ensue which may indeed put us one step closer to an Armageddon. But will it be the one Scripture describes?

Holy terror seems new to us, but prior to the French Revolution it was the dominant, perhaps the only, form of terror, and holy terror, whenever it appears, is linked usually to messianism. Two well-known historical examples are the Assassins or *Fidayeen* of Islam and the Jewish Zealots and *Sicarii*. The Assassins emerged in the eleventh century, persisted for two hundred years and are the first known example of an international conspiracy organised by a state, a conspiracy which threatened the governments of several Islamic realms. The Zealots who lived earlier, in the first century, survived for a shorter period, some sixty years, but they had enormous significance.

They successfully provoked a massive rebellion against Rome, one which ended in catastrophe. The Second Temple—the ritual centre of Judaism—was destroyed, and the final act in the rebellion was a gruesome mass suicide at Masada. The revolt subsequently inspired two more massive uprisings in successive generations. Large Jewish centres in Cyprus and Egypt, then under Roman dominion, were decimated; Judea itself was de-populated; and then the final tragedy, the Second Exile or Diaspora, occurred, an exile which had a traumatic impact on Jewish consciousness and became the central Jewish experience for the next two thousand years, one which altered virtually every insitution of Jewish life.

No single messianic terror group has occupied such a prominent place in the Christian world. Messianic movements there have been numerous, episodic and have had comparatively less effect, perhaps because of the decentralised character of the Christian world. Still, the Christian examples are much better documented than those in Islam and Judaism, and they are important, for the terror of the Christian world is instructive because it is not so intimately connected to underground organisations. The Crusades, for example, had an essential messianic component which produced some extraordinary bizzare practices especially in the People's Crusades. And in the late medieval period for brief moments the Taborites and the Anabaptists created public arrangements which could be called systems of state terror.

My question is, why does messianism produce terror or, better still, what are the psychological and logical links between messianic motifs and terror? It is common knowledge among the historians and sociologists of messianic movements that those movements often produce terror. Norman Cohn (*Pursuit of the Millennium*) and Bryan Wilson (*Magic and the Millennium*) have given us rich studies of violence in particular millennial movements. But we still lack a general analysis of the issue, particularly the question of terror. The focus here will be on the Jewish and Christian experiences, but I will use some examples from Islam and from primitive societies too. My concern is more with the internal logic or internal dynamics of movements and not with their external circumstances, though I do recognise the latter as being important.

Let us begin by making clear how I shall be using the two key terms, terror and messianic belief. Most academics see the terrorist as one who uses violence unlawfully for political purposes; and there is a strong tendency to describe terrorists as members of small underground rebel groups which employ hit and disappear (i.e., guerrilla-like) tactics.[5] I prefer the more traditional conception, one which, as we shall see, is especially appropriate to messianic experiences. In this view terror is understood as extranormal or extramoral violence, a type which goes beyond the conventions or boundaries particular societies establish to regulate coercion. Such conventions identify justifications, establish limits and immunities and through these conventions, one is able to distinguish between the appropriate and inappropriate social responses to criminal as opposed to belligerent activities.

Sometimes, rebels accept the same restraints governments do. It would be very difficult, for example, to distinguish the methods of the major protagonists in our own Revolutionary and Civil Wars. But other times they do not. The distinguishing characteristic of the terrorist therefore, is a deliberate decision to abandon those restraints or to refuse to accept as binding the prevailing moral distinctions between belligerents and neutrals, combatants and non-combatants, appropriate and inappropriate targets, legitimate and illegitimate methods. The terrorist *knows* that others will regard his actions as shocking or as atrocities, and that is one reason he acts as he does, for his object in using terror for messianic ends is to create a 'new consciousness' by methods which provoke extreme emotional reactions—panic, horror, revulsion, outrage and sympathy. In this respect, any person or group may commit terrorist acts; certainly rebels may do so but so can large armies and established authorities, as the cases of the Crusades and the Zealot–*Sicarii* revolt illustrate. The nature of the act not the status of the persons who commit it is the critical feature.

What do we mean by messianic belief? A messianic belief is one which visualises a day in which history or life on *this* earth will be transformed totally and irreversibly from a condition of perpetual strife which we have all experienced to one of perfect harmony that many dream about, where there will be no sickness and no tears, where we will be wholly *liberated* from all rules, a condition of perfect freedom. History ends *because* God has promised us that it would; and at His appointed time He will intervene in our affairs saving only those who deserve to be saved.[6] This particular concept of messianism is often known as millenarianism or millenialism, but I prefer to reserve these two terms for particular Christian cases where they seem more appropriate.

The details or the content of various messianic beliefs differ. Some may be conducive to terror while others do not seem to be. But no matter what the content of a doctrine may be, its significance depends initially on two conditions. Believers must think that the day of deliverance is near or imminent, and they must also think human action can help consummate the process. When these conditions are fulfilled, six substantive elements of a messianic doctrine will shape decisions to employ terror: (a) the nature of the desired action, (b) the cause or character of the messianic aspiration, (c) the proof that believers think may be necessary to demonstrate sufficient faith, (d) the moral qualities ascribed to participants in the messianic struggle, (e) the 'signs' or 'portents' of a messianic intervention and, finally, (f) the character of the deity's involvement. Messianic doctrines, it should be stressed, rarely form a coherent whole, and are usually sufficiently ambiguous to allow participants to choose between alternatives or abandon one course for another when that other appears more productive.

IMMINENCE AND HUMAN AGENCY

Clearly, one can believe that a messianic era is predestined and also be confident that the day of deliverance is neither near nor predictable. But it does not seem reasonable to think that in all times in all circumstances those who believe in a day of reckoning will remain content with a doctrine that this day is always very far off and/or unknowable. The histories of religions with messianic components seem to confirm both propositions. While a sense of imminence is not present usually, it does appear intermittently and sometimes after very long periods of absence. Eight centuries after the messianic vision first took root in Jewish consciousness, a sense of imminence was aroused, finally, in the generation before the Zealot–*Sicarii* revolt shortly before the development of Christianity. The first five centuries of Christianity exhibited numerous Christian and Jewish messianic episodes, activities which ceased until the time of the Crusades in the eleventh century when they began again. A third period then occurred in the sixteenth and seventeenth centuries.

The hope which a messianic vision supplies is obviously important for the orthodox revealed religions, because without it the rest of the religious tradition may seem onerous or meaningless. Without the component it is even conceivable that some of the revealed religions might not have survived. Judaism had good reason, therefore, to retain its belief that a messiah would come, and the conception was passed on to Christianity and to a lesser extent Islam, where it is known as Mahdism and is especially significant among the Shia.

While the value of a messianic belief may be self-evident, when a sense of imminence takes over, when some believe that the world will end tomorrow or within a forseeable future, a variety of dangerous reactions are likely to occur just because so much anxiety will be generated concerning who will be saved and how. Hugh Schonfield's description of the Jews in the first century does not seem far-fetched. 'The whole condition of the Jewish people was psychologically abnormal. The strangest tales and imaginings could find ready credence. ... Almost every event was seized upon to discover how and in what ways it represented a Sign of the Times and threw light on the approach of the End of the Days.'[7] Such anxieties can uproot the orthodox religion itself, for the religion is the ultimate source of the disappointments which occur when the messiah does not appear.

Orthodox religious leaders attempt to forestall messianic anxieties and explosions in a variety of ways. The Council of Ephesus (431) went right to the root of the matter; it denounced the doctrine of salvation on earth as heretical error and fantasy, asserting that the messianic promise pertains to life after death, an event in the spiritual world. Normally, most Christians have accepted this view; but the relevant Biblical passages can be interpreted in very different ways too, and no Council could prevent Christians from believing those interpretations upon occasion. The Jewish tradition never could deny that messianism pertained to this world, and it attempted to defuse potential tensions by making the Jew's primary responsibility to attend to ordinary living even in the face of clear evidence of a messianic presence.[8] 'If you have a sapling in your hand' Rabbi Yochanan Ben Zakkai taught, 'and they tell you that the Messiah has come, first plant the sapling and then welcome the Messiah'. Sound advice, but not advice always followed.

The orthodox religions find it necessary even to deny the possibility that one could ever know the time for a messianic epoch, and they sometimes make strenuous efforts to prevent individuals from thinking or publicising contrary views. In England during the Restoration it was a criminal offence to speculate on the date of the Second Coming.[9] Shia authorities in the ninth century denounced the 'time determiners' as 'liars' who spread 'disillusionment and despair'.[10] And an early medieval rabbi wrote, 'May the curse of heaven, fall upon those who calculate the advent of the Messiah and thus create political and social unrest among the people'.[11] Each of these cases provides evidence that as soon as the speculation about the date of the great event becomes a popular activity, there is an inevitable tendency (based I suppose on wishful thinking) to believe that it will happen sooner and sooner or become more and more imminent.[12] In England that speculation was an integral part of seventeenth-century upheavals, just as it was an essential element of the ninth-century insurrections among the Shia and in the three disastrous rebellions which Jews waged against the Romans much earlier.

Under what circumstances does a messianic appearance seem imminent? This, of course, is a crucial question. But the problem of the chapter is the relationship of messianic motifs and terror, and it would divert us too much to tackle the question directly. Still, since we are living in a period where many believe the messiah to be imminent, a very brief comment stressing only that which is relevant in logic of the revealed religions is appropriate.

We shall focus on the contemporary situation as illustrative. While its features are unique, they are in some measure present in earlier experience also. A most conspiciuous characteristic of our world since the 1950s[13] is a general revival of religious enthusiasms and that revival necessarily draws attention to the messianic component in the revealed religions, a component which is usually ignored. Clearly, religious enthusiasm is not messianism, but each religious revival probably stimulates dormant sentiments that a messianic delivery could be imminent.[14]

Messianism is always associated with the presence of 'signs', and in our day it is easy for the believer to see two of the most prominent signs in messianic eschatology. In most Jewish, Christian and Islamic messianic visions, the 'Last Days' emerge in the context of world catastrophe, and the spectre of such a possibility has haunted everybody's imagination ever since the Second World War, most of all in the form of nuclear holocaust, but also as ecological, technological and population disasters etc. Indeed, 'end of the world' thinking has become so striking in secular circles that the apocalyptic theme in religious thought has gained a kind of intellectual respectability.[15] Never before has the end of the world seemed so feasible, and since messianism functions as a device to explain catastrophe, one would expect it to emerge naturally whenever catastrophe is experienced or anticipated.[16]

A second sign is the restoration of the state of Israel, a common theme in apocalyptic prophecies. The re-establishment of Israel, especially after the Six Days War when the holy places were regained, has had an enormous impact on various American Christian millenarian groups loosely lumped together as 'Fundamentalists'. Their interest goes back to the early nineteenth century, when the extraordinary and humiliating failures of millenarians to predict the Second Coming compelled them to abandon their reliance on Biblical dating schemes to emphasise instead the significance of signs or portents, the most important being the restoration of Israel to its ancient homeland.[17] The return to the Land has also been, of course, the primary reason for the recent appearance of the first important Jewish messianic movement since the seventeenth century, the Gush Emunim. Indeed, anticipated possession of the Land is a *sine qua non* of Jewish messianic movements, and its actual possession in the past has had enormous consequences. In the First and Second Commonwealths messianic sentiments were immensely stirred, and, hence, it is conceivable that every restoration of Israel will always generate messianic movements.

Islam, too, has been experiencing religious revivals which must also contribute to anticipations that a Mahdi will come, and the spectre of world catastrophe must stimulate those anticipations as it does in the other revealed religions. Expectation concerning the Second Coming among Christians has probably had an effect too, because in some traditions the Mahdi is supposed to appear soon after Christ returns. Contemporary Islam also seems greatly influenced by dating schemes. One particularly relevant for us today is the tradition that the Mahdi will emerge at the beginning of a new century according to the Islamic calendar. The startling attack (1979) on the Grand Mosque of Mecca—Islam's holiest shrine—which staggered the Saudi dynasty occurred in the first hour of the first day of the Islamic year 1400. The assailants (who came from twelve countries including the US) named one of their number the *Mahdi*, and every detail in the assault seemed contrived to follow a well-known Islamic prophecy.[18] There are other examples which seem related to this particular tradition. A century ago Chinese Gordon's army was massacred in Khartoum by the Sudanese Mahdi who had staked his claim to be the Mahdi on the first day of the Islamic year 1300. A few years before and after that date several Mahdi movements emerged utilising the same general expectation that that century was *the* century. In Egypt today three messianic groups (one of which assassinated Sadat) have appealed to this dating tradition.[19] (It is conceivable that the Iranian revolution is linked to it too.)

We now return to our principal concern in the section, the relationship of imminence and action. If the obstacles to making imminence credible are overcome, there is still no reason to think action must ensue unless the believer thinks that he can influence messianic events, which means he must deny the teachings of the religious establishments on this issue. Among the Jews, for example, a rabbinic tradition persists that the Messiah's advent was fixed in the creation of the world, and even God therefore cannot hasten or retard the process.[20] The contradiction is that messianism makes sense or is attractive only if we believe that the righteous and the wicked have different fates, and, consequently, in opposition to what authorities want us to think, some believers will conclude that what we do must count after all. When a sense of imminence takes root, some believers must find it psychologically impossible to regard their actions as irrelevant, simply because the consequences of being mistaken are so urgent and momentous. *At the very least*, they will act to secure their own salvation. And once the initial barrier to action has been overcome, it will only be a matter of time before different kinds of action make sense too. Soon they may think they can shape the speed or timing of the process.

RANGE OF CONCEIVABLE ACTIONS

Clearly, there can be no one prescribed way to accomplish these purposes. Messianic speculators have suggested various possibilities not all consistent with each other, and in the past different movements have tried different courses. One can speak of a range of actions which seem to make sense recognising that believers make choices, swinging sometimes radically from one alternative to another.

Some activities are obviously non-violent. Proselytising is common. One may give property away to discharge debts, finance proselytising and show one's love for humanity as the Millerites did, an American messianic movement (predecessor of the Seventh Day Adventists) in upstate New York in the 1840s. Messianic groups sometimes travel great distances to a sacred site where redemption is supposed to begin. After the Jews were dispersed in the wake of the Second Temple's destruction, Jewish messianic episodes for the next nineteen centuries normally induced a collective exodus to the Holy Land. Groups of Indians in Brazil periodically would peacefully migrate to find 'The Land of No Evil'. Numerous Melanesian cargo cults in the twentieth century awaited deliverance in designated spots. In Jamaica several decades ago the Ras Tafari, a black messianic group, organised to go to Ethiopia. Those who have seen the film *Close Encounters of the Third Kind* may recall the migration to the site of messianic deliverance was its central theme.

Action to signify a change of identity or the purification of community often accompanies migration: crops, livestock and all means of gaining livelihood may be destroyed in a holocaust. Because those objects are mechanisms we use to discharge normal or daily obligations, their destruction symbolises or represents the emergence of the 'new' form of humanity.

The purification and migration processes are more familiar as part of the Western experiences in another form. When believers think that an advent is not immediate they often create a sacred community which tries to separate itself completely from the profane world and is characterised by hypernomian behaviour, i.e., asceticism, excessive self-discipline and a stringent observation of rules which comprehend every aspect of the individual's life. The ethos of this hypernomian community gives messianists cause to identify themselves as the 'righteous remnant' which all the prophecies proclaim will be saved.

In Islam where the term *mahdi* connotes 'rising from concealment' and/or 'rebellion against constituted authority',[21] the groups which withdraw almost invariably intend to find a better and more secure base to organise their violent onslaught on society. The pattern is reflected in Muhammad's own career which probably provides the archetype or model. When he failed to convert his own people in Mecca, he fled to primitive, remote but more receptive Medina from which he returned later in triumph. So expected is the messianic recourse to violence in the Islamic world, that even Jewish messianism there is often violent too, though in the diaspora circumstances of the Christian world, Jewish messianism rarely is.

The fate of hypernomian groups which withdraw seems more complicated in the Christian world than is the case in Islam. If society does not leave them alone or compels them to participate, they may resist, usually by pacifist methods, even accepting martyrdom—perhaps to remind God of the price being paid for His tardiness! Sometimes, after a difficult period, the groups change their course and actively engage the larger society, moving in the process directly from pacifism to terror. The Anabaptists and Taborites of medieval Europe are examples which come to mind,[22] and they were apparently preceded by the Jewish Essenes in the first century.

The striking change is puzzling but there are several good reasons. Whether one chooses pacifism or terror, one still is rejecting the existing conventions governing coercion and thus there is some consistency in the dynamic. A second argument is more particular to the messianic doctrines of the revealed religions which suggest several possible courses of action. Believers, thus, can choose to do different things or different things at different phases of the process. The two dominant images in those doctrines are of the 'suffering servant' and of the 'avenging angel', the latter most often representing the final days or the days of destruction. Pacifism then can be understood as activity appropriate only while waiting for messianic activity to begin, behaviour which in the Christian case also seems to embody the spirit of original religion. To usher in the new age another kind of behaviour is necessary. It is not surprising, therefore, to find that when messianists who abandon pacifism become convinced that they were mistaken about the timing of the process, they often revert to pacifist traditions. Anabaptist history reflects this rationale; the group returned to pacifism after a gruesome experience with terror during the Reformation. Islam provides at least one striking parallel case. In nineteenth-century Iran, the Babi messianic movement began in a terror campaign but upon defeat transformed itself into the Bahia, a pacifist group.

Bryan Wilson's study of the Christadelphians, a contemporary British messianic movement, emphasises something else as well, namely, that pacifism sometimes can be nourished by a profound hatred and not simply by love.

> Christadelphianism is basically a revolutionary organization, vigorously opposed to the social order. . . . But this attitude is not translated into social action although at the appointed time, there would be disposition to do so. . . . The Christadelphian is in conflict with the prevailing social order but powerless to organise its overthrow. . . . Reform [is] useless . . . he [does] not want the world to get better; he [is] opposed to peace, and he want[s] war. Misery was the world's lot and his pronouncement of the fact [falls] little short of active rejoicing. He was emotionally involved in his predictions for disaster out of which he alone would emerge triumphant.[23]

A study of the sequence of events in the Zealot–*Sicarii* uprisings, which were preceded by an extensive passive resistance campaign, reveals another consideration. Angry unarmed demonstrations can tax superbly disciplined troops as the Romans learned. When that discipline breaks down, the atrocities which result, especially when women and children participate, may so disturb a community that virtually any countermeasure seems justified. There are comparable instances in the modern world (i.e., Northern Ireland, Cyprus etc.) which suggests a connection between passive resistance and terror which is independent of the messianic ethos.

THE CAUSE

If a messianic believer thinks that he must participate in a struggle to 'force the end', the nature of the messianic aspiration itself or the cause will become a factor conductive to terror; and this is our *second* doctrinal condition. When the stakes of any struggle are perceived as being great, the conventional restraints on violence diminish accordingly. One expects, for example, that wars which threaten the very existence of the belligerent parties to be much more savage than those for territory or for trade; and it is common knowledge that the appearance of revolutionary states in an existing international order introduces a new level of ruthlessness in world politics. If nothing else were involved, the extraordinary image messianists sketch of the future—the transformation of human existence itself—can induce one to waive limits.

Unreal expectations necessarily create bitter disappointments, which lead in their turn to a variety of responses. A very common one is to believe that that traitors are responsible. The Zealots–*Sicarii* and the Anabaptists had their Reigns of Terror which bear some resemblance to those which came later in the great revolutions of France, Russia and China. Another disappointment results when a group decides that the messianic date is not imminent as it had thought initially. It, accordingly, adopts a more uncompromising attitude towards the world which sometimes encourages a dissenting element to engage in desperate actions against the larger society hoping that the latter's response might compel the messianic group to resume its initial stance. This *may* have been the motive behind the frenzied mutilation murders of Whites in San Francisco, (1973–1974) by the Fruit of Islam, an element which broke away from the Black Muslim movement when that movement began moderating its extraordinary militancy. Similarly, the origin of the Italian Red Brigades has been usually understood in a similar way, as an attempt to make the Communist Party believe in revolution again. The very recent case of American hijacked hostages taken by a Shia faction in Lebanon (June 1985) *may* have been inspired by a similar concern, namely a desire to goad the main Shia body back into increased militancy towards parties outside Lebanon.

PROOF

A *third* doctrinal element is the 'evidence' needed to demonstrate faith. If hypernomian behaviour seems ineffective, new 'tests' or new attempts to prove moral worthiness are contrived. Recently, in Israel when the Camp David Accords were struck it seemed to a few members of the Gush Emunin that a process of relinquishing the Land had begun because the people had sinned in allowing Muslims to have certain sacred shrines. 'It [Camp David] was a direct signal from Heaven that a major national offense was committed, a sin that was responsible for the political disaster and its spiritual consequences. Only one prominent act of desecration could match the magnitude of the setback: the presence of the Muslims and their shrine on Temple Mount, the holiest Jewish site, the sacred place of the first, second and third (future) Temples.'[24]

In the first century some believed the condition of God's intervention would be His conviction that the believer's faith was unshakable, and perhaps the most striking action in this regard occurred when the Zealots decided to burn their own food supplies after Jerusalem was taken, to signify that they had indeed placed all their trust in Him. He had to act for He was bound by His Promise to rescue the righteous remnant. While the Zealots thought that there was no better way to demonstrate commitment, most rabbis considered this an effort to blackmail God which could not possibly succeed.

Josephus, who is our only source, suggests that the rebels often acted as though they thought that faithfulness was being measured by the taboos one was willing to violate or by one's ability to deny limits. When the *Sicarii* mounted their assassination campaign against Jewish priests who they charged had succumbed to Hellenistic influences, the attacks normally occurred on the most holy days. The clear message was that even the most sacred occasion or circumstance could not provide immunity.[25] Josephus' description of the deplorable fate of a Roman garrison illustrates this point. After receiving a safe passage agreement secured by a covenant, the most inviolable pledge Jews could make, the troops surrendered.

> When they had laid down their arms, the rebels massacred them; the Romans neither resisting nor suing for mercy but merely appealing to the Covenant! ... The whole city was a scene of dejection, and among the moderates everyone was racked with the thought that he should personally have to suffer for the rebels' crime. For to add to its heinousness, the massacre took place on the sabbath, a day on which from religious scruples Jews abstain from the most innocent acts.[26]

As the assailants obviously understand, the aggrieved will perceive such violence as atrocities, and are likely to respond in kind, providing the original assailant in turn with a fresh justification for new atrocities. Hence, when the news of the massacre reached the Greeks of Caesarea, the Roman capital of Judea and a major source of military recruitment, they massacred the entire Jewish population 'perhaps 20,000 in a single hour'. Jews revenged themselves by indiscriminate attacks on Greeks elsewhere, and by such means the conflict involved more and more participants who were pulled into an ever-escalating struggle by atrocities which manipulated their fear, outrage, sympathy and guilt.

The antinomian ethos suggested by these acts is a strikingly common feature of messianic movements,[27] and these acts usually have other meanings as well. When, for example, primitives consign their means of subsistence to a holocaust, they are signifying that they have taken an irrevocable step into the new world,[28] one in which *all* existing moral standards will be destroyed as well.

Gershom Sholem's analysis of the Sabbatian movement which rocked seventeenth-century Jewry, for example, demonstrates that its participants believed that the condition of liberation was the systematic violation of every sacred precept.

> When fulfilling each commandment the pious Jew says a blessing. But according to the new messianic formulation introduced by Sabbatai Zevi himself, he says: 'Praised be He who permits the forbidden,' a formula which the defenders of the Jewish tradition rightly regarded as the epitome of this revolutionary heresy.[29]

> Through a revolution of values what was formerly sacred became profane and what was formerly profane [became] sacred. ... More than anything else ... the 'radicals' insisted on the potential holiness of sin. ... The Gordian knot of the exilic Jew had been cut and a vertigo that ultimately was to be his undoing seized the newly liberated individual: genuine desires for a reconsecration of life mingled indiscriminately with all kinds of destructive and libidinal forces tossed up from the depths by an inexpressible ground swell that undulated wildly between the earthly and the divine.[30]

The process reminds one of the term coined by the French theologian Jacques Ellul to describe the more bizarre activities of student radicals in the 1960s, 'desacrilisation'—the pressing need for those who see themselves involved in the creation of a new world to profane all the sacred symbols and norms of the old.[31] Nineteenth-century Russian anarchists were engaged in an identical effort, and those familiar with the works of Issac Bashevis Singer will remember that the desacrilisation process among the Sabbatians is the major theme of his novel *Satan in Goray*.

The Sabbatians did not employ terror; their antinomianism was a secret affair. But a doctrine of this sort must create an interest in terror under appropriate circumstances; and the Frankists, a Sabbatian offshoot, did preach that terror was holy and their language strikingly resembles that of the Russian anarchist Nechaev, usually considered the creator of modern revolutionary terror.[32]

Medieval Christian antinomianism was practised more publicly. The Brethren of the Free Spirits and the Adamites, who moved from a phase of hypernomianism during which they were known as Flagellants, believed that they had entered into a state of grace or had literally become gods incapable of sin. 'A man who has a conscience is himself Devil and hell and purgatory.'

The Adamites declared that 'blood must flood the world to the height of a horse's head. ... From their island stronghold' they 'waged what they called a Holy War. ... They set villages on fire and cut down or burnt alive every man, woman, and child they could find', justifying their acts 'with a quotation from Scripture: "And at midnight there was a cry made—Behold, the bridegroom cometh".'[33] In the First Crusades the Tafurs who 'represented' the poor, and as such 'exhalted as a Holy People worth far more than the knights', normally massacred all the inhabitants of places captured. One incident bears a striking resemblance to Josephus' description of the fate of the Roman garrison which surrendered to the *Sicarii*; and perhaps it was no accident that it took place on the same spot in Jerusalem. Among the Tafur atrocities reported by Christian sources were instances of cannibalism to signify superior commitment or to prove themselves free of sin.[34]

SIGNS OR PORTENTS

The *fourth* doctrinal element is the 'signs' or visible proof that a deliverance is in process. Most messianic visions associate the destruction of the old order and the birth pangs of the new with a series of cataclysms so profound and so unique that they appear to dissolve both the laws of nature and of morality. The world appears to be in the grip of uncontrollable forces: earthquakes, floods, volcanic eruptions, falling stars, widespread famines, raging epidemics, revolutionary wars, gruesome massacres, the dissolution of the most elementary social units and, above all, the unprecedented persecution of the righteous. The terror and horror described is meant to distinguish this struggle from those which have always engaged men. When we believe that a sign of deliverance is a period of inconceivable woe and that the period has not yet occurred, there will be some eager to do their part; and both the commission and provocation of atrocities seem to be means admirably designed for that end. If the road to Paradise runs through Hell, if the fulfilment of the Promise depends upon life becoming as unbearable as possible, violence can have no limits because it cannot be associated with a principle that tells us when to stop because we have either succeeded or we have failed. When disasters do not bring redemption, the obvious remedy is to make the suffering even more profound, and in principle there is no way to demonstrate that our situation is as horrible as it can be.

THE PARTICIPANTS

The *fifth* doctrinal element is the description provided of the participants' moral nature, for our picture of the enemy always shapes our view of the kind of struggle we must wage. In the language of Dead Sea Scrolls, the struggle is seen as a 'War between the Sons of Light and the Sons of Darkness', or in other messianic contexts between Ormazd and Ahriman, God and Satan, Christ and Anti-Christ. The enemy is wholly evil, always dangerous or, in short, something other than human. Binding agreements are impossible to make, because the restraints which the enemy accepts or proposes are designed for the sole purpose of lulling us into complacency. The temptation becomes overwhelming to argue that against such an antagonist everything is permissible. He must be mercilessly destroyed, though perhaps in some cases his evil nature may be purged by terror.

Justifications for unlimited violence are strengthened when we see *ourselves*, and not simply our cause, as wholly righteous, an essential feature of antinomianism, indeed, part of its very definition. The medieval Christian Free Spirits and Adamites literally believed themselves to be gods, and hence able to commit acts which were grotesque by conventional moral standards. Similar phenomena are central issues of Dostoyevski's novels *Crime and Punishment* and *The Possessed* which concern the nineteenth-century anarchists who are the architects of modern terror. The picture of the participants in both the Christian and Dostoyevski cases reminds one of claims often made by contemporary terrorists that the enemy is a symbol or beast not a person and that the freedom fighter cannot be a terrorist regardless of the methods employed.[35]

GOD'S ROLE

The *sixth* and final element is the character of divine intervention. Will God participate in the struggle? In ancient Israel the wars in which God participates are different always from those between human forces only. Whether we are talking about messianic activities or of the earlier wars to gain the Promised Land, which seem to be a model for the messianic conflict, these differences are sustained. The simple fact of divine participation produces a paralysing terror or dread which dissolves the enemy's resolution and negates his advantage of superior numbers and equipment. God fights by means of famine, pestilence and other natural disasters which spread devastation indiscriminately. At its worst, a violent conflict between humans gives the victor a choice concerning the lives and fortunes of the defeated; and normally conquerors preserve in order to possess. At their best, such wars may be subject to conventions concerning the dispositions of populations and properties never engaged or no longer involved in the conflict. But in sharp contrast to this practice, the enemy and his properties had to be exterminated completely in Israel's early holy wars, lest continued existence corrupt Israel. In the later messianic wars terror seems to be violence without restraint or violence which transcends those limits which ordinary concerns for utility and morality dictate.

Let me conclude quickly. Once a messianic advent appears imminent, doctrine guides the expectations and, therefore, the actions of believers, doctrines which, for the most part, are the creation of the dominant or orthodox religious cultures—Judaism, Christianity, Islam and so on. When the doctrines are vague and conflicting, believers must make choices and may abandon some for others more promising and equally legitimate. This also means that there will be differences between single movements and distinct phases which seem contradictory within a single movement. Yet in every case powerful impulses towards terror are inherent in the beliefs of a world to be destroyed, the gains imagined, the character of the participants and God's methods. Beyond all this, and I cannot emphasise the point enough, terror is attractive in itself to messianists just *because* it is outside the normal range of violence, and for that reason represents a break with the past, epitomising the antinomianism or complete liberation which is the essence of the messianic expectation.

NOTES

1 DC Rapoport, 'Fear and Trembling: Terrorism in Three Religious Traditions', *American Political Science Review*, 78(3) Sept. 1984, pp. 658–677.

2 The somewhat panicky concern to protect government buildings in Washington after Shia suicide attacks in Lebanon is indicative. In December 1983 the *Los Angeles Times* reported that a four-minute bomb warning in Coast Guard headquarters provoked a mass exodus of officers while the enlisted men were left behind. In several TV interviews after the US Embassy in Kuwait was destroyed in 1984, I was struck by the fact that all my interviewees seemed convinced that there never could be a defence against suicide attacks.

3 The most thorough account of the plot I know is contained in Ehud Sprinzak's paper 'Fundamentalism, Terrorism and Democracy', *Colloquium Paper*, Woodrow Wilson International Center for Scholars, 15 September 1986. A later version of this paper will be published in *Journal of Strategic Studies*, May 1987.

4 The allegations are made by Janet Aviad, 'Israel: New Fanatics and Old', *Dissent*, Summer 1984, pp. 338–343; Barbara and Michael Ledeen, 'The Temple Mount Plot', *The New Republic*, 18 June 1984, pp. 20–23, and Eti Ronel, 'The Battle Over Temple Mount', *New Outlook*, Feb. 1984. But the identified parties have denied all these allegations.

5 The earliest contemporary discussion of terrorism emphasised the extranormal character of the violence as its distinguishing feature. (See TP Thornton, 'Terror as a Weapon of Political Agitation', *in* H Eckstein (ed.) *Internal War*, New York: Free Press, 1964; EV Walter, *Terror and Resistance: A Study of Political Violence*, New York: Oxford University Press, 1969; DC Rapoport, 'The Politics of Atrocity', *in* Y Alexander and S Finger (eds.) *Terrorism: Interdisciplinary Perspectives*, New York: John Jay, 1977; and H Price Jr. 'The Strategy and Tactics of Revolutionary Terrorism', *Comparative Studies in Society and History*, 1977, 19, pp. 52–65. Recently, the more common definitions do not distinguish between violence and terror. See, for example, CA Russell, *et al.* 'Outinventing the Terrorist' *in* Y Alexander, *et al.* (eds.) *Terrorism, Theory and Practice*, Boulder, Colorado: Westview, 1979.

6 Clearly we have excluded two other messianic forms, one which is wholly secular (i.e., Marxism) and one which posits salvation as an event in the spiritual or unseen world, the orthodox Christian doctrine. My characterisation corresponds roughly to Yonina Talmon's description of millenarism. But because she speaks of movements not beliefs, she specifies imminence as a necessary feature. See 'Millenarism', *Encyclopedia of the Social Sciences*, New York: Macmillan, 1968. While the notion of a personal saviour was once an essential part of the definition, the term, as it is now used, is interchangable with millenarism and chiliasm.

In this chapter I have not distinguished between 'pre-messianic' and 'post-messianic' doctrines. The first visualises a single sudden dramatic destructive advent while the other sees an initial advent which is spiritual and/or gradual, one which is displayed in the unfolding of history which may or may not be followed much later by a violent one. The post-messianic view, which is a doctrine of progress, was characteristic of nineteenth-century messianic groups like the Mormons. See Stow Persons, *American Minds*, New York: Henry Holt, 1958, pp. 176–177. The Gush Emunin, an Israeli messianic group, which has a fundamental concern to settle the West Bank, has a post-messianic view but one which reserves an essential role for violence.

7 Hugh J Schonfield, *The Passover Plot*, New York: Geis, 1965, p. 19.

8 The place of the messianic hope in Jewish liturgy is discussed in Julius Greenstone, *The Messiah Idea in Jewish History*, Philadelphia: Jewish Publication Society, 1906, Appendix.

9 Christopher Hill, 'Till the Conversion of the Jews', UCLA Clark Library Lecture, 30 October 1981.

10 Wilson D Wallis, *Messiahs: Their Role in Civilization*, Washington, DC: American Council on Public Affairs, 1943, pp. 85–86.

11 *B.T. Sanhedrin* 97a.

12 A leader's description of how the Millerites, an American messianic movement in the 1840s, were impelled by the demands of their followers to fix a date for the Secomd Coming is interesting in this regard.

'At first a definite time was generally opposed; but there seemed to be an irresistible power attending its proclamation, which prostrated all before it. It swept over the land with the velocity of a tornado, and it reached hearts in different and distinct places almost simultaneously, and in a manner which can be accounted for only on the supposition that God was (in) it.

The lecturers among the Adventists were the last to embrace the views of the time ... [but ultimately they] could but exclaim, "What were we, that we should resist God." It seemed to us to have been so independent of human agency that we could but regard it as a fulfilment of the midnight cry.' Quoted in Leon Festinger, *et al. When Prophecy Fails*, Minneapolis: University of Minnesota Press, 1958, p. 20.

Raphael Patai's explanation of the hostility to time speculators is similar, 'The results of all these efforts in widely different periods to discover a method of calculating the date of the advent had a common conclusion—that the Messiah would come soon, not in a distant and indefinite future but in their [the calculator's] own lifetime.' *The Messiah Texts*, New York: Avon, 1979, XXXVIII.

13 In 1973 Gottfried Osterwal wrote 'Contemporaneous history is to a large extent the history and growth of new religions and cults. There is hardly a region in the world that in the last two or three [decades] has not given birth to a new religious movement or that has not seen the sudden revival of some old messianic belief. And hardly a week passes ... somewhere where another prophet arises whose

message of a soon coming "messiah" and the imminent destruction of the "present world" becomes the basis of a new messianic movement or religious awakening. Over 6000 of such new religious movements have been reported from Africa. Since the Second World War hundreds of new religions arose in Japan and a similar number has been reported from the Philippines. The thousands of cargo cults and prophetic movements in New Guinea and Oceania are well-known, Southeast Asia ... Latin America ... North America and Europe [show] that the expectation of the soon coming Messiah ... is a universal phenomenon.' *Modern Messianic Movements as a Theological and Missionary Challenge*, Elkhart, Indiana: Institute of Mennonite Studies, 1973, p. 7.

14 'Millenarian enthusiasm [has] always flourished when men thought and cared deeply about religion and when political convulsions tempted them to deduce that the Time of the End was approaching.' PG Roger, *The Fifth Monarchy Men*, London: Oxford University Press, 1966, p. 132.

15 Michael Barkun, 'Divided Apocalypse: Thinking About the End in Contemporary America', *Soundings*, 66(3), pp. 257–280, Barkun's perceptive essay is the source for the themes in this paragraph.

16 In the eyes of those who experienced it the fall of Rome probably provided an early parallel to our sense that the world can be destroyed.

17 Timothy P Weber, *Living in the Shadow of the Second Coming: American Premillenialism 1875–1982*, Grand Rapids: Zonderwan, 1983, Ch. 6.

The restoration of Israel has, of course, been interpreted in different ways at various times. In the Crusades it was understood as the conquest of the holy places. In the late medieval period, groups like the Taborites and Anabaptists imagined themselves to be the new Israel, and among the seventeenth-century English Protestants there was great agitation to send the Jews back to Zion.

18 The tradition is discussed in Sachedina, Abdulaziz Abdulhussein, *Islamic Messianism: The Idea of the Mahdi in Twelver Shiism*, Albany: SUNY Press, 1981, pp. 150–180.

19 Edward Mortimer, *Faith and Power: The Politics of Islam*, New York: Vintage, 1982, pp. 75–79, 181–182.

20 *B.T. Sanhedrin* 97b.

21 DS Margoliouth, 'On Mahdis and Mahdism', *Proceedings of the British Academy*, London: Oxford University Press, ND, p. 213.

22 Norman Cohn, *The Pursuit of the Millenium*, Revised edn. New York: Oxford University Press 1970, pp. 198–281.

23 *Sects and Society*, Berkeley: University Press, 1961, p. 351.

24 Sprinzak, 'Fundamentalism ...' *op. cit.* p. 8.

25 *Antiquities of the Jews*, transl., H St Thackeray, *Loeb Classical Library*, London: Heinemann, 1962, XVII, p. 23.

26 *The Jewish War*, *ibid.*, II. p. 457.

27 The *OED* defines an antinomian as 'one who maintains that the moral law is not binding upon Christians under the law of grace' and the word generally refers to persons who do not believe themselves bound by social rules or standards.

28 In nineteenth-century Russia the Skoptsi (who numbered tens of thousands including nobles, officials, rich merchants and peasants) believed that the messianic period would be populated by sexless beings, and therefore, the condition of joining the movement was castration for the men and the cutting of the breasts for the women.

29 Gersom Scholem, *The Messianic Idea in Judaism*, New York: Schocken Books, 1971, p. 75.

30 *Ibid.* p. 112.
31 *The New Demons*, London: Mowbray, 1975, pp. 48–87. Nineteenth-century anarchists often 'desanctified' themselves by committing acts that they regarded as personally obscene, the object being to break the hold of society's moral conventions over their feelings. A similar process took place among Weathermen and the Japanese Red Army. See my 'Politics of Atrocity', *op. cit.*
32 *Ibid.* pp. 126–134, 'The annihilation of every religion and positive system of belief—this was the "true way" the "believers" were expected to follow. Concerning the redemptive powers of havoc, Frank's imagination knew no limits: "Wherever Adam trod a city was built but wherever I set foot all will be destroyed for I came into the world only to destroy and annihilate."' *Ibid.* p. 130. Compare this with Nechaev's picture, 'The revolutionary ... knows only one science: the science of destruction. ... He enters the world ... only because he has faith in its speedy and total destruction. ... He must not hesitate to destroy any position, any place, or any man in this world—all must be equally detested. ... If he has parents, friends, and loved ones; he is no longer a revolutionary if they can stay his hand.' 'Revolutionary Catechism' in my *Assassination and Terrorism op. cit.* pp. 79–81.
33 N Cohn, *Pursuit*, *op. cit.* pp. 148–163.
34 *Ibid.* pp. 65–67.
35 The parallels between revolutionary and messianic experiences are striking but a discussion of them would require another essay.

Martyrdom as Legitimacy: Terrorism, Religion and Symbolic Appropriation in the Armenian Diaspora

K Toloyan

It is imperative to begin by acknowledging two facts that may seem to disable at the outset the project implied by my title. Armenian terrorists virtually never refer, in their published writings about their motivation and agenda, to their religious beliefs, if any. On the whole, they see themselves as resolutely secular nationalists and leftists, and they would in all likelihood be indignant even at the suggestion that mediated and indirect connections might exist between their acts and world view, on the one hand, and Armenian religion, on the other. Conversely, the Armenian Church has disapproved of terrorism, and would be as horrified at the suggestion of even an indirect relationship between its faith and terrorism as the Pope is by the claim of some Catholic activists and theologians that the Church's teachings can be interpreted to legitimate liberation theology, Philippine guerrilla priests or Sandinista priest-ministers. Yet Robert W Taylor's description of the relations between the Catholic Church and Latin American politics corresponds even more closely to the situation of the Armenian Diaspora. Namely, there is a 'dynamic and dialectical relationship' between religion and politics, 'both mutual and multi-faceted: mutual because religion and politics have evolved together, taking material and symbolic support from one another, and multi-faceted because they both embrace inter-institutional conflict and accommodation ... as well as more subtle exchanges whereby religious and political orders give legitimacy and moral authority to one another'.[1] In the American context, terrorism is a form of violent political conduct which is not given, but rather must rhetorically and symbolically seize and appropriate legitimacy and authority. It is only in such a perspective that the actions of Armenian terrorist groups become fully comprehensible.

This chapter cannot be—as a study of Shiite religiosity and terrorism may legitimately aspire to be—about any *explicit* causal relation between Armenian religion and terrorism. More than most, Armenian terrorism is best understood as a cultural, and not simply political, phenomenon. While I do not discount the importance of the political agenda of the terrorists, or of their ideology, or above all of the conditions obtaining in the Middle East in the period 1965–1975 that re-animated this long-dormant phenomenon, I do believe that Armenian terrorism can only be properly understood in a broader cultural context. In that context, religion and popular narrative are very important factors.[2] Of necessity, my study focuses on the culturally privileged concepts and discourses that are essential to what Richard Martin, writing on Islam, has called 'world-view formation'. The 'cosmography' of what he calls 'textual communities' is 'constituted by those for whom a paradigmatic text or texts is employed in shaping discourse'.[3] Such a shaped discourse, shared by all Armenians, and important to both the Church and the terrorists, is at the core of this chapter.

More than most Christian churches, the autocephalous Armenian Apostolic Church is a *national* church; it has been intimately involved in, and indeed central to, the self-definition of the Armenian nation ever since its conversion to Christianity in AD 301. Just as Moses and Exodus, according to David Rapoport, are associated with 'the establishment of a new order, one in which religious and political elements are inseparable',[4] so also the Armenian Church has been a potent force in shaping Armenian national and political culture since its founding. Few significant phenomena of Armenian history have been independent of its influence. We must therefore be patient in teasing out the workings of the intricate cultural apparatus which mediates the implicit, indirect connections between religion and politics, including terrorism. Our most urgently felt disciplinary impulse has been to 'politicise' terrorism, that is, to interpret complex cultural phenomena such as Armenian terrorism as mere, or only, or just political acts and facts, motivated by and motivating other political acts in a direct chain of causation composed only of political elements, ideologies and agendas. Despite occasional gestures that acknowledge the complexity of sociocultural determination, studies of terrorism end by 'politicising' religion, reducing it to one more motive in the familiar chain of causation. What I shall be discussing in this chapter are, precisely, relations that cannot be appropriated or assimilated into a vectorally direct model of motivation or cause. The Armenian Church is related to Armenian terrorism in that it shapes, or at least contributes substantially to, a cultural web which both enables and limits the thoughts and actions of Armenian terrorists. I hasten to add that the latter are eager to join political scientists in declaring themselves as political men.

These men of political violence are not an altogether new presence in Armenian life. Armenian terrorism began in the mid-1890s, in the Ottoman Turkish Empire, as a response to the extraordinarily repressive measures of the Sultan Abdul Hamid II, and was used to retaliate against government officials, Armenian informers in Turkish service, and most spectacularly, to attract the attention of the European powers and to persuade them to intervene in the internal affairs of the Ottoman Empire so as to insist on reforms to relieve the burdens of the Armenians. Historically, Armenian terrorism was less consequential in fulfilling these externally aimed ambitions than as part of a larger organised effort at village-based self-defence, the limited success of which brought a measure of legitimacy to the secular groups that created self-defence units in Armenian villages. Two political organisations, the Social-Democratic Hunchag party (founded in 1887) and especially the hesitantly socialist but intensely nationalist Hye Heghapokhaganneri Dashnagtzootyun, the Federation of Armenian Revolutionaries or ARF (founded in 1890), were the organisers of this entire range of activities, and its chief beneficiaries as well. In the eyes of the oppressed population, though rarely in the view of the conservative Istanbul-based leadership, the martyr-giving and martyr-avenging underground political organisations began to achieve a legitimacy equal to the Church's, which had historically founded its claims to dominance, in large part, on its own martyr-saints. The figure of the martyr was both an instrument in and the site of a peculiar form of cultural struggle for legitimacy in Armenian history and remains so at the present time. The complex cultural formation that created such an instrument cannot be fully discussed here. But since Armenian terrorism is not merely a struggle against Turkey but also part of a struggle for legitimacy within the Armenian communities of the Middle Eastern Diaspora, we must briefly examine the salient features of this cultural formation.

Armenian society developed in volatile political circumstances: the ancient and medieval Armenian kingdoms were often buffer or vassal states, rarely lasting more than a few centuries. As a result, the nation was most commonly administered by a loose coalition of elites and institutions which functioned as intermediaries between the Armenian population and its foreign overlords. These elites constantly competed for the acquiescence of the population and for legitimacy. For reasons I discuss elsewhere,[5] over the centuries Armenian culture has tolerated only a few, highly specific strategies for achieving that legitimacy: elites must claim to be warriors for the nation; caretakers of its all-too-numerous needy; or guardians of the immortal souls of Armenian individuals and the equally transcendent soul or spirit of the Nation. Such claims are formulated, disseminated and perpetuated principally in narratives which are part of the fabric of the culture, shaping individual and collective self-conceptions. For my argument in this chapter, what matters is that since the establishment of the Armenian Church, the 'warrior' claim has come to imply martyrdom as a necessary correlate, or has been replaced by it outright. The militant martyr has become a substitute for the warrior in the cultural struggle for validation and legitimacy. An institution whose tenets could not inspire martyrdom or other specific forms of sacrifice did not, and still cannot, command much allegiance in the Armenian Diaspora. While the Armenian terrorists are not and never have been practitioners of 'sacred terror' in David Rapoport's sense of this term, many of his remarks can be applied to them with very litle modification: 'Martyrdom, the voluntary acceptance of death in order to demonstrate the truth [of a belief or cause] to man, is a central, perhaps critical method of message-giving ... used both to dispel the doubts of believers and *to aid proselytizing efforts.*'[6]

My point is that terrorism and the martyr-giving which accompanied it was not a minor aberration of political practice but rather part of a larger struggle for the right to lead the Armenian nation that developed in the nineteenth-century and has continued unabated since. Terrorism was in abeyance from 1923 until 1973; the names of the best-known terrorists (avengers of the Genocide) were ritually invoked in public life, as counters in a rhetorical and occasionally armed struggle for entitlement and legitimacy in the Diaspora, but all concerned preferred the rhetoric of memory to terrorist action.

In 1973, Kourken Yanikian, an old man acting on his own, killed two Turkish officials in California to 'avenge' the loss of his entire family in the Genocide of 1915–1922. His action was the subject of furious debate in Armenian public and private life; it came to add urgency to a controversy begun in Lebanon in 1965, on the fiftieth anniversary of the launching of the Genocide.[7] After a period of incubation, the controversy erupted in terrorist action in January 1975, when the Armenian Secret Army for the Liberation of Armenia (ASALA) bombed the Beirut headquarters of the World Council of Churches (WCC). The site was not chosen for religious reasons. The ASALA communiqué and subsequent analyses argued that the WCC, in which bishops of the Armenian Church have held important administrative posts, was citing Christian and allegedly humanitarian reasons to speed the emigration of (Christian) Armenians to the (Christian) West. ASALA claimed that this movement of Diaspora Armenians away from Middle Eastern countries close to the borders of historical Armenia encouraged both the development of historical amnesia and the dissolution of the communal life possible only in the Muslim Middle East and especially in confessional Lebanon, where religious difference matters enormously in the definition and maintenance of separate and cohesive communities.

Since 1975, the Armenian terrorist movement has changed tremendously: it has grown, splintered, engaged in fratricidal warfare and declined. Throughout, while the terrorists have competed with the more established Armenian organisations for the support and allegiance of the community, they have very rarely criticised the Church directly, even if they have done so indirectly, often using symbols made effective by centuries of ecclesiastical rhetoric and practice. The terrorists have not declared themselves pro- or anti-ecclesiastical; nor have they explicitly signalled their awareness of using ecclesiastical traditions. But they have used them. To invoke a parallel, native informants cite only certain sets of social rules and meanings when they explain their motives or behaviour to inquiring anthropologists. However, the anthropologist does not constitute his social model additively, by simply compiling informants' reports. By analysing their reports and actual behaviour, he constructs a model of society which identifies unarticulated, unacknowledged, even unknown rules and relationships, which go further than, and often differ from, that set of social rules cited by the native informant. I shall argue that the structural causes and the cultural, *collectively* constituted codes that enable and constrain terrorist behaviour include religious elements either not recognised or not mentioned by them.

Finally, let me take note of an objection to my argument that some readers would eventually advance anyway. We know that of the approximately 1.5 million Diaspora Armenians, no more than eighty-five have ever been active in the ASALA, and many fewer than fifty in the Justice Commandoes and the Armenian Revolutionary Army. Of these, all but two have come from Lebanon, Syria, Iran and Turkey; one from France; and an interesting maverick from the USA. If the vast majority of Armenians are consciously or unconsciously touched by the religious and cultural institutions and phenomena under discussion, one might ask, how is it that only such a trivially small number become terrorists? I will offer several answers. First, only two religiocultural influences are truly pan-Diasporic; two others that I consider essential to the rise of terrorism are peculiar only to certain parts of the Middle East.[8] Second, the political and social conditions of the Middle East sine 1967, and especially of Lebanon and Iran after 1975, have evolved in such a way as to facilitate the development of terrorism in a community possessed of certain indigenous traditions that potentiate a terrorist response when it is under stress extreme enough to be called crisis, and is frustrated when it seeks to respond in more peaceful ways. Thirdly, I would ask whether any social scientist can answer a similar question : for example, why is it that out of millions of poor Americans, only certain ones commit crimes again and again, while others from identical social circumstances suffer deprivation without turning to crime? Fourth and finally, I would say that I don't know why. This chapter is about what I do know.

It is best to begin tracing the relations between the Church and terrorism at the level of explicit language. The terrorists have successfully appropriated Armenian locutions that are also found, with varying degrees of frequency, in the rhetoric of the older political parties and institutions. All originate in the language and traditions of the Church. The two most ubiquitous locutions are drawn from narratives to which Armenians everywhere in the Diaspora, and in particular in the Middle East, tend to be exposed. These are the narratives of the Genocide and the story of Saint Vartan and the martyrs who fell with him at the battle of Avarayr. The latter is literally a story of martyrdom; the former uses the imagery and vocabulary of martyrdom and Christ's passion.

Of the 1.5 million Armenians who died in the Genocide, around half died of thirst, starvation and disease in the course of forced marches under brutal conditions from the Armenian highlands to the Syrian desert, in particular to the region of Deir ez Zor, west of the Euphrates. These events are the referent for two locutions, one drawn from the Passion of Christ and the other from stories of martyrology and Christian Witness. The narratives and commemorations describe the death march as a 'Golgotha', and all those who fell in it as martyrs. The event is frequently described as the 'crucifixion' of the Armenian nation which, it is fervently recalled, was the first to accept Christianity formally as the religion of prince and people. Occasionally, the indifference of Allied nations to the plight of the Armenians is described, like Pilate's act, as a 'washing of hands'. Of the idioms of Armenian Christianity, the synonyms for 'martyr' are used so commonly to refer to the notable and ordinary victims of genocide as to amount to cliché.

The Genocide scarred virtually every Armenian family in the Diaspora and has remained unacknowledged by the Turkish government. It is therefore not surprising that it remains a psychological wound, and its vocabulary passionate. The ubiquity and rhetorical power of a second Armenian narrative, that of Saint Vartan, is more surprising, since the referent is a set of events that took place in the years AD 450–451. These are commemorated by a Saint's Day in the calendar of the Armenian Apostolic Church. Armenian children encounter the story at Church, in Sunday School, in kindergarten and elementary school. More advanced students in the parochial school systems of the Middle East study it in extended narrative form, usually in contemporary Armenian but sometimes even in the classical Armenian in which it was written down by the monk Yeghishe. This narrative has been ably translated and controversially edited by the Harvard scholar Robert Thomson,[9] who believes that the historically accurate residue in the narrative is small and that the model for the heroic resistance and martyrdom of Vartan and his men derives more from the Biblical books of the Maccabees than from reality. However, the debate about the historical accuracy of the work is beside the point. The invocation of the model of the Maccabees only serves to underscore the ways in which the Saint Vartan story enables and sanctions certain kinds of resistance, endowing it with a mantle of traditional and religious authority. Warriors and terrorists have been able to 'find their rationale in [this] past . . . [and] in the interpretation of [such] precedents from founding periods of the parent religion'.[10]

While this religious dimension was vital in the period extending from the fifth to the nineteenth centuries, it has steadily become less so since. In the nineteenth century, the increase of literacy, the revival of Armenian literature and the increasing accessibility of secular education combined to spawn a dozen versions of the tale. The first major Armenian Romantic poet composed one of his most important poems about the battlefield where Vartan and his followers fell fighting the Sassanid Persians. Two of the most important early romantic-historical novels authored by Raffi, the Armenian equivalent of Victor Hugo, invoke Vartan as a model, while a third takes related figures from the same era for its heroes and villains. In the process of secularisation of the tale and proliferation of its versions three words have remained in play: *v'gah*, or witness, important in the earlier versions; *martyros*, from the Greek martyr; and *nahadag*, its Armenian synonym. In many recountings of the tale, in speeches, sermons, laments and funeral orations, the formulaic line most frequently invovked is *mah imatzyal anmahootyun e*, that is, 'death knowingly grasped is immortality'. The line is pivotal to Yeghishe's book, and refers to the willingness of Saint Vartan and his followers to risk all in defence of Armenian Christianity, conceived then (as now) as a crucial component of national identity.

What the ecclesiastical narrative and the Saint's Day liturgy acknowledge and what later poets, novelists, revolutionaries and now terrorists point to is the fact that Vartan was no mere soldier of the faith, but the *sbarabed*, the hereditary commander of the nation's military forces, what the French would later call the 'Constable': in other words, the premier warrior of the nation, about whose noble family, the Mamikonyans, most Armenian children educated in the Middle East know at least two other stories, and sometimes more. The emblematic warrior of the Armenian nation is also its paradigmatic martyr, perfectly combining secular and religious virtues. The contemporary interpretation retains the vocabulary and imagery of the Church's tradition, but regards as a Vartan-figure any layman willing to risk all for the nation; the religious aura envelops such figures without requiring a confession of religious faith or motive. Vartan's life and death are endlessly narrated in formulaic language, with a passion that establishes them as models of exemplary courage and virtue. Today, even in Sunday schools in the USA, the grandchildren of pacific third-generation Armenian–Americans, many of them members of the Knights of Vartan, still learn to recite a rhyme that declares: *Hye em yes, hye em yes/Kach Vartanin torn em yes*, namely, 'I am Armenian, I am Armenian/the grandchild of valiant Vartan'. The first and second statements are equal, and they imply a regulative autobiography: to be Armenian is to acknowledge Vartan as ancestor. To acknowledge as ancestor one who is not a blood relative is to acknowledge his moral and symbolic authority. In an ethnically pluralist America, the lines and the tradition have no further import. In the Middle East, where Armenians are less assimilated and much beset, the statement and the Vartan stories as a whole come into play as projective narratives that not only tell a story of the past, but also map out future actions that can imbue the time of individual lives with transcendent collective values.[11] Like the narratives of the Genocide, the Vartan stories enrich Armenian rhetoric with words, clichés, phrases, clusters of metaphor and analogy that together constitute a lexicon of highly charged locutions.

The third locution commonly appropriated by the terrorists and involving the Church derives from the tale of Khrimian Hyrig; its kernel is encapsulated in an endlessly repeated reference to the *yergateh sherep*, 'the iron ladle'. There is no element of legend in this tale. In 1878, when representatives of the Ottoman Empire and the various European powers met in Berlin to discuss a peace treaty between the Ottomans and Tzarist Russia, the treatment of the Armenian subjects of the Empire was an issue. Significantly, the Armenians were represented not by their secular leaders, who were not recognised as a specifically political elite by the Ottoman Empire, but by the Patriarch of Constantinople, Megerdich Khrimian, who is still known by the affectionate nickname *Hyrig*, 'little Father'. The Empire acknowledged Khrimian as the head of an Armenian community, the *millet*, defined strictly by its adherence to the Armenian Apostolic faith; Catholic Armenians, for example, were not recognised by Ottoman Turkey as members of the Armenian *millet*. Unable to obtain for his flock any of the consideration he had hoped for, Khrimian returned from Berlin to meet leaders of the community, and described the conference in a folk parable: all met round a huge kettle of *herisa* (a quintessentially Armenian folk dish for festive occasions), but while the representatives of the Powers came with iron ladles, he had only a paper ladle (a memorandum of worthless promises authored by the very states who had invited him to come), so he got no *herisa*. It would be useless to go back to such banquets, he added, until the Armenians, too, had an iron ladle. This utensil became a transparent symbol for armed force, and has become both a cliché to all Armenians and a logo for some: the official organ of the Armenian Popular Movement of Lebanon (which is the political front for ASALA in that country) is called 'Yergateh Sherep'; its logo is a hand poised above a kettle of stew from which it is plucking a morsel shaped like the map of Armenia. The instrument of extraction is a Kalashnikov whose stock is twisted and beaten into the shape of an iron ladle.

The terrorists use the locution of the iron ladle in three ways. First, they invoke it to address the surprisingly large number of Armenians who, like the Maronite Christians of Lebanon, retain the belief that the Christian West will some day intervene on their behalf. The cliché reminds such Armenians that the most famous clergyman of their recent history specifically advised them to abandon that hope; the Great Powers did not care if Armenia got no *herisa*. Second, the terrorists imply that they are the true heirs of a militant wisdom that contemporary Armenian clergymen do not preach, and (by implication) should. Third, they invoke the authority of a revered clergyman to call Armenians to armed struggle. With the locution of the 'iron ladle', the terrorists mobilise this whole complex of political argument euphemistically, yet potently and economically, to address an audience that is steeped in the language of its Church. They communicate much as Mao communicated with Chinese audiences by alluding to centuries-old poems or adages derived from Confucian tales.

The Armenian Church is unable to intervene against linguistic appropriations such as these. In the first place, it lacks the means to resist actively the re-interpretation and re-direction of rhetorical practices which it has historically done so much to disseminate and to make a part of the ordinary discourse of its people. Secondly, by virtue of its role as an authoritative institution involved in attempts to influence and even direct many aspects of Diaspora community life, it cannot help but generate new rhetorical and symbolic practices which terrorists and their sympathisers can again turn to their own use. We must now consider those aspects of the institutional and rhetorical life of the Church which have made it vulnerable to re-interpretation by the terrorists and their propagandists.

Theologically, the Armenian Church is one. Administratively, it is both fragmented and decentred. There are two 'Catholicos'-es, who rank above Patriarchs, Archbishops and the rest of the episcopacy. One Catholicos, based in Soviet Armenia, administers the See of Echmiadzin, which controls the religious institutions still tolerated in the Soviet Union, as well as those in most of Europe, Australia, South America and portions of North America. The other Catholicos, based near Beirut, administers the See of Cilicia-Antelias, which extends to Lebanon, Syria, Iraq, Iran and many communities in North America and Venezuela. This is the See most directly relevant to our discussion. The Patriarchs of Jerusalem and Constantinople control their own small spheres of virtually autonomous administration.

In addition to this tangle of jurisdictional fragmentation and episcopal conflict, we must take into account the more healthy administrative decentring of the Armenian Church within the See of Cilicia-Antelias: namely, married priests are not appointed to parishes, or celibate clergy to larger, diocesan units except by the consent of councils in which civilians dominate. Bishops, and even the Catholicos, are elected by a council in which laymen's votes outnumber the votes of the clergy, in sharp contrast to, say, the Catholic Church. This has two results: it brings clergymen and laymen into constant contact; and even though the Church unquestionably remains the most legitimate and authoritative institution of Diaspora Armenian life, clergymen make few decisions without having to take into consideration the opinions of lay leaders. Secondly, because laymen belong to different political groupings which are unevenly distributed, specific parishes and even entire dioceses can pressure or persuade their priests and bishops into adopting positions that differ remarkably from those adopted by other clergymen. Thus, while perfect theological amity and accord reigns between the Armenian bishops of, say, New York and Beirut, they and the priests subordinate to them may take diametrically opposed positions on matters concerning certain Diasporan realities.

At last count, in 1978, there were 287 parishes of the Armenian Apostolic Church in the Diaspora: 226 parish priests, 89 celibate priests below the rank of bishop, 21 bishops and 13 archbishops. Few of these commit themselves to public pronouncements concerning terrorism, but as we shall see, they address political issues indirectly relevant to it. It is also fair to say that in close-knit communities like those of the Armenian Diaspora, the private opinions of religious or other notables, while not always public, are also not secret, and that the range of opinion found in the clergy is nearly as large as among laymen; such opinions have a way of becoming known without ever being officially articulated. However, in this instance we will consider only public pronouncements.

Since a number of Armenian clergymen have held positions in the World Council of Churches, and since the Catholicos of the See of Cilicia-Antelias has played a significant role in writing some of he WCC's declarations, the Armenian Church has also drafted position papers on issues of general concern to practising Christians. The most recent draft of a still-tentative position paper describing the See's position[12] is closely modelled on the WCC's position concerning the place of Christianity in the public sphere of social life and politics. Following the WCC, the Armenian statement portrays Christ as devoted to 'the value of the individual, the sanctity of human life, and the principles of human freedom'. It also represents Christ as condemning those who transgress against these principles, 'exploit other human beings' or practise various sorts of discrimination. Citing Galatians 3:27–28 ('Baptized into union with him, you have all put Christ on as a garment. There is no such thing as Jew or Greek, slave and freeman, male and female; for you are all one person in Christ Jesus'), the Church condemns inequality and discrimination (Article I). In other articles, specifically invoking the activity of the WCC and Vatican II, the statement further declares the urgency of a Christian commitment to oppose a variety of oppressions, among others the 'violation of human rights and the killing of individuals and nations' (Article II). Finally, in a passage devoted more specifically to the Armenian condition in the Diaspora, the statement adds: 'To all Armenians, it is a truth as plain as day that *the Armenian Church is inextricably intertwined with the life of the Armenian people*, [and has been] spiritually, educationally, culturally and *when necessary politically active* in that life' (my emphasis). It is therefore essential, the statement concludes, that 'the Armenian Church ... motivated both by Christian and broad human principles, give an important place to ... the pursuit of Armenian rights, of compensation and of justice' (Article IV).

It is necessary to put such statements in proper perspective. In the normal course of events, the positions articulated here are highly unlikely to have practical consequences. Even if the draft of this position paper is adopted by the Armenian Church, its *direct* consequences will be negligible. Like others that participate in the WCC, the Armenian Church will continue to interpret this statement to mean that more must be done for refugees (including those from Lebanon and Iran, who include many Armenians) and for human rights. It will not lead to an advocacy of un-Christian acts, let alone to any acceptance of terrorism. Nevertheless, the endorsement of political struggle in the pursuit of justice, even—under some circumstances—for the Church itself, stands as an invitation to interpretation. Armenians of all political convictions will not have difficulty responding to it. The rhetoric of the position paper gives Christian validation to a struggle for the rights of collectivities and against nation-killing; this latter term can be taken to refer both to the Genocide of the Armenians and the seizure of their lands by Turkey. All existing Armenian political groups claim to be struggling for a recognition of that Genocide; some, including the terrorists, for a restoration of the land as well. While the Church's explicit distancing of itself from terrorism is real, so is the problematisation of that distancing which results from the explicit sanctioning of political struggle in religious terms, and in a language that is the *lingua franca* of Armenian political discourse. In fact, it may be useful to reverse the order of emphasis: above all, the Church continues to privilege the discourse of Christian duty and Christian martyrdom as it speaks to the need to struggle for human rights; to a less specific degree, it valorises certain kinds of political struggle, even as it wholly diassociates itself from terrorism as a form of such struggle.

The position is not an acute problem for the Church in most of the Diaspora. But it can become consequential in areas, such as Lebanon, where the indirect but very real pressure of parishioners' beliefs pushes clergymen in the direction of declarations and commitments that have more open political content. The difficulties this can cause are reflected in a preface written by Dr Paul Loffler, a theologian who directs the University of Hamburg's Academy of Mission. Introducing Bishop Aram Keshishian's *The Witness of the Armenian Church in a Diaspora Situation*,[13] Loffler writes:

> One is taken aback at first to find preservation of cultural heritage and of national unity or the survival of a people included in [the concept of] witness. Thinking of the inevitable political consequences of such a witness, one, as a Western Christian, wants to raise all sorts of fingers warning of non-theological factors, unspiritual entanglements and of all the dirty political business which must follow. Yet who

> can contradict the statement that the Christian Church cannot be apolitical? ... To bring back to our consciousness the risky, yet overpowering wholeness of witness, which radiates into all areas of life and society, is part of the ecumenical impact of the Armenian Church.

Loffler's reluctant acquiescence to Keshishian's broadening of the concept of witness perhaps gives us a hint of what the Armenian interpreter can make of the Bishop's statements. He will view it in three contexts: as symptomatic of the situation of all serious Christians and clergymen in a world full of injustice; as directly relevant to the situation of the Middle East, where the involvement of Islamic clergy in non-religious life is common and Shiite theocracy on the rise; and as especially significant in the context of the near-despair which the Armenian Diaspora of the Middle East is experiencing as its cultural identity is threatened by bureaucratic persecution in Turkey, religious pressures in Iran and civil war in Lebanon. The stresses and temptations created by the latter two contexts are obvious, and the role of the Armenian Church in responding to them predictable to some extent. But the Bishop's view of the broader obligations of the Armenian Christian and his Church requires further interpretation.

Bishop Keshishian's book indicates that he, the prelate of the Armenians of Beirut, is responsive, as are most literate Armenians, to the claims made in Latin America by liberation theology and to the parallel claims, stripped of theological elaboration, constantly hinted at by the Armenian press. The Armenian press, especially that section of it which is controlled by the ARF, frequently refers to the struggle in Nicaragua, which it sees as a battle for national self-determination in which sectors of Christianity are for once playing the right role. One need not share this specific political affiliation, of course, in order to hold the viewpoint. Bishop Keshishian's formulation of the issue is significant precisely because of its religious and not merely political conception of the issue. In a section of his book titled 'A Peculiar Theology of Witness', he writes:

> The content of the Church's witness is to proclaim in word and sacrament the definitive breaking into history of the Kingdom of God in Jesus of Nazareth (*Kerygma*) ... [to become] a sign and anticipation of the Kingdom on Earth (*Koinonia*), and to realize the Kingdom through service in the socio-political order (*Diakonia*). ... [The content of the Church's witness] is the announcement of God's offer of salvation in Christ, through identification with the oppressed, the struggle for liberation, and service among the poor. ... The Church does not *have* a witness, she *is* the witness. In fact, the witness is the raison d'etre of the Church's very being and existence. With such a theology of *martyria* the Armenian people understood the Church as the living presence of God in the midst of their life and history. (pp. 26–27)

Such a statement both clarifies a certain kind of Armenian understanding of the role of the Church and demonstrates how inextricably what some Westerners think of as the political can be intertwined with the religious. In particular, the concept of *Diakonia* poses a dilemma that has existed since

Christ's own time: was he heralding a Kingdom of Earth or of Heaven? The New Testament is notoriously ambivalent on the matter: it is not even clear whether the Romans crucified him because he was a religious challenger of the dominant Jewish leadership or because they regarded him as a zealot in politics and a potential danger to their own imperium. Nor is it certain that such a distinction could have been made then. It is clear that the distinction is very hard to maintain today, both in Nicaragua and in the Middle East. The Armenian Church, Bishop Keshishian declares, is heir to a divine intervention in human history, to which it has born witness with its martyrs and a 'theology of *martyria*' which is not written in ink but in blood. That witness *is* the Church, or, in terms of popular religion, the Church over the centuries has so successfully appropriated sacrifice for major Armenian causes as an aspect of martyrdom for the Church that the two remain impossible to separate.

In turn, the Armenian terrorist movements have appropriated the language of martyrdom from the Church and have made it an essential part of the narrative apparatus by which the lives of terrorists are reclaimed and valorised. They have borrowed both the language of the Church and the style of hagiographic narratives of martyrdom, and have adapted these to produce projective narratives and regulative biographies that portray their own militants as true contemporary martyrs for the Armenian cause. Furthermore, in the publications of terrorists and even in writings by others who have only a very limited sympathy for them, terrorism has sometimes been regarded as a '*Kerygma*, a definitive breaking into history', not by God but by the hitherto passive Armenian Diaspora.

Such an appropriation of martyrdom is in fact a claim for legitimacy within the realities of the Armenian Diaspora; the Church has had to counter with moves that are (in the last analysis) also political. Bishop Keshishian not only re-affirms the Church's heritage of witness, but re-defines it further, in a chapter entitled 'The Politicization of Witness':

> The political involvement of the Armenian Church has been and still is, indeed with a renewed impetus, so deep and extensive that it is often quite difficult, if not impossible, in any given stand or function of the Church to distinguish between faith and politics, theology and ideology. The Church is a political factor par excellence in the Armenian Diaspora. (p. 42)

Affirming that the Church has a decisive role to play in the survival of the Diaspora, which is after all its flock and raison d'être, the Bishop goes on to propose: 'The Church should initiate a process of *conscientization*. This involves the revolutionization and politicization of the Armenian Diaspora in its very foundations and structures' (p. 43; emphasis in original).

Two *caveats* concerning the interpretation of these remarkable passages. As Bishop Keshishian elaborates, it becomes clear that the 'revolutionisation' he is referring to is a revolution in consciousness. He wants the Church to 'become the avant-garde of this process of self-discovery and self-assessment, and to mobilize the Armenian Diaspora with this end in view' (p. 45). The call to witness becomes a diffuse call, addressing both self-consciousness and self-image, as well as human rights, which are pointedly said to include 'concern for human rights in general and the violated rights of her people in particular, especially on the international scene' (p. 46). At no point in his text does 'revolutionisation' retain its specific political meaning. Indeed, the relatively middle-class Armenians of Lebanon or most of the Diaspora incline towards conservatism in every aspect of the economic and political sphere but one: that which concerns 'the violated rights' of the Armenian Diaspora, the same rights in the name of which Armenian terrorism was launched, tapping a reservoir of rage and hopelessness that remains undiminished in parts of the Middle East. The Bishop has, in a sense, learned from the terrorists' rhetorical strategy. Whereas the latter have seized the once Church-controlled language of martyrdom for secular purposes, he has appropriated the locutions of 'revolution' for ecclesiastical purposes. He manages simultaneously to respond to his Lebanese–Armenian parishioners' need to hear promises of radical change to ameliorate their parlous situation *and* to evacuate from the concept of 'revolution' its most radical political implications, replacing them with a vision of cultural renewal in the realm of consciousness. In the realm of rhetoric, Church and terrorism thus become mirror images: each defines its task in terms of essentials (to guard Armenian culture and its Christian spirit; to lead armed struggle until the ancestral lands are regained, the Genocide is acknowledged and Armenian society is revolutionised), but each appropriates rhetorical locutions, narrative devices and metaphors from the other (in summary, the terms clustered around martyrdom in one case, around revolution in the other). In doing so, each hopes to claim the loyalty of the largest possible number of people in the heterogeneous Diaspora communities.

This leads us to the second *caveat*. In a sense, the Bishop's words are inconceivable outside of the Lebanese situation: no Armenian Bishop elsewhere in the Middle East and especially in the peaceful Western sections of the Diaspora, would describe the Armenian Church as he does, let alone generalise as he does. Yet it is worth noting that his book is available in English, not the language of his Lebanese–Armenian parishioners, and is made available to the whole Diaspora. His flock exerts a daily and powerful influence on him, as he on it, and due to emigration from Lebanon, remnants of that group are now to be found everywhere in the Diaspora.

One of the many ways in which such influence has manifested itself is in the realm of ritual. Both in Lebanon and in certain isolated parishes elsewhere in the Diaspora, where recent emigrants from Lebanon have been numerous, parish priests have been requested to perform masses for the souls of dead martyrs, members of the Armenian Revolutionary Army who died in a suicide commando raid on the Turkish embassy in Lisbon, Portugal, in 1983. Some clerics have agreed; others have resisted. The entire situation invites comparison with that which has prevailed in Nicaragua for some time now. The Sandinistas are not terrorists, of course, but the challenge they represent for the Pope and the traditional church is multifaceted. The 'words' "the Kingdom of God" crop up in speech and in print with a frequency disquieting' to the clergy, Conor Cruise O'Brien reported recently.[14] The Christian supporters of the Sandinistas, as well as many of the Sandinistas, regard their struggle as one for the 'earthly Paradise', themselves as the 'Pueblo de Sandino, Pueblo de Cristo', and have developed a 'cult of the revolutionary dead', who 'are invariably referred to in countless official statements and inscriptions as "heroes y martires": not merely national heroes but also martyrs—witnesses, through their death, to their faith in the God of the Poor' (p. 55). This fusion of secular heroism and religious martyrdom, so troubling to the Pope during his visit to Nicaragua, was accomplished in Armenian life by the fifth century AD, *by the Church itself.* It is that fusion which has enabled Armenian terrorists to tap an enormous reservoir of emotion in certain portions of the Diaspora, and to turn that emotion both into various passive sorts of support and, most importantly, into an instrument of self-conception and self-validation. The terrorist can see himself not as a marginal outcast from his society but as a paradigmatic figure of its deepest values—as martyr, *nahadag* and witness—living and dying in the central martyrological tradition of the culture, while remaining resolutely secular, disdaining the promise and reward of any paradise.

NOTES

1 Robert W Taylor, 'Liberation Theology, Politics and Violence in Latin America', paper presented at 'Terrorism: An International Conference', University of Aberdeen, Scotland, 15–17 April 1986, p. 2. In large part, Taylor paraphrases Daniel Levine's excellent essay, 'Religion and Politics, Politics and Religion', *Journal of InterAmerican Studies and World Affairs*, 21(1), February, 1979, pp. 5–7. For RW Taylor's paper see above, pp. 45–54.

2 For an extended discussion of the cultural roots of the phenomenon, see my 'Cultural Narrative and the Motivation of the Terrorist', forthcoming, *Journal of Strategic Studies*, May 1987.

3 Richard C Martin, 'Striving in the Path of Allah: Toward an Understanding of Religious Violence in Text and Context', paper presented at 'Terrorism: An International Conference', University of Aberdeen, Scotland, 17–19 April 1986, p. 5. For Revised Version see above, pp. 55–71.

4 David C Rapoport, 'Moses, Charisma and Covenant', *Western Political Quarterly*, June 1979, p. 123. My emphasis.

5 Khachig Tololyan, 'Institutions and Legitimacy in the Armenian Diaspora', MS in preparation.

6 David C Rapoport, 'Fear and Trembling: Terrorism in Three Religious Traditions', *APSR* 78(3), September 1984, p. 665.

7 I discuss the events which fuelled this debate, and the nature of the debate itself, in an essay concerning the decade (1965–1975) immediately preceding the onset of Armenian terrorism: 'Incubating Terrorism: Memory, Commemoration and the Sense of Crisis in the Armenian Diaspora, 1965–1975, MS in preparation.

8 These four factors are analysed in my essay on 'Cultural Narrative', *op. cit.*

9 Robert Thomson, tr. and comm. [The Monk] Yeghishe, *History of Vartan and the Armenian War*, Cambridge: Harvard University Press, 1982.

10 Rapoport, 'Fear and Trembling', *op. cit.*, p. 674.

11 Projective narratives and regulative biographies are discussed in my essay on 'Cultural Narrative', *op. cit.* In effect, projective narratives plot out how ideal selves must live out significant lives: they dictate biographies and autobiographies to come, and instruct individuals in how they would ideally have to live, act and die in order to contribute properly to their collectivity and its future. They prescribe not static roles but dynamic shapes of the time of our lives. In the Armenian instance, individuals or segments of the community frequently understand routine experiences of injustice in the terms of earlier narratives of oppression and resistance. Such narratives are projected upon both the present and the future as morally privileged patterns for interpretation and action. Furthermore, the system of Armenian cultural narrative not only projects actions and lives through narratives, it also appropriates them. A regulative biography retains biographical details which can be assimilated into the paradigms and ethical models of the ideal life as these are articulated by projective narratives. Taken as a whole, then, the system functions diagnostically by identifying and interpreting certain forms of danger and injustice as worthy of resistance, plots out ideal lives and actions for heroes and martyrs and prescribes patterns for regulative biography as a form of secular hagiography.

12 'Hye Zhoghovoorti Iravoonkneroo Hedabentman Hartze' ('The Issue of the Quest for the Rights of the Armenian People'), no date, but as of early 1986, this document was circularing among the episcopacy of the See of Cilicia-Antelias.

13 [Bishop] Aram Keshishian, *The Witness of the Armenian Church in a Diaspora Situation*, New York: Press of the Prelacy of the Armenian Apostolic Church of North America, 1978, pp. 9–10.

14 Conor Cruise O'Brien, 'God and Man in Nicaragua', *The Atlantic*, 258(2), August, 1986, p. 55.

III

Trends and Patterns in the History of Terrorism

Terrorism in Early Modern Europe: The Camisard Revolt

L and M Frey

At the Diet of Ónod (1707) two of Rakóczi's adherents, Counts Bercsényi and Károlyi, drew their swords and murdered Melchior Rakovszky, a nobleman who opposed the continuance of the war; they did so in full view of the assembly. On the Feast of the Holy Innocents (28 December 1705) the Spanish assaulted and murdered the French troops who were passing through the city of Saragossa. In the Cévennes, French peasants, dubbed Camisards, seized a number of pregnant Catholic women and slew them, tearing the fetuses from their wombs (1702). A cold-blooded execution, frenzied mob violence and ritualistic murder marked the insurrections which shook Europe during the War of the Spanish Succession (1702–1714). We will focus on the revolt in the Cévennes.

What differentiated the violence of this insurrection from common crime was its motivation. These acts were political crimes. In the Cévennes the rebels repudiated basic norms and conventions; they engaged in terroristic activities, as did the government. Both sides resorted to 'the systematic use of extreme violence and threats of violence in order to achieve public or political objectives'.[1] The rebels did not engage in systematic terrorism as Laqueur defines it because they only used terror as a subordinate strategy.[2] What they shared with modern terrorists was their antinomianism, that is, their conviction that the promotion of their cause exempted them from traditional mores, from humanitarian considerations. They engaged in 'sub-revolutionary' terrorism for they protested governmental interference with a way of life and the destruction of the Huguenot community. The government through men such as Bâville engaged in repressive terrorism aimed at suppressing the insurgents.[3] Even before the revolt in the Cévennes broke out, Bâville had advocated terror in the conviction that it would discourage rebellion. Such violence was both instrumental in the sense that it was used as means to another end and expressive in that it stemmed from feelings of anger or fear. On their side the rebels also used violence, such as the castration or execution of Catholic priests to dramatise their grievances. Terrorism became a hallmark of this insurrection.

The Camisard revolt began with a murder and escalated into a series of atrocities.[4] The murder had been foretold. From the gallows on 16 January 1702 Françoise Brès prophesied the death of the prosecutor, the abbot François de Langlade du Chayla.[5] Du Chayla, a man who had tortured and executed Protestants and whose name was a byword for cruelty, was an obvious target. The religious frenzy that would tinge his murder can be seen in the personality of Abraham Mazel, a visionary and a predicant or lay preacher. In the early spring of 1702 Mazel dreamt that he drove a number of fat black steers who were devouring the cabbages from the garden. For him the dream was a portent—the garden the church of Christ, he the chosen one, the steers Catholic priests. So began a crusade against the Catholic Church. After joining a band of prophets in the mountains, Mazel was commanded by the Holy Ghost to free his brothers imprisoned at Pont-de-Montvert.[6]

The time for vengeance had come. Directed down to the smallest detail, the prophet, joined now by a group of peasants, walked to Pont-de-Montvert on 24 July 1702 singing psalms. They broke down the door and set fire to the house where the abbot had hidden. The speed of the flames which soon engulfed all of the house except the prisons was interpreted as a sign of divine vengeance. Again, the rebels thought, God had intervened sparing the neighbouring homes, as well as the occupants of the house, who escaped through the windows. The fleeing abbot was captured and killed. The official autopsy revealed that his body had been pierced fifty-two times. Any one of twenty-four wounds would have been fatal.[7] The group then proceeded to cut off the ears and nose of another priest, Boissonade, throwing him from the church tower, and to castrate yet another, who died a few days later. Not only did Mazel and his cohorts attack the clergy, they also murdered the family of a Catholic seigneur. Fearing further atrocities, the curés buried the abbot in haste, wearing civilian garb, and quickly fled to the chateau, protected by soldiers. The intendant voiced his unease, 'Voici un temps de tribulations ou il faut veiller'.[8] The Cévennes was rapidly becoming an armed camp. One of the prophets was soon caught and condemned to having his hand cut off before being burnt alive at Pont-de-Montvert. He died chanting the psalms. A portent, a dream, a convulsion, a murder, a castration. Thus began what has been called the last war of religion. It has also been known as the *camisard* revolt because the insurgents wore a kind of blouse, or *chemise* (in French), *camiso* (in Languedoc dialect) over their clothes to identify themselves or over their heads to disguise themselves. Did this fearsome appearance frighten their enemies? The word *camisard* might also have originated from *camisade* meaning night attack.

Had the fiscal demands of a society at war helped to ignite the rebellion? Louis XIV's wars caused an increase of approximately fifty per cent in the incidence of taxation and threatened to destroy the agrarian economy.[9] The fiscal charges, especially taxes, combined with existing indebtedness and the burden of usury, only deepened an existing agrarian depression. Contrary to all economic dictates or logic, the government instead of curtailing its demands increased them by levying additional taxes on an already impoverished land, on a populace facing a crisis in living standards. The pressures of war exacerbated the economic crisis and perhaps affected the timing of the revolt.

What was remarkable was not that the revolt began, but that it had not begun earlier. Despair had armed the people: persecution and massacre had galvanised the Huguenots, who adopted the cry 'Liberty of conscience or death!' For many it became just that—a struggle to the death. The government's attempts to eradicate Calvinism had begun in 1661 and culminated with the Revocation of the Edict of Nantes in 1685. Louis XIV had moved from limited toleration to legal and finally violent persecution. Louis' representative in Languedoc argued that 'if subjects have a different religion from that of their prince, his dominance and their subjection cannot be complete'.[10] Protestantism caused divisions within the state; the spiritual schism could only produce civil schism. This intolerance produced civil war; this belief became self-fulfilling. Louis' policy of establishing Catholicism as the only religion of the state had disastrous consequences in the Cévennes. It led to the destruction of all Calvinist churches, the prohibition of all assemblies and forced attendance of all children at Mass. The edict was strictly enforced in Languedoc, a bastion of Protestantism.

The attempts to extirpate Calvinism in the mountainous Cévennes, where ninety per cent belonged to the Reformed faith, meant an attack on the culture of the area. Religion and the synodal structure had forged a communal spirit. The Huguenots formed a highly cohesive, even insular, sub-culture, a society within the larger one, *un contre-état calviniste*.[11] Calvinism had permeated the life of the people to such an extent that it had virtually eliminated the native folklore. Psalms replaced the old folk songs and were even sung to lull children to sleep. The use of the *langue d'oïl* in the Bible, in the Protestant texts and in the church services further reinforced the Protestant sense of community and accentuated the differences with their Catholic neighbours. When the Huguenot mystics spoke in tongues, they spoke in French, not in the *langue d'oc* of the region. Ironically, these Protestants, whom contemporaries viewed as fighting the absolute state, unified the realm through their adoption of the French language. Not only language but also names distinguished the Huguenot community. The Protestants chose names from the Old Testament, such as Elie Marion, Abraham Mazel etc.[12] Even jewellery divided the two worlds. The Catholics wore a cross; the protestants, who considered the wearing the cross idolatrous, adopted a symbol of the Holy Spirit. The very insulation of the Calvinists protected their core values and bred an isolationist mentality. The revocation then meant a de-culturation, a de-culturation enforced by an occupying army.

The military occupation initially ensured that the resistance to the government's edict would remain passive. Many Calvinist ministers insisted on obedience to the sovereign, arguing that the harsh winter and difficult summer preceding the revocation presaged the persecution. The persecution itself was seen as a sign of the punishment of God. At the outset, the opposition, albeit clandestine, centred in the family, for Protestants the school of faith. It was here that the father read the Bible, intoned the psalms. The parents reinforced the children's faith. Elie Marion, one of the leaders of the revolt, later reported that the secret instructions of his parents deepened his 'aversion for the idolatry and for the errors of Papism'.[13] Some of these children, burdened by feelings of guilt, resented the outward conformity to the edict. Many carried books to church which were ostensibly Catholic texts but which actually were Calvinist prayers. Others practised free marriage rather than go through the Catholic ceremony; they married by mutual consent, without priest, without witnesses. Catholic baptism was often followed by another, a Protestant baptism. The dying often refused Extreme Unction. But Catholic revenge did not stop at death. Those who had refused the last sacrament were dragged through the mire, face to the ground, and thrown on a refuse heap. Often bodies, secretly buried, were disinterred. Such posthumous vengeance proved so unpopular that more and more Protestants were allowed to die in peace. Only threats filled the churches.

At this time in 1685 the King appointed a new intendant for Languedoc, Nicolas Lamoignon de Bâville, a man of inflexible severity, of missionary zeal, who soon filled the prisons and the galleys. Bâville was unlikely to repeat the mistakes of his predecessor, who had been accused of weakness.[14] The Huguenots, in his eyes, were guilty of both heresy and rebellion. For him Protestantism was a 'source of dissension and discord'. Thus he rigidly adhered to the governmental policy of assimilation, *'un même roi, une même loi, une même foi'*. After expelling eighty-five pastors in order to ensure that the Protestants would remain leaderless, he would report that 'There is no parish which has not been cleansed'.[15] Bâville advocated terror in the conviction that it discouraged rebellion, seizing children, billeting troops, closing churches, executing entire families, interning many in prisons or galleys. In an ironic way Bâville became another victim of the Revocation. As the insurrection continued, he became disillusioned with 'this sad life'.[16] The government's policy exasperated the population and contributed to the spirit which fostered prophetism.

Resistance, nonetheless, became more open. People refused to attend the Catholic Church and turned instead to the clandestine church, to what became known as the church of the desert. The desert served as a two-edged metaphor indicating both the geography and the spiritual desolation of the Huguenots in France.[17] In 1700 one observer counted sixty regular assemblies.[18] This alone attested to the failure of the Catholics to win over the majority in this region. The clandestine church encompassed both the violent and the resigned; some congregated together to pray, others to arm themselves against the royal dragoons.

The active struggle of the Huguenots against oppression began in 1688 and was influenced by various prophets, including one Jurieu in his *Pastoral Letters*. His vision was a millenarian one that followed the successive stages of the Apocalypse. For him the revocation represented the persecution of the righteous. Papism, he predicted, would end between 1710 and 1720. The Second Coming would follow. His writings were widely disseminated throughout the Cévennes. Just such prophetic logic would dominate the revolt. To those living in expectation of a miracle, the reports of miracles were easily believed—psalms falling from the sky, drums mysteriously beating, trumpets sounding. Natural credulity made them even more receptive to such reports. Their interpretation of the Bible, particularly the Apocalypse, reinforced their belief that God would miraculously intervene. The initial prophecies often spoke of agricultural calamities. The subsistence crisis then helped fulfil expectations of an apocalypse. The faithful spoke of destroying the empire of the devil, of the Beast, of the false prophet; they denounced the Catholic authorities in Apocalyptic language as 'followers of the Beast'. Mazel, the prophet in our initial murder, had prophesied the destruction of the Empire of the Beast in 1702, by which time the Apocalyptic mentality had spread throughout the Cévennes. The authorities, especially the rational Bâville, were stupefied by the religious hysteria, convulsions and so on which they had unleashed. The forced de-culturation led to traumatic shock. In the words of Le Roy Ladurie,

> The traumatism of a people deprived of its ministers and its spiritual leadership, tormented by a sense of guilt (for having accepted the Revocation and temporarily repudiated its faith) and oppressed in the bargain by hard times and taxes was so severe that it engendered cases of anxiety, neurosis and even hysteria which would turn into bloody fanaticism.[19]

The first visionary was a young shepherdess of sixteen, Isabeau Vincent of the Dauphiné. Baptised a Catholic, she how returned to the original faith of her parents. Her mother had died and her father had become a *nouveau converti*. While asleep in 1688 she sang the ten commandments in rhyme and then a psalm and finally enjoined the Huguenots to remain true to the faith in the belief that God would save not only her but others as well. Her imprisonment came too late to stop the spread of imitators. These prophets went through the traditional stages of fainting, swooning, convulsions, temporary paralysis, stiffness or rigidity. Such manifestations convinced not only the visionaries, but others as well that they were protected by the Holy Spirit. The visionaries of the Vivarais believing themselves invulnerable met a tragic end. Protected by tiny, white and, needless to say invisible, angels, they met the soldiers' muskets with bare chests, shouting 'Tartara, back Satan'. They were killed where they stood, three hundred strong in February 1689. Even such massacres did not stop the movement or destroy the faith which existed in families and in isolated villages and hamlets. The prophecies of a Marie la Boiteuse reflected the resiliency of a faith that had not died. In 1700 she announced that the day of deliverance had arrived. She was a little early.

This messianism spread southwards to the Cévennes. Most prophets were young, illiterate men and women, who turned away from the apostasy of their fathers. We can hear them denounce the treason and cowardice of their parents in the words of one of the leaders, Cavalier, who resolved to 'defend the cause of the law that our fathers have unhappily forsaken by cowardice'.

Among the prophets were the future leaders of the revolt, Cavalier, Mazel, Rolland.

The serious disorganisation of the society induced by de-culturation resulted in considerable stress which interfered 'with the normal processes of maturation and a secure sense of personal identity'.[20] Religious conversion represented one way of overcoming such stress. The feeling of oppression and helplessness so characteristic of adult conversions was also present in the Cévennes. The very experience of religous conversion often produced strong leaders.

Prophetism, present since 1685, became contagious as did both individual and collective hysteria. The role of the prophets in the insurrection was central.[21] As 'vessels of the Spirit', they aroused the Protestants from 'the sleep of the dead'.[22] None doubted their missionary zeal. The forced abjuration of faith and culture induced a traumatism, a canalising or channelling of violence into other outlets. The rituals of the assembly both expressed community cohesion and created it. Rituals 'in the sense of a stereotyped sequence of actions' were not only symbolic; they also highlighted the grievances and legitimated the violence, transforming murders into executions.[23] Such actions were but another part of a multifaceted reaction to forced de-culturation, to apostasy. The visionaries were but the most visible manifestation of this crisis.

Such visions, such public hysteria, not only engendered courage and confidence, but strengthened the rebels' conviction that they were on the side of God. After the murder of the abbot, resistance crystallised around a group of young chiefs and the number of insurgents multiplied. As summer became autumn, the agitation became a revolt. The priests fled to the protection of the cities. The clandestine church buttressed the Camisards, whose fighting faith, strict discipline, prophecy and inspiration earned their movement the sobriquet: 'Théâtre sacré.' One royalist commander on being surprised cried out, 'A vous voici, messieurs les fanatiques!'[24] When fighting they would often intone the psalms, especially psalm 68:

> Save me, O God, for the waters have come up to my neck. I am stuck fast in the mire of the deep, and there is nowhere to set my foot. I am come into deep waters, and the waves overwhelm me. I have grown weary of crying, my throat has become hoarse; my eyes have failed while I await my God. More numerous than the hairs of my head are they who hate me without cause, stronger than my bones are they who unjustly oppose me: shall I return that which I took not away?

The psalm which begins with this catalogue of misery then advocates punishment for the persecutors.

> Let their eyes be darkened that they see not, and make their loins continually to shake. Pour out the indignation upon them and let there be none to dwell in their tents. ... Let them be blotted out of the book of the living and let them not be enrolled among the just.

These visionaries, unlike the Muggletonians of England, preached war, not peace. 'Burn the churches, kill the Catholics.' It became a holy war. The primitive savagery and ritual murders, which characterised the revolt, led contemporaries to label it the savage rebellion. Rebels, for example, tore the fetuses from the wombs of Catholic peasant women and threatened to burn alive peasants who attended Mass. Under God's name they pillaged without scruple and murdered priests without compunction. The rebels could not be ignored as their numbers mushroomed from an initial eighty to twelve hundred in 1700 and ultimately to five thousand.

The king dispatched four regiments to quell the insurrection, but the terrain of the area and the complicity of the populace made the intendant's task a formidable one. Bâville, for one, complained that the inaccessibility and the remoteness of this land, 'the most wretched in the world', made the populace more likely to rebel.[25] The Rhône and the mountains isolated the movement, delineating an area where wild highlands rose to central mountains, a region particularly suitable to guerilla warfare. The raiders would disappear into villages and gather supplies at night. In most battles the rebels did not number more than 1500 but their realisation that the punishment they faced if caught was worse than death inspired them to fight on ferociously and give no quarter. When outnumbered they would melt into the countryside. Their mobility, their knowledge of the area gave them an enormous advantage. Divided into several groups, each had its own secret cache of provisions. Not united in any formal way, they proved an elusive enemy. The commander of the government troops thought it 'un espèce de miracle' to encounter them. It was no use, Montrevel said, to try and find those 'invisible demons'.[26] To put down what had become a popular and peasant uprising the government attempted to intimidate through execution or through razing several villages. The government's repression merely cemented the solidarity between the Camisards and the population. The authorities found themselves caught in a vicious cycle; increasing the number of troops might only add to the number of insurgents. Government troops could not distinguish the innocent from the guilty. The guerilla became a peasant by day. The rebels replied in kind with other atrocities.

By 1703 the beleaguered Montrevel was proposing desperate solutions, such as a scorched earth policy. He intended to destroy the countryside, to level the villages, to demolish the ovens and the mills in order to ensure that the rebels died of cold and hunger, to rid the country of this 'vermin' which continued to multiply. Bâville, however, insisted on following the law, keeping the distinction between the innocent and the guilty. He rejected Montrevel's proposal to take hostages and execute two for every one Catholic killed.[27] Meanwhile some of the Catholics, who decided to defend themselves, sewed onto their garments small white crosses. These *Camisards blancs*, *Cadets de la Croix* or *florentins* soon began to kill and rob those not involved in the insurrection. Even Montrevel turned against this brigandage and issued an edict against them. In September 1703 he launched a programme of deportation, massacre, summary judgement and destruction of homes and provisions. After razing 466 villages, he re-grouped the people in walled areas or strategic hamlets, threatening them with death if they attempted to return to their former villages. Many died of starvation or fatigue en route; others died in cells or galleys. Finding one prophet and his followers, the royalists executed all seventy of them. Bâville was appalled at the summary execution of unarmed men. 'I have never seen anything more horrible than this butchery in cold blood.'[28] They could well have intoned 'Save me, O God for the waters have come up to my neck'.

Too late to save his brethren, Jean Cavalier counterattacked at Sommières, burning inns, massacring Catholics, stealing supplies and destroying granaries, mills, sheds, even sheep pens. The young Cavalier, general of the *armée des fidèles* swore vengeance before a bloody trophy, the head of one of the rebels. 'Let their dwelling be devastated and let there be none to dwell in their tents.' The 'vengeance of heaven' was heavy, forty churches burned or pillaged, between two hundred and three hundred abandoned, two hundred inhabitants killed. The misery of the countryside was aggravated by the early harsh winter; the snow and the frozen rivers made provisioning difficult and increased the desperation of the insurgents. Atrocities followed atrocities. Royalists killed prisoners taken. In one engagement, rebels pulled a royalist from his horse and beheaded him. On 26 February 1703, yet another rebel, André Castanet, avenging the death of his mother and sister, took the village of Fraissinet-de-Fourques and executed all the inhabitants, including women and children. 'Let them be blotted out of the book of the living.'

By 1704 the rebels had no refuge, they faced cold, famine, despair, a descent into hell. 'I am stuck fast in the mire of the deep and there is nowhere to set foot.' The Cévennes had been systematically devastated by fire. In March 1704 the rebels, by now reckless, ambushed a group of royal troops killing 22 officers and 300 soldiers. Thier commander had enjoined them, 'My brothers double your prayers and we will be the victors'.[29] They were. They despoiled the dead taking the plumed hats and embroidered jerkins and donning them. 'Let their eyes be darkened that they see not.'

The appointment in April 1704 of Claude Louis Hector de Villars signalled a new policy of pacification. He might well have commented, as had his successor, that he 'came not as a persecutor, nor as a missionary, but in the resolution to render justice equally to all the world'.[30] To him the cruelty had only prolonged the conflict. In March the revolt was at its height but three months later the most important rebels had submitted and two months after that the majority of the Camisards. Villars continued to pursue the rebels vigorously while at the same time extending offers of amnesty. Fortunately for Villars, just before his arrival, a soldier spotted an older woman carrying food. Threatened with hanging, she finally divulged the location of the rebels' provisions. The royalists then proceeded to the cache, surprising some thirty rebels, killing them and sticking their ears upon bayonets. They went on to massacre the population of the neighbouring villages. 'I am come into deep waters and the waves overwhelm me.' By 19 April Villars had encircled the partisans, surprising Cavalier's men in a skirmish, killing one-third, including three prophetesses. None asked for quarter. They sought death, the royalists reported, 'With an extraordinary ferocity'.

Now with a stronger hand, Villars could play the role of pacifier. He removed the scaffolds and the torture-wheels from the villages. If the rebels came down from the forest and the mountains, they would be offered an amnesty. They could leave the country or join the king's army on the condition that they be dispersed throughout the royal forces. Louis was certainly anxious for a settlement. Although the royalists had succeeded in isolating and in containing the revolt, the war had threatened Louis' position. He was forced to commit troops to a rearguard action at the same time he was fighting most of Europe in the War of the Spanish Succession. In May 1704 Cavalier signed a humble letter to the king requesting pardon and asking that the partisans be allowed to leave the realm. As he signed, did he remember another abjuration, an earlier one, signed by his father, one he had so vigorously denounced? 'I have grown weary of crying, my throat has become hoarse.' Cavalier was offered a command in the royal army and vague promises of toleration for his co-religionists, promises later violated with impunity.[31] The majority, however, did not survive. Many, knowing only violence, continued the fight. 'More numerous than the hairs of my head are those who hate me.'

The rebels continued the fight until 1710 with no munitions, no allies, no friends to aid them. It was a desperate and doomed struggle. Mazel, our initial murderer, who had obtained an amnesty and gone into exile in 1705, returned in 1709 to rejoin his comrades and to instigate a new insurrection. He did not live a year. In 1710 he was captured and killed. His head was burned in the public square at Vernoux. 'I have become disheartened and have waited for someone to take pity, but there was no one, and for comforters, but I found none.'

How can one explain the Camisard revolt? It was part of a long line of movements inspired by religious visions. It occurred in a society in which religion 'determines and dominates the total world outlook' and in a period 'when the political and religious aspects of society were still largely undifferentiated.'[32] Religious ideas permeated the ethos of the Camisard society. When the existing structure of society, in the case of the Camisards, the Huguenot community, was undermined, the members become less able to face calamity. Cohn argues that 'revolutionary chiliasm has flourished only where the normal familiar pattern of life has already undergone a disruption so severe as to seem irremediable'.[33] The collapse of the traditional value system created a sense of disorientation, frustration and guilt. The Camisards were haunted by the guilt of apostasy. With the disintegration of the religious community, the Camisards found themselves deprived of the material and emotional support to which they had become accustomed. At the same time, many faced poverty and/or famine. Such calamities caused by little-understood forces, Cohn argued.,

> may then produce an emotional disturbance so widespread and acute, such an overwhelming sense of being exposed, cast out and helpless, that the only way in which it can find effective relief is through an outburst of paranoia, a sudden, collective and fanatical pursuit of the Millenium.[34]

Persecuted minorities, such as the Camisards, who do not have the power to change the social situation or relieve the strain imposed on them typically adopt value-oriented beliefs, such as Millenarianism. These beliefs acted as an alternative means to modify the society.[35] The movement answered the search for a sense of community. The government persecution radicalised the movement and enabled the Camisards to interpret their suffering in apocalyptic terms. Their sufferings heralded the Millenium. The coincidence of persecution with the economic and demographical crises made the Camisards open to a millenarian movement. The stress of de-culturation combined with their economic woes created a sense of alienation from life as it then was and induced a feeling of escapism. The peasants were vulnerable to millenarian movements because their Judaeo-Christian *Weltanschauung* (apperception) predisposed them to view history in teleological terms, that is to imagine that history has an inherent purpose, pre-ordained to be realised on earth, the Second Coming.

This belief galvanised individuals, infusing them with confidence, energy and, as we have seen, ruthlessness. It also isolated them from the reality of the king's power and made them impervious to ineluctable limitations, assured of their ultimate triumph. The leaders were filled with a spirit of heroic action, a spirit which pitted them against the forces of evil. Their sense of mission imbued the rebellion with an undoubted ruthlessness and brutality. The tale of the revolt echoes that of a fifteenth-century sect, the Taborites, who preached total chiliastic war. The faithful were enjoined to 'plunge the swords into the enemies of Christ and to wash their hands in the victims' blood'.[36] The enemies of God were to be exterminated. 'The enthusiasm of these groups, the spirit of total dedication to a cause of overriding importance, the conviction of doing God's will, often lead to a dehumanisation of the opponent who is conceived as all evil and all depraved.'[37]

The religious dimension heightened the intensity of the conflict and enabled them to create a reality different than that forced on them.[38] The Camisard revolt makes most sense interpreted as a collective effort to cope with a situation of strain. Prophetic visions and an apocalyptic mentality dominated the revolt. The commitment to a future world led to a certain antinomianism, a rejection of traditional norms.

The insurrection ended as it had begun, with violence. The rebels were hunted down and ritualistically executed. Violence elicited counterviolence, terror, counterterror. In early modern Europe authorities customarily reacted with repression, the violence of which dehumanised and traumatised the populace. Violence gave to the rebel, however temporarily and however illusorily, a sense of control; it freed him from a sense of inaction and despair. This was not surprising in a society accustomed to a high level of violence.

The past conditioned the prospects for future violence.[39] The indestructible past, the historical traditions and beliefs, increased the likelihood and subsequent magnitude of violence. The levying of new taxes or the raising of old ones could ignite revolt as could a rise in the price of that basic commodity, bread. An even more fundamental cause of revolt was the State's attack on local liberties and privileges. During the French religious wars Languedoc, a privileged province and a *pays d'état*, had resisted centralisation. As late as 1632, the peasants had joined with their lords in defending the province against the central government whose most visible agent was the tax collector. Religious issues too could ignite revolt; even earlier the Waldensians and the Albigensians had fought Catholic orthodoxy.

Earlier insurrections pre-figured the revolts that would erupt during the War of the Spanish Succession. The tradition of violent protest was reinforced by the identification of concrete targets which helped to mobilise support for the insurgents and increased the normative justification for violence. Such targets were vulnerable to attack for they provided a tangible enemy, unlike the distant and divinely sanctioned King. The peasants could be stirred to act against the tax collector, an alien element in the rural world and the most visible agent of the central government. The increasingly bitter and sustained resistance meant that taxes could only be collected by force or by threat of force. Concrete symbols, such as the *camiso* in France, reinforced the sense of community, the 'we versus them' mentality. Slogans such as 'liberty of conscience or death' mobilized the masses by articulating grievances and goals. The government's repression could only increase popular support for the rebels. The new ideational justifications for violence were so effective because they were based on a historical tradition of resistance. Furthermore, they appealed to the people in terms of specific deprivations such as the loss of traditional liberties. The liberties they sought were not 'powers of themselves but merely an exemption from the abuses of power'.[40] What they sought were safeguards against the encroaching power of government. In France they fought for freedom of conscience.

In France autonomous organisations threatened the centralised State. The Huguenot communities became independent foci of 'social orientation and political loyalties', independent forces in society not only because of their separate organisational identity but also because of their value systems.[41] The Huguenots had an independent ideological system, a system which shaped the world according to a given set of values. The Camisards, living in a Bible-based culture, were oblivious of the secular values which buttressed the absolute state. Faced with the destruction of the local community and their way of life, they fought back desperately, even appealing to France's enemies, the Protestant powers of England and the United Provinces for help. The very existence of the Huguenots then threatened the basis of the absolute state. Identification with religious activity often meant loyalty to transcendental values rather than to a political community. The meaningful distinction was between the elect and the unregenerate, not the native and the foreigner. The fellowship of the Church extended across borders. We are, as one Huguenot supporter wrote, in the same body, that of Christ. The group referent of the Huguenots, wider than that of territorial France, extended to Calvinists and even to other Protestants throughout Europe. Because their main referent was the religious, not the political community, those who did not actively join the rebellion hid and aided the rebels in the Cévennes.[42] The possibility that the Huguenots would undermine actively or passively the absolute state troubled rulers like Louis XIV, who did not want independent sources of power within France and who consciously tried to limit their development.

In a state where religious authority seconded in a certain measure the civil power, where the legitimation of the ruler was couched in religious terms, dissent could only be viewed as potentially if not actually seditious. The Huguenots, therefore, represented a very real threat in a state validated by religious sanctions, a theocratic state where God not only sanctified the King but the social order as well. The authorities could not but view Protestantism as a source of division, of rebellion.[43] The revolt had confirmed many in their belief that Protestantism should be equated with sedition and disorder. Even after the rebellion was suppressed, the persecution continued, but not with the same intensity. Only the fear of igniting another war dissuaded the authorities from harsher measures.

The Camisard revolt can only be understood as the clash of 'two radically different cultural universes'.[44] Although it was not a *jacquerie*, the revolt harnessed the energies of the most exploited order, the peasantry. The gulf between the propertied and the propertyless had widened; the inflationary spiral, dubbed the price revolution, coupled with technological backwardness worsened the plight of the peasant. Peasant unrest was as old as the servile order and indeed an integral part of that order. Traditionally such violent protest was directed against concrete targets, especially those outside the community. This revolt followed that tradition. The rebels did not attempt or even envisage altering the aristocratic framework of the State. They suffered from a type of 'imaginative poverty, an incapacity to conceive of alternative social worlds ... the result of narrow horizons, limited social experience'.[45] Nonetheless, this revolt reveals much about the extent of disaffection in early modern Europe and the response of the absolute state to unrest.

The revolt was a local and historically conditioned reaction to and manifestation of great social dislocation. A study of this revolt may provide insight into both earlier and later conflicts. Undoubtedly this revolt is more similar to medieval insurrections than to modern revolutions. Yet studies of the transformation of traditional rural communities may aid in the understanding of contemporary transformations. In Third World countries, for example, major social and political issues 'arise from the continuing transformation of the peasantry'.[46] The Camisard revolt vividly illustrates—if one needs reminding—the tragic consequences of forced de-culturation. In another context, another era, another continent, Jean-Paul Sartre would criticise the French in Algeria for 'wiping out their traditions, for substituting our language for theirs, and destroying their culture without giving them ours'.[47] This revolt also addresses another problem, modernisation and its breakdown in some contemporary societies. These early modern societies, like various modern ones, were being 'de-traditionalised', that is, 'drawn into wider, more differentiated and specialised institutional frameworks'.[48] The central government extended its legal, administrative and political activities. The local community fought back and with tragic consequences. It was a fight they could not win.

NOTES

1 WT Mallison and SV Mallison, 'The Concept of Public Purpose Terror in International Law: Doctrines and Sanctions to Reduce the Destruction of Human and Material Values', *in* M Cherif Bassiouni (ed.), *International Terrorism and Political Crimes*, Springfield, Illinois: 1975, p. 67, hereafter cited as Bassiouni, *International Terrorism.*
2 Walter Laqueur, *Terrorism*, Boston: 1977.
3 See Paul Wilkinson, *Political Terrorism*, London: 1974.
4 A number of contemporary accounts illumine the revolt; Jacques Bonbonnoux, *Mémoires de Bonbonnoux, chef Camisard et pasteur du désert*, Cévennes: 1883; Jean Cavalier, *Mémoires sur la guerre des camisards*, Paris: 1973; Maximilien Misson, *Le Théâtre sacré des Cévennes*, Marseilles: 1977; *Mémoires inédits d'Abraham Mazel et d'Elie Marion sur la guerre des Cévennes, 1701–1708,* Vol. 34 of *The Publications of the Huguenot Society of London*, Paris: 1931; *Meslange de Literature, historique et critique sur tout qui regarde l'état extraordinaire des Cévennois*, London: 1707; *Nouveaux mémoires pour servir à l'histoire des trois Camisars*, London: 1708; *Examen du Théâtre Sacré des Cévennes* (in English), *Cry from the Desert*, London: 1708.
5 H de Villenoisy, 'L'Abbé du Cherla, monstre sadistique ou martyr de la foi', *Almanach cevenol*, 5, pp. 73–87.
6 Emmanuel Le Roy Ladurie, *The Peasants of Languedoc*, Chicago: 1974, p. 283.
7 The Catholics compared him to St Sebastien and the revolt to a new *jacquerie*, led by bandits without faith, without law. *Précis historique de la guerre des Camisards, 1702–1710,* Nîmes: 1892, pp. 14, 47, 62.
8 Jean-Robert Armogathe and Philippe Joutard, 'Bâville et la Guerre des Camisards', *Revue d'histoire moderne et contemporaine*, 19, 1972, p. 51; hereafter cited as Armogathe and Joutard, 'Bâville'.
9 Robin Briggs, *Early Modern France, 1560–1715*, New York: 1977, p. 52.
10 Quoted in Pierre Miquel, *Les guerres de religion*, Paris: 1980, p. 487.
11 Janine Garrisson-Estebe, *L'Homme protestant*, Paris: 1980, p. 7.
12 Joutard, *La Légende*, p. 39.
13 Miquel, *Les guerres de religion*, p. 495.
14 'Si les voies douces sont tournées en poison, il faut bien, malgré l'inclination naturelle en reprendre de sévères ou laisser tout perdre.' Armogathe and Joutard, 'Bâville', p. 61.
15 Miquel, *Les guerres de religion*, p. 419. See Nicolas Lamoignon de Bâville, *Mémoires pour servir à l'histoire de Languedoc*, Amsterdam: 1734, hereafter cited as Bâville, *Mémoires.*
16 'Le métier d'intendant est si triste maintenant ... je n'y ai trouvé que veritables sujets d'inquiétude, des difficultés a surmonter sans fin, aucun moment de repos et de tranquillité et j'ai oublié entièrement la douceur qu'il y a posséder son âme en paix qui devroit être le seul bonheur de la vie.' Bâville, 25 May 1708. Quoted by Armogathe and Joutard, 'Bâville', p. 62.
17 Hillel Schwartz, *The French Prophets: The History of a Millenarian Group in Eighteenth-century England*, Berkeley: 1980, p. 14, hereafter cited as Schwartz, *The French Prophets.*
18 Miquel, *Les guerres de religion*, p. 495.
19 Le Roy Ladurie, *The Peasants of Languedoc*, p. 272.
20 Lewy, *Religion and Revolution*, p. 262.

21 Daniel Vidal, *L'ablatif absolu, théorie du 'prophetism', le discours camisard en Europe (1706–1713)*, Paris: 1977.
22 Robert P Gagg, *Das Leben der sudfranzösischen Hugenottenkirche nach dem Todesurteil durch Ludwig XIV*, Zurich: 1961, p. 165; hereafter cited as Gagg, *Die Hugenottenkirche*.
23 *Ibid.*, pp. 14–19.
24 Maurice Pezet, *L'épopée des Camisards, Languedoc, Vivarais, Cévennes*, Paris: 1978, p. 112.
25 Bâville, *Mémoires*, pp. 77–81; Joutard, *La Légende*, p. 59.
26 Armogathe and Joutard, 'Bâville.'
27 *Ibid.*
28 *Ibid.*, p. 63.
29 Miquel, *Les guerres de religion*, p. 504.
30 Berwick, *Mémoires*, 1, 179.
31 Hillel Schwartz, *The French Prophets and Knaves, Fools, Madmen, and that Subtile Effluvium: A Study of the Opposition to the French Prophets in England, 1706–1711*, Gainesville, Florida: 1978.
32 Guenther Lewy, *Religion and Revolution*, New York: 1974, p. 251.
33 Norman Cohn, *The Pursuit of the Millenium*, London: 1957, p. 310.
34 *Ibid.*, p. 314.
35 Neil J Smelser, 'Structural Conduciveness', *in* Ronald Ye-lin Cheng (ed.), *The Sociology of Revolution*, Chicago: 1973, pp. 21–22.
36 Lewy, *Religion and Revolution*, p. 109.
37 *Ibid.*, p. 243.
38 Harvey Mitchell, Preface in *Rural Revolt*, p. 73.
39 Gurr, *Why Men Rebel*, p. 171.
40 James Fennimore Cooper quoted in Arendt, *On Revolution*, pp. 141–142.
41 For a general discussion of this question see SN Eisenstadt, *The Political Systems of Empires*, London: 1963, pp. 62–64 and 140–191.
42 For the basic autonomy of religious organisations see SN Eisenstadt, *Tradition, Change and Modernity*, New York: 1973, p. 193.
43 Ernest Albaric, *Essai sur l'esprit national du protestantisme français au XVIe et au XVIIe siècle* 1853, reprint, Geneva: 1969, pp. 2–3 and Gabriel LeBras, *Etudes de sociologie religieuse*, New York: 1975.
44 Joutard, *La légende*, p. 39.
45 Peter Burke, *Popular Culture in Early Modern Europe*, New York: 1978, p. 176.
46 Henry Landsberger, (ed.), *Rural Protest: Peasant Movements and Social Change*, New York: 1973, p. ix.
47 Fanon, *The Wretched of the Earth*, p. 13.
48 SN Eisenstadt, 'Breakdowns of Modernization', *Economic Development and Cultural Change*, 12, July 1964, pp. 346.

The Dynamics of Terrorism During the Transition to Democracy in Spain

Fernando Reinares

The detonator which precipitated the change of the political system in Spain from authoritarianism towards a liberal democracy was set off in December 1973, when the then President of the Government, Admiral Luis Carrero Blanco was killed in a bomb attack. Though General Franco was still alive, postfrancoism became inevitable. A regime so leader-orientated had lost the person who could guarantee continuity. Although there did exist an institutional heir, Prince Juan Carlos, political succession had been granted to the victim of what soon would be known as 'Operación Ogro'. In this way terrorism made its mark at the very beginning of the transition and became a part of the sordid legacy of the dictatorship: a poisonous inheritance which would finally turn out to be one of the major obstacles to the granting and the consolidation of freedom. Despite all of the self-justification, the practical reality of terrorism has developed into a relentless attack on those forces working towards a peaceful and pluralist re-organisation of society. A brief look at the events resulting from this transition requires some preliminary notes on the genesis and evolution of terrorism during the last years of the Franco regime.

Political violence is a constant feature of Spain's historical development. Francoism itself emerged from its most scandalous form: the Civil War. Francoism in its turn was soon attacked by the communist guerrilla fighters of the *maquis*. Sporadic actions either of an anarchist character or by groups like DRIL (Iberian Revolutionary Directorate of Liberation) were also indications of violent resistance to the dictatorship. It was in 1959 that the organisation which would become the fatal protagonist of terrorism during the political transition began its activities, on a small scale at first. Because of its importance it will receive preferential treatment in this brief chapter. This organisation is ETA, *Euskadi ta Askatasuna* or Euskadi and Freedom. Emerging from a generational changeover in Basque nationalism and carrying out a radical re-defining of this nationalism, ETA planted their first bomb on July 1961. Both men and material were limited. However, in May

1962 it celebrated its first assembly, where it defined itself as 'the Basque revolutionary movement of national liberation created in patriotic resistance'.[1] Soon an intense debate arose within the organisation on the use of violence. In 1964 ETA published a document with a significant title: *La insurrección en Euskadi* [Insurrection in the Basque Country]. In it is set down the basis for what it calls the armed struggle. It argues in favour of armed struggle as the only option against francoist repression. Insurrection can be, in fact, a rational weapon, when the oppression eliminates all the other means. However, some data reveal that we are faced with the elaboration of a theory of terror in whose delirium the arguments used against an authoritarian regime will be perpetuated into the democracy. The ingredient which produces such a confused distortion is none other than the nationalistic mystique. The author of the texts which would serve as the ideological structure of ETA, wrote: 'It is obligatory for all the sons of the Basque Country to oppose denationalisation even if revolution, terrorism and war have to be used to obtain this.'[2] We are faced with one of the typical formulas of the critical moment in nationalism: millenarism. This is the attitude which attributes an absolute value to the political objective of national independence. As Raymond Aron would observe[3] it is precisely this conception of the absolute which brings with it the cynicism of one exclusive *end* which justifies all the means. The recourse to violence and terrorism finds here its ideological justification. In the end, using it in the context of a dictatorship or of a democracy is irrelevant, nothing must change until the day of final paradisical liberation.

Throughout the tortuous evolution of ETA it is clear that there was an irreconcilable difference between the theories of separatist millenarism and political pragmatism. Such was the culture mix of successive splits. The first did not take long to happen. At the end of 1965 circumstances caused the political office of ETA to fall into the hands of the most pro-worker sector of the organisation. This sector was traditionally the least nationalistic and the most inclined to political action of the masses rather than placing emphasis on the prime importance of a strategy based on armed struggle. In fact, it was not Marxism which induced the violence—this emanated directly from nationalist fanaticism. As an analyst has pointed out, 'it is not difficult to see here the confirmation of the aggressive character which nationalism always has. The great nationalisms usually result in imperialism, little nationalisms often end up in terrorism'.[4] However, this does not oblige us to offer a gratuitous exemption to the voluntaristic face of Marxism; as is known, Marx forged his theory not only as a science of society, but also as a doctrine for the revolutionary assault on power, that is to say, as a doctrine of violence.[5] Not in vain did the pro-worker tendency still accept the use, though restricted, of violence. Its only fear was that the complete organisation would become polarised by an activity of a military character. This pro-worker executive was soon questioned, formally accused of Spanish deviation and expelled in 1966 during the fifth assembly of ETA. The nationalist fraction, much more disposed to the use of arms, ended up taking control of the group, which it then re-structured. From this point onwards ETA accepted the principle of the action-repression spiral, a strategy which materialised with the initiation of terrorist operations in the full sense in 1967, and in 1968, with the first murders. However, in 1970 ETA was again divided and in a critical state. The repression had caused ravages among the militants which together with the lack of internal cohesion, provoked a situation almost of final agony. Following the Burgos trial, however, francoism made ETA rise from its ashes.

The Burgos trial, held at the end of 1970, tried sixteen Basque nationalists accused, among other presumed crimes, of banditry, military rebellion and terrorism. Owing to the internal situation of the Franco regime, the national and international repercussions of the event were extraordinary. The publicity surrounding, and propagandistic character of, contemporary terrorism ensured that the trial became an important triumph for ETA: it was the spur which allowed the organisation to re-build itself. Political violence in our time would be pointless without the coverage given by the mass media. Francoism became ETA's *protector* while quite a large part of Spanish public opinion felt a vague sympathy for the clandestine organisation, in the false conviction that it was a group of youths carrying out a strong resistance against the ominous dictator. The organisation itself had contributed to this with its practice of selecting only police as targets. However this myth was only a mirage which, like ballast, accompanied the misfortunes of a society where the majority was convinced that the disappearance of the dictatorship and the establishing of democracy would inevitably bring about the disappearance of terrorism. However, ETA was not fighting against Franco, but against that political community we call Spain. Already in September 1964 in the official bulletin of the organisation, *Zutik*, this warning had appeared, 'anti-francoism fights against Franco as if there was no Spanish repression on the Basque Country. We fight against the Spanish oppression as if there was no Franco'.[6] Following the Burgos trial, the social and political dynamics of ETA were changed and became much more lethal. However, the problems of internal cohesion remained.

Some months after the sixth assembly, ETA claimed responsibility for the surprising and enigmatic attack which killed Admiral Carrero Blanco. In the winter of 1973 the possible exhaustion of the regime caused certain sectors of the organisation to reflect. Thinking is very often a subversive act in associations held together almost exclusively by a hierarchy and the imperative emphasis on the gun, and once again it motivated a schism. Although the armed struggle was still not questioned within ETA, the growing autonomy and importance of the military sector became unendurable for the pro-worker sector. At the top of the executive there predominated the thesis disposed to reconcile the armed activity with political action of the masses. The military sector criticised such positions harshly and finally transformed the complete machine into a military structure. In this way, by the autumn of 1974, the break between ETA political–military (ETA p–m) and military ETA (ETAm) became final. For the latter the armed struggle was the exclusive method whereas for the former this was combined with other types of political action. Perhaps the trigger for the split can be found in the massacre caused by a bomb which exploded in September of that same year in a cafeteria in Madrid. Despite all the evidence pointing to ETA, they denied responsibility, perhaps having realised the serious mistake they had made. That attack would confirm for the first time that its policy of selecting targets had finished. Once violence is unleashed, restrictions do not exist. The armed struggle surprisingly leads inexorably to indiscriminate terrorism. Self-imposed limitations are only the ingenuous projection of a subjective wish. The terrorists know how and where their terror begins, but they do not know how and where it ends. With democracy, the extraordinary terrorist threat may not only destroy our lives but may lead to the destruction of our liberties. Thus the certainty that there exists no justification for violence in a context of tolerance.

Terrorism in Spain was not limited to ETA. In 1974 FRAP (The anti-fascist and patriotic revolutionary front) proclaimed its existence. It had arisen from the Communist Party of Spain (Marxist–Leninist). It carried out three murders in 1975. In a similar way anarchist-inspired and short-lived organisations arose, such as the MIL (Iberian Liberation Movement), one of whose members was condemned to death and executed. Together with these groups, and at a time when it might seem paradoxical (that is during an authoritarian and dictatorial regime), there emerged numerous groupings of the extreme right who used terror under various labels: Warriors of Christ the King, ATE (Antiterrorism ETA), Triple A, Spanish Basque Batallion. During this flood of violence, two members of ETA and three of FRAP were executed by the regime in September 1975.

With the transition came the conflict among various interests for privileged access to the new re-distribution of power and influence. The background was made up of a civic culture which demonstrated its sensitivity for liberties and amnesty. As a study by José Maria Maravall has revealed[7] the transition was possible in the synergy of two concomitant processes: *reform*, agreed by the established power and *pressure* from a civil society which was more or less articulated. Faced with this polemical situation the two branches of ETA which had sprung from the original organisation, made different assessments which *a posteriori* are antithetical. It is at this point that the ideological and political matrices crystallise and shape their evolution. Military ETA has not changed its strategy; on the contrary, it shows signs of evolving towards a more systematic terrorism. The blindness of the armed struggle whose confused primacy cuts off any spark of critical reflection contributes to this, together with the radicalisation which sprang from the tragic events which happened in the city of Vitoria in March 1976 where five workers died in a repressive action against demonstrators. During the first three months of that year, the political–military faction—which had been on the verge of breaking up—charged its special commandos, *talde bereziak*, with two important kidnappings that had purely economic objectives. However, one of the hostages, an industrialist, was murdered. This led to a serious controversy within political–military ETA resulting immediately in the resignation of some of its top leaders. Among these was Eduardo Moreno Bergareche, better known by his nickname 'Pertur'. Within the organisation there was already speculation that Spain was on the threshold of a liberal democracy. The reasoning behind this was to continue along a path of giving as much relevance to armed activism as to the political aspect of their actions. Pertur was convinced that the possibility of an eventual establishment of democracy would necessitate the subordination of the armed struggle to the political activities. In this way he elaborated his thesis of 'doubling' or the functional separation between political action requiring greater capacity, and the armed struggle, which he believed should shed its offensive character and serve as cover and support for popular conquest. What is significant about this is that it proposed the creation of a political party. This constitutes the beginning of a process aimed at regulating the uncontrolled violence which emanated from the nationalist conflict. The party that came about was EIA (*Euskal Iraultzarako Alderdia* or Party for Basque Revolution), the germ of what later became *Euskadiko Eskerra*, a group dedicated to peaceful action through its presence in the institutions including the Spanish Parliament. It also mediated for the abandonment of violence and the self-dissolution of the seventh assembly of political–military ETA, between 1981 and 1982. It was at that seventh assembly, held in 1976, that the thesis of Pertur triumphed.

The differences between political–military ETA (ETApm) and military ETA (ETAm) are often either minimised or ignored. These were clarified in the aforementioned period. The responses are totally distinct from the tension generated between the political activity and armed action. The dynamics of political–military ETA mean the adoption of institutional channels with the resulting disappearance of all armed cover. This came about as the collective demands, generated within the Basque population, found legitimate and formal procedures for their free expression. The existence of such channels is the condition which facilitates the slow social and political isolation of violence: isolation which determines the existence of any terrorist organisation. Perhaps because of this, military ETA saw that the effective consolidation of a democratic regime in Spain would mean its own extinction. It therefore inverted the binomial so that it would form a social support, amorphous and without any other political content apart from the simple, radical nationalist claim, very far from the back-up to action of a political character. Later this would be known as *Herri Batasuna* (United People). Terrorism would be perpetuated through the treacherous dissolution of the political wing and its sublimation to an elitist use of violence. The prominence of the means leads to granting them the title of ends in themselves. There exists an inherent tendency in the terrorist community to persist beyond the conditions which have provoked its formation. The organisation becomes the unconfessed ultimate reason for terror.[8] Political violence in the Basque Country would appear more and more connected, not with movements which propose social–political change but with an organisation which appears to be more and more openly military. Nevertheless, it does not lack certain social support. The definitive separation between the two fractions of ETA came about when the party, supported by the political–military branch, decided to present itself at the constitutive general elections, called for June 1977. Because of this the special commandos (*bereziak*) decided to leave and integrate with military ETA, although some of the militants renounced such an incorporation and created a new terrorist group: Los *Comandos Autónomos Anticapitalistas* (Autonomous Anticapitalist Commandos). This group added to the terror along with another separatist group, MPAIAC (Movement for Self-determination and independence of the Canarias Archipelago), and to the terror promulgated by GRAPO (Anti-fascist revolutionary group Primero de Octubre) and the extreme right. The gangster-like activity of these last mentioned included a plan for political de-stabilisation which reached its maximum point with the murder of five lawyers, specialists in labour cases, in Madrid. This was in January 1977. With FRAP virtually broken up, GRAPO emerged at the end of 1976 when the central committee of the Reconstituted Communist Party of Spain ratified its decision to carry out by means of armed force what it blindly perceived as the revolutionary needs of the population. This decision was taken in the mistaken belief that it had the support of the population. The movement claimed to emulate the Uruguayan tupamaros and showed signs of harsh cruelty. The small organisation, numbering not much more than thirty militants, took their name in memory of the murder of four policemen carried out by the PCE(R) on 1 October 1975 in supposed revenge for the executions of September of that same year. The GRAPO struck at important moments of the political transition. Its declared objective was to prevent the perpetuation of Franco. But the real result was to generate a tension which hindered governability during the passage to democracy.

The stage for the transition had the actors in position for an unprecedented political innovation: the peaceful emergence of democracy out of a despotic regime. Unequivocally Spanish society opted for conciliatory moderation.[9] Violence was more and more the bunker of intransigents. However paradoxical it might appear, terrorism—minority, symbolic and maximalist—confirmed the generic bloodlessness of the change that took place. This does not detract from the magnitude of the violence as a political problem or from its human impact and social consequences. Politically organised violence against the State grew in virulence as the transition concluded with the promulgation of the Constitution. In December 1978, the Spanish political system fell into line with the industrially advanced Western democracies. In the words of Professor Luís Rodríguez Zúñiga: 'In a very short time, and with minimum social costs in comparison with the size of the change, a historical project so often attempted and frustrated and always until now in blood and horror has been carried out'.[10] With the basis for Spanish political life set up, a new process began: that of consolidation.[11] The chronicle of its difficulties is well known and necessarily involves terrorism which during the constitutive period had begun a bloody escalation.

Democracy did not turn out to be the longed-for exorcism of terrorism. After the first free general election, despite the amnesty and the concession of a pre-autonomic regime for the Basque Country, the number of ETA victims grew (see Table 1). Terrorism became more frantic as political transformations accelerated. The growing activity of the Basque terrorist organisation profited from a broadening of the machinery for economic extortion

Table 1. Victims of ETA (Killed), 1968–1980

Year	Victims killed	Political events
1968	2	
1969	1	
1970	—	Burgos Trial
1971	—	
1972	1	
1973	3	
1974	6	
1975	17	Death of Franco
1976	16	First Amnesty
1977	9	First General Elections
1978	67	Constitution
1979	76	Second General Elections: Statute of Autonomy for the Basque Country
1980	96	Elections to the New Basque Parliament

and from some other changes in its methods of operating. The 'legal commandos' appeared and extended their area of activity to include all Spanish territory, where ETA can count on an infrastructure and logistic support. But the new offensive also took a sudden and important qualitative leap. On 21 July 1978, while in the Congress of Deputies the discussion of the Constitutional bill was drawing to a close, military ETA machine-gunned General Juan Manuel Sánchez Ramos. It was the first time that an army general had died in a terrorist attack. Thus began a strategy of provocation directed against the army and aimed at feeding the involutionist temptations which nestled in certain sectors of the army bureaucracy. Military ETA had asserted that the first elections of June 1977 'were no more than a trap to legitimise as democratic a regime which fundamentally was a military dictatorship'.[12] It needed to demonstrate this but was never able to. Its illusory insistence produced successive serious crises in the governability of the political system.

As has repeatedly been pointed out, the terrorism of ETA is inseparable from the Basque question. From Basque nationalism ETA extracted a delegitimising vision of the State, and the hostile attitude necessary for the will to fight. ETA proclaimed 'in it there will not be any non-belligerents, only patriots and traitors'.[13] The constitutional referendum turned out to be insufficient to regulate the nationalist conflict in the Basque Country, the only place where the democracy did not receive the approval of the majority of the population (Table 2). Moderate Basque nationalism had proposed abstention which meant the beginning of a confused attitude regarding the legitimacy of the new democratic State. As the problem of political violence is inseparable from the disharmony which appears in the legitimacy of the institutions, such ambiguity becomes an implicit and tacit support for terrorism. In practice, the main difference between terrorism which is essentially nationalistic and other forms is found in the behaviour of the population,

Table 2. Results of the Constitutional Referendum of 1978 in the Basque Provinces of Spain (% of electoral roll)

	Basque provinces				
Results	Guipúzcoa	Vizcaya	Alava	Navarra	Total Spain
Yes	27.7	31.1	42.3	50.4	58.8
No	13.0	9.5	11.4	11.3	5.3
Blank	2.2	2.5	4.7	4.3	2.4
Total participation	43.4	43.9	59.3	66.6	67.7
Abstention	56.6	56.1	40.7	33.4	32.3

Source: Juan J Linz *et al.*, *Informe sociológico sobre el cambio político en España, 1975–1981*, Madrid: Euramérica, 1981, p. 315.

Table 3. Results of the Referendum of the Statute of Autonomy (1979) for the Basque Country provinces* (% of electoral roll)

Results	Guipúzcoa	Vizcaya	Alava	Total
Yes	55.1	53.6	52.9	54.0
No	2.4	2.9	5.7	3.1
Blanks/others	2.4	2.5	4.6	2.7
Total participation	59.9	59.0	63.2	59.8
Abstentions	40.1	41.0	36.8	40.2

* The province of Navarra was not included within the Basque Autonomous Community.

Source: Spain Ministerio del Interior, Quoted from Juan J Linz, 'De la crisis de un Estado unitario al Estado de las automomías', *in* Fernando Fernández (ed.), *La España de las Autonomías*, Madrid: IEAL/Ministerio de Administración Territorial, 1985, p. 548.

that is, in the different ways of approving the violence which is generated by the connection of the nationalist community: active support, passive support or ambiguous neutrality.[14] Thus democracy arrived in the Basque Country with a deficit in its legitimacy which was only overcome in 1979 with the approval of the Statute of Autonomy (Table 3), accepted by political–military ETA and rejected by military ETA. Meanwhile, terrorism had been the violent symptom of a still unfinished transition.[15] After the 'Statute of Guernica', violence would no longer be a rational method to be used to reach political objectives but a blind machine used to create and re-create the myth of national identity. Any attempts to analyse and identify the technical, political, economic and social circumstances under which terrorism persists, will always find one variable beyond control: fanaticism.

NOTES

1 The not inextensive literature on ETA is either journalistic or devoted to political apology. Some exceptions are: George Hills, 'ETA and Basque Nationalism',

Iberian Studies, Vol. 1, No. 2, pp. 83–90; John Llewelyn Hollyman, 'Basque Revolutionary Separatism: ETA', *in* Paul Preston (ed.), *Spain in Crisis*, London: The Harvester Press, 1976, pp. 212–233, Gurutz Jaúregui, *Ideología y estrategia política de ETA*, Madrid: Siglo Ventiuno, 1981; and Robert Clark, *The Basque Insurgents*, Madison: University of Wisconsin Press, 1984.

2 Fernando Sarrailh de Ihartza (psed. of Federico Krutwig), *Vasconia: Estudio dialéctico de una nacionalidad*, Buenos Aires: Norbait, 1963, p. 30.

3 Raymond Aron, *Polémiques*, París: Gallimard, 1955.

4 Alejandro Muñoz Alonso, *El terrorismo en España*, Barcelona: Planeta, 1982, p. 29.

5 See Alvin W Gouldner, *The Two Marxisms: Contradictions and Anomalies in the Development of Theory*, London: Macmillan, 1980.

6 *Zutik*, No. 24, September 1964. Cited in Jaúregui, *op. cit.*, p. 212.

7 José María Maravall, *La política de la Transición, 1975–1980*, Madrid: Taurus, 1981.

8 Salvador Giner, 'La conquista del caos', *in* Fernando Reinares (ed.), *Terrorismo y sociedad democrática*, Madrid: Akal editor, 1982, p. 15.

9 A summary of social and political attitudes of Spanish civil society during this period can be found in the study of Professor Juan Diez Nicolás, 'Evolución de la ideología de los españoles en el proceso constituyente', *in* Club siglo XXI, *Constitución, economía y regiones*, Madrid: Ibérico de Ediciones, 1978, Vol. III, p. 146 and ff.

10 Luis Rodriguez Zúñiga, 'Sobre la sociedad española actual', *Rēvista de Occidente*, No. 50, June 1985, p. 109.

11 See José María Maravall and Julián Santamaría, 'Political Change in Spain and the Prospects for Democracy', *in* Guillermo O'donell, Philippe C Schmitter and Laurence Whitehead (eds.), *Transitions from Authoritarian Rule: Comparative Perspectives*, Baltimore and London: The Johns Hopkins University Press (forthcoming).

12 Public declaration of ETA(m) quoted in Alejandro Muñoz Alonso, *op. cit.*, pp. 112–113.

13 'Manifiesto de ETA al pueblo vasco', quoted *in* José María Garmendia, *Historia de ETA*, Vol. 1, San Sebastián: Haranburu, 1983, p. 285.

14 On the question of social support for terrorist organisations, see: Luciana Ballini, 'Who Supported the Red Brigades? A Model for the Analysis of Support for Left-wing Terrorism in Contemporary Italy', Paper presented at the 1985 British Sociological Association Annual Conference, University of Hull, April 1985.

15 For further discussion on political violence in Basqueland, see Fernando Reinares (ed.), *Violencia y Política en Euskadi*, Bilbao: Desclée de Brouwer, 1984.

Contemporary Terrorism and the Intellectuals: The Case of Italy

R Drake

In the immediate aftermath of Aldo Moro's death, during the spring of 1978, I began to think about writing a book on Italian terrorism. Until then I had been content to labour in the field of my graduate training, late nineteenth-century Italian intellectual and political history, but Moro's violent end at the hands of the Red Brigades struck me as an event of such profound significance for the people of Italy that I soon resolved to investigate it. This resolve was inspired by personal considerations as well. Several years earlier I had been honoured to receive the first Aldo Moro fellowship for study in Italy, and that connection heightened my interest in his fate.

I wanted to know why he had been killed, a seemingly simple and straightforward question, but the path of knowledge in this case led into a wilderness of political and historical riddles. To even try and answer them it became necessary to recount the history of the terror which claimed Moro's life. More than this, at a very early stage of my research I realised that to understand the Moro tragedy the inner workings of an entire epoch would have to be laid bare and then placed in a meaningful relationship with the historical themes of which terrorism, the distinctive scourge of Italian life during the past decade and a half, is a culmination. That realisation changed the form of my study, from an investigation of a particular episode to a general history; what began as the source of my interest in Italian terrorism became a symbol of the whole.

The tragedy of contemporary Italian terrorism had its concrete beginnings in December 1969 with the Piazza Fontana bombing in which sixteen people were killed and ninety were wounded.[1] For the next five years Italian terrorism was perceived to be essentially a right-wing phenomenon of bank and train bombings. Then from 1975 to 1979 right-wing terrorism yielded the headlines to such left-wing terrorist groups as the Red Brigades and Front Line. The Bologna train station massacre of August 1980, with seventy-nine killed and one hundred and eighty-eight wounded, signalled yet a third phase, characterised by a resurgence of right-wing terrorism.[2] For the last several years both left-wing and right-wing extremists have contributed to Italy's toll of political violence. After 1982 there was a sharp statistical decline in terrorist acts as a whole, but Italy has not yet entered the postterrorist era of her history.

In no other contemporary European society have so many people been maimed and killed as sacrificial victims to the tyranny of both left-wing and right-wing ideology. More than twelve hundred deaths and injuries can be directly attributed to terrorist actions in Italy since 1969.[3] What has caused such an enormous volume of terrorist violence? Who are its exponents, and who supports them? What do they hope to achieve and at whose expense?

I approach these questions along a line of investigation that is theoretically eclectic, with thinkers as diverse as Weber, Mannheim, Gramsci, Namier and Tocqueville illuminating my understanding of how a history of this particular kind should be written. What they all have in common is an insistence on the crucial role of the intellectuals in the history of revolutionary politics from which terrorism is never absent. For the actual structure of my model of terrorism I have been deeply influenced by Fernand Braudel and other *Annales* school historians, particularly by their view that history is to be explained in terms of long-, medium- and short-range forces.

As for long-range forces, Italy is always in crisis because of what Braudel would call 'the slow but perceptible rhythms' of her history; that is to say, for the Italians there is always a difficult rapport between population, space and resources.[4] This difficulty has been accentuated by the burden of Italy's past, on which the French historian Jacques Le Goff has commented in the following way: 'It seems to me that the exceptional gravity of the weight of history in the Italian collective consciousness derives from the explosive combination of three elements—the consciousness of being a very old people, the sentiment of decline between the glory of [their] origins and present state, and the inquietude of existing [as a nation] for only a short time.'[5] Despite the artistic and spiritual genius of the Italian people, centuries of miserable conditions in a land impoverished and degraded by the occupying armies of foreign countries did nothing to prepare Italy for a civic life of peaceful and orderly progress.

It is from this socioeconomic premise and its cultural ramifications that the country's heavily ideological political tradition derives. In combination these forces have made Italy a laboratory of what Karl Mannheim calls 'the politics of utopia' where the revolutionary mystique casts a powerful spell.[6] From the inception of the country's modern history, with the coming of the French Revolution, Italian politics have been inflamed by revolutionary rhetoric of the left and by counterrevolutionary rhetoric of the right. Both of these ideological developments have resulted repeatedly in terrorist action. Filippo Buonarroti, the Italian comrade of Gracchus Babeuf in the 1796 Conspiracy of Equals and a long-time professional revolutionary in Italy, stands out as the archetypal left-wing politically active intellectual fanatic. The other end of the ideological spectrum was simultaneously in ferment. After their brutal liquidation of the revolutionary legacy in the Kingdom of Naples, Cardinal Fabrizio Ruffo's *Sanfedisti*, or Army of the Holy Faith, developed—subsequent to his own disillusioned removal from politics—into a network of reactionary societies in opposition to the underground radical societies of the Restoration period.

Indeed, throughout her modern history Italy has been the promised land of ideologically driven thinkers and activists. It was not an accident that Bakunin, Marx, Sorel and Lenin found vast stretches of fertile ground in Italy for their theories of class hatred and class war, anymore than it was purely fortuitous for fascism to be invented and carried to triumph in Italy. The historical juxtaposition of desperately poor and exploited people on the one hand and constantly insecure elites on the other severely impedes centrist politics, as the annals of the Italian people convincingly illustrate.

Mannheim's approach to the history of ideas has been augmented by those *Annales* historians, particularly Jacques Le Goff, and by the precursors of that school, such as Lucien Febvre, who have made distinguished contributions to our understanding of *mentalités*, i.e., long-term cultural forms and categories, and of how such forces condition the temper of society.[7] We learn from them that each society has its own mental inventory of words, symbols and concepts which are formed and preserved through long periods of time. These cultural schemes and principles become internalised and almost unconscious in a culture, providing coherence and meaning for certain ways of thinking. Every society is characterised by these habit-forming idea-forces which become categories of fundamental thought for its members whose specific attitudes and actions are inevitably coloured by some aspect of the *mental collectif*. The collective mentality orders the past in a way comprehensible to the present without having to make these fundamental values explicit. Thus, the emotional response of a people—that is, their spirit or *conscience collective*—is formed by a unique historical environment outside of which their value structures, belief systems and cultural norms as well as their particular patterns of interaction would remain unintelligible. These distinctive modes of thinking and acting which we ascribe, for the sake of convenience, to national character, Machiavelli conceived in terms of *necessità*, or the limitations placed on human choice by the society in which political decisions are made.

Of course, modern societies inherit not one, but several competing visions of the world, including one which is hegemonic. For these visions people engage in every activity from debating to murder. Therefore, discontinuity is as important in this history of *mentalités* as continuity.[8] However, some societies are more fully integrated from an ideological point of view than others, with relatively little disagreement over fundamental political and moral values. In such historically favoured societies the citizens can get on undisturbed with the routine business of politics, family and work. Acts of violently deviant behaviour will be identified as criminal and lunatic, even though the actors may think of themselves as the revolutionary vanguard of one ideological cause or another.[9] Tragically this degree of integration has never been achieved in Italy, a country where the belief in revolution as the most efficacious way of adjusting society to desirable changes has been invincible.[10]

Medium-range forces in Italian history have aggravated and intensified the country's long-term problems. Since the Second World War the migration from countryside to city and from south to north has continued at a prodigious rate, initially fuelling the phenomenal economic boom of the 1950s and early 1960s, but thereafter, with public expectations soaring, progress slowed and then stopped.[11] The double effect of this epic migration was to injure agriculture seriously and to create an enormous mass of deracinated workers in the cities. The Italian solution to the problems of modernisation has left the countryside dangerously depopulated, the cities dangerously overpopulated and the economy victimised by a nearly total dependence on imported oil as well as by a growing dependence on imported grain.

Throughout the rest of the 1960s the cost of living rose along with unemployment and inflation. Although wages rose, too, the distribution of wealth and power was widely perceived to be unequal. Despite the efforts of the shrewd and able Moro, political sagacity was not a hallmark of the era; in vain did Italy seek a stable coalition to guide her through the difficult passage from a largely traditional past to a consumer society. On the whole Italian culture reflected the stresses of modernisation and was all but powerless to withstand their deep, unsetting thrust into the nation's psyche and mores. As the cities of the north, swamped by an alien population from the south, lost their traditional character, a new mass society rapidly came into existence, with almost no period of adjustment. Socially and culturally, the country was in the deepest turmoil, and this condition left a mark on every feature of national life.

These difficulties came to a head with the 'hot autumn' of 1969 when Italy experienced the worst and most numerous strikes in her postwar history as more than one-quarter of the labour force—5.5 million workers—walked off the job.[12] Never before in all Italian history were so many man-hours of work lost as in 1969, with a total of five hundred and twenty million.[13] Encouraged by their dramatic economic gains of 1959–1963, these multitudes of workers balked at the modest increments won for them by their unions during the mid-1960s. Now in the late 1960s they raced far out in front of their union leaders in demanding better wages and factory conditions. To gain these ends they paralysed the country with wildcat strikes and random work stoppages. Frightened and outraged, employers demanded government action, but this was not forthcoming. With the centre-left Christian Democrat–Socialist coalition in ruins because of fierce Socialist in-fighting, only a minority Christian Democratic cabinet could be formed, under Mariano Rumor. His *monocolore* government was too weak to deal effectively with the escalating violence, which also included a vast outpouring of student protest.

It was against this background of Italy's collapsing fortunes in the late 1960s that the protagonists of contemporary right-wing and left-wing terrorism appeared. In terms of short-range forces affecting Italy's 'age of lead' the crucial developments can only be understood in connection with dramatic policy shifts occurring at the opposite poles of Italy's parliamentary life. At about the same time and for similar political reasons Giorgio Almirante's Movimento Sociale Italiano (MSI) and Enrico Berlinguer's Partito Comunista Italiano (PCI) began a forced march towards the centre. The MSI abandoned its *coup d'état* mentality inherited from the fascist tradition.[14] The PCI did the same thing with its revolutionary beliefs, including revolutionary rhetoric, on the Eurocommunist grounds that Italy would have to find an alternative to Bolshevism in her search for a just society.[15]

These moderate policies created a furore on the extreme right and on the extreme left. With a greater vehemence than ever before, right-wing radicals said 'no' to Almirante and to official neofascism. The dissidents, led by unreconstructed members of such radical neofascist organisations as Ordine Nuovo and Avanguardia Nazionale, continued to hold out for the revolutionary strategy. The dominant personalities among the extreme commando types were Clemente Graziani, Franco Freda, Stefano Delle Chiaie, Adriano Tilgher and Juni Valerio Borghese who dismissed Almirante as a temporiser and a politician; even Pino Rauti, the erstwhile leader of Ordine Nuovo, was condemned by the radicals upon his return to the MSI fold in 1969.

To understand their viewpoint it must be realised that the year 1922 is an *annus mirabilis* for them, an emotional inspiration for their own dreams of the future. Believing that history will repeat itself, they view the fascist march on Rome, not as the nebulous myth of some vanished or utopian civilisation, but as an historic fact of living memory. The *tanto peggio, tanto meglio* (the worse things are, the better things are) lesson of that history has not been lost on them: chaos in the streets and the fear of social dissolution engendered powerful political emotions in 1922, creating the necessary preconditions for Mussolini's rise to power. In its post-Second World War incarnation the strategy of tension was originally designed to achieve the traditional goals of the radical right: to discredit and to supplant liberalism by making the government look as ridiculously impotent as possible and to use the spectre of a Marxist revolution as a pretext for taking power in order to save the country. From this violent historical tradition in Italian politics such neofascist terrorist groups as Ordine Nuovo, Ordine Nero and the Nuclei Armati Rivoluzionari evolved. Trying to cause enough confusion and anarchy in order to provoke a nationwide call for the radical right-wing dictatorship of their dreams, their members blow up banks, trains and stations.

The connecting ideological link between these diverse neofascist leaders and groups is Julius Evola (1898–1974). They all recognised him as their *maestro segreto* and essentially agreed with Almirante's earlier characterisation of him as 'our Marcuse, only better'.[16] A fringe fascist intellectual during the period of Mussolini's dictatorship, Evola had gained fame after the Second World War as the arch guru of radical neofascism, with such books as *Gli uomini e le rovine* (1951) and *Cavalcare la tigre* (1961). In this last book he surveyed modern society and dolefully proclaimed, quoting his adored Nietzsche, that 'the desert is growing'.[17]

For those youths who believed that only a violent rejection of the status quo would enable Italy to escape a dual enslavement, to Marx and to Coca-Cola, Evola was a beacon in the long night of Italy's spiritual crisis. They turned to him for instruction on how to validate themselves in a worthless age. What they learned, particularly from Evola's final homilies, was the paramount need to do battle against the forces of darkness, i.e., against Christian Democrats and Communists. 'Nothing in this system deserves to be saved', Evola exhorted, and the implications of his exhortation were not very subtle.[18] For example in 1970 he wrote, 'It is not a question of contesting and polemicising, but of blowing up everything'.[19] Three years later Evola was warning his followers about the imminent 'decisive hours' as the left, emboldened by the 'undoing of Italy's government, prepared to take power'.[20] Only armed resistance would offer the right any hope of victory, he counselled—an analysis that fitted the radical neofascist mood exactly.

At the opposite ideological pole the Red Brigades and related terrorist groups originated in the protest movements of the late 1960s when the country's radical Marxists said 'no' to the PCI policy of compromise and pluralism. Most of the protestors were content merely to talk about revolution, but the Red Brigades and their fellow terrorists followed the path of revolutionary Marxism to its logical conclusion, in a violent campaign to overthrow the capitalist state. The Red Brigades contended that by abandoning the revolutionary project, the PCI had abandoned Marx. Renato Curcio, the founder of the Red Brigades, claimed to be the true upholder of Marxist–Leninism in Italy because his group alone seriously wanted to provoke the holocaust of capitalism. Thus, as the PCI moved steadily towards the centre, such terrorist groups as the Red Brigades claimed to be filling the vacuum on the revolutionary edge of Italian politics.[21]

Left-wing terrorists in Italy started out with no more apparent advantages than those of the Weather Underground in the United States or the Baader–Meinhof Gang in Germany; but whereas the Weather Underground quickly faded out in America because of the unconquerable indifference of the American people, and the Baader–Meinhof Gang stagnated at a handful of members, such groups as the Red Brigades flourished in Italy well into the 1980s, attracting a thousand militants and more than two thousand external supporters in their heyday around 1978–1979.[22] It is one of the purposes of my study to determine why in Italy terrorism proved to be such an attractive proposition for left-wing radicals and such a resistant foe for the government. The case of Toni Negri, the charismatic radical professor at the University of Padova who for years was at the centre of revolutionary activity in Italy, brings this problem into sharp focus.

While never a member of the Red Brigades, Negri has candidly admitted his moral responsibility for some of the excesses associated with Autonomia operaia, his radical Marxist organisation, which for years functioned, in part, as a revolving door for extraparliamentary left militants on their way to the terrorist underground. Moreover, in the numerous journals that he edited and books that he wrote during the 1960s and 1970s Negri uncompromisingly defended the revolutionary rationale for sabotaging and undermining the capitalist state.[23] In Negri's mind Marxism implied a strategy of tension in the war against capitalism. The struggle between capital and labour had not, in its essentials, become any more complex or less implacable since Marx's time: what is good for the capitalist state is bad for the worker. As he expressed this point in *Il dominio e il sabotaggio: sul metodo marxista della trasformazione sociale* (1978), 'the self-valorization of the proletarian class is above all the destructuralization of the enemy totality'.[24] There could be no compromise, no dialogue, no commerce of any kind with the representatives of the money system. In the capitalist world, the state structured and the workers de-structured; that was all. Shootings, sabotage, strikes, absenteeism, deviant behaviour, criminal behaviour and the refusal to work all contributed to the de-structuralisation of the capitalist economy.[25] Wherever capitalist valorisation broke down, proletarian valorisation was augmented: 'And no pity for the enemy.'[26] For Negri, properly politicised violence fostered the ultimate good of humankind. Hence, as he wrote in *Proletari e stato* (1976), 'the necessity of a militant avant garde force, capable of deepening ... and continuing the crisis and of blunting ... the violence of the bosses'.[27]

The terrorist potential in Negri's Autonomia programme was always sizeable, and later he would confess that his books—the most violent of them at any rate, the ones he has referred to as 'bad literature'—nurtured the tearing passion of the age. For this he apologised during his 1983 trial, but Autonomia Operaia never retracted its policy of diffuse violence.

Neither Negri nor his extremist associates, such as Oreste Scalzone and Franco Piperno, could have had the enduring impact they did without the support of a vast approving audience in Italy. Although the University of Padova was the unexcelled hotbed of this sedition, Negri did manage to establish a substantial Autonomia presence in the factories as well. By contrast, campus radicalism in America during the late 1960s and early 1970s was connected in a serious way to only one major issue: the war in Vietnam or, more accurately, the draft which affected college-age students. Not imperialism, but the obligation to defend imperialism created an atmosphere of extreme unrest which vanished overnight when the apparatus of the student draft was dismantled. Thereafter, radicalism continued to exist on college campuses, as it still does, but more as an exercise in cultural nostalgia than as a serious political movement with a well-developed awareness of how the neocapitalist establishment is to be transformed into a classless society.

Anyone who worked or studied on an American university campus during the late 1960s and early 1970s will recall the conspicuous presence of professors and graduate students *à la* Negri, i.e., ardent radicals in love with the idea of revolution. That the American Negris either disappeared by the mid-1970s or only managed to survive as easily recognisable specimens from a bygone era suggests a condition of infertility in the humus of American culture for this kind of radicalism. In a morally integrated society such as the United States, revolutionary ideas face a virtually invincible challenge from the combined forces of cultural inheritance and of existing political and economic power structures.[28] For this complex of forces to be neutralised will evidently require a far greater shock than even so desolating a blow to American civic and psychic life as the Vietnam War.

However, in Italy Negri's revolutionary ideology was already anticipated in the minds of his multitudinous admirers, some of whom found their way into terrorist groups. In Negri the revolutionary generation of the 1970s found a spokesman of supernal brilliance for its hammer, sickle and rifle version of an alternative society—a latter-day sequel to other visions of the same general character which had seized previous generations of Italian radicals. Negri was speaking a political language in which his audience was completely fluent, and his success depended not on an issue or a moment, but rather on his extraordinary ability to convey the traditional message of revolution in a way that made it come alive for thousands of young Italians.

The professor only pointed in the direction of a brave new world, but, as in every revolutionary movement, not all who were inspired by the quest for paradise came equipped with a discriminating intellect, a highly developed sense of irony and firm convictions about the sanctity of human life. Some only heard the call to revolutionise and then let their instincts do the rest. The history of left-wing terrorism in contemporary Italy is about such individuals, but we must ask ourselves why so many Italians heeded this call in the first place. The answer must be that for an audience of many thousands Negri and his fellow intellectuals on the radical left succeeded in giving expression to the genuine anxieties and hopes of a political culture suffering from a deep historic crisis.[29]

Negri and Evola, who played leading roles in the ferment of contemporary Italy by acting as transmitters of the country's revolutionary traditions which inevitably contain a terrorist component, by no means exhaust the possibilities for research on the connections between theories of violence and violent action. Ten years before his death during the terror, on 28 May 1980, the journalist Walter Tobagi wrote a perceptive and justly acclaimed study, *Storia del movimento studentesco e dei marxisti-leninisti in Italia*, which dealt with the increasingly revolutionary ferment in Italy on the far left.[30] His book is an encyclopedia of the hundreds of revolutionary parties, newspapers, journals, committees, study groups and personalities that appeared during the 1960s. I have explored only a small portion of these materials. Moreover, numerous other figures on the right were eligible for the kind of investigation I have undertaken for Evola.[31] As it is, however, I hope to have shown that Italy's cultural and political traditions have exerted a decisive influence on the present, as exemplified in the careers of these two intellectuals who inherited ways of radical thinking, from Marx and Nietzsche, as well as precedents for radical action, from Bolshevism and Fascism, which they then developed further along the lines of their own revolutionary aspirations.

If long-range, medium-range and short-range forces have combined to produce the unusually severe problem of terrorism in Italy, the intellectuals have given voice to these forces and communicated them to the present generation. This is not to say that the Italian terror of our time can be explained by referring to the biographies and intellectual itineraries of certain radical ideologists. It would be fruitless to try and make generalisations about a social phenomeon of so vast an extent as Italian terrorism on the basis of a few individual portraits.[32] However, it seems reasonable to proceed from Max Weber's assertion that social phenomena involve the action of agents who themselves attach a sense to what they are trying to do. According to this line of reasoning, the historian of Italian terrorism would be obliged to try and determine what the sense of terrorist action is, what the intentions of those involved in terrorism are. In other words, the task of Weber in *The Protestant Ethic and the Spirit of Capitalism*, to identify the historical sources of 'bourgeois consciousness', became for me a matter of identifying the historical sources of 'revolutionary consciousness'.[33]

For this reason I included in my study some representative specimens of radical ideology, right and left. I certainly did not mean to suggest by my choice of figures that any or all of them were necessarily terrorists or even pro-terrorist in their thinking. However, history established connections in these cases, between thought and action, which the historian must attempt to illuminate with as much impartiality as human nature allows.

The precise political function of radical intellectuals can never be stated with absolute certainty. Such questions as which terrorists read or followed them do not lend themselves to clear-cut answers, as the Italian courts have been and are now in the process of discovering. Nevertheless, Antonio Gramsci was surely correct in his assertion that the intellectuals are 'the specialised representatives and standard-bearers of society', i.e., they articulate the political and cultural aspirations of certain groups in society and, to some extent, influence them.[34] When these groups belong to what Arno Mayer calls the 'crisis strata' of society, the function of ideology becomes a crucial part of the revolutionary process, whether on the left or the right.[35] Tocqueville illustrated this point in *The Old Régime and the French Revolution*: 'the vapourings of the *littérateurs*', he noted, had created the essential preconditions for the events of 1789 by undermining respect for traditional values and customs, or, in the idiom of Gramsci, by furnishing the shock troops for the assault of an enlightened counterhegemony against the Bourbon hegemony of Crown and Altar.[36] In *Anatomy of Revolution* Crane Brinton documents the same 'transfer of allegiance of the intellectuals' in revolutionary Russia.[37]

As is true of all important developments in history, human consciousness had to be prepared for the coming of terrorism before it appeared as an actual fact in contemporary Italy. In Richard Weaver's words, 'The theoretical considerations always precede and, in a figurative way of speaking, grade the land for what is to follow'.[38] Historically, intellectuals help to create a state of mind for revolutionary violence, and this mental world of radical utopianism is the starting point for a historical understanding of Italy's age of lead, 1969–1986. Then, of course, other steps must be taken if the analysis is to bear fruit. 'No ideas, no revolution', to be sure, but abstractions can only herald a protracted campaign of revolutionary terror if society has already created an expectant audience for them. For radical intellectuals to be effective, the minimal requirement is that a portion of the population must be suffering from varying degrees of disequilibrium, as in the Italy of our time.

NOTES

1 Arnaldo Giuliani, 'Orrenda strage a Milano', *Corriere della sera*, 13 December 1969. Two additional bombs went off in Rome on 12 December: at the monument

of the Unknown Soldier in Piazza Venezia and in an underground passageway connecting the two buildings of the Banca Nazionale del Lavoro on via Bissolati. In this last explosion sixteen people were wounded, though none seriously.

2 Francesco Fornari, 'Un medico, "Per ore ho medicato gente che aveva perso le gambe e le braccia",' *La Stampa*, 3 August 1980.

3 Richard Drake, 'A Chronicle of Italian Terrorism: 1969–1986', Pt. 1, *The Revolutionary Mystique and Terrorism in Italy: 1969–1986*, Bloomington: Indiana University Press, forthcoming.

4 Fernand Braudel, *The Mediterranean and the Mediterranean World in the Age of Philip II*, New York: Harper and Row, 1972, Vol. 1, pp. 20–21.

5 Jacques Le Goff, 'Il peso del passato nella coscienza collettiva degli italiani', *in* Fabio Luca Cavazza and Stephen R Graubard (eds.), *Il caso italiano*, Milan: Garzanti, 1974, p. 536.

6 Karl Mannheim, *Ideology and Utopia: An Introduction to the Sociology of Knowledge*, New York: Harcourt & Brace, 1936. See also his *Essays on the Sociology of Culture*, London: Routledge & Paul, 1956.

7 Jacques Le Goff, *Time, Work, and Culture in the Middle Ages*, transl. by Arthur Goldhammer, Chicago: University of Chicago Press, 1980.

8 Michel Foucault, *The Archaeology of Knowledge*, transl. by AM Sheridan Smith, New York: Pantheon, 1972. See p. 144 for a blistering critique of historians who misrepresent history as the teleological unfolding of a grand theme.

9 Chalmers Johnson, *Revolutionary Change*, Stanford, Stanford University Press, 1982. See Ch. 4, 'The Disequilibrated Social System'.

10 Nando Dalla Chiesa, 'Del sessantotto e del terrorismo: cultura e politica tra continuità e rottura', *Il Mulino*, Jan–Feb 1981. See especially p. 172.

11 Norman Kogan, *A Political History of Italy: The Postwar Years*, New York: Praeger, 1983, Ch. 16, 'The Changing Social Climate'.

12 Joanne Barkan, *Visions of Emancipation: The Italian Workers' Movement Since 1945*, New York: Praeger, 1984, p. 75.

13 *Ibid.*

14 For Almirante's views on political violence, see his *Autobiografia di un 'fucilatore'*, Milan: Borghese, 1974: 'I invite all Italian youths, but I invite above all the men of thought and culture, the newspapermen and the writers, to a crusade against horror' (p. 136). In this same book he categorically denied the charge that acts of violence were ordered by the MSI. See Ch. 10, 'La mia gente'. On 18 February 1982 he called for the death penalty to be imposed on convicted terrorists. See Giorgio Battistini, 'Sul terrorismo nel MSI è subito polemica', *La Repubblica*, 19 February 1982.

15 See Enrico Berlinguer, 'Imperialismo e consistenza alla luce dei fatti cileni', *Rinascita*, 28 September 1973; 'Riflessioni sull'Italia dopo i fatti di Cile: Via democratica o violenza reazionaria', *ibid.*, 5 October 1973; 'Riflessioni sull'Italia dopo i fatti di Cile: Alleanze sociali e schieramenti politici', *ibid.*, 12 October 1973.

16 Cited by Giorgio Galli, *La crisi italiana e la destra internazionale*, Italy: Mondadori, 1974, p. 20.

17 Julius Evola, *Cavalcare la tigre*, Milan: Vanni Scheiwiller, 1961. 'Introduzione.'

18 Cited by Franco Ferraresi, 'La destra eversiva' *in* F Ferraresi (ed.), *La destra radicale*, Milan: Feltrinelli, 1984, p. 76.

19 Evola, in a 15 January 1970 *Conciliatore* interview with Gianfranco de Turris, republished by de Turris (ed.), *Omaggio a Julius Evola*, Rome: Volpe, 1973.

20 Evola, 'L'esercito e l'obbedienza', *Il conciliatore*, April 1973.

21 Drake, 'The Red Brigades and the Italian Political Tradition' *in* Yonah Alexander and Kenneth A Myers (eds.), *Terrorism in Europe*, New York: St Martin's Press, and London: Croom Helm, 1982.
22 *Terrorism and Security: The Italian Experience*, Report of the Subcommittee on Security and Terrorism of the Committee of the Judiciary United States Senate, Washington DC: US Government Printing Office, 1984, p. 20.
23 See especially the journals *Potere operaio* and *Rosso*. Among Negri's books in which the theme of political violence is central, see *Proletari e stato: per una discussione su autonomia operaia e compromesso storico*, Milan: Feltrinelli, 1976; *La fabbrica della strategia: 33 lezioni su Lenin*, Padova: CLEUP, 1976; *Il dominio e il sabotaggio: sul metodo marxista della trasformazione sociale*, Milan: Feltrinelli, 1978; *Marx oltre Marx: quaderno di lavoro sui Grundrisse*, Milan: Feltrinelli, 1979; and *Dall' operaio massa all' operaio sociale: intervista sull'operaismo*, *in* Paolo Pozzi and Roberta Tommasini (eds.), Milan: Multhipia, 1979.
24 Negri, *Il dominio e il sabotaggio*, p. 12.
25 *Ibid.*, p. 43.
26 *Ibid.*, p. 45.
27 Negri, *Proletari e stato*. Proposition 11 'Ora subito: appunti sul programma'.
28 On the idea of moral integration, see Johnson, *Revolutionary Change*, *op. cit.*, Ch. 2, 'The Social System: Coercion and Values'.
29 Drake, 'The Red Brigades and the Italian Political Tradition', *op. cit.*
30 Walter Tobagi, *Storia del movimento studentesco e dei marxisti-leninisti in Italia*, Milan: Sugar Ed., 1970.
31 For an inventory of right-wing ideological extremism, see Ferraresi (ed.), *La destra radicale*, *op. cit.*
32 However, Johnson notes that micro information is relevant to the sociology of revolutions when it is used in conjunction with a macro model. In fact, the macro model depends on micro information for verification. See *Revolution and Social System*, Stanford, Hoover Institution Press, 1964, p. 50.
33 Max Weber, *The Protestant Ethic and the Spirit of Capitalism*, New York, Scribner, 1958.
34 Antonio Gramsci, *The Modern Prince and Other Writings*, transl. by Louis Marks, New York: International Publishers, 1957. See 'Critical Notes on an Attempt at a Popular Presentation of Marxism by Bukharin' and 'The Formation of the Intellectuals'.
35 Arno Mayer, 'Domestic Causes of the First World War', *in* Leonard Krieger and Fritz Stern (eds.), *The Responsibility of Power: Historical Essays in Honor of Hajo Holborn*, Garden City, New York: Doubleday and Co., Inc., 1967, and reprinted *in* Dwight E Lee (ed.), *The Outbreak of the First World War: Causes and Responsibilities*, fourth edn., Lexington, Massachusetts: DC Heath, 1975.
36 Alexis de Tocqueville, *The Old Régime and the French Revolution*, Garden City, New York: Doubleday and Co., Inc., 1955.
37 Crane Brinton, *Anatomy of Revolution*, New York, Random House, 1965. See Ch. 2, 'The Old Regimes'.
38 Richard Weaver, *Visions of Order: The Cultural Crisis of Our Time*, Baton Rouge: Louisiana State Press, 1964, p. 93.

Terrorism in Germany: 1985

H J Horchem

During the past twenty years, the majority of the Western European countries have been subject to attempts and actions committed by politically motivated terrorists. The international terrorism of Middle East organisations constituted a specific problem in this context. Terrorists involved in these activities are still operating with the certain knowledge that they will be offered a refuge where they will not be pursued in connection with their activities. If they are apprehended, a new action will be planned and organised to free them.

Terrorism of a non-international character in Western European countries has essentially different roots and is born of different motives than international terrorism, although there are corresponding phases of development. Terrorism of autonomistic movements, as for instance in Great Britain and Spain, has similar roots, but differs in the historical background. Terrorism as encountered in the Federal Republic of Germany and in Italy is motivated by similar revolutionary ideas, but still has different motives.

Motivation, ideology and the justification of violence are influenced by the environment of the terrorist organisations and are in turn reflected in the environment and initiate in this way new motivations.

THE 'RED ARMY FACTION' (*RAF*)

IDEOLOGY AND STRATEGY

Until recently, German terrorism consisted of three main groups: the RAF, the '2 June Movement' and the 'Revolutionary Cells' (RZ). At the beginning of 1980 the '2 June Movement' abandoned the 'armed struggle'. The RAF took over its rest-cadre in June 1980.

The RAF is the oldest and most brutal terrorist organisation in Germany. It was born with the violent release of Andreas Baader from prison on 14 May 1970. Ulrike Meinhof and Horst Mahler took part in this action. Meinhof justified the operation in a statement during her trial on 13 September 1974, calling it an exemplary action. She said that the action comprised all the elements of the strategy of the armed anti-imperialistic struggle.

The armed anti-imperialistic struggle aims at destroying the imperialistic feudal system, politically, economically and militarily. The anti-imperialistic struggle is being conducted in international actions against the defence allies of the United States—in particular NATO—and the German Federal Armed Forces. Nationally, the struggle is conducted against the armed forces of the state apparatus, which represents the monopoly of power of the ruling class, that is, the police, the Federal frontier police and the security services. Also as targets are the power structures of the multinationals, that is, state and non-state bureaucracies, the parties, trade unions and the media. These theses of Meinhof can still be found in the latest publications of the various commandos of the Red Army Faction. Wherever such political aims are mentioned, so-called US imperialism is mentioned as well.

The tracts of Mahler and Meinhof are of considerable importance to the political motivation and justification of all the German terrorists—not just for the Red Army Faction. The three main tracts (the concept of the earlier guerilla armed struggle in Western Europe, urban guerilla warfare and the class struggle) appeared between April 1971 and April 1972. The language of Meinhof has affected the linguistic style of the various commandos to this day.

Between 11 May and 24 May 1972, the Red Army Faction commandos carried out six serious bomb attacks in Frankfurt, Munich, Augsburg, Hamburg, Karlsruhe and Heidelberg. Four people were killed and nineteen injured. This escalation of violence led to an intensive search for the terrorists. The public were encouraged to pass on information to the security authorities. As a result of information passed on by the public, the following members of the Red Army Faction were arrested between 1 June and 15 June 1972: Baader, Meinhof, Holger Meins, Jan Karl Raspe, Gudrun Ensslin and Gerhard Muller.

A year later, in the summer of 1973, the Red Army Faction began to build a follow-up group. This group founded other groups in Hamburg, Frankfurt and Amsterdam. It intended, through the creation of sufficient logistical measures, to prepare for the main aim of the Red Army Faction, namely, to release their members being held prisoner. They raised the necessary money through bank robberies. On 4 February 1974, this group was destroyed by the concerted action of the security authorities in Hamburg, Frankfurt and Amsterdam. Nine members were arrested and have been condemned to long prison sentences.

A year later, a new follow-up group was formed, which carried out the attack on the German embassy in Stockholm on 24 April 1975, during which two officials, the military attaché and the commercial attaché, were shot dead. The terrorists were attempting, by way of these murders, to press for the release of the Red Army Faction prisoners.

In 1976, it became clear that the Red Army Faction had built up a further follow-up group. On 30 November 1976, the lawyers Siegfried Haag and

Roland Mayer were arrested during an autobahn check. Papers found on the two arrested persons showed that new actions were being planned. The bank notes they carried had been stolen during bank robberies in Cologne and Hamburg.

Despite the arrest of the group leader, Haag, the group became strong enough to carry out serious violent actions in 1977, the zenith of terrorism in Germany up to the present day.

This is the list of the RAF-connected operations carried out in 1977:

(a) 5 January, Basel/Lörrach frontier: the attempted murder of a Swiss customs official.
(b) 7 April, Karlsruhe: the murder of Attorney General Siegfried Buback and his guards.
(c) 3 May, Singen: the attempted murder of police officials during the capture of Verena Becker and Gunter Sonnenberg.
(d) 25 August, Karlsruhe: an attempted rocket attack on the Federal Justice offices.
(e) 5 September, Cologne: the kidnapping of Hans-Martin Schleyer and the murder of his three guards and his driver.
(f) 19 September, The Hague: the attempted murder of a Dutch policeman.
(g) 22 September, Utrecht: the murder of a Dutch policeman during the arrest of Knut Folkerts.
(h) 13–18 October, Majorca/Mogadishu: the hijacking by Palestinian terrorists of the Lufthansa plane 'Landshut' with ninety-one hostages and the murder of pilot Jürgen Schumann.
(i) 18 October, Mulhouse: the murder of Hans-Martin Schleyer.
(j) 10 November, Amsterdam: the attempted murder of a Dutch official during the arrest of Christoph Wackernagel and Gerd Schneider.

Nineteen terrorists, ten of them women, were sought in connection with these crimes. While preparing the crimes, the terrorists used twenty apartments, at least twenty-three bought, rented or stolen vehicles, several semi-automatic guns, machine pistols and regular pistols, a dozen typewriters, tape recorders, video recorders, copying machines and more than thirty forged documents for apartments, hotels and the acquisition of vehicles.

The Red Army Faction was able to continue its armed struggle even after the arrest of its most important members. They could rely on a circle of supporters who kept up the link between the arrested terrorists and the 'operational' ones. Several lawyers played an essential role in these links. They also succeeded in recruiting new, mostly young, lawyers to their cause.

The Red Army Faction succeeded, with the help of supporting groups, in carrying out propaganda actions designed to portray West Germany as a fascist state and to justify the aim of the terrorists.

During the campaign, the supporters of the Red Army Faction alleged that the imprisoned Red Army members were subjected to 'isolation torture'. In reality, they enjoyed and still enjoy considerable privileges over other prisoners. Their cells are bigger. They have radio, television and as many as several thousand books in their cells. The campaigns of their supporters often produced understanding for the Red Army cause in Germany, and in neighbouring countries anti-German standpoints were mobilised, especially in Marxist and neo-Marxist circles.

The campaigns were organised by 'committees against torture'. Out of these committees developed the Red Army supporting groups, which still exist, though no longer in name. These included the Anti-fascist Group and the Solidarity Committee for Political Prisoners, or Red Help. Their supporters still exist however, and provide the reservoir for illegal activities in the future. Groups of this kind exist in Hamburg, Wiesbaden, Berlin, Frankfurt and Kaiserslautern.

In view of the RAF, terrorist violence is always 'propaganda of the deed'. This part of their terrorist activities was and still is aimed above all at the German student movement. The RAF believes that the leading force and the avant garde of the class struggle is not the working class but the 'revolutionary intelligence'. By 1971, the RAF had already stated in a publication 'Close the Loopholes of the Revolutionary Theory—Build up the Red Army': it is not the organisations of the industrial working class but the revolutionary sections of the student bodies that are today the bearers of the contemporary conscience.

The association between the RAF and the student movement lasted for years. In fact, the protest movement of the German students in the late 1960s and early 1970s was one of the most important roots of the RAF. This movement formed the basis—the 'legitimate fringe'—of the RAF until the early 1980s. Marxism–Leninism and a simplified interpretation of Maoism became the ideology of the RAF.

In the last few years the attitude of the large majority of German students has changed. Students of today are more pragmatic and job oriented than they were before. Besides that, Maoism has lost its persuasion as a theory, because capitalistic rules seem to have improved the economic situation in China.

The second part of the theory of the RAF is not convincing either anymore. The RAF claimed and still is asserting that it can solve the problems of the Third World by armed struggle in the Federal Republic of Germany. But after the Soviet occupation of Afghanistan and the neo-colonialistic policy of the USSR in Africa even left-wing people are realising that the ills of the Third World do not stem from capitalist extortion and that European unemployment cannot be cured by Latin American style solutions.

STRUCTURE AND ACTIVITIES IN 1984/1985

The RAF consists of a hard core of 'commandos', a 'legitimate' fringe and thirty-six terrorists in custody. The fringe amounts, as in the past, to about two hundred people. The hard core is a 'commando' of fifteen people. Inge Viett (born 12 January 1944 in Steinwarde) and Henning Beer (born 30 September 1958 in Hamburg) are the only remnants of the RAF of the 1970s. The other members joined the 'commando' in the last year. They came out of the 'legitimate' fringe of the supporters.

There are arrest warrants out for twenty-five German terrorists, among them several members of the '2 June Movement' (who in the meantime have given up 'armed struggle'), such as Hans-Joachim Klein. Two others are probably dead. Four women have left the RAF and joined Middle Eastern terrorist organisations. Of these the whereabouts of Ingrid Siemann (born in 1944) and Sigrid Sternebeck (born in 1949) are unknown. Susanne Albrecht (born on 1 March 1951 in Hamburg) was for a long time in a PLO camp in South Yemen and now lives in a PFLP camp in Damascus. Friederike Krabbe (born on 31 May 1950 in Bentheim) was initially a member of the Palestinian terrorist organisation '15 May' (Abu Ibrahim), and now works for the Special Command (Wadia-Hadad Group) in Baghdad.

The RAF had a long period of decline before it started new operations at the end of 1984. The change of the political climate and the change of character of the RAF is illustrated by the fact that the RAF has not been able to produce new strategic papers since 1980. And even the last strategic concept, the 'Heidelberg paper' from summer 1980, was more a cry for help to the left-wing environment than an analysis of the political situation in Germany.

On 25 June 1979, members of the RAF attempted to assassinate Alexander Haig, the head of the NATO forces in Europe, on his way from his home to the headquarters of NATO in Casteau near Brussels. The bomb which was intended to kill him exploded only a split second after he crossed the bridge where the bomb was hidden.

However, setbacks have not thwarted the RAF. After failing to create a 'revolutionary situation' as a result of an attack against the headquarters of the NATO Air Force at Ramstein, and the attempted assassination of the US Army Commander in Europe, General Kroesen, it limited itself in 1982 to 'logistical' operations. On 15 September 1982 Christian Klar, Adelheid Schulz, Brigitte Mohnhaupt and Inge Viett raided a bank in Bochum. The first three were arrested in November and caches of weapons, ammunition, money and forged papers were seized. On 26 March 1984, four other RAF members held up a bank in Würzburg. So the RAF again had success despite the absence of its leading members. This provoked thoughts about giving priority again to armed struggle over 'logistical' operations.

The arrest of six key members of the RAF in July 1984 in Frankfurt and Karlsruhe showed how far these thoughts had developed. Documents seized included an assessment of the current political situation in the Federal Republic, and operational plans to be put into effect in three phases. At the end of 1984, key NATO establishments were to be blown up; simultaneously, RAF detainees were to begin a hunger strike with the demand that they should be held together in the same detention centre (nothing was said about freeing them); the third stage was to be the execution of 'representatives of repression'. The paper showed that the preparations for this plan, which indeed was realised in December 1984, were incomplete. The paper showed too that the plan was not only the work of the hard core of the RAF, but of the organisation as a whole.

On 5 November 1984, five RAF members broke into the shop of a gunsmith near Ludwigshafen and stole revolvers, rifles and ammunition.

In the first days of December 1984 the imprisoned RAF members started the hunger strike. On 18 December a RAF commando attempted a bomb attack against a NATO school in Oberammergau. The operation only failed because the detonator of the car-bomb did not work; the terrorists had not taken account of the frost. On 15 January 1985 RAF and the French *Action Directe* (AD) issued a joint statement announcing the formation of a united front to combat NATO imperialism. On 25 January AD terrorists assassinated General René Audran, a top French defence official, outside his home near Paris. On 1 February two RAF terrorists murdered Ernst Zimmermann, a leading German arms manager, at his home near Munich. After this killing the RAF detainees ended their hunger strike.

On 8 April other attacks were carried out by the 'legitimate' fringe of the RAF.

An 'illegal militant commando Jonas Thimme' detonated a bomb at the building of the 'Internationale Schiffs-Studiengesellschaft' (ISS) in Hamburg. Another explosive charge in an office of the ISS in an adjacent house was deactivated in time. Jonas Thimme belonged to the fringe of the RAF in southern Germany. He killed himself on 20 January 1985 while transporting a bomb to a computer centre in a baby buggy. His co-assailant, Claudia Margarete Wannersdorfer, was badly hurt.

A 'Militant commando Ulrike Meinhof' damaged the NATO pipeline near Iggingen in southern Germany.

Three members of the RAF, wearing uniforms of the Bundeswehr, tried to get access to an ammunition depot in Neukirchen near Traunstein. They failed because the guards started to check their identity. The RAF members fled.

On 8 August 1985, the RAF aimed again at 'US imperialism'. It exploded a car-bomb in a parking area at the US air base in Frankfurt. Two bystanders were killed, twenty injured.

The terrorists gained access to the air base with an identification card of an American soldier. To get the identification card they assassinated the soldier with a shot in the neck.

THE 'REVOLUTIONARY CELLS' (RZ)

THEORY AND STRUCTURE

The policy of the RZ was from the beginning to distinguish their strategy from the political concept of the RAF. They opposed the theory of the RAF that only student elites should guide the revolution. They emphasised that each action should be fed back to the 'masses'. Each single revolutionary activity should be linked up with existing conflicts in society. Operating from these principles the RZ developed the so-called 'contact-theory' (see the publication of the RZ, *Revolutionärer Zorn*—Revolutionary Anger—Nr. 1, May 1975, p. 6, and Nr. 4, January 1978, p. 17).

They evaluated the present political situation as a period in which multinational corporations would dominate almost all governments in the Western world. 'US-multis' particularly (e.g., oil industry) would represent true imperialism by exploiting the Third World. The task of the RZ therefore had to be to attack US targets everywhere in Germany.

Until 1980 these attacks were directed only against objects. With the killing of Hans-Herbert Karry (Minister of Finance of Hessen) on 19 December 1980, the RZ policy changed. In a letter claiming responsibility, the murders stated that the attack against Karry was meant only as a 'punishment'. They had intended to shoot him in his knees. They killed him only because it was too dark to aim correctly. The RZ obviously intended to imitate Italian examples.

The security forces were able to gain some insight into the structure of the RZ only after the arrest of Hermann Terling in June 1978. Terling lost his legs and his eyesight when a bomb which he was constructing in his flat exploded.

Differing from the concept of the urban guerillas of the RAF, the RZ members are trying to stay 'legitimate' as long as possible. They are not living permanently 'underground', but are organised in small groups ('cells') of five to eight members only, each group operating independently. The members of each cell know each other only by cover names.

ACTIVITIES 1984/1985

In May 1984 the West German authorities regarded the RZ as potentially the most dangerous terrorist organisation since it had been responsible for more terrorist actions since 1973 than either the '2 June Movement' or the RAF, though without reaching their level of brutality. The fact that it operates in small units also makes it much more difficult to combat. Although the RZ's publication, *Revolutionärer Zorn* (Revolutionary Anger), has not appeared since January 1981, four of its policy papers have appeared in the leftist press since mid-1983: 'Working against the West-Runway' in Frankfurt (August 1983), an assessment of the Peace Movement (December 1983), a Discussion Paper on the 35-hour-week (March 1984) and an interview on the women's section of the RZ in the magazine 'Emma' (June 1984).

The discussion paper on the future of the Peace Movement was quite intelligent and included criticism of developments in the Eastern bloc. It took the view for example, that the Soviet Union's lack of economic power in the Third World would soon force it to either abandon its worldwide revolutionary objectives 'in the name of friendship between peoples', or resort to 'purely military means of ensuring zones of influence'. It argued that although the Soviets could continue supplying arms for national liberation movements both before and after victory (as in Nicaragua), they could not afford any more Cubas. It also argued that after the stationing of Pershing-II, the radical left's influence within the Peace Movement would collapse because of the increasing influence of the Greens, the Churches, elements within the SPD opposition, traditional Communists and others. Revolution is not only not wanted but is even increasingly rejected by the radical left itself.

This analysis provoked a noticeable reduction in terrorist operations. Official sources reveal that this gave way to a phase of internal debate over the question of whether a campaign of political and subversive action would not in the long term—at least in the prevailing political situation—promise greater success than revolutionary action. Consequently the RZ did not support the latest RAF operations.

In the last two years—probably because of the debate about the future possibilities—the membership of the RZ has shrunk from two hundred, with five to eight combatants per cell, to a maximum of eighty.

After the RAF abandoned the hunger strike the RZ started operations again.

With four bomb attacks they 'punished' corporations which through their business politics had allegedly 'Fought against the striking miners' in the United Kingdom.

On 28 April the RZ detonated several bombs with time fuses at the building of the employers unit and an office of a chemistry factory in Cologne and at the building of the 'Deutsche Bank' in Düsseldorf.

On 30 May the RZ made a bomb attack against a subterranean NATO pipeline near Frankfurt/Main.

'GUERRILLA DIFFUSA'

This movement tries to give terrorist activity a 'revolutionary' rationale. Sometimes it is impossible to decide whether the political phraseology used is not simply a camouflage for straightforward crime. For example, last September four young men from Berlin were arrested after a raid on a bank in Westphalia. A search produced written political and ideological material which was intellectually worthless. But it also revealed that the Berlin 'terrorists' had committed arson on five occasions with Molotov cocktails. In one case the culprits had falsely claimed to belong to the RZ.

In October 1984, four young people from Hamburg were arrested for their part in a raid on an insurance office, also in Westphalia. They came from a 'social-revolutionary' so-called 'job-centre' and from the hard left Hamburg 'Aid for the Unemployed'.

In November 1984, three people arrested for breaking open vending machines in Rheda admitted to Molotov-cocktail attacks on installations of the British Army in Germany. But there was in fact no political link; it was simple vandalism.

Guerrilla Diffusa is largely a collection of ordinary criminals, with no discernible links with the RZ or the RAF.

THE EFFECT OF THE PEACE MOVEMENT AND GREENS ON LEFT-WING TERRORISM

All left-wing terrorist groups are suffering from the fact that potential supporters in the last two years have been seeking and still are looking for careers in politics, administration and journalism, opting for institutional reform rather than revolution to 'change society'.

Besides that, the new movement for peace and ecology, represented by the Greens in the German parliament, is attracting more political interest from the former terrorist sympathisers than the cause of RAF and RZ can do. Until 1981 the Peace Movement was strongly influenced by Communists, but since 1982 it has broadened its base within the SPD opposition and the Greens. Politically it is close to becoming a new middle-class movement with new social objectives.

In the elections for the parliaments of the 'Länder' in spring 1985 the Greens failed to top the five per cent margin in North Rhine–Westphalia and in the Saar. In Berlin they got an astonishing 10.6 per cent success. In Hessen the SPD government offered a coalition.

The party rally in Hagen on 23 June 1985 agreed that the Greens should be open for 'all possibilities of the political spectrum'—from governing alone to forming a coalition with the Social Democrats.

The new middle class with its new social objectives (peace, ecology etc.) is regarding the efforts of the Greens in the parliaments of the Federal Republic, the 'Länder' and the cities with sympathy. Part of this middle class are also the forces which in the past supported the theories of the RAF or the RZ. Today they are more pragmatic than a few years ago. They believe in possible coalitions between SPD and Greens and hope for a chance to change society with reforms rather than by revolution. To this extent they are diverting support from terrorism. This new evolution is accompanied by a growing sentiment of anti-Americanism.

RIGHT-WING TERRORISM

ROOTS AND OBJECTIVES

German right-wing terrorism has two roots. One is the NPD which still is the strongest force in German right-wing extremism, at least as far as numbers are concerned. The NPD (National Democratic Party) is experiencing a continuing process of decline. In the last twenty years it has lost twenty-five thousand members. Today it has only four thousand members. This process of decay acted as a boost to some small Neo-Nazi groups which are the second root for present-day German right-wing terrorism. Young members of the NPD joined the ranks of these Neo-Nazi groups and brought into their organisations more militancy.

Neo-Nazi groups which became a hot-bed for terrorism are the 'Aktionsgemeinschaft Nationaler Sozialisten' ('Führer' is the former lieutenant of the Bundeswehr, Michael Kühnen, now in jail) and the 'Deutsche Aktionsgruppen' (the head of this organisation is the former lawyer Manfred Roeder, now in jail too).

Two other German right-wing extremist organisations which went into terrorism later were the 'Wehrsportgruppe Hoffman' and the 'Volkssozialistische Bewegung Deutschlands/Partei der Arbeit' (VSBD/PdA).

ORGANISATIONS AND ACTIVITIES

Right-wing terrorists are today much more ready to use violence than was believed to be the case in the past. Killings happened for the first time in 1980. On 21 August 1980 members of the 'Deutsche Aktionsgruppen' murdered two Vietnamese in a boarding house for foreigners in Hamburg. On 26 September the Neo-Nazi Gundolf Köhler, a lone wolf without an organisation, killed himself and twelve visitors at the Oktoberfest in Munich; he wounded seventy-two people. On 24 December 1980 the Neo-Nazi Frank Schubert from Frankfurt killed two Swiss custom officers at the Swiss–German border and committed suicide afterwards. On 28 May 1981 Friedhelm Enk, a member of the 'Aktionsgemeinschaft Nationaler Sozialisten' murdered another member of his group who was believed to be a 'traitor'; Enk was obeying the order of a vehmic court in Hamburg.

Responsible for the murder of the Jewish publisher Levin and his friend Mrs Frieda Pöschke on 19 December 1980 was the 'Wehrsportgruppe Hoffmann'. Hoffmann himself gave the order. He is now awaiting sentence at the tribunal of Nuremberg. The killer was Uwe Behrendt. He was in Germany in December 1980, then took refuge in a camp of the Al Fatah. He committed suicide.

Neo-Nazi groups have suffered a number of setbacks. Six Neo-Nazis of the now defunct 'Kexel/Hepp Group', arrested after a bank raid in Hessen, revealed that they had blown up the cars of American soldiers in Darmstadt, Butzbach and Frankfurt. Walter Kexel was under suspicion of having taken part in an attempt to blow up a Jewish restaurant in Paris on 9 August 1982. On 13 February 1985 the trial against the members of the 'Kexel/Hepp Group' started in Frankfurt. On 15 March 1985 Kexel was sentenced to thirteen years of imprisonment. On 17 March he committed suicide.

On 25 January 1985 the Frankfurt Court sentenced Michael Kühnen, leader of the Neo-Nazi 'Action Front of National Socialists and Activists' (ANS/NA), to three years and four months of imprisonment because of Neo-Nazi propaganda. On 7 December 1983 the Minister of the Interior, Friedrich Zimmermann, had banned the ANS/NA. Kühnen had fled in March 1984 to Switzerland and subsequently to France. On 2 July 1984, the magazine *Stern* had interviewed Kühnen in Paris. In the accompanying article Kühnen was described as a 'Führer' who had deserted his comrades. The members of his organisation in the Federal Republic began to ask themselves why they were having to lead an underground existence whilst their Chief was wining and dining in Paris. Kühnen sought to parry these attacks by 'Letters from Exile' which he published in his illegal magazine *The New Front*. He argued that he would re-organise ANS/NA from France and return to Germany in 1985. Kühnen was expelled by the French authorities on 5 October 1984 and arrested on his arrival in Cologne. On 14 November 1984 the criminal court in Frankfurt started a trial against him, which led to his sentencing and imprisonment. He is also due to face charges from courts in Hamburg, Flensburg and Brunswick.

Since September 1984 the trial against the Leader of the 'Wehrsportgruppe Hoffmann', Karl-Heinz Hoffmann, and his lifetime companion Franziska Birkmann has been going on. Hoffmann is accused of having given the order to kill the Jewish publisher Shlomo Lewin and his mate Frida Poeschke.

Other Neo-Nazi leaders either have completed their sentences or are still in jail (Thies Christophersen, Dr Manfred Roeder).

The Neo-Nazis failed to obtain support from potential thugs outside the political arena. In October 1983, Neo-Nazis from all parts of the Federal Republic travelled to West Berlin with Rockers, skinheads and drop-outs, to break up a football match between Turkey and Germany and turn it into a battle with the Turkish immigrant workers present during the match. This was prevented by the presence of three thousand policemen. Several Neo-Nazis were arrested.

The links between the German Neo-Nazis and Middle Eastern terrorists have collapsed. The worldwide publicity given to their links with the PLO and their training in the Al Fatah camps, has deterred even terrorists like Abu Iyad, responsible for the 1972 Munich massacre. Neo-Nazi organisations in Denmark, Belgium, France and the United States have had their communications severed by the success of the German security services.

Extreme right-wing terrorism has lost its motivation and no longer represents any real danger in the near future. But the courts treat the Neo-Nazis rather more gently than their extreme left-wing counterparts. This may be because the Neo-Nazis respect the juridical forms. They stand up when spoken to, address the judge correctly, are properly dressed and have inoffensive hairstyles. Some judges behave as if hygiene is a sign of patriotism.

However, the terrorist activities of Neo-Nazis have decreased decisively in the last year.

INTERNATIONAL CONNECTIONS

TRAINING OF RAF MEMBERS IN THE MIDDLE EAST, RZ MEMBERS AS MERCENARIES

Andreas Baader was released on 14 May 1970, after a bank robbery that took place in Berlin. In June, members of the hard core of the Red Army

Faction went via Damascus to Jordan to be militarily trained in a Fatah camp. At this time, there was a struggle between the armed Fatah Palestinians and the Jordanian troops, who eventually removed the Palestinians from Jordan. The stay by the Germans did not prove to be a success. The group only indulged in discussions.

Horst Mahler, who, after his return in August 1970, only remained free for another two months, concluded in an essay on the armed struggle that 'a fighting group can only exist through struggle itself. All attempts to organise and train a group outside real conditions lead to ridiculous results, often with tragic consequences'.

Since the Red Army Faction has always operated independently, the hijacking of the Lufthansa plane in Majorca, whose passengers were eventually freed in Mogadishu, was not planned and coordinated in advance with the Palestinians. The latter only wanted to use the situation that existed after the kidnapping of Schleyer to try to secure the release of two members of PFLP, who had been arrested in Turkey, as well as to obtain a ransom.

German terrorists were also involved in the logistical preparations for the attack on the Israeli Olympic team in Munich in 1972, which ended in a massacre. They came from the Revolutionary Cells.

Direct cooperation in operations did not occur until 1975. Ilich Ramirez-Sanchez ('Carlos') recruited German terrorists for the attempt to shoot down an Israeli airplane at the Paris Orly Airport with a rocket. The German terrorists, Gabriele Kröcher-Tiedemann and Hans-Joachim Klein, were also involved in the commando raid against the OPEC conference in Vienna (led by Carlos). Brigitte Kuhlmann and Wilfried Böse were recruited by Carlos in 1976 and were members of the commando that hijacked an Air France airplane to Entebbe.

All German terrorists who cooperate with international terrorist organisations either come from the Revolutionary Cells or offer their services to the foreign organisations after they have left their own or after their own groups have been destroyed. The Red Army Faction had, as an organisation, not worked together with international terrorist units until 1984. This is possibly explained by the fact that the Red Army Faction has its own style of operating. The Palestinians do not, for instance, involve their leaders directly in their operations; in the Red Army, every leader must participate in the attacks.

There has only been one attempt at a large-scale international operation. A group of fifty international terrorists from seven countries wanted to kidnap the former Swedish Minister of Labour, Anna-Greta Leijon, in an attempt to secure the release of terrorists in prison in Germany. This operation was led, however, by the Red Army Faction.

Contacts between the RAF and the Italian Red Brigades were never organised, and they have ceased as a result of the decisive losses by both organisations.

A year ago, two leading RAF representatives sought to establish links with the Basque ETA terrorists. Attempts to set up joint operations failed, however, because whereas the ETA sought a 'full amnesty' for its combatants, the RAF had as its objective the liberation by force of its comrades in custody.

In the last year the RZ and the RAF have both shown an increasing interest in the operations of the French Action Directe (AD). Left-wing extremists in Germany regarded the AD as the only effective Marxist–Leninist terror organisation in Europe, and this finally led to a cooperation between the RAF and AD.

One hour before Jean Audran was assassinated, a female voice with a strong German accent called his home asking at what time the General would return. After the murder the commando Elisabeth Van Dyck from Action Directe claimed responsibility. Van Dyck was an RAF terrorist suspected of having participated in the assassination of General Attorney Siegfried Buback, the banker Jürgen Ponto and Hanns Martin Schleyer (all murdered in 1977). She was killed during a police raid in Nuremberg in May 1979. The claim letter appears to have been translated from German thus providing further evidence of AD/RAF cooperation.

The links of the RAF to AD could enhance the capabilities of both terrorist organisations. At least this is the hope of the leading personalities of the RAF and of AD who wish to establish a 'West European Urban Guerilla'. But language problems and differences in character and behaviour will restrict future cooperation to propaganda rather than to joint action.

The operations of the Belgian 'Communist Combattant Cells' (CCC) were thought to support the cause of the RAF but they were not coordinated with the RAF in advance. The CCC did however use the situation that arose as a result of the hunger strike of the RAF as a lever for their own propaganda.

It is remarkable that the CCC came into the open only after the demonstrations against the deployment of Pershing-II failed to succeed. Besides that the CCC are lacking the environment and the fringe support that other terrorist organisations have. Nobody knows the names of the combatants of the CCC and how many they are. Finally the manifestos of the CCC look like the old manifestos of the Italian Red Brigades, a terrorist organisation which had links with the Soviet Union.

The CCC seem to be an investment of the KGB with the purpose of sabotaging NATO installations.

A KGB influence could also be behind two other terrorist incidents which happened during the hunger strike period of the RAF. In Portugal on 28 January 1985 'FP 25', a new terrorist movement with strong links to the Moscow-oriented former officers around Colonel Carvalho, shelled NATO warships in Lisbon harbour. On 1 February it attempted a bomb attack against NATO barracks in Beja.

In Greece a bomb in a bar frequented by US servicemen injured seventy-eight people on 28 January, the same day of the attack against NATO ships in Lisbon. A hitherto unknown group, the 'National Front', claimed responsibility.

The only success the RAF had during the latest 'revolutionary activities' was to establish a new relationship with the Palestinians. After the hunger strike had started, the 'legitimate' fringe of the RAF attempted to approach the PFLP headquarters in Damascus. On 16 January 1985 Ingrid Barabass, Regine Nicolai and the lawyer Adler met the spokesman of the PFLP, Bassam Abu Sharif, in the 'Hotel Berlin' in East Berlin. As a result of this meeting Abu Sharif gave an interview to the West German left-wing daily *Tageszeitung* (taz) on 19 January 1985 in which he strongly supported the cause of the RAF.

Barabass and Nicolai are two of the five female terrorists who were arrested in Paris on 25 July 1980. They were sentenced to imprisonment in Germany. After completing their sentences they again joined the supporter fringe of the RAF. Adler is defending Brigitte Mohnhaupt, the former leading terrorist of the RAF, in her trial in Stuttgart–Stammheim.

When looking at the possible cooperation between the RAF, AD and Middle Eastern terrorist organisations the attempts to coordinate French and German countermeasures are looking rather weak. Partners on the German side are the Federal Office for Criminal Investigation (BKA) and the Federal Office for the Protection of the Constitution (BfV) with their advanced computer equipment. The French government sent to the first meeting with the German authorities a mammoth delegation representing six institutions which claim all to be responsible for counterterrorism. The French do not have the necessary data banks to exchange information with the German offices. Besides that the French attitude towards foreign terrorists is still more gentle than that of the other governments of the European Community. About three hundred former members of the Italian Red Brigades took refuge in France. The Italian Interior Minister, Oscar Scalfaro, is convinced that they are carrying on their work and have not, as the French maintain, renounced the use of violence. The Italian government has sent at least one hundred requests for extradition which were unanswered up to the present.

TRAINING OF RIGHT-WING TERRORISTS IN THE NEAR EAST, THE INTERNATIONAL NEO-NAZI NETWORK

Right-wing terrorists have had contacts with Palestinian terrorist organisations for years.

Already in spring 1967 after the Six Days War the right-wing organisation 'Bund Heimattreuer Jugend' (association of young people loyal to their homeland) founded a 'Hilfskorps Arabien' to support the cause of the Palestinians against Israel. The cooperation of a few members of this 'Hilfskorps' with the Al Fatah did not succeed.

The initiator of more successful operations was Udo Albrecht who came in the late 1950s from the German Democratic Republic into the Federal Republic of Germany. He founded a 'Freikorps Adolf Hitler' and fought in 1970 with twelve members of his organisation on the side of the 'Black September' group against the troops of King Hussein in Jordan. Albrecht is an ordinary criminal, an adventurer and perhaps an agent of influence of the Soviet Union. Since 1958 he has spent a total of seventeen years in jail. He broke out of jail eight times. The last time he escaped from the German authorities was whilst showing them an alleged hideout of weapons near the border with East Germany. He fled into the GDR. The first time it was known that he had any connection with the PLO was when he was arrested in Zurich in Switzerland with an identification card of the Al Fatah. He escaped to Austria. In 1975 he attempted to go with three comrades (Weil, Bernburg and Pahl) in a Mercedes car to the Lebanon. The car was intended to be a gift for the PLO. At the Italian/Yugoslav border the car was seized because the Yugoslavian authorities found Neo-Nazi pamphlets in it. The three comrades were arrested and later expelled. Albrecht escaped. In 1976 four Germans, hired by Albrecht as mercenaries for the PLO, deserted to the Lebanese falange. They testified to the press that they as German right-wing people were trained by the PLO to fight against the Israelis.

They got passports from the German embassy to leave the country. On their way to the airport in Beirut they were captured again by the PLO. They were interrogated, their hair was cut and they were 'expelled'. After the press conference of the falange the PLO also attempted to hold a press conference with alleged defectors of the falange. The journalists attending this meeting very soon realised that the defection was a fake: the supposed former fighters of the falange did not even know the emblem of the falange, the palm tree.

In the early 1970s Albrecht also approached Manfred Roeder, head of the 'Deutsche Aktionsgruppen'. He suggested that Roeder should contact the Palestinians. Between 1976 and 1978 Albrecht was imprisoned on remand in Hamburg. In this time Roeder went to Lebanon and there met Abu Jihad, deputy of Yassir Arafat in Al Fatah, responsible for the Western section of the Middle East. Abu Jihad refused to cooperate with Roeder. Meeting Abu Jihad was quite unfortunate for Manfred Roeder. Had he met Abu Iyad instead, a cooperation would have been guaranteed.

Abu Iyad was removed by Abu Jihad on 15 May 1980 as deputy of Al Fatah. He is still a member of the central committee of the Al Fatah and head of the 'Joint Security Services' of the PLO. He is opposing the 'appeasement politics' of Yassir Arafat very strongly. He supported Karl-Heinz Hoffmann even after it became obvious that cooperation between the PLO and German right-wing extremists was bad propaganda for the Palestinian cause.

At the end of 1979 Karl-Heinz Hoffmann went to Beirut with fifteen members of his organisation. They were trained by PLO officers who were under the command of Abu Iyad. The training was very hard and the discipline which Karl-Heinz Hoffmann demanded was very rigorous. In September 1980 four members of the group deserted and fled back to Germany. This happened after Hoffmann had beaten heavily a member of his group named Bergmann. After the beating Bergmann was put into jail and didn't get food. He was tortured because Hoffmann thought Bergmann was a traitor. Bergmann probably died after this treatment. In spring 1981 he was still alive, but since then he has 'disappeared'.

On 19 December 1980 the Jewish publisher Levin and his partner Frau Pöschke were murdered in Erlangen. The assassin was Uwe Behrendt who committed the murder under orders from Karl-Heinz Hoffmann. He then returned to Lebanon from Germany. He committed suicide later.

In the meantime ten members of the 'Wehrsportgruppe Hoffmann' came back to Germany. They were investigated by the police and now are on trial. Hoffmann himself came back in spring 1981 and was arrested in summer 1981 when he tried to leave the country with his girlfriend via Frankfurt airport. He is awaiting sentence from a law court in Nuremberg.

Manfred Roeder—after failing to establish contacts to the PLO—went to Itatataja in Brazil. There he met members of the German colony, most of them old Nazis. He gave lectures and got money for this. He didn't collect money for Neo–Nazi organisations in North America, but he went to the United States to meet Mr Duke from the 'Knights of the Ku Klux Klan' and Mr Wilkinson of the 'Invisible Empire'. He made speeches to audiences of the Ku Klux Klan and got money for this too.

In 1980 he went to Syria and to Iran. His attempts to gain an agreement for cooperation with Al Fatah, PLO and PFLP failed. In Iran he wanted to meet Khomeini but he was able to meet only Ayatollas of the third rank. The Iranian Government did not want to cooperate with Roeder.

On 20 January 1982 two members of the 'Wehrsportgruppe Hoffmann', Hubel and Bojarski, were arrested in Avezzano near Rome in Italy. They were extradited to the German authorities. A third member of the 'Wehrsportgruppe Hoffmann', Paul, escaped.

On 10 January 1982 four members of the 'Volkssozialistische Bewegung Deutschland/Partei der Arbeit', Klaus and Kristian Hewicker, Gerhard Töpfer and Ernst Balke, were given to German authorities by the Belgian police. They were sentenced for their membership in a terrorist organisation and for bank robbery.

Other members of the 'Volkssozialistische Bewegung Deutschlands/Partei der Arbeit' found refuge in France. Klaus Ludwig Uhl, Kurt Wolfgram and Peter Fabel lived for some weeks in the house of M Loubet in Metz and in the house of M Iffrig, Doctor of medicine, in a village near Strasbourg. On 20 October 1981 they met Friedhelm Busse, the head of their organisation, in Munich. During an attempt to arrest them Uhl and Wolfgram were shot, Fabel was wounded.

The 'Volkssozialistische Bewegung Deutschlands/Partei der Arbeit' had contacts with the French Neo Nazi organisation 'Fédération d'Action Nationale et Européenne' (FANE) and to the Belgian 'Vlaamse Militante Orden'. The Fane has been prohibited in the meantime and declared illegal. It had about one hundred members.

THE GOVERNMENT RESPONSE

COUNTERMEASURES OF THE SECURITY FORCES

The search for German terrorist organisations is extremely difficult. Their members, particularly the Red Army Faction members, are intelligent, work conspiratorially, have the support of ideological sympathisers, can operate openly in an open society and are determined to resist any official action by the use of lethal weapons.

The success of the security authorities depends to a large extent on support and information from the person in the street. There was a lack of this sort of information during the logistical build-up of the Red Army Faction between 1970 and 1972. When the State showed itself to be determined to counteract terrorism through large-scale searches, information from the public became more forthcoming. After the escalation of violence in 1975, the willingness of the population to help the security authorities decreased. Between 1975 and 1977, the number of 'wanted lists' on show in West Germany diminished considerably. The police were only able to put up a quarter of the previous number of posters in small shops. This example proves that a democratic state can be shaken when the population begins to believe that it is more dangerous to do something for the State than against it.

The arrest of about one hundred German terrorists has shown that such groups can be sought out and destroyed by democratic means. The general search measures available to the police do not as a rule suffice. The police have to rely on intelligence information so that their searches can be conducted on a more selective basis. Intelligence work in terrorist organisations has its limitations, however; there is the danger of agents of intelligence services becoming agent provocateurs or, at least, becoming involved in criminal activity themselves. In addition, these agents are risking death if they are exposed.

The violent actions of the terrorists have led to an increase in the personnel and material strength of the West German security authorities. The number of jobs in the Federal Criminal Office has increased from 933 in 1969 to over 2500 in 1977. There are about 22,000 members of the Federal Frontier Protection Force, of which the GSG 9 commando, which operated in Mogadishu, forms a part. (There are approximately 150,000 policemen in West Germany.)

The Federal Criminal Office has been extended to act as the central information and communication office for counteracting terrorism. The collection and collation of intelligence is done with the most modern forms of electronic data machinery. The Federal Frontier Protection Force has been extended as a strong addition to the police force. The GSG 9 commmando unit has been developed into a special unit for supporting the police in combating violent crime. The Länder have similar special police units. In addition, the Federal Frontier Protection Force is required to safeguard airports, government departments and diplomatic missions abroad.

The Federal Office for the Protection of the Constitution now has the task of studying all aspects of terrorist activity. It uses electronic methods to collect and evaluate information it receives. The considerable amount of personnel and technical aids available to the security authorities obliges them to use and weigh up their resources selectively. On the one hand, they have to discover the terrorist organisations and arrest the violent criminals; on the other hand, the temptation to cover West Germany with a search net reminiscent of George Orwell's 1984 has to be resisted. An overreaction by the State would play straight into the hands of the terrorists.

NEW LAWS TO COMBAT TERRORISM

Following a 1971 law, the hijacking of a plane or attacks on a plane carry a penalty of not less than five years imprisonment. Manslaughter in this context carries imprisonment of not less than ten years. In the same year, the law was extended to include kidnapping of adults. A law against taking hostages was also introduced. In 1976, a law was introduced against those supporting and encouraging serious violent crime.

The right of defence was also partly changed. There is now the possibility of excluding a defence lawyer from a trial if he is suspected of being involved in the crime of the defendant. It is now no longer possible for one defence lawyer to defend several accused persons standing trial. The possibility of carrying on the trial in the absence of the accused (for example, during a hunger strike) was extended in 1974.

In 1976, a law was passed that introduced greater penalties for membership in a terrorist organisation. The law concerning the arrest of terrorists was strengthened, and a control of written communication between the defending lawyer and his client was made possible.

In 1977, a law was passed preventing contacts between arrested terrorists and their defending lawyers if the chances of thereby freeing a prisoner were increased. A new law was passed in 1978 allowing for the search of all apartments in an apartment building. During a large-scale police search, control points are allowed on roads. Also, defending lawyers can be disbarred if there are indications that the lawyer is planning a crime together with his client. Dividing panels have been authorised for discussions between the accused and his or her lawyer to prevent the handing over of any objects.

GOVERNMENT, TERRORISM AND THE MEDIA

Publicity is part of the terrorist action itself. The terrorist operation is 'propaganda of the deed'. The resonance the terrorists hope to find in the media is calculated. Therefore government adherence to a firm attitude is made more difficult by the publicity the terrorist expects and which indeed is given to terrorist actions in the media.

During the Stockholm embassy attack, Swedish Television had a camera focused on the embassy for several hours.

After the kidnapping of Hans-Martin Schleyer in 1977 the first ultimatum of the terrorists contained two demands on the media: at 10 a.m. one of the prisoners was to inform the commando unit, via television, of the departure of the prisoners who were to have been set free and the announcement was supposed to be broadcast during the main news at 8 p.m. In their third message the kidnappers demanded that a video-tape of Schleyer reading a letter be broadcast. Video-tapes and polaroid photos with ultimatums and announcements were constantly sent to the domestic and foreign press.

The German press, at the government's request, conducted itself with remarkable restraint in its treatment of information during the Schleyer case. The terrorists therefore lost the publicity they had expected.

Almost immediately, after the Federal Government and the Federal Office of Investigation got hold of the news of the kidnapping of Schleyer and the assassination of his driver and his three bodyguards, they decided on a news blackout. Three days later, they requested the press to comply with it in such a way that they would use utmost discretion if news from the terrorists reached them directly. The media were asked to cooperate with the Federal Government in relating the news in the papers or radio stations, television stations and so forth. And they were also asked not to endanger the investigation by the police. This was supported by the National Press Council in Germany, a professional organisation, which suggested that the press abide by these rules. So there was a twofold action; the decision by the Federal Government not to give out news immediately when it emerged but to use it selectively when they thought it was helping the investigation or protecting the life of the hostage. And on the other hand there was the press, which could not, of course, be ordered not to investigate on its own, which in fact it did. It made its own research, and many communications reached the press. But the editors decided to use the news according to certain standards, namely saving the life of the hostage, not hindering the investigation and not giving a theatre to the terrorists and their propaganda.

This took an unusually long time, exactly forty-five days. As the report of the Federal Government showed, there were twenty-five communications from the terrorists to the Federal Government and equally twenty-five communications back to the terrorists using at some time the help of the Swiss lawyer, Denis Payot. In this figure are not included the communications after the hijacking of the Lufthansa plane 'Landshut'.

Eight deadlines passed in the meantime—deadlines at which the terrorists had said that the life of Schleyer would be ended.

The government could not, of course, ask the foreign press to abide by this self-discipline. So when the terrorists, who had asked for the release of eleven convicted terrorists of the Baader–Meinhof group, tried to undercut the news blackout and went directly to news organisations or papers in France or in Holland or television stations, some of them picked it up and broadcast or published it, and then of course some of the German papers picked it up themselves, quoting the foreign sources.

But there were two breaks that were crucial in many ways. At an early stage, in its issue of 19 September, which hit the streets around 15 September, the magazine *Der Stern* published an account of the conversations between the Federal Government and its so-called big advisory board, which contained members of the parliamentary opposition, various organisations who were concerned, as well as law-enforcement people.

In this conversation, so the magazine related, there was a unanimous decision not to release the prisoners but to try to gain time by negotiating with the terrorists. It sounded very credible and, of course, could immediately have endangered the life of the hostage. At a later stage, there was a second event where the German news agency *dpa* published an account that the son of Hanns Martin Schleyer was ready to pay the $15 million that were asked for by the hostage takers. That was already after the Lufthansa jet had been brought to some Arab countries. The news agency also mentioned the place and the time where the $15 million would be given to the terrorists. What the government did not know at that time was that the hijackers had called the Schleyer residence directly and asked for these $15 million. The effect of the news release, of course, was that at the given time at the Hotel Intercontinental in Frankfurt hundreds of journalists were around, including two TV teams, and the payment of the $15 million never took place.

It is debatable whether the life of Hanns Martin Schleyer could have been saved by the payment alone, withholding the release of the prisoners.

A third break was outside of the German press. It was a television story in Israel, which is ironic in many ways because the successful rescue of the hostages in Entebbe relied solely on the secrecy of the operation. The fact that Israeli TV later apologised to the Federal Government showed that again there was some soul-searching done and that they came to the conclusion that at that point in the development it was very wrong to go public on the air. It was exactly five hours before the rescue operation in Mogadishu happended.

The editor of *Die Welt* said later that he, like most of the other editors, thought that it was an exception, but that it was justified. All the same, he said, 'It was a monster because every news blackout goes against the grain of every journalist. And also it cannot mean that the editors give up their responsibility to the government. To ascertain what is newsworthy or not should be their responsibility. A news blackout should not have the effect that journalists will not be able to check out news stories by themselves. That would mean censorship and cannot be accepted.'

The editor of the radio station 'Sudwestfunk' was very critical about the length of the news blackout (forty-five days) and said that it was very questionable whether you can uphold a news blackout for such a stretch of time. This was and should be an exception but not the rule.

An opinion poll was carried out by the opinion institute in Allensbach about how the population felt after being kept totally without any knowledge of what had happened to Schleyer, what the terrorists wanted and so forth, for quite some time. Astonishingly, seventy per cent of the people said that they found the news blackout reasonable and justified and did not demand gory stories or blow-by-blow-reporting.

Despite this cooperation between government and press, the life of Schleyer could not be saved.

The effect of the restrictions on the press was nil. There was no loss in circulation or in profit. It could not affect the broadcast stations or television stations in West Germany because they are not commercial, but public. None of the papers lost in any way. The news blackout after the Schleyer kidnapping did not save his life, but the blackout around the Lufthansa hijacking and the rescue operation of Mogadishu definitely helped to save eighty-six lives.

GOVERNMENT RESPONSE DURING TERRORIST ASSAULTS

The improved personnel and technical resources of the security authorities, even if they reach optimal conditions, will not prevent terrorists from committing crimes. The new laws help state institutions to combat terrorism, but they are only one of several means that can contribute to the solution of the problem. The guiding principle for the realisation of new legal solutions must be the individual assessment of, and response to, each problem. All generalised responses should be viewed with scepticism. They easily become routinised. Terrorists have always been ingenious enough to deal with generalised laws and can adapt to them easily.

Apart from the search apparatus, there are three important factors that can be used to combat terrorist crime successfully: (a) security for vulnerable persons and institutions, (b) constant attention being paid to terrorist organisations and their arena with intelligence resources and (c) a decisive attitude on the part of the government towards the terrorists, especially during and after a terrorist attack.

A successful action by terrorists is usually followed by new violent crimes. Nothing is as successful as success. The occupation of the German embassy in Stockholm and the murder of two German diplomats, in an attempt to release terrorists from German prisons, resulted *inter alia* from the government giving in to the demands of the terrorists in the kidnapping of Lorenz. The resolute attitude by the government during the attack on the Stockholm embassy contributed to the fact that there were no further serious attacks for the next one and a half years.

When a Palestinian commando in an attempt to exploit the situation during the Schleyer kidnapping hijacked a Lufthansa plane, thereby putting pressure on the government, the government reacted offensively. They ordered the GSG 9 special unit to try to release the hostages. This succeeded in Mogadishu after discussions with the government in Somalia. This led to the suicide of Baader, Ensslin and Raspe in prison in Stuttgart/Stammheim. Schleyer was murdered.

Each single terrorist attack requires a special defence and reaction determined by the situation. Experience to date has shown that reactions must be determined by one rule: the responsible organs of State must not during an attack react in the way the terrorists expect them to. Such a reaction would be the success that would breed a repeated attack. The state institutions must always show that they will not give in to blackmail and that violence will not be tolerated. Otherwise a problem, which is essentially a problem of security, could well become a question of the future existence for free societies and states.

CONCLUSIONS

Neo-Nazi terrorism has lost its leaders and ideologists for some time to come. Consequently there is no sign of any significant political comeback, as opposed to straightforward crime.

Guerilla Diffusa is without political significance. It is tied up with the desire for prestige through vandalism and respresents no real danger to public safety.

Protection against terrorism originating in the Middle East is not possible. Terrorist activities from this quarter will happen again and again—as long as the political situation in the Middle East (particularly between the Arab states) is as unstable as it is today. Some Arab organisations use Europe as a battlefield to fight their wars against each other.

The RZ went through a process of self-examination. Now they have once more started terrorist operations. Because of their insistence on 'feedback from the masses', their activities depend on general political developments in West Germany. Therefore they will try to exploit the anti-nuclear feelings, the motivations of the Peace Movement and the revived anti-American sentiment in Germany. The sounding-board of their actions are the Greens. The motivations of the RZ meet the attitude of the peace-oriented and neutralistic forces of the Green party. They hope that their bombings could support strategy and tactics of Green policy. And the Greens in some cases indeed are benefiting from these activities ('only aimed against objects'), claiming that the bombings are caused by grievances in the present society. These grievances only the Greens would be able to do away with.

For the foreseeable future the attacks of the RZ will be pointed at US facilities, NATO installations and the nuclear industry. Concerning US and NATO installations the RZ will avoid attacking barracks and weapon depots because they have to reckon with intensified security measures there. They will concentrate on logistical equipment like energy-supply systems, oil depots and pipelines.

Since 1977 the RAF has again and again suffered setbacks. In the last year it has been widely criticised by the left. It lost its international links. In spite of these defeats, the RAF could retain its objectives and its criminal energy and organisation intact. In 1984 the RAF was able to recruit new fighters.

The leaders also realised the limits of the present possibilities for the 'armed struggle'. The RAF did not demand anymore the release of their prisoners. They only claimed that their comrades should be brought together in one prison.

Despite this restriction, the 'revolutionary activities' of the RAF did not succeed. The government did not give in to the demands of the terrorists. The protest demonstrations in favour of the RAF were rather small. The supporting activities of the environment of the RAF (about forty attacks with explosives and arson) ended after the hunger strike broke down.

By means of their new contacts with the French terrorists and the Palestinians the RAF has regained some kind of prestige in the world of international terrorism. On the other hand, it is still lacking a new convincing theory for the present political situation and theoreticians who could formulate a new strategy. Because of this the members of the RAF are today without a motivating vision for their fight. They always postulate, of course, that the 'armed struggle' must be pursued, come what may. But the new generation of the RAF is almost without hope of winning the 'armed struggle' in the end. They are becoming desperate. The RAF may consequently develop a Kamikaze mentality.

Targets of the attacks of the RAF are NATO and 'US imperialism'. The RAF will not restrict its future operations to objects of logistics only. It will try to kill American soldiers.

Middle Eastern Terrorist Activity in Western Europe in 1985: A Diagnosis and Prognosis

D A Pluchinsky*

INTRODUCTION

From 1980–1985 Middle Eastern terrorist groups have carried our over 233 attacks in Western Europe which have resulted in 155 deaths and over 1232 injuries.[1] Thirty-two per cent of these attacks, forty-two per cent of these fatalities and forty-three per cent of these injuries occurred in 1985. Middle Eastern terrorist activity has been and continues to be a major security and political problem for most countries in Western Europe. Many of these countries (West Germany, Spain, the United Kingdom, France, Italy, Greece, Portugal and Belgium) are also confronted with a serious indigenous terrorist threat from various separatist and Marxist revolutionary groups.

The more active and dangerous of these groups are the Red Army Faction (RAF) and the Revolutionary Cells (RC or RZ) in West Germany; the Red Brigades (RB) in Italy; Action Directe (AD) and the Corsican National Liberation Front (FLNC) in France; the Popular Forces of 25 April (FP-25) in Portugal; the Popular Revolutionary Struggle (ELA) and the 17 November Group in Greece; the Basque Fatherland and Liberty movement (ETA-M) in Spain; the Communist Combatant Cells (CCC) in Belgium; and the Irish Republican Army (IRA) in the United Kingdom.

The level of threat posed by any of these groups in their respective countries at a particular time varies, depending primarily upon the number and impact of police arrests and the ideological and operational unity within the groups.

---

* Dennis Pluchinsky is the European analyst in the Threat Analysis Division of the Bureau of Diplomatic Security in the US Department of State. The opinions expressed in this chapter are solely the author's and should not be interpreted in any way as representing the views or policies of the US Department of State.

While the short-term threat posed by these groups varies, the long-term threat remains high. All of these groups have, at one time or another, been dealt crippling operational blows by police and security forces. The fatal blow, however, has been missing. Many of these groups are already into their third or fourth 'generation'—both in terms of membership and leadership. The security threat posed by these indigenous groups will not dissipate at any time in the immediate future.

Compounding the indigenous terrorist problem for the European police and security forces is the activity of foreign, primarily Middle Eastern, terrorist groups. It is a problem of 'spillover' terrorism. Unfortunately, Western Europe has proven to be a preferred operational area for these groups. More attacks by Middle Eastern terrorist groups take place in Western Europe than in any other region, excluding of course, the Middle East. Moreover, there are certain Middle Eastern terrorist elements that prefer operating in Western Europe rather than in the Middle East. The Abu Nidal group and those entities responsible for assassinating Libyan and Iranian dissident elements are more active in Western Europe. For example, two-thirds of the Abu Nidal group's nearly twenty attacks in 1985 took place in Western Europe.[2] And over ninety-five per cent of the terrorist attacks directed since 1980 at dissident Libyan exiles have taken place in Western Europe.[3]

Why this preference for Western Europe? What does this region offer that these groups can't find in other regions like Latin America, Africa, the Far East, North America and, in some cases, even in the Middle East? There are five factors which I believe make Western Europe an attractive operational area for Middle East terrorist groups.

(a) *Western Europe provides these groups with a potential manpower pool which facilitates the building and maintenance of a logistical infrastructure.* There are large communities of Palestinians and Arabs in most West European countries. This also includes the large student populations. Moreover, Middle Eastern businessmen and tourists frequently travel to Western Europe. This makes it easy for Middle Eastern terrorist groups to send in operational elements which can not only blend into the environment but can also receive logistical aid from sympathisers and in-country support elements.

(b) *Western Europe offers these groups geographical proximity and compactness, excellent transportation facilities and relatively easy cross-border movement.* In other words, it is easy to get to Western Europe and, once there, move around between countries.

(c) *Western Europe offers these groups abundant, easy and attractive targets.* Middle East terrorists carry out attacks against three targeting sectors: Israeli or Jewish, Western and Arab or Palestinian. There is a large quantity of these targets in Western Europe.

(d) *Western Europe offers these groups immediate worldwide publicity when they carry out an attack in the region.* The publicity spotlight is broader and brighter in Western Europe than in most other regions. With regard to the Middle East, attacks carried out by Middle Eastern groups in

Iran, Syria, Iraq and Libya receive little publicity because of the state-controlled press in these countries. In Lebanon, the level of political violence in that country literally buries, from a publicity standpoint, all but the most spectacular and lethal incidents.

(e) *Western Europe provides these groups with a 'substitute battleground' in which to carry out their intra-Palestinian and inter-Arab feuds.* The majority of the attacks carried out by Middle Eastern terrorist groups is aimed at other Arab and Palestinian targets. The authoritarian nature of such states as Libya, Iran, Iraq and Syria makes it difficult for these groups to operate effectively within these states. Israeli security measures also make it difficult for these groups to operate within Israel. It is less risky and operationally easier to attack Libyan, Syrian, Iranian, Iraqi and Israeli targets in Western Europe.

DIAGNOSIS

Middle Eastern terrorist activity in Western Europe is a product of the numerous antagonistic relationships which exist in the Middle East between states, ethinic and religious groups and Palestinian and Arab personalities. More and more of these conflicts, feuds and disagreements are evolving into 'mini-terrorist wars' which are being fought not in the Middle East, but in Western Europe—a substitute battlefield. Who are the adversaries in these mini-terrorist wars? What are their motives? What effects do these terrorist attacks have on the security environment in Western Europe? I hope to answer these questions in the following brief assessment of Middle Eastern terrorist activity in Western Europe during 1985.

Last year, Middle Eastern terrorist groups carried out 75 attacks in Western Europe which caused 65 deaths and over 529 injuries.[4] In 1984, the figures were 47 attacks, 18 deaths and 63 injuries. These 75 Middle Eastern attacks in 1985 were carried out in 14 West European countries. Only Portugal, Luxembourg, Finland, Ireland, Belgium and Norway were spared. The countries selected most frequently for these attacks were Greece (14), Italy (13) and Cyprus (9) (see Figure 1).

Of these 75 attacks in 1985, 42 were directed at Arab and Palestinian targets, 13 against Israeli and Jewish targets and 20 against 'Western' targets, including 5 aimed at the United States.[5] These are the three major targeting sectors for Middle Eastern terrorist groups. The most significant development was the fact that 20 attacks were directed at Western targets. I will discuss this targeting sector later.

A breakdown of the 42 attacks aimed at Arab and Palestinian targets indicates that:

8 were directed at Libyan exiles
7 against Jordan
6 against PLO moderates and Arafat supporters

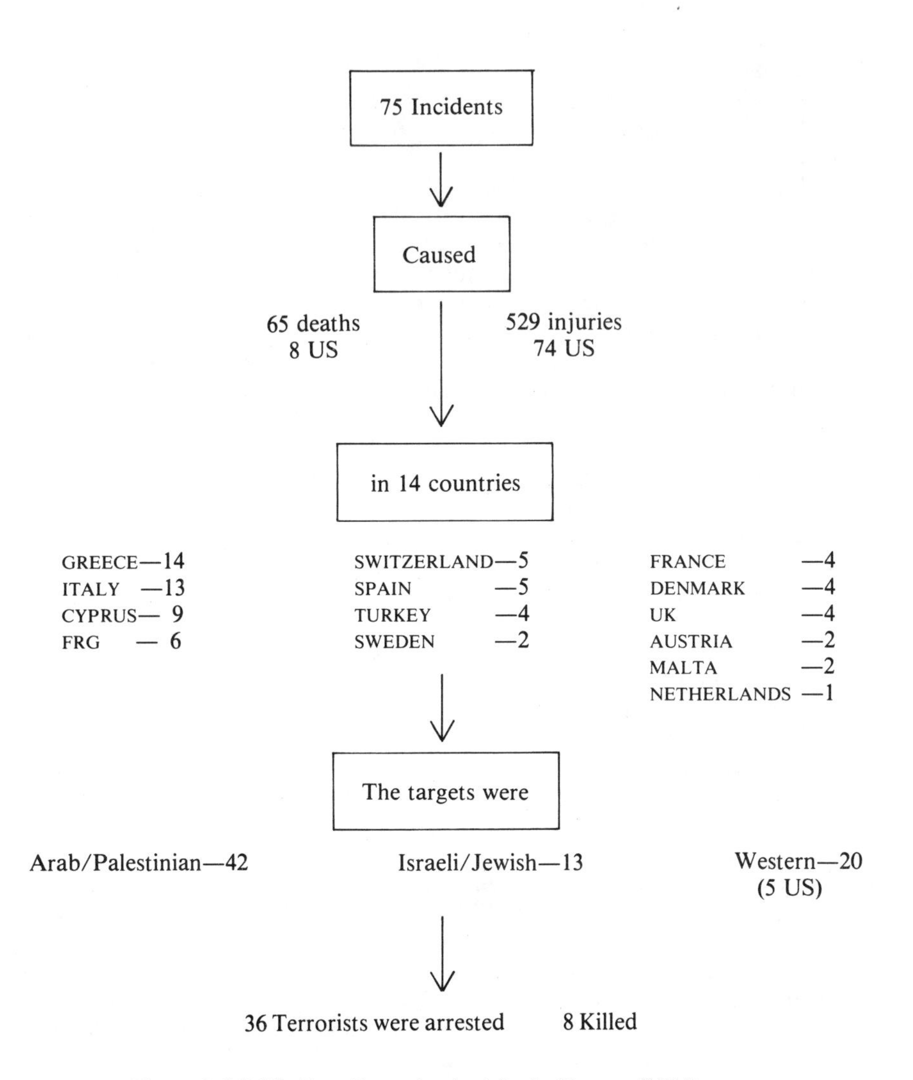

Figure 1. Middle East Terrorist Activity in Europe (1985).

6 against Libya
5 against Iran
4 against Syria
2 against Iraq
1 against an Iranian exile
1 against an Iraqi exile
1 against Tunisia
1 against a Palestinian student.

The suspected or stated motives for the above attacks are as varied as the targets. The ten attacks directed at Libyan, Iranian and Iraqi political exiles were carried out in order to silence or intimidate exiled opponents of these regimes. Libya and Iran are particularly active in these types of intimidation campaigns. These opposition elements, however, occasionally retaliate against Libya, Iran or Iraq—sometimes with the support or encouragement of other Arab states which also oppose these regimes. For example, Iranian dissidents and former supporters of the Shah of Iran are believed to have been responsible for five attacks against Iranian targets in Western Europe in 1985. Iraqi dissidents, operating under the name of the 'Organization of the Iraqi Islamic Vengeance', and with the suspected support of either Syria or Iran, carried out two attacks against Iraqi interests in Nicosia. Moreover, Libyan opposition elements—occasionally with the suspected support of Iraq, which obviously opposes Libya's support for Iran—carried out six attacks last year against Libyan targets in Western Europe.

The catalyst for the seven attacks against Jordanian targets and the four against Syrian targets appears to have been the Jordanian–PLO agreement signed on 11 February 1985 in Amman. This agreement, which sought a negotiated Middle East peace settlement, was opposed by Syria. Syria was also displeased with Jordan for re-establishing diplomatic ties with Egypt in September 1984 and for agreeing to host the Palestine National Council (PNC) meeting in Amman on 22 November 1984. President Assad had warned Arafat not to convene a meeting of the PNC. The February 1985 agreement and the November 1984 PNC meeting most likely provoked Syria into contracting with the Abu Nidal group to attack Jordanian targets, as a show of 'displeasure'. The Abu Nidal group has apparently been based in Damascus since November 1983 when the Iraqi government banished it from Baghdad. This symbiotic relationship between the Abu Nidal organisation and Syria consisted of Syria providing the group with resources and a safe haven and the Abu Nidal group in turn providing Syria with a 'terrorist option' when developing and implementing its foreign policy. Ironically, this is the same type of relationship the Abu Nidal group had with Iraq when Baghdad used the group to attack Syrian targets in the mid 1970s.[6]

The Abu Nidal organisation has a history of creating commando names for specific terrorist campaigns. The name 'Black June' was used in the late 1970s when the group attacked Syrian targets; the 'Arab Revolutionary Brigades' was used when the group hit moderate Arab states like Kuwait, the United Arab Emirates and Jordan; the 'Revolutionary Organisation of Socialist Moslems' has been used primarily against British targets; and the more formal name for the Abu Nidal organisation, 'Fatah-Revolutionary Council' is used primarily in attacks against Israeli targets. For the Syrian-backed terrorist campaign against Jordan, and, to a lesser extent against moderates within the PLO, the Abu Nidal group used the name 'Black September Organisation' or BSO—a parody on the name used by the PLO when it sanctioned terrorist attacks in the early 1970s.[7] Abu Nidal's use of this commando name first appeared on 4 December 1984—two weeks after the start of the Palestine National Council meeting in Amman—when the BSO killed a Jordanian political counsellor in Bucharest. The BSO attack communiqué denounced Jordan for plotting with PLO leader Yassir Arafat.

After the signing of the February 1985 PLO–Jordanian agreement in Amman, BSO attacks against Jordanian targets increased. In March, the BSO attacked Jordanian airline offices in Rome, Athens and Nicosia. In April, anti-tank rockets were fired at the Jordanian embassy in Rome and at a Jordanian airliner in Athens. In July, the BSO carried out a machine-gun and grenade attack on the Jordanian airlines office in Madrid, and assassinated a Jordanian diplomat in Ankara. In September, the BSO killed a supporter of Yassir Arafat in Athens. This has been the last attack carried out by the BSO. The PLO–Jordanian agreement was eroding. King Hussein went to Damascus on 30–31 December for discussions with President Assad, and on 19 February 1986, Jordan ended political coordination with the PLO in working towards a Middle East peace settlement. The PLO–Jordanian accord no longer threatened Syria's premier position in Lebanon, and the BSO attacks against Jordan have stopped—for now.

I previously stated that there were four terrorist attacks registered against Syrian targets in 1985. In April, the Syrian airline office in Rome was bombed and in Geneva, a bomb exploded in a vehicle driven by the Syrian Charge and another bomb was found in front of a Syrian diplomat's residence. In June, a bomb was found outside the Syrian embassy in London. These attacks appear to be retaliatory attacks against Syria by PLO elements for the Syrian-backed Abu Nidal attacks against Jordan and PLO moderates. As a result, the Syrian–Jordanian–PLO conflict in late 1984 and 1985 was the catalyst for twelve terrorist attacks involving Jordanian, Syrian and PLO targets in Western Europe. This is a classic example of a Middle Eastern political feud, fought in the terrorist mode, spilling over into Western Europe.

It should also be pointed out that there were six terrorist attacks against moderate PLO members and supporters of Arafat in Western Europe in 1985. One of these attacks was claimed by Abu Nidal's 'Black September Organisation'. Another was claimed by the 'Eagles of the Palestinian Revolution'—a suspected Syrian-backed Palestinian group. Consequently, these two attacks were most likely linked to the above-mentioned Syrian–Jordanian–PLO conflict. The remaining four attacks were probably carried out by dissidents from Arafat's 'Fatah' organisation and other anti-Arafat elements from the 'Palestine National Salvation Front—a Syrian-supported counterweight to the PLO.

This concludes my discussion on the forty-two terrorist attacks directed at Arab and Palestinian targets in Western Europe in 1985 by Middle Eastern groups. I would now like to briefly survey the thirteen attacks directed against Israeli and Jewish targets in Europe.

Attacks against Israeli and Jewish targets are a standard part of Middle Eastern terrorist activities in Western Europe. Stringent security measures in Israel make it difficult for these groups to carry out attacks in Israel so Western Europe is an attractive alternative. The number of attacks per year varies, depending primarily on the number of 'trigger events' which take place in the Middle East. Any increase in the number of attacks can usually be attributed to specific events like the Israeli military incursion into Lebanon and the massacres at the Sabra and Shatila refugee camps in 1982 or Israeli retaliatory bombing attacks against PLO targets. The unusually high number of attacks against Israeli and Jewish targets in 1985 can be traced to several events which took place in the Middle East. Of the thirteen attacks which took place in 1985, I believe that six of these attacks were terrorist retaliations for three specific events: (a) the Israeli bombing on 21 July 1985 of a small Lebanese village called Kabrihka, (b) the Israeli interception in late August 1985 of two yachts off the northern coast of Israel which contained thirteen Fatah and 'Force 17' terrorists and (c) the Israeli bombing of the PLO's headquarters in Tunis on 1 October 1985. The six attacks and these three events combined to produce a dialectical spiral of violence between Israel and Middle Eastern terrorist groups.

The third and last targeting sector for Middle Eastern terrorist groups is 'Western targets' and by this I mean attacks against US and West European facilities and personnel. Of the 75 terrorist incidents carried out by Middle Eastern groups in Europe in 1985, 20 were directed at Western targets. It was these attacks that attracted the most publicity for the groups, caused the most casualties and had the greatest impact on the political and security environment in Western Europe. The primary reason that these attacks had more of an impact on the security environment in Western Europe than those directed at Arab, Palestinian, Israeli and Jewish targets, is that the attacks aimed at Western targets were more indiscriminate in nature and clearly designed to cause mass casualties. These attacks caused 45 deaths, or 66 per cent of all the fatalities caused by Middle Eastern attacks in 1985, and 439 injuries or 83 per cent of the injury total. The objective of these attacks was to cause shock and then induce fear. This in turn was to translate into pressure on the European countries to release imprisoned Middle Eastern terrorists. This was the primary motive for 13 of the 20 attacks directed at Western targets.

These thirteen attacks involved the following terrorist campaigns designed to release imprisoned comrades:

(a) Three incidents directed at Swiss targets by suspected PLO terrorist elements to pressure the Swiss to release two Palestinian terrorists arrested on 26 April shortly after bombing two Syrian diplomatic targets in Geneva.
(b) Two attacks against French targets in Paris by suspected Iranian-backed Shiite groups to force the French to release the terrorist involved in the

attempted assassination of former Iranian Prime Minister Bakhtiar in Paris in 1980.

(c) The hijacking of TWA flight 847 out of Athens by Lebanese Shiite terrorists to force the US to put pressure on the Israelis to release some 700 Lebanese Shiite Muslim prisoners.

(d) The 27 December attack on the airport in Vienna by Abu Nidal to pressure the Austrian government into releasing three Abu Nidal members arrested in Vienna for a 1981 attack on a Vienna synagogue.

(e) Four attacks by the Abu Nidal group, operating under the name of the 'Revolutionary Organisation of Socialist Muslims', against British targets in Greece, Spain and Italy in order to force the British to release the three Abu Nidal terrorists being held for the attempted assassination of the Israeli ambassador in London in 1982.

(f) Two attacks by the Abu Nidal group against Italian targets in Italy in order to pressure the Italian government into releasing an Abu Nidal member arrested in Rome in April 1985 for firing an anti-tank rocket at the Jordanian embassy and because of Italy's request to the Greek government to extradite an Abu Nidal member for the October 1982 attack on a Rome synagogue. Both attacks, the Café de Paris bombing in September and the attack on Fiumicino airport in December, had secondary objectives. The Café de Paris attack was also aimed at the British and the US, and the Fiumicino attack was also directed at Israel and the US.

The remaining seven attacks directed at Western targets in Western Europe in 1985 were either carried out for other motives, such as support for Iran in the Iran–Iraq war or in retaliation for the Israeli bombing of a small village in southern Lebanon, or were simply not claimed. In fact, there were five attacks in 1985 which have not been attributed to any specific Middle Eastern group or state. However, it is generally agreed that Middle Eastern groups were involved. The first took place on 12 April when a bomb exploded in the El Descanso restaurant near the Torrejon air base outside of Madrid. This particular restaurant is frequented by US military personnel and their dependents. Eighteen Spaniards were killed and eighty-two were injured, including fifteen Americans. Several groups, including the 'Islamic Jihad' organisation, claimed credit for the bombing. However, no viable claim has been received. The second unclaimed incident took place on 19 June when a bomb detonated in the check-in area of the Frankfurt international airport. Three people, including two children, were killed and forty-two others were injured. Although some twenty groups claimed credit for the attack, no viable claim has been received.

Another attack occurred on 1 July when a bomb exploded in the transit luggage section of Fiumicino airport in Rome. Twelve people were injured in this bombing. No terrorist group claimed credit for this attack. The possibility exists that in both the Frankfurt and Rome incidents, the bombs detonated prematurely. The targets may not have been the airports but aircraft departing from these airports. A fourth unclaimed attack took place on 24 November when a car bomb exploded in a US military commissary area in Frankfurt. Some thrity-six people, including thirty-two Americans were injured during this attack. Once again, no group claimed credit, but Middle Eastern terrorists are the primary suspects.

Of all the terrorist developments which took place in 1985, I believe the intensified activities of Middle Eastern terrorists against 'Western' targets in Western Europe were the most significant. This assessment is based on several factors:

(a) 1985 marked a dramatic increase in the number of attacks against 'Western' targets and in the casualties caused by these attacks.[8] In 1984, we recorded only six attacks against 'Western' targets which resulted in two deaths and twenty-six injuries. In 1985, there were 20 attacks, 45 deaths and 439 injuries. The attacks last year clearly indicated a trend towards more indiscriminate attacks designed to cause mass casualties.

(b) There was a significant increase in the number of attacks directed at US targets. In 1984, there was only one attack carried out against a US target. This was the attempted assassination of the US Consul General in Strasbourg on 26 March by the Lebanese Armed Revolutionary Faction. In 1985, we recorded five attacks which caused eight US deaths and seventy-four injuries. These attacks signal a trend of increasing Middle East terrorist attacks against US targets in Western Europe.

(c) The attacks by Middle Eastern groups against 'Western' targets in 1985 signalled the beginning of a terrorist campaign by certain groups to focus on a perceived 'Achilles heel' of West European governments—tourism.[9] One of the groups, the Abu Nidal organisation, implied as much in its communiqués. After the 16 September grenade attack on the Café de Paris on the Via Veneto in Rome, an Abu Nidal group warned tourists, especially Arabs, to stay away from Britain, Spain and Italy to avoid 'operations by our heroic strugglers'. This warning was repeated after the group bombed the British Airways office in Rome on 25 September. This communiqué warned 'tourists to avoid British, Spanish and Italian institutions because they will be targets of our operations'. These warnings were possible indicators that attacks, like the airport attacks in Rome and Vienna, were being planned.

Middle Eastern terrorist activity has been a security and political problem for Western European governments since the early 1970s when Palestinian airplane hijackings dominated the terrorist scene and the massacre at the 1972 Olympics in Munich testified to the bloody and desperate nature of Middle Eastern terrorism. Over the years, the threat of Middle Eastern terrorism in Western Europe has generally oscillated between the low and moderate levels with an occasional peak into the high level. Such peaks are most often triggered by a particularly lethal or well-publicised Middle Eastern terrorist attack, such as the Carlos-led raid on the OPEC Ministerial meeting in Vienna in 1975, the seizure of the Iranian embassy in London in 1980, the attack on the Rue Copernic synagogue in Paris in October 1980, the Carlos threat to the French government in February 1982 and the massacre at the 'Jo Goldenberg' restaurant in Paris in August 1982.

In general, Middle Eastern attacks in Western Europe have been directed at other Arab or Palestinian targets or against Israeli or Jewish targets (see Figure 2). Historically, there have been few attacks against Western targets in Western Europe. In fact, we have recorded only twenty-eight attacks during 1980–1984. However, the twenty attacks which took place in 1985 indicate that these groups are beginning to concentrate more of their attacks on Western targets. Moreover, it appears that these groups are intentionally designing their attacks to scare tourists away from certain countries in Western Europe. I do not believe that this is a targeting aberration, but the signal of a dangerous and growing trend. The February and March 1986 bombings in Paris, the 2 April bombing of TWA flight 840 over Athens, the 5 April bombing of a disco in West Berlin frequented by US servicemen and the 8 April threat by the Lebanese Armed Revolutionary Faction that 'Italian streets will witness tragedies like those in France', would appear to support this assessment.

PROGNOSIS

I would now like to offer some projections concerning Middle Eastern terrorist activity in Western Europe in 1986. While these projections are free, they do come with a limited warranty.

(a) There is a good possibility that a Middle Eastern terrorist group and a European terrorist group will carry out a joint operation sometime in 1986.

(b) Middle Eastern groups should carry out somewhere between sixty and seventy terrorist attacks in Western Europe this year. As of 6 April we have already recorded thirteen attacks. I expect the number of attacks to significantly increase during the summer or tourist months.

(c) The radical Palestinian groups under the protection of Syria and Libya will continue to focus on indiscriminate bombings designed to cause mass casualties. Iranian-backed groups and certain Lebanese terrorist groups will also select this tactic—more so than in the past. I believe that Middle Eastern groups have realised that they can put more pressure on a West European country by carrying out indiscriminate bombings in the capital of that country than by kidnapping its citizens in Lebanon. Such bombing campaigns have a significant, negative influence on tourism—a potential 'Achilles heel' for the governments of certain West European countries.

(d) While Middle Eastern groups will continue to primarily target other Arabs and Palestinians, I believe that, proportionately, more attacks will be directed at 'Western' targets. The fact that Middle Eastern terrorists are still imprisoned in France, Great Britain, Spain, Italy, Greece,

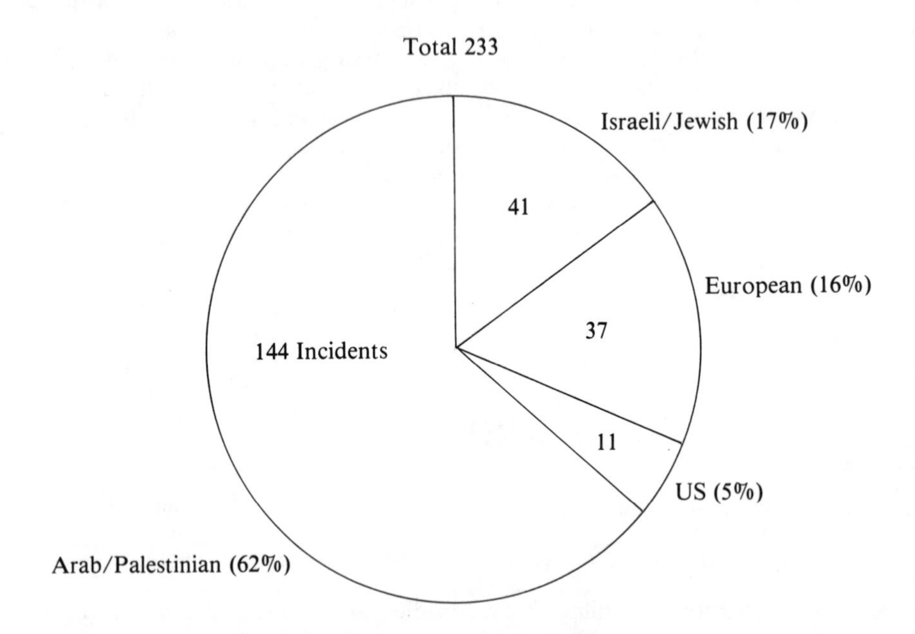

Figure 2. Middle East Terrorist Attacks on Targets in Europe (1980–1985).

Cyprus, Turkey, Austria and Switzerland, and the recent Libyan threats of retaliation over the 23 March Gulf of Sidra incident, only underlines this targeting trend.

(e) As airport security around terminal buildings is tightened and security checks on hand and checked luggage intensifies, I believe there is a growing possibility that some Middle Eastern groups will utilise the SA-7—a Soviet-made surface-to-air missile—to attack commercial aircraft. This weapon was found in Palestinian terrorist conspirative apartments in Western Europe in the mid 1970s. These groups have access to these weapons. Any group which is willing to blow up an airliner in mid-air, bomb a disco packed with over four hundred people, or throw hand grenades at airline passengers in an airport check-in line, would have no moral problem firing a missile at a commercial airliner.

(f) I would also anticipate the increased use of anti-armour weapons, such as the M-72 LAW, RPG-75 or RPG-7, by these groups. The high terrorist threat level in Western Europe for US and European dignitaries has dictated increased security measures for buildings and for vehicular travel. Some of these measures can be defeated with anti-armour weapons, both those which are shoulder-fired and those fired from automatically timed, makeshift launchers. It should be noted that the Abu Nidal group used an anti-armour weapon in two attacks last year—at the Jordanian embassy in Rome and at a Jordanian airliner at Athens airport.

(g) At this point, there are five interesting developments to monitor in 1986. First, now that the Abu Nidal group has publicly threatened Iraq because Iraq confiscated some $50 million worth of Abu Nidal's property, equipment and weapons in November 1983 when it banished the group from Iraq, will we see more attacks against Iraqi interests in Western Europe?[10] Will it replace Jordan as the most targeted Arab country by Middle East terrorists operating in Western Europe? Secondly, how will Abu Aba's 'Palestine Liberation Front' react when several of its members are put on trial in Italy in late 1986 for hijacking the Italian cruise ship the *Achille Lauro* and charged with kidnapping and murder? Thirdly, how will the Lebanese Armed Revolutionary Faction (LARF) respond when and if France puts George Ibrahim Abdalah, the suspected LARF leader, on trial? It is generally believed that the LARF has been behind the recent spate of bombings aimed at key tourist and public areas in central Paris.[11] Fourthly, will Qadafi be satisfied with one or two retaliatory terrorist attacks against US targets in an attempt to recapture his lost 'prestige' or has he initiated a dialectical spiral of violence which will develop its own momentum? An obvious corollary of this fourth development would be whether or not the United States decides to carry out any further military actions against Qadafi? And finally, has Great Britain's resolve finally deterred Abu Nidal from further attacks against British targets in Western Europe in order to free his members imprisoned for the attempted assassination of the Israeli ambassador in London in 1982?

The answers to these questions will determine the level and lethality of Middle Eastern terrorist activity in Western Europe in 1986.

NOTES

1 This figure includes explosive devices discovered by police before they could detonate and devices which failed to detonate due to mechanical failure. The majority of these attacks were either claimed by a Middle Eastern group or subsequent investigation linked a Middle Eastern group to an attack. Some incidents, however, were attributed to a Middle Eastern group through 'analysis', that is, the suspected link was made based on the target of the attack, method of operation, area of operation and the timing of the attack (did it occur just after a 'trigger event' in the Middle East?).

The annual figures for the number of Middle Eastern terrorist attacks in Western Europe and the fatalities and injuries caused are:

	Incidents	*Fatalities*	*Injuries*
1980	33	28	65
1981	20	11	214
1982	34	23	248
1983	24	10	113
1984	47	18	63
1985	75	65	529

The above figures are subject to minor changes as further investigation and subsequent arrests lead to responsibility being attributed for past attacks which, at the time, were not attributed to Middle Eastern terrorist groups.

2 Paper released by the US Department of State in Washington, DC in January 1986 entitled 'Libya Under Qadafi: A Pattern of Aggression', p. 13.

3 Based on my files. See also DA Pluchinsky, 'Political Terrorism in Western Europe: Some Themes and Variations' *in* Yonah Alexander and Kenneth Myers (eds.), *Terrorism in Europe*, London: Croom Helm, 1982, p. 61.

4 This figure *does not* include the fifty-eight passengers killed during the Egyptian counterterrorist attack on the hijacked Egyptian Air plane in Valletta, Malta on 24 November 1985. For comparative purposes, indigenous terrorist groups in Western Europe (including the IRA and the ETA) were responsible for one hundred and eighteen deaths in 1985. If the IRA and the ETA were excluded, the figure would be twenty-seven.

5 The five attacks against US targets in Western Europe in 1985 were: the 14 June hijacking of TWA flight 847 out of Athens, the bombing of a TWA office in Madrid on 1 July, the 22 July bombing of the Northwest Orient airline office in Copenhagen, the car bombing at a US military shopping area in Frankfurt on 24 November and the attack at the El Al and TWA ticket counters at Rome airport on 27 December. This year, as of 6 April 1986, there have already been three Middle Eastern terrorist attacks against US targets in Western Europe: the 2 April bombing of TWA flight 840 out of Rome, the 5 April bombing of the 'La Belle' disco in West Berlin, and the 7 April bombing of the Northwest Orient airline office in Stockholm.

6 The Abu Nidal organisation used the commando name of 'Black June' (after

June 1976 when Syria fought the Palestinians in Lebanon) to attack several Syrian targets during the latter half of 1976. For example, on 26 September Black June terrorists attacked a hotel in Damascus which caused four deaths and thirty-four injuries. Three of the terrorists were captured and publicly hung in Damascus the next day. On 11 October the Syrian embassies in Rome and Islamabad were attacked by Black June. On 1 December, Black June terrorists attempted to assassinate the Syrian Foreign Minister in Damascus. The Abu Nidal organisation was based in Baghdad at the time of these attacks. For an excellent article on the Abu Nidal group and its relationships with radical Middle East states, see Aaron D Miller, 'A Portrait of Abu Nidal: The Man Who Loves to Kill Americans', *Washington Post*, 30 March 1986, p. D1.

7 It is possible that the Abu Nidal's use of the commando name 'Black September Organisation' is a commemoration of the 17 September 1982 massacre in the Sabra and Shatila refugee camps in Lebanon.

8 The number of Middle Eastern terrorist attacks against Western targets in Western Europe from 1980 to 10 April 1986 is as follows:

1980	1
1981	4
1982	8
1983	10
1984	5
1985	20
1986 (as of 4/10)	10.

9 With the concurrent fall of the dollar it is difficult to accurately assess the effect on tourism of recent Middle Eastern terrorist attacks in Western Europe. However, it would appear that these attacks have had a major, negative impact on tourist travel to Western Europe, especially the Mediterranean countries. Since the hijacking of TWA flight 847 in June 1985, there has been a dramatic increase in the number of press and magazine articles and TV programmes dealing with the effect of terrorism on tourism. Various polls indicate that Americans are afraid of travelling to Western Europe. A recent *Newsweek* poll taken between 26 and 27 March 1986 (before the bombing of TWA flight 840 and the bombing of the disco in West Berlin) indicated that sixty-one per cent of the Americans interviewed, if they had the opportunity to travel overseas this summer, would refuse to go because of the threat of terrorism (Newsweek, 7 April 1986, p. 23).

10 UPI reported on 6 March 1986 that a statement published in *As Safir*, a leftist Beirut weekly, by Abu Nidal's 'Fatah Revolutionary Council' made public for the first time the group's two-year dispute with Iraq. The group accused the Iraqi intelligence services of trying to kill three Abu Nidal members. It also accused the Jordanian, Iraqi and PLO intelligence services of collaborating and passing data about the group to other countries. The Abu Nidal group gave Iraq two weeks to return $50 million worth of the group's 'property, equipment and weapons' in Iraq which was confiscated by Baghdad in November 1983 when it banished the group from Iraq. If Iraq does not return the materials, the Abu Nidal group warned that it would have to 'face the consequences'.

11 A group calling itself the 'Committee for Solidarity with Arab and Middle East Political Prisoners' has claimed credit for several bombings of tourist areas in central Paris in February and March 1986. The group is ostensibly seeking the release of three terrorists being held in France: a suspected leader of the Lebanese

Armed Revolutionary Faction (LARF), an Armenian terrorist and a pro-Iranian terrorist who attempted to kill former Iranian Prime Minister Bakhtiar in Paris in 1980. In communiqués issued on 20 March and 7 April this group also demanded that Italy release two imprisoned members of the LARF or else the group would 'make the streets of Rome and its people subject to what is being witnessed in Paris'. This group is believed to be a commando of the LARF.

Terror in Ireland: Observations on Tynan's *The Irish Invincibles and Their Times*

C Townshend

The stabbing to death of the newly appointed Chief Secretary for Ireland, Lord Frederick Cavendish, and the Permanent Under-Secretary, Thomas Burke, on 6 May 1882 in Phoenix Park, Dublin, was labelled by a contemporary journalist 'the greatest political crime of the century'.[1] A general view of its impact may suggest that it was indeed such. Another writer compared its effect to that of the Clerkenwell explosion of 1867 which had precipitated Gladstone's first great Irish reforms.[2] A major political initiative in 1882, the Kilmainham Treaty between Gladstone and Parnell, was killed at birth by it, and the following three years saw Ireland governed under repressive legislation while Britain struggled with a 'dynamite war' conducted by Irish–American terrorists. This difficult period culminated in Gladstone's acceptance of the need for Irish autonomy.

Yet closer examination reveals formidable difficulties in interpreting the 'political' deed of the Irish Invincibles. What political effect was it intended to have? What precisely was Invincible policy, and how did the organisation prepare to carry it out? What, indeed, did the organisation consist of, beyond the twenty-six men eventually arrested for their part in the Phoenix Park assassinations, and the few others 'known to the police'? Answers to these central questions—important to the study both of Irish history and of terrorism—must be based on evidence of exiguous quantity and doubtful reliability. In part this is a necessary consequence of the secrecy natural to underground groups; in part, too, it is due to the short life of the Invincible organisation between the late autumn of 1881 and late spring of 1883. The taciturnity of its members, untypical of Irish nationalists, was broken only by the trial evidence—in particular the testimony of James Carey—and by the publication over ten years later of Patrick Joseph Percy Tynan's *The Irish National Invincibles and their Times*. Even if, as a cursory glance will show, most of his book concerns the Times rather than the Invincibles, Tynan offers the only substantial picture of the group's outlook.

Tynan achieved celebrity as 'No. 1', the linkman between the headquarters of the Invincibles in London and the subordinate 'directory' and its forces in Dublin. In his own account he appears as the operational commander of the latter. Unfortunately his real position is not so certain. A 'needy and seedy commercial traveller', who in the astringent view of the journalist Moir Bussy was 'not even a blatherskite or a silly ass until a silly mistake enshrouded him in a blaze of execrable notoriety'.[3] Tynan had been an inactive member of the Irish Republican Brotherhood (IRB), and a more active member (whether or not he saw himself as a Fenian infiltrator) of an English militia battalion, the Queen's Own Westminster Volunteers.[4] He was able to escape to America when the Invincibles were broken up, because he was unknown to the police. Did this reflect his real unimportance, or merely the limitations of the much-vaunted 'great Irish detective' John Mallon? No firm evidence exists on which to base an answer. Tynan remains an obscure figure.

The circumstances of the book's publication in New York are likewise shadowy, though it is clear that the body of the text was written in 1887, six years after the creation of the Invincibles. A short addendum carries the account up to 1893. In the original edition, whose balance was quite seriously altered in the edited version published a few months later in London by Chapman and Hall, it forms an extended account of 'three decades of struggle against the foreign conspirators in Dublin Castle'. Despite its fluent savagery and its capacity for striking paradox, Tynan's writing is not for the most part the work of an original thinker. It is symptomatic rather than seminal. As an illumination of the Fenian *Weltanschauung*, however, it is outstanding. (One British intelligence officer conceded reluctantly that despite its repetitiveness it was 'worth the attention of the criminologists or those interested in the psychology of fanaticism'.)[5] Tynan's pre-occupations, like his torrid style, are unmistakably Fenian.

Two themes dominate: the futility of argument or 'moral suasion', even by mass movements, as a means of inducing the British to halt their genocidal war against the Irish; and the immorality of the 'provincialist' (home rule) policy pursued by Irish parliamentarians. Physical force is the only possible means and an independent Irish republic the only moral end. Seven chapters (VI–XII) are devoted to an account of the attempted IRB rebellion of 1867 and its aftermath, presenting classical Fenian insurrectionism—from which the Invincibles were so strikingly to deviate—as the ideal. As Tynan despairingly repeats, the emigration forced by British maladministration in Ireland was causing vastly greater losses than the most bloody war of independence. This extensive section was omitted from the London edition of the book, which thus takes the misleading shape of a history of Irish parliamentarism.[6] Also consistently edited out of the remaining chapters are Tynan's most incisive formulations of the basic Fenian analysis. For instance, 'British interests ... make a peaceful solution of the Irish question *impossible*'; 'Ireland's bloody struggle with her enemy can only cease with the destruction of the Irish race or the creation of an Irish republic'; 'Ireland has no alternative between victory and extermination'; 'Ireland has no need of politics'.

Tynan's tireless denunciation of parliamentarism as both morally demeaning and practically futile is the essence of Fenianism, with added personal venom from the shocking moment at which the parliamentary leaders publicly condemned the Phoenix Park murders as a 'cowardly and unprovoked atrocity' which had 'stained the name of hospitable Ireland'.[7] Indeed, one of his main concerns is to demonstrate that the Invincibles were a natural outgrowth of the older physical-force organisation, or rather the 'wing of the Irish party more active than the other'. His constant stress on the integral unity of the Irish national movement, and the regularity of the Invincibles' position within it, was a counter to the known view of some IRB leaders that 'the Invincible conspiracy was merely a form of agrarianism transferred to the city, and its members were seduced from the principles of the IRB by the grossest misrepresentations and made parties to a treacherous attempt to break up the great secret organisation'.[8] Undoubtedly most of the Invincible rank and file, like Tynan himself, were former IRB men. But Tynan further sought to demonstrate that the Invincibles were not simply countenanced but actually financed and directed by the highest level of the 'Parnellite government' (for instance his remark that 'to say that Parnell was not in sympathy with and did not sanction the removing of Cavendish and Burke is to say that he was not leader of the Irish party'). What is to be made of this contention? Even Parnell's enemies on the *Times* Special Commission never charged him so directly with complicity. The most judicious account of the whole affair concludes that Tynan's charges 'must be assessed as, in the main, the hysterical bitterness of an underling who has been misled and, to his own mind, betrayed'.[9]

It is obvious that, like earlier Irish secret societies and agrarian 'associations', the Invincibles recruited by exaggerating their own power and legitimacy. But is equally obvious that some of the connections with higher levels were not altogether exaggerated. The IRB view that the Invincible campaign was 'agrarianism transferred into the city' can be sustained in some degree. The leadership of the Land League was directly involved in the creation of the new secret society. Finance was undoubtedly supplied, though the quantity cannot be ascertained.[10] The results were mixed. The widespread impression that 'money was plentiful among the Invincibles' may have had an impact on recruitment. Tighe Hopkins found it hard to believe that the ill-favoured rank and file Invincibles 'had in them the stuff that patriotism is made of'. There were surprisingly few fanatics: Hopkins names Joe Brady and Tim Kelly, and one may add the veteran Fenian John Walsh, the quiet Dan Curley, and, surely, Tynan himself. Many others were not uninterested in the financial benefits of activism.

The other consequence of plentiful money should have been abundant weaponry—a commodity at least as vital as membership. Yet Tynan's account shows that the Invincibles found it impossible to obtain enough arms—especially explosives—for the projected attack on Lord Spencer. They never acquired bombs, and Tynan shows himself a restrained supporter of the Clan na Gael's dynamite campaign and O'Donovan Rossa's 'skirmishing'. They carried revolvers (which were easy to smuggle into Ireland) and even, according to one account, bought two Winchester rifles. But the weapons chosen for the assassination of Burke were the simplest possible. Twelve-inch surgical knives were brought across from London to Dublin in the skirts of Mrs Frank Byrne, wife of the Secretary of the Land League of Great Britain. Tynan's account claims that he himself decided on the use of 'the weapon immortalised by Palafox' but others agree that the idea was Carey's. (Carey, significantly, later regretted the destruction of the knives on 'No. 1's' orders: he thought that they should be exhibited publicly as a monument to the historic deed.)[11]

If Tynan's account is at times tendentious on the subject of the Invincible organisation, it is uniquely interesting on Invincible policy. No concrete information was produced by the police investigation of the trial evidence about the intention behind the Invincible operations. Carey merely said that the society aimed 'to make history'. Brady and Kelly, who actually drove the knives into Burke and Cavendish, never enlarged on their reasoning. Observers may have recognised that 'the policy of direct assassination' as distinct from armed insurrection was a new departure in political violence.[12] But they seem to have been incurious about its intended effect. They regarded Invincible jargon for killings as repellent euphemisms, rather than as clues to intention. There was, for instance, some carelessness in reporting the content of the black-edged cards sent to newspaper editors on the day after Phoenix Park: according to several accounts these read 'Executed by the Irish Invincibles' (or 'by order of the Irish Invincibles'); others read them as saying 'This deed was done by the Irish Invincibles'.

Tynan is quite forthcoming on this issue. He consistently employs a term, 'suppression', which seems to reflect a wider awareness of terrorist ideas in other countries. Attacks were made not upon individuals but on the offices of the British State. These offices were to be 'suppressed' by the repeated killing of their incumbents. The most obvious targets were the Viceroyalty, the Chief Secretaryship and the Under-Secretaryship. There is here an echo of early Russian terrorists' hopes that the state structure might be undermined by the elimination of its chief functionaries. It remains muted, however, amidst more familiar ideas. The Fenian *Leitmotiv* of insurrection always recurs: the Invincible attacks are 'the advance courier of a war of independence'; 'Enslaved peoples require to be educated as the advance guard to freedom; street fights are the forerunners of revolution'; from *émeutes* might spring insurrection'. Such pious hopes are tempered by a hint of new realism. Tynan often speaks of a 'guerrilla war' which was 'to harrass and in some measure destroy', or still more prophetically 'paralyse', the enemy. (Although he is less prophetic when he contemptuously dismisses the idea of boycotting the British government and its forces as 'the delusion of an imbecile'.) When the Invincibles were set up, 'a species of guerilla warfare was determined on (it was the future making its appearance on the scene)' ... and again, 'these guerilla attacks might eventually lead up to a war for independence'.

Tyrannicide and harassment might have some effect, but would it be enough? He is vague about the positive hopes reposed in these policies. In the end it is the most primitive of all motives, revenge, which underpins the war of reprisals. Again and again Tynan demonstrates this. Irish people 'imbibe hatred of the English invaders with their mother's milk', yet they 'are not seeking revenge to satisfy any appetite of hatred'. Revenge becomes in itself a moral imperative. He quotes Rossa's wish to 'hurt England', to 'make her feel that Irish vengeance is something to be feared'. He declares that 'Ireland seeks an eye for an eye and a tooth for a tooth'. 'The blows dealt by the British invader are incessant; they are answered back by prostrate Ireland only in a sporadic and intermittent manner.' Physical force thus appears not so much as a rational stategy as a psychological necessity. No proof is adduced, or considered necessary, that the suppression of British offices will produce a measurable effect on British policy.[13] For Tynan this leads to the important conclusion that the republican soldier was beyond politics. It was not his business to follow 'the intricate details of statesmanship. His was the plain duty of the soldier to try and destroy the murderous foe'.

This overlaying of complementary, and even contradictory, motives in Tynan's account undoubtedly mediates the reality of Invincible thinking. It is especially relevant to the question whether the Phoenix Park murders were intended as a decisive rejection of the Kilmainham initiative. Such an interpretation would, it is clear, be too simple. The slipshod reconnaissance for the failed *attentats* against Forster in the six months between November 1881 and May 1882, the surprising inability of the Invincibles to ascertain the appearance of the most notable Irish public official (who was, it must be said, a very easy target), together with Tynan's own account of his very casual planning for an attack on Spencer in the summer of 1882, all sustain the belief that the timing of the 6 May operation was fortuitous. Here the question of the victims arises. The death of the 'Castle rat' Burke, a Catholic well known as the lynchpin of the administration, and from the nationalist standpoint a renegade, was to most people at least comprehensible albeit deplorable. Cavendish, however, appeared doubly innocent. Not only was he a reticent man who could not hope, with a Viceroy like Spencer, to occupy the position of power held by Forster, and who, in any case, had not had a chance to exercise a single administrative function; but his appointment was seen as an earnest of a new conciliatory policy. His assassination thus appeared monstrous on both personal and political grounds. Tynan was careful to demolish the resulting theory that his death had been a ghastly accident, and to point out—with his capacity for brutal paradox—that Cavendish became automatically guilty the instant he assumed 'the scarlet robe of Ireland's assassin'. For good measure he adds that Cavendish was 'on the threshold of fresh crimes'. (A form of legal reasoning more arbitrary than any of which Tynan accused the British.)

The assassination was thus both vengeance and prevention. Two further dimensions are hinted at, though the reader may feel that they are later superimpositions rather than original motivations. Imagining the scene of Lord Spencer's death, Tynan reflects that this 'supreme effort to crush out in blood and carnage' the tyrant's life, might require 'the sacrifice of the whole sacred band'. Here surely is a pre-echo of Pearse's exaltation of blood-sacrifice, the inspiration of the 1916 Rising. The sacrifice is a quasi-religious one: the national cause is 'sacred', as is the national soil; to 'smite the foe' is a 'sacred duty' or a 'sacred mission', and the missioners a 'sacred band'.

The final idea that emerges is that of propaganda. Tynan does not explicitly speak of 'propaganda of the deed', but this central terrorist concept is implicit in his approach. It comes closest to expression in an unusual paragraph which leaps beyond conventional Fenian thinking:

> The multitude have a tendency to accept a master. Their mass deposits apathy. A mob easily totalises itself into obedience. Men must be aroused, pushed, shocked by the very benefits of their own deliverance, their eyes wounded with the truth, light thrown in terrible handfuls.

How revolutionary is this idea? Elsewhere Tynan's reasoning is more traditional, as when he holds that 'the sight of cold steel, and blood smoking hot' (at Spencer's assassination) would 'inspire the people'. Here the fatal imprecision of Fenian—and most insurrectionist—thinking re-appears. Yet Tynan does seem to put his finger on a new mysticism in political violence whose consequences were to be profoundly destructive.

In this sense Tynan's work casts more light on the future than on the events of 1882. One must continue to doubt whether Brady and Kelly were consciously actuated by the more sophisticated of the ideas elaborated in his book. The Phoenix Park murders as such remain an isolated act whose true political message is indecipherable. At the same time, the underlying simplicity beneath Tynan's verbal barrage directly reflects the convictions of straightforward 'patriots' like Brady. The unshakable belief in the truth of the nationalist vision and the right of the nationalist to use force to educate the masses, the uncompromising antagonism towards England and the intolerance of politics, together form the mental armoury of Irish republicanism.[14] As has become clear, violence would be used with or without any hope of positive effect. It becomes a justification, and almost an end, in itself. An ethical function is added to the pragmatic strategies of other terrorist groups. The self-protection of the fighters; the politicisation of the people; the disorganisation of the State; all these strategies can be traced amongst the Irish Invincibles as amongst, say, the Socialist Revolutionaries in Russia.[15] But the inner force of Irish terrorism was of a different order.[16] If the Invincibles had no immediate offspring, their successors were to emerge in the twentieth century. Their legacy was never more apparent than at the centenary of their creation.

NOTES

1 Tighe Hopkins, *Kilmainham Memories*, London: 1896.
2 FM Bussy, *Irish Conspiracies*, London: 1910, p. 7. In both cases violence brought the Irish question 'within the sphere of practical politics'.
3 Bussy held that the label 'No. 1' was attached to Tynan by misreporting of the

trial of Michael Kavanagh, during which a photograph of Tynan was produced as 'exhibit No. 1'. This seems to go too far, however, and most others—including the investigating magistrate—accepted that 'No. 1' was an Invincible functionary.

4 Volunters were in fact distinct from militia, having been established to meet the anti-French scare of 1859, and continuing to provide a part-time outlet for popular patriotism.

5 Capt HBC Pollard, *The Secret Societies of Ireland*, London: 1922, p. 85.

6 Although the full text, it will be noted, goes as far as to print the Irish Government Bill of 1886 *in extenso*. The other sections omitted from the London edition are the excursions into British crimes in South Africa (Chs XX, XXVI). The most crucial chapter, XXXIII, is detached to form 'Part II'.

7 *Freeman's Journal*, 8 May 1882.

8 FJ Allen, *Weekly Irish Independent*, 12 May 1893, quoted in EC Houston, *Number One's Book*, London: 1894, appendix. The President of the IRB Supreme Council, Kickham, made the same point, while John Devoy protested that 'the Celtic nature revolted at the bare idea of assassination'.

9 T Corfe, *The Phoenix Park Murders*, London: 1968, p. 137.

10 It is frequently suggsted that £108,000 was unaccounted for in the Land League funds. No sum of anything like this order could have been disbursed without Parnell's knowledge.

11 See Carey's evidence reprinted in JA Curran, *Reminiscences*, London: 1915, pp. 184–192.

12 Pollard, *op. cit.*, p. 86.

13 Apart, be if said, from observation of the British reaction to the 1867 explosion. But no effort was made to analyse the mechanics of public panic.

14 For an insider's presentation of republican 'ideology', see S Cronin, *Irish Nationalism*, Dublin: 1980.

15 Cf. M Hildermeier, 'The Terrorist Strategies of the Socialist Revolutionary Party in Russia, 1990–1914', *in* WJ Mommsen and G Hirschfeld (eds.), *Social Protest, Violence and Terror in Nineteenth and Twentieth Century Europe*, London: 1982, pp. 82–83. This collection also contains an essay by P Alter, 'Traditions of Violence in the Irish National Movement', which misleadingly suggests that the Invincibles used dynamite.

16 To this extent W Laqueur's categorisation, in *Terrorism*, London: 1977, p. 69, of Irish terrorism as 'empirical' seems a misnomer. Its lack of doctrinal concern might be better expressed by labelling it 'opportunist' terror.

The Irish Republican Army and Terror International: An Inquiry into the Material Aspects of the First Fifteen Years

M McKinley

Many times since 1968 the circus of carnage which the situation in Ulster has often resembled has left observers so alienated that they were unable to explain what their senses described. In general this resulted from a confrontation with conditions to which they were unaccustomed, to the point of being foreign, as this 1980 account illustrated.

> Anyone accustomed to wandering around the countries of the Third World would find little in Ulster that is unfamiliar. Guerrillas, suspended democracy, armies and gunmen on the streets, unthinkable behaviour in prisons, questionable and questioned frontiers, squalid housing, grinding poverty, indifferent multi-nationals, once vibrant economies in visible decline—these are the essential characteristics of much of the contemporary world. The uniqueness of Northern Ireland is that it lies, not south of the equator, but just off the shores of Britain.[1]

In particular it was a consequence of the inability to understand why the United Kingdom—its political system stable and democratic, its wealth distributed reasonably well, its society open and obsessively moderate—should include within its boundaries organisations, commonly denoted terrorist and paramilitary, which displayed an almost autistic fury across their whole range of actions. Many observers, therefore, adopted the habit of mind which Joseph Conrad so clearly manifested in *The Secret Agent* over seventy years ago in relation to an act of anarchist terrorism:

> A blood-stained inanity of so fatuous a kind that it was impossible to fathom its origins by any reasonable or even unreasonable process of thought.[2]

Since 1968, it is obvious that the 'circus' and the concomitant refusals to countenance rational explanations for certain violent phenomena in Northern Ireland have been matched by extravagant propositions concerning the international dimensions of the conflict. And in turn these propositions have struck an answering chord in many putative strategists and others who were attracted to studies of violence which have earned the appellation 'international terrorism'. This is not to claim that the conflict in Northern Ireland was, or is, without its influences from outside the Six Counties—the 'American dimension' refutes this—but the evidence to hand suggests a far different picture than Walter Laqueur's multinational, corporate view of an international terrorist operation:

> planned in West Germany by Palestine Arabs, executed in Israel by terrorists recruited in Japan with weapons acquired in Italy but manufactured in Russia, supplied by an Algerian diplomat, and financed with Libyan money.[3]

Indeed, it is the purpose of this chapter to challenge the assertions that there existed in Northern Ireland an international terrorist network as evidenced by the contacts, supply of arms and operations of the paramilitary organisations involved in the conflict, particularly the Irish Republican Army (IRA). The reality, it will be argued, supports this view only selectively and provides but a poor basis for a general proposition of this type.

I propose therefore, to confine this chapter in accordance with the following four terms of reference. First, the period under discussion is, for the most part, 1968–1983. Second, this period has seen two paramilitary organisations under the banner 'Irish Republican Army'; however, the principal focus will be upon the Provisional IRA, as it is both the most active and the one about which the greatest number of claims are made in respect of international affiliations and operations. To this end, unless otherwise stipulated, the initials IRA will denote the Provisionals. Third, the 'American Dimension' of the troubles is treated as a separate section of this chapter: because of its special significance it is, in my opinion, worthy of being distinguished from the generality of the other international dimensions of the IRA. And fourth, the linkages or aspects which will be examined will be only those which relate *materially* to terrorist operations conducted by the IRA. I stipulate this because in the matter of the international contacts of the IRA, for example, there is a *prima facie* case for classifying them according to two levels. The *lower or less important* of these questions the sense of the term 'contact' because in very many cases it denoted no more than loose association, or close proximity of (mainly) left-wing groupings which occasionally and temporarily matured into an actual meeting. It was as though the various organisations were agitated, as in Brownian motion, and that they were therefore subject to the probability of contact by virtue of existing somewhat like particles in a common and restricted universe. When their paths, which seldom if ever obeyed the same compass, coincided, there was generally cause for concern as though it signified the conjunction of evil when in most instances a less sanguine conclusion was justified. As Peter Janke wrote of this phenomenon:

> The point about these links and one could go on adducing evidence of contacts is that it is not at all an international revolutionary conspiracy, but rather a network of tiny groups acting illegally that comes across one another in their search for arms and are prepared to help when called upon for a meal, a night's shelter, an overcoat, a hair dye or a railway ticket.[4]

Furthermore, it should be appreciated that this judgement applies not only to contacts with groups (or governments) in Africa, Asia (including China), Latin America and very often, Western Europe, but also Eastern Europe and would cover even the rather erratic ventures made by the Soviet Union into the 'troubles'. To say that Soviet propaganda organs have consistently distorted events in Northern Ireland to conform to a pre-conceived pattern of a popular uprising by an oppressed community against 'British imperialism', is an understatement. Indeed they so grossly misrepresented the situation that their pronouncements were ludicrous.[5] Notwithstanding this, and the need to develop friendly relations with Ireland (with which it established diplomatic relations in 1974), Moscow has maintained a cautious public attitude towards the Official IRA and a critical one in relation to the Provisionals.

There were, of course, exceptions, but there were of a different, higher, order of significance than those previously considered. It seems that once the situation in Northern Ireland had established its credentials as a conflict—i.e., as a shooting match—it attracted the attention and, it is alleged, the attendance of the acolytes of war. The appeal of some of these rested upon their past exploits, as with Otto Skorzeny, a former Nazi SS Colonel who was wanted for war crimes in his native Austria, and whose principal claim to notoriety was his leadership of the raid to rescue Mussolini after the fall of the Fascist Government in 1943. Twenty-eight years later he was linked with Ruairi O Bradaigh of Provisional Sinn Fein. Despite Skorzeny's apparent sympathy, however, the significance of his interest in the Northern Ireland conflict existed very largely in the collective imagination of the editorial staff of the *Sunday Telegraph*. All that that publication could muster to justify its article on him was an unconfirmed report of a meeting with O Bradaigh in Spain.[6]

Much later in the period under review, Protestant militants also came up with a Second World War figure in support of their cause. In 1977 John McQuade, a former Chindit, claimed he had formed a secret 'army' that would 'seek out and destroy' the IRA in Ulster.[7] Evidently he was unsuccessful; indeed his only success may have been in securing a lengthy two-column coverage in the *Daily Telegraph*. McQuade in any case was a Northerner and his enterprise was probably more notable for what it negatively emphasised—that reports of foreign interest generally related to the IRA. But they did not always concern themselves with figures from the past.

According to Father O'Neill of St Eugene's Roman Catholic Cathedral in Derry, two North Koreans and an Algerian (not to mention a number of Englishmen), were present among the Provisional gunmen of Creggan and the Bogside in 1972.[8] In 1977 a further measure of notoriety was added to the Republican cause with disclosures made in the Old Bailey of approaches made to a former member of the Parachute Regiment and Angolan mercenary recruiter, John Banks, for the supply of arms. As with so many of the instances cited in this and the following chapter it was, for the IRA, an indiscriminate move. Everybody and everything ended up in the wrong place: Banks in the service of the Special Branch; British Provisionals in the Old Bailey and later, gaol; and the arms in (probably) Antwerp.[9]

However the IRA has not been without its 'successes'. According to David Barzilay, it was 'known' that the organisation had attracted two 'foreign' electronics experts to work upon sophisticated trigger mechanisms for a bombing campaign to be conducted in Northern Ireland. He also claimed that these experts were not to be found in the North but 'in the South', an allegation which appeared to be based on unspecified information provided to him by the British Army. Nevertheless, for those who were convinced that the Republic was a 'haven for terrorists' one subsequent allegation put the matter beyond doubt and confirmed Barzilay's cryptic reference to such people being 'very well protected'.[10]

In his machinations to avoid a United States deportation order, a former Provo 'active', Peter McMullen, stated to the *Boston Globe* that the IRA had received training and encouragement from a regular Irish Army colonel in precisely the same type of explosive devices (photo-cell and radio-controlled) to which Barzilay referred to the previous year. He also claimed that some of the electronic components were provided by an Irish television manufacturer sympathetic to the cause.[11] Naturally the Irish Army rejected these allegations out of hand, while McMullen, for his part, denied knowledge of the officer's identity. It is difficult, therefore, to draw from the evidence a conclusion of any strength. Hence the most balanced view which could be stated, of the period 1969–1974 anyway, may be that of Lieutenant-Colonel George Styles, the commander of the British Army bomb disposal teams in Northern Ireland in that period:

> really we never could prove or disprove the rumours about foreign mercenaries. But, pressed to an opinion, I'd say it's more than likely they existed ...[12]

Notwithstanding this, one conclusion which may be drawn is that it is not always helpful to look beyond the borders of the United Kingdom, nor even the island of Ireland, for instances of external links to the 'troubles'. Strictly speaking, of course, the Republic of Ireland is a foreign country in relation to the United Kingdom, but given the unique relationship which exists between it, Great Britain and Northern Ireland, it seems a contrivance to classify as international, or external, linkages from the Republic and Great Britain into Northern Ireland. Also, I would argue that, in this instance, North–South distinctions are meaningless. Provisionals on either side of the Border belong to the same organisation, and both the British and Irish Governments have recognised this. Further, that it would involve an unnecessary and meaningless division of labour to impose a North–South framework upon an analysis of the contacts between both wings of the IRA and various organisations in Britain.

This is not to claim that the *role* of such contacts was any greater than those excluded from this analysis under Janke's dismissal, rather that their involvement signified two aspects of the support network of the paramilitary organisations. The first was that these were often of a domestic or relatively local origin and that to ignore this fact results in a distortion of any study of the external links. Second, the more significant links are those with people or groups that have demonstrated a willingness either to supply, or engage in, sustained campaigns of violence.

According to this criterion, of the almost kaleidoscopic selection of the terrorist and separatist/nationalist spectrum with which the IRA established contacts in the early and mid-1970s, the most important appears to have been with various Basque organisations. In April 1972, the IRA, the Basque *Euskadi Ta Askatasuna* (ETA)—Basque People and Liberty—and the Breton FLB were reported to have signed a political agreement which was followed some two years later by a statement which embraced other, smaller national minorities such as Piedmontese. Via the auspices of the appropriate Sinn Fein, the officials and various ethnic groupings followed suit with a socialist equivalent, in September 1974, known to initiates as 'The Brest Charter'.[13] What this duality of contacts suggested was confirmed by a deeper study. The ETA, like the IRA in 1969–1970, was subject to splits. Hence the officials, in keeping with their 29 May 1972 unilateral declaration of a ceasefire, lined up with a 'socialist revolutionary party' in which the operative term was 'socialist'. The Provisionals, on the other hand, by 1979 anyway, found more common ground with *Euskal Izaultzarako Alderia* (EIA)—the Basque Revolutionary Party—an ETA breakaway which supported 'armed actions' and 'refuse[d] reformism'.[14]

Although there were further similarities in their respective stands on national sovereignty and independence, and other areas besides,[15] it was the willingness of both the IRA and the (then) ETA to reciprocate with firearms and technical (explosives) expertise that placed this link in an altogether different category from those covered previously. Contact between the two organisations dates back at least to 1972 when Jose Echebarrieta, one of ETA's most influential members, was reported to have made two secret visits to Dublin to seek contact with both the Officials and the Provisionals. According to Maria McGuire, Basque leaders met Provisional Chief of Staff, Sean MacStiofain, and in exchange for training in the use of explosives, provided fifty revolvers.[16] For years, however, this was the sole item of substance upon which wild speculations were made of an IRA–ETA network. Yet the resemblance in the technical field, between the assassination of the Spanish Prime Minister, Admiral Luis Carrera Blanco, in December 1973, and that of the British Ambassador in Dublin, Christopher Ewart-Biggs, three years later,[17] gave further credence to the Spanish Police's 1974 claim of the existence of a secret pact between the two.[18]

Whether, as was alleged (but denied by the ETA), the IRA supplied the explosives used in the former, or as Albert Parry implies, the IRA trained the ETA on a continuing basis[19] is, like so many questions in this area, undetermined. Both were possible but neither necessarily followed. As to the former, explosives appear not to have been an overly difficult material for terrorists to obtain in the last decade, and with regard to the latter, a training in explosives was surely within the range of competence of the ETA once they had learned the first lessons. Besides, there is no record of further 'quid pro quo' exchanges after that mentioned by McGuire. Since the time of Ewart-Biggs' death, the IRA–ETA–EIA link has been somewhat less substantial and confined to an exchange of visits and congratulatory statements. In all, given that this link appears to have been the most significant, there is little to justify other than the most modest claims being made as regards the paramilitary organisations in Northern Ireland and their place within an international terrorist network.

At first sight this was in sharp contrast to the supply of arms from external sources to the same groups. If the information relating to the discovery of arms—be they actually in their possession, or intended for same—is correct, the paramilitaries could have foregone few opportunities to obtain them from every quarter. By 1973, at least 282 types of weapon had been discovered[20] representing fifteen countries of origin (manufacture).[21]

Later disclosures were equally impressive. Official figures released on the eighth anniversary of the British Army's involvement in the Northern Ireland conflict showed that it had by then recovered 902,554 rounds of ammunition, 257,489 lb. of explosives, 297 machine-guns, 2667 rifles, 2962 pistols, 881 shotguns, 18 rocket launchers, 57 rockets, 427 mortar tubes and 441 mortar shells. In addition, Army personnel had defused 2828 bombs.[22] (And this does not include the amounts recovered from paramilitary sources by the Irish and other Governments.) From a closer examination of arms-recovery information it became clear that not only had the numbers of weapons increased, but also they had become both more modern and sophisticated as well.[23] From the presence in the Provisional IRA arsenal of various semi–automatic weapons, a historian of the IRA, J Bowyer Bell, concluded that:

> basically the Provos were better armed for their business than the British Army for theirs. Equally significant by the end of 1977, the Provos were far more elegantly armed than the loyalist paramilitaries or the militias-in-being ...[24]

These figures and reports notwithstanding, it is important to treat the following discussion of the actual supply of arms to the conflict in the North with caution. First, it must be emphasised that it is concerned only with the estimated (maximum) 40–50 per cent of arms which originated from sources *outside* of the USA.[25] Second, in relation to these countries of origin, there is considerable merit in the repeated *caveats* given by British Ministers of State for Defence, to the effect that the place of manufacture of arms and explosives was not necessarily the place where the terrorists obtained them.[26]

Third, it is necessary to be sceptical of claims that some suppliers of arms, by virtue of that fact, were exerting a *controlling* influence over the conflict. As Richard Rose wrote:

> Probably the outsiders who have benefited most from the Troubles have been dealers and brokers in arms from Hamburg to Libya. To continue to benefit, however, they must maintain their distance. Otherwise, they too will find themselves tagged as Catholic arms dealers, whether they are actually Christian, Muslim or atheist.[27]

And finally, the scale of the operation must at all times be borne in mind. By the standards of many conflicts the above inventory of recovered weapons was modest. Nevertheless no one would deny the effectiveness of the IRA campaign since 1968, even if it has not been successful in its own terms. The point to be made, of course, in relation to arms, was simply but accurately expressed by Peter Janke: 'very, very few suffice'.[28]

From the seven Western European countries which produce one-quarter of the world's weapon supplies, came the bulk of the arms that is the concern of this chapter.[29] Having stated that, it must also be repeated that it is in this part of the discussion that the cautions mentioned before are particularly apposite. Thus a common feature to be noted was that the city in which the negotiations took place, the port of loading and the city of origin of the arms were almost invariably different *within* each venture. Furthermore the distinction between Eastern and Western Europe was blurred to the point of meaninglessness.

Maria McGuire, for example, wrote of accompanying Daithi Ó Connaill (Dave O'Connell), a member of the Provisionals' Army Council, between Dublin, Zurich and Amsterdam, for the latter to negotiate a deal in Prague with Omnipol, the sales organisation for the Czech arms factory at Brno, for a shipment ex Rotterdam.[30] It was, for all that, a not unusual episode in which the elements of foreign venues, intrigue and (frequently) failure were to be repeated on numerous occasions.

Unfortunately for a work such as this most of the publicly available information has been derived from the successful interception of illegal arms intended for Northern Ireland. The reports of such operations were, therefore, subject to security considerations and devoid of virtually all mention of the politics of both purchase and apprehension. Furthermore, in many cases the arms in question appeared to be part of an independent arms dealer's stock on hand, from which information the conclusion to be drawn was that the deal was made on financial rather than political criteria.[31] And this becomes more compelling in the common knowledge that no government in Western Europe has permitted either its state or private enterprises to sell arms to the paramilitary organisations in Northern Ireland. Consequently, in those instances where only an antiseptic collection of facts were reported such as that Browning pistols (and matching ammunition) had been imported from the Continent, or that French arms, ammunition and chemicals were discovered, there are but poor grounds for deducing more than that the Provisionals (in the foregoing cases) took advantage of the international commercial availability of weapons and supplies.

Furthermore, nothing in the foregoing cases seriously challenges previous judgements in respect of Communist intervention by Czechoslovakia or the Soviet Union. There remains of course, a residue of uncertainty arising from Ó Connaill's apparent success in, to use McGuire's words, 'making an arms deal with a *Communist country*'[32] (emphasis added). Subsequently, further doubt was added by the recovery of Czech pistols so new that they did not appear in any standard works of reference.[33] Yet no matter how suggestive these facts were of an active and substantial Czech interest in the North, they must also be tempered by accounts which supported a contrary interpretation.

The first is that Ó Connaill, his negotiations with Omnipol in Prague notwithstanding, was required to work through an American intermediary *and* an arms dealer. As both were regarded by him as untrustworthy, and as the latter was to be contacted in Brussels,[34] there are grounds for inferring that Omnipol did not agree to supply arms direct to the Provisionals.

The second concerned Ó Connaill's certainty that he was shadowed in Switzerland by the 'Czech or Russian secret police'[35] which, if true, and taken in conjunction with the first reason, may have indicated that the manufacturers were in some doubt as to the wisdom of supplying those he represented.

The third was Jones' (presumably) expert opinion that the Browning pistols mentioned earlier, and the Czech pistols discovered at the same time, may well have represented arms obtained by a *single* purchase.[36] If so, the case alleging Czech intervention would be weakened correspondingly, since the supply of arms of differing national origin would (again presumably) have been the prerogative of an independent dealer.

Finally, the absence of any further body of evidence which could implicate the Czech Government or its agencies since the time of Ó Connaill's 1971 approach to Omnipol, must question the resolve with which Prague was prepared to act, if at all.

The same is true of the Soviet Union, but in its case the conclusion is less equivocal. This does not mean that Soviet-made weapons have not been in evidence—they have—in the form of rifles, hand-grenades and even rocket launchers, but the numbers involved have been small, and there was no serious suggestion that they signified Russian intervention.[37] However, the discovery of Soviet weapons in transit for the Provisionals did signify that Soviet weapons were quite widely available on the international market (see the following discussion of the *Claudia* affair).

The case which perhaps best illustrated this was the celebrated affair surrounding the use of Soviet-designed, but Bulgarian-made, RPG-7 rocket launchers in November 1972.[38] Although the Soviet Government rejected a Foreign Office request for its help in investigating the matter, and although it seems certain that it could have assisted, the opinion in Whitehall was that there was no direct connection between the Soviet Union and the Provisionals.[39] Indeed, the likeliest source of weapons was a group of Middle

East states (discussed in the following), at least four of which had been Russian clients for the RPG-7.

In turn this underscored the Provisionals' logistics dilemma. Close cooperation between American, British and Irish law enforcement agencies ensured that attempts to supply arms from the United States were made at high risk and could be successful only in odd lots.[40] Hence a reliance on that source meant that the IRA would be slow to re-arm. The alternative, it appears, was to expedite this objective by recourse to sympathetic organisations and regimes, but at even greater risk. The RPG-7s, despite their successful debut, are to be seen within the latter category. It is necessary, therefore, to turn to a consideration of a small number of revolutionary regimes/movements.

With but tolerable distortions, 'small number' is easily reduced to two in descending order, the Libyan Government of Colonel Mu'ammar al-Qaddafi and the Palestine Liberation Organisation (PLO). Basically, Qaddafi's interest in the Northern Ireland situation stemmed from his perception of it as a nationalist revolution in which the IRA for the most part, represented the progressive forces. Anti-colonialism, his self-appointed role as an instrument of God and an understanding of the whole Ulster Question which bordered on fantasy were contributing factors.[41] And even then this may not have covered them all. Robert Fisk probably captured the essence of his motivation when he wrote 'The nature of the struggle seems to be of less importance than the fact it exists ...'.[42]

While the aforementioned disposition would not necessarily preclude it, the suggestion that Qaddafi was acting as a proxy for the Soviet Union in this period seems unlikely. Apart from the fact that his country was not receiving Soviet arms, the President was also known to have directed his displeasure towards Egyptian leaders for their overdependence on such supplies, and to have attacked the Soviet Union during the 1973 conference of non-aligned nations in Algiers.

Notwithstanding Qaddafi's outlook it was March 1973 before it found a tangible expression. On the 28th of that month, the *Claudia*, a 298-ton coaster, was intercepted by the Irish Navy off Helvick Head, Co. Waterford, and was found to contain five tons of arms intended for the IRA.[43] It was an operation which not only provided an illustration of the propensity for the conflict in Northern Ireland to exceed the boundaries of the Province, but also allowed brief glimpses of the complexities which have increasingly attended it.

It was complex because the voyage of the *Claudia* had been the subject of another one of those international deals, initiated in Germany and negotiated in two foreign capitals, Tunis and Tripoli. The vessel itself had taken considerable pains both to conceal its route—by re-tracking—and to disguise the immediate origins of its cargo—by loading it in international waters. It was, moreover, registered in Cyprus by the German Giromar Shipping Company (for which Lloyds had no address), a company ninety per cent owned by Gunther and Marlene Leinhauser, the former of whom had been convicted in 1967 for attempting to smuggle arms from Czechoslovakia to Kurdish rebels in Iraq.[44]

The concern that the IRA had been able to negotiate such a relatively large arms purchase was only heightened by persistent reports that the *Claudia* had delivered between one and three arms shipments to Ireland in the previous fifteen months.[45] Furthermore, there were questions which remained unresolved, although dismissed by the Irish Government, as to whether the five tons of arms recovered were the entire shipment or but part of a very much larger one which had been either trans-shipped earlier or dumped overboard when the crew of the *Claudia* realised their predicament.[46] The belief that the Soviet Union, despite the appearance of arms of its manufacture in the cargo, was probably not involved was of little consolation to the British and Irish authorities. The evidence all too clearly pointed to the fact that Libya was.

One prior development in this general period prompted speculation that another state (or organisation) had adopted a similar role. The introduction of the Soviet-designed RPG-7 rocket launcher to the IRA's arsenal in November 1972 did much to give this suggestion currency some months before the *Claudia* affair. At that time, the general suspicion which attached to Qaddafi as a supplier of arms to the IRA was of a low order: Libya was not an arms client of the Soviet Union, whereas Algeria, Egypt, Iraq and Syria were reported to have received recent shipments of RPG-7s.[47] As best as can be ascertained from available sources, however, these four client states were not directly implicated and the IRA's possession of the weapons in question is still put down to an undetected arms deal negotiated in the Near or Middle East sometime in 1972.[48]

While the *Claudia* incident appeared not to dampen Qaddafi's enthusiasm for the Northern Ireland conflict, his subsequent attitude towards it was somewhat erratic. From being a benefactor of the IRA in 1972–1973, he became, in 1974, the willing host for supplicant parties from the other side of the province's paramilitary divide. Early that year the Libyan Government began to consider whether, in addition to the Provisionals, some extreme 'Loyalist' groups which favoured an independent Ulster might not also qualify for support as 'anti-imperialistic'. Qaddafi himself was reported to have expressed admiration for the Ulster Workers' Council Strike of May 1974 which, according to his Irish education adviser, Eddie O'Donnell, the Libyan leader viewed as a 'valid mechanism' that reminded him of his own non-violent coup in September 1969.[49]

Thus, in late 1974, the Ulster Defence Association (UDA) was invited to participate in a visit to Libya arranged for the Development of Irish Resources organisation (DIR), a previously little-known group suspected of being subject to 'Republican' influences. However, according to DIR's chairman, Walter Hegarty, the organisation was not aligned with any political cause, and it had cooperated with the UDA's involvement because of a common interest in the development of Ireland's offshore oil and gas resources.[50]

This was a credible position as it was a motive equally attributable to those seeking a united Ireland and those contemplating an independent Northern Ireland (as the UDA were known to favour if the British link could not be maintained to its satisfaction).[51] But it was not entirely consistent with Eddie O'Donnell's claim that he secured the UDA invitation so that the Libyans could meet the men behind the Protestant strike, nor with the reports that the UDA had made representations to Qaddafi, particularly concerning his patronage of the IRA, and certainly not with the simultaneous presence of a Provisional Sinn Fein delegation at the same hotel in Tripoli at which the UDA were staying.

The reasons given were plausible, but in relation to the representations by the UDA and the presence of the Provisionals, incomplete. Whatever the truth in UDA spokesman Tony Lyttle's claim that his organisation had been invited to Libya 'to enlighten [the Qaddafi regime] on the truth of the Northern Ireland situation' it was surely to be expected that every opportunity would be taken to do so in any case. In turn, the arrival of the Provisionals some five days after the Loyalists was guaranteed by the anxiety on the former's part that an attempt was under way to disrupt their arrangement with Libya, and that this should be strenuously resisted.[52]

In the ensuing period it was possible, without putting too fine a point on it, to conclude that the IRA had not been successful. The first indication that Qaddafi may have undergone a change of heart was provided by a statement made in November 1974 by Glen Barr, a leading UDA figure on the visit.

> the Libyan Government appeared to be under the impression that the IRA were Freedom Fighters. ... We were able to show them the other side of the coin. They were interested in our proposal for an independent Northern Ireland and I think we were successful in putting our case across ...[53]

From the time of this announcement until late 1977 there was no further evidence of arms reaching Ireland from Near or Middle East sources. Yet in the month following the UDA visit, Qaddafi was reported as having told senior Maltese Government officials that his aid to the IRA to that point was £5 million, although he did not specify whether this was in cash or in kind.[54] November 1974 also saw the report of a similar statement from Kuala Lumpur, Malaysia, made in this instance by the Libyan Prime Minister, Major Abdul Jalloud.[55]

After April 1975, however, the equivocal nature of the Libyan attitude became more pronounced. After receiving an Irish parliamentary delegation in that month a Libyan spokesman disclaimed any further interventionary role for his government.[56] From further statements by the delegation leaders on their return this was taken to imply that Libya would no longer aid any illegal organisation in Ireland, including the IRA.[57] Yet, in so far as the supply of arms was concerned, further developments suggested that the Libyan Government, while it had come to a realisation that the Irish question was not as simple as it first believed, was not about to embrace a practice of self-denial with regard to Northern Ireland. In September 1975, two of its representatives, including Eddie O'Donnell, met with UDA leaders in Northern Ireland and, it was understood, discussed in general terms the potential for Libyan investment in the event of British withdrawal.[58] If this was true then the core of Libyan interest in Northern Ireland was still derived from, and defined in terms of, Qaddafi's Anglophobia. By extension, he was seeking, through discussions with the UDA, to manipulate the Province's tensions, if not to his advantage, then certainly to Britain's embarrassment and discomfort. Furthermore, given the strength of his hatreds, and the fact that his government's (then) recent pronouncements eschewing support for 'illegal organisations' left much to be desired in Dublin and London, some residual doubt remained whether Libya had actually desisted from supplying arms to the IRA. Indeed, Qaddafi's statements in this time were, without being too specific as to how, so strongly supportive of the IRA that its propaganda in early 1976 continued to proclaim the affinity between Libya and the Provisional cause.[59] Presumably this would not have been the case had Libyan support been withdrawn.

From then until the close of the period under review, any assessment of Libyan involvement in the affair of Northern Ireland must be based on developments of an indeterminate and sometimes conflicting nature. Following the December 1977 arrest of Provisional Chief of Staff, Seamus Twomey, in Dublin, there were unofficial reports of IRA leaders once more visiting Tripoli. In this period the IRA received both a military and a psychological boost with the introduction of the M60 machine gun to its arsenal, a weapon then suspected in some quarters of being supplied from the Middle East. A 1979 report by Peter McMullen, a former member of both the Parachute Regiment (from which he deserted), and the IRA (from whom he defected), tended to confirm this suspicion. McMullen claimed that in 1977–1978 the Provisionals had received seven tons of arms from Libya, including 'Russian surface-to-air missiles, RPG5s and RPG7s'.[60] By his account the major obstacle to their use had been the prospective operators' inability to understand the Russian text of the instruction manuals![61] Finally, it was alleged that Thomas McMahon, convicted in early 1980 for the murder of Lord Mountbatten, had perfected his remote-control bomb-making skills (under Russian supervision) in Libya.[62]

Against such 'evidence' three contra-indications should be taken into account. The first was that it was later held, with near certainty, that the origin of the M60 machine guns brandished by the Provisionals in early 1978 was a National Guard armoury in Danvers, Massachusetts, from where they were stolen in August 1976.[63] The second was that, in the period late 1977–mid 1980, which presumably was sufficient time for a translation of instruction manuals to be effected, there was no recorded instance of an attack involving an RPG-7 or a surface-to-air missile. Both indications were therefore consistent with, and supportive of, the third, which was a report of discussions held in Libya between Qaddafi and the British Conservative Party's Shadow Foreign Secretary, John Davies. According to Davies, the Provisional IRA had ceased to be regarded as among the world's liberation movements, from which it was inferred that Libya was no longer prepared to support the Provisionals.[64]

As on previous occasions when Qaddafi had given assurances to this effect there was much unsaid that encouraged doubt as to his real intentions. Davies was not then regarded as being within the top echelon of the Tory opposition's hierarchy, even less could he have been regarded as a representative of the British Government. Thus Qaddafi's choice of messenger was curious. Davies' report moreover, suffered not only from being based on inference but also from being given *ex parte*. (In combination, these considerations may have accounted for the poor attention given to it in the press.) Even then its contents provided no answer to whether Libya had recently supplied the Provisionals with arms, or more importantly, whether it was absolutely committed to not supplying them in the future. Furthermore, two additional reasons to doubt Qaddafi's sincerity were afforded by the knowledge that at the time of Davies' visit, a sale of trucks, aircraft and spare parts worth more than £200 million was being held up by the United States Government in an attempt to dissuade Libya from harbouring international terrorists.[65]

Given Qaddafi's outlook and record of erratic behaviour it could not be assumed that any action he took in the face of American pressure was likely to become an established feature of Libyan policy. And even if to all appearances it did, there remained a distinct possibility that one or more of the numerous Arab liberation movements he gave considerable backing to—such as the PLO—might act as his proxy with the IRA.[66] Indeed, there was evidence that this organisation had been so involved for some years, albeit in a secondary and shadowy capacity. To be precise this activity was carried out by two of the PLO's constituent groups, the Popular Front for the Liberation of Palestine (PFLP), and Al Fatah.

One commentator on Middle East affairs, Yonah Alexander, dates IRA–PFLP cooperation from as early as 1968.[67] Certainly, by May 1972, it was more widely acknowledged, even heralded, as in Radio Cairo's exultant report of the massacre at Lod Airport, near Tel Aviv, by three members of the (Japanese) Red Army specially recruited for the occasion.

> The participation of three Japanese members in the suicide action at Lod proves that the PFLP succeeded in obtaining international support as a truly revolutionary movement. Strong bonds exist between the Palestinian resistance organisations and other liberation movements in Africa, the IRA, the Vietnamese revolutionaries.[68]

But as evidence of a substantial nexus with the IRA, this was very thin as the contacts then in evidence appeared to be at the ideological level and almost exclusively concerned Official Sinn Fein.[69] Thus there was no suggestion that Irish revolutionaries were willing to emulate the Japanese example and be sacrificed for the Palestinian cause; ironically, only the night before the above broadcast, the Official IRA had ordered an immediate cessation of all hostilities other than those of a defensive nature.

Subsequently, whether as a result of this unilaterally declared ceasefire or some other reason, the PFLP liaison with Ireland was expanded to include the Provisional IRA.[70] In May 1972, at Baddawai in Lebanon, the PFLP and Black September hosted a meeting attended by representatives of numerous terrorist and nationalist/separatist organisations including the IRA.[71] In the same year subsequent meetings in Algeria, Japan and Dublin gave rise to reports not only of a closer liaison between such groups, but also of agreements 'to supply each other with arms and information and to carry out operations on behalf of and in the name of a brother movement'.[72] Furthermore, McMullen claimed in 1979 that a young Arab woman living in Dublin was the liaison officer between the PLO and the IRA.[73]

To date, the IRA–PFLP cooperation has allegedly found a tangible expression in three areas. The first concerns the provision of training facilities. If testimony given in an Old Bailey trial by mercenary-recruiter, John Banks, was to be believed, an IRA training camp had existed in Algeria, in 1973, on the edge of the Sahara Desert.[74] While doubts as to Banks' reliability as a witness were raised by his admission that he had previously lied on two counts to the London *Evening Standard*, the substance of his claim received confirmation the following year.

In a BBC documentary on terrorism, Abu Maher, a member of the PFLP team, which attacked an El Al aircraft at Athens airport in 1968, told of a camp run by his organisation at which people from several nations, including Ireland, were being trained. (Neither the location of the camp nor a more detailed description of the Irish members was provided.) In the same programme an IRA presence at a training camp in Aden was reported by Israeli Colonel Elihu Lavite, who claimed that this information was forthcoming from his interrogation of terrorist Lidwina Janssen.[75] McMullen also claimed that in more recent times (after 1977), the IRA leadership was able 'to attract money, arms and training from the Palestine Liberation Organisation and representatives of Libyan Leader Colonel Qaddafi'.[76]

Substantially similar accounts were provided following the deployment of the United Nations Interim Force in Lebanon (UNIFIL) in 1978. While covering its activities *Irish Times* correspondent, Conor O'Cleary, interviewed a PLO colonel in Beirut who advised that a small number of IRA members had received instruction in explosives and guerrilla warfare techniques, in Lebanon, until just prior to that time (June 1978).[77] O'Cleary also noted that UN observers in UNIFIL were in agreement that such an arrangement had been in existence for a period of years.[78] In some quarters this was held to be a disingenuous assessment: Alexander, for example, contended that the training continued through the course of 1978 'apparently with the full knowledge of the UN officers serving in the area', and that at least ten IRA members arrived for training in each of the following fifteen months.[79]

Subsequent accounts not only confirmed this aspect but were also more specific. In 1979, for example, *Corriere della Sera* of Milan carried a report which claimed, *inter alia*, that members of the IRA had received training at a camp 'in the locality of Sebhah [Libya]'.[80] The following year, a NATO report estimated that forty-four members of the IRA had received training at Palestinian camps in the previous year—at Burj Al-Barajna and Damour in Lebanon, and Socotra in South Yemen.[81] Notwithstanding the differences as to place, quantity and time which were to be found between the foregoing accounts, they were sufficiently consistent to establish the IRA's client relationship with the PLO/PFLP for the provision of services.

McMullen's 1979 claim would extend this to a second area. According to him two IRA operations—the murder of Sir Richard Sykes, British Ambassador to the Netherlands, in March 1979, and the explosion at the Grand Palace in Brussels the following August—were undertaken in partnership with the

PLO.[82] Unfortunately (again) for this inquiry, there were other conflicting accounts as to who might have been responsible for the former: in Holland, spokesmen for the IRA and for the Italian Red Brigades on behalf of the IRA claimed the deed.[83] And further doubt must be attached to McMullen's claim as, by the time of the incident in question, he had been *persona non grata* with the IRA for at least a year, and might not, therefore have been speaking with authority on either instance.[84]

If either of these 'arrangements' also included the provision of arms it was not readily apparent from the available information. However a case may be made that this third area was the subject of a separate understanding with another PLO constituent, Al Fatah. In the literature on terrorism, Al Fatah (Yasser Arafat's group) was cited as the source of IRA-intended arms on three separate occasions since 1972. The first appears to have existed only in the mind of Alexander:[85] there are simply no records of a seizure of such a consignment in Antwerp in December 1972. (Perhaps he meant the 1977 episode, as follows.) There was also some doubt as to the second, which was John Barron's unsubstantiated claim that the *Claudia*'s captured shipment had been supplied from Al Fatah, *and not Libyan stocks*.[86] The remaining instance concerned a consignment of arms which was discovered in Antwerp, but in December 1977, and which led to the trial of Seamus McCollum in Dublin in July 1978. While his testimony in no way implicated Al Fatah, the markings on several of the boxes did.[87] Of themselves they were less than conclusive evidence of its involvement, but in the context of the RPG-7s used in 1972, the *Claudia* interception and Qaddafi's interest in Ireland, they were sufficient to encourage the belief that Al Fatah, or an organisation closely aligned with it, was a likely source of some of the IRA's arms shipments.[88] Whether it justified the *Daily Telegraph*'s claim that over half a million dollars in arms had passed through it previously remains an open question.[89]

Views on the significance of the Al Fatah link varied—from numerous commentators on the right who, irrespective of the evidence, saw the Middle East suppliers as mere agents for what was fundamentally a Soviet enterprise of sowing disaffection where it could—to the official and frequently expressed view of Her Majesty's Government, which was somewhat less sanguine. During one period of Question Time in the House of Commons in 1978 a number of Members who were inclined to the former view were assured by the Northern Ireland Secretary, Roy Mason, that the IRA's contacts with 'Palestinian terrorists' were neither 'significant' nor even 'a real link'.[90] Indeed, Mason extended his assessment to cover not only organisations in the Middle East but 'international terrorist' organisations in general.[91]

In support of his Government's position the Secretary relied in part upon the relative ease with which arms could be purchased in the Middle East and seemed to imply that such deals were commercially rather than politically inspired.[92] In part though, he relied upon a form of wishful thinking which was controverted by evidence cited earlier in this chapter, namely that

> The appalling record of the Provisional IRA within the Province and its lack of political support do not enable it to establish any significant international links.[93]

He thereby left unanswered why it was that such organisations as the Red Army and the Red Brigades were seemingly able to operate on an international scale while enjoying considerably less political support than the IRA. Equally, Mason was ignoring the substantial support which had been lent the Provisionals from the United States, and even their ability, demonstrated over some eight years, to operate in Northern Ireland in the face of the very difficulties he described. However, his position was arguably reinforced by none other than Yasser Arafat who, when asked if the PLO supplied arms to the IRA, replied, 'No, I am searching for weapons myself'.[94] But in the same interview the Al Fatah leader was also reported to have denied that the PLO had 'any links' with the IRA which, in the light of the foregoing, questioned his credibility.

Whether Mason's assessment could be held to apply between 1978 and 1982 depends on the significance attributed to developments in this period. It would depend, for instance, on the basis for Coogan's 1980 claim that not only was the PLO cooperating with the IRA and the INLA, but that it was also in league with the Russians to provide the latter with arms.[95] It would also depend upon how many PLO-trained IRA personnel it took for the link to be upgraded to 'significant'. If the NATO estimate of forty-four for 1979 was *accurate* then the issue is almost beyond doubt: that number of trained operatives flowing into the IRA's active service units, even on a one-off basis, can only be regarded as substantial in the context of Northern Ireland. And if the NATO assessment was *accurate and typical*, then the PLO training connection must in every sense be seen as significant.

As of late 1982, however, one final consideration is forced upon this analysis. With the June Israeli push into Lebanon, the PLO's training programmes for foreigners in that country were at an end, at least in the short term. Indeed, among the first to appreciate this fact were four members of the INLA who were captured by the Israeli Army at a training school outside Sidon.[96] Notwithstanding the availability of training venues in other Middle East countries, the early indications were that the PLO in Lebanon had suffered massive disruption to its operations across the board, and concomitantly, its ability to assist and host foreign groups such as the IRA at anything like the previous levels, if at all.

These Middle East sources excepted, the only other source of arms outside the United States that warrants inclusion here is Canada, because of several attempts in that country to supply arms and finance to both Loyalist and Republican paramilitary organisations in Northern Ireland. The first evidence of this supportive activity was seen in August 1969 with an announcement by some one hundred and fifty Toronto Irish–Canadians that they intended sending money, which could be used to buy guns if necessary, to the women and children of the (Catholic) Bogside in Derry.[97] Thereafter the networks of the US-based Irish Northern Aid Committee (NORAID) and the Irish Republican Clubs were extended to Canada but support activities on behalf of both the Official and Provisional movements were thought by observers to be limited by the mainly Protestant complexion of the estimated two million Canadians of Irish descent. Nevertheless, in 1972 (admittedly a 'high' year in relation to international interest in Northern Ireland), it was reported that 'about $40,000' had been forwarded by NORAID.[98] (It has not proved possible to obtain other reliable estimates of financial aid.)

In the matter of supplying arms the available record is slightly more forthcoming. Judging by this, 1973 and 1974 were the years in which would-be gun-runners were most active. And the police most diligent. Three arms shipments intended for the Irish Republican Army (IRA) were intercepted—one on the Canadian side of the Canada/United States border,[99] and the other two as part of a combined operation involving Canadian and Irish authorities, in Toronto and Dublin, respectively.[100]

The total amount of arms involved was small, but in each case consistent with the numbers recorded in several other seizure operations originating in the United States:[101] 15 rifles and ammunition in the border case;[102] 5 sten guns, 12 hand guns, about 18,000 rounds of ammunition and 10 hand grenades in Toronto; and 17 rifles, 29,000 rounds of ammunition and 60 pounds of gunpowder in Dublin.[103]

Of particular interest in the border interception were the American affiliations of Joseph Myles, a resident of Michigan, who was described by the Canadian authorities as an 'executive officer of an American organisation Northern Irish Aid' (sic).[104] For his pains he, and at least three accomplices, were sentenced to jail terms ranging from seventeen months to two years.[105]

As regards the combined operation, two aspects were notable. The first concerned the cooperation between the Canadian and Irish authorities over a three-month period, while the second was that the shipment was intended for the *Official* IRA. This was somewhat curious, because that organisation had unilaterally declared a ceasefire on 29 May 1972. However, it appeared not to denote a renewed campaign of violence by the Officials.

According to Commissioner Edward Lysyk of the Royal Canadian Mounted Police (RCMP), investigations revealed that the man responsible for the attempt, one John Patrick Daniel Murphy, was engaged in a 'lone operation'.[106] His efforts, therefore, were probably to be explained by the Official IRA's need, as a paramilitary organisation, to maintain an armoury for self-defence and in case a situation arose in which it would need to reconsider engaging once more in an armed struggle. There is no evidence that it has done so since. Thus, with regard to both wings of the IRA, the influence of the Canadian connection upon their ability to operate in Northern Ireland was minimal.

(The same was true in respect of the Loyalist paramilitary organisations, although official estimates do concede that 'one or two' successful attempts have been undertaken to supply arms out of Canada.[107] In addition, at least two attempts were unsuccessful. Both were related and both involved consignments which were destined for the Ulster Defence Association, either for the purpose of training members on the Yorkshire moors, or for use in Northern Ireland itself.)[108]

Subsequent to these events, there is little *evidence* of Canadian involvement in the affairs of Northern Ireland. In 1977 a claim was made by one Jim Kennedy that Canada was being used by Loyalist extremists as a base for gun-running *with* the knowledge of the Canadian authorities. However, since Kennedy was at the time in an immigration jail in Vancouver and was thought not to be Kennedy, but James McCann, an IRA fugitive, the accuracy of his statement was open to considerable scepticism.[109] Yet it—or at least not that part of it which referred to the continuing role of Canada as an arms source—could not be dismissed out of hand. In Dublin, just three months later, Donald C Jamieson, the Canadian Secretary of State for External Affairs, made a statement in which he admitted that, because of his country's long undefended border, it was possible that illegal arms movements to Northern Ireland were taking place. As he put it, 'sometimes these things do happen'.[110]

Mention will be made of just one other source of external support which the IRA might have received. Although there is no reference to it in any published documents, the possibility—more the probability—that the IRA occasionally obtained the services of professional assassins from outside Ireland, for service in Northern Ireland, has been suggested.[111] Because of the sensitive nature of security operations in the North, no further information was forthcoming, and it is therefore not possible to elaborate on the matter beyond this paragraph.

THE AMERICAN DIMENSION

1968–MARCH 1976

The awakening interest evinced by Irish–Americans in events in Northern Ireland in 1968–1969 was hardly a new development. Neither was it unusual that it should be expressed by some in cash and kind. In times of strife in Ireland since last century it has virtually defined the relationship between the Irish at home and those in the United States to the point where, in the Declaration of Independence of 1916, the support of Ireland's 'exiled children in America' was especially recognised. In December 1969 the breakaway Provisional Army Council, in the face of overwhelming evidence that the Irish Republican Army (IRA) which had existed prior to that time was unable to provide the maximum defence for the Republican population of Belfast, made a plea which, although less specific, was clearly directed at the USA.

> We call on the Irish at home and in exile for increased support towards defending our people in the North and the eventual achievement of the full political, social, economic and cultural freedom of Ireland.[112]

The message was clear: it was a call to provide aid for military action. However, the likelihood that it would produce an effective and immediate response in military terms was not overwhelming. This was a consequence of a number of factors, perhaps the most important being the attrition due to Americanisation of the ethnic Irish. But it also reflected the overall inability of the Northern Ireland conflict itself to inspire and mobilise, in any *sustained* fashion, groups (journalists, civil libertarians, American radicals, the Democratic Party etc.), which by tradition and/or their principal interests, might have been expected to have provided sympathy and assistance.[113] This meant that no more than an 'emaciated framework' was available upon which to build an aid network in 1968–1969.[114]

The organisational malaise was exacerbated by the fact that, despite the claimed predominance of those with North of Ireland ties within it, it also included what Clark observed as an '... estrangement, confusion of view points, and a general perplexity about what could be done in any practical way'.[115] In turn, this determined the essentially negative character of the support network which resulted, and its aversion to any cognitive effort with regard to the future of Ireland—as instanced by its recourse to slogans such as 'England Get Out of Ireland' (or its equivalent).

It was probably no surprise then, that James Bowyer Bell's 1971 edition of his standard history of the IRA should have contained the following passage:

> Any kind of armament acquired in Ireland is very dear indeed (a revolver may cost eighty pounds), and outside Ireland there are *few sympathetic sources or sponsors. American money flowing into Dublin in response to the troubles in the North was far less than the English Sunday papers liked to believe* ... [emphasis added].[116]

The amount which Bell thought fit to dismiss thereby was of the order of 'hundreds of thousands of pounds'.[17]

It was a surprise, therefore, to find that the English papers were in fact closer to the mark in their estimate of a general American willingness to contribute funds to relief programmes in Northern Ireland, and, more particularly, to the IRA. In late August 1969, Bernadette Devlin, then visiting the United States on behalf of the Northern Ireland Civil Rights Association (NICRA) claimed to have received 'pledges' totalling US$650,000 for the 'homeless' of the Six Counties.[118] In October of the same year the actual amount estimated to have been raised was a considerably less, but still substantial, US$92,000.[119] The following year, total US funds for a multiplicity of uses was estimated at US$450,000,[120] an amount which was consistent with Mick Flannery's claim that, for the three years to October 1972, the organisation which he represented (the Irish Northern Aid Committee) had been responsible for forwarding some US$500,000 to the North.[121]

Evidently, the IRA did not miss out on the bonanza. In Bell's 1974 edition of *The Secret Army* his 1971 opinion was noticeably changed in respect of the US financial response to the Provisional's appeals of 1970:

> Already some money had begun to flow through a variety of pipelines, in some cases to independent defence groups in the North but increasingly through overt or covert conduits to Dublin GHQ or various Republican aid committees. *The response from America was like nothing since the Troubles* ...[122]

Exactly how much the Provisional IRA received Bell did not divulge. Indeed, apart from the inference that the financial aid it received was substantial, the only conclusion which can be drawn with any certainty, even at this time, is that stated by Clark—that 'the full record of assistance to the Catholic minority and to the IRA will ever remain obfuscated'.[123]

Nevertheless, there were patterns and influences clear in those early years which were were to govern American influence upon the Northern Ireland conflict until the mid-1970s. First, despite Bernadette Devlin's fund-raising success of August 1969, the socialist views she professed were anathema to the essentially conservative Irish–Americans who were the large majority of contributors.[124] Indeed, in view of subsequent events, the latter's generosity at that time must be seen as an indiscriminate outpouring of sympathy for the plight of the Northern Catholic community. The measure of American opposition for Devlin's goals may be gauged from a report that a visit by her in 1971, during which she met Black Panthers and hippies, and after she had given birth to a child out of wedlock, yielded only some £150 after expenses.[125]

Second, it followed that the Official IRA, with its openly socialist orientation, was unlikely to be popular with the Irish–American community, and this was, and remains, the case to this day. By the same logic the Provisionals should also have been excluded from the financial benevolence of that community. But they weren't, and the reason was to be found in their not entirely deserved appearance as a more 'traditional' Republican organisation. While the Provisionals were certainly closer to the mainstream of Republic tradition than their Official counterparts, their philosophy and policies, such as they were, admitted some of the same left-radical elements which the Irish–American community found so unacceptable.[126]

The Provisionals, however, were possessed of more forethought, guile and dishonesty. They contrived, and quite cynically at that, to enhance their appeal to those who lived in the past while muting their adherence to socialist principles—both being undertaken in the belief that the end, however ill-defined, justified the means, however disagreeable. It worked, as Maria McGuire testified:

> There should be copious references to the martyrs of 1919 and 1920–22—the period most of the audience would be living in. Anti-British sentiment, recalling Cromwell, the potato famine, and the Black and Tans, could be profitably exploited. By no means should anything be said against the Catholic Church. And all references to socialism should be strictly avoided—tell them by all means that the Ireland we were fighting for would be free and united, but say nothing about just what form the new free and united Ireland would take.
>
> The formula was in general, very successful ...[127]

Indeed, so successful was it that the Official's network of support in the United States could not be described as other than modest. Unless specifically excepted, all references to the IRA in the succeeding pages of this chapter are to its Provisional wing.

The financial broker for the Provisionals' trans-Atlantic fund-raising is the

Irish Northern Aid Committee—NORAID, also known as INAC. According to its statement of registration with the US authorities under the Foreign Agents Registration Act, 1938 (FARA), it was founded in New York City in April 1970 by three IRA veterans of the civil war period, Mick Flannery, Jack McCarthy and John McGowan,[128] 'in response to an urgent call from its foreign principal, the Northern Aid Committee, Belfast'.[129] Accordingly, since its foundation, NORAID's record has been consistent in four aspects. It has:

(a) boasted of the large amounts it was remitting to persons such as Joe Cahill[130] in Northern Ireland;
(b) insisted that while these funds were intended for 'relief', it was up to 'the people on the other side' to decide how to spend them;
(c) agreed that part of the money was used for the purchase of arms; and
(d) repeatedly, and without reservation, supported the Provisionals' campaigns.

The organisational structure upon which NORAID's efforts are based has been variously estimated at one hundred chapters (in 1972, by Flannery) and eighty chapters (in 1975, also by the NORAID source).[131] The latter is generally regarded as the more reliable figure. Similarly, the NORAID claim of 80,000 members throughout the US has been discounted by official sources as an absurd exaggeration which was probably based on a paper estimate of members attending social functions over a period. The estimate which is favoured is 'several thousand ... possibly upwards of 2000', who are sufficiently numerous and active to have a considerable effect on most Irish–American organisations in the United States.[132] Of this number the largest concentration is in New York and the National headquarters is in the Bronx. Otherwise the most important centres are Chicago, Boston, Philadelphia, San Francisco, Los Angeles, Baltimore and various towns in New Jersey and Connecticut.[133] Among those who have spent some time observing its activities, NORAID has acquired a reputation, based on an apparently high level of visible coordination, as a close-knit and disciplined group.[134]

In support of its activities NORAID appears to command the full-time attention of its President and Vice-Presidents.[135] It also runs to a weekly newspaper, the *Irish People*, with a full-time editor. In addition, in 1975 Flannery (then President) was known to have a telex machine in his home in the Bronx and, according to journalists who visited him there, received continuous reports on it from Provisional sources in Ireland.[136] Unfortunately the use of modern technology has frequently failed to advance NORAID's understanding of the issues in Northern Ireland: for example, one report carried in the *Irish People* claimed that the Irish Special Branch had attempted to break an IRA ceasefire by organising sectarian murders in collusion with the Northern Ireland Social Democratic and Labour Party.[137]

To further sustain the fund-raising and lobbying operations, NORAID has played host to a number of prominent Provisionals such as Billy Kelly[138] and Ruairi O Bradaigh,[139] but they and others were hampered by the US Immigration and Nationality Acts which exclude aliens 'connected with organisations which advocate the killing of government agents or the unlawful destruction of property'. While this provision undoubtedly had an effect on the guest-of-honour lists for money-spinners such as dances and dinners, it probably had little impact on the other main source of finance, direct subscriptions.

To judge by reports and the schedules attached to NORAID's more recent six-monthly returns under the FARA, most contributors are working-class Irish–Americans. In some cases the arrangements are institutionalised: a number of Locals of the Transport Union and the Longshoremen's Union in New York are said to contribute fixed weekly amounts to the organisation (NORAID has close links with the national presidents of both unions).[140] In addition, a small number of wealthy Irish–Americans, such as hotelier Billy Fuller, are known to be contributors,[141] as are some Irish-born owners of chains of bars in New York who both contribute funds themselves and allow their establishments to be used as collection centres. However, it is understood that the larger contributors in America, like those in Ireland, try to maintain anonymity by insisting that their contributions be 'laundered' secretly.[142]

The results of these combined efforts have been summarised in Table 1. As may be seen in Table 1, Flannery's October 1972 claim (cited earlier) that NORAID had sent close to US$500,000 to Northern Ireland in the three previous years was probably not excessive;[144] in just the eighteen month period ended 29 July 1972 the total remitted was US$452,299. *But there were, and remain, reservations about accepting many of NORAID's claims.* The above, for instance, mentions a three-year period—presumably from October 1969—yet NORAID's statement of registration also claims that it was founded some seven months later in April 1970.[145] Furthermore it is obvious from the table that, in default of *income* figures for the first three reporting periods, and of a complete absence of reliable information before that time, even the most informed estimates of NORAID's financial dealings could be hopelessly wrong.

In this regard it is useful to refer to the return for 29 January 1973, in which it will be found that nearly US$20,000 *in excess of reported receipts* was remitted. This suggests that latter figures detailed under 'Surplus' appear to confirm that part of each six months' takings are retained, to bolster poor performances, aid special projects in the future or establish a capital fund.

For undefined reasons this latter question of a steadily accumulating NORAID fund has received no attention from commentators, yet it is, potentially, of some significance. At the very least it could, if NORAID chose to falsify its returns, be used for a period of one to two years to disguise the falling away of financial support from the average level since 1976. On the other hand, there is a widely held belief that 'blood on the streets' (of Northern Ireland), or what are euphemistically termed 'spectaculars' (particularly daring IRA operations), induce the sympathetic Irish–American community to renew or increase its contributions, and the suggestion cannot be discounted that some of the surplus has been used in sustaining or enhancing this.[146] And if it should be thought that such suggestions unwarrantedly impugn the honesty of NORAID's officials, there is always the caveat provided by the

Table 1. Irish Northern Aid Committee Reported Details of Financial Undertakings.[143,196]
(All amounts in US dollars)

Six month period ended		Income	Expenditure	Disbursements to NI	Surplus
29 July	1971*	no information	4,575	11,500	not known
29 January	1972	no information	12,738	128,099	not known
29 July	1972**	no information	25,440	312,700	not known
29 January	1973	172,000	41,388	150,438	–19,826
29 July	1973	159,617	19,581	121,723	18,313
29 January	1974	129,968	10,826	99,966	19,176
29 July	1974	121,822	8,193	110,833	2,796
29 January	1975	115,522	11,620	102,648	1,254
29 July	1975	130,852	44,472	70,977	15,403
29 January	1976	no information	24,955	64,205	not known
Minimum six year total:		$829,781	$203,788	$1,173,089	$56,942
29 July	1976	80,201	20,278	55,500	4,423
31 January	1977	81,262	12,342	48,000	20,920
29 July	1977	84,017	12,914	60,115	10,988
29 January	1978	68,713	11,985	39,000	17,728
29 July	1978	84,091	19,179	73,857	8,945
29 January	1979	83,417	17,672	59,200	6,545
31 July	1979	74,550	21,653	61,616	–8,719
31 January	1980	140,074	15,625	105,230	19,219
Four year total:		$696,325	$131,648	$502,518	$80,049
Minimum ten year total:		$1,526,106	$335,436	$1,675,607	$136,991
31 July	1980	90,056			
31 January	1981	105,124			
31 July	1981	250,511	(See note 16)		
Minimum eleven year total:		$1,971,796			

* Information taken from document entitled 'Supplemental Statement'.
** Information taken fron hand-written draft.

attorney responsible over some years for the monitoring of the organisation's compliance with the FARA, that they were of a type who 'just can't treat straight with any government'.[147]

Thus it is only prudent to conclude that the figures produced in the foregoing represent less than accurate accounts of NORAID's transactions. Indeed NORAID personnel were reported, in 1975, to have boasted in private of much greater sums than those found in the table—up to US$4 million per year—being remitted to Northern Ireland.[148] As these claims were generally held to be more in the nature of romantic speculation, the conservative 'official' figures remain as the best available, albeit probably understated, indication of the intensity and fluctuations of popular Irish–American support for the Provisionals.

By way of comparison, it is interesting to note the extent to which the potential of Irish-America was not realised, as illustrated by the following examples. Throughout the entire period 1968–1983 the best NORAID appeared capable of, in so far as attracting public figures in support of its fund-raising, was to interest actor Richard Harris, thriller-writer Len Deighton and Longshoremen's President Teddy Gleason, in attending a dinner for which the Provisional Republican faithful paid US$18 per head.[149] Yet an Ireland Fund Dinner, organised by Tony O'Reilly, probably the most prominent and successful Irishman living in the United States,[150] could count on the presence of leading members of the Irish–American establishment—such as Speaker 'Tip' O'Neill—and would command US$175 per plate.[151]

The distinctions, needless to say, were only superficially of a culinary nature. What they attested to was the failure, foreshadowed at the outbreak of the troubles, of the aid network to expand its following beyond the narrow confines of the sectional 'Old Irish' (Republican) interests. In general, neither the politicians nor the wealthy Irish–Americans, nor the Catholic Church found the prospect of associating with NORAID worth the opprobrium it would have earned them.[152] It was to be expected, therefore, that the isolation of the activists should have extended to non-Irish–American organisations and the higher reaches of the US Federal Government, although the former was the more difficult to account for. After a promising beginning in which specialised groups of humanitarians concerned themselves with Northern Ireland, their interest withered; groups working in the fields of foreign policy, interreligious understanding and anti-colonial concerns generally avoided the issues of Northern Ireland with a consistency that was quite inconsistent with their stated objectives.[153]

If there was any one reason for this behaviour it was to be found in Northern Ireland and in the terror bombing campaigns of the IRA. As Clark wrote of these other, influential and many 'friends of Ireland' and their view of the network:

> they saw it as tied to more of the same murderous violence without solution that they recoiled from in Vietnam.[154]

In this they were perceptive. While NORAID spokesmen were wont to pretend that its funds were used purely for relief, there were far too many instances in which the lie was given to this claim. As one anonymous representative explained in 1971:

> Our job is to get up the money and send it to the people over there. What they use it for is up to them. We attach no strings. Everything we do in this country is aimed at assisting the final phase of the struggle for freedom in Ireland.[155]

Moreover, there is irrefutable evidence that several of NORAID's officers were implicated in numerous arms offences which led to trials in Canada and the United States. The following year the same manifestation of support without responsibility was clear in Mathew Higgins' (Vice President of NORAID) statement that:

> We're involved in supporting the activities of the Provisional IRA and that Branch of Sinn Fein which supports the Provisional IRA. We provide what funds we can and the people on the other side have to decide what has to be used for what purpose.[156]

In 1975 he was even franker:

> We have no objections to it [the purchase of guns] if they have money to spare. They've got to get them from somewhere. If the overall kitty is big enough to buy weapons that's their business. We were formed for the purpose of supporting the Irish Freedom movement. We still support the Provisional IRA—no ifs and buts about that ...[157]

For some time, however, there was no irrefutable evidence that NORAID, *per se*, engaged in activities other than *fund-raising and supply*. On the other hand, there appeared to be little refuge for the organisation in Mick Flannery's protestations that allegations of gun-running were 'terrible' and 'vicious' lies, and in his appeal to the Scottish juridical prerogative that 'no one has ever proved a thing'.[158] Indeed, by the end of 1982 Flannery's cover was particularly transparent with his admitted involvement as a conspirator in an unsuccessful venture to smuggle arms to the IRA from the United States.[159]

According to a report of testimony given in the trial of Frank Grady, convicted in New York in March 1976 for illegally exporting arms and falsifying documents, the organisation's intentions were clear from the earliest days of its existence.

> Shortly after the formation of the [Yonkers] branch, they [Grady and others] were approached by Martin Lyons, then a senior official at Northern Aid headquarters and one of the founders of the organisation and asked to assist in the purchase and export of guns for use by the Provisional IRA in Northern Ireland.[160]

Thereafter, the most notorious case involved the 'Fort Worth Five' in 1972. This became a *cause celèbre* in both Irish–American and US civil rights circles because, from the viewpoint of the former, the issue of the supply of arms and ammunition to the IRA and, from the latter perspective, constitutional and civil rights questions. Among other cases which came to light were those of Charles Malone, a NORAID member living in San Francisco, and James O'Gara, a New York NORAID official, both of whom were convicted on arms charges in 1973.[161] And within a year, four people—two Irish and two Irish–Americans—were convicted in Baltimore, Maryland, of conspiring to smuggle one hundred and fifty-eight semi-automatic rifles (worth about

US$30,000), plus armour-piercing shells and other explosives from New York to Ireland. According to reports this was the United States biggest case of gun-running,[162] and although there was no indication in the course of the trial as to who or what provided its financial backing, the Baltimore District Attorney, Jeff White, left little doubt as to what inference should have been taken:

> The statements [at the trial] didn't actually mention the Irish Northern Aid Committee, but it was clear who was meant. ... We didn't make radical distinctions between the two groups [NORAID and the IRA]. Statements made at the trial in reference to the group which came up with the money were to 'Irish' and 'IRA', but we considered them to mean the Irish Northern Aid Committee.[163]

Further grounds supporting this conclusion were provided by three instances in the two succeeding years. The first concerned the 1975 conviction of Joseph Myles, described by the police as 'an executive officer of a US organisation, Northern Irish Aid' (sic), on a charge of conspiracy to export arms to Ireland.[164] The second was the Grady case, already mentioned, while the third related to two Philadelphians—Neil Byrne and Daniel Cahalane[165] (head of NORAID's Delaware County Chapter)—who were found guilty of illegally exporting arms to the IRA.[166]

Such examples not only highlighted the value of the United States as an armoury to the IRA, but also pointed to the potential which existed for a widening of the conflict by involving American citizens in ancillary, or actual, fighting roles—or at least the *fear* of this development. Early on, there were reports that a group calling itself the United Ireland Committee of New York had enlisted volunteers to fight in aid of the Catholic population in the North but these seem now to be either overstated or simply patriotic fiction.[167] Scepticism, also, was attached to reports that the IRA had obtained the services of 'former American servicemen'[168] and that some of them were under investigation by the Army Council for spying and treachery.[169] They relied heavily on the judicious use of statements (by unidentified British military and IRA personnel) which did not necessarily confirm the claim of the articles, and they appear to have been carried only in the papers of the Berry group.[170]

The same dismissive attitude was not appropriate to, nor was it adopted by, any of the governments concerned, in respect of the Trans-Atlantic traffic in arms for the IRA. According to Stanley Orme, a Minister of State at the Northern Ireland Office, the evidence from recovery operations conducted by the security forces in the Province indicated that eighty-five per cent of the Provisionals' weapons originated in the United States,[171] thus establishing that country as its most important single source of supply.[172]

The American Government notwithstanding the seriousness with which it viewed this matter, disputed the British estimates. One agent of the Bureau of Alcohol, Tobacco and Firearms, Don Zimmerman, countered that a claim of even seventy-five per cent was 'a ridiculous exaggeration'.[173] Moreover, the available data appeared to support his position, although certain juxtapositions of time are required to do so. In the same June 1975 article which carried Zimmerman's statement, it was reported that 1581 'guns of American manufacture' had been found in Northern Ireland connected with the IRA. This figure, when compared with the overall (Ulster-wide) total of 4974 *for the period 1971–1975*,[174] represented a proportion of approximately thirty per cent. (And this appeared to be a steadily decreasing ratio over time: when figures to 1979 were taken, it fell as low as twenty-three per cent, for weapons which were 'said to be of US manufacture'.)[175]

If allowance is made for the fact that the 1971–1975 percentage was artificially high because the figure of 1581 included recoveries of US arms for 1969 and 1970 as well, but omitted *total* (Ulster-wide) recoveries for the same period which must have increased the figure of 4974, then it would seem that there was a wild divergence between the competing British and American estimates. And irrespective of the interpretation given to the statistics of arms recoveries, they confirmed in a rather obvious way the relative ease with which the IRA was able to replenish and maintain its fighting requirements in Ulster, a point made by Bell and Jones.[176] Indeed, some arms were reported to have travelled the greater part of their journey in style—aboard the Cunard liner, *Queen Elizabeth II*.[177]

It is possible, however, to effect a reconciliation between the American and British claims by reference to the impressive record of the actual weapons which the IRA came to use. In 1969 it was poorly armed, where it was armed at all. By 1971 it had introduced the Armalite AR130 (the civilian, semi-automatic version of the selective fire AR 1S) and the M1 Garand into its arsenal. From 1972 on, these were supplemented by military surplus and commercial variants of the M1 carbine, the AR 1S, and the M3 SMG ('Grease Gun').[178] As from 1974, recoveries in Northern Ireland included the above weapons plus small quantities or single examples of the following:

AG 42b semi-automatic rifle (Swedish Army surplus).
NATO MIA semi-automatic rifles (commercial name for M 14 US Army rifles).
GA1/42 semi-automatic rifles (Wehrmacht surplus).
SAFN semi-automatic rifles (Venezuelan Army surplus).
M 62 semi-automatic rifles (current Finnish Army rifle).
NATO Beretta 59/69 semi-automatic rifle (current Italian Army rifle).[179]

According to RD Jones of the British Intelligence Corps, the above list was 'very significant'. Apart from the M3 SMG, all the weapons listed were available over the counter in the United States—with the last two having the names of firearms dealings engraved upon them.[180] If to this is added the knowledge that until 1973, the AR 180 was made under licence in Japan, and thereafter by the Stirling Armament Co Ltd of Great Britain, for sale and distributions by the Armalite company at Costa Mesa, California, and hence forwarded to the IRA from the US, the grounds for a considerable divergence of views were well established. They became even more so in the light of the claim made by (US) Assistant Attorney-General, William Olsen, that some Americans were involved on behalf of the IRA in attempts in Mexico to illegally purchase, *inter alia*, this same weapon.[181] Whether or not such factors fully accounted for the conflicting views is not clear, but it may be inferred that they were substantially a consequence of the British Government's position that the term 'American arms' should be interpreted so as to encompass those which were 'modern' (as per note 61) and to include weapons which were not only of US manufacture, but also of a loosely defined US origin. And this despite the fact that the AR 180 (according to Bell the 'IRA's favourite weapon') by virtue of being made by Stirling, was in effect also a British weapon![182]

But the list also indicated that the IRA possessed a multiplicity of types and calibres among both their longarm and pistol weaponry. In Jones's opinion this reflected the success of the security forces in repeatedly depriving the IRA of its weapons, and its subsequent recourse to piecemeal procurement. The further consequence was that insoluble problems of maintenance were created, which in turn exacerbated the supply situation by rendering useless weapons with relatively simple faults.[183] Thus despite its success in obtaining arms and ammunition in quantity, it was evident by 1978 (the year of Jones's article) that, in the period 1968–1976, the IRA had probably failed in its objective of obtaining them according to its criterion of '*identical* ... and recent manufacture'.[184]

From the vantage point of 1986 this conclusion is confirmed only more so. The record of US financial and material assistance of the early and mid-1970s now appears as a guttering of a candle rather than the advent of a truly transnational movement. Although the figures do not show it, it is Clark's contention that 'apathy reconquered the spirits of many' in the Irish–American support network after the Ulster Workers' Council Strike in mid-1974.[185] Certainly NORAID's reported disbursements to Northern Ireland show a dramatic tumble in 1975, and by that time, too, there was an apparent hiatus in gun-running sufficient to suggest that major attempts were a matter of history. American interests in Ireland were to be revived, but as a result of initiatives which are beyond the scope of this chapter. For the most part, these were undertaken by those whose motivations might be classified as other and better than those which coloured this early period.

MARCH 1976–1983

If this chapter was to address the 'American Dimension' in its fullest sense the above period would concentrate on the significance of political developments which eclipsed the importance of the support network in the period 1976–1980. It would feature the role of certain prominent Irish–American politicians—Hugh Carey, Edward Kennedy, Daniel Patrick Moynihan and 'Tip' O'Neill—and their efforts to move a President in what culminated, in 1977, as the 'Carter Initiative'. Thus it would consider the emergence, at the highest political levels in the United States, of more pragmatic, and ultimately, a more responsible approach to the Irish Question than had been in evidence before. This, however, is outside the present terms of reference but, for all of that, this second period of review needs to be understood in its context.

In order to understand the decline to which reference has been made it is necessary to consider, first, the standing and effectiveness of the Northern Ireland support network in the US after 1976. In so far as the supply of arms was concerned, the record provides a *qualified* confirmation of the optimistic assessment given in 1977 by the US Ambassador to the Court of St James, Kingman Brewster, that it was on the wane.[186] The reason for this caution is that there were a number of claims which, when set against the available evidence, appear exaggerated, if not contradictory.

On one hand there is the IRA claim, inspired it seems by low-grade science fiction, that it had shot down a British Army Air Corps *Gazelle* helicopter using a US-made M60 machine gun firing 'specially developed magnetic bullets'. This was almost certainly a fabrication. Indeed, reports of the Army inquiry into the loss of this aircraft pointed to a structural or dynamic failure after a 'beyond-limits manoeuvre'.[187] Nevertheless, it was true that the IRA was in possession of a small number of belt-fed M60s, which it is now generally believed were stolen from a National Guard armoury in Danvers, Massachusetts.[188] Exactly who stole them and how they were obtained is not clear. In any case, the possession of this weapon, a somewhat cumbersome one for the urban type of operations which are the mainstay of IRA actions, was more important for the psychological boost it gave its owners than for its military value. One the other hand, US explosives were in good supply: according to Bell and Coogan, IRA sympathisers working on the construction of the New York City water tunnel diverted sizeable quantities of this material to Ireland in the course of the project.[189] Also acquired from the US were useful field aids such as stolen US Army electronic binoculars which made worthless the infra-red torch surveillance of the Northern Ireland security forces.[190]

None of these indications, however, provided a clear image of the extent of supply of arms and associated equipment from the US to the IRA. Nevertheless, there were facts and figures which suggested that the arms traffic was being reduced in this period. By September 1979, American-made arms comprised only twenty-three per cent of arms recovered by the security forces in Northern Ireland—down from approximately thirty per cent in 1975 (based on the analysis undertaken in the previous Section).[191] Even allowing for the basis upon which it computed its estimates of the national origin of recovered arms, the British Government, in 1981, reduced its estimate of American arms to forty-seven per cent, down from eighty-five per cent in 1976.[192] And finally, in late 1981, NORAID was placed on the defensive with the arrest in New York of four Irish–Americans including founder Mick Flannery and a branch treasurer on arms-smuggling charges. In the same period NORAID itself was required to amend its registration under the Foreign Agents Registration Act of 1938 to show as its foreign principal, not the 'Northern Aid Committee, Belfast, Ireland', but the Irish Republican Army. Legal action with a similar objective was also taken by US federal authorities against the organisation's newspaper the *Irish People*.

Against these developments which pointed to a contraction of the American Dimension in respect of weapons there were two further developments which suggested the contrary. The first was that reports of the use of 'US arms' by the IRA continued throughout the period under review. And this was despite the recovery of such arms in search operations by the security forces.[193] The second was provided by information made available after the successful interdiction of an IRA arms supply route in February 1982. According to Federal immigration officials, a conduit from the US to Dublin and Belfast had been in operation from as far back as 1974.[194] Furthermore, in the eighteen months prior to the interdiction, at least twelve smuggling operations had been allowed to pass unhindered in order to piece together precise details of the IRA's network—which extended from Dublin through Amsterdam and Toronto to Buffalo.[195]

By these accounts, therefore, the IRA was operating a regular and relatively sophisticated system of regular weapons procurement out of North America. (In the absence of any reference to the quantities involved it is not possible at this stage to assess the full significance of this system, nor is it possible to extrapolate merely from its existence and international extent to the alleged operation of a French Connection through Brittany discussed earlier.) Nevertheless, on balance this would apppear to be a system which was not only operating under pressure, but at a reduced scale compared to its earlier performance.

Financial support, as reflected in the bi-annual returns of the Irish Northern Aid Committee (NORAID), and set out in Table 1, is also difficult to gauge.

The foregoing figures, however, are subject to the same qualifications and reservations which were made in respect of NORAID's returns in the preceding section. According to information provided by IRA defector Peter McMullan, the discrepancy between reported and the actual income of NORAID could have been staggering. Whereas the organisation claimed to have raised some US$1.5 million between 1971 and 1980, his claim was that, between 1969 and early 1981, nearly US$5 million had been received by NORAID.[197]

But if official figures are the criterion, a different, seemingly confused, picture is painted. For the most part (8 out of 11), the level of NORAID's six-monthly receipts post-1975 is down in comparison with that of the earlier period. The confusion stems from the three exceptions to this pattern. However, it is instructive to approach them with a knowledge of events within each return period. Thus, in the return for 31 January 1980, the increase coincides with a period that included the murder of Lord Mountbatten and the killing of eighteen British soldiers at Warrenpoint, Co. Down (August 1979). The second un-characteristic return is that filed for the period ended 31 January 1981—a period which also brackets the IRA bombings in Britain of December 1980.[198] And the third, and by far the largest amount of income reported by NORAID, was for the period ended 31 July 1981, during which time the H-Block hunger strike campaign by Republican prisoners in the Maze Prison outside Belfast reached its peak.[199] What emerges, then, is a reinforced belief in the criminally perverse power of 'blood-in-the-streets' ('spectaculars') to loosen the purse strings of Irish–Americans sympathetic to the Provisional cause. In the absence of such stimuli, however, the financial reports of NORAID suggest that Northern Ireland gradually slipped as a priority from 1976 onwards. (Regrettably, for both the relevant US Government agencies and students of the Irish Question, NORAID, in the early 1980s refused to file details of its financial undertakings so more recent figures are unavailable for interpretation.)

In other respects, too, it was apparent that the support network was faced with reduced interest. In September 1978, Teddy Gleason, a Vice-President of the Irish National Caucus, a pro-Provisional lobby group, and President of the International Longshoremen's Association, called for a worldwide boycott of British goods in support of demands being made by four relatives of Irish prisoners in Long Kesh (the name by which the Maze Prison was formally known). Despite the fact that Gleason expected full support for the measure from the Executive of the American Federation of Labor-Congress of Industrial Organisations, seven of whom were first-generation Irish–Americans, British commerce was not endangered. (This should not have been a surprise to anyone, least of all to Gleason: he had, in 1975, disavowed boycotts as being unlikely to either save lives in Ulster or bring the sides to the bargaining table.)

Furthermore, when American intervention by those associated with the network became more direct, lack of interest at home was replaced by hostility in Northern Ireland. Thus in 1978, the Deputy Leader of the Social Democratic and Labour Party (SDLP), John Hume, denounced the *American* Ancient Order of Hibernians for their crude attempts to sabotage US investment initiatives. According to him, there was evidence that the latter, under the sway of some of its leadership who sympathised with the IRA, had resorted to suggesting that, in general, there should be no American investment in the North as this would result mainly in Protestant employment, and that one US company in particular should be 'concerned about the possible safety of its plant'. As Hume was quick to observe, the notion that a lack of investment would somehow contribute to political change was not only 'misguided', but also difficult to reconcile with the (American) Hibernians' recent resolution at a conference in Killarney which purported to offer friendship to Protestants.[200]

Overall, the situation in the US could be attributed to five factors although their relative weight may be difficult to ascertain. The first and most obvious of these factors was political development, or rather their lack of it, in Northern Ireland. The Ulster Workers Council Strike in 1974 gave birth to a political stalemate which effectively remains to this day. Furthermore it was followed by a decrease in the level of violence (as compared with the early 1970s). In combination they served to deprive the support network of what Clark termed 'the energising effect [of] constant headlines'.[201]

The second, also a Northern Ireland factor, compounded the effect noted above. This was the erosion of support by conservative Irish–Americans as a consequence of their increasing awareness of the IRA's socialist orientation—evidenced by its assassination campaign against Northern businessmen.[202] The third and fourth were internal circumstances. Weariness from years of activity had so sapped the movement that much of it, even before 1976, was pervaded by apathy.[203] And it now appears that, by 1979, at the latest, a breach had developed between NORAID and the Irish National Caucus as a result of personality clashes and a conflict over which group was to provide the leadership for Irish–American supporters of the Provisionals.[204]

Fifth, the network and those associated with it were out of touch with the prevailing mood which, from March 1976, and in both Northern Ireland and the US, embodied a firm rejection of violence, and hence of the Provisionals. In the former it rose from the courageous stand taken by the Peace People and the promise and inspiration they provided across the sectarian divide.[205] To many around the world, accustomed to being informed only of the carnage which was sweeping Northern Ireland, they were the best hope for a solution that had emerged in eight years of conflict. Even when the promise which the Peace People represented proved illusory, and the Provisional movement subsequently grew in popularity, the above impediments were sufficient to militate against any notable rejuvenation or re-energising of the support structure.

At this point it is appropriate to return to the perspective of what is being discussed in this chapter. It principally concerns the supply of arms to a relatively localised conflict which between 1968 and 1983, claimed the lives of some 2200 people. Sadly, in terms of the natural and man-made hazards to which the world is accustomed, it is frequently regarded as a small toll of a small war in the north-eastern confines of a small country. Other indices confirm this: according to a Foreign and Commonwealth Office authority on the situation in Northern Irleand, ballistic signatures indicated that in 1978, only about 1000 weapons were in *active use* in the Province.[206] This, and the relatively small quantity described in virtually all of the IRA's attempts to acquire arms, both frustrated and successful, is a caution against taking too expansive a view of the current 'troubles'.

The record of paramilitary operations related to the conflict reduced its international dimensions even further. By far the greatest number of incidents were the responsibility of one organisation—the Provisional IRA—although on a few occasions its pre-eminence was challenged by the Officials,[207] some unnamed Protestant extremists[208] and latterly the Irish National Liberation Army (INLA).[209] Even then, in the context of some of the more spectacular or news-generating activities associated with *international terrorism*, the IRA's could only be described as modest. It had not, for example, ever attempted to hijack an aeroplane, nor has it, the Niedermayer incident notwithstanding,[210] been noticeably drawn to kidnapping.[211] In other fields, however, such as those of ambush, assassination and bombing, the IRA demonstrated an ability to sustain a virtual urban guerrilla war which, in 1978 and in Northern Ireland alone, continued to occupy a regular British garrison of over 13,000, the part-time Ulster Defence Regiment of some 8000 and a considerable proportion of an expanded Royal Ulster Constabulary.[212] Across the Border the comparable figure was less than 5000.[213] As a 1978 British intelligence report concluded:

> [The IRA] has the dedication and the sinews of war to raise violence intermittently to at least the level of early 1978, certainly for the foreseeable future . . .

Its 'campaign' of violence is likely to continue while the British remain in Northern Ireland.[214]

Although statistics are but poor indices of the suffering and disruption to daily life which have been caused by the conflict in Northern Ireland, they do at least reveal that its more violent manifestations have been contained within the Six Counties. Whereas, by 1983, over 2200 lives had been lost in the Six Counties, less than 160 in total had been lost in Britain, the Republic of Ireland and Western Europe in Northern Ireland-related violence. What these statistics suggest, then, was the intention on the part of the antagonists not to expand, or perhaps the inability to expand, the conflict beyond the borders of Northern Ireland under 'normal' circumstances.

A close inspection of the records of out-of-state incidents lends considerable support to this interpretation. They appeared to have arisen out of various ulterior, as opposed to central, motives which otherwise governed the conflict in the North. And there were sound reasons for the general avoidance of foreign battlegrounds, as McGuire explained:

> it was our [the Provisional IRA's] definite policy then not to take the war to England. We knew we would not be able to sustain operations there: on classic guerrilla theory you might only where the population will support you and give you refuge. Previous attempts to carry the war to England had been ... disastrous and counter-productive.[215]

Thus revenge,[216] the need of a bargaining chip[217] and the desire to dramatically re-focus British attention on the Province[218] were the motivating forces behind British operations when they were undertaken. It was as though the paramilitaries had decided upon a fundamental distinction—regarding the war in Northern Ireland in the classical Clausewitzian sense of the practice of diplomacy by other means, and the terrorist operations further afield as the gruesome arm of public relations.

Essentially, neither English nor European operations were the main thrust of the campaign conducted by the Provisional IRA, or any other paramilitary organisation in Northern Ireland for that matter. In the final analysis the conflict remained, throughout the period under review, essentially within the dimensions of the questions from which it sprang. Although the antagonists garnered supplies from external parties, the fight itself never seemed likely to include, to any significant level, other than the Irish and the British in Ireland. For that reason, Sir Walter Scott's description of it all was as accurate in 1981 as it was in 1825.

> Their factions have been so long envenomed, and they have such narrow ground to do their battle in, that they are like people fighting with daggers in a hogshead.[219]

NOTES

1 Richard Gott, 'A Foreign Land', *Guardian Weekly*, 24 February 1980, p. 4.

2 Joseph Conrad, *The Secret Agent: A Simple Tale*, London: JM Dent, 1947, p. x.
3 Walter Laqueur, *Guerrilla: A Historical and Critical Study*, London: Weidenfeld and Nicolson, 1977, p. 324 (hereafter cited as Laqueur, *Guerrilla*).
4 Peter Janke, 'The Response to Terrorism', Royal United Services Institute for Defence Studies (RUSI), *Ten Years of Terrorism: Collected Views*, London: RUSI, 1979, p. 25.
5 See Dev Murarka, 'Moscow Takes A New Look At Ulster', *The Observer* Foreign News Service, No. 30023, 24 March 1972; and 'Soviet Distortions On Northern Ireland', February 1977, a paper held by the International Institute for Strategic Studies, and noted 'Source Not Known'. In the writer's opinion, this second paper, which juxtaposes Soviet comment with verifiable fact was produced by British Government authorities for general distribution to offices and personnel who might have a need to refute Soviet allegations.
6 *Sunday Telegraph*, 31 October 1971, pp. 1 and 3.
7 *Daily Telegraph*, 8 February 1977.
8 BBC Radio 4 Programme, 'Today', as cited in Clutterbuck, *Protest and the Urban Guerrilla*, London: Cassell, 1973, pp. 217–218.
9 *Daily Telegraph*, 7 April 1977, and *Guardian*, 7 April 1977.
10 *Irish Times*, 28 September 1978.
11 *Boston Globe*, 7 September 1979, p. 2.
12 George Styles, *Bombs Have No Pity: My War Against Terrorism*, London: William Luscombe, 1975, p. 111.
13 Galician, Breton and Welsh groupings were represented in company with Official Sinn Fein and Herriko Alderi Socialista Iraultalea—People's Revolutionary Socialist Party—to sign a 'Declaration on the struggles against colonialism in Western Europe' (Roger Faligot, 'Basques, Sinn Fein and the Brest Charter', *Hibernia*, 20 January 1978, p. 12, hereafter cited as Faligot, 'Basques, Sinn Fein and the Brest Charter').
14 *Ibid.*
15 *Ibid.*
16 Maria McGuire, *To Take Arms: A Year in the Provisional IRA*, London: Macmillan, 1973, pp. 71 and 110 (hereafter cited as McGuire, *To Take Arms*).
17 Both were killed by the detonation of an under-the-road explosive device as their respective motor vehicles passed over it.
18 Roger Faligot, 'Basques, Sinn Fein and the Brest Charter', p. 12.
19 Albert Parry, *Terrorism: From Robespierre to Arafat*, New York: Vanguard Press, 1976, pp. 171–172.
20 Parliamentary Debates, House of Commons, *Official Report*, Vol. 811, 15 February 1971, col. 1237 (hereafter cited as House of Commons, *Official Report*).
21 Austria, Belgium, Czechoslovakia, Finland, France, West Germany, Hungary, Italy, Japan, New Zealand, Spain, Sweden, The United Kingdom, the USA and the USSR (House of Commons, *Official Report*, Vol. 851, 20 February 1973, col. 47). Later a sixteenth was added—Venezuela (RD Jones, 'Terrorist Weaponry in Northern Ireland', *British Army Review*, April 1978, p. 19 (hereafter cited as Jones, 'Terrorist Weaponry in Northern Ireland').
22 *Times*, 15 August 1977.
23 For examples, see the reports of a mortar attack on Belfast's Aldergrove Airport using electrical ignition devices (*Guardian*, 8 March 1975), and the hijacked beer train episode in which it emerged that the Provisionals had become skilled

in the use of light-sensitive circuits and what are known as radio-controlled improvised explosive devices (*Times*, 23 November 1978).

24 J Bowyer Bell, *The Secret Army: The IRA 1916–1979*, revised and updated edn. Dublin: Academy Press, 1979, pp. 439–440, (hereafter cited as Bell, *The Secret Army*).

25 Even this figure is subject to considerable doubt. In the 1970s there was some disagreement in Anglo–American relations as to exactly what constituted arms of US origin, and hence, the proportion of total arms that were classified accordingly. British estimates were as high as 85%—a claim that the US Government found quite unacceptable. The figure of 40–50% is the writer's estimate, based on both an analysis undertaken elsewhere and recent British estimates: see my 'The Ulster Question in International Politics, 1968–1978', unpublished PhD thesis submitted in the Australian National University, Canberra (hereafter cited as McKinley, *PhD Thesis*); and *International Herald Tribune*, 30 July 1981.

26 House of Commons, *Official Report*, Vol. 850, 13 February 1973, col. 321; and Vol. 851, 20 February 1973, col. 47.

27 Richard Rose, *Northern Ireland: A Time of Choice*, London: Macmillan, 1976, p. 68.

28 Peter Janke, 'The Response to Terrorism', Royal United Services Institute for Defence Studies (RUSI), *Ten Years of Terrorism: Collected Views*, London: RUSI, 1979, p. 25 (hereafter cited as RUSI, *Ten Years of Terrorism*).

29 Conor Brady, 'Provisions of Violence', *Irish Times*, 25 March 1977. The seven countries were given as: Belgium, France, Italy, Sweden, Switzerland, the UK and West Germany.

30 McGuire, *To Take Arms*, pp. 42–49.

31 This for example, appears to have been so in the case involving the mercenary recruiter, John Banks (*Guardian*, 22 February 1977 and 7 April 1977).

32 McGuire, *To Take Arms*, p. 45.

33 Jones, 'Terrorist Weaponry in Northern Ireland', p. 21. See n. 21.

34 McGuire, *To Take Arms*, p. 44.

35 *Ibid.*, pp. 43–44.

36 Jones, 'Terrorist Weaponry in Northern Ireland', p. 21.

37 House of Commons, *Official Report*, Vol. 908, 30 March 1976, col. 472, and Albert Parry, *Terrorism: From Robespierre to Arafat*, New York: Vanguard Press, 1976, p. 379.

38 *Guardian*, 29 November 1972; and *Times*, 30 November 1972. In 1981, Boris Shtern, a former Russian journalist, claimed that he was on board a Soviet trawler when it stopped off the Irish coast one night in 1971 and unloaded a secret cargo to waiting boats. Unfortunately, Shtern's certainty on the matter goes no further than reporting that the cargo was concealed in a crate and that it was received by two Irishmen from the KGB officer on board the trawler. Exactly who they were, or what they represented, was not reported; similarly it was only Shtern's (and others of the crew) opinion that the crate contained arms. (*Times*, 30 April 1981, p. 7). If it did, the quantity involved was obviously quite small.

39 House of Commons, *Official Report*, Vol. 848, 21 December 1972, cols. 470–472; and *Daily Telegraph*, 11 December 1972.

40 J Bowyer Bell, *A Time of Terror: How Democratic Societies Respond to Revolutionary Violence*, New York: Basic Books, 1978, p. 135.

41 This is a conclusion drawn from material which appears elsewhere—see McKinley, *PhD Thesis* (n. 25 above).

42 *Times*, 21 April 1975.

43 *Guardian*, 30 March 1973. The arms recovered were 250 Russian-made (AK 47) self-loading rifles, 247 Webley .38 revolvers, more than 20,000 rounds of Belgian and Russian ammunition, 100 anti-tank mines, 100 cases of anti-personnel mines, 600 lb. of TNT, 500 lb. of gelignite and 300 hand grenades (see also *Guardian*, 31 March 1973; *Sunday Telegraph* 1 April 1973; and *Times*, 21 April 1975).

44 Leinhauser had been caught at an intermediate point, on the French–German border, with a consignment of American, German, Italian and Yugoslav pistols and revolvers (*Daily Telegraph*, 31 March 1973).

45 *Guardian*, 30 March 1973; and 6 April 1973.

46 *Guardian*, 3 April 1976; and *Times*, 3 April 1973. Similar reports were to be found in other British newspapers throughout the two weeks after the operation and were also repeated by the above at different times in this period.

47 *Foreign Report*, No. 1277, 3 January 1973, p. 5.

48 In its attempts to locate the origin of the rocket launchers, British Intelligence sent samples of the dust and sand found inside one of the weapons to scientists of all the leading petroleum companies in Britain in the hope that it could be geographically identified. But it wasn't (*Times*, 21 April 1975).

49 *Times*, 22 April 1975; and *Belfast Telegraph*, 4 December 1974.

50 *Irish Times*, 15 November 1974, p. 1.

51 In view of the unionist orientation of the UDA, this may seem a contradictory statement. Basically, it arose because although the UDA demanded that Ulster remain British, it also came to the conclusion that the British may not wish to retain Ulster. Hence, the UDA's response was to opt for an Ulster identity, independent of Britain and the Republic of Ireland, which would preserve the Protestant character of the Province. For a brief exposition of this view see Andy Tyrie (supreme commander of the UDA), 'Independence is the Only Alternative', *Guardian Weekly*, 24 February 1980, p. 5.

52 The late arrival of the Sinn Fein delegation might also have suggested that the DIR was either an inefficient conduit or less 'Republican' than imagined.

53 *Belfast Telegraph*, 15 November 1977.

54 *Sunday Telegraph*, 22 December 1974. This claim was consistent with former IRA member Peter McMullen's 1979 claim that Libyan 'arms and *loans*' ran to $5 million per year (emphasis added). See *Boston Globe*, 2 September 1979, p. 12.

55 *Times*, 21 April 1975.

56 *Financial Times*, 23 April 1975.

57 *Irish Times*, 28 April 1975.

58 *Daily Express*, 26 August 1976; and *Financial Times*, 15 September 1975.

59 McKinley, PhD Thesis (see n. 25).

60 *Boston Globe*, 7 September 1979, p. 1.

61 *Ibid.* The abbreviation RPG stands for Rocket Propelled Grenade. Although the existence of the RPG-7 has been known since 1962, there is no such weapon as the RPG-5, or even an SA 5 or SAM 5 (both would refer to surface-to-air missiles). However, the urge to dimiss McMullen's account out of hand may be resisted in the knowledge that there is a weapon of similar appearance to the RPG-7, designated SA 7 [FWA Hobart (ed.), *Jane's Infantry Weapons 1975*, London: MacDonald and Jane's 1974, pp. 779–781.

62 A *Daily Mail* report, as cited in *Encounter* LIV, February 1980, p. 25.

63 *Irish Times*, 21 September 1978.

64 *Times*, 24 June 1978.
65 *London Sunday Times*, 25 June 1978.
66 Edward S Ellenberg, 'The PLO and its Place in Violence and Terror', *in* Livingston, Kress and Wanek (eds.), *International Terrorism in the Contemporary World*, Westport: Greenwood Press, 1978, p. 175.
67 Yonah Alexander, 'Terror International: The PLO–IRA Connection', *American Professors for Peace in the Middle East, Bulletin*, October 1979, p. 3 (hereafter cited as Alexander, 'The PLO–IRA Connection').
68 As cited in Yonah Alexander, 'Terrorism and the Media in the Middle East' *in* Yonah Alexander and Maxwell Finger (eds.), *Terrorism: Interdisciplinary Perspectives*, New York and Maidenhead, Berkshire: John Jay and McGraw-Hill, 1977, p. 177.
69 *Financial Times*, 11 December 1972.
70 According to Dr Garret Fitzgerald, it was just possible that the PLO did not altogether understand the nature of their association with the IRA. During Ireland's Presidency of the Council of Ministers of the European Community in 1975, he toured the countries of the Maghreb as one of his official duties, but in Algiers took the opportunity to hold discussions with a PLO spokesman. In the course of this Fitzgerald gained the impression that the PLO regarded the IRA as the 'Irish Government's underground army', and hence, Dublin's condemnation of their activities as no more than *pro forma* statements intended to placate (say) the British Government! With some difficulty, he attempted to persuade the PLO otherwise. Among his measures were the withholding of Irish Government support for various PLO demands, which were otherwise considered just, for as long as the organisation continued to support the IRA (Interview, 1978).
71 Paul Wilkinson, *Terrorism: International Dimensions*, Conflict Studies No. 113. London: Institute for the Study of Conflict, 1979, p. 8.
72 *Ibid.* Wilkinson claims that, in May 1972, the West German Embassy in Dublin was bombed by the IRA with the Baader–Meinhof gang claiming responsibility for the attack.
73 *Boston Sunday Globe*, 2 September 1979, p. 12.
74 *Guardian*, 25 March 1977.
75 'Terror International', BBC 1, 30 January 1978.
76 *Boston Sunday Globe*, 2 September 1979, p. 1.
77 *Irish Times*, 19 June 1978, p. 1.
78 *Ibid.*
79 Alexander, 'The PLO–IRA Connection', p. 3. He also claimed that others were being trained in Libya and Syria.
80 As cited in Charles Horner, 'The Facts About Terrorism', *Commentary*, June 1980, p. 42. This report also mentions three camps in South Yemen where members of 'terrorist groups from all over the world' receive training from Cuban, Russian and East German instructors, but it is not clear whether this description was intended to cover the IRA.
81 Robert Moss, 'PLO Trainees for Terror', *Daily Telegraph*, 1 December 1980.
82 *Boston Sunday Globe*, 2 September 1979, p. 12.
83 *International Herald Tribune*, 24–25 March 1979.
84 By his own account he faced an IRA court of inquiry (for refusing an assignment) in February 1978, and flew to the US in April 1978 to escape an IRA squad charged to kill him (*Boston Globe*, 6 September 1979, p. 2).
85 Alexander, 'The PLO–IRA Connection', p. 3.

86 John Barron, *KGB: The Secret Work of Soviet Secret Agents*, New York: Reader's Digest, 1974, p. 255. Bell claims they were 'donated to the anti-imperialist struggle by Colonel Qaddafi' (*The Secret Army*, p. 398).
87 *Irish Times*, 19 July 1978.
88 Bell, *The Secret Army*, pp. 437–438.
89 *Daily Telegraph*, 19 July 1978, p. 2.
90 House of Commons, *Official Report*, Vol. 949, 11 May 1978, col. 1378.
91 *Ibid.* (see also House of Commons, *Official Report*, Vol. 947), 13 April 1978, col. 1653.
92 *Ibid.*, col. 1388.
93 *Ibid.*, col. 1378.
94 Interview of Yasser Arafat by Barbara Walters for ABC Television News, 9 September 1979, as reported in the *Irish Times*, 10 September 1979, p. 1.
95 Coogan, *The IRA*, p. 543.
96 *Australian*, 15 July 1982.
97 *Daily Telegraph*, 20 August 1969.
98 *Irish Independent*, 13 May 1974.
99 *Times*, 7 June 1975.
100 *Toronto Star*, 17 July 1973, pp. 1 and 2. The Dublin seizure was made at the docks, upon containers loaded from a British freighter, the *Manchester Vigour*.
101 See McKinley, PhD Thesis (n. 25).
102 *Times*, 7 June 1975.
103 *Toronto Star*, 17 July 1973, pp. 1 and 2.
104 *Times*, 7 June 1975.
105 *Ibid.* According to information received from official sources, seven 'Irish immigrants' went to trial in Toronto in 1975 on charges of conspiring to export, and attempting to export, a machine gun, 20 semi-automatic rifles, 10 sten-guns and more than 8000 rounds of ammunition. Unfortunately, the writer has not been able to establish for certain whether the Myles *et al.* case was part of this general attempt, or a separate attempt entirely. But in the writer's opinion, it was probably the former.
106 *Toronto Star*, 17 July 1973, p. 1. In England, the *Daily Telegraph* was not impressed with Lysyk's modest assessment—it ignored his comments and carried the headline, 'Canadian Arms Ring Broken', *Daily Telegraph*, 18 July 1973.
107 Jones, 'Terrorist Weaponry in Northern Ireland', p. 21.
108 *Irish Times*, 19 August 1974.
109 *Daily Telegraph*, 11 June 1977.
110 *Irish Times*, 7 September 1977.
111 One source was of the opinion that certain shootings in Derry, because of the circumstances surrounding them, were either the work of a freelance operator, or hired killer who visited the city specifically for the operation and left again.
112 *Irish Times*, 29 December 1969.
113 Dennis J Clark, *Irish Blood: Northern Ireland and the American Conscience*, Port Washington, New York: Kennikat, 1977, pp. 31–33 (hereafter cited as Clark, *Irish Blood*).
114 *Ibid.*, p. 34.
115 *Ibid.*
116 J Bowyer Bell, *The Secret Army: The IRA, 1916–1970*, New York: John Day, 1971, p. 369.
117 *Ibid.*, p. 372, note 12.

118 *Times*, 26 August 1969, p. 2.
119 *Sunday Telegraph*, 19 October 1969. This may be an understated figure; Clark (*Irish Blood*, p. 19) claimed Devlin raised US$200,00 from her American visit.
120 *Financial Times*, 24 June 1970.
121 *Daily Telegraph*, 26 October 1972.
122 J Bowyer Bell, *The Secret Army: A History of the IRA*, Cambridge, Massachusetts: MIT Press, 1974, p. 373 (hereafter cited as Bell, *The Secret Army*). An even later edition of this work was published in 1980 by the Academy Press, Dublin, and covers the period to 1979.
123 Clark, *Irish Blood*, p. 39.
124 *Ibid.*, p. 19.
125 *Daily Telegraph*, 9 September 1971.
126 The clearest exposition of Provisional Republican socialist principles is to be found in a document published by (Provisional) Sinn Fein, from whom the Provisional IRA is only notionally separate, i.e., *Eire Nua* [*New Ireland*]*: The Social and Economic Programme of Sinn Fein*, Dublin: Sinn Fein, 1971.
127 Maria McGuire, *To Take Arms: A Year in the Provisional IRA*, London: Macmillan, 1973, p. 108 (hereafter cited as McGuire, *To Take Arms*).
128 Irish Northern Aid Committee, Registration No. 2239, two public files designated Section I and Section II respectively, held by the US Department of Justice at the Federal Triangle Building, 315 9th Street, Washington, DC (hereafter cited as US Department of Justice, NORAID files).
129 *Focus: The Irish Question*, by NORAID, 1975.
130 A Provisional IRA leader, who had barely escaped hanging for his part in the murder of a policeman in 1942, and who in 1973 was convicted of gun-running for his part in the *Claudia* affair (Cahill was the ranking Provisional on board the vessel when it was intercepted).
131 See the *Sunday Telegraph*, 10 December 1972, and *New York Times*, 16 December 1975, respectively.
132 Confidential Briefing Paper, Embassy of Ireland, Washington, DC, dated 17 April 1975 (hereafter cited as Embassy of Ireland, Briefing, 12 April 1975).
133 *Ibid.*
134 *Ibid.*
135 Higgins was McGowan's successor on the death of the latter in 1974.
136 Embassy of Ireland, Briefing, 17 April 1975.
137 *Irish People*, 26 April 1975. For an account of Dr Conor Cruise O'Brien's Comments on such 'infamous inventions', see the *Irish Times*, 30 April 1975.
138 Described as being the former 'commander of the Provisionals' Third Belfast Battalion' and also the 'first Chief of Staff of the Provisionals in Belfast' *Sunday Times* 'Insight' Team, *Ulster*, Harmondsworth, Middlesex: Penguin, 1972, pp. 25, 189.
139 IRA Chief of Staff in 1958–1959 and 1961–1962. In the period with which this discussion of NORAID is concerned (1970–1976), O Bradaigh was President of the Provisional Sinn Fein.
140 Embassy of Ireland, Briefing, 17 April 1975.
141 Christopher Dobson, 'How IRA gets guns and cash', *Sunday Telegraph*, 26 January 1975.
142 Embassy of Ireland, Briefing, 17 April 1975.
143 US Department of Justice, NORAID files.
144 *Daily Telegraph*, 26 October 1972.
145 US Department of Justice, NORAID files.

146 Daring as opposed to stupid—although the difference very often escapes the writer: the term murderous could be applied with equal validity to many of the operations in either category. Nevertheless, if the distinction is made, it might be noted that following the Birmingham bombings of 21 November 1974, the amounts reported by NORAID decreased and this trend may have been assisted by the narrow escape of Miss Caroline Kennedy from a London car-bombing in October 1975. On the other hand the murder of Lord Mountbatten in August 1979 evidently met with approval, if the returns are any indication (see next section). It is likely, of course, that other influences contributed to these results, but these appear not to have detracted from the strength of the perception noted in the above text.

147 Interview, United States Department of Justice, Washington, DC, 1979 (hereafter cited as Department of Justice Interview, 1979).

148 Embassy of Ireland, Briefing, 17 April 1975. Publicly (in 1975), Deidre Ó Connaill, wife of Daithi Ó Connaill (then a member of the Provisional's ruling Army Council), admitted that NORAID was sending US$36,000 *per week* (US$1,872,000 per year) to Northern Ireland (*Daily Express*, 4 February 1975).

149 *Daily Express*, 4 February 1975.

150 Anthony John Francis O'Reilly, an outstanding international rugby footballer in the mid-1950s and early 1960s, whose achievements in business matched those in sport. His life and business interests require him to live both in Ireland and the United States—in the latter of which he is widely known as President of the Heinz Foods conglomerate. According to an associate editor of *Fortune*, 'O'Reilly, . . . figuratively speaking, has the longest reach of any living Irishman'. See Thomas J O'Hanlon, *The Irish: Sinners, Saints, Gamblers, etc.*, New York: Harper and Row, 1975, p. 256.

151 David McKittrick, 'Irish Everywhere in the Land of Immigrants', the first of four major articles on the Irish in America, *Irish Times*, 3 September 1979, p. 10. The proceeds of such functions go towards Irish charities and, according to McKittrick's report, 'O'Reilly's efforts raise much more than those groups associated with Republican causes'.

152 Clark, *Irish Blood*, p. 40. Although the Catholic Church in America was one of the principal agents in breaking down the ethnic identity of Irish–Americans since the late nineteenth century, and although it avoided taking up the issue of Northern Ireland after 1969, certain clerics within it have provided what might be termed 'moral' support which may have been sufficient, when viewed through some eyes, to have countered any residual qualms about supporting organisations which subsidised or engaged in violence. In this, three clerics were prominent: Bishop Drury of Corpus Christi Diocese, Texas, who appeared publicly with Ruairi O Bradaigh and was a frequent speaker at NORAID functions; Fr Sean McManus, national chaplain to the Ancient Order of Hibernians, and National Co-ordinator of the Irish National Caucus in the US; and Sister St Hugh of NORAID, New York, who was at one time editor of the *Irish People* (Embassy of Ireland, Briefing, 17 April 1975).

153 *Ibid.*, pp. 33 and 67.

154 *Ibid.*, p. 75.

155 As reported in the *Irish Times*, 20 October 1971.

156 *Washington Post*, 16 March 1972.

157 *New York Times*, 16 December 1975.

158 *Daily Express*, 8 January 1976, in conjunction with *International Herald Tribune*, 14 January 1976.

159 Radio Telefis Eireann Transcript of Radio 1 programme, 'This Week', Report No. N. 149 of 7 November 1982.
160 *Dublin Sunday Independent*, 14 March 1976.
161 Embassy of Ireland, Briefing, 17 April 1975. It is regretted that, in relation to the above trials, it has not proved possible to obtain evidence from official US sources. Unfortunately, the writer's written and verbal requests to the Bureau of Alcohol, Tobacco and Firearms (BATF), Department of the Treasury, met with no success in this regard. Information concerning Malone, O'Gara and two others not cited, was refused under the general provisions of the Privacy Act 1974, and by the specific requirement that the written consent of those whose record was to be examined, be obtained. [Letter to the writer, from the Assistant to the Director (Disclosure), BATF, 12 October 1979.]
162 Embassy of Ireland, Briefing, 17 April 1975.
163 *Sunday Herald Advertiser*, 9 June 1974.
164 *Times*, 7 June 1975.
165 Cahalane had previously spent five-and-a-half months in jail in 1973 for refusing to testify to a Federal Grand Jury.
166 For a brief reference to this case, the recovery by the British authorities in Northern Ireland of almost half the arms in question, and the subsequent loss of Byrne and Cahalane's appeal to the Supreme Court, see the *Times*, 24 January 1978.
167 *Times*, 16 August 1969.
168 *Sunday Telegraph*, 18 February 1973. A denial by the IRA was reported in the *Daily Telegraph*, 30 March 1973.
169 *Sunday Telegraph*, 1 April 1973.
170 Proprietors of the *Daily Telegraph* and *Sunday Telegraph*.
171 As reported in the *Daily Telegraph*, 10 January 1976. Prime Minister Harold Wilson made a similar claim at this time which deserves inclusion because of the different inferences, emphasised in the following, which he appeared to draw from recovery information: 'The fact is that most of the *modern* weapons now reaching the terrorists in Northern Ireland are of American origin, possibly as much as eighty-five per cent of them. They are *bought in the United States* and they are bought with American donated money', London Press Service, Verbatim Service, 'IRA Fund Raising', 243/75, 17 December 1975, an extract from Wilson's speech to the Association of American Correspondents, Savoy Hotel, London, 17 December 1975.
172 Parliamentary Debates, House of Commons, *Official Report*, Vol. 901, 4 December 1975, col. 1924 (hereafter cited as House of Commons, *Official Report*). See in conjunction with Jones, 'Terrorist Weaponry in Northern Ireland', p. 17.
173 As reported in the *London Sunday Times*, 2 November 1975.
174 Jones, 'Terrorist Weaponry in Northern Ireland', p. 24 (see Table 1).
175 *International Herald Tribune*, 25 September 1979, p. 3. According to this report 2300 of a grand total of 10,000 weapons conformed to the above description.
176 Bell, *The Secret Army*, p. 373; and Jones, 'Terrorist Weaponry in Northern Ireland', p. 24.
177 Interview with William V Shannon, United States Ambassador to Ireland, Dublin, 24 April 1978 (hereafter cited as Shannon Interview). The Ambassador also mentioned the involvement of some stewardesses of Aer Lingus in smuggling small quantities of arms into Ireland.
178 Jones, 'Terrorist Weaponry in Northern Ireland', p. 17.

179 *Ibid.*, p. 19.
180 *Ibid.*, *Note*: the M3 SMG was capable of automatic fire and hence illegal in the United States; nevertheless it was believed by the British authorities that this weapon was also obtained in the US, probably on the Black Market (*Ibid.*, p. 17).
181 *New York Times*, 14 March 1973.
182 Bell, *The Secret Army*, pp. 439 and 446n, and Coogan, *The IRA*, p. 538n.
183 Jones, 'Terrorist Weaponry in Northern Ireland', p. 24. As this is not a technical discussion, specific reference to calibre types has been omitted, but they (eight pistol and nine rifle calibres) are to be found in the article cited. *Note*: Jones makes no mention of *where* the IRA's pistol inventory was obtained from, but it is clear from his account (when used in conjunction with a small arms reference manual) that it was predominantly of non-US manufacture.
184 McGuire, *To Take Arms*, p. 40.
185 Clark, *Irish Blood*, p. 69.
186 *Irish Times*, 21 June 1977.
187 *Flight International*, 18 March 1978, p. 756. The helicopter in question crashed close to the village of Jonesboro, Co. Armagh, in February 1978, killing the Commanding Officer of the 2nd Battalion, Royal Green Jackets, Lieutenant Colonel Corden-Lloyd. *Note*: The above explanation of the crash is not universally accepted: one respected historian of the IRA accepts its claim that the *Gazelle* was shot down—see Tim Pat Coogan, *The IRA*, rev. and exp. edn. London: Fontana, 1980, pp. 481 and 510 (hereafter cited as Coogan, *The IRA*).
188 *Irish Times*, 21 September 1978.
189 J Bowyer Bell, *The Secret Army: The IRA 1916–1979*, rev. and updated edn. Dublin: Academy Press, 1979, p. 438; and Coogan, *The IRA*, p. 476.
190 *Guardian Weekly*, 19 October 1980, p. 5. This report also records that another American-made countersurveillance device was acquired at this time, but from Dublin where it was openly available—cheap receiver which could detect the man-detecting radar used by the Special Air Services at observation posts along the border.
191 i.e., approximately 2300 of 10,000 weapons were said to be of US manufacture (*International Herald Tribune*, 25 September 1979, p. 3).
192 *International Herald Tribune*, 30 July 1981.
193 *Guardian Weekly*, 9 August 1981, p. 16.
194 *International Herald Tribune*, 2 March 1982, p. 5.
195 *Times*, 10 February 1982, p. 6.
196 Irish Northern Aid Committee, Registration No. 2239, two public files designated Section I and Section II respectively, held by the US Department of Justice at the Federal Triangle Building, 315 9th Street, Washington, DC (hereafter cited as US Department of Justice, NORAID files). The figures for 31 July 1980 onwards were supplied by the Registration Unit, Internal Security Section, Criminal Division, US Department of Justice, Washington, DC, in answer to the writer's letter of inquiry; unfortunately the extracts from NORAID's returns did not show the additional data concerning expenditure and disbursements. As of July 1982, NORAID had failed to provide its returns for January the same year.
197 *Times*, 23 February 1982, p. 24.
198 The month-by-month breakdown of income by NORAID supports this interpretation: of the $105,000 subscribed, over $55,000 was received in December and January. The targets attacked were the Hammersmith Territorial

Barracks, the Royal Air Force base at Uxbridge and the Bromley-by-Bow gas works (*Guardian*, 18 January 1981, p. 4).

199 In the campaign itself ten Republican prisoners (IRA and INLA) starved themselves to death; on the streets civilians and members of the security forces died as the violence increased.

200 *Irish Times*, 3 July 1978.

201 Dennis J Clark, *Irish Blood: Northern Ireland and the American Conscience*, Port Washington, New York: Kennikat, 1977, p. 69 (hereafter cited as Clark, *Irish Blood*).

202 Conor O'Clery, 'US Is Watching Provisional Fund-raising', No. 2 of a series entitled Report from Washington, *Irish Times*, 19 January 1978.

203 Clark, *Irish Blood*, p. 69.

204 *International Herald Tribune*, 8–9 September 1979, p. 1; and Interview (in 1979) at Consulate-General for Ireland, New York.

205 An organisation, composed mainly of women founded in 1976 and generally associated in the public eye with the work of Betty Williams and Mairead Corrigan, who introduced a note of hope, based on Christian love and tolerance, into the otherwise violent atmosphere of Northern Ireland. In 1977, Corrigan and Williams were recognised by the award of the Nobel Peace Prize for the preceding year. It should be noted, however, that the Movement had, by 31 March 1978, received only £900 in donations from the US (*Daily Telegraph*, 24 April 1978). See also Dalry O'Donnell, *The Peace People of Northern Ireland*, Camberwell, Victoria, Australia: Widescope, 1977.

206 Interview, FCO.

207 The bombing of an Army Officers' Mess at Aldershot, on 22 February 1972, which killed six civilians and a Roman Catholic chaplain was claimed by the Officials.

208 Persons so described were generally held to be responsible for the Dublin and Monaghan car bombings which claimed 28 lives in the space of three hours on 17 May 1974.

209 In March 1979, the INLA murdered the Conservative Party's principal spokesman on Northern Ireland as he was leaving the House of Commons car park. According to McMullen, Provisional IRA cooperation was provided (*Boston Sunday Globe*, 2 September 1979, p. 12). However, David O'Connell (Daithi Ó Connaill), then of Provisional Sinn Fein, denied this (*International Herald Tribune*, 27 November 1980, p. 4).

210 A fatal kidnapping undertaken by a small group of volunteers without official approval of the IRA command. See Bell, *The Secret Army*, pp. 406–407.

211 However, the Provisionals have, on at least two occasions, hijacked a goods train on the main Belfast–Dublin railway and blown it up. See *Daily Telegraph*, 30 December 1975; and *Times*, 21 November 1978.

212 In 1978 approximately one-quarter of the UDR's strength was on full-time duties.

213 In the absence of official figures in the last few years the figure of 5000 was estimated by the writer, perhaps generously, to allow for the increase in the numbers of the security forces on Border duties since mid-1974, when it was nearly 3000 (Dail Eireann, Parliamentary Debates, *Offical Report*, Vol. 273, 26 June 1974, col. 1576). Even if the estimated figure is inflated, the order of comparability is not greatly affected.

214 *Guardian*, 19 October 1980, p. 5. The report cited was a private assessment stolen from military intelligence *by the IRA* in 1979, and released by it. However,

the authenticity of Document 37, as it was formerly titled, was admitted by the British Government (*Canberra Times*, 12 May 1979).

215 McGuire, *To Take Arms*, p. 92.

216 This motive, a consequence of Bloody Sunday, was clearly behind the Aldershot bombing of 22 February 1972 (see Bell, *The Secret Army*, p. 385).

217 The rash of bombings in London and Manchester in January 1975 was designed specifically for this purpose (Whale and Ryder, 'Decade of Despair', p. 15).

218 Two incidents in 1974, the bombing of a coach on the M62 carrying servicemen and their families (12 dead), and explosions at Army barracks at Guildford and Woolwich (7 dead) were timed to coincide with the British election campaign of February and October/November of that year respectively (*Ibid.*, p. 16).

219 As cited in ATQ Stewart, *The Narrow Ground: Aspects of Ulster, 1609–1969*, London: Faber and Faber, 1977, p. 12.

Terrorism in the United States during 1985

B Hoffman

INTRODUCTION

Events throughout 1985 demonstrated repeatedly the threat posed to United States interests and citizens by terrorists abroad. During a year in which there were record highs both in the number of terrorist incidents worldwide and their resultant fatalities, the hijacking of a TWA airliner in June, the murder that same month of four American servicemen in El Salvador, the pirating of an Italian cruise ship in October, seizure of an Egypt Air plane in November and the massacre of American travellers in Rome and Vienna the following month underscored a long-standing pattern of international terrorism. The United States is—and has long been—the number one target of a variety of foreign terrorist organisations. Indeed, of the approximately four hundred and fifty acts of terrorism during 1985 recorded in the Rand Corporation's terrorism chronology,[1] a quarter (111) were directed against American targets.

At the same time, however, the United States itself—as has also long been the case—remained relatively insulated from these escalations of terrorist violence. Moreover, a preliminary examination of 1985 statistics from Rand's chronology reveals that there was a decline in the number of terrorist incidents in that country from fifty-one incidents in 1984 to twenty-four during the past year.

However heartening this development may be, or however small this total appears in comparison with the worldwide figure, we should not be lulled into thinking that the United States is either immune to violence from political extremists within its own borders or that the terrorist acts which occur there do not warrant attention.

But before I discuss what I see as some sources of concern, let me briefly consider first, why there has been comparatively so little terrorism in the United States and, second, some of the likely reasons behind last year's decline in terrorist incidents.

TERRORISM IN THE UNITED STATES: AN OVERVIEW

Although the United States is the country most frequently targeted by terrorists abroad, it is near the bottom of the list in terms of the number of terrorist attacks within its own borders.[2] Moreover, despite the fact that the United States has the highest crime and homicide rates in the industrialised Western world (as well as the greatest number of both legal and illegal weapons in the possession of its citizenry), politically motivated crimes are relatively infrequent.[3] The terrorist statistics compiled annually by the Federal Bureau of Investigation (FBI) indicate that only 29 incidents were recorded in that country in 1980, 42 in 1981, 51 in 1982, 31 in 1983 and 13 in 1984.[4] By comparison, France had 102 reported terrorist incidents in 1980, 59 in 1981, 56 in 1982 and 122 in 1983; Italy experienced 118 terrorist attacks in 1980, 72 in 1981, 26 in 1982 and 9 in 1983; and West Germany recorded 21 acts of terrorism in 1980, 37 in 1981, 28 in 1982 and 6 in 1983.[5]

There are several possible reasons for the relatively low incidence of politically motivated violence in the United States. First, the United States is not a politically polarised country. Unlike France, Italy or Germany, where a variety of political parties represent the extremes of the ideological spectrum in national politics, the United States has traditionally been a two-party country. Moreover, the two parties differ little in actual substance from one another. Another possible factor inhibiting terrorism in the United States may be that country's unparalleled upwards economic and social mobility, which provides opportunities for social and economic advancement. In addition, the United States is a politically absorptive society. Since the turn of the century, American politics have been to a great extent ethnic politics, and immigrants have been readily absorbed by the major political parties and integrated into the American political system. Finally, while other Western nations have violent irredentist groups,[6] there are none in the United States, except for a Puerto Rican faction.

Three types of terrorist organisations, however, do exist in the United States:

Ethnic separatist and émigré groups.

Left-wing radical organisations.

Right-wing racist, anti-authority, survivalist-type groups.[7]

Approximately two-thirds of all terrorism in the United States is carried out by ethnic–separatist or émigré terrorists.[8] Their causes and grievances often have little or nothing to do with domestic United States politics; the United States is simply the battleground where their foreign quarrels are fought. Of the three types of terrorist organisations in the United States, the ethnic/émigré groups have generally shown themselves to be the most persistent and violent (in other words, their operations tend to inflict the highest numbers of casualties). These groups also spawn successor generations of younger terrorists. However, despite the potentially wide appeal of these organisations within their own communities, the narrow focus of their parochial, ethnic-centred causes means that they have a far smaller political constituency than ideological terrorist groups have. Support comes only from other ethnic/émigré groups in scattered, tightly knit communities around the country.

In contrast, left-wing radicals and other issue-oriented groups have a much wider constituency because of the broader political nature of their causes. They are also usually less lethal than their ethnic/émigré counterparts. They engage mostly in symbolic bombings to call attention to themselves and their causes, but they are generally careful not to undertake actions that might alienate potential supporters or their perceived constituency. Although some of the leftist groups justify their existence and operations with vague references to Marxist–Leninist dicta, others are quite specific in their reactions to various contentious political issues.

Radical leftist groups have existed in one form or another since the late 1960s. They originated in student movements that were organised to protest United States involvement in the Vietnam War (such as the Students for a Democratic Society or SDS). When the war ended and the United States withdrew from Southeast Asia, the related protests and terrorist violence declined. In recent years, US involvement in Central America and South Africa's apartheid policy have given new life to left-wing groups such as the Weather Underground and the Black Liberation Army (BLA). These issues have also led to the creation of new, more narrowly focused, leftist-leaning groups, including the Revolutionary Armed Task Force, the United Freedom Front and the Armed Resistance Unit.

The right-wing terrorists appear to embrace traits of both the ethnic separatists and left-wing terrorists. They are extremely violent, have no reservations about killing, spawn successor generations, and are often oriented towards specific political issues. Right-wing groups can be divided into specific, issue-oriented terrorists (for example, anti-abortion crusaders in amorphous entities like the 'Army of God') and traditional hate-groups. In recent years, several racist and reactionary groups have surfaced in the West, the South and the Midwest. Their members include anti-federalists, anti-Semites, racists, survivalists and Christian fundamentalists. Although related to the Ku Klux Klan and various American Nazi groups, the newer organisations—the Aryan Nations, the Posse Comitatus, the Order, the Covenant, the Sword and the Arm of the Lord—not only champion the old dogmas of a racially pure, Christian United States with no Jews, Blacks, communists, Catholics or atheists, they are also violently opposed to any form of government above the county level, are militantly anti-abortionist, publicly advocate the overthrow of the US government and in many cases, advocate the extermination of Jews.

The tactic most commonly used by US-based terrorists (like terrorists worldwide) is bombing. Bombings provide a dramatic, but relatively easy, means of drawing attention to the terrorists and their causes. Most of the explosions take place at times or in places chosen to cause as few casualties as possible. Emphasis on the use of bombs usually indicates that a terrorist group is at a somewhat 'primitive stage' in its development and lacks the organisational expertise, logistics or knowledge to engage in more complicated or coordinated operations. Few skills are required to manufacture a crude bomb, or to plant one in the dead of night and then be miles away when it explodes.

The emergence of new extremist right-wing groups, however, may herald a new type of American terrorism. The members of these groups are considerably more skilled with weapons than other terrorists in the United States. Many, in fact, are accomplished armourers for whom converting semi-automatic weapons to fully automatic machine guns is not difficult. They have large stockpiles of sophisticated weapons, are well-trained in survival techniques and outdoor living and possess an apocalyptic vision of the future, in contrast to the more neatly defined political aims of the other types of terrorist groups in the United States.

REASONS FOR THE DECLINE

One reason, undoubtedly, is the continuing success achieved by the FBI as well as state and local law-enforcement agencies in tracking down and arresting wanted and suspected terrorists. For example, in September 1985, thirteen key members of two Puerto Rican separatist groups, the FALN (the Spanish acronym of 'Armed Forces for National Liberation') and the *Macheteros*, were arrested in Boston, Dallas, Puerto Rico and Mexico. This was but the latest in a series of blows dealt to the separatists by government agencies that began with the capture of eleven FALN members in 1980, the group's premiere bomb-maker, William Morales, in 1983 and four other group members that same year. Thus, whereas Puerto Rican separatists had been the most active terrorists in the United States—having committed some one hundred and sixty-one acts of violence between 1977 and 1984—they were responsible for just one incident in 1985.

Widespread arrests of members of other ethnic terrorist organisations, such as those in the United States large Armenian and Cuban exile communities, have similarly undermined these two movements. Between 1980 and 1982, for instance, fifteen attacks were staged by Armenian terrorists, with no further terrorist operations since. The abrupt suspension of Armenian violence is undoubtedly due in part to the harsh prison sentence handed down to Hampig Sassounian, who was convicted of murdering the Turkish Consul-General in Los Angeles, and the arrests in October 1982 of five other Armenian youths who were en route from Los Angeles to Philadelphia on a bombing mission.

At one time, anti-Castro Cuban militants were among the most active terrorists in the United States. During 1980 and 1983, they are credited with thirty-two acts of terrorism. However, the apprehension of six key members of the Omega-7 group during 1982 and of their leader, Eduardo Arocena, in

1983, so severely crippled the anti-Castro terrorist movement that no further incidents have occurred.

In the case of all three of these ethnic/émigré terrorist movements another reason for their respective declines may be simple disillusionment and exhaustion among old members and the waning enthusiasm of potential recruits. One of the distinguishing characteristics of ethnic/émigré terrorism in the United States has been their ability—unlike issue-oriented, left-wing terrorists, for example—to spawn successor generations. Young members of these ethnic communities, inculcated with the folklore of past acts of heroism and daring by their elders, once formed an eager pool of recruits to the terrorist organisations. It appears, however, that as the goals of the terrorists have become increasingly distant despite years of effort—either to bring about the creation of an independent and sovereign Puerto Rico, obtain recognition from Turkey for Armenian claims of events that took place over seventy years ago or overthrow Castro and liberate Cuba from communism—and their violence has brought no tangible results, the ardour of both old members and potential recruits has waned.

Continuing friction in relations between the United States and Libya has recently been cited as increasing the likelihood of Libyan 'hit-squads' being deployed to the United States. On at least two occasions in the past, state-sponsored terrorist acts—allegedly carried out at the behest of Libyan leader Mu'ammar Qaddafi—have in fact occurred. It should be emphasised that Libyan actions in the United States have been restricted to attacks on Libyan nationals and not directed against American targets there. Nevertheless, in October 1980, a Libyan graduate student in Colorado was seriously wounded and the following July another Libyan student was found murdered in Utah. Further assassinations, however, were probably prevented by the arrest of two Libyan students in August 1984 when they attempted to purchase silencer-equipped small arms from undercover FBI agents.

Indeed, continuous monitoring of Libyan student activity here resulted in the creation of a special federal grand jury in June 1985 to investigate evidence of other assassination plots directed against at least three Libyan opponents of the Qaddafi regime. Some fifteen Libyans resident in the United States were subpoenaed to appear before the jury. Whether by coincidence or not, shortly after the grand jury began to hear testimony, a Libyan diplomat attached to his country's UN delegation was deported on grounds of his involvement in planning the assassination of Libyan dissidents here.

Inroads have been made against left-wing terrorists as well. On 11 May 1985, federal authorities arrested Marilyn Jean Buck, one of the handful of suspects still at large from the botched hold up of a Brinks armoured truck in Nyack, New York in 1981. Evidence discovered in the safehouse used by Buck linked her and two accomplices to sixteen bombings that had occurred in the New York and Washington DC areas since 1982—including the US Capitol building in November 1983. In March 1985, seven members of the United Freedom Front (UFF), another leftist group, were indicted on charges of bombing a total of ten businesses and military installations in the New York metropolitan area. The arrest of the seven seriously undermined their organisation as evinced by the fact that the last action claimed by the UFF was in September 1984—just two months before the first wave of arrests which resulted in the March indictments.

Unlike ethnic/émigré terrorists, domestic left-wing radicals have always had trouble recruiting new members to their organisations. To a great extent, the majority of the left-wing organisations are simply recycled versions of radical groups that first surfaced in the late 1960s and early 1970s to oppose United States involvement in Southeast Asia. The apprehension of the seven UFF terrorists is a case in point, as it was discovered that the group was in fact an almost identical—but renamed—version of the decade-old Melville-Jackson Group. In this respect, then, arrests of members have a particularly devastating effect on the leftist groups since they are unable to replenish their ranks easily. Hence it is not surprising that there has been a dramatic decline in left-wing terrorist activity in the United States. The lone attack in 1985 credited to a left-wing group (the Red Guerrilla Defence) was the February bombing of the Police Benevolent Association offices in New York City.

INCREASES IN DOMESTIC TERRORIST ACTIVITY AND OTHER SOURCES OF CONCERN

JEWISH TERRORISM

The only increase in domestic terrorist activity came from Jewish extremists—who, according to the FBI, are associated with the Jewish Defence League (JDL). Despite the fact that the JDL is a perfectly legal entity—incorporated under New York State law and enjoying tax-exempt status because of its religious affiliation—the group has not only long been classified as a terrorist organisation by the FBI, but has been cited as the United States second most active one.[9] Indeed, between 1977 and 1984, thirty-seven acts of terrorism were attributed to the JDL by FBI officials. Moreover, during the past decade or so, at least fifty indictments have been handed down to JDL members of whom at least thirty have been convicted in United States courts of committing, or conspiring to commit, terrorist offences.

During the past ten years, as the JDL experienced a decline in membership and influence, the threat that it posed appeared to be primarily symbolic. The group used terrorism to draw attention to itself and its causes, to maintain momentum and perpetuate its image as an 'action-oriented', non-traditional, Jewish pressure group. Recent events, however, suggest that this view requires revision. The recent increase of militant Jewish terrorism represents not only an escalation of violence but a significant change in targeting patterns, as well as a dramatic shift in tactics.

Twelve times as many terrorist acts have either been claimed by or are alleged to have been carried out by Jewish extremists in 1985 as in either 1983 or 1984 (one incident occurred in each of the two earlier years). Whereas Soviet property and diplomatic personnel were previously the terrorists' primary targets, only two attacks in 1985 were connected with the Soviet Union. Rather, it now appears that the terrorists primary focus has shifted to organisations and individuals perceived by them as hostile to Jewish interests.

This is not an entirely new development. As far back as 1976 the JDL had already begun to expand its scope of activities to include Iraqi, Iranian, Egyptian, Palestinian, Lebanese, French and German targets. But these operations were isolated and infrequent and were consistently overshadowed by the group's pre-occupation with the issue of Soviet Jewry. There appears now to be a concentration of effort against persons and institutions considered to be enemies of Jews and Israel. Targets now include alleged former Nazis and war criminals, Palestinian and Arab individuals and institutions, and persons and so-called research centres promoting views about the Holocaust that minimise the dimensions of Jewish suffering.

Perhaps the most far-reaching change, however, is the increasing use of assassination, both to draw attention to the terrorists' causes and to eliminate perceived enemies of the Jewish people and Israel. This is an ominous development. Political violence does not occur in a vacuum and is responsive to both internal and external stimuli. In the case of the JDL, the internal stimulus undoubtedly comes from the decline in membership and financial contributions that the group has experienced in recent years. By expanding its targets, Jewish extremists—as other terrorists have attempted—may also be trying to appeal to a larger and more diverse constituency. This could represent a bid to regain the momentum and duplicate the JDL's successes of the 1970s.

External stimuli probably include the growing sense of unease felt by Jews in the United States as a result of the anti-Semitic insinuations and proclamations issued by the Reverend Louis Farrakhan, leader of the Black Muslim Nation of Islam; the growing evidence of a widespread network of right-wing and Neo-Nazi extremists in the United States; the hijacking of a TWA aircraft in June 1985 by radical Shi'as in which Jewish passengers were separated from Gentiles; and the murder of Leon Klinghoffer (an American Jew who was a passenger on the Italian cruise ship seized by Palestinian terrorists in October 1985). All of these developments have alarmed Jews, and more important, they may have convinced the terrorists that the Jewish public has become more amenable to and supportive of militant Jewish activity.

RIGHT-WING EXTREMISM

Another significant area of concern is the growth of right-wing extremist activity in the United States. Although organised hate-groups such as the Ku Klux Klan and various incarnations of Hitler's National Socialist (Nazi) party have existed in the United States for decades, the advent of extremist White supremacist/paramilitary groups oriented towards 'survivalism', outdoor skills, guerrilla training and outright sedition—such as the Aryan Nations, the Order, the Covenant, the Sword and the Arm of the Lord (CSA) and the Posse Comitatus—is a newer phenomenon. Although the geographical locus of the movement is in the West, Mid-West and South of the United States, the extremists' network extends as far east as North Carolina and Georgia, west to California and the Pacific northwest states and on a north–south axis embracing Texas and Canada.

The members of these groups are, for the most part, not full-time terrorists as is often the case with their leftist counterparts.[10] Rather, they see themselves as 'minutemen': the inheritors of the tradition of the American Revolution's 'minutemen' who were available at a moment's notice 'to fight for their inalienable rights'. They are bound together by their shared hostility to any form of government above the county level; their vilification of Jews and non-Whites as children of Satan; their obsession with achieving the religious and racial purification of the United States; their belief in a conspiracy theory of powerful Jewish interests controlling the government, banks and media; and their advocacy of the overthrow of the US government, or 'Zionist Occupation Government', as they call it.

During 1985, twenty-three members of the Order were apprehended in twelve states, eleven of whom were convicted of a variety of offences under federal racketeering statutes in December. But the incarceration of what appears to have been the nucleus of the Order and the death thirteen months earlier of the group's founder and leader, Robert Matthews, does not, however, mean that the group has been completely neutralised. There are indications that throughout 1984 and 1985 members of the Order were busy establishing a network of safehouses and support cells in the southwestern and southeastern regions of the United States. Indeed, the organisation of the group was such that the identities of many members still at large are not known. Security measures used by the Order included requirements that members carry false identification (often names taken from headstones at local cemeteries) at all times, and the use of disguises and code-names.

Another potential threat from the right comes from the organisation calling itself the Posse Comitatus. The basic *raison d'être* of the Posse Comitatus is anti-federalism. Its members are opposed to the federal and state income tax, the existence of the Federal Reserve System and the supremacy of the federal judiciary over local courts. Federal and state taxes in particular are decried as 'Communist and unconstitutional'; and a return to the gold standard and abolition of the Federal Reserve Bank are advocated.

Throughout the 1970s, local chapters of the organisation were founded in almost every state in the United States. According to one observer, 'The group maintained a low profile, concentrating on passive tax protest activities, such as providing legal counsel for tax evaders and prompting constitutional justification for local county rules and powers'. However, during 1984 and 1985, Posse Comitatus 'has become more violent, particularly in the midwest and far northwest'.[11] To some extent this trend has been fuelled by the plight of financially depressed farmers in those regions. Searching for an answer to their economic predicament, these persons become susceptible to facile political and religious interpretations of their problems and responsive to grandiose conspiracy theories of secret cabals composed of Jews, bankers and the US Federal Government to explain their situation. As Dixon Terry, chairman of the Iowa Farm Unit Coalition, explained, 'Farmers are victims of the hate propaganda and phony schemes of a surprisingly strong, organized right-wing element'.[12]

Reports of increasing extremist and White supremacist recruitment activity and propaganda efforts aimed at Midwestern farmers have surfaced throughout the past year. Ku Klux Klan publications such as *The White Patriot*, the fledgling Populist Party's organ, *The Spotlight* and the extremist National Agricultural Press Association's (now discontinued) *Primrose and Cattleman's Gazette* have appealed to farmers to stop paying taxes, ignore state and federal judicial authority, abjure from using US currency and arm themselves. The present farm crisis is blamed on 'bankers and Zionists operating through the Federal Reserve System'. As the KKK publication declared, 'To put it simply, the Jew plan is to steal your land'.[13]

There is also evidence of growing right-wing extremist involvement in the anti-abortion issue. The Posse Comitatus, in particular, has stated in its publications that abortion is part of the global conspiracy 'masterminded' by the Jews.[14] Nor is this type of twisted thinking isolated in the poorer, rural and less cosmopolitan regions of the United States. The recorded telephone message of an Orange County, California group, the White American Resistance, informed callers that:

> Almost all abortion doctors are Jews. Abortion makes money for Jews. Almost all abortion nurses are lesbians. Abortion gives a thrill to lesbians. Abortion in Orange County is promoted by the corrupt Jewish organization called Planned Parenthood. ... Jews would do anything for money, including the rape of innocent children followed by the ripping and tearing of the living child from the young mother's womb, while it is still forming. Jews must be punished for this holocaust and murder of white children, along with their perverted lesbian nurses who enjoy their jobs too much.[15]

Moreover, despite a decline in the number of abortion clinic bombings in 1985 (five as compared to twenty-one during 1984), there appears to have been a significant change in the anti-abortionist terrorists' tactics. In December 1985, for example a small bomb exploded in a New York City abortion clinic that was 'full of patients and staff'. A last-minute call to police warning of the bomb enabled the building to be evacuated shortly before the explosion took place. As Faye Wattleton, president of the Planned Parenthood Federation of America, explained, 'Until recently, all attacks have occurred under the cover of darkness during times when there was some hope that no one would be hurt by bombs or arson. [This] bomb exploded in mid-afternoon, with clinic patients and staff on the premises'.[16]

Far more disquieting, however, was the *large* parcel bomb mailed to a Portland, Oregon clinic that was designed to explode upon opening. A clinic staff member, instructed to look for suspicious packages, alerted police who safely defused the device. Postal authorities in Portland subsequently discovered three other mail bombs addressed to two abortion clinics and a Planned Parenthood clinic that does not, in fact, perform abortions. This incident, the first demonstrating a deliberate intent to kill someone—along with the New York incident—suggests an alarming change in militant anti-abortion tactics.

CONCLUSION: FUTURE PROSPECTS IN DOMESTIC TERRORISM

Despite an overall decline in terrorism in the United States during 1985, there remain sources of concern that merit continued attention and vigilance. Among them is the upsurge in violence by Jewish militants, the existence of a widespread network of volatile, right-wing extremist organisations and the ominous apparent shift in the nature of anti-abortion terrorist operations.

The increase in Jewish terrorism does not necessarily imply a continued escalation of such activity in the United States. Past events have demonstrated how periodical outbursts of concentrated violence are often followed by dramatic declines in terrorist operations because of heightened attention from federal and local law-enforcement agencies. Nevertheless, terrorist incidents that occur abroad and specifically target or indirectly involve Jews from the United States or elsewhere, may provoke deliberately retaliatory or revenge-minded strikes and create a dangerous cycle of international terrorism and domestic, vigilante, responses.

Although there is an almost natural inclination to dismiss right-wing extremists and White-supremacists as intemperate hot-heads, uneducated 'country bumpkins' or mentally unstable alarmists, they have demonstrated that they are serious in their beliefs and dedicated to their causes and, moreover, are willing to use violence in pursuit of their goals. The Neo-Nazis, anti-Semites, racists and 'survivalists' who comprise this geographically widespread network of groups are not the isolated, technically unsophisticated, crude pipe-bomb manufacturers who have dominated most of the US-based terrorist groups in the past. They are well-trained in the use of arms and explosives, are skilled armourers and bomb-makers and are adept at guerrilla warfare techniques and outdoor survival. They are violent and, more confounding to the analyst, they are mercurial and unpredictable.

Further, the right-wing terrorists embody many of the traits typical of both ethnic/émigré and left-wing terrorists. The rightists, like the ethnic/émigré groups, are more violent than their leftist counterparts, have been able to replenish their ranks with new recruits and, like the left-wing terrorists, are motivated in some cases by controversial, popular political issues (such as abortion) to enlarge their power base.

One of the difficulties faced by the analyst attempting to forecast terrorist trends in the United States is the small number of incidents that annually occur here. This paucity of data—combined with the volatile and dynamic character of terrorism itself—attaches a pre-eminent qualification to analyses of future prospects. Suffice it to say, that while the number of terrorist incidents in the United States is relatively small compared with those overseas and, moreover, is statistically insignificant compared to the amount of violent domestic (non-political) crimes, they nevertheless merit continued attention and should not be dismissed completely.

NOTES

1 As of 7 January 1986, 438 terrorist incidents had been recorded in the Rand chronology. Past experience, however, suggests that by the time the final figures are available that number will have increased by 10 per cent.
2 According to The Rand Corporation's Chronology of International Terrorism, between 1968 and mid-1985, the United States was the country most often targeted by terrorists abroad (1257 incidents), followed by Israel (293), France (278), the United Kingdon (203) and Turkey (117).
3 See Bonnie Cordes *et al.*, *Trends in International Terrorism, 1982 and 1983*, The Rand Corporation, R-3183-SL, August 1984, pp. 2–3.
4 Federal Bureau of Investigation, Terrorist Research and Analytical Center, *FBI Analysis of Terrorist Incidents in the United States* (see reports for 1981, 1982, 1983 and 1984, published annually in March of the succeeding year). The 1984 figure is somewhat misleading, since attacks on abortion clinics were not included in the FBI count. According to The Rand Chronology of Terrorist Activity in the United States, there were 50 attacks during 1984, of which 21 were abortion related.
5 Statistics from Risks International, Inc., 1980–1983.
6 For example, the Irish in the United Kingdom; the Corsicans, Bretons, New Caledonians and assorted Caribbean separatists in France; and the Basques and Catalonians in Spain.
7 Anti-authority survivalist groups include some specific, issue-oriented movements of the left as well as the right.
8 Cordes *et al.*, *op. cit.*, p. 3.
9 *Orange County Register*, 18 November 1985.
10 The group known as the Order appears to be the main exception.
11 David Audsley, 'POSSE COMITATUS', *TVI Journal*, Summer 1985, p. 13.
12 *New York Times*, 21 September 1985.
13 *New York Times*, 20 September 1985.
14 James Ridgeway, 'Unholy Terrorists', *Village Voice*, 25 January 1985.
15 *Ibid.*
16 *Associated Press Wire Service*, 18 December 1985.

The 'Doping' of America: The Ambivalence of the Narco-terrorist Connection and a Search for Solutions

R Ehrenfeld and M Kahan

INTRODUCTION

Narco-terrorism is a particularly sinister manifestation of the international terrorist phenomenon because its unique effects are insidious, persistent and more difficult to identify than are the sporadic, violent outbursts of the armed assailant.

The manufacture and delivery of narcotics is part of the terrorist portfolio for various reasons. The most obvious is that drugs are a source of revenue to support the general activities of terrorist organisations. Another reason is that the use of drugs in target countries, such as the United States, is part of the terrorists' programme to undermine the integrity of their enemies. This is achieved by weakening the moral fibre of society, by encouraging widespread addiction and by nurturing the socially enervating criminal activities that flourish around the drug trade.

There is no lack of evidence of connections between the international narcotics trade and terrorist organisations. For example, we can produce nearly one hundred references since 1974 to the narcotics operations of the PLO, linking that organisation through Syria, Bulgaria and Cuba—all of which are, of course, acting in concert with the Soviet Union—to drug traffic to the United States. Many of these examples include organised crime networks as the effective distribution mechanisms, and also involve drugs-for-arms transactions.

There is also a very large body of evidence collected by various US government Administration agencies, by the US Congress in open hearings and in Federal court proceedings. Much of this material is publicly available, albeit in the form of thick, closely printed verbatim transcripts in which there is no synthesis, analysis or codification of the material.

We recently did some analysis of this publicly available information and published an article in the *Wall Street Journal* on the narco-terrorist phenomenon.[1] Among the people who contacted us for more information and for the identification of our sources were offices of two Members of Congress who sit on committees that had held the very hearings we used. When we expressed our surprise that they did not recognise their own work, one reaction was: 'Thank God for Academicians'.

However, despite this evidence and despite the daily impact of its deadly and depraved operations, narco-terrorism receives insignificant public exposure. This is particularly so in the United States which, while not the only national target of the narco-terrorist network, is from all available evidence a more frequent target than all others combined. This chapter, then, focuses on the United States, but its arguments could apply to other target nations.

In contrast to evidence gathered by the government about other problems, the information on the narco-terrorist connection has been given very little official publicity. These other problems include investigations of illegal immigration, organised crime, political corruption and Japan's penetration of the US car market—to mention only a few examples from recent years. In these cases, the evidence was converted into popularly accessible summaries and widely disseminated through the media with the support of government spokesmen.

Yet, the Federal government remains almost entirely silent on the issue of the narco-terrorist connection. Now and then, here and there, a statement or a reference to the phenomenon is made, but there is no trace of any commitment to enlighten the public in a systematic way.

These occasional, sporadic attempts to expose the issue for a specific purpose can actually discredit the evidence and undermine attempts to bring the larger problem of narco-terrorism to public attention. One recent example of this was President Reagan's televised appeal for support for his proposal to give the Nicaragua Contras $100 million in military aid. At one point in that speech, Mr Reagan held up a photograph and made the statement:

> The Sandanistas have been involved themselves in the international drug trade. I know every American parent concerned about the drug problem will be outraged to learn that top Nicaraguan Government officials are deeply involved in drug trafficking. This picture, secretly taken at a military airfield outside of Managua, shows Frederico Vaughn, a top aide to one of the nine commandantes who rule Nicaragua, loading an aircraft with illegal narcotics, bound for the United States. No, there seems to be no crime to which the Sandanistas will not stoop—this is an outlaw regime.[2]

For most viewers, this was their first exposure to the links between international drug traffic and America's political opponents, and to the concept that drug traffic finances military activities. For the few informed observers, it appeared that the President was trivialising a very complex and not easily accepted phenomenon. In fact, among those of us who follow the narco-terrorist connection, Nicaragua is seen as a weak case study, and the Federal

Drug Enforcement Agency (DEA) issued a disclaimer against the conclusiveness of the President's assertions. Two weeks later, on 1 April, Attorney General Edwin Meese appeared on ABC–TV's 'Good Morning America' programme, stating that the DEA disclaimer was mistaken.

As a result of this, the credibility of the narco-terrorism argument in the United States is being tied to the specifics of the Nicaraguan situation. We fear that future efforts to educate the public about narco-terrorism will be challenged on the narrow grounds of the Nicaragua debate, and the credibility of those small bits of evidence.

The US government has, then, failed to accept its responsibility to systematically inform the public about the huge and growing body of evidence on connections between international narcotics trafficking and international terrorism. On those occasions when the government made attempts, however ill-managed, to bring these issues to the public, the media seemed to fail in fulfilling *its* obligations.

Why has the US government not devoted more resources to educational campaigns publicising the narco-terrorist connection? How could a campaign be mounted? What could it do?

Before we attempt to address those questions, we will explore some of the reasons we believe have so far hindered the adoption of any comprehensive programmes to educate the general public about the extreme threat that narco-terrorism represents.

This failure to inform the public represents *fear* on the part of government officials: fear that their inability to control this narco-terrorist situation will lead the public to lose faith in the ability of their leaders to protect the society from a dangerous environment.

From another perspective, we observe that the very leadership groups to whom we turn for guidance have become part of the problem. The evidence about domestic distribution of drugs shows that use and addiction have spread into and through the middle and upper middle classes of the United States, to the extent that those who are responsible for preventive measures (including media attention) may well be in the prime user groups. In other words, the available evidence on the characteristics of drug users allows us to postulate, through their matching demographic characteristics, that they could be the very people who manage our major institutions.

The narco-terrorist takes further advantage of the middle-class failure to fulfil its leadership role by enlarging the existing demand. This *embourgeiosement* of the drug phenomenon in the United States was summarised by Dr Arnold M Washton in testimony before the President's Commission on Organised Crime:

> It [cocaine use] has permeated virtually every geographic area and socioeconomic group. Cocaine is no longer uniquely the drug of the very rich and famous. It is now the drug of choice of middle class America—those who hold responsible jobs—those who perform vital services—those we most rely upon their judgement, skill and experience.[3]

The drug problem may have gotten so out of hand in the United States that public officials and the media find it increasingly difficult to comprehend, or to communicate it to the public in credible terms. To the extent that this is part of the problem, bureaucratic rivalries and jurisdictional jealousies between foreign policy agencies, law-enforcement officials and health and welfare institutions—to name a few—could prevent the development of solutions or of educational programmes. In the words of Elliott Abrams, Assistant Secretary of State for InterAmerican Affairs:

> [The drug problem] is not just a health problem, not just a foreign aid problem, not just a police problem. It is a moral challenge and a national security matter. It threatens democracy in our hemisphere and children in our homes.[4]

As the problem grew and became manifest among America's 'ruling class', government and corporations have had to introduce programmes to test employees for drug use. The perceived necessity of having such testing programmes—in order to prevent the dangers, inefficiencies and breaches of security associated with drug use—is greeted with indignation and suspicion over the ulterior motives of the testers. These issues quickly spill over into concerns about civil rights and liberties and, in this way, the narco-terrorists implicitly achieve another goal: Americans begin to distrust each other, and to argue in favour of legalising drug use as a means of protecting their rights and liberties.

The argument has now shifted very far away from the main stream. Not only do we talk about narco-terrorism as an external threat, but we focus on our own political and economic institutions as the 'enemy' because they 'violate' our rights; this sets up the distinct possibility that future attempts by these very institutions to educate the public about narco-terrorism and its direct links to the growing addiction problem in the United States will fall on suspicious ears.

The inability of social scientists to closely and reliably identify the characteristics of terrorists or of potential drug addicts is partly responsible for the failure of government to deal with these problems. In the end, as we will see in the next two sections of this chapter, we are left with fiction, basic political philosophy and political rhetoric.

OUR PURPOSE

There has been no previous effort to sort through these scattered elements of the narco-terrorist phenomenon and the responses to it from its main target, the United States. We know, but do not fully understand why, there is not a concerted effort to define the phenomenon and to devote significant public resources to eradicating it at its sources. We also know that there has been no effort to mount a public education programme to make the target population—the American people—aware of the narco-terrorist threat. This is even more difficult to understand.

In this chapter we explore some of the possible reasons for this, and we identify what we believe are some key variables. At the end, we reach for some ideas and hypotheses about where to begin a systematic investigation of why the narco-terrorist phenomenon has received so little public exposure.

THE OBLIGATIONS OF THE STATE

In the latter part of his book, *Terrorism: A Study of National and International Political Violence*, Walter Laqueur concludes:

> Thus the results of the application of political science to the study of internal conflict, far from proving anything, have been quite negative and no truly scientific (that is, predictive or explanatory) theories have emerged ... even if there existed a valid theory of political instability and civil violence in general, it would still be a long way from a theory of terrorism. ... There should be no illusions about what can be discovered about the origins and the character of terrorism: all that can be established is that terrorism is more likely to occur in certain circumstances than in others and that in some conditions it cannot take root at all. ... Fiction holds more promise for the understanding of terrorism than [does] political science ...[5]

Laqueur's review of the political science literature on violence, terrorism and domestic upheavals reveals the general weaknesses in 'scientific' approaches to the problem. These approaches attempt to quantify the circumstances under which terrorism appears, and to establish the argument that a set of objective environmental factors determine (or create a likely atmosphere for) the emergence of terrorism. Laqueur is testifying to the failure of our search for predictive power over terrorism.

This failure is certainly not due to an insufficient data base: several thousand terrorist acts have been chronicled in the past fifteen years, and they represent enough variety to permit stratified sampling and for the manipulation of a variety of background factors in the search for the best 'fit' of the data to statistical models. We can deal similarly with the many noble attempts to draw psychological profiles of terrorists. On these scores, in fact, terrorism provides excellent opportunities for the barefoot empiricist to run amok in the slag heaps of raw data.

We did learn a great deal from these attempts to reduce terrorism to systematic variables. We find, for example, that terrorism occurs under so many different sets of conditions that there seem to be relatively few circumstances under which these acts are *not* likely to occur.

We begin to understand that the essence of terrorism is its very unpredictability. It is the randomness, the sheer unannounced violence of the terrorist act that penetrates directly to our deepest fears of a chaotic world.

Terrorism defies our science as it also defies our Western concept of civilisation.

Laqueur's turn to fiction for significant insights into terrorist phenomena is, although not finally satisfying of our need to understand, a useful step in the direction of acknowledging that these acts are essentially subjective events. We can glimpse at what he is aiming by imagining, if we can, what it would be like to *be* a terrorist—to actually commit an act of extreme violence against other human beings, chosen by coincidence and subjected to the full fury of our most violent urges.

Perhaps even more instructive is to conjure up the idea of being the *victim* of terrorism (although we note that the fiction cited by Laqueur almost never depicts the situation from this side). It is somewhere in the interstices of these realms of our imagination and our fears that we will find our answer to 'what is terrorism?'

Somewhere in our deepest fears we find the definition of terrorism and of the fears that stem from the narco-terrorist connection. It is here also, perhaps, that we can identify the reluctance of our leaders to confront this phenomenon. This aspect of narco-terrorism was defined by Elliott Abrams in his 10 February 1986 speech before the Council on Foreign Relations:

> For I believe that few issues we face in the areas of foreign policy and national security have a greater and more immediate relevance for the well-being of the American people than international narcotics. The sooner all of us who ponder foreign policy issues recognize the extreme threat posed by international narcotics trafficking to the health of our nation and its neighbors, the sooner will this danger to our families and our children be reduced and eliminated.[6]

This perception and the atmosphere of urgency it conveys are a good start in the direction of seeking solutions. Unfortunately, despite their sense of urgency, these remarks have not received very wide circulation. Why are they being expressed only now, when the fundamental facts about narco-terrorism were known and available inside the government fifteen years ago—during the Nixon Administrations of the early 1970s—and had been accumulating for at least a decade before that?

We did not hear about these things back then because our political leaders were pre-occupied with other problems and issues that they perceived to be—and which did become—fundamental challenges to their legitimacy. One more issue like that—such as the narco-terrorist threat—could have finally undermined their ability to keep the public trust.

In fact, when we asked a number of officials and foreign policy experts who were active in those earlier years why the narco-terrorist issue was not brought to public attention then, the composite answer was:

> What did you expect the United States to do? To interfere with other countries' internal affairs, because they couldn't solve their own problems? *Besides, we had our own problems to deal with: Vietnam, Watergate, the Civil Rights Movement, etc.*

In saying this, they admit that things were already somewhat out of control, that the Government's authority was being challenged on a number of fronts and that another problem was simply too much for the leadership to handle. They denied the problem, and in doing so they denied the obligation of the State to provide its citizens with the fundamental protections that are its major rationale.

We have to go back only to the seventeenth century to find the philosophical underpinnings of the modern State. Thomas Hobbes, trying to rationalise through the chaos of England's civil wars and the justification for the legitimacy of State authorities who were not in place through Divine Right, thought:

> every one is governed by his own Reason; and there is nothing he can make use of, that may not be a help onto him, in preserving his life against his enemies; it followeth, that in such a condition, every man has a right to every thing; even to one another's body.[7]

This is the condition that Hobbes supposes pre-exists the civilised State, which is born of the selection of the Monarch to whom each person pledges some part of his right—in particular giving over his 'right to every thing; even to one another's body'. These individual pledges are accumulated into the Social Contract. Hobbes was, in fact, positing the situation that would obtain if this fundamental pledge of the civilised man were to be abandoned by all.

In this pre-State situation, one's fellow creatures are likely to invoke this right: we would find it incumbent to protect ourselves against the ravages and incursions—real or supposed—of others against our persons. Hobbes stresses that, in the absence of the civilising Contract, we each have the right to kill:

> To this warre of every man against every man this also is consequent; that nothing can be unjust. The notions of Right and Wrong, Justice and Injustice have there no place. Where there is no Common Power, there is no Law; where no Law, no Injustice. Force and Fraud, are in warre the two Cardinal vertues.[8]

It is, then, in the State of Nature, where the 'warre of every man against every man' is fought, that we find the ultimate definition of terrorism: the primordial, pre-civilised but fundamental right of each person to kill. This is chaos, the war of each against all in which life is 'nasty, brutish and short', and in which no advancement of sensibility is possible. It is a time of darkness. It is only the 'Common Power', in the form of the Monarch who is the elected holder of the only legitimate right to kill, to whom we turn for security and through whom we sanctify the Contract that ends the war.

In Hobbes' conception, it is this decision, and the resultant faith that we place in the Monarch (the State) that keeps order by providing the means to resist human urges to return to the state of Nature. This is the ultimate rationale for the surrender of some of our freedom, and for the construction of the machinery of government to provide for our safety and to protect our ability to make a living in a predictable environment.

The relative peace of the new order is an artificial construct, always ready to be challenged by the more basic passions:

> The desires and other Passions of man are in themselves no Sin. No more as the Actions that proceed from those Passions till they know a law that forbids them, which till lawes be made they cannot know: not can any any law be made till they have agreed upon the person that shall make it.[9]

We can recognise these challenges to the civilised order at the interpersonal level—in common criminal activities, for example. We can also recognise them in the perspectives of twentieth-century revolutionaries—of the right and the left—where we find ideological justifications for using 'any means at our disposal' to further the ends of the movement. Lenin, Hitler, the Weather Underground, Baader–Meinhof, the Arab League, LEHI and the British Mandate authorities, M19, the Red Brigades—among many others—are all in the long line of challengers who have employed various versions of terrorism. They have used various kinds of terrorist tactics to further national liberation movements and to support internationalist goals, but always to threaten the legitimacy of the established order in their target States. The narco-terrorist, connected to drug traffic and employing the method of random killing of innocent bystanders, is a very special hybrid, and the latest in this long line.

PUBLICLY AVAILABLE EVIDENCE

The Federal Government has known for quite some time about the narco-terrorist threat to the integrity of the State. In its own recently released, but extremely difficult to obtain, report, *America's Habit: Drug Abuse, Drug Trafficking and Organized Crime*, the Government asserts in a section titled 'Government Complicity':

> A number of hostile foreign governments, motivated either by a need for hard American currency, or by a more ideological desire to undermine governments in Europe and the United States, actively facilitate drug trafficking activities. Cuba and Nicaragua blatantly aid traffickers smuggling drugs from Colombia to the United States; the Bulgarian government assists traffickers transporting drug shipments from Southwest Asia to Western Europe. All three countries are geographically well-positioned to service transshipment points for drugs en route to Europe or the United States, and all allow trafficking routes to cross through their sovereign territory, thus providing a way for traffickers to circumvent drug-interdiction authorities.[10]

This citation is buried, on page 144, amid the body of evidence, collected over a thirty-two-month period, and the appendices to the report. In the face of the evidence and testimony contained elsewhere in the report, this summary is actually a very mild depiction of narco-terrorist phenomena and motives. That is, for those who look for conclusions under the indexed heading, 'Government Complicity', they will find the above bromide, instead of the more pointed accusations buried even more obscurely in the body of the report. There, we find statements such as:

> The links between terrorist and insurgent groups and traffickers are most substantial in drug source countries, including Colombia, Peru, Burma and Thailand. In Colombia, four major insurgent organizations work in collaboration with cocaine traffickers. ... One FARC (Revolutionary Armed Force of Colombia) front reportedly obtained over 3.8 million dollars per month by assessing ... (a) protection tax. Collected monies are used to buy weapons and supplies which are often shipped into Colombia on return drug flights.[11]

This funding method serves specific ideological purposes as well, as explained elsewhere in the report by Professor Michael Ledeen, a recognised authority on terrorist activities:

> Running drugs is one sure way to make big money in a hurry. Moreover, the directions of the flow are ideologically attractive. Drugs go to the bourgeois countries, where they corrupt and they kill, while the arms go to the pro-Communist terrorist groups in the third world.[12]

An even harsher definition of the narco-terrorist ideological purpose is found in the testimony of Antonio Farach, before Senator Paula Hawkins' Senate Drug Enforcement Caucus in 1983. This testimony was certainly available to the President's Commission. Farach is the former Minister Counselor of Nicaragua's Embassies in Venezuela and Honduras. He defected to the US in September 1983 and appeared at hearings in Miami, where he said:

> In the first place, drugs did not remain in Nicaragua. The drugs were destined for the United States. Our youth would not be harmed, but rather the youth of the United States, the youth of our enemies. Therefore, the drugs were used as a political weapon because in that way, we were delivering a blow to our principal enemy ... in addition to a political weapon against the United States, the drug trafficking produced a very good economic benefit which we needed for our revolution ... we wanted to provide food for our people with the suffering and death of the youth of the United States.[13]

Thus, in response to those who say 'Well, after all, the government *did* publish its findings and that constitutes informing the public', our reply is:

(a) The report is difficult to obtain, and generally can be found only by those who already follow these issues very closely. We were able to obtain a copy of the report only through personal contacts on Capitol Hill in

Washington, who had to personally photocopy the only copy of the report available to Congressional offices and return it the same day.

(b) The report is seven hundred pages long, with a one-page conclusion. It is another example of the government's failure to communicate in accessible language or format.

(c) The major headings which are meant to offer sub-conclusions, such as the 'Government Complicity' section that we cite above, do not vividly enough depict the testimony and other evidence on which they are based.

(d) There is no cross-referencing or indexing between the summaries and their supporting evidence in the report, so that conclusions can be easily tested against the evidence.

The government, in short, failed to honestly reveal to the public what it knows—and has known for some time—about the threat to the United States from narco-terrorist activities.

Before and besides the report from the President's Commission on Organized Crime, there are many similarly difficult to access examples of collections of testimony, statements in evidence and hearings on the subject of narco-terrorism. The Congress is also responsible. Two fairly recent examples are:

(a) *The Cuban Government's Involvement in Facilitating International Drug Traffic.* Joint Hearing before the Subcommittee on Security and Terrorism of the Committee on the Judiciary and the Subcommittee on Western Hemisphere Affairs of the Foreign Relations Committee and the Senate Drug Enforcement Caucus, United States Senate, 30 April 1983. 687 pages. No summary, no conclusions, no index.

(b) *Legislation to Combat International Terrorism: 98th Congress.* Hearings and Markup before the Committee on Foreign Affairs and its Subcommittee on International Security and Scientific Affairs and on International Operations, 9 November 1983, 7, 13, 19 June 1984, 26 September 1984. 418 pages. No summary, no conclusions, no index.

If narco-terrorism is such a concerted threat to the integrity of our society, why is the subject treated in this obscure way? Imelda Marcos' buying habits received more attention and definition from the government and the media than has narco-terrorism.

The media joins the government in what looks like a conspiracy to minimise our knowledge of the narco-terrorist threat. All the information about narco-terrorism has been available to the media for many years, and it is curious that they have done so little to inform the public about what seems to be potentially sensational news, and subject matter worthy of deep investigative reporting.

Presented with the President's Commission report, for example, the media focused on some rather subsidiary questions, such as the right of government agencies to require urinalysis of key employees—a recommendation that was even more obscurely placed in the report than was the 'Government Complicity' section that we mentioned earlier. In a one-page section titled simply 'Guidelines', the report suggests that:

> The President should direct the heads of all Federal agencies to formulate immediately clear policy statement, with implementing guidelines, including suitable drug testing, expressing the utter unacceptability of drug use by Federal employees. Government contracts should not be awarded to companies that fail to implement drug programs, including suitable drug testing.[14]

This issue is what the media exploited to the exclusion of almost everything else in the report.

Although the question of drug use by Federal employees and drug testing of them do have a valid place in our public forums, they should not *replace* the question of the penetration of American society by the narco-terrorist network.

As so often happens in the United States, the media seized on the narrowest, most immediate and most clearly domestic aspects of the reports. In this case, the question of urinalysis—its legitimacy and its personal implications.

We noted earlier in this chapter that encouraging internal suspicion and Constitutional in-fighting is actually one of the goals of the narco-terrorist network: the focus on drug testing fosters domestic disputes and mistrust, and occasionally leads to serious discussions about legalising drug use. The way the media dealt almost exclusively with the urinalysis issue shows, once again, that we fell into this trap.

The pro-legalisation argument has several damaging elements to it. We find most of them in the perspective of Arnold Trebach, Professor of Justice at American University in Washington DC, who has made a career of advocating the legalisation of drug use in the United States. Typical of his approach are the following excerpts from an interview in which Trebach participated. He argues, first, that preventing drug use is virtually impossible:

> Sure, we can curb some of the drug traffic. But we will never be able to prevent those Americans who want to use drugs from doing so—without, that is, massive invasions of our constitutional freedoms ...

Then he simplifies the issue by reducing the implications of drug traffic to a matter of individual preference:

> We are moving toward increasingly revolting methods of preventing people from doing what they want to do.

Next, these implications are treated to the imagining of an absurd conclusion:

> It won't be long before legislators will be required to bring in a warm bottle of urine before every important vote. This is the road we are on; if we continue down it, I see a very bleak future ...

Then, the entire issue of the international drug trade and of the narco-terrorist connection is obviated by adopting a position advocating legalisation:

> So, I'm suggesting new approaches to dealing with drugs. Otherwise, we'll need greatly increased law enforcement in the face of constantly increasing demand, and we will inevitably invade the liberties of our people.[15]

This argument accepts the inevitably of addiction and fails to understand who is responsible for the spread of drug use and addiction is this country—and the political and ideological motivations behind their activities. It is an avoidance of the real issue similar to the rationalisations, noted earlier in this chapter, that we heard from public officials for why the narco-terrorist problem was not dealt with many years ago when it first became manifest: 'What did you expect the United States to do? To interfere with other countries' internal affairs because they couldn't solve their own problems?'

There are legal and rhetorical considerations on both ends of the narco-terrorist connection: we cannot interfere at the source because that entails entanglement in the affairs of other states, and we cannot interfere at home, because that requires compromise of individual rights. There must be another way.

SUMMARY AND CONCLUSIONS: BEGINNING THE SEARCH FOR SOLUTIONS

While the rhetoric flies, evidence about the narco-terrorist connection continues to accumulate, and the spread of drug use and addiction becomes a more serious drain on our national resources. The narco-terrorist looking at the accumulating evidence would find reason to believe that he is winning the war of attrition.

We must think much more systematically about solutions to the narco-terrorist threat. At the beginning, and at the very least, we must think seriously about why our responses so far have been misdirected, ineffective and riddled with internal conflicts and contradictions.

This chapter is an attempt to outline our thoughts on these issues, and to generate the ideas and hypotheses that will guide the next stages of our work.

This is part of what we have developed so far:

(a) Narco-terrorism is a unique phenomenon, and it must be dealt with in a unique way. Narco-terrorism connects the drug problem with the terrorist problem, and it is both a multinational and a domestic problem. Neither the Government nor the media approach it from this perspective. Rather, the Government and the media continue to treat the drug issue and the terrorist problem on separate agendas. A systematic review of available Government publications and speeches on the topic, and of media treatments of the information made available by the Government, would demonstrate this.

(b) The Government's approach is due in part to the fears of elected officials and of high-ranking bureaucrats that their inability to deal effectively with the problem could undermine the legitimacy of their positions, and could lead to a loss of public faith in the ability of the State to protect its citizens from danger. In-depth interviews with key decision makers could help to determine whether this is an explicit consideration, or whether it remains implicit in their behaviour and explanations.

The Government cannot articulate a systematic approach to narco-terrorism. There is no clear assignment of the issue to a specific authority. Instead, information gathering and dissemination and policy formulation about narco-terrorism and how to confront it are subject to overlapping and competing jurisdictions. The various agencies, commissions and nooks and crannies to which parts of the narco-terrorist problem have been assigned should be catalogued, and their work collated to see exactly what is known and where the gaps are in our knowledge. We will find that we know quite a lot—and this includes only unclassified information, the kind that we have used to take us this far in our work.

(c) The media take their clues on this issue from the Government. This is not the only issue on which the media allow the Government to set the public information agenda. Indeed, it could become a classic case study of this phenomenon : educating the public about the narco-terrorist problem requires some in-depth research and penetrating analysis. It is not 'news' in the sense that our media prefer exclusive, sensational, immediate and, preferably, scandalous angles with which to attract mass attention.

The media do devote a great deal of space to some aspects of the drug problem—particularly to the distribution and use of drugs in the United States. We do question the effectiveness of this exposure, however. From the evidence we have seen so far, public opinion polls and other forms of attitude and knowledge data gathering seem to indicate that the public, while aware of a general drug 'problem', is still very unsophisticated about such things as the difference between various kinds of drugs, their effects and their sources. We propose, in our further research, to more closely investigate the extent to which information and knowledge has permeated the public consciousness in the more than two decades since the drug problem became a public issue.

The search for 'news' also often distracts the media into important but subsidiary issues, which we can categorise as 'localisations'. Some recent examples of this are major feature articles in national weekly news magazines about drug use, addiction and testing programmes—written anecdotally—but without any space given to the narco-terrorist connection.[16]

The diversion into subsidiary issues often fulfils the media's roles of acting as the public conscience and the monitor of official behaviour. However, these watchdog requirements could also be fulfilled by criticisms of the Government's failure to properly deal with the narco-terrorist phenomenon and its threat to the society. Why do the media not perceive the problem this way?

(d) There are other aspects of the narco-terrorist phenomenon that should be wound into the story—including the Soviet connection and the activities of some specific international terrorist organisations (such as the PLO) against whose activities the US Government already is publicly opposed. We noted some of these aspects in our *Wall Street Journal* article. Why, even in these clear-cut cases, is there no systematic discussion of narco-terrorism, and no attempt to educate the public?

(e) When all of the research on these issues and problems has been done, and we more clearly understand why narco-terrorism has not yet been usefully discussed in the public forum, then we will be able to propose a practical and workable programme through which to expose the narco-terrorist phenomenon and its dangers.

NOTES

1 Rachel Ehrenfeld and Michael Kahan, 'The Narco-terrorist Connection', *Wall Street Journal*, 10 February 1986, p. 20.
2 President Ronald Reagan, 'Speech to the American People', 16 March 1986 as recorded in the *New York Times*, 17 March 1986, p. A12.
3 Testimony of Dr Arnold M Washton before the President's Commission on Organized Crime, 27 November 1984, p. 2.
4 Elliott Abrams, 'Drug War: The New Alliances Against Traffickers and Terrorists', speech before The Council of Foreign Relations in New York, 10 February 1986. Published as Current Policy No. 792, United States Department of State, Bureau of Public Affairs, Washington, DC. No date.
5 Walter Laqueur, *Terrorism: A Study of National and International Political Violence*, Boston, Massachusetts: Little, Brown and Co., 1977, pp. 144–146.
6 Elliott Abrams, *op. cit.*
7 Thomas Hobbes, *Leviathan*, Ch. 14, p. 64. (All page numbers are from the original 1651 edition.)
8 *Ibid.*, Ch. 13, p. 63.
9 *Ibid.*, Ch. 13, p. 62.
10 *America's Habit: Drug Abuse, Drug Trafficking and Organized Crime*, The President's Commission on Organized Crime, Report to the President and the Attorney General, March, 1986, p. 144.
11 *Ibid.*, p. 155.
12 *Ibid.*, p. 135.
13 *The Cuban Government's Involvement in Facilitating International Drug Traffic.* Joint Hearing before the Subcommittee on Security and Terrorism of the Committee on the Judiciary and the Subcommittee on Western Hemisphere Affairs of the Foreign Relations Committee and the Senate Drug Enforcement Caucus, United States Senate, 30 April 1983, pp. 45–46.
14 *America's Habit, op. cit.*, p. 419.

15 'What is Our Drug Problem?', *Harper's Magazine* Forum, December, 1985, p. 45.

16 *Newsweek*, 17 March 1986; *Time Magazine*, 17 March 1986. Both were cover stories, and both followed the publication of *America's Habit* by the President's Commission on Organized Crime.

State Policy and the Cult of Terror in Central America

H E Vanden

Let's face it, our people are teaching people how to kill people, how to set up ambushes, how to set up a claymore so it can kill the most people.[1]

Terrorism, it has been suggested, is a poor man's political violence, a way in which the oppressed and the downtrodden have of gaining some modicum of revenge against the rich and wealthy. As such it is often seen as a weapon to be used against the State, particularly the advanced capitalist State of the Western world. Political terrorists are often equated with the anarchists of the last century whose object it was to bring down the State itself and whose actions went beyond the bounds of 'civilised' conduct. As suggested by the *In Re Meunier* case in International Law, British courts were loath even to classify anarchist violence as legitimate political activity because 'The party of anarchy is the enemy of all governments', and because its activities were 'primarily directed against the general body of citizens'.[2] Much the same attitude seems to have developed in many countries with respect to political terrorism, particularly since so much of the terrorist activity reported in the Western press does indeed seem aimed at innocent civilians. Terrorist bands were considered beyond the pale and were thought to be composed of the lunatic fringe of deviant political movements. Although often convenient for state policy makers, this explanation tended to see political terrorism as an activity that, like anarchism, was directed against states if not against society itself.

Lamentably for those of use who would study this phenomenon from an academic perspective, the reality is a little more complex. Terrorism is not only practised by fringe groupings such as Black September (Palestinian) or Sendero Luminoso (Peruvian), but by major state actors as well. Many experts believe that states such as Libya and North Korea are involved in terrorist activities in many areas of the world. Others see the hand of the KGB behind the most diverse forms of political violence in widely different locations.[3]

Nor is the origin of the word terrorism found in the actions of isolated extremist bands.

> The word 'terrorism,' derives from the era of the French Revolution and the Jacobin dictatorship which used terror as an instrument of political repression and social control. The so called Reign of Terror during the early 1790's was thus a *state-directed* activity, domestic in inspiration and in execution.[4]

The first modern use of the term was thus employed to describe state policy, not the actions of individuals. By conceiving of terrorism as a possible instrument of state policy one is much less constrained in one's understanding and use of the term. Likewise, it is possible to be more objective in the employment of the term since the focus is now shifted to the action itself and is not premised on the status of the agent.

Terror is not solely the instrument of leftist guerrillas, radical national insurgents or ultra-violent right-wing groups. It is practised by a variety of actors, ranging from isolated bands of zealots to major state actors. The targets are sometimes governments, sometimes their people and sometimes the rebels and their supporters. One of the most horrifying aspects of terrorism is that it differs from classical military activity in one fundamental aspect. Far from distinguishing between combatant and non-combatant, terrorism is often designed to strike at the very core of a society or a particular group—at the defenceless civilian population. If such activity is untenable for small, loosely organised groups of irresponsible extremists, it is even less defensible for large, sophisticated states that—unlike small groups of individuals—do have a vast array of options open to them to achieve their policy objectives. Nor do they usually lack the resources or administative capability to pursue more civilised means of policy implementation. A further problem is presented because the definition of what constitutes political terrorism is often subjective.[5] It is at least partially dependent on the political values we derive from those states or political movements with whose policies and/or ideologies we identify. Thus care must be taken in the way in which events and actions are classified.

In that much of the academic research on terrorism is done by those of us who come from or reside in Western or pro-Western states, we need to take special pains to apply our definitions of terrorism even-handedly. We should strive to be able to categorise political terrorism on the basis of the event itself, not the status or orientation of the perpetrator.

As is suggested by Grant Wardlaw in his recent work *Political Terrorism*, the problem of defining what actually constitutes terrorism, 'is further complicated by the unwillingness of many to acknowledge that terrorism, whatever the definition may be, is as much a tool of states and governments as of revolutionaries and political extremists'.[6] States—even those we support—may be engaged in terrorism or may back those who do. Indeed, Wardlaw goes on to suggest that 'it is all too easy to focus on outlandish activities of small groups to the exclusion of institutionalized, "official" terrorism practiced by a number of readily identifiable regimes'.[7]

Defining terrorism or classifying an act as terrorist is not a simple task, particularly in light of the arbitrary way in which the term is used by political leaders and the mass media. Without a clear understanding of what the phenomenon constitutes, one could easily be at the mercy of those who intentionally use the term for some political end or according to some unstated political agenda. For instance, in a recent work on political terrorism by a group of Soviet writers, the authors suggest that while Communists accept revolutionary violence, 'they reject terrorism as a means of obtaining political objectives'.[8] Yet later in the same work one finds a very curious application of the term terrorism to events in Afghanistan. The authors state that the main perpetrators of terrorism in that country are the US-backed guerrillas. No mention is made of the fact that there are widespread reports to suggest that at least some of the Soviet forces seem involved in the rather extensive employment of their own forms of violence to terrorise the civilian population in that country.[9] A more even-handed investigation of all the instances of the reported use of terror in Afghanistan might render very different results, particularly if it were not premised on the inherent correctness of revolutionary violence or the wrongness of that practised by the counter-revolutionary tribesmen. Likewise, some attempt to distinguish between combatants and civilians might have been helpful.

Terrorism, then, is the intentional use of violence to create a sense of intense anxiety or extreme fear (terror) in the general civilian population or some specific segment of it.[10] It is 'a method of action by which an agent tends to produce terror in order to impose his domination'.[11]

It is not the monopoly of one group, one ideological orientation or one state. Rather it is an instrument of policy that is employed by a variety of different actors to achieve their objectives. If we are to understand it we must be able to isolate it from any particular pre-conceptions—conscious or unconscious—and view it with less passion and more objectivity. We must try to see it as it is, not as we think it should be.

CENTRAL AMERICA

> The president's rule of conduct is never to give grounds for hope, and everyone must be kicked and beaten until they realize the fact.[12]

The case of Central America is illustrative of the varied use of terrorism in the actual social context. Looking at the three Central American countries that are currently experiencing the greatest levels of violence, we find that terrorism is used to describe the acts of rebels and government alike in Guatemala, El Salvador and Nicaragua. President Ronald Reagan has taken perhaps the greatest liberty with the term when he suggests that the guerrillas both El Salvador and Guatemala are indeed terrorists while the counter-revolutionaries (*contras*) are 'the moral equivalent of the founding fathers' of the United States.[13] While those readers outside the United States who have secretly harboured doubts about George Washington all along may find this statement of some amusement, one imagines that this statement obfuscates more than it illuminates. The reality of Central America is clearly much more complex.

Poor and not developed economically, Guatemala, El Salvador and Nicaragua have for some years been striving to change the nature of their societies. It is an intense struggle that has frequently witnessed the extensive use of violence. Recent history suggests that violence has become a common tool for all too many political groups. But the culture of violence is not new to Central America. The masses have been brutalised since the time of the conquest, if not long before. Violence, if not terror, became a means of ensuring the domination—or at least acquiescence—of the common people. During the early colonial period in Guatemala, the Spanish military authorities has a special method for treating an Indian village that rebelled against Spanish rule. The authorities found those whom they thought were responsible for the uprising. They impaled some on large, pointed staffs and placed them on the path to the village. The heads of the principal leaders were cut from their bodies, placed on pikes and displayed at the entrance to the village. This was meant as an object lesson to all who would challenge colonial authority. It was an attempt to instil an intense fear in a target population so as to modify their behaviour. The use of political terror is not a recent phenomenon in Central America. It has been used as a means of spreading fear among the civilian population for centuries and continues to be an instrument of policy down to the present. It is employed by governments and guerrillas alike, but not always to the same degree.

No doubt in large part influenced by the relatively high levels of support enjoyed among certain segments of the civilian population, the highly motivated leftist revolutionaries that have been operating in mostly poor, mostly peasant El Salvador and mostly poor, mostly Indian Guatemala have been more sparing in their use of political terror than have the forces of the governments they oppose. But they too have employed political violence to create fear, if not panic, among members of very specific target populations. For instance, in the early 1980s both the guerrillas of the Faribundo Martí National Liberation Front in El Salvador and the Guatemalan National Revolutionary Unity were kidnapping members of the conservative oligarchies and ransoming them for large sums of money that were used to finance further guerrilla activities. The 1985 kidnapping of Salvadoran president José Napoleon Duarte's daughter suggests a return to this type of activity. Also beginning in early 1985 one guerrilla faction (the Revolutionary Army of the People, a member of the FMLN in El Salvador) began to kidnap local mayors who supported the Government. At least one was killed after being taken.[14] Although condemned by most of the FMLN leadership, this suggests the extent to which the intensifying nature of the conflict has influenced some fringe groups to resort to terrorism to intimidate the local government officials.

GUATEMALA

Despite the revolutionaries' best efforts, the old politics still dominate in Guatemala and El Salvador. Violence often becomes an end in itself—a direct means of achieving a policy outcome.[15] Guatemala managed to evolve to a new, more humane type of political system from 1944 to 1954, but was thrown back into the old brutality in 1954 when a CIA-organised coup toppled Jacobo Arbenz, the constitutional president.[16] In the introduction to *Dialectica del terror en Guatemala* the widely respected Guatemalan social scientist, Edelberto Torres-Rivas, notes that 'the terror has been permanent' for more than twenty years in his country and that more than fifty thousand people have been killed.[17] The authors go on to argue that it is state-sponsored terror that is creating the vast majority of the victims in Guatemala. Terror, it seems, has become a specific tactic in the counterinsurgency campaigns that have become a major thrust of Guatemalan governmental policy in recent years. Like the earlier Spanish authorities, the Guatemalan government would not tolerate any challenge to its rule. Any political opposition from the left or centre was perceived as subversive and thus liable to the most severe punishment. Death squads—a byproduct of the counterinsurgency campaigns of the 1960s—continued to operate freely. Thousands of people were killed outright or 'disappeared', and their tortured, often mutilated, bodies then appeared days or weeks later to re-inforce the fear that the general population was already experiencing. Although the US had helped to set up the counterinsurgency programme and had continued to give Guatemala large amounts of military aid, it finally proposed a cut-off in military aid in 1977 because of the magnitude of the human rights abuses.[18] Guatemala reacted by suspending the US Military Assistance Program and seeking arms elsewhere. 'The "Frankenstein Monster" had taken on a life of its own. The Guatemalan regime rejected Washington's prodding on human rights. It had to, such methods were intrinsic to its method of rule.'[19] State terrorism had been institutionalised.

By the early 1980s, guerrilla groups like the Revolutionary Army of the Poor had begun to grow and to find increasing support among the long-exploited highland Indian peasants. This led to even more brutal attacks by the security forces. Whole villages that were thought to support the guerrillas were destroyed and many of their inhabitants massacred. There were repeated claims that the army was practising genocide against the Indian population.[20] Urban intellectuals and university students and professors were also prime targets. The worst abuses occurred under the rule of military dictators General Efraían Ríos Montt (March 1982 to August 1983) and General Oscar Humberto Mejía Víctores (August 1983 to January 1986), but the pattern remained the same. Even members of centrist parties like the Christian Democrats were assassinated when they criticised government abuses.

The record as to who is actually so brutally employing violence to intimidate the population is all too clear.

> In fact, Amnesty International has concluded after study of thousands of cases over a period of many years that the majority of political abductions have been

> carried out by currently serving and reservist members of all branches of the Guatemalan military and security forces, acting under the orders of their superiors in the guise of so-called 'death squads'. These squads were originally developed in the 1960's counter-insurgency strategy and since then have provided a convenient fiction for successive administrations who could claim that massive instances of 'disappearances' and extrajudicial executions of those who oppose the government policies had actually been the work of 'extremist groups' who were out of government control.[21]

The fear was so great that thousands fled the country. In the meantime, the Republican Administration has gradually increased military assistance and now seeks to restore full military aid. It is hoped that the recent installation of civilian president Vinicio Cerezo (a Christian Democrat who was himself the target of several assassination attempts) will curb most abuses. It is, however, unclear if the powerful military leaders will bend to the will of a civilian politician who many see as more window dressing than ruler.

EL SALVADOR

El Salvador presents another interesting case of how the prolonged use of violence may affect the civilian population. The history of the republic is replete with popular uprisings against elitist rule. There was a major Indian peasant revolt in 1832; another took place one hundred years later in 1932. Such attempts at change were brutally resisted by the regimes in power and the wealthy landowners who constituted the dominant political group. Indians and peasants were second-class citizens who had to be kept in their place by whatever means necessary. Paternalism, legalistic manoeuvring or even a demonstration election were often sufficient, but violent repression was at no time precluded. After Faribundo Martí and the small group of mostly Marxist leaders of the 1932 uprising were arrested in the early hours or days of the rebellion, some 60,000 insurgents were left at the mercy of the military and security forces, who soon initiated a massive wave of indiscriminate repression. No quarter was given, and in the resulting massacre ('*La Matanza*' or killing as it is now called) some 30,000 men, women and children were killed to ensure that El Salvador's rulers would not soon be confronted with another uprising, and to intimidate the lower classes generally.[22] Up until 1979, even reformist movements like the Christian Democratic Party were kept from power by electoral fraud (as in José Napoleon Duarte's first bid for the presidency in 1972) and continued military intervention. The most conservative sectors of the oligarchy worked closely with reactionary sectors in the armed forces to maintain a death grip on the economic and political system.[23]

Reformist elements in the military finally cooperated with some moderate politicians to stage a progressive coup in October of 1979. However, progressive officers were soon out-manoeuvred by right-wing military interests, and the civilian politicians who joined the junta soon found that the promised reforms were not forthcoming and that they too could be targeted by the rightist groups who resisted these initiatives.[24] An even higher level of brutal repression developed and most of the civilian politicians who had initially joined the junta resigned in protest, with many—including the present head of the FDR, Guillermo Ungo—moving to the ranks of the Revolutionary Democratic Front (FDR). It was under these conditions that José Napoleon Duarte first returned and agreed to join the military rulers as President in a reformed junta. Like his civilian predecessors, he was never able to control the increasing repression that some of his fellow junta members used to try to control the growing opposition forces. The killing—*La Matanza*—was being repeated once again.

From late 1979 through most of 1984 the killing increased in El Salvador. Amnesty International believes over 40,000 Salvadorans were killed in political violence from the time of the 1979 coup through 1983 and that 'a large portion of those killed were the victims of extrajudicial executions by government and security forces'.[25] Anyone who advocated reform or better conditions for the masses was suspect. The massacre of large numbers of unarmed civilians became commonplace as the governmental forces attempted to use terror to intimidate large segments of an increasingly hostile population. The US Government continued to support the regime, blaming the violence on independent right-wing forces and on the leftist insurgents themselves. The continuation of US military assistance to the Government prompted Archbishop Oscar Romero to call for an end to US aid to the government. He and a growing number of church activists became very critical of the first Duarte Government because of continued human rights violations. Amnesty International went so far as to suggest that 'reports of stepped-up aid to El Salvador's internal security forces coincided with reports of repression'.[26] Romero continued to speak out, even though he received several death threats. He refused to be intimidated by the growing terror the regime was unleashing. In his Sunday, 23 March 1980 homily that was broadcast to the nation, he accused the security forces of 'sowing terror' in the countryside and called on soldiers not to kill their own people.[27] A military spokesman immediately labelled his call a 'crime'. He was assassinated the following day while offering mass. The following month, the US Government approved an additional $5.7 million in military aid to El Salvador. The nature of the violence was also demonstrated by the rape and murder of three American nuns and an American religious worker in December of 1980. Although Government involvement was initially denied, subsequent revelations (resulting from intense pressure from the US Congress rather than any internal pressure) established the fact that the killings were actually carried out by Government soldiers. Whether or not they were acting on orders from their superiors was never clarified. Elections in 1982 did not modify the regime's behaviour. Roberto d'Abuisson, a rightist politician with links to the death squads, emerged as an important leader in the new assembly. d'Abuisson and his ARENA party continued to be important power contenders, despite d'Abuisson's reputed involvement in the assassination of Archbishop Romero.[28]

When former president Duarte managed to defeat d'Abuisson in a high turnout run-off election in May of 1984, El Salvador witnessed a return to nominal democratic civilian government. Despite strong backing from the US, President Duarte was not able to make the security forces relinquish the use of political violence to terrorise large numbers of civilians. This was particularly true for those who stayed in areas where the rebel forces were the most active. Here the civilians were viewed as real or potential rebel supporters. A series of reforms do, however, at least seem to have reduced the incidence of human rights violations. Nonetheless, some critics suggest that the US supplied and trained Salvadoran Air Force is now dropping large numbers of bombs on civilian areas to achieve the intimidation that was formerly supplied by the death squads and government patrols.

In 1985, Amnesty International noted that it received continuing reports that the Security Forces in El Salvador had been involved in 'a systematic and widespread programme of torture, "disappearance," and extrajudicial execution of men, women and children', and that the victims included real or perceived opponents of the government: 'priests, trade unionists, leaders and members of peasant organizations, church workers, human rights activists, people working with relief organizations, medical personnel, and persons being treated for their wounds abducted from their sick beds. ...'[29] The report goes on to state that the aforementioned abuses are continuing to take place despite the steps the Salvadoran Government has taken.[30] Meanwhile, the US Government has continued to increase its military aid to El Salvador. It provided a total of $196.6 million in military assistance to that country in 1984.[31]

One is here presented with a difficult situation. Although the opposition forces in El Salvador are clearly guilty of the selective use of terrorism, the vast preponderance of the political violence that has been used against the civilian population is executed by Government forces. The United States continues to give those forces more and more military aid. El Salvador has practised a policy of state terrorism and the Reagan Administration, all the while denouncing terrorism, has increased its aid to the very forces that regularly employ it.[32]

NICARAGUA

Another civil conflict in Central America brings this apparent paradox into even sharper focus. The policies promulgated by the Sandinista regime in Managua have created a great deal of controversey among Nicaraguans and in many other parts of the world. Since July of 1979, a regime made up of Marxist rebels, Catholic priests and bourgeois politicians has been trying to forge a new society to replace an old one that was the result of fifty years of Somoza dictatorship. The United States, it seems, never wanted the Sandinistas to come to power and tried until the last days of the old regime to ensure the continuation of the only force powerful enough to resist them—Somoza's National Guard. When that strategy failed an American operative went so far as to charter a plane, paint it with the Red Cross emblem and use the ruse to rescue Colonel Tinto Pérez, a key National Guard Officer, from the Guatemalan Embassy where he had taken refuge when the FSLN triumphed.[33] Other remnants of Somoza's hated *Guardia* (National Guard) managed to make their way out of Nicaragua to Honduras, El Salvador, Guatemala and even Miami. Their initial support came from Nicaraguan and Cuban right-wing groups in Miami, and from the far right politicians and military men who were responsible for so much of the terror in Guatemala and El Salvador.[34] In 1980, while many of the guardsmen were still in Guatemala, they organised their first group, the 15 September Legion. More raids into northern Nicaragua were organised. From the outset, this and subsequent *contra* groups seemed to adopt the same rules of engagement they had employed in Somoza's fight against the Sandinistas. Anyone who was a Sandinista, a potential Sandinista or a supporter of the movement was a target, as were those around him. Summary execution, torture and mutilation were considered to be acceptable means to deal with such people. The standard rules of war were not, it seemed, operative. Thus several of the teachers and students who went to remote areas of the country as part of the massive literacy campaign in the first year of the revolution were assassinated.

Even during the 1980 presidential campaign, Ronald Reagan and his conservative supporters had made it clear that they were no friends of the Sandinistas. In March 1981 the Republican White House issued an initial policy paper for stepped-up covert action in Central America.[35] That same year William Casey, the new head of the Central Intelligence Agency started to organise the 'secret war' against the Nicaraguan government.[36] In the meantime, the budding counterrevolutionaries had found some other supporters.

Through their contacts with the Guatemalan military, the ex-guardias were introduced to a group of Argentinian advisors who the Argentine military had sent to Guatemala to aid that country in its fight against 'subversives'.[37] Veterans of Argentina's dirty war that claimed thousands of civilian lives, they found they had much in common with their Nicaraguan counterparts. Soon the Argentine Army's Batallion 601 was being use to train and organise a force that could be used to attack the new government in Managua. Many Nicaraguans were even sent to Argentina for special training. None seemed to have any qualms about the way the Argentine military had used its own brand of state terrorism to silence dissent in that nation. While US–Argentine relations were warming, the Argentine military was setting up a military organisation that would operate out of Southern Honduras to attack Nicaragua. This was the structure the US Government bought into when they started to supply covert funding for the Nicaraguan counterrevolutionaries. William Casey evidently took an interest in the project from the first and flew to Honduras in 1981 to check on its development. The remnants of the old National Guard were combined with a few other Nicaraguans to form the FDN, the Nicaraguan Democratic Force. As support from the United States increased, they began to mount larger attacks in Nicaragua. After their humiliating defeat in the Falklands War, the Argentine military eventually withdrew its advisors and the US began to take a more active role in the 'secret war' against the Sandinista regime. They could find a few Nicaraguan politicians who were not closely tied to Somoza or the *Guardia* and integrate them into the FDN leadership to give it some façade of civilian democratic leadership. Those who were actually doing the fighting were another story. Most of the initial troops were ex-guardsmen as were virtually all their officers. People like Suicida (suicide), Cancer, El Muerto (the dead one) led the fighters into the field. They seemed to have little or no respect for human life, often killing their own men for some infraction. They hated the Sandinistas and all who worked with them. They seemed to believe that they could reduce support for the regime by brutalising all who were connected with it. As civilian casualties reached the thousands, more and more reports of their abuses began to come out of Nicaragua. The Government had also committed some abuses like the killing of Miskito Indians in a poorly conceived attempt to move them from their traditional homelands to areas where the Government could better protect them from the roving *contra* bands and any influence they might wield.[38] However, the government admitted its mistakes and soon changed its whole policy of relocation. Abuses of the laws of war by the Nicaraguan Government declined drastically even while the fighting intensified.[39] However, abuses by the *contras* continued to increase. Gang rapes, emasculation and eye-gouging were common practices. A well-publicised report about the persistent attacks on Nicaraguan civilians suggests that this was part of a campaign of *contra* terror against the Nicaraguan population.[40] The counterrevolutionaries and their American supporters first denied and then minimised these actions. However, in a 1985 Americas Watch report on violations by both sides in the Nicaraguan conflict, the human rights organisation concluded that:

> In combination, the *contra* forces have systematically violated the applicable laws of war throughout the conflict. They have attacked civilians indiscriminately; they have tortured and mutilated prisoners; they have murdered those placed *hors de combat* by their wounds; they have taken hostages; and they have committed outrages against personal dignity.[41]

A recent report on Nicaragua by Amnesty International expresses concern about 'the frequently reported torture, mutilation, and execution style killing of captives by irregular military forces opposing the Nicaraguan Government'.[42] The FDN and MISURA (a misquito Indian force) are cited as the two groups responsible for these violations. The *contras* had developed a policy of terrorising the civilian population so they would be afraid to support the Government, help produce the badly needed export crops or simply abandon the countryside and flee to the cities where they would need to be maintained. Crops could not be harvested in northern areas of the country because of the danger to the farm workers. Cooperative farms, private farms, schools and even health clinics became prime targets in the increasingly violent attacks. Workers, teachers and health-care personnel were frequent targets. Trucks, buses and cars were shot up or simply blown up as they drove along isolated stretches of road. But the old politics of violence and intimidation did not work the way they had under Somoza. The counterrevolutionaries had not been able to take or hold any areas of the country as they and their American advisors had hoped. But they were able to make the population pay for their resistance. By 1983 and 1984 terror had once again become an end in itself. Although often times irrationally used, it was not completely isolated from Reagan Administration policy. Reports of a CIA Manual surfaced in October of 1984. *Psychological Operations in Guerrilla Warfare* had been prepared by a Central Intelligence Agency employee and distributed to the troops of FDN fighters. In a section on 'Implicit and Explicit Terror', the manual reminds the reader that 'A guerrilla force always involves implicit terror because the population, without saying it aloud, feels terror that the weapons may be turned against them'.[43] In another section on the 'Selective Use of Violence For Propagandistic Effects', the manual is even more explicit: 'it is possible to neutralize selected targets, court judges, *mesta* judges, police and state security officials, CDS chiefs, etc ...'.[44] Many *contra* forces seem to have assassinated just such people in the ways suggested by the manual. American advisors were teaching the counterrevolutionaries how to use their violence more precisely to achieve a sense of terror in the civilian population in Nicaragua. The revelation of the existence of the manual and its apparent call for assassination created quite a furore and underlined an inherent problem in US policy: the Central Intelligence Agency and the Republican Administration had to obscure the obvious. Even those in the US Congress who did not want the Sandinistas in power, 'did not want to sign on to the tactics needed to get rid of them'.[45] Thereafter the counterrevolutionaries would be described as freedom fighters and those fighting to restore democracy in Nicaragua. Their clear practice of terror would be masked by rhetoric that was increasingly hostile to the Sandinistas.

Not all were convinced. Edgar Chamorro had been recruited by the CIA to form part of the civilian leadership of the FDN and to act as their public relations spokesperson. But as time went on he became more and more troubled by the frequent reports of atrocities committed by FDN troops against civilians and Sandinista prisoners. As he talked to the unit commanders after they returned from the field, he concluded that

> The atrocities I had heard about were not isolated instances, but reflected a consistent pattern of behavior by our troops. There were unit commanders who openly bragged about murders, mutilations etc. ... they told me it was the only way to win the war, that the best way to win the loyalty of the civilian population was to intimidate it and make it fearful of us.[46]

Later in the same document he is explicit about the relation between the main *contra* organisation and the United States.

> The FDN turned out to be an instrument of the US Government and, specifically, of the CIA. It was created by the CIA, it was supplied, equipped, armed and

trained by the CIA and its activities—both political and military—were directed and controlled by the CIA.[47]

This same view is borne out in Christopher Dickey's book, *With the Contras* and even in the Americas Watch report on violations of the laws of war.[48] The conclusion seems clear. The terrorists operating in Nicaragua are not the Sandinistas (although their human rights record is clearly wanting), but the US-backed counterrevolutionaries.

Terrorism lends itself to subjective definition. It can continue to be 'used almost entirely as a pejorative term to refer to the actions of some opposing organization',[49] or it can be used as a means of identifying certain types of action irregardless of who is committing them. Applying the second criterion to the data at hand one might reach conclusions very different from those championed by some of the large Western states or the news media they have been able to influence. A careful analysis of the situation in Central America suggests that the use of terrorism is not the sole preserve of leftist guerrillas or the poor and the disenfranchised. It has become a consistent policy tool for the pro-Western regimes in Guatemala and El Salvador and is frequently employed to protect the interests of the rich and powerful. It has also become one of the principal methods of operation for the main *contra* force operating out of Honduras. Further, anti-terrorist rhetoric aside, the Reagan Administration seems quite willing to support regimes that have consistently waged terror against their own people and is now engaged in a clear example of state-supported terrorism against Nicaragua.[50] The cult of terror in Central America is not just a function of local conditions or a political culture that tolerates high degrees of violence. It is equally a function of the policies of some pro-Western Central American states and the policy the Reagan Administration has devised for the region.

NOTES

1 Christopher Dickey, *With the Contras in Nicaragua*, New York: Simon and Schuster, 1985.
2 *In re Meunier*, Great Britain, High Court of Justice, Queens Bench Division, 1894. L.R. (1894), 2, Q.B. 415.
3 See Claire Sterling, *The Terror Network*, London: (Weidenfeld & Nicholson, 1981.
4 Robert A Friedlander, 'The Origins of International Terrorism', *in* Yonah Alexander and Seymour Maxwell Finger (eds.), *Terrorism: Interdisciplinary Perspectives*, New York: John Jay Press, 1977, p. 31.
5 See Paul Wilkinson, *Terrorism and the Liberal State*, London: Macmillan, 1977.
6 Grant Wardlaw, *Political Terrorism, Theory, Tactics, and Counter-measures*, London: Cambridge University Press, 1982, p. 9.
7 *Ibid.*
8 Yu Pankov (ed.), *Political Terrorism, An Indictment of Imperialism*, Moscow:

Progress Publishers, 1983, p. 20. See also I Blishchenko and N Zhdanov, *Terrorism and International Law*, Moscow: Progress Publishers, 1984.

9 Yu Pankov, *Ibid.*, pp. 189–194.

10 The 1937 Convention on Terrorism defines the purpose of terrorism as that 'calculated to create a state of terror in the minds of the primary target'. See Jordan J Paust, 'A Definitional Focus' *in* Alexander and Finger (eds.), *Terrorism: Interdisciplinary Perspectives, op. cit.*

11 Jerzy Waciorsky, *Le Terrorism Politique*, Paris: A Peldone, 1939, p. 71. See also G Wardlaw's definition, 'political terrorism is the use, or threat of use, of violence by an individual or a group, whether acting for or in opposition to established authority, when such action is designed to create extreme anxiety and/or fear-inducing effects in a target group larger than the immediate victims with the purpose of coercing that group into acceding to the political demands of the perpetrators'. *op. cit.*, p. 16.

12 Miguel Angel Asturias is a Nobel Prize winning Guatemalan novelist who gained fame for his portrayal of the brutal methods that a prototypical Central American dictator used to terrorise his own people into submission.

13 *The Washington Post*, 2 March 1985, p. 1.

14 Amnesty International, *Amnesty International's Current Concerns in El Salvador*, June 1985, Amnesty International, London, p. 1.

15 For a general discussion of this phenomenon, see Julio Barreiro, *Violencia y política en América Latina*, Colección Minima, No. 42, 4th edn. Mexico City: Siglo Veintiuno, 1978.

16 See Stephen Schlesinger and Stephen Kinzer, *Bitter Fruit, The Untold Story of the American Coup in Guatemala*, New York: Anchor Books, 1983.

17 Edelberto Torres-Rivas, *in* Gabriel Aguilera Peralta, Jorge Romero Imery *et al.*, *Dialectica del terror en Guatemala*, San José: Editorial Universitaria Centro-americana, 1981, p. 9.

18 Aguilera, Romero *et al.*, p. 123.

19 Gorden L Bowen, 'Guatemala: The Origins and Development of State Terrorism', *in* Donald E Schulz and Douglas H Graham (eds.), *Revolution and Counter-revolution in Central America and the Caribbean*, Boulder, Colorado: Westview Press, 1984, p. 287.

20 See Washington Office on Latin America's collected testimony of massacres committed in the Indian highlands. Found in George Black, *Garrison Guatemala*, New York: Monthly Review, 1984, pp. 181–183.

21 Amnesty International, 'Disappearances in Guatemala under the Government of General Oscar Humberto Mejia Victores (August 1983–January 1985)', New York: Amnesty International, March 1985, pp. 1–2.

22 See Thomas Anderson, *Matanza, El Salvador's Communist Revolt of 1932*, Lincoln: University of Nebraska Press, 1971 and Roque Dalton, *Miguel Marmol, los sucesos de 1932 en El Salvador*, San José: Editorial Universitaria Centro-americana, 1972.

23 See Tommie Sue Montgomery, *Revolution in El Salvador*, Boulder, Colorado: Westview Press, 1982.

24 Richard Millet, 'The Politics of Violence: Guatemala and El Salvador', *Current History*, 80, No. 463, February, 1981, p. 7.

25 Amnesty International, 'Extrajudicial Executions in El Salvador', New York: Amnesty International, 1984, p. 3.

26 'Testimony on El Salvador', submitted by Amnesty International to the Sub-committee on Inter-American Affairs of the Committee on Foreign Affairs of the US House of Representatives. (Hearings held on 5 and 11 March 1981.)

27 *Amnesty International 1980 Annual Report*, New York: AI, 1981, p. 131.
28 Raymond Bonner, 'Despite Salvador Vote, Killings Go On', *New York Times*, 25 April 1982.
29 'Amnesty International's Current Concerns on El Salvador', mimeo, London: AI, June 1985, p. 1.
30 *Ibid.*, p. 3.
31 US Department of State, *Country Report on Human Rights Practices, 1984*, Washington: US Government Printing Office, 1985, p. 530.
32 See, for instance, Robert W Taylor and Harry E Vanden, 'Defining Terrorism in El Salvador: "La Matanza"', *The Annals of the American Academy of Political and Social Sciences*, 463, September 1982, pp. 106–118.
33 Christopher Dickey, *With the Contras, A Report from the Wilds of Nicaragua*, New York: Simon and Schuster, 1985, p. 51.
34 Dickey is able to link early support for the *contras* to people like Mario Sandoval Alarcón (a rightist Guatemalan politician considered to be one of the organisers of *La mano blanca*, the original death squad in Guatemala) and Major Roberto d'Aubuisson, the Salvadoran politician with links to the death squads in his country. See Dickey, *Ibid.*, pp. 86–88.
35 Dickey, p. 104.
36 *Ibid.*, p. 102.
37 *Ibid.*, p. 126.
38 Americas Watch, *Violations of the Laws of War by Both Sides in Nicaragua, 1981–1985*, New York: Americas Watch, 1985, p. 4.
39 *Ibid.*
40 See Reed Brody, *Contra Terror in Nicaragua, Report of a Fact-finding Mission: September 1984–January 1985*, Boston: South End Press, 1985.
41 Americas Watch, *Violations of War*, p. 6.
42 Amnesty International, *Nicaragua: The Human Rights Record*, London: Amnesty International, 1986. This report is also critical of the Nicaraguan Government because of its short-term imprisonment of prisoners of conscience, prolonged pre-trial incommunicado detention of political prisoners and restrictions on their right to a fair trial, and poor prison conditions (p. 1).
43 *Psychological Operations in Guerrilla Warfare*, translation by Congressional Research Service, 15 October 1984, p. 11.
44 *Ibid.*, p. 4.
45 Dickey, p. 210.
46 Affidavit of Edgar Chamorro, submitted to the International Court of Justice, *in re* Nicaragua vs United States of America, 5 September 1985. Obtained through the Central American Historical Institute, Georgetown University, Washington, DC, p. 23.
47 *Ibid.*, p. 23.
48 See Dickey, *op. cit.*, and Americas Watch, *Violations of War*, p. 5.
49 Wardlaw, *op. cit.*, p. 9.
50 The US government has already given more than $100 million to the *contras* and Ronald Reagan is now seeking a second $100 million from the US Congress. See 'Contras Kill Four, Wound 13 in Truck Ambush', a UPI story printed in the St Pete Times, St Petersburg, Florida, 18 February 1986, p. 14a.

Terrorism and Insurgency in South Africa

F McA Clifford-Vaughan

THE USE OF VIOLENCE

Studies of terrorism commence with difficulties over nomenclature. This is especially true of the activities of those groups in Southern Africa whose proclaimed aims are 'national liberation', 'freedom' and 'justice'—and whose opponents are thus presumed to resist these desirable states. Such terms as 'freedom fighters' (with or without inverted commas), 'guerrillas', 'liberation forces' and 'democratic, progressive, peace-loving movements', would seem to preclude any discussion of their aims. However, at least as far as this chapter is concerned, any debate as to what to call the perpetrators of bomb and other outrages in South Africa may perhaps best be settled by using their methods rather than their stated aims as the criterion. The placing of landmines on public roads, the setting of limpet mines in shopping centres, the murder of local government officials and the destruction of their homes are all elements in a series of terror tactics and part of a larger strategy of revolutionary war.

The South African Government judges the 'active propaganda' methods of Lenin to be terrorism. Terrorists are considered to be criminals, who are arrested and tried in the courts when possible. To this end, the Government uses the complicated provisions of the Internal Security Act and other legal rules to prosecute individuals arrested by the South African Police.[1]

It should be mentioned here that the South African police force is a paramilitary gendarmerie which is legally the 'first line of defence' in the security of the Republic. From time to time, the South African Defence Force (SADF)—mainly the Army—assists the Police in this task but the SAP is the real responsible force.

A point worth making at this juncture concerns the attitude towards violence *per se* in Africa, especially when compared to Western European norms of civic behaviour.[2] Violence is endemic in African political life and there are many examples of this in existing political regimes throughout the continent.[3] A tolerance of violence is also characteristic of a frontier or settler society, which means that all communities are affected. What would be considered by governments and electorate in Europe to be unacceptable force is commonplace in Africa.[4]

Violence is thus, unfortunately, a fact of life and the use of terror is part of the apparent norm of political action. The possibility that, under certain conditions, the aim may become lost sight of and violence (hence terror) unleashed, is not confined to any one race group or community within the Republic.

Terrorism, as part of the overall attack on the existing Government and social system, may also be seen as an outcome of a lack of inhibitions regarding the use both of violence and of the established tactics now known as revolutionary warfare. (This latter, based on the theories of Mao Tse Tung, Lenin and Clausewitz concerning the political dimension of war, is perceived as a threat to the security of the state and is the principle security preoccupation in South Africa.)

Terrorism is included among the tactics being used to force the surrender of the present government and the installation of a 'progressive', radical, political group. One's perception of its aim—'liberation' and/or 'capitulation'—is not necessarily based on one's racial origins[5] but depends on many factors, including one's terrorism toleration quotient.

The terror campaign in South Africa is carried out, by their own claim, by the African National Congress (ANC), through its military wing, Umkhonto we Sizwe (MK)—'Spear of the Nation'. Its stated strategy is to destroy the existing political, economic and social structure of South Africa by means of (a) political subversion and propaganda; and (b) sabotage and terrorism.[6] Such tactics, in effect, amount to a revolutionary-war strategy, as will be demonstrated in this presentation.

The term 'revolutionary war' has been widely interpreted as the forcible attempt by politically organised groups to gain control of a country's decision-making structure through unconventional warfare and terrorism, which is integrated with political and social mobilisation on the premise that 'the people are both the targets and the actors'.[7]

ARMED ACTION

The year 1976 is generally regarded as the time when the ANC managed to operationalise its 'second Umkhonto Campaign' of armed action against South Africa.[8] The independence of Mozambique provided a contiguous area for infiltration into South Africa and also opened up Swaziland as an infiltration conduit. Widespread domestic troubles throughout South Africa, epitomised by the unrest in Soweto, succeeded in radicalising many Blacks. A large number of radicalised, comparatively well-educated, young Blacks fled from South Africa—many joining the ANC. By the latter half of 1978, official security police estimates calculated that some 4000 fugitives were undergoing insurgency training in Angola, Libya and Tanzania.[9]

The most sustained insurgency operation during this period took place along the northeastern border with Mozambique and Swaziland. In the ten months leading up to April 1978, nearly one hundred suspected insurgents carrying military equipment and more than two hundred recruits were captured in these border areas.[10] Special police units seized large quantities of arms, ammunition and explosives which were to have been arms caches designed to support future infiltration. The insurgent groups involved in these actions were based in Mozambique, in a camp close to the Swaziland border, whence they infiltrated South Africa through Swaziland into the triangle of South African territory bounded by Mozambique and Swaziland. The area is mountainous, undeveloped and geographically ideal guerilla territory.[11]

These ANC operations caused South Africa to deploy police and military forces in increased strength along South Africa's landward borders.

According to Hough,[12] there were 12 incidents of violence attributed to the ANC in 1979, 19 in 1980, 55 in 1981 and 32 in 1982. In his estimate, the organisation's armed attacks were the tip of the iceberg, the extent of which was almost impossible to measure from the 'legal surface' of South African politics.[13]

Lodge recorded 210 instances of terrorist activity between 1977 and 1983 and divided them into ten main categories,[14] in order of frequency:

(a) The sabotage of railroad communications, mainly in urban areas, and of links between Black residential areas and the city centre. There were thirty-eight reported instances of this form of action.
(b) Assassination and attempted assassination aimed at perceived opponents. There were thirty-seven reported instances.
(c) Attacks on industrial installations such as electricity substations and oil refineries. There were twenty-eight such incidents.
(d) Contacts between insurgents and security forces totalled twenty-three.
(e) Attacks on Administration offices: twenty-three.
(f) Pamphlet bombs: eighteen.
(g) Attacks on police stations: eighteen.
(h) Bomb explosions in city centres or public areas: fifteen.
(i) Attacks on military targets: five.
(j) Attacks on the diplomatic offices of Homeland States: two.

The main attacks occurred (in order of frequency) in African townships, in central business districts and in the countryside. Most incidents tended to cluster around the urban–industrial complexes of Johannesburg and Durban and in other areas of the Transvaal and Natal.[15]

Sabotage included a number of spectacular incidents, designed to achieve wide national and international media coverage in order to fulfil the aim of a strategy of armed propaganda:

(a) The successful sabotage of eight oil tanks at Sasolburg in 1980.
(b) A rocket attack on the Voortrekkerhoogte military complex (South Africa's Aldershot), just outside Pretoria.
(c) The successful infiltration of four bombs into South Africa's top-security Koeberg nuclear power station in December 1982.[16]

Other important incidents served to illustrate the simple fact that there is a manifest 'terrorism' potential in any strategy of urban-guerilla warfare:

(a) The Gooch Street shooting of 1977, in which two Whites were killed by terrorists.
(b) The 1980 Silverton bank seige, which led to the death of two White civilians after three well-armed terrorists took hostages in a bank in a White suburb of Pretoria.
(c) The bomb explosion in an administrative building in the Batho township of Bloemfontein, on 18 February 1983, which injured seventy-five Blacks and killed another.
(d) The car bomb attack against the SA Air Force Headquarters in Pretoria, on 20 May 1983, which led to nineteen fatalities, plus more than two hundred injuries and included a number of civilian casualties.[17]
(e) On 4 April 1984, three civilians were killed and twenty-two injured when a car bomb exploded in rush-hour traffic near the offices of the Department of Internal Affairs in Durban.[18]
(f) On 15 July 1984, a second car bomb exploded in Durban, killing five people and injuring twenty.

Attacks on police stations increased, along with the use of more advanced weapons. Petrol bombs were thrown at police stations in 1976. More sophisticated bombs damaged three police stations on the Witwatersrand in late 1977 and early 1978. In May 1979, the ANC attacked the Moroka police station in Soweto, with AK47 rifles and Russian hand grenades, killing one Black constable and wounding five others. In November of the same year, another armed attack was launched against the Orlando police station, also in Soweto, killing two Black policemen and wounding another two. In January 1980, three heavily armed ANC insurgents attacked the Soekmekaar police station (a small White town in the Northern Transvaal), wounding a Black constable and escaping by car. On 4 April 1980, some eleven ANC insurgents, using RPG-7 rocket-launchers and AK47 assault rifles, attacked the Booysens Police Station in a White residential section of Johannesburg and made their escape in two motor cars.

In summary, the period since 1976 has seen an escalation of the ANC's armed activity, albeit of limited scope and intensity. Unable by its nature to challenge the State's control of power, the campaign is characterised by armed propaganda, as one step in a multidimensional, multiphased, protracted people's war.[19]

OVERT TERRORISM

While the ANC has attempted to increase its participation in mass-based Black local action and to extend its insurrection-type tactics, it has also developed a stronger inclination towards terrorism, as enunciated at the Kabwe Conference and the Lusaka Press Conference and as manifested in incidents of rural and urban terrorism.

RURAL TERRORISM

The Kabwe Conference consciously included South Africa's White farmers as legitimate targets of ANC insurgency. Beginning in November 1985, barely five months later, a series of landmines were detonated by civilian vehicles on farm roads in the Messina district, close to the Zimbabwean border. One civilian was killed, two civilians and four soldiers were injured, when six landmines were detonated in late November.[20] This was followed, on 15 December 1985, by the death of six more civilians (five others being injured) when a light truck detonated a landmine on a game farm some thirty kilometres from Messina.[21] On 12 February 1986, another landmine was detonated by a civilian truck in the same district, the sole occupant escaping serious injury.[22] On 4 January 1986, a landmine was detonated by a light truck, killing its two civilian occupants,[23] in the Ellisras area, more than two hundred kilometres southwest of Messina. It would appear that the insurgents who planted this mine, originated from Botswana, while those responsible for the Messina explosions came from Zimbabwe.

The dislocation and damage caused underscores the potential of such a strategy in disrupting the rural areas of South Africa—especially considering that the tactic was effected by a small group and that the SADF follow-up involved large numbers of troops who had no apparent success in apprehending those responsible.

However, such operations are dependent upon external bases for their continuing success. At this stage, it would appear that neither Zimbabwe not Botswana are prepared to host large terrorist camps of the type found in Zambia and Mozambique during the Rhodesian insurgency. Indeed, even the isolated incidents mentioned brought about heavy diplomatic signals from South Africa to the countries concerned, including threats of offensive action if these routes were not closed.

URBAN TERRORISM

To the earlier chronology of urban bomb explosions[24] must be added a further forty-two between August and December 1985. Death and injury to innocent civilians often resulted. On 23 December 1985, a bomb exploded in the middle of a shopping centre in the coastal resort of Amanzimtoti, south of Durban, killing five civilians and injuring another sixty-one people, many seriously.[25] The target was clearly civilian and the timing of 10.45 a.m.

suggests an unequivocal intent to kill, maim and terrorise. *The Times*, London, stated: 'The Durban bomb is arguably the most indiscriminate act of terrorism to date, except insofar as it seems to have been aimed mainly at whites.'[26]

MOBILISATION OF THE MASSES

The 'mobilisation of the masses' in South Africa has been a major function of front organisations for the banned African National Congress/South African Communist Party, at least since 1970, when the explosive power of youth groups was realised.[27] This has developed into the politicisation of Black and Coloured schools, and other educational centres. A direct result is school boycotts, also burning of classrooms, books and the occasional teacher. Throwing of stones at motorcars on the highway has increased, too.

'Black Consciousness' has also been fostered and groups adopting this philosophy or psychological attitude[28] are playing a large part in politicising that majority group of the population, especially students at tertiary establishments. The South African Student Organisation (SASO) was formed as a result of the efforts of Steve Biko and others at the University of the North, Turfloop, in 1969 and was a conscious effort to break away from the all-White National Union of South African Students (NUSAS). Most of the followers of SASO were supporters of the Pan-African Congress. Indians and Coloureds were also admitted, giving a new dimension to the concept 'Black African'. After 1975, Biko adopted the view that the ANC was the primary revolutionary movement and that the Black Consciousness Movement should amalgamate with the ANC. Other groupings with Black Consciousness principles and ANC leanings include the Azanian Peoples Organisation and the Azanian Student Organisation, to name but two. All are actively engaged in mobilisation and politicisation, if not in 'active measures'.

Incidentally, the overdue admission of Black students to English-medium White universities has now brought Black activism to what were formerly the seedbeds only of White radical activism. The more visible results of mobilisation include mass attendances at funerals and at gatherings to mark anniversaries of violent occurrences. Whipped-up emotions often result in further violence. In some areas, mass boycotting of White-owned shops demonstrates the latent power of the Black consumer, to both Black and White.

As a central tenet of ANC strategy, the mobilisation of the masses aims to draw the 'politicised' individuals into the ranks of the ANC.[29] To this end, the ANC has also attempted to infiltrate and organise itself in anti-government bodies such as the United Democratic Front and the trade union movement.[30]

TOWNSHIP UNREST

The current wave of unrest and rioting sweeping across South Africa, the often harsh, repressive response by the State, the severe economic recession and unemployment, have provided the ANC with a firm basis for action in this field. Slovo believes that the upsurge of ANC incidents in 1984 and 1985 played an important inspirational role in heightening revolt and unrest.[31]

While the ANC has been partly responsible for the unrest, it would appear that it, like the government, has been reactive rather than initiatory in the situation. The State itself has acknowledged this reality. In an address to the President's Council in February 1986, the Minister of Law and Order, Louis Le Grange, outlined the complexity of the causes of violence:

(a) The crisis of legitimacy and credibility of local authorities, which are unable to live up to Black moderates' expectations.
(b) Grievances over influx control.
(c) Atrocious physical conditions in many of the townships, and unpopular township removals.
(d) A lack of say in political decision-making processes.
(e) Real/perceived inequalities in education and facilities.[32]

According to Schlemmer, in trying to understand the unrest one has to consider: 'a complexity of interacting conditions—a matrix of conditions.'[33] He argues that any pattern of political unrest must be analysed at two levels: 'One level is that of the manifest goals and objectives among leading participants. Another level is that of the conditions, frustrations and motivations existing among the rank and file members of communities, which create the propensity for unrest or the inclination to participate in the pattern of behaviour prescribed by the leading figures.'[34] Most objective studies of township unrest point to such propensity prior to any intervention by either the ANC or the UDF.[35]

The ANC attempts not only to utilise and take credit for the unrest but also, if possible, to control the situation. Indeed, the widespread violence has forced the ANC to re-formulate its strategy, to encompass a more closely ordered perspective on insurrection, for use in the specific conditions of the South African situation. Clearly, because of the powerful nature of the South African state, unrest and revolt alone will not overthrow the system, but the ANC contends that such tactics can certainly be used as part of a protracted strategy of revolutionary warfare. Insurrection (mass unrest and revolt) can weaken the State and serve as a radicalising and recruiting agent for the ANC's people's army.[36] Insurrection, then, fits into the wider rubric of revolutionary warfare:

> Between the anvil of united mass action and the hammer of the armed struggle we will crush Apartheid and white minority rule.[37]

In fact, the mass unrest and industrial action of insurrection can be used to actively develop more mature revolutionary conditions:

It is an imperative task of the revolutionary and democratic forces to compound and deepen the crisis, by ever intensifying the struggle for national and social emancipation.[38]

As mentioned by Tambo, democratic forces have facilitated mass mobilisation for the ANC by increasing political awareness and activism amongst the population. Thus, for example, the ANC regards the UDF as a major tool in promoting its aims, because the UDF's affiliates represent disparate groups such as workers, students, churches and community or social welfare associations. The UDF's appeal to a wide spectrum of 'liberals' makes it an ideal and typical front organisation:

Revolutionary groups are not in the business of just setting up front organisations, but also of penetrating and trying to take over groups that are still legal and which have roughly identical aims. Some of the affiliates of the UDF, for example, have ideologies indistinguishable from the ANC's.[39]

DESTRUCTION OF LOCAL GOVERNMENT

Facilitated by local grievances and popular enmity towards the Administration, insurrection and armed action have been used in attempts to render the urban Black areas ungovernable by destroying local government.

To this end, there have been numerous petrol-bomb, hand-grenade and rifle attacks on policemen and town councillors and their property.[40] Administrative structures and their associated personnel have also been attacked, along with police stations and personnel carriers (Casspirs). The detonation of a Soviet landmine by a police vehicle near Pretoria in February 1986, and the subsequent discovery of five anti-tank mines carried by a terrorist killed by police in the Eastern Cape, portend an ominous escalation of attempts to make the townships 'no-go' areas for the Security Forces.[41] In short, township administration has, in many cases, all but collapsed and the situation has been militarised by the inability of the police to operate in many townships, except in armoured personnel carriers, in strength.

This 'strength' has not prevented the murder of eleven Black policemen in the first two months of 1986 alone. Other adjuncts to insurrection, such as the firebombing and murder of moderate Black councillors and other perceived collaborators, are a 'classical' form of terrorism. The method known as 'necklacing' adds a horror dimension.

The ANC has thus been implementing the early stages of a protracted insurgency, under cover of a widespread insurrection. This has led a senior Washington journalist to conclude that:

The ANC, since early last year, ordered cadres to eliminate all blacks who assist the white government in administering black townships. The instruction to terrorise or kill black councillors, civil servants, policemen and other collaborators has been carried out with startling ferocity.

The technique should be familiar to veterans of the Vietnam War, where the systematic assassination of village leaders was used by the VietCong to collapse the adminstration of the Saigon Government. Terror succeeds where minor officials go unprotected.[42]

The ANC has recently called on township residents to move from the stage of ungovernability to one where people's political committees are set up.[43] The creation of 'parallel hierarchies' is a technique known to be part of communist revolutionary warfare tactics.[44] The similarity with Vietnam is again evident, as pointed out in *The Washington Post*, 26 February 1986:

If the Vietnamese pattern holds true, these block committees will collect rents and fees that the government cannot collect, conscript guerillas whose loyalty the government cannot win, determine the curriculum of schools the government cannot control and generally take over local administration.

In the townships of Lamontville and Chesterville, near Durban, this is already happening and people are being persuaded and threatened by 'cadres' or 'street committees' not to pay rent to official township authorities.[45] No doubt, similar is happening elsewhere.

These are lessons which the ANC has also learned from the Rhodesian experience of ZANU and ZANLA. Perhaps as such they are even more relevant to South Africa than is Vietnam.[46]

IDEOLOGICAL DIMENSIONS

All revolutions are about state power—ours is no exception.[47]

The aim of the banned African National Congress, in formal alliance with the South African Communist Party[48] is a closely organised seizure of state power. To this end, they visualise a protracted struggle against the presently constituted incumbents of state power, embracing all forms of struggle, violent and non-violent, in a totalist revolutionary warfare strategy. Once state power has been captured, the aim of the ANC/SACP alliance may be defined as the radical re-structuring of South African society, on the politcal basis of majority rule, in a unitary state, within an economic framework of Marxist socialism.

The ANC's 'Strategy and Tactics'[49] postulates a two-stage process of revolutionary transformation for South Africa, where confrontation in the early stages of the conflict will be based primarily on race. A 'nationalist liberation struggle' is defined by the ANC as its primary strategeic objective.[50] It has been consistently stressed in ANC literature that the nationalist liberation struggle will be followed by a process of 'social and economic emancipation':

In our country more than in any other part of the world, it is inconceivable for liberation to have meaning without a return of the wealth of the land to the people as a whole. It is therefore a fundamental feature of our strategy that victory must embrace more than formal political democracy. To allow the existing economic forces to retain their interests intact is to feed the root of racial supremacy and does not represent even a shadow of democracy.[51]

This viewpoint has been reinforced in contemporary ANC thinking. ANC President, Oliver Tambo, has laid greater stress on the revolutionary role of the Black working class and the aims of socialism. In 1981 Tambo praised the alliance with the Communist Party and the reciprocal influence the two organisations have had on one another.[52] The Communist Party, for its part, has always been clear on the question of a 'socialist' revolution, as in the following statement by Slovo, a high ranking official of the SACP:

It is precisely because, in South Africa, capitalist production relations are the foundation of national repression that the nationalist struggle itself has an objective co-incidence with the elimination of all forms of exploitation. ... If every racist statute were to be repealed tomorrow, leaving the economic *status quo* undisturbed, 'white domination' in its most essential aspects would remain. *National liberation*, in its true sense, must therefore imply the expropriation of the owners of the means of production and the complete destruction of the state. *There can be no halfway house*.[53]

For radical opponents of the government and the present socioeconomic system, the objective of armed and revolutionary struggle is the seizure of state power and the subsequent transformation of the economic and social system to a Marxist or Marxist–Leninist model:

For the ANC there is no alternative. We reject all reforms and concessions designed to sustain white rule and exploitation in our country. The struggle is not for minor tinkering with the exploitative socio-economic system but *for the seizure of power*.[54]

Limited reform that falls short of a complete transfer of power to the ANC will fail to satisfy the revolutionary who is seeking state power. Says Slovo: 'To create conditions in which insurgency can take root in the South African context means nothing less than to set the stage for an immediate advance towards majority rule.'[55] Slovo rejects as 'anti-historical' any prospect of a real transformation in the power structure based on reform:

Those then who maintain that a substantial shift in political power could eventually come through changes by and within the system can only base their prophecy on the faith that the SA ruling class will set a precedent in history and abandon the real source of its power without a fight.[56]

Radical opposition to the South African government sees the pragmatic reforms instituted by P W Botha and his administration as little more than a tactical re-disposition, calculated to streamline apartheid's machinery and to rationalise and strengthen both White control and, more importantly, the control of the dominant interests of capitalism over the economy. Insofar as reform attenuates injustices in the system, it is seen as dangerous by the insurgent since it serves to erode popular sympathy and active support for the revolution and to strengthen the power base of the Government.

The continuing schism between the South African government and the ANC is illustrated by the recent conditions laid down by the ANC as basic pre-requisites before 'negotiations' can begin:

(a) The lifting of the ban on political organisations in South Africa.
(b) The regime's acceptance of and commitment to universal adult suffrage in a united and non-fragmented South Africa.
(c) Unconditional release of Nelson Mandela and all other political detainees.
(d) Abolishment of all Bantustan 'homelands'.[57]

Given the latent structural flaws in the South African system, as well as the respective positions of the South African Government and the radical opposition (ANC/SACP, UDF, AZAPO, PAC etc.), it becomes clear that the structural determinants of the situation (coupled with the subjective and objective positions of the antagonists, and their support bases within these structures) are such that neither side will accept a political solution that does not include the control of state power at the expense of the material interests of the other side.

Reforms instituted by the government will, almost by definition, fail to satisfy the demands and aspirations of the radical opposition. This is not because the government fails to comprehend this fact but because acceding to these demands would mean nothing less than the destruction of the whole system the government is committed to maintaining and defending. A solution that does not include within itself the destruction of the State and its replacement by the insurgent's model, cannot be found in the 'civil' dimension alone. The State and its socioeconomic order is threatened by revolutionary violence. To argue, in this context, that the military role can be eschewed and peaceful change brought about at the negotiating table—without capitulation—is to misunderstand the dynamics of the situation. The struggle between the South African Government[58] and the ANC/SACP is a struggle for state power between antagonists lacking social, economic and political consensus; a struggle which apparently cannot be accommodated in any pluralist, liberal, democratic concept of political relationships.

The use of armed violence is the basic tenet of revolutionary warfare. Mao Tse Tung argued that the seizure of power by armed force is both the central task of revolution and its highest form. In the South African context, 'national liberation' movements started off by seeking to achieve change peacefully but soon found that this route was blocked to them. According to Wallerstein: 'each concluded that the only road to national liberation open to them was the road of armed struggle.'[59]

Furthermore, he argues: 'It was not that they rejected dialogue, rather they found regretfully that it was only through armed struggle that one day a real dialogue of coloniser and colonised would be rendered possible by the equalising impact of military combat.'[60]

In an address to the court during the Rivonia trial, Nelson Mandela put forward a similar line of argument:

> We felt that without violence there would be no way open to the African people to succeed in their struggle against the principle of white supremacy. All lawful methods of expressing opposition to this principle had been closed by legislation and we were placed in a position where we had to accede to a permanent state of inferiority or defy the government.[61]

In 1968, Tambo argued, in a 'Call to Revolution', that:

> Africans and other oppressed people could not hope to achieve their freedom except by organising their own liberation army and arming the masses to fight a revolutionary war of liberation. We in the ANC do not imagine that the defeat of imperialism in Southern Africa will be quick or easy. We realise that it will be longdrawn and bloody.[62]

The role of revolutionary warfare was formalised at the 1960 Morogoro Consultative Conference and statements by ANC officials since then have continually re-asserted the validity and correctness of the path of armed struggle. Despite the Nkomati Accord between South Africa and Mozambique, the ANC re-affirmed its belief in the validity of armed struggle and terrorism. In May 1984, *Sechaba* argued, as a result of Nkomati: 'Our principle aim, therefore, is and must be to intensify our political and military offensive inside South Africa.'[63]

For its part, the SACP has always been a committed advocate of violent forms of struggle. The April 1977 SACP plenum confirmed that current actions have as their ultimate aim an attempt by force of arms to overthrow the Government of the Republic. 'Soweto closed the debate about the legitimacy of resorting to armed struggle, while acting as a precursor which has brought closer than ever the possibility of an effective beginning to the armed struggles.'[64]

FUTURE PLANS

At the 1985 Kabwe Conference of the ANC, decisions were taken to attempt to both broaden and escalate the range and application of violence. The ANC describes the conference as having been a 'Council of War'. Delegates to the conference did not see any point in negotiations with the South African Government, nor did they see a 'national convention' as a victory for the ANC:

Victory as far as the ANC is concerned means the revolutionary seizure of state power. It does not mean a national convention.[65]

The ANC plan a substantial escalation of the armed struggle as well as an increase in 'permissible' targets for sabotage and terrorist attack:

They argue that the government has shown no willingness to distinguish between 'hard' and 'soft' targets over the past ten months of serious unrest or in the raid on refugees in Gaborone. They point to the assassination of activists. They say the increasing militarisation of South Africa, particularly of the white bloc, the inclusion of white farmers in rural security networks, the organisation of urban whites into civil defence units, and the anti-union and anti-worker actions of some companies has made the distinction between 'hard' and 'soft' a blur.

But the ANC has added a wide range of people involved in some way in defending, promoting and justifying apartheid's national or class inequalities to its list of targets. In adition, that indications are clear the Umkhonto we Sizwe guerillas will no longer be under instructions to take quite the same care about avoiding casualties among civilians in strikes against specified targets.[66]

According to Slovo, this change in tactics was brought about by the increased radicalisation of the ANC's support base inside South Africa:

The vital element now is the combat willingness of the majority. We need to respond to the mood of the people—that we must take the lives of the other side as well.[67]

APPRECIATION OF ANC TACTICAL PROBLEMS

It is clear, then, that over the past twenty years the ANC has increased its commitment to the seizure of state power. Nevertheless, its implementation of aspects of revolutionary warfare against South Africa remains at a relatively immature level of development.

An analysis of ANC insurgency against South Africa since 1960 points to the fact that, alongside the successful mobilisation of the population, there are other indispensable requirements for the successful development of a strategy of armed violence against the South African state—and indeed for the survival of the ANC itself.

The early period between 1960 and 1964 (when the ANC attempted a sabotage campaign and the implementation of Operation Mayibuye), proved conclusively that the particular situational context of contemporary South Africa makes any internal organisation highly vulnerable to state counteraction. Indeed, the experiences of this period and later point to the manifest and intractable problems of attempting to establish 'base areas' or 'liberated zones' inside South Africa, in the face of the State's preponderant coercive apparatus (administrative, legal, social, the police and military). Throughout the past twenty-five years, the entire geographical area of South Africa has firmly remained a military zone of control in which the SADF has freedom of movement. The same has held true inside southwest Africa (Namibia). The insurgent may attempt to contest a given area, or operate in a given area through the conduct of covert operations, but he is unable to control any area in the conventional sense of a 'liberated guerilla zone'. The implications of these facts for the insurgent are profound.

If a 'guerilla army' is to operate, it has to have easy source of supply, food and ammunition, a safe area to rest and receive medical aid, and finally a safe area to train new recruits in order to convert mass mobilisation and power support into usable military currency. For strategic viability and effectiveness—as opposed to merely the ability of small tactical groups to operate over short periods—the organisation must have organisational coherence, an operational infrastructure and superstructure (control and command), which is relatively free from the counterforce of the target state. An organisation can, after all, suffer only a limited number of Rivonias before it becomes disorganised and disordered. Furthermore, if it hopes to escalate the conflict beyond the lower levels of political mobilisation and agitation, sporadic sabotage and terrorism, it must have large base areas capable of hosting the nucleus of a real 'people's army'. For Mao Tse Tung, this was indispensable to the success of a 'people's war'.[68]

Faced with the reality of the post-Rivonia domestic environment, the ANC was forced to seek an exile condition in which to develop these necessary assets. The period between 1964 and 1975 served to demonstrate the problems contained in any attempt to develop insurgency against South Africa from external base areas that were not contiguous with South Africa's northern borders. The experience highlighted the almost insurmountable obstacles posed by the geographically intervening zone of buffer states which were actively hostile to the aims and intentions of the ANC.

Conversely, the period between 1970 and 1984 showed that, given access to facilities in neighbouring states, infiltration and insurgency could begin to develop actively. It must be remembered, of course, that this development was attenuated by the conditional, restricted nature of the access provided by Black states unwilling to allow the development of large guerilla bases.

Angola is, perhaps, the exception in that it has allowed SWAPO to build large-scale military bases on its soil and has aided in their defence. SWAPO's dependence on external bases in Angola and Zambia, and on Soviet arms and equipment is well documented. The escalation of SWAPO's armed campaign after the independence of Angola serves as conclusive proof of the vital aspect of such bases in the development of insurgency.

Court trials of ANC insurgents in this period highlight their dependence on foreign bases. Most attacks were carried out by cadres, trained and armed externally, who entered South Africa from external bases, more often than not returning to them after fulfilling their missions.[69] Training and administration of the ANC/SACP and SWAPO remains an almost entirely external function. The ANC's secretariat is based at Lusaka, Zambia, while cadres are given 'civilian' training in Tanzania and military training in Angola. Further specialised military training is provided at bases and locations in the USSR and East Germany. Military equipment is provided by donor states (especially the USSR) for both the ANC and SWAPO. Indigenous sources of modern military hardware are thus almost non-existent. According to Stuart Menaul, by 1983 the ANC had some 10,000 trained guerillas, the majority of whom were based outside South Africa.

THE STANDING OF THE ANC

There is considerable ignorance and misunderstanding about the real objectives of the ANC, both inside and outside South Africa.

INTERNALLY

Within the Republic, the important factor of information and misinformation is largely controlled by governmental regulations, which means considerable limiting of what can be reported for public consumption. Within this situation, the English-language media is accused of left-wing bias, the Afrikaans press of complicity with the Government, the Black and Indian press with much of the misinformation and speculation regarding the origins and motives of terror acts—a position which is exploited, quite naturally, by cadres of ANC/SACP and by UDF, AZAPO and other front organisations engaged in subversion. This state of affairs is not helped by the banning of publications and people. For example, most of the sources quoted in this chapter—and certainly *Sechaba*, Tambo and Slovo—are legally prohibited from being quoted in the Republic. This creates uncertainty among the literate population, Black and White, as to the intentions and objectives of the insurgents. Businessmen and students naively clamour to have meetings with the ANC, in Zambia or Zimbabwe, 'to find out their aims'!

Universities are allowed to possess banned material for research purposes but its reading is again controlled by Government regulation. Academics with access to such information who prefer the notion of evolution to revolution and who condemn the methods and aims of the ANC/SACP and their front/support organs, are accused by the ill-informed student body of being 'reactionary fascists'. The gutting by firebombs of the departments of Political Science and Social Studies at the University of Natal on 21 March 1986 (in which this author lost all his documentation, books and academic possessions, except for the manuscript of this chapter, which had been removed for correction) caused an outburst of ignorant speculation as to the perpetrators. Opinions varied between 'police agents' and 'unknown left-wingers'. The obvious conclusion would have been ANC, since such action is in keeping with past track-records and the terrorisation of 'liberal' academics is known to be on the agenda.

Marighella rather than Mao seems to be the tactic utilised, but someone has obviously also read his Sun Tzu on the subject of winning without actually fighting!

The State's response, one feels, should be to make all this information freely available, or at least not to impede its propagation. Since the general view seems to be that the ANC, even after twenty-odd years of activity, is really no nearer to gaining the Clausewitzian final victory, it might be a good notion to allow this fact to be widely disseminated by those who wish to do it. After all, propaganda and information, together with intelligence, are important factors in insurgency operations ... for both sides!

INTERNATIONALLY

Outside South Africa, the ANC seems to be regarded in many quarters as worthy of assistance in their noble fight against the evils of apartheid. As has been shown, their methods and objectives go considerably further. It is well to point out that examples abound of mistaken perceptions by outsiders as to the intentions of African 'liberation' movements. They are quite prevalent elsewhere, too. The ANC/SACP alliance, by its own claim, is aiming for revolutionary seizure of state power and subsequent transformation of South Africa's economic and social system to a Marxist or Marxist–Leninist model. The significance of this for the West is obvious.

CONCLUSION

That change is taking place is undeniable, throughout the whole spectrum of South Africa's internal policies, its social, economic and political life. This process now started cannot be stopped, except by a major cataclysmic revolutionary uprising, and it will eventually produce results, unforeseen at the moment. Whether these will be viewed as beneficial to the people of South Africa will depend, no doubt, on the ideological framework within which one is operating.

What is certain is that the results of terrorism of the type now occurring in South Africa will lead to disaster for all Blacks, Whites, the economy and the progress of future development. For this, if no other reason, the international community should cease its aid to terrorist-orientated groups, no matter how noble their stated aims. Their kind of change cannot result in anything other than total chaos ... chaos which will be exploited by those who would use such conditions for their own ideological purposes.

NOTES

1 The narrow legalistic view of terrorism is not shared by all Security Forces

engaged in counterinsurgency operations (COIN OPS). The Army, for example, pays great attention in its training programme and in its operations to the political aspects of terroristic acts. Troops are taught the elements of revolutionary warfare techniques and the aims of the 'enemy'—a term used generally by SF officers when referring to ANC/SACP cadres. Civic Action and other socioeconomic programmes are also carried out by Security Force personnel as part of COIN OPS.

2 Western European studies of the phenomenon of political terrorism are extensive and are probably based upon a view that 'le terrorisme est un moyen politique, une manifestation de violence collective, une force'. G Bonthoul and R Carrere, *Le Défi de la Guerre, 1740–1974*, Paris: PUF, 1976. G Wardlaw, *Political Terrorism*, Cambridge, 1982; P Wilkinson, *Political Terrorism*, London: Macmillan, 1974; and W Laqueur, 'The Anatomy of Terrorism', *Ten Years of Terrorism*, London: RUSI, 1970; offer explanations for terror based on political culture and democratic permissiveness, as well as national character.

3 Cf. e.g., DT Kunert, *Africa: Soviet Strategy and Western Counter-strategy.* Occasional Paper No. 1, SA Forum, 1981, pp. 6 *et seq.*

4 Cf. EV Walter, *Terror and Resistance: A Study of Political Violence*, Oxford: OUP, 1969, p. 12 *et passim.*

5 The terms 'White', 'Black', 'Indian' and 'Coloured' (mixed race), as used in this chapter, are not an attempt to perpetuate previous governmental racial classifications. They are used as a means of differentiation throughout South African society. For example, institutions like the Black Students Society identify themselves as such. Tribal names are also used as a means of identification—for example, Inkatha is described (by its own members) as a Zulu cultural movement. The ANC appears to consist mainly of people of Xhosa origin. Whether these facts are significant can be debated.

6 'ANC Strategy and Tactics, 1969' in *Sechaba*, 1970.

7 Cf. R Taber, *War of the Flea*, 1974. P Wilkinson, *Terrorism and the Liberal State*, London: 1977; and G Wardlaw, *op. cit.*, pp. 3–17 *et seq.*; have similar definitions.

8 T Lodge, 'The ANC in 1982' *SA Review* (*One*), Johannesburg: Ravan Press, 1983. Lodge is seen in some quarters as an apologist for the ANC (e.g., *Aida Parker Newsletter* (*APN*), Johannesburg, No. 71, December 1985).

9 *Rand Daily Mail*, Johannesburg, 2 June 1978.

10 *Daily News*, Durban, 30 April 1978.

11 *Daily News*, Durban, 16 April 1978.

12 Professor M Hough, Director, Institute for Strategic Studies (ISSUP), University of Pretoria.

13 *The Star*, Johannesburg, 5 January 1983.

14 T Lodge, *The ANC and Violence in South Africa*, Public Lecture, University of Natal, 29 September 1983. Official sources give similar figures.

15 T Lodge, *op. cit.*

16 *Keesing's Contemporary Archives*, 1984; also confidential interview with Security Force officers.

17 The myth propagated by pro-ANC supporters that bombs were selective and that the ANC/SACP attacks and resulting deaths were 'accidents' was firmly laid to rest in this incident and in the indiscriminiate bombings which followed.

18 *Daily News*, Durban, 5 April 1984. According to Lodge (*op. cit.*), bomb attacks in the 1977 to 1983 period were intended to inspire confidence amongst the dominated population rather than terror within the White community.

19 J Slovo, *South Africa and the New Politics of Revolution*, London: Penguin, 1977, pp. 195 *et seq*.
20 *Natal Mercury*, Durban, 16 December 1985.
21 *Ibid.*
22 *Natal Mercury*, 13 February 1986.
23 *The Daily News*, 6 January 1986.
24 See earlier in chapter.
25 *Natal Mercury*, 24 December 1985.
26 *The Times*, London, 23 December 1985.
27 'Primary objectives for infiltration during the 1970s were Black youth organisations, Black trades unions and certain specifically created 'front organisations', as well as the 'liberal, White, English-speaking universities'—*Interview with a Security Force Officer*, 1986.
28 *Black Consciousness*, unpublished paper by FMcA Clifford-Vaughan.
29 'Our task is to find ways of harnessing the combat potential and exploiting the new strength of the people in political motion'—Joe Slovo (SACP/ANC), 1985.
30 A massive disinformation programme has been launched to sell the idea that detained Communists are actually oppressed nationalists. A poll held recently in Soweto revealed that 90 per cent of high-school students in the town thought Mandela had been convicted for supporting the rights of Blacks; none knew of his membership of the SACP and only 2 per cent had heard of Rivonia.—Conversation with Security Force Officer, 1986.
31 J Slovo, *The Guardian*, London, 11 August 1985.
32 Research undertaken in South Africa by social scientists has underlined the complexity of the causes of urban unrest, as contained in *Indicator SA*, published by the University of Natal:

1. 'Black Urban Unrest: How Serious Is The Problem?'—Schlemmer L, in Vol. 1, No. 2, 1983.
2. 'Administration Boards Still Rule—Fick M, in Vol. 1, No. 2, 1983.
3. 'Political Unrest and African Rights', Parts One and Two—Schlemmer L, in Vol. 2, No. 3, October 1984.
4. 'Township Unrest by Township Residents'—Schlemmer L, in Vol. 2, No. 4, January 1985.
5. 'Resistance to African Town Councils'—Laurence P, in Vol. 2, No. 4, 1985.
6. 'South Africa's Urban Crisis: The Need for Fundamental Solutions'—Schlemmer L, in Vol. 3, No. 1, 1986.

33 L Schlemmer, 'South Africa's Urban Crisis', *Indicator SA*, Winter 1985, p. 3.
34 *Ibid.*
35 David Nbaba, secretary of the ANC observer group at the UN, said in *The Black Scholar*, November 1984: '... Tambo called on the South African people to make themselves ungovernable ... institutions unworkable ... a number of black stooges have been killed, many heads of black townships have been petrol bombed ... people are now challenging these collaborators ... this is a phase of the people's war ... you have to mobilise for such actions ...'
36 According to standard texts on insurrection, mass unrest, strikes and armed activity from below, coordinated with seizure of the Government's strategic arms, often from above, occurring at a historical juncture where the threatened state is faced with a serious political, economic and/or military crisis, is enough to provide the short, sharp move needed to overthrow the *status quo*. This would clearly not apply in the South African case.

37 N Mandela, quoted in *Sechaba*, March 1984.
38 O Tambo, quoted in *Sechaba*, March 1984.
39 Dr Simon Baynham, quoted in *The Sunday Tribune*, 10 November 1985.
40 Writing in late 1985, Schlemmer contended that since August 1984 some 160 public buildings and some 300 homes of Black councillors and policemen had been destroyed and that about 240 urban councillors had resigned, following the deaths of five councillors and numerous attacks on councillors and property. L Schlemmer, *op. cit.*, p. 2. See also note 35.
41 *Sunday Times*, Johannesburg, 23 February 1986. Police have expressed concern about apparently well-equipped arsenals in the townships and the prospect of armed attack by dissidents every time they enter these areas. 'Liberal' opinion has joined Black protests against the presence of Security Forces in townships, for whatever purposes.
42 *The Washington Times*, 26 February 1986.
43 *Business Day*, Johannesburg, 29 May 1985.
44 Cf. FMM Clifford-Vaughan, *Force and Peace*, Durban : 1979 ; and 'Some French Notions on Revolutionary War' *Assegai*, Salisbury : 1969 ; as well as the literature on this phenomenon cited therein.
45 Confidential conversation with academic sociologist who conducts research in the townships named, March 1986.
46 P Pandya, *An investigation into the application of Mao's ... theory of insurgent warfare by ZANU during the campaign in Rhodesia*, unpublished MA thesis, University of South Africa, 1985.
47 Oliver Tambo, President of the South African National Congress, in *Sechaba*, March 1984. *Sechaba* is the official publication of the African National Congress.
48 While analysts dispute the relative strengths of the ANC and SACP within the alliance, what cannot be disputed is the relative importance of the SACP within the elite structures. At the June 1985 Kabwe Conference of the ANC, the National Executive Committee of the ANC was reconstituted. In its present form, 19 of its 30 members are concurrently members of the SACP.
49 'ANC Strategy and Tactics, 1969' in *Sechaba*, 1970, was the exposition and summation of ANC strategy, which came out of the 1969 consultative conference at Morogoro, Tanzania.
50 At the Kabwe Conference, June 1985, the ranks of the ANC internal underground and National Executive Committee were opened up to Whites, Coloureds and Indians. This has been referred to as the stage of full organisational unity between the ANC and proven 'non-African' progressives.
51 'ANC Strategy and Tactics, 1969' in *Sechaba*, 1970. This point was developed by Michael Schatzberg in *The Political Economy of Zimbabwe*, New York : Praeger, 1984, qv. He argues that, in the context of the Zimbabwean insurgency, national liberation has not been followed by a successful economic transformation.
52 *Sechaba*, 1981. The date 30 July 1981 marked the 60th anniversary of the SACP.
53 J Slovo, *South Africa : The New Politics of Revolution, op. cit.* Joe Slovo is also concurrently a member of the National Executive Committee of the ANC and top strategist of the ANC's armed wing.
54 *Sechaba*, 1977, p. 34.
55 J Slovo, *op. cit.*, p. 115.
56 J Slovo, *Ibid.*, p. 112.
57 JM Makatini, ANC, at the OAU Defence Commission, 8th Session, Accra, 1984, as quoted in *Africa Research Bulletin*, January 1984. Makatini was coordinator

of ANC terrorist training in Algeria in the 1970s; and later ANC representative at the United Nations, New York. He is at present international affairs director of the ANC.

58 As pointed out already, the government represents a particular social and economic system. This analysis would thus apply *inter alia* to any change in government which did not include a transformation of the socioeconomic order and the accession to power of the ANC. 'Our Nationalism must not be confused with chauvinism or the narrow nationalism of a previous epoch. It must not be confused with the classical drive by an elitist group among the oppressed people to gain ascendancy so that they can replace the oppressor in the exploitation of the mass' 'ANC Strategy and Tactics, 1969' in *Sechaba*, 1970.
59 I Wallerstein, *The African Liberation Reader*.
60 *Ibid.*
61 R Price, *The Apartheid Regime* (Cape Town: David Phillip, 1980), p. 78. Mandela was leader of the ANC. On 11 July 1963 the police raided the ANC headquarters in Rivonia and the subsequent trial of ANC leaders began in October 1963. Mandela was found guilty of attempting to overthrow the State by force and was sentenced to life imprisonment. See note 30.
62 *Sechaba*, 8 January 1968.
63 *Sechaba*, May 1984.
64 *The African Communist*, No 70, 1977, p. 14.
65 H Barrell, 'All For the Front', *Work in Progress*, 38, Johannesburg, 1985, p. 12.
66 *Ibid.*, p. 13.
67 *The Guardian*, London, 11 August 1985.
68 Pandya, thesis *op. cit.*, nevertheless, states that in spite of the failure of ZANU to develop a conventional Giap people's war, ZANU succeeded in its aim of overthrowing White power in Rhodesia. In this case, outside diplomatic interference may have played a bigger role than is admitted.
69 Analysis of evidence presented at the trials of captured ANC insurgents shows the dependence of the insurgency campaign on external base facilities. Arms and ammunition were smuggled in most of these cases, from Lesotho, Mozambique (using Swaziland as a conduit), Botswana and, to a lesser degree, Zimbabwe. Captured insurgents revealed training in Angola, Tanzania, Mozambique, East Germany and the USSR. Significantly, although attempts were made to establish local cells and 'safe houses', insurgents tended to operate on a mission-orientated basis, entering South Africa for a terrorist raid and exfiltrating after its conclusion to a neighbouring state.

IV

Behavioural Aspects

Theories on the Efficacy of Terrorism

N O Berry

It would be a very useful task to detail for each alleged purpose or function the actual mechanism of operation of the terror process leading to the supposed result. To our knowledge this has never been attempted.[1]

The task is to explain why terrorism works. If it did not produce intended results—at least some of the time—then it would cease to be a political strategy. Terrorism without efficacy would then only be an expression of some destructive pathology.

Terrorism is here defined as the threat or use of illegal violence to weaken a hated political authority.[2] The political authority can be a government, party, minority, class, race, religion, region or any combination of the above. By definition, terrorism works when the target of terrorism acts in such a manner that it either loses public support for its political position or it lessens its own political capabilities. Terrorists cannot weaken the hated political authority by their own actions.

Terrorism is a strategy of the weak.[3] If those wanting to weaken a hated political authority were strong, they would not use terrorism as their main strategy because successful terrorism depends entirely upon the actions of the target. The target, in effect, has control of the situation. So if those wanting to weaken a hated political authority are strong, they *will use strategies for which the outcome is more within their own control.* The outcomes of coups, revolutions and guerrilla wars are in some measure in the hands of plotters, revolutionaries and guerrillas. Not so with terrorists. Theoretically, every terrorist action can be defeated by the target of terror.[4]

If successful terrorism depends on the target's action, then to explain successful terrorism one should study the behaviour of the target and not the behaviour of the terrorists. The key question, therefore, is why does a target act in such a way as to weaken itself and thereby make terrorism efficacious?

To answer this question, I will describe precisely what the terrorists want the target to do to weaken itself. Then it will be possible to analyse why the target responds that way. Presented here are five responses that targets can take that will weaken their political authority.[5] They are labelled: (a) over-reaction, (b) power deflation, (c) failed repression of moderates, (d) appeasement of moderates and (e) massive intimidation. For each of the five responses a hypothesis will be offered to explain why the target responds in such a way as to weaken itself. Three key variables appear to explain each of the five responses: the target's perception of (a) self, (b) the terrorists and (c) the relative capabilities between self and terrorists.

The value of this exploratory study is twofold. On one hand, the findings will help terrorists to be more successful. If terrorists know how a target is pre-disposed to respond, then they can tailor their terrorism to manipulate the target's perception so that the target will respond in a way that weakens itself. Knowledge, alas, is a basis of power. This knowledge, on the other hand, can also be used by the targets of terrorism to thwart terrorism. If a target knows the perceptions which will lead to the response that coincides with the purpose of the terrorists, it can alter its perceptions and respond in a different way. By doing so it 'wins' because the terrorists have utterly failed to elicit the desired response from the target. The behaviour of the terrorists will be seen as irrational violence or a hollow threat and they will have been weakened themselves. They are the losers. The only way to make terrorists losers is to understand when, how and why terrorism works.

THE THEORY OF OVER-REACTION

Over-reaction by a target, whether subject to regime or insurgent terrorism, is a familiar pattern of behaviour. The loss of public support is inevitable.

The target's indiscriminate use of force injures the innocent. The innocent believe that the injury is unjustified and, whether overtly or nor, condemn the target. This condemnation makes the injured innocent receptive to recruitment by the terrorists. In January 1984, the Amal in Lebanon used terrorism to provoke the Christians into shelling Shiite villages in order to further politicise the Shiite population, to de-legitimise the Christian regime and to recruit fighters.

Even those not directly injured will see the target's over-reaction as violating the legitimate rules of politics. The use of force on others will be seen as a threat to oneself. As Carlos Marighela has written, the target has acted 'to transform a country's political situation to a military one'.[6] The denial of civil rights without cause, another over-reaction, will be interpreted as protecting the target and not the people.[7] And if the target over-reacts with ostentatious protective measures, it magnifies the political stature and threat from the terrorists. It sets the stage for a drama where the protective measures become a challenge for the terrorists to overcome. Symbolically, overcoming even one person gives great prestige to terrorists.[8] Qaddafi's defiance of the US and the Sixth Fleet off his coast in January 1986 has made him a folk hero to many Arabs and had made the Palestinian cause more salient. If the target can be made to over-react by bringing into the struggle a repugnant third party, then terrorists can reap the public's disaffection. It did not help Idi Amin's legitimacy to bring in Libyans and Palestinians to be his praetorian guard when provoked by the initial insurgent violence encouraged by Tanzania. Here, Amin was the target and he over-reacted.

In the eyes of the public, these over-reactions make the target the enemy and, in comparison, the terrorists friends.[9]

Over-reactions can also result in the target lessening its own capabilities. Counterterrorism can be very expensive in terms of money, attention, equipment and labour. Over-reaction usually entails even greater costs. And it can turn a target away from the political, economic, and social activities that would bring it accomplishments and more popular support.

Why does a target over-react?

> Hypothesis 1. When a target perceives itself to be righteous, the terrorists to be the epitome of evil, and the relative capability in terms of force as overwhelmingly favouring itself, then a target is likely to over-react.

The perception of good versus evil provides the motive for a great effort at crushing the terrorists. Stereotyping and de-humanising an enemy, as Lifton and other psychologists have analysed, permits massive counterforce.[10] One often heard among American GIs in Vietnam, 'the only good gook is a dead gook'. Such perceptions excused free-fire zones, the burning of villages and worse. The Soviets in Afghanistan likewise see the contest as being one between good and evil. The 'progressive' and 'popular' forces confront those labelled 'reactionary', 'feudal' and 'agents of American imperialism'. No wonder they consider the all-out use of force to be justified. Note also how Israelis and Palestinians perceive each other, producing a history of constant over-reaction by both parties.

While self-righteousness and a challenge by the forces of evil provide the motive for indiscriminate strikes at those who dare to use violence, perceptions of great relative capability permit the target confidently to order the massive use of force. This may seem obvious when the regime is the target, less so when insurgents or potential insurgents are the target. Regimes usually have an overwhelming advantage in force. Again, terrorism is the strategy of the weak. So when insurgents are the target, regime terrorism denotes that it is the regime that is weak. The regime then uses terrorism to provoke the opposition to over-react, to use its robust capabilities so as to reduce its popular support or to deplete its own force capabilities. For example, until recently, Israel successfully provoked the mainline Palestine Liberation Organisation (PLO) groups to engage in indiscriminate action in order to discredit the Palestinian cause and to expose PLO forces to 'justified' retaliation. Growing international support in the 1970s had given the PLO a feeling of great and growing power.[11]

Regardless, over-reaction is made more likely when the target sees itself as powerful and able to inflict a lesson upon so unworthy a foe.

Another illustration of this point comes from Benedict J Kerkvliet's excellent study of the Huk rebellion in the Philippines. In the early stages of the rebellion in the 1930s the peasants protested, raided granaries of landlords and began to organise.

> Peasants . . . viewed their movement in terms of mutual protection against landlords and government officials. When they protested alone or in small numbers, peasants were liable to be evicted, be arrested, or suffer other reprisals; when they acted in large numbers, they were less vulnerable.[12]

At this stage the peasants did not want the landlords and government officials to over-react. The peasants themselves would be the victims. Yet it does illustrate that a vast power imbalance induces over-reactions.

The Huk case also illustrates that a perception of good versus evil provides a basis for over-reaction. 'A common belief among local and national government officials', Kerkvliet relates, 'was that the peasant movement was subversive, communistic, and manipulated by a few clever leaders'.[13] Orders were given more than once to shoot peasants during strikes and to demolish their houses. These over-reactions, though not provoked by a conscious peasant strategy at this point, did stimulate a loss of political support for government authorities, a quickening of peasant mobilisation and a weakening of the Philippine Constabulary's legitimacy.

THEORY OF POWER DEFLATION

A target that is incapable of responding to terrorism will lose public support and lessen its capabilities and confidence to thwart terrorism in the future.

The inability of a target to respond is manifested a number of ways. If the target, usually a regime but it can also be an insurgent group, cannot protect its people, then it will lose legitimacy. The same result occurs when terrorists can choose the timing and victims of their strikes without hindrance, and then successfully collect ransom, release prisoners, have manifestos read or printed in the media, destroy symbols or injure or kill victims. If they can completely avoid retaliation, especially if the target goes through all sorts of anti-terrorist motions and proclamations, the success of the terrorists is even greater and plain for all to see. What Thornton calls 'disorientation' is clearly seen in the behaviour of the target.[14] It is bad theatre for the target. The terrorists, supposedly the weak, seem to be in control.

The British had great difficulty dealing with the Sons of Liberty who perpetrated the Boston Tea Party in the early stages of the American Revolution. The same target exhibited disorientation to the always symbolic and sometimes brutal attacks by the Irgun Zvai Leumi in Palestine. One of the most spectacular terrorist acts occurred in 1978 in Nicaragua. Eden Pastora and a handful of Sandinista fighters seized the National Legislative Palace in Managua, kidnapping almost the entire congress. President Somoza believed he had no choice but to fulfil Pastora's demands. With released prisoners,

Pastora and his men made a triumphant exit through the streets to the airport and a safe departure.

The above are examples of successful insurgent terrorism against target regimes. Examples exist of the reverse. Che Guevara, for instance, found himself unable to shake the role of the hunted as the Bolivian military, assisted by the CIA, did the hunting. Che, the target of regime terror—for Bolivian authorities violated rules of warfare including the murder of Che himself—found that he was incapable of protecting his people or of fulfilling his task of organising a revolution.

Since the function of political authorities centres on protecting people and controlling the policy-making process, those authorities who fail in these tasks lose their legitimacy as authorities. The more failures, the more their power deflates.

What makes targets of terrorism incapable of dealing with the terrorists?

Hypothesis 2. When a target perceives itself doing its duty while both harassed by its enemies and lacking the public support it thinks it deserves; perceives the terrorists as a clever, formidable foe with some logic, legitimacy or justice on its side; and perceives the relative capability in terms of force as generally favourable overall to itself but in this particular case weakened by a lack of intelligence or viable military options, then a target will likely be unable to act against the terrorists.

Paul Wilkinson sees terrorism '... to be a strategy most suited to national liberation struggles against foreign rulers used by relatively small conspiratorial movements lacking any power base.[15] In these cases the target, often relying on civilian and military bureaucrats, sees itself doing a dirty, difficult job without the public support it merits. This, alone, makes definite policy difficult to formulate. Bold policy may out-pace fragile public support by incurring huge costs, such as by killing innocent bystanders. Combine this rather debilitating plight of the target with a perception that the terrorists are a rather clever, resourceful lot who firmly believe in their cause and tactics. A further reason for caution exists. The terrorists are serious, dedicated fighters who will skilfully match the target's action with spectacular reaction. To act is to invite embarrassment and danger. Reprisals would be swift. And to over-react may further enshrine their cause. Finally, the terrorists create situations where options for action all have greater costs than benefits. The first difficulty may be identifying and finding the terrorists. Usually the intelligence service is hampered by a public who gives the terrorists sanctuary and anonymity. This allows the terrorists to surprise the target, striking where the target is the least prepared to respond and where the terrorists enjoy multiple options while the target does not.

These points are illustrated by the British experience in Palestine. Menachem Begin, in his book *The Revolt*, gives one of the most forceful legitimisations for terrorism.[16] Irgun violence would force the British to confront the plight of the Jews, unite the Jews in revolt and provoke Arab violence in order to impose substantial costs upon the British for social control, and so disorient British policy in Palestine that they would quit the scene. By February 1947, the British found Palestine 'increasingly out of control', with Arabs and Jews polarised and themselves without the power either to resolve the dispute or to partition the land.[17] Britain had run out of options, save one: it turned the problem over to the United Nations.

THE THEORY OF FAILED REPRESSION OF MODERATES

The terrorists' target chooses to attack not only the terrorists but the moderate, non-violent opposition as well. If the target is a regime, it can ban political parties, institute censorship, increase surveillance, arrest and incarcerate protestors and even kill moderates as an example to others of the costs of opposition. If the target is an insurgent group, it can kidnap, bomb and assassinate the moderates both in the regime and in the non-violent opposition to the regime. The repression does not paralyse the moderates if insufficient or inefficient force is used. Instead of moving away from the terrorists, the moderates do the opposite. They conclude that moderation is untenable and to protect themselves from the target they go to the side of the original terrorists, usually as the lesser of two evils. The target has converted mild opposition into militant opposition and weakened itself by absorbing the physical and mental costs of repression.

The Shah of Iran increasingly repressed moderates in the 1970s. It did not work. One reason, among many, for its failure was the Shah's vacillation in carrying through with either reforms or repression. In part, this can be attributed to US human rights opposition to the Shah's personal weakness and to an inept SAVAK intelligence service. Vacillation made the Shah appear weak and allowed a large coalition to form against him. Eventually the bazaar, the mosque, the modern business sector and the intellectuals united in militance with the small existing terrorist groups against the monarchy.

Repressing moderates had actually worked for the Shah on earlier occasions. As Barry Rubin described it:

> The shah must have remembered his success in riding out the 1962–63 upheaval over the White Revolution and, earlier, in co-opting opposition elements after Mossadegh's fall. On these two occasions, he had cracked down hard and then proceeded to separate moderates from radicals, winning over some of the former, eliminating the latter. That strategy would fail this time, first because the charismatic Khomeini was able to keep the moderates in line and second because the fence sitters gradually became convinced that the shah would fall. On the earlier occasions, the hopelessness of dissent had led the protestors to surrender. This time, the hopelessness of the shah's position caused those in the middle to cast their lot with the revolution.[18]

The same pattern occurred roughly during the same time period with Anastasio Somoza in Nicaragua. When the Chamber of Commerce and the Catholic Church, suffering repression, aligned with the FSLN, it was apparent that Somoza's legitimacy had all but vanished.

Examples of insurgent targets repressing moderates include the Tupamaros in Uruguay. Although they succeeded in militarising the regime after a number of successful power deflation operations, the Tupamaros' own response to regime terror disaffected moderates. Their excesses of violence brought the non-violent, moderate opposition and the military into a strange arrangement that eventually resulted in the restoration of democracy. The Sendero Luminoso (Shining Path) of Peru, target of the counter-terrorism of the Guardia Civil, characteristically repressed the moderate peasant opposition and thereby widened support for the regime. A very unusual case involved the Black Panther Party in the United States. Targeted by the FBI and local police authorities, Black Panther violence and militant rhetoric so disaffected moderate Blacks that the Panthers found themselves increasingly isolated. In 1971 the Black Panthers disavowed violence, in effect, recognising that repressing moderates divided and weakened themselves and the Black movement.

Why do targets attempt to repress moderates, weakening themselves and strengthening the terrorists or counterterrorists?

> Hypothesis 3. When the target perceives itself to be absolutely beseiged to the point where it must act to preserve its authority; perceives the terrorists or counterterrorists as threatening all that the target holds dear—with the main source of the threat the duping of moderate elements to ally with the extremist aims of the terrorists; and perceives the relative capability as favourable in terms of force but on the brink of a radical reversal if the moerates are allowed to combine with the terrorists; then the target is likely to repress moderates in order to prevent this coalition.

Repressing moderates is an eleventh-hour gamble to preserve authority. The target believes reforms or buying off the opposition will not suffice. Repression is an act of desperation, and as such, has a high probability of failure. But at this point there seems to be no other option. The terrorists or counterterrorists are on the brink of victory. They have duped the moderates.

Again, the Iranian case illustrates this perception. Rubin reports the Shah's view of the protestors in mid-1978. 'There are people everywhere who are easily instigated. They hear a few words and immediately they are electrified and stop thinking.'[9]

Frustrated that neither reforms nor mild repression seemed to work, and bolstered by Zbigniew Brzezinski's personal assurances of US support, the Shah approved a full-scale assault on the moderate opposition. On 8 September 1978, 'Black Friday', the military massacred about 1000 protesters in Tehran's central Jaleh Square.[20] The moderate opposition, led by Shariat-Madari, declared it would no longer cooperate with even reformist officials of the Shah's regime.[21] A revolutionary situation crystallised.[22]

Whereas target over-reaction may be seen as an act of omnipotence and self-confidence, repressing moderates stems from frustration, anger and anxiety. These emotions lead to irrationality and desperate actions.

THEORY OF APPEASING MODERATES

Vigorous political reforms, which appease moderates, alienate the avid supporters of the old order. These supporters can move into the camp of the irreconcilable opposition. For example, when Prime Minister Pierre Trudeau made major reforms on behalf of French Canadians on the issues of language and political appointments, a substantial number of English-speaking Canadians considered these actions as nothing more than a dastardly appeasement of the Front de Liberation du Quebec (FLQ). Concessions seemed to be a reward for planting bombs and blowing up Canadians. Similarly, allowing the unionisation of workers and collective bargaining in the nineteenth and early twentieth centuries was viewed by doctrinaire capitalists in many industrialised countries as surrendering to the perpetrators of strikes and labour violence.

Reforms also result in political devolution that weakens the old order because power is given up or diffused through sharing it with former opposition elements. Granting self-rule or sovereignty to a province or colony, enfranchising the lower class, granting minority rights, establishing welfare programmes and instituting a functioning legislature all reduce the political power of the *ancien regime*. How different the power of the current Spanish Government from that under the rule of Franco! How much hope is placed upon the Anglo–Irish Agreement on Northern Ireland as the start of altering its one-sided political authority? The history of the growth of democracy is the history of reforms induced by violence and the threat of more violence.

Why appease moderates through reforms?

> Hypothesis 4. When a target perceives itself as a legitimate political authority but one which has made mistakes in the past; perceives the terrorists as capitalising on these mistakes and attracting growing popular support for radical solutions that go far beyond remedying past mistakes; and perceives the relative capability as overwhelmingly favourable to itself but liable to deteriorate the longer the struggle continues; then targets are likely to appease moderates.

The target that appeases moderates is usually a regime, although, as the Black Panther case illustrates, insurgents can appease a moderate opposition through reforms as well.

The target institutes reforms partly because it is just, but mainly because reforms coopt the potential or actual mass base of the terrorists. Reforms remove the injustices that stimulated the terrorism in the first place. They remove the cause. As Walter Laqueur points out, removing grievances will not end terrorism.[23] However, it will isolate the radical and habitual terrorists from the mass of the people who do not like the risks of disorder and violence, especially if they bear them for no apparent cause. Isolated and desperate, the terrorist leaders can be hunted down, tried, convicted and incarcerated. They lose their sanctuary provided by the moderates, if not their belief that they still represent the true interests of the masses.

Perhaps this process seems mislabelled when it is referred to as successful terrorism. Yet the hated political authority is weakened and weakened in line with the professed aims of the terrorists. Terrorism has worked even though the terrorists are dead, in jail or struggling to stay alive in basements or in the mountains.

Historians of the history of Canada will undoubtedly celebrate the skill and determination of Prime Minister Trudeau in defusing the terrorism on behalf of French Canadians. Eventually his policies defused separatism as well.

Trudeau was fully aware of the injustices inflicted upon French Canadians. As he said:

> In the matter of education as well as political rights, the safeguards so dear to French Canadians were nearly always disregarded throughout the country, so that they came to believe themselves secure only in Quebec. Worse still, in those areas not specifically covered by the constitution, the English-speaking majority used its size and wealth to impose a set of social rules humiliating to French Canadians.[24]

He instituted a classic two-pronged attack on militant separatism. The passage of the Official Languages Act, introduced in October 1968, allowed all Canadians to use either English or French in their dealings with the Federal Government. It facilitated French Canadians being able to operate politically in all of Canada. Almost as important for appeasing French Canadian moderates were reforms in the area of political recruitment. Trudeau opened up the public service to more French Canadians. From an insignificant number, Trudeau had over twenty per cent of public-service officials having French as their first language by 1976.[25] The best and the brightest of French Canadians were appointed to high political positions in Ottawa so that the Federal Government truly *represented* Canada.

The other prong was the firm suppression of the FLQ, especially after the 1970 kidnappings of British Trade Commissioner James Cross and of Deputy Prime Minister Pierre Laporte (who was assassinated in captivity). Trudeau invoked the War Measures Act and approved arrests. 'It is more important to maintain law and order', said Trudeau, 'than to worry about those whose knees tremble at the sight of the army'.[26] This firmness induced the moderates to renounce violence and his reforms helped the moderates to be loyal Canadians. Pursuing one prong without the other would have been a disaster. Reforms without firmness would have made Ottawa seem cringing and without authority. Firmness without reforms would have made Ottawa appear unjust and brutal.

Isolated, many FLQ members abandoned terrorism in favour of continuing the separatist struggle at the electoral level. That, too, failed. The Parti Quebecois won the 1976 provincial election but it had no mandate for separation.

It must not be forgotten that terrorism and the French Canadian issue created a political climate that helped put Trudeau in office and mobilised support for his reforms. Wise political authorities take terrorism seriously and take it to indicate that a legitimate problem exists that requires immediate attention. Terrorists are not crazy. Terrorists do not risk their lives without an initial cause. Therefore, terrorism can spark needed reform and weaken an over-bearing target.

THEORY OF MASSIVE INTIMIDATION[27]

Those who are intimidated into inaction or obedience will not keep or build public support because those who do not act cannot serve others—cannot protect, provide or promote. Fewer and fewer young communists rallied to the side of the old Bolsheviks when they were intimidated by Stalin's great purge and terror beginning in 1936. The SA under Ernst Röhm ceased being a political force after Hitler's terror of 1934 liquidated its leadership. Insurgent terrorists can use intimidation too. When Castro and his 26th July Movement demoralised Batista's police and military forces and compelled them to leave alone the area around their base in the Sierra Maestra in late 1958, Batista's regime lost legitimacy. For those in the immediate area, Castro was the one who determined who got what, when and how. He had authority. For Cuba at large, Castro appeared to be the force to be reckoned with in the future.

As Abram de Swaan points out in his 'Terror as Government Service', the target *weakens itself* by deciding not to act.[28] Unlike power deflation, where the target is unable to respond to terrorism, intimidation comes when the target is able to respond but does not. The target exhibits the absence of any political energy.

Why?

Hypothesis 5. When a target sees itself as uncertain in his or her convictions and risking a chance of extreme punishment for political actions in an unpredictable situation; perceives the terrorists as dedicated in their aim and more than willing to use violence in its pursuit; perceives relative capability as favouring reasonable people like themselves under normal conditions but perceives the conditions to be abnormal because the terrorists can kill or out-manoeuvre at whim; then the target will be intimidated and not act even though it may have great or potentially great capabilities.

De Swaan sees torture by regimes as designed

[to] spread an ever-present fear, of arrest, of ill-treatment, of mutilation, of betrayal, of death. The purpose of all this is that people will ask themselves with every action whether their deeds do not create risks for themselves and for the people around them, that they will not just abstain from what is forbidden, but will avoid whatever has not expressly been allowed. They really must continually

> try to imagine what the rulers would want them to do, they must become vicarious rulers for themselves. Only then the completion of the terrorist regime has been achieved.[29]

This analysis is so perceptive that it is worth continuing at some length.

> If everyone would know [for certain] what acts would lead to arrest and torture and which would go unpunished, most people would refrain from the first and without worrying, commit the others. But the purpose of an intimidation apparatus is precisely to impose so much fear in people that of their own account they will abstain from things that otherwise would be hard for the regime to detect or prevent. Not even a police state can always keep under surveillance all people in all their doings. And because the regime cannot enforce its own commands and prohibitions, fully or even partially, it must create a negative game of chance, which leaves it to the citizens to avoid the risks.[30]

Intimidation works when the target experiences fear and feels vulnerable. That is not enough, however. What explains martyrs? What explains the behaviour of those who stand up to overwhelming force or a credible threat of violence even when they are certain they will suffer the consequences? Strong convictions, notably when upholding them has public witness, inhibit intimidation. In de Swaan's words, those with strong convictions do not 'become vicarious rulers for themselves'. They are self-ruled.

One of the great ironies of history is that Stalin had to kill so many people in his attempt to intimidate opponents or potential opponents. He could induce fear; he could make them feel vulnerable; but he was dealing with people who were believers in Marx and Lenin. Many had firm convictions. The show trials and false confessions hid the fact that the overwhelming majority of the old and some new Bolsheviks went to their deaths defiant and unintimidated. Eventually, the new generation who filled the shoes of the purged knew enough to take their convictions from Stalin's cues. These people were easily intimidated and did what they were told.

CONCLUSIONS

Each theory demonstrates that terrorism is efficacious only if the target makes it so. Terrorism demands that the target perform. It induces a test of the target's competence, whether the target is a regime or an insurgent group. The behaviour of the target is the key to understanding why terror works because terrorism's purpose is to illicit a particular kind of behaviour, namely, behaviour that weakens the target. The target's perceptions, as the five hypotheses have illustrated, provide the bases of the target's behaviour. So while the causes of terrorism, that is of the terrorist's behaviour, are largely sociological, the success or failure of terrorism, which is determined by the target's behaviour, is largely psychological. Terrorists must know or manipulate the target's psychological perceptions to induce it to act in the way it is predisposed to act. For example, a powerful, self-righteous target confronting terrorism perpetrated by the forces of absolute evil can be best made to over-react, but not easily made to power deflate, repress moderates, appease moderates, or be intimidated.

Of course, a powerful, self-righteous target confronting terrorism perpetrated by the forces of absolute evil does not have to over-react. Knowledge of one's own perceptions and how they can be manipulated informs oneself of the propensity to make particular mistakes. Prudent targets do not behave as automatons.

Successful terrorism leads to a different kind of political struggle because it changes the relative capability of the contestants. The target is weakened and the terrorists strengthened. Political strategies are always dependent upon relative capabilities. Those who have developed substantial relative capabilities will not continue to rely on a strategy of terrorism. Terrorism is not only a strategy of the weak, it is also a weak strategy. Rarely can it 'finish off' an opponent, cannot overthrow a government, cannot bring national liberation, cannot reform a culture, or do anything else by itself except shift the power balance. At this point, strategies more under the control of the former terrorists, such as negotiating, revolting, making a coup d'état or electioneering, are able to produce substantial political results.

Finally, the development of theories on the efficacy of terrorism reveals a strategy which puts some targets into impossible dilemmas. A large, moderate, non-violent opposition movement in tandem with a terrorist movement forces the target to deal with the issues behind the opposition. With only a large, moderate, non-violent opposition, the target can ignore it or grant it meaningless concessions without much fear of retribution. With only a terrorist movement, the target can crush it. But in tandem, the target must either repress or appease the moderates. Repression risks driving the moderates to the terrorists. Ignoring the moderates here will be seen as repression because it will be difficult to compartmentalise anti-terrorist actions as only being directed at the terrorists. The moderate will feel the chill along with the terrorists. Repression then radicalises and militarises the moderates. The only other option is to appease the moderates via reforms. As Gandhi and King well knew, the rejection of non-violent mass action by the target is really a preference by the target for a violent struggle and all the costs and risks that that entails. Targets who usually avoid using strategies of violence are then forced to reform. Targets that like violence, of course, will not be moved to reform by non-violent protests. They will repress. In 1933 and 1934, the non-violent strategies of Hitler's opponents failed because Hitler, in control of the Government, had few inhibitions against using violence any way he chose. The British in India, on the contrary, had some major inhibitions.

The literature on terrorism has principally dealt with either its causes or, in the popular press, with its immorality. There has been a reluctance to examine its usefulness as political strategy. This study is a preliminary effort to analyse its efficacy.

NOTES

1 Alex P Schmid, *Political Terrorism*, New Brunswick: Transaction Books, 1983, p. 96. It is subtitled *A research guide to concepts, theories, data bases and literature* and it has proven invaluable for this study.
2 Nicholas O Berry, 'Dealing with Terrorism', *USA Today*, 113, July 1984, pp. 40–42. A political authority is one that commands followers.
3 See *Schmid*, p. 41.
4 Schmid and others rightly distinguish between the 'target of violence', that is the victim, and the 'target of terror'. Quite often a non-political 'innocent' party or symbolic object is the target of violence, but that is not the political authority whose weakening is sought. *Ibid.*, p. 92.
5 See *Schmid*, pp. 97–99 for a listing of twenty purposes and functions of terrorism as defined by theorists and terrorists. Among the twenty, many overlap. In our analysis, the weakening of the target includes its transformation from dictatorship towards democracy.
6 *Ibid.*, p. 185.
7 Grant Wardlaw, *Political Terrorism*, Cambridge: Cambridge University Press, 1982, p. 58.
8 This was the point of my op-ed piece in *The New York Times*. 'Good Fences, Bad Idea', on 19 December 1983, as well as a point of my testimony before a congressional subcommittee. US Congress, House, Subcommittee on Civil and Constitutional Rights, *Hearings, Domestic Security Measures Relating to Terrorism*, 89th Congress, 2nd Session, 1984, p. 97.
9 Berry, *Hearings*, p. 94.
10 Robert J Lifton, *Home From the War*, New York: Simon and Schuster, 1973. See chapter 7, 'Gooks and Men'.
11 When the PLO realised in 1985 that its international support did not significantly alter the balance of power with Israel, it stopped over-reacting to Israel's provocations and began a tortuous strategy to lay the groundwork for negotiations. Nevertheless, some Palestinian factions still believed in the availability and efficacy of violence and saw Arafat as selling out. Their terrorism continued on the *Achille Lauro*, at the airports in Rome and Vienna and elsewhere.
12 Benedict J Kerkvliet, *The Huk Rebellion*, Berkeley: University of California Press, 1977, p. 45.
13 *Ibid.*, p. 57.
14 Cited in *Wardlaw*, p. 34.
15 Paul Wilkinson, *Political Terrorism*, London: Macmillan, 1974, p. 126.
16 Menachem Begin, *The Revolt*, New York: Nash Publishing Co., 1977.
17 Richard Allen, *Imperialism and Nationalism in the Fertile Crescent*, New York: Oxford University Press, 1974, pp. 375, 380. Allen makes the point that Zionist violence was not responsible for Britain's departure. Britain, he asserts, would have left anyway. Perhaps so, but high costs and no options got Britain out in 1948, in time for Israel both to provide a home for Jewish refugees before they settled elsewhere and to win the war with the yet unorganised Arab states.
18 Barry Rubin, *Paved With Good Intentions, The American Experience and Iran*, New York: Penguin Books, 1981, p. 205.
19 *Ibid.*, p. 212.
20 *Ibid.*, p. 214.
21 *Ibid.*, p. 216.

22 *Ibid.*
23 Cited in *Schmid*, p. 167.
24 George Radwanski, *Trudeau*, New York: Taplinger Publishing Co., 1978, p. 314.
25 *Ibid.*, p. 342.
26 Walter Stewart, *Trudeau in Power*, New York: Outerbridge and Dienstfrey, 1971, p. 50.
27 I am grateful to Richard and Sharon Cleghorn and Janet Berry for helping to conceptualise the difference between power deflation and massive intimidation.
28 Cited in *Schmid*, p. 167.
29 *Ibid.*
30 *Ibid.*, p. 175.

Group and Organisational Dynamics of Political Terrorism: Implications for Counterterrorist Policy

J M Post

> The purpose of terrorism is to terrorize.
>
> Lenin

> The principal motivation for becoming a terrorist is to belong to a terrorist group.
>
> Post

As the cancer of political terrorism has spread, the debate over effective counterterrorist policy has intensified. From the situation room at the White House to the conference room at the University of Aberdeen to the op-ed pages of *The Times*, the debate rages. The answers offered to the question—what will deter terrorists from their acts of violence?—range from surgical military retaliatory strikes to redressing the legitimate grievances of the terrorists.

Let us examine that question: what will deter terrorists from their acts of violence? It contains an implicit premise, a premise which all too often is left implicit. For the purposes of this discussion, I should like to make that premise explicit and re-phrase the question as it should be asked. Based upon a clear understanding of the psychological framework of terrorists, what acts will impact upon them in such a way as to deter them from their acts of violence?

It will not be a surprise to readers to observe that one of the embarrassing reasons that the premise is usually left implicit is that our understanding of terrorist psychology is primitive at best. Nevertheless, behavioural scientists attempting to understand terrorist psychology are making encouraging—if halting—progress in developing an evidence-based knowledge base concerning the psychology of terrorists. In the balance of this chapter, I will attempt to integrate some of the disparate materials bearing on terrorist behaviour and suggest the outlines of a psychosocial theory of terrorist psychology. Having made the premise explicit, I will then suggest implications for counterterrorist policy.

Another reason the psychological premise is usually left un-examined is the understandable reluctance to penetrate the minds of individuals who could commit such heinous acts. The typical lay assessment of the Shiite suicide bomber willing to give his life for a cause is that he must be a crazed fanatic; the act must be the product of a deranged mind, it is so difficult to comprehend, so illogical. Yet most terrorists are psychologically normal, and there is a particular psycho-logic, the understanding of which makes their actions explicable.

In dissecting terrorist psycho-logic, it is necessary to utilise three different levels of analysis: individual psychology, group psychology and organisational psychology.

INDIVIDUAL PSYCHOLOGY

Comparative studies of terrorist psychology do not indicate a unique 'terrorist mind'. Terrorists do not fit into a specific psychiatric diagnostic category. Indeed, most would be considered to fit within the spectrum of normality. Nevertheless, individuals with particular personality dispositions are drawn to the path of terrorism. A feature in common among many terrorists is a tendency to externalise, to seek outside sources to blame for personal inadequacies. Without being frankly paranoid, there is an over-reliance on the ego defence of projection. Other prominent traits were a defensive grandiosity, an exaggerated self-absorbtion with little regard for the feelings of others. On the basis of psychodynamically oriented interviews with a small group of Red Army Faction (RAF) terrorists, Bollinger found psychological dynamics resembling those found in narcissistic borderlines. He was particularly struck by the history of narcissistic wounds, which led to a deficient sense of self-esteem and inadequately integrated personalities. The terrorists he interviewed demonstrated a feature characteristic of individuals with narcissistic and borderline personalities—splitting. He found they had split off the de-valued parts of themselves and projected them onto the establishment which then became the target of their violent aggression.

These psychological characteristics are associated with certain psychosocial features, a pattern of psychosocial vulnerabilities which renders those who become terrorists especially susceptible to the powerful influences of group and organisational dynamics. In particular there are data which suggest that as a consequence of troubled family backgrounds many terrorists have an incomplete psychosocial identity and an exaggerated need to belong.

The major study sponsored by the Ministry of the Interior of West Germany is illustrative. In their study of the epidemiology of terrorism, they found twenty-five per cent of terrorists had lost one or both parents by age fourteen. Fully a third had been convicted in juvenile court. There was a high frequency of job and educational failure. The lives of the terrorists before joining were characterised by social isolation and personal failure. For these lonely alienated individuals from the margins of society, the terrorist group was to become the family they never had.

Among the welter of terrorist groups, I find it useful to distinguish two major categories, which have quite different psychosocial dynamics—the 'anarchic-ideologues' such as West Germany's Red Army Faction (RAF) and the Brigate Rosse (BR) of Italy, and the 'nationalist–secessionists' groups such as ETA of the Basques and the Armenian Secret Army for the Liberation of Armenia (ASALA). Alienation from the family is characteristically found among the 'anarchic-ideologues'. They have turned against the generation of their parents, which is identified with the establishment. They are dissident to parents loyal to the regime.

In apparent contrast, the 'nationalist–separatists' are carrying on a family mission; they are loyal to families dissident to the establishment. But while they are not estranged from their families, as are the 'anarchic-ideologues', they are not at one with their societies. Thus they too have fragmented psychosocial identities. Thus for both classes of terrorists—for both the 'anarchic-ideologues' and the 'nationalist–separatists'—joining the terrorist group represents an attempt to consolidate a fragmented and incomplete psychosocial identity, and, most importantly, is an expression of an extremely strong need to belong.

To recapitulate, from the perspective of individual psychology, terrorists are not in the main suffering from serious psychopathology. They do not suffer from mental illness which could lead to the profound distortions of motivation and reality testing one would expect to be associated with the driven motivation to carry out an act of terrorist violence. But while essentially normal psychologically, there are psychosocial wounds which predispose them to seek affiliation with like-minded individuals who share their tendency to externalise and blame society for their own personal shortcomings.

GROUP PSYCHOLOGY

This combination of a strong affiliative need coupled with an incomplete personal identity, provides the foundation for especially powerful group dynamics. This suggests that the terrorist group would be an unusually powerful setting for producing conforming behaviour. Insofar as the individual psychosocial identity is incomplete or fragmented, the only way the member feels reasonably complete is in relation to the group. Belonging to the terrorist group becomes for many the most important component of their psychosocial identity. Indeed, data from terrorist memoirs and from interviews with terrorists suggest that there is a tendency to submerge the individual identity into a group identity, and to subordinate their own judgement to that of the group. The strong need to belong, to which we have referred earlier, becomes a major level ensuring compliance of group members. Andreas Baader, a founder of the Baader–Meinhof gang, by threatening expulsion was able to ensure compliance. In response to members who expressed doubt concerning the violent tactics of the group, he indicated that 'whoever is in the group simply has to be tough, has to be able to hold out, and if one is not tough enough, there is not room for him here'. Professor Baeyer-Kaette, who had unusual access to members of the Heidelberg cell of the Red Army Faction, cites the example of a new recruit discussing an operation which had a high probability of producing a high casualty rate. When he questioned whether it was ideologically proper to conduct an operation where innocent blood would be shed, a heavy silence fell over the room. It quickly became apparent that to question the decision was to be seen as disloyal. Moreover, to question the group judgement was to risk losing his newly won place in the group.

But the risks may be much more consequential than losing his membership. Several conveyed the fear that once in the group, the only way out was feet first, so that to disagree actively with the group and be perceived as dissident was to risk not just membership but life itself. Baumann stated that withdrawal was impossible except 'by way of the graveyard'. Boock, a former RAF member, described the intensity of the pressures 'that can lead to things you can't imagine ... the fear of what is happening to one when you say, for example, "No, I won't do that, and for these and these reasons." What the consequences of that can be'.

Thus there are great pressures for compliance and conformity, for muting dissent. Consider the dilemma of the doubting group member, at once desirous of belonging, yet uncomfortable about an action which runs counter to his principles. For him, the ideological rhetoric plays an especially important role, providing a justification for the contemplated anti-social act. Indeed, as Baeyer-Kaette has noted, there is a remarkable upside-down logic found in group discussions. But there is a psycho-logic to the reasoning if one accepts the basic premise that what the group defines as good is desirable, and what the group defines as bad is evil. If the group cause is served by a particular act, no matter how heinous, the act is, by definition, good.

This explains the extent of violence and viciousness which terrorists can justify. The standards of the group take over and become the norm; the standards of the world outside of the group have become ego-alien. It is onto this outside world that the members have projected their own hateful aggressive impulses. This is the world which must be destroyed.

The rhetoric of terrorism is absolutist, idealising and de-valuing—polarising 'us versus them', good versus evil. What is within the group is not to be questioned—is ideal. What is without—the establishment—is the cause of society's ills. 'It's not me, it's them'—the motto of the failed youth on the margins of society, seeking to find an external cause for his difficulties. How attractive, for such an individual to find he is not alone, that there are others like him, and that there is a codified body of ideas, a belief structure, which explains systematically how 'they' are responsible for the problems he and his underprivileged cohorts are suffering.

Throughout the broad spectrum of terrorist groups, no matter how diverse their causes, the absolutist rhetoric of terrorism is remarkably similar. The absolutist rhetoric of terrorism is characterised by splitting. Splitting is an important psychological characteristic of the borderline personality, a personality disorder which is disproportionately represented in the terrorist population. As was noted earlier in the discussion of individual psychology, Bollinger, who has had the unusual opportunity of conducting in-depth psychoanalytic interviews of RAF terrorists, found a striking preponderance of borderline mechanisms—especially splitting and projection. These mechanisms in our judgement contribute powerfully to shaping the terrorist group dynamics. The terrorist group members project onto the establishment the split-off de-valued aspects of the self, while concomitantly idealising the group. To the extent that the terrorist ideology de-values and de-humanises the establishment, and identifies it as the cause of society's (the terrorists') problems, it is not only not immoral to attempt to destroy the establishment, it is indeed the highest order of morality, for by the terrorist's upside-down logic, destroying the establishment is destroying the source of evil, and only good can result.

What is being suggested then is that the substantive content of terrorist rhetoric is not what attracts the aspiring terrorist. It is not the articulation of the Palestinian, or Armenian, or Basque cause. *The cause is not the cause.* Rather it is the structural logic of the rhetoric which is so compelling, providing as it does a psychological rationale for striking out against society, refashioning an internal, individual crisis into a shared hatred of society. This externalising ideo-logic is the glue which holds the group together, providing the rationale for striking out against the outside enemy.

A brief excursion into indirect evidence provides further insight into terrorist group dynamics. Studies of the membership of the Unification Church of Reverend Moon are particularly instructive. They indicate that the more isolated and unaffiliated in terms of family and friends the individual was before joining, the more likely he was to find membership in the church attractive. And, the greater the emotional relief he found upon joining, the more likely he was to accept instruction to participate in anti-social acts. For the purposes of this comparison, we refer to the remarkable mass engagement ceremony in Madison Square Garden, where Reverend Moon assigned fiancés to 1410 members. The individuals who found in the Unification Church their entire self-definition were willing to accept blindly the assigned marital partner, surely contrary to the social mores to which these individuals had been socialised.

A further major contribution to the power of the group over its members derives from the relationship between the group and its surrounding society. In particular, for the underground group isolated from society, group cohesion develops in response to shared danger. In the words of a member of RAF, group solidarity was 'compelled exclusively by the illegal situation, fashioned into a common destiny'. 'The group was born under the pressure of pursuit' according to the testimony of another RAF member, who considered the pressure to be 'the sole link holding the group together'.

Thus the terrorist group represents an almost caricatured version of the 'fight–flight' group described by Bion. The 'fight–flight' group defines itself in relation to the outside enemy which it sees as bent on destroying it. (This perception is not without a foundation in reality, but the group rarely recognises its own role in provoking that societal response.) The 'fight–flight' group acts oppositionally to the outside world which both threatens its existence and justifies its existence—the only way for the 'fight–flight' group to preserve itself is by fighting against or fleeing from the enemy out to destroy it. Feracutti has conceptualised this as a fantasy war, but the belief that the enemy is out to destroy it is not merely a paranoid delusion. While initially it may derive from internal psychological assumptions, as a consequence of terrorist acts the psychological assumption becomes a self-fulfilling prophecy as the terrorist group successfully creates an outside world which is indeed out to destroy it—the fantasy war has become a war in reality.

Whatever psychological pressures are within the individual terrorists, whatever psychological tensions are within the group—these tensions are externalised. Terrorist groups require enemies in order to cope with their own internal tensions, and if such enemies do not exist they create them. For if they cannot act against an outside enemy, they will tear themselves apart.

As the foregoing review indicates, there is a pattern of behaviour which indicates that *the predominant determinant of terrorist actions is the internal dynamics of the terrorist group*. If the terrorist group does not achieve recognition as a feared opponent of the establishment, it has lost its meaning. A terrorist who does not commit acts of terrorism is not a terrorist; if the terrorist group does not commit acts of terrorism, it has lost its meaning. A terrorist group needs to commit acts of terrorism in order to justify its existence, and it needs to be recognised as a feared opponent in its fantasy war against society.

If this characterisation of the psychology within the pressure cooker of the terrorist group is apt, what are the implications for decision making? In addressing this question, it is important to emphasise that in most decision making groups, for reasons elaborated above, individual judgement tends to be suspended and subordinated to the group process. This is exactly the climate in which the phenomenon identified by Janis as 'groupthink', can flourish. Occurring when groups make decisions under crisis conditions, it is defined as: 'high cohesiveness and ... an accompanying concurrence-seeking tendency that interfered with critical thinking ... a mode of thinking that people engage in when they are deeply involved in a cohesive in-group, when the members' strivings for unanimity override their motivation to realistically appraise alternative courses of action ... a deterioration of mental efficiency, reality testing and normal judgement that results from in-group pressures.'

The symptoms of groupthink include:

(a) Illusions of invulnerability leading to excessive optimism and excessive risk-taking.

(b) Collective rationalisation efforts to dismiss challenges to key assumptions.
(c) Assumption of the group's morality.
(d) Unidimensional perception of the enemy as evil (thereby denying feasibility of negotiation) or incompetent (thereby justifying risky alternatives).
(e) Intolerance of challenges by a group member to shared key beliefs.
(f) Unwillingness to express views which deviate from the perceived group consensus.
(g) A shared illusion that unanimity is genuine.
(h) The emergence of members who withhold adverse information from the group concerning the instrumental and moral soundness of its decisions.

This cluster of traits which Janis has labelled 'groupthink' would seem to epitomise the decision making of the terrorist group. Of particular importance are the reduction of critical judgement, the assumption of the group's morality and the illusion of invulnerability leading to excessive risk-taking.

Semel and Minix have specifically investigated the effects of group dynamics on risk-taking. In a group-problem-solving task, they found that US army groups shifted in the direction of riskier policy choices than the individual members had preferred privately. Individual tendencies were strongly reinforced and intensified as a result of interactions within the group. Moreover, the tendency of group members to conform to the preferences of the group was found to increase with the length of interactions with the group.

The phenomena described by Janis and by Semmel and Minix occur with psychologically healthy mature adults. If mature adults with healthy self-esteem and appreciation of their own individuality can slip into such flawed decision processes under the pressures of group dynamics, what of groups composed of individuals with weak self-esteem who depend upon the group for their sense of significance? Does this not suggest that such groups would be subject to such distorted decision processes in magnified degree?

But a distorted decision process is not equivalent to total irrationality. To look at the world through distorted lenses is not equivalent to being blind or being subject to visual hallucinations. Is there a 'psycho-logic' which under the pressure of distorted decision processes could lead a terrorist group to opt for weapons of mass destruction? Jenkins has noted that 'terrorists want a lot of people watching, not a lot of people dead. ... Mass casualties may not serve the terrorist goals and could alienate the population'. But are there circumstances where the upside-down logic of the terrorist could lead them to want a lot of people dead, where they could be drawn to a conclusion that mass casualties could serve their goals and would not alienate the population? If there is a psycho-logic which could lead a group down that path, might not the distorted decision process described above make the difference in a close decision?

A proposition advanced by Ariel Merari is useful to invoke here. He has made the important distinction between domestic terrorists acting on their own territory and those acting on the soil of other nations. Such groups as the Red Army Faction and the Red Brigades believe they are in the vanguard of a social–revolutionary movement. They aspire to persuade their countrymen to join their fantasy war against the establishment. They depend upon their countrymen for both active and passive support. In attempting to draw attention to their cause through their acts of terrorism, it is their countrymen they are trying to influence. The same is true for ETA when it is acting in the Basque region. In vivid contrast, when a group operates across borders, the rules of the game in terms of target of influence are quite different. As Merari has emphasised, when Palestinian terrorists operate in Israel, the horror and disapprobation of the population in the target country is not a disincentive—it is a reward. But here too, the issue of audience comes into play, and in the media age each act has multiple audiences. If the contemplated act would invoke international opprobrium, it could be construed as a setback to the Palestinian cause. A similar logic could be applied to radical Shiite terrorism, but here different weights are probably attached to sectors of the international audience. The degree to which the West is alienated by a particular act is probably not a major disincentive. The group acting across borders is significantly less constrained than one operating within its own national boundaries, and we believe it is with such groups that the greatest danger lies.

Another class of terrorist groups which pose great danger for raising the stakes of violence are the losers. The primary requirement for any group is to survive. And surviving means committing acts which justify and call attention to its existence. What of the terrorist group or faction on the way out, which has lost its support, lost the headlines and in a factional struggle has lost its influence to a rival group? Desperate for success, might not such a group in its deliberations ask 'What have we got to lose?' Could the pressures of group decision-making coupled with the requirement for group survival not argue for a terrorist spectacular as a way of regaining prominence? While the constraints raised earlier would continue to operate, in the circumstances outlined above, we would suggest they would be significantly weakened. In our judgement, it is with such a group that the greatest danger of nuclear terrorism lies.

INFLUENCES OF ORGANISATIONAL PSYCHOLOGY

The foregoing discussion of the group dynamics of political terrorism is particularly apposite for the autonomous cell—where the group is relatively small, simple and undifferentiated—and plans and conducts its own operations. The dynamics of such a group, where leadership and authority reside within the group, differ in significant ways from those of terrorist groups which are elements of a larger organisational structure. For the latter, the authority is perceived as being located outside of the group. In this circumstance, the member is prone to vest this unseen authority with absolute wisdom and power.

Moreover, for the differentiated terrorist organisation, there is a clear separation of the leadership echelon from the cadre, of the decision makers from the actors. The perceived locus of authority has a major impact upon the internal dynamics of the group. Where the leader is physically available within the group, complete with all his warts and blemishes, he is available as a target for the anti-authority feelings of the members. Indeed, the genesis of multiple factions within terrorist organisations is more often than not the consequence of personalistic rivalries within groups which lead to splitting off of factions. As an example, the ideological differences among the many factions within the PLO with similar titles are more often than not a matter of nuance. Historically, the reason for the difference was usually an impatient deputy or follower wanting to do his own thing.

This provenance has an important impact upon organisational decision-making, when the leaders of factions within an organisation come together to make decisions bearing on overall organisational goals. Interpersonal rivalries and resentments regularly can be expected to come into play. Given the premium placed on 'revolutionary heroism', in a council of rival faction leaders, it is difficult to imagine an advocate of prudence and inaction. In such a setting, the pressure to outdo one's rival in terms of boldness and courage would be intense, and pressures towards risky decision making by the leadership group would be strong.

While many of the basic features of organisational life are found in the terrorist organisation, there are special characteristics which have major impact upon both structure and communication. In particular, *terrorist organisations are secret organisations*. Students of organisational psychology regularly emphasise the importance of clear and effective communication between the leadership, middle-level management and the members (or workers). In a complex terrorist organisation, clear and effective communication between the leaders and the terrorists would pose a grave security risk. Yet without such communication, there is lack of effective control by the leadership. In contrast to the hierarchy of the Red Army Faction, the Revolutionary Cells chose a flat organisational scheme, composed of relatively autonomous cells. While security and feelings of personal involvement in decision making were stronger, the organisational coherence, and ability to develop a common strategy towards shared goals, were decidedly weaker.

The forms of terrorist organisations vary in another important respect. While some terrorist organisations have as their sole objective pursuit of their political goals through terrorist tactics, for others the terrorist organisation is the illegal corporate entity operating in parallel with a legal entity as components of an overall organisation dedicated to the particular cause. As examples of this complex structure, Crenshaw cites the IRA and ETA, observing that the IRA is the military wing of Sinn Fein, which is a legally constituted political party. By the same token, ETA is closely linked to a network of committed sympathisers and active supporters striving legally for Basque autonomy. Thus the overall corporate goal is not obtaining its political goals through terrorism per se, but the diversified corporation in effect can flexibly shift tactics in support of its overall objectives. But while profit centres within a corporation may quarrel with headquarter's management, ultimately they will comply with headquarter's directives. But the terrorist wing of an overall political organisation may not accept guidance instructing temporary cessation of terrorist activity, for guidance does not equate to control, and terrorists do not lightly cease being terrorists.

Just as the primary goal of the terrorist group is to survive, so too for the terrorist organisation. A basic principal of organisational psychology—that the survival of the organisation is the highest priority—applies fully to terrorist organisations. Organisational theorists are fond of citing the example of the cavalry, which persisted anachronistically long after the advent of the gas combustion engine which rendered it obsolete. Considering that perhaps eighty-five per cent of the objectives of the Basques for autonomy have been achieved, how striking that ETA persists as a viable terrorist organisation. If their goals were truly Basque autonomy, they might well have declared victory and folded up shop, indicating they were no longer necessary. That ETA persists suggests that the goal of self-preservation has a higher priority than the ostensible political cause, that ETA is in effect the cavalry of the terrorist world. In an apparent, but not actual, paradox, then, success in achieving its espoused goal can threaten a terrorist organisation, depriving it of its rationale. We have already noted in the discussion of 'groupthink' the consequences of failure. If survival is paramount, as we have suggested, and a terrorist organisation becomes identified as a 'loser', no longer attracting new recruits, unable to attract public attention, this circumstance is one which may push an organisational faction into a particularly dangerous posture, to cross previously inviolate thresholds and consider acts of mass destruction in order to regain the limelight, reverse the slide downhill and ensure organisational survival: the paradox of destroying in order to survive. What is being described is a kind of organisational homeostasis. Both success and failure threaten the terrorist organisation's primary goal—survival—which is viewed as the major determinant of terrorist actions.

IMPLICATIONS FOR COUNTERTERRORIST POLICY

As we observed in the introduction to this chapter, actions designed to deter terrorists should be based on a clear understanding of the individual, group and organisational psychology of terrorism. Identifying the locus of authority is crucial in estimating the effects of particular tactics. As a general proposition, the more autonomous the terrorist group, the more counterproductive reactive retaliation is likely to be. It will strengthen group cohesion, exaggerate the importance of the group, reduce internal tensions and justify its world view. Our understanding of the importance of the role of belonging to the terrorist group to its members suggests that even the threat of death will not persuade the terrorist to give up his violent trade, for to cease being a terrorist is to give up a fundamental aspect of his social identity. The intensity of the personal rivalry and tension within such groups argues for a policy of benign neglect, for without the external threat, such groups can self-destruct.

For the terrorist organisation, too, retaliatory policies can magnify a sense of importance and significance. The terrorists' perception that they are involved in a fantasy war has been justified by reality. But the external decision-making group in the corporate organisation may respond to retaliation temporarily at least by laying low or backing off its activist course. It cannot be coerced into giving up terrorism, for, as for the terrorist group, to do so would be to give up its raison d'être. For the complex terrorist organisation, like ETA or the IRA, wed to a legal political organisation, retaliatory policies can lead the superordinate leadership to inhibit terrorist actions in the service of the larger political goal.

For the state-supporting terrorism, a similar argument concerning effects of retaliation follows. On the one hand it magnifies the importance of the actor and justifies the perception of being the victim of outside aggression, while dissolving internal dissent. Yet, the primary goal of the state is survival and furthering national interests, and if the pursuit of terrorism threatens those goals, it can be reduced or abandoned in the face of outside threat. Thus we are arguing that the higher the level of authority, including complex corporate organisations and states supporting terrorism, the greater the rationale for the retaliatory tactic in carefully selected circumstances being efficacious. The more autonomous and self-sufficient the terrorist group, the greater the likelihood of retaliation being counterproductive.

Our understanding of the powerful effects of group and organisational dynamics upon terrorist behaviour suggests the utilisation of other tactics which thus far have been under-utilised as elements of a longe-range strategy. For terrorism promises to be a feature of the political landscape for the foreseeable future, and there is no quick fix. In the long run, a policy which renders the path of terrorism unattractive is the most effective counter-terrorism. The goals should be to inhibit potential terrorists from joining, which leads to disenchantment within the group and weakens support to the group. To accomplish these goals, a multifaceted programme is required, of which a central element must be a much more effective programme of public information. Terrorism is, after all, a form of psychological warfare waged through the media. Thus far we have not effectively countered the terrorist's primary weapon. In the service of this challenge distorted propaganda is not necessary. Effective communication of the vicious reality of terrorism—unmasking the murders posing as heroic leaders of a noble cause for what they are—these are the tasks of effective public education. The most effective psychological warfare for civilised society is the propagation of the truth.

Euroterrorists Talk about Themselves: A Look at the Literature

B Cordes

INTRODUCTION

Much research has been devoted to examining what terrorists have done in the past and identifying trends for predicting what they might do in the future. Less attention, however, has been focused on terrorist motivations or indeed, on *terrorists*' self-perception. By using the primary materials provided by the terrorists themselves, i.e., memoirs, statements, interviews and communiqués much information about the terrorist mindset and decision making can be gleaned.

What terrorists say about themselves is often more revealing than they intend. Although terrorism is often described as a form of communication, terrorists are rather poor communicators. Like many poor writers what they lack in clarity they often make up for in quantity. The purposes of terrorist communications can be analysed from two different aspects: how they persuade (or intend to persuade) others (what I call the *propaganda aspect*) and how they persuade themselves (the *auto-propaganda aspect*.)

The fundamental contradiction for terrorists is that while they are deliberately employing what we in fact regard as terrorist violence, they characterise their actions as something else.[1] While a criminal accepts that he is indeed a criminal, a terrorist goes to extraordinary lengths to deny that he is a terrorist. This denial may consist not only of semantic denial but of re-characterising themselves as freedom fighters, revolutionaries, etc., 'Because it is necessary,' declares a left-wing Belgian intellectual shortly before his own trip to the underground, 'in the face of the wall of silence, the lies and the provocations, to state that these groups struggle for communism and not because of their propensity for terrorism, as is so insistently asserted by the media of those who preserve themselves with occupation, war and legal assassination . . .'[2]

To comprehend the terrorist mindset it is crucial to uncover the rationale, motivations and mechanisms for such denial. By listening to what the terrorists say, this analysis assesses how they see themselves, what they think they are doing and what they think their actions will accomplish.

As late as 1979 Nathan Leites recognised that, although much work of varied nature is being conducted on what terrorists do and on what makes them do it, very little considers 'what they thought they were doing', or precisely 'what good [they thought] it would do'.[3] There are several reasons for this gap. First of all there is a paucity of data or relevant material provided by the rebels themselves. When terrorists write or speak about themselves it is usually after a particular terrorist action, i.e., declaratory communiqués, occasionally explanatory political tracts, patchy interviews with often sympathetic journalists, or the *very* rare occasion when a terrorist lives long enough to write his memoirs. Material of this kind which does exist is rarely published and is often difficult to obtain. Last but not least, the terrorist literature that is available provides very ponderous, and often repetitive reading. Consequently, a valuable primary source is being neglected.

This chapter takes a look at some of the dynamics of terrorism and proposes a simple framework for examining the terrorists' view of themselves and their actions. Terrorist violence is meant to carry a message that is not always heard or understood as the terrorists would like it to be: rather than communicating 'mayhem and destruction' with a particular bombing for instance, they would prefer that their audience read 'solidarity with the oppressed peoples of the Third World'. So, not only do they throw bombs, but they often have to write, and, it seems, in greater volume than previously. Often unconsciously, it appears, the purposes of communiqués are not only to explain their actions to others but to persuade the terrorists themselves that what they have done was justified, was appropriate, and carried sufficient weight in the pursuit of their cause. Keeping these two ostensible purposes in mind when reading terrorist literature we can perhaps address Leites' question '... how do they make it plausible to themselves that their acts serve the attainment of their goal?'[4]

FOCUS

The existence of several different types of terrorist groups, many with differing aims and sociopolitical contexts further complicates the study of terrorist literature and thwarts most attempts at generalisation. Part of the complexity of terrorism is the fact that it is conducted by a variety of idiosyncratic individuals with widely divergent national and sociocultural backgrounds. Efforts to provide an overall 'terrorist profile' are misleading, for as Post cautions, 'there are as nearly as many variants of personality who become involved in terrorist pursuits as there are variants of personality'.[5] To mitigate the errors inherent in making overly sweeping generalisations, this study limits itself to an examination of terrorists from a particular geographical area, with the assumption that, although a number of nationalities are represented, they probably share the concept or worldview of being 'Western' and 'European'. Additionally, the groups chosen share similar ideological frameworks of the radical left.

Post makes a useful distinction between 'anarchic-ideologues' such as the Italian Red Brigades or the German Red Army Faction and 'nationalist-secessionist' groups such as the Spanish Basques of ETA or the Irish Republican Army, stating that

> There would seem to be a profound difference between terrorists bent on destroying their own society, the 'world of their fathers,' and those whose terrorist activities carry on the mission of their fathers. To put it in other words, for some, becoming terrorists is an act of retaliation for real and imagined hurts *against the society of their parents*; for others, it is an act of retaliation against society *for the hurt done to their parents*. ... This would suggest more conflict, more psychopathology, among those committed to anarchy and destruction of society, ...[6]

Accordingly, this study examines a variety of material written and spoken by European 'anarchic-ideologues'—specifically, the major left-wing groups found in France, West Germany, Italy, and Belgium, frequently categorised in very general terms as anarchist/millenialists (for it is recognised that such distinctions have very specific connotations for the left), or, more recently, 'Euroterrorists'. Hence, this analysis employs material from Belgian groups such as the Communist Combatant Cells (CCC) and the Revolutionary Front for Proletarian Action (FRAP); from French groups such as *Action Directe* (AD); from German groups such as *Rote Armee Fraktion* (RAF), Revolutionary Cells (RZ), and *Rote Zora*; and from Italian groups such as *Brigate Rosse* (RB) and *Prima Linea* (PL).[7]

Although these particular groups are of differing ages all trace their roots and initial inspiration from the student revolts in Europe in 1968, originating in the protest movement against the Vietnam War. Focusing most of their energies on changing or overthrowing the governments of their respective countries, they share a common hatred for the United States and claim allegiance to a revolutionary brotherhood dedicated to solidarity with Third World liberation movements. It was in 1981 that the Red Brigades, considered purely an Italian problem, first struck out at NATO with its kidnapping of US General Dozier. Shortly after, other anti-NATO attacks occurred throughout Europe, culminating in 1984 and 1985 with a declaration of unity announced by the German Red Army Faction and the French *Action Directe*. Joint actions by these groups, with implied Italian inspiration, as well as continued and apparently coordinated attacks against American NATO, and Israeli targets by the entire spectrum of radical left groups throughout Europe (from Greece, to Portugal, to Belgium), led to the coining of the phrase 'Euroterrorism' and the suggestion that an international master cell was in place guided by a single strategy of destroying the Western alliance. European terrorist groups enjoyed an increase in stature as European countries scurried to work together on countermeasures as they imagined the terrorist groups were already doing successfully.

Although cultural and national differences exist, typologies of terrorist groups frequently categorise by ideological bent and stated aim. Within the spectrum of left-wing organisations, the anarchist groups are considered the most extreme in a number of ways. Terrorist doctrine often differs considerably from terrorist practice, but it is with the anarchist groups that this gap is most strikingly evident. What these terrorists say and what they actually do are usually two entirely different things. A May Day bombing, for instance, is an 'intervention on behalf of the workers' or an 'affirmation of the proletarian value of the world holiday of the oppressed'. Their words and actions involve a fair amount of high-sounding but inflated and deluding concepts. Imbued with Marxist–Leninist explanations for their actions, the terrorists' words reveal that they may actually derive their impetus from other, often more personal sources. It is for these very reasons that an examination of this type of terrorist literature may be so valuable. Alongside the conflict and contradiction of words and actions is a corresponding need to justify and explain: 'we believe that we should first attempt to clarify what happened ... to fight against the disgusting campaign of the bourgeois politicians ...'.[8] Or the need may be to self-criticize in a magnanimous manner: 'We must criticize ourselves first because we did not make the political step forward that we counted on with the attack ..., and then because there were reasons for this!'[9] Lastly they must clarify because although the terrorist actions carry much communicative weight and 'speak by being', it is true that there are those 'fact[s] that [are] known by everyone, even if in only a hazy way.'[10] It appears that the larger the gap to be filled between words and actions, the more elaborate are the mechanisms developed to rationalise one's existence and persistence in a course of violence.

FREQUENCY AND TYPES OF TERRORIST LITERATURE

The violence of terrorism is rarely understood by the public as well as the terrorists would like; frequently they choose to express themselves in written and oral forms—particularly if they are provided with a platform. Some groups it seems, write more than others. The Belgian Communist Combatant Cells (CCC) has been quite prolific since its inception, while the French Action Directe (AD) was never able to sustain a flow of written materials. Save for some interviews and a few short papers, AD's communiqués have been often rather short and brutally to the point, while the CCC will take five pages or more to explain a particular action. The Italian Red Brigades (RB) are known for their voluminous works and painfully detailed documents, while the German Red Army Faction (RAF) wrote about itself and its actions consistently in the early years, but only sporadically since then. Indeed, the absence of any significant declarations by the RAF since 1982 led authorities to believe that this was one more indication that the movement was in disarray and weakened.

A necessary caution in analysing written materials of terrorists is that while we tend to impute the declarations to the entire group, the individual author or authors certainly imbue the text with personal elements. It is usually unknown to what extent the texts are approved or censored by other members, although such practices undoubtedly exist. The frequency and quantity of writing may, as mentioned, indicate the health of the group, yet much written material is issued from prison cells by incarcerated members. More likely, it appears that the frequency, quantity and style of writing depends as much on the availability of an intellectual-type member prone to written expression as on the overall condition of the group, although it may be this very lack of intellectual leadership that also indicates a group in decline. Without the 'proper' justification and explanation of the group's violence and periodic assessment and/or re-alignment of strategy, terrorist activity tends to deteriorate into mindless or self-serving violence. 'Communication and discussion are necessary because they are the prerequisites for all to learn ...[11] but at the same time, 'Communism does not develop via radical positions in texts. It expresses itself in a precise analysis of the situation and in a transfer to actual practice ...'[12] Similarly, during the early days of the RAF, then leader Ulrike Meinhof dedicated herself to espousing revolutionary doctrine for the group, concluding however, that 'Writing is shit, now let's make the revolution.'[13] With Meinhof's death, Brigitte Mohnhaupt took over the pen as well as the intellectual leadership of the RAF rather effectively, but with her demise 'on the whole, at least toward the outside, the RAF has become less verbal, and the men and women now prominent in it make very few statements. For example, we have no statements at all ... from current co-leader Christian Klar. But that does not mean he is not a true fanatic.'[14] Actually Klar has written some rather unintelligible material from his prison cell in Germany, accompanied by some superficially theoretical treatise from Brigitte Mohnhaupt—it appears that some individuals simply choose to write more than others.

Certain personalities carry the weight and responsibility for writing for the group. Pierre Carette, presumed leader of the Belgian CCC and probable author of their extensive communiqués, has a history of radical activity and as printer by profession, has an intimate association with the written word. The Red Brigades owes its literary debt to figures such as Curcio and Moretti, and the Germans to Mahler, Mohnhaupt and Meinhof.

An additional caution is necessary in such an analysis of terrorist literature. Each type of material presumably has a particular purpose: Policy papers are for internal as well as external consumption to outline strategy and rally support; communiqués are to explain and persuade a larger public, and a perceived constituency; while memoirs are therapeutic autobiographies to justify and critique the past. Yet all this material can be seen as focusing on several audiences and as serving the purpose of denial. The very need, even compulsion to explain and justify, is to deny the real appearance the violent actions portray. And this denial is directed as much at an outer audience as it is to an inner one. Not only need they convince themselves, but other terrorist groups as well. They have a 'constituency' they must answer to, be it fringe sympathisers or potential recruits or the terrorists of other groups. A certain prestige and intellectual sophistication is required to be considered legitimate. Least important audience of all, it appears, is the state itself, although the communiqués are often directed to the authorities. The group and the individual author(s) require the written and spoken exercise to build conviction amongst the members and in its audience. There is no greater fan of the terrorist, however, than the terrorist himself. Analysing the material from these two different aspects should separate one fiction from another and perhaps even provide some useful facts.

THE PROPAGANDA OF VIOLENCE

Terrorism is a dynamic, not static concept. It is the particular use of violence for effect, 'speaking with action' rather than with words. Obviously, terrorists want to get a message across. Often, however, they are like absent-minded professors who have forgotten whether they had told this terms' students about the significance of this or that, and simply assume that they know—to the students' complete mystification. Often this is the case following a terrorist action that the terrorists intend should speak loudly for itself.

Modern explanations of the phenomenon of secular terrorism range from the psychological to the sociological to the historical. From an additional perspective, however, it is useful and instructive to listen to what the terrorists have to say. How they characterise themselves, their chosen enemy, their actions and their goals, provides us with a unique view.

The act of choosing the targets for terrorist violence is an important component of terrorist activity. The attacks, contrary to popular belief, are not normally random and indiscriminate, but carefully calculated, measured and debated as to the appropriateness and the propaganda value of the target. For example, on 1 May 1985, the CCC carried out an attack against a Belgian Employers' Association building in Brussels. The bomb was made powerful enough to kill but warning notices were sprinkled liberally at the scene. Yet when the device did 'inadvertently' kill, the group regretted the deaths of the two firemen, declaring its solidarity with the country's workers.[15] The press explained that the CCC had claimed that the explosive device malfunctioned. The attack itself was meant to 'speak' on behalf of the workers on May Day, a fact reiterated by the communiqué 'saluting international workers' solidarity against the exploiters.'[16] The auto-propaganda effect of the communiqué, however, was to state that the use of violence was somehow to protect workers from a worse evil and to reassure themselves, along with their audience, that the deaths were *unintended*, regardless of the amount of explosives placed. Numerous similar examples abound in communiqués following terrorist actions involving 'unintended' deaths.

Aside from the message of violence directed against particular kinds of targets, the terrorists thus also use written and spoken language to legitimise, rationalise and justify their actions. It appears that although there are ample historic examples of appealing causes and precedents for terrorism, the rationales for terrorism today undergo severe strain. For in the 1980s violence is directed against societies with more ample means than ever available to their citizens to express and attempt to redress their respective grievances. Such a phenomenon requires extensive explanation by the terrorist to rationalise and justify his actions not only to himself but also to an audience of perceived or potential sympathisers.

MOTIVATIONS AND MORALITY: HOW DO THE TERRORISTS SEE THEMSELVES?

Much suggestive but inconclusive work has been done on the psychological mechanisms of terrorism exploring the personalities and backgrounds of those drawn to political violence,[17] and the dynamics at play within a terrorist group.[18] It is tempting but impracticable to review a number of these to explain what the terrorists are saying when they write—one analysis however, deserves special consideration because of the weight of its explanatory power. Franco Ferracuti points out that the curious tendency of terrorists to always invoke war as the reason for and the intentions of their actions has a particular and not completely obvious purpose for the terrorists. It is in war Ferracuti suggests, that aggression is permitted and thus, 'The "normal" [not insane] terrorist is therefore like a soldier outside of time and space living in a reality of war that exists only in his or her fantasy'.[19] Comparing real war with the terrorists' fantasy war he discovers that the terrorists are actually attempting to replicate certain conditions which must exist for such war to take place. The process involves identifying a crisis (or creating one), building an organised collectivity of opposition, transforming the 'enemy' into something 'alien and hostile', and building a reciprocal 'maniacal feeling of increasing power and invulnerability'. Elements such as these are abundant in terrorist literature with constant references to the 'armed struggle', 'war on imperialist war' and characterisations of themselves as 'soldiers', and 'militants', and 'revolutionaries.'

> BUILD UP THE POLITICAL-MILITARY FRONT IN WESTERN EUROPE AS PART OF THE WORLDWIDE STRUGGLE BETWEEN THE INTERNATIONAL PROLETARIAT AND THE IMPERIALIST BOURGEOISIE.
>
> NEVER BE DETERRED BY THE ENORMOUS DIMENSIONS OF YOUR OWN GOALS.
>
> THE WEST EUROPEAN GUERRILLAS ARE CONVULSING THE EUROPEAN CENTER.[20]

To maintain the 'war footing' it is at the same time necessary to discredit legal or peaceful attempts to fight the battle. In the following excerpt, the italicised words (my emphasis) demonstrate this fascination with imagining that the terrorists are 'at war' because of the imminence of war, and the futility of other non-violent means, in a declaration of responsibility for a bombing of a computer office of the French Ministry of Defence:

> *Wars, war economy*, a continuing economy based on *arms*: This is the central characteristic of the economy of imperialism, the constant stimulus it needs to stay afloat. Whether it be a question of *the two great wars, the cold war of the 1950s, the some 250 armed conflicts* the world experienced from 1945 to 1984, the intensification of *weapons* spending ... *militarism* clearly appears as the lifesaver to which capitalism systematically clings whenever the forces inherent in its own system risk sinking it in the abyss of *crisis*. Confronted with the need inherent in the system, *it is ridiculous to look to peaceful pacifism.*[21]

It may be that violence, terror, *illegal* actions breed more satisfaction and *possible* results despite the higher risks. Expounded as the strategy of last resort, terrorism it appears often serves personal motives; expediency determines the decision cited above, to take up arms. Regardless of the cause, it is the propaganda of violence, transmitted through the media, which creates an awesome enemy we normally would hardly recognise. The auto-propaganda effect of these messages is persuasion that the enemy is real, the cause just and the terrorist's existence not only justified, but called for due to the 'urgency' of the moment. The enemy, in this case, members of an international conference on technological developments and applications; the purpose for striking them is unclear. The subsequent communiqué explains that, as the gathering itself demonstrates 'the period of small steps [by the imperialists] and of hitting individual targets is over; the acceleration of the process of reconstruction is now proceeding with the regularity of a steam roller ... [over the bodies of the workers]'.[22] An attack against them makes perfect sense, and the self-appointed radicals are the ideal candidates. They are endowed with particular qualities that allow them to carry on the struggle, 'to work towards a strategy of communist liberation of the proletariat' because they can 'regard the present with the insights of tomorrow...'. Indeed, the 'historic task of the communists—both as a faction and as an organized avant garde of the proletariat—is to understand the movement of capital in its entirety ... to understand ... the development of the revolutionary consciousness of the proletariat ...'[23] Above all, these representatives possess the means to support the development of their struggle, one of them being 'Marxist analysis in order to understand reality'.[24] Without violent action however, somehow 'Marxist methodology would deteriorate to a static theorizing about reality', while with the two they can 'really develop the dynamic of construction/destruction'.[25]

Terrorism is a rational and at times, for certain actors, an efficient strategy in which the benefits exceed the costs for its employers. The motives stem, however, from a variety of sources. Although they are framed in rationality and utility, the justifications are often moral ones. Thus, the 'just' war is the battle against evil, or in self-defence. Going against the prevailing system and mores, using violence in a 'legitimate' fashion can provide individuals with personal satisfaction (or frustration) far beyond the stated 'cause'. Obviously there are many motives for engaging in such unconventional activities. The point here is that the terrorism has become so accepted as an inevitable facet of international affairs that its use is contemplated and undertaken by even those with purely criminal motives.

As the activity is 'corrupted' more rationalisations are needed. That is when the communiqués are generally issued, when the media 'misrepresents our combat' by introducing 'questioning and suspicion'[26] and even because they are branded as 'anarchists'. They treasure their commitment to the people, believe the feelings are reciprocal and fashion themselves as adventurous young people, who with little trouble and much ingenuity, are able to make an impact on the state. Intrigue is part of the game and 'intelligence is not a shameful disease ... but a necessary practice ...'.[27]

Terrorist memoirs of defectors and depositions given by repentant terrorists reveal that terrorists themselves have debated the issues of the morality of violence and just what constitutes 'terrorism'. Generally living underground, such individuals slowly become divorced from reality, descending into a make-believe world where they wage Ferracuti's 'fantasy war'. They take great satisfaction in noting the US rallying for 'the war against international terrorism' because it validates their view of the enemy and their view of themselves as soldiers. They can never rest or withdraw from the struggle however. The defector Klein describes the misery of his life, still underground, but this time without his comrades, living in fear of them as well as of authorities. His attempts to publish material about his terrorist life are resisted by the group; Klein has swapped one struggle for another.[28]

The active terrorists must continually justify their actions to themselves as well as to their real and perceived constituencies. Because of the indefinite boundary between political terror and crime there is a need to elevate the terrorist motive above the criminal, a need which becomes elemental to the terrorist's perception of his success. Through 'demonisation' of the enemy comes 'heroisation' of the rebel.[29] This need to justify and validate his violent actions becomes a consuming part of his existence, for indeed, even the terrorist is *aware* of the moral, legal boundaries he oversteps. Not only is he a soldier, but a victim who must prevail: 'Not those who cause the most suffering will be victorious, but rather those who suffer the most!'[30]

Violent, extra-legal activity is justified in the minds of the terrorists by their stated conviction that all legal processes are to no avail, since the cards are stacked against them. The reigning system of 'capitalism' has built-in mechanisms for 'pacification of the antagonism of the masses' while 'the bell jar of state security that is in place over society does not disappear, but rather is felt by increasing numbers of the people, the screw of impoverization that they have applied begins to take hold'.[31] The terrorist is not deluded.

THE ENEMY

Much effort goes into characterising the enemy. The David and Goliath theme is prevalent—there is nobility and honour in the courage and determination of an oppressed party who dares to strike out at the 'oppressor'. Dehumanising the enemy becomes automatic with practice. Klein, in an interview given from hiding after his defection from the RAF, spoke of his fear of having a weapon with him *now* because he was unsure of his control over it. Possession caused what he called an 'over-estimation of your opponent' with subsequent use being easily justified with little forethought.[32] To justify acts of violence, the situation must be black and white, with little room for hesitation. Often using the claim of conspiracy, the groups build the evil enemy, explaining here why violence is necessary and why it is necessary *now*:

> We arrive at this step from the objective situation: The central importance of Western Europe for the reconstruction of imperialism which has become weakened as the result of the liberation struggle of the peoples of the South ... which in turn has resulted in a collision between the growing forces of productivity and the limitations of the world markets. This has led to a global political, economic, and military crisis in the imperialist chain of states, and has now touched the entire imperialist systems.[33]

The tone of alarm communicates the necessity of the organisation while the murky, sometimes confused explanation portrays the revolutionaries as dedicated, hard-working intellectuals who have clearly thought all of this out. It is hard to imagine the average man on the street getting this message from the widely distributed flyer. Rather, looking from the auto-propaganda aspect, the tract certainly impressed its writer, making him *feel* this generation of the Red Army Faction had been created in response to this threat. Characterising the enemy as a conspirator has its advantages. The terrorist plays the part of self-appointed detective with a superior ability to recognise and decipher the state's *real* intentions.

Although he may pose himself as particularly knowledgeable about the purposes of the 'imperialist conspiracy' it is evident that much internal group friction results over these debates. The discussions themselves can lead to disagreement wherein splits occur, with factions following a new, self-determined rationale. All revolutionary groups—terrorist or guerrilla—have had their internal critics. Sometimes these critics, like Hans Joachim Klein and Michael Baumann of the German millenialist groups for example, have left the underground and written or talked about how the clandestine life of terrorist violence had gone wrong. Debates over the justification for violence, the types of targets, the issues of indiscriminate versus discriminate killing, are endemic to a terrorist group. Differences of opinion evidenced within terrorist groups have on occasion misled authorities into believing that a schism existed. Because of the new 'internationalist' focus of AD communiqués and yet the continuation of AD anti-establishment actions, French authorities appear convinced of a group split.

Apparently, the auto-propaganda aspect of words and actions can at times become too powerful and dominating, to the point that the group loses touch with reality. Popular support is hardly to be gained by a group which did not become a symbol of justice and liberty. Between 1980 and early 1984, limited to avoiding arrest and running from police, and occasional seemingly meaningless bombings, the European terrorist groups lost what minor public support and interest they had previously enjoyed. There was a tendency to lose sight of their strategic needs to mobilise the masses and open up the 'path' to their goal. AD, RAF, and new CCC communiqués corrected this situation with a stream of written material during the summer and autumn of 1984. Even to the terrorists, violence carried out with the proper goal and strategy is more acceptable, and thus somehow justified, while aimless violence, regardless of the rightness of the cause for it, is deprecated, and far more difficult to rationalise. The need for intellectual discussion was neglected but finally reformulated in the wake of the European peace movement and the addition of nuclear missiles to the continent.

What had actually occurred was that the 'enemy' could now be characterised on a grander, more evil scale, and its 'true character' was more evident than before. While 'this situation is understood by all workers . . .', it provides an augmentation of 'the capital of sympathy and unification which we were in the process of accumulating . . .'[34]

Name-calling is profuse throughout the communiqués of every group (i.e., 'pigs', 'imperialist exploiters', 'carrions and their consorts', etc.), but frequently the State is labeled *terrorist*, particularly with regard to treatment of the rebels themselves, such as 'the terrorist programme against the prisoners' and infrequently or secondarily with regard to actions seen as directed against the rest of the people in general: 'the major power of NATO has raised state terrorism against the anti-imperialist guerrilla groups, the liberation movements and the population, which are refusing their loyalty, to an official government policy.'[35] Some analysts would label this technique as a projection on the part of the rebels but they are not the only ones to do so:

> The demonizing of the guerrillas, the witch hunt, the *projection of terrorism* onto the guerrillas are losing their effectiveness, and no longer mobilize on behalf of the state. On the contrary, terror is the concept that clings like tar to a system that only destroys, suppresses and stands in the way of any kind of human development. (My italics).[36]

WHAT THEY THINK THEY ARE DOING

Violent action serves multiple purposes. It is meant to communicate, but it also serves as an example of what can be done. According to Fanon's argument violence is good because it liberates; similarly the terrorists believe that a violent act will speak for itself. It awakens, making the people aware of the 'inherent contradictions of the state', and demonstrates that resistance is possible, 'showing in practice the real possibilities of the confrontation with the police state in the strategy for socialism.'[37] An act can have remarkable results according to the terrorists:

> Attacks on the multinational structures of NATO, on its bases and strategists, on

> its plans and propaganda, are bringing about a transformation of the awareness and practices of the proletariat, going beyond its national characteristics and bringing about an international organizational advance.[38]

The spectacular act gains access to the media, thus breaking the 'barrier' to the people. They take for granted that the 'present order cruelly frustrates the interest of most' and if the people are only made aware through violent acts that exposure will bring conversion to the terrorists' point of view.

Unfortunately, sometimes the exposure given to the terrorists is not to their liking. When actions have unintended consequences, groups have been known to withdraw their claims, but if that is not practical, elaborate explanations are required. A good example can be found by returning to the CCC May Day bombing that claimed the lives of two firemen at the scene of the burning van containing explosives. Shortly after the incident, another bombing took place at the 'head financial and logistics office' of the Brussels gendarmerie. According to the CCC, 'The entire world will understand the selection of this target for attack because of the responsibility of the gendarmerie ...'.[39] The firemen's deaths were the first to result from the extensive bombing activity of the CCC since October 1984. The media and government response was outrage, but presumably the CCC experienced a severe reaction to the event as well. Rather than feeling remorse or guilt however, 'the deaths of these two men shock us deeply and arouse our rage at those responsible ...'[40] Several pages are dedicated to explaining how the responsibility for the firemen's deaths could and should be placed at the doorstep of the 'gendarmerie' and not at their own. Their dismay lies more in the fact that 'the deaths of these public servants has destroyed and obviated the power of our initiative, has concealed the correctness of the attack ...' and that 'the police campaign which is being carried out in the media concerning our so-called "contempt for human life" is a despicable falsification of our political texts ...'[41] Although they regret the deaths, they are convinced of the appropriateness of the target. It is the deaths which 'in a tragic way' made the act 'incomprehensible and inaccessible to the population as a whole'.[42] The explanation is that the 'pigs' sent the firemen to their deaths, probably because of the 'scorn that the bourgeoisie has for the workers ...' and so that the authorities could 'exploit' the accident.

Without saying so directly, the remorse of the terrorists is expressed, particularly in one passage that nearly sounds like a plea for forgiveness: 'We bow down before the victims and respect the pain of their families and comrades. We understand their rage, but we ask them in view of our explanation to consider against who this rage should be directed ...'[43]

What has been called 'Euroterrorism' actually developed as a concept years before its manifestations in joint communiqués and action. The shift from clearly indigenous groups to a 'West European guerrilla' was more an expansion of a state of mind than a radical change in type of operations. The European groups involved, to one extent or another, had always been 'anti-imperialist' and anti-US (some having previously attacked American targets).

Additionally, however, the newly declared association of the French AD and German RAF (in January 1985) has not kept either group, or the newly formed Belgian CCC, from persisting in their purely national-minded attacks or statements.

Although the document stated that 'It is now necessary and possible to open a new phase in the development of a true revolutionary strategy in the Imperialist Centres ...' with the purpose of creating 'a West European guerrilla',[44] each of the European groups was to continue acting on its national program. Keeping in mind the shared struggle where 'Each one must fight in the sector where he has the most strength,' the rebels were at the same time 'always offensively [link] the fight to those of other proletarians involved in other sectors of the same struggle'.[45] The campaign of joint actions and communiqués was credited, rightly so, with having tremendous impact:

> There is a specter going around in Europe: the specter of 'Euro-terrorism'. All forces of old Europe have aligned themselves in a holy crusade in order to hunt down this specter: the pope and NATO, Paris and Washington, Scelfaro and Barrionuevo, Fabius and Kohl, etc. The entire repressive apparatus of old Europe, the Europe of the alliance, has placed itself in a state of emergency in view of the rise of revolutionary guerrillas.[46]

An educational process is necessary they state, part of which is done through writings, part through joint actions. The union is envisaged by the terrorists as a requisite step in revolutionary strategy where 'Today it is important to regard Western Europe as a homogeneous territory, where the formation of a unified revolutionary pole is possible ...',[47] but not to be accomplished overnight. 'Concretely put: we regard the process of the new-formation of the totality of the European proletariat into one single proletarian faction as a process that has not yet been concluded.'[48]

This union or 'internationalization of the proletariat' is necessary because the *enemy* is unified, But the unification of the European terrorist groups into a 'metropolis proletariat' will not be 'a soup in which all experiences are blended ...'.[49] but will recognise national differences. Although the very idea of a 'front' is called an 'open concept', it is insisted that there must be resistance to any purely independent structures.

Ironically, the union of revolutionary groups into an 'anti-imperialist front in Western Europe' is required to fend off the unification of Western Europe, which is considered the next step in 'imperialist domination'. The most 'aggressive of the capitalist factions' is the military-industrial complex, considered responsible for the impetus to militarise, homogenise, and 'Americanise' Western Europe into 'one counterrevolutionary bloc'.[50] The crisis is imminent and action, not pacifism, is necessary *now* because of 'the reality' of the coming 'imperialist war' and the risk of being 'damned to be "cannon fodder" in the coming conflicts and, until that point, to be "profit fodder" in the Near East, Africa, etc.'.[51] Exhorting to action is not to take the offensive, however. Revolutionary acts are in response to what is characterised as another offensive threat. Thus, an action is justified if it is accepted that, 'That which is destroying us must itself be destroyed . . .'.[52]

WHAT THEY THINK IT WILL ACCOMPLISH

Whatever the terrorists believe they will accomplish is fairly well hidden, but the fact that they believe they are successfully moving towards this unknown is often stated and with confidence. According to one imprisoned terrorist, 'It is fairly certain that the extent of the armed actions and the massive actions in solidarity with the revolutionary militant prisoners *justify the fear* that has been unleashed on the governments of the member states of NATO . . . the success of all of this activity is undeniable.'[53] In piecing together allusions to this future a picture emerges of destroying one society so as to replace it with a new one. This new social system is to be based on the free development of the individual, the emancipation of the proletariat and 'can only come about through the destruction of capitalism and the opening of a path to communist liberation'.[54] Not one of the terrorist authors seems to be able or interested in specifying what the new social system will be like, but all are agreed that 'We want to destroy this society in order to build up' another, one that will be 'a just and classless society, in which production meets the needs of all, not only the needs of a privileged few . . . a society in which "equality for all" no longer has to be demanded, because it has already been realized'.[55] The European terrorist groups of Italy and Germany have histories stretching back to the late 1960s, where as purely indigenous terrorists they held programs to overthrow their respective establishments. Such actions are now considered 'utopian presumptiveness' where 'detaching one's own territory from the imperialist chain' is not only impracticable but selfish.[56] Within the new concept, it is admitted that each national struggle is equally necessary and must take place simultaneously. In practice, however, the groups remain greatly concerned with anti-establishment actions, with political developments in their own country, and particularly with the fate of their own comrades and the treatment of 'political prisoners'. Such concerns are reflected in page after page of communiqués explaining the failure of operations, and condemning actions by authorities against incarcerated comrades.

Frequently quotes from illustrious revolutionary figures—Marx, Lenin, Che—are used to validate and inexplicably explain that 'The present belongs to the struggle; the future belongs to us' (Che).[57]

CONCLUSION

Although idiosyncratic differences emerge from group to group because of different writers, different nationalities, and different national programmes, the basic characteristics of the European 'anarchic-ideologues' are the same. The groups share (1) obviously, but importantly, a common use of terrorist violence; (2) denial that they are terrorists; (3) the need to portray themselves in a favorable light in order to attract support; (4) the need to rationalise and justify what they do; (5) the tendency for self-criticism.

A number of basic conclusions consequently emerge. According to the memoirs of defectors and the depositions of repentant terrorists, a life of violence tends to harden or defeat its adherents. Once in the underground it is nearly impossible to leave it intact. Those who do escape are more demoralised than renewed, as Klein indicates in his written work from hiding.

Another impression, but certainly not conclusion from terrorist literature, is that it may be true that European anarchists may belong more to the 'province of psychologists than political analysts . . .'.[58] The ability to see our reality in their terms, to us is dramatically unreal; but to continually convince themselves and try to convince others of this abstract vision is remarkable in its energy and persistence.

Difficult as it is to systematically gauge the frequency and quantity of writing by terrorists the impression is that not only do the groups appear to write less frequently as they age, but by deduction we can say that this suggests they may care less about the consequences of their acts. These observations are less evident in the communiqués than in the memoirs or statements of repentants.

The stress of life underground and the continous struggle to survive often distorts the already 'strange' perceptions of terrorists, according to members of terrorist groups who have defected or recanted. Although another form of 'underground life', the prison appears to have similar effects on the terrorists. After several years of incarceration, virtually cut off from the outside world, the images they conjure of the people and of the enemy become more and more bizarre.

What about 'Euroterrorism?' This 'Internationalist anti-imperialist Front' is actually what Bell has characterised as 'quarrelling brothers'.[59] From small references sprinkled throughout these communiqués, it can be gathered that this is exactly what these European terrorist groups are. Declarations of 'unity', 'comradeship', 'brotherhood' etc., are in fact elusive. The 'Western anti-imperialist front' is more a loose confederation of like-minded groups than an actual organisational structure. Intuitively, this failure can be attributed to idiosyncratic group rationales and strong, uncompromising personalities. Attempts at cooperation with each other appear difficult to execute in practice and, if achieved, are often short-lived.

Despite the claims of union, the real focus of these groups is the problems they see in their own countries and political systems. It is not a matter of aging as a group and expanding their horizons. On the contrary, the older and more sophisticated the group, the stronger appears to be the revelation that because of the inherent imbalance between the group and its chosen enemy the state, no notable changes can be forced into the international environment. The prospect for change at home can be nearly as futile, but time and again these groups have felt they made an impact, if only by the attention they generated from the security services of the state and media coverage. A recent document put out by remnants of the Red Brigades of Italy makes this sentiment clear when its author thanks all the other European revolutionaries for their actions and declarations of solidarity, but insists that the Red Brigades not be distracted and continue with the business at hand—the problems of politics at home. It appears that the union of the European groups remains more in the mind of authorities than in the minds of the terrorists.

Such conclusions derived from terrorist literature need to be confirmed by continued examination of this neglected area. Not only is the quantity and quality of such literature a measure of the health and cohesion of a group it can also be a window into their otherwise clandestine, underground life.

BIBLIOGRAPHY

BELGIAN GROUPS

'Fighting Communist Cells Communique', dated 26 November 1984, *Open Road*, Vancouver, Canada, Spring 1986.
'Concrete Answers to Concrete Questions', CCC Communique, David Schiller translator, May 1985.
'Communique of CCC', 1 May 1985.
'CCC on May 1 Action', 6 May 1985, in *Zusammen Kaempfen* July 1985.
'CCC Communique No. 3 from the Karl Marx Campaign', 4–5 November 1985.
'CCC Communique and Addendum', 28 January 1986.
'FRAP Communique' David Schiller translator, May 1985.
'Communique by FRAP', in *Zusammen Kaempfen* July 1985.

FRENCH GROUPS

'Interview with "Action Directe" Leader Rouillan' *Liberation*, Paris, 17 August 1982, p. 3.
'Action Directe Leader Rouillan on Attacks, Goals', *Le Matin*, Paris, 5 October 1982, p. 19.
'Un Manifeste d'Action directe', excerpts of long AD communique, *Le Monde*, Paris, 21 October 1982.
'Action Directe Communique, Anti-Apartheid Bombings', 4 September 1985, *Open Road*, Vancouver, Canada, Spring 1986.

GERMAN GROUPS

RAF Texts, Bo Cavefors Publishers, Malmö, Sweden, 1977.
'RAF 8 August 1985 Communique', David Schiller translator.
Baumann, Michael, *Terror or Love? Bommi Baumann's Own Story of His Life as a West German Urban Guerrilla*, Grove Press, NY, 1978.
——, 'The Mind of a German Terrorist', *Encounter*, Vol. LI, No. 3, September 1978, pp. 81–88.

Horchem, Hans, 'The Development of West German Terrorism After 1969: An Overview', *TVI Journal* Vol. 5, No. 4, Spring 1985.

Kellen, Konrad, unpublished 'Primer' on the Red Army Faction, 1982.

Klein, Hans-Joachim, *La Mort Mercenaire: Temoignage d'un Ancien Terroriste Ouest-Allemand*, Editions du Seuil, Paris, 1980.

——, 'Les Memoires d'un Terroriste International', *Liberation*, 8 October 1978.

'Revolutionary Cells Communique', dated both 24 April 1985 and 2 September 1985, in Spring 1986 issue of *Open Road*, Vancouver, Canada.

'Revolutionary Cells and Rote Zora, Discussion Paper on the Peace Movement', *Open Road*, Vancouver, Canada, Spring 1986.

ITALIAN GROUPS

Court Depositions of Three Red Brigadists, Sue Ellen Moran, editor, Rand Corporation, February 1986.

'Document 142', excerpts of Red Brigades communique in *Le Point*, 2 April 1984.

Prima Linea, 'Des deserteurs du terrorisme temoignent', *Liberation*, No. 2072, Paris, 13 October 1980.

Silj, Alessandro, *Never Again Without a Rifle: The Origins of Italian Terrorism*, translated from the Italian by S Atanasio, Karz Publ., NY, 1979.

Zoppo, Ciro, '"Never Again Without a Rifle," by Alessandro Silj: A Review of a Book and a Situation', *Terrorism*, Vol. 2, Nos. 3 & 4, 1979, pp. 271–81.

NOTES

1 Issues of definition, of course, have presented a problem to many seeking a clear boundary for what should be considered terrorism. The label has become so burdened with value connotations that even the actors themselves reject it, a distinct change from the turn of the century when anarchists and revolutionaries proudly adopted it. Terrorism in this essay refers to a definition first used by Thornton in 'Terror as a Weapon of Political Agitation', *Internal War: Problems and Approaches*, Harry Eckstein (ed.), 1964, p. 73; 'Terror is a symbolic act designed to influence political behaviour by extranormal means, entailing the use or the threat of violence.' Additionally, it is determined by the nature of the act and not by the nature of the perpetrator. See also Brian Jenkins' *The Study of Terrorism: Definitional Problems*, December 1980, Rand Corporation.

2 Pierre Carrette in an undated excerpt from *Documentation Communiste*, cited in *Action Directe*, by Alain Hamon and Jean-Charles Marchand, Editions du Seuil, Paris, 1983, p. 246.

3 Nathan Leites, 'Understanding the Next Act', *Terrorism*, Vol. 3, 1979, p. 1.

4 *Ibid.*, p. 2.

5 Jerrold Post, 'Notes on a Psychodynamic Theory of Terrorist Behavior', *Terrorism*, Vol. 7, No. 3, 1984, p. 242.

6 *Ibid.*, p. 243.

7 The sources enlisted in this study do not constitute a comprehensive compilation (the attached bibliography is the optimistic beginnings of one) of all such primary source material but are probably representative.

The French AD for instance was created in 1979, and the CCC not until 1984, while the Italian Red Brigades and the German RAF were well into their 'second generation' by that time. Many current groups are the result of the decline and splitting of previous groups.

8 'CCC Comments on 1 May Action', 6 May 1985.
9 *Ibid.*
10 *Ibid.*
11 Unknown author for 'Anti-Imperialist Front', *Zusammen Kaempfen*, July 1985.
12 'Communiqué of Action Directe', June 1985.
13 Quoted in Leites, p. 32.
14 Konrad Kellen, Unpublished 'Primer' on the Red Army Faction, 1982.
15 'CCC on 1 May Action', 1 May 1985.
16 *Ibid.*
17 Examples are A Kaplan, 'The Psychodynamics of Terrorism', *Terrorism*, 1978, or Jerrold Post, 'Notes on a Psychodynamic Theory of Terrorist Behavior', *Terrorism*, 1984.
18 Konrad Kellen, *On Terrorists and Terrorism*, The Rand Corporation, December 1982.
19 Franco Ferracuti, 'A Sociopsychiatric Interpretation of Terrorism', *The Annals of the American Academy of Political and Social Science*, September 1982, p. 136.
20 'Communique of Action Directe', June 1985.
21 'Communique from Direct Action', *Ligne Rouge*, 13 July 1984.
22 'Communique from Direct Action', *Zusammen Kaempfen*, July 1985.
23 *Zusammen Kaempfen*, July 1985, pp. 3–6.
24 *Ibid.*
25 *Ibid.*
26 'Concrete Answers to Concrete Questions', CCC Communique, David Schiller translator, May 1985.
27 *Ibid.*
28 Hans-Joachim Klein, 'Les Memoires d'un Terroriste International', *Liberation*, 8 October 1978.
29 A Kaplan, 'Psycho-Dynamics of Terrorism', *Terrorism*, 1978.
30 Brigitte Mohnhaupt quoting Irish hunger striker, Patsy O'Hara, 26 March 1985, cited in Spring 1986 issue of *Open Road*, Vancouver, Canada.
31 Brigitte Mohnhaupt from prison, 26 March 1985.
32 'Interview with Hans Joachim Klein,' *Liberation*, 8 October 1978.
33 'For the Unity of Western Europe's Revolutionaries', RAF communiqué approximately early 1985.
34 'CCC communique', 6 May 1985.
35 'Christian Klar from prison', 26 March 1985.
36 *Ibid.*
37 *Zusammen Kaempfen*, July 1985, pp. 14–16.
38 'Communique from Action Directe', claiming credit for the assassination of General Rene Audran, 25 January 1985.
39 'CCC on 1 May Action', 6 May 1985.
40 *Ibid.*
41 *Ibid.*
42 *Ibid.*
43 *Ibid.*
44 'For the Unity of Western Europe's Revolutionaries', RAF communique approximately early 1985.

45 'Communique from Direct Action,' *Ligne Rouge*, 13 July 1984.
46 *Zusammen Kaempfen*, July 1985, pp. 14–16.
47 'Internationalization of the Struggle', author unknown, *Zusammen Kaempfen*, July 1985, pp. 3–6.
48 *Ibid.*
49 *Ibid.*
50 *Zusammen Kaempfen*, July 1985, pp. 8–9.
51 *Ibid.*
52 'Communique by FRAP', April 1985.
53 *Zusammen Kaempfen*, July 1985, pp. 14–16.
54 *Ibid.*
55 'Communique of FRAP', April 1985.
56 *Ibid.*
57 *Zusammen Kaempfen*, July 1985, pp. 28–31.
58 B Bell, 'Old Trends and Future Realities', *Washington Quarterly*, Spring 1985.
59 *Ibid.*

Victims of Terrorism: Dimensions of the Victim Experience

E E Flynn

Modern society has come to experience terrorism in a variety of ways: (a) as a form of political expression or action by political dissidents striving to overturn an existing government; (b) as a cataclysmic way of seeking redress for real or imagined grievances; (c) as a method of gaining publicity for causes or grievances; (d) as surrogate warfare against governmental entities; (e) as a means for gaining local, national or international leverage for causes or issues; and (f) as a novel rationalisation for the commission of essentially apolitical, ordinary crimes. Terrorism purposively uses fear as a means to attain particular ends. Terrorism is by nature coercive, dehumanising, a theatre of the absurd, and designed to manipulate its victims, and through them, a larger audience. Definitions of terrorism are notoriously difficult and imprecise. A nosology includes (a) *non-political terrorism*, defined as the deliberate creation of fear for coercive purposes with an end goal of collective or individual gain, or terrorism engendered by seriously mentally disturbed individuals; (b) *quasi-terrorism*, defined as the application of terroristic techniques in situations that do not involve terroristic crimes as such. Examples of this type abound and include the taking of hostages in derailed bank robberies or prison riots as bargaining leverage to secure freedom or concessions; (c) *limited political terrorism*, which involves ideologically or politically motivated terroristic acts, such as assassinations or the bombing of public buildings, but which fall short of seeking to overthrow established governments; (d) *official or state terrorism*, defined as governmental rule based on fear, oppression and persecution, and finally; (e) *political terrorism*, defined as violent, criminal behaviour designed to create fear in a society—or in a substantial segment of it—for political purposes.[1] When fully developed, political terrorism is revolutionary in character and seeks to subvert or overthrow an existing government.

Even though the data on the incidence and severity of terrorism, in all its forms, are sketchy, fragmented and therefore suspect, it appears that terrorist activity is rising the world over, that there is a trend towards more lethal incidents and injuries compared to years past and that US citizens (diplomats, the military and business personnel) and US property are being increasingly targeted.[2] The October 1983 suicide bomb attack that killed two hundred and forty-one US marines is but an example of the growing risk of terrorism and its increasing costs. Given these trends, an increasing number of officials and private citizens will find themselves involved in terroristic crime, as victims of abductions and hostage-holding incidents or as targets for destruction. Some victims are deliberately targeted on the basis of their personal or professional characteristics or because they symbolise whatever has become the object of terrorist hate and annihilation. Other victims are chosen randomly and become victims strictly by chance.

There is a growing body of literature on the subject of terrorism and its victims, but it is scattered and reflects many points of view, as well as many disciplines.[3] The diversity of research methodologies used, such as retrospective studies of hostage experiences or laboratory studies of stress and sensory deprivation, presents major problems for generalising from the information we do have. In the absence of epidemiological studies and base line data, it is difficult to chart psychological, social or physiological changes, much less predict future effects of terrorisation on the victims of these crimes. Given the complexity of the issues, starting with the acute trauma surrounding the terrorist event, the peculiar interrelationship that may develop between the terrorist and his victim, the variety of psychological and physiological response mechanisms that are involved, it is obvious that any holistic understanding of the victim experience can only be derived from an interdisciplinary perspective. It is the purpose of this chapter to synthesise and critically assess our knowledge of the victim experience in terrorism. Drawing on the contributions of the disciplines of medicine, psychology, psychiatry and sociology, general principles are identified to further the understanding of the phenomenon, aid in the preparation for the experience of victimisation of persons at risk and to assist in the development of an improved system response to victims.

THE EFFECTS OF TERRORISM ON SOCIETY

Any examination of recent history clearly shows democracy's peculiar vulnerability to terrorism. Bound by the rule of law and due process, a democratic regime cannot resort to the same bloody methods used against it in combating terrorist crime. It is surely no accident that we do not hear much of revolutionary violence in totalitarian countries, where autocracies with limitless powers terrorise ethnic, religious or racial groups, and sometimes brutally subject entire populations. Terrorism is by definition anti-democratic for at least two reasons. First, sustained incidents of terrorism will inevitably produce governmental countermeasures for the purpose of self-defence. These, in turn, can also become oppressive, thereby alienating the population from their government. Second, terrorist movements are clearly elitist, in spite of their alleged glorification of and identification with the masses. By seeking to coerce duly elected governments into concessions or even abdication, terrorists exert great stress on a country's institutionalised legal mechanisms and wholly circumvent the democratic process established to bring about orderly social and/or political change. While there are no systematic studies of the effect of terrorism on the quality of life in nations experiencing sustained and serious assaults, there is growing evidence of encroachments of the civil liberties in such nations. Great Britian, for example, one of the oldest and more stable democracies in the world, in its struggle with sectarianism and periodic armed insurrection in Northern Ireland, has instituted such basically undemocratic measures as internment, in-depth interrogation, as well as arrests, searches and seizures without the benefit of warrants. There is also censorship. There has even been a relaxation of the rules of criminal procedure, such as trials without juries, the admission of hearsay evidence, a shift in the burden of proof from government to defendant, as well as an increase in penalties for activities classified as terrorism. West Germany and Italy, under sustained assault, have made comparatively benign procedural changes but have also significantly increased the penalties for terrorist-related crimes.

Governmental countermeasures such as these are not only understandable as mechanisms for self-defence, but are also demanded by the public. No form of political authority can long expect to survive continued, serious assaults on its institutions, and people, under the long-recognised concept of 'social contract' do have a right to protection. Public outrage and demand for harsh action against terrorists seems to be the norm in nations experiencing serious problems with terrorism. Jenkins, commenting on public opinion polls conducted in Western Europe during the 1970s, notes that a majority of people polled supported military reprisals, the killing of terrorist leaders, capital punishment for offenders and summary executions, even if these measures seriously violated civil liberties or endangered innocent civilians.[4] European nations are not alone in terms of public resentment of terrorism and in succumbing to questionable control mechanisms. When in the early 1970s the city of San Francisco experienced the so-called 'Zebra' killings, in which White persons were randomly shot on the streets by a small band of profoundly disturbed Blacks, public fear led to public approval of search and seizure tactics that were clearly in violation of the probable cause requirements of the US Constitution. In addition, states and federal governments perennially resort to military force to quell domestic violence, whenever they deem it necessary. These and similar developments justifiably raise serious questions as to the future of democracies as democracies.[5] How does one properly balance the protection of the public with the requirements of constitutionally guaranteed civil liberties? The collective evidence clearly points to an erosion of these liberties, whenever counterterrorist controls are applied, and to a public only too willing to trade its freedom for a modicum of law and order. It can therefore be stated that to the degree that terrorism succeeds in changing a democracy into a facsimile of a garrison state and thereby into a totalitarian regime, the foremost victim of terrorism is democracy itself.

THE EFFECTS OF TERRORISM ON THE QUALITY OF LIFE

Looking at the impact of terrorism on individual citizens in countries that have consistently borne the brunt of terrorism, such as Italy, Northern Ireland, Spain and West Germany in Europe; Egypt, Israel and Lebanon in the Middle East; Turkey; and Argentina, El Salvador, Nicaragua and Uruguay in Latin America, one notes a serious erosion in the quality of life of those affected. Terrorism is exacting a heavy toll on international diplomacy and on the life styles and work habits of political leaders, diplomats and business executives the world over. Political assassinations disrupt the conduct of governmental affairs and can overthrow existing state authorities; international relations are strained when diplomats are killed or imprisoned and their embassies sacked; officials and representatives of criminal justice systems must carry out their work under well-advertised death threats; and corporate executives cannot operate their businesses without persistent threats of kidnappings, bomb threats, extortion attempts and similar terrorist activities.

Concerns for personal safety are affecting a widening circle of people the world over. For example, air travel is encumbered through the scanning and frisking procedures for travellers who must endure a serious invasion of their privacy. Sally-ports and waiting areas separate passengers from family and friends. The transport and storing of luggage is increasingly difficult. Airports, banks, industrial complexes, private and public institutions and even penitentiaries have been affected by terroristic actions. The fear generated by terrorism and by the possibility of victimisation in an ever-widening arena is raising the social costs of the problem, in addition to the economic costs. They do so by weakening the social and political fabric of affected countries and by diverting scarce economic and criminal justice resources from other vital areas.

THE EFFECT OF TERRORISM ON ITS VICTIMS

SETTING THE STAGE

The circumstances under which individuals may become victims of terrorist acts are as varied as the causes of terrorism and depend upon the particular objectives and targeting tactics of the terrorists. Victims may be chosen selectively or at random. In selective terrorism, specific groups, such as police, judges, soldiers or prison personnel are targeted. In randomised terrorism, victims are chosen indiscriminately, a method guaranteed to instil maximum fear among the public. Variations in the objectives of terrorists affect the degree of threat posed to the victim. As a result, victims may be killed, maimed or injured. They may also be taken prisoner or hostage. Further, the specific form of terrorist victimisation also varies widely. There may be face to face contact, such as during state-sanctioned torturing of prisoners or concentration camp inmates, the brainwashing of prisoners of war, skyjackings or other hostage-taking events. There may also be anonymity between victims and terrorists. Letter bombings, car bombings or similar explosive devices, randomly or purposively placed, fall into this category. Some incidents may be brief ranging from minutes to a few hours, while others may be of long duration, lasting weeks, months and sometimes years. As seen earlier, some incidents may involve political hostage takings and others may be instigated by criminal or mentally deranged persons. Yet, in spite of the formidable diversity of the circumstances and form terrorist incidents can take, there is evidence of similarities in the effect of victimisation.[6] These similarities persist to a considerable degree, even when unexpected terrorist captivity is compared with victim experience of natural disasters.[7] Given this evidence, exploration of that experience is warranted, independent of its causes and forms. The exclusive focus on victims is merited, both for its own sake, and because a cumulative systematic assessment and evaluation of the victim's knowledge and experience can increase the effectiveness of treatment, improve society's responses and thereby reduce the harm to victims of future events, and finally, to the small degree that it may be possible, facilitate prevention.

Before proceeding with the detailed analysis of the victim experience, it is useful to note that our knowledge of this subject is based on a gradually accumulating body of information about the pathology connected with trauma-induced stress. It includes retrospective studies of torture victims and concentration camp survivors, and information on such psychologically coercive techniques as the 'brainwashing' of prisoners of war in North Korea, first collected during the 1950s and 1960s.[8] Szu-hsiang kai-tsao, also known as Chinese thought reform or ideological re-moulding is also included in this genre, since it exploits so-called brainwashing techniques on a mass scale. Since these earlier years, more data have been added from studies of former prisoners of war in Viet Nam and from the examination of torture and other abusive treatment of political prisoners in Northern Ireland, Portugal, Greece, South Africa and several Latin American nations, to name a few.[9] The most recent efforts have examined hostage experiences in Ireland, Iran, Canada and the United States.[10] While much empirical research remains to be done, the cumulative effect of this knowledge base is helpful in defining the parameters of the issue and in pinpointing critical areas where more data will be needed.

THE SOCIAL PSYCHOLOGY OF THE TERRORISTIC EXPERIENCE: KEY ELEMENTS OF THE PROCESS

Regardless of the objectives and format of terrorisation, its basic process involves an unpredictable, powerful force, threatening the victim with annihilation. The experience is immensely stressful and generates in the victim feelings of anomia, total helplessness and powerlessness. Terrorisation denies the victim's ability to control his behaviour. Psychological and physical shock, characteristic of any severe trauma, follow. The degree of horror involved is perhaps best described by Weiss, who coined the term idiocide.[11] It means 'death of self', and constitutes an almost universal crime characterised by many degrees. Weiss defines the term as a crime, committed against an individual, which 'reduces, extinguishes, or precludes the presence or exercise of vital human powers'. Idiocide contains two elements: denial of status and denial of stature:

> There is a denial of status when an individual is brought down or kept from the position he normally or rightfully occupies, turning him into a victim, a hostage, a prisoner, a neglected or alienated member of society, cut off from the opportunity to survive, to maintain a level already achieved, or even to grow—thereby making his promise meaningless. ... Where a loss in status precludes the carrying out of some role, a loss in stature affects an individual as a single unit. Starvation, torture, and murder have it as an inescapable consequence. Indeed, every means of human destruction, from genocide to war, no matter what the occasion, excuse, explanation, or benefit, is inevitably idiocidal, radically reducing the stature of an individual, making him less than a human can be and should be.[11a]

Ochberg, on the basis of systematic hostage interviews, offers a more operational, yet remarkably parallel definition of terrorist victimisation: '... when somebody who is bigger and stronger or better-armed than I am assaults and damages me, and as a result of that aggression I feel less powerful, more fearful, in essence knocked down a couple of rungs on a dominance hierarchy, then I've been victimized.'[12]

Since the choice of victims in many terrorist attacks (as well as in most criminal assaults) is determined by chance, they can neither anticipate nor control the event. The victim's experiential repertoire contains little, if anything, to prepare him for such an incident, on the basis of which he can try to predict what may happen next or how he should best conduct himself. The multiple threats to life, security, bodily integrity and self-esteem precipitate in most victims a crisis reaction in which the emotions and behaviour of the threatened person are significantly disrupted.[13] A victim suddenly faced with the very real possibility of imminent death, finds himself unable to muster the necessary physical and mental resources to rise against the assault on his person. Such feelings of impotence shatter the self-image, dissolve the self-confidence and set in motion sequelae of complex and interrelated social–psychological and physiological response mechanisms. Some of these involve conscious efforts on the part of the victim, others are deeply submerged in the subconscious. The primary purpose of these efforts is to assure the survival of the victim. The remainder of this chapter focuses, in detail, on these response mechanisms, to see how they may be affected by the crisis situation and modified by the victim's life experiences and character traits.

EXPERIENCING TERRORISM: ACUTE VICTIM RESPONSE

The Psychodynamics of Experiencing Terrorism. In his informative work on victimisation, Symonds identifies four distinct phases of psychological responses of victims to violent crimes.[14] While the duration and intensity of each phase varies according to the nature and quality of contact between the criminal and his victim, the responses seem to hold for such diverse victimisations as kidnapping, hostage takings, rape, robbery and even burglary, where there is no contact with the criminal at all. The first two phases constitute the acute victim response, the last two the delayed victim response.

The first phase of the victim response to terrorisation is concerned with the immediate situation and its experience. It consists of shock, disbelief, denial and delusion. It is characterised by a paralysis of action and the denial of sensory impressions.[15] Only when the victim begins to perceive the reality of the situation and feels hopelessly entrapped, the second phase begins. It is characterised by a paralysis of affect. Symonds calls this terror-induced, pseudo-calm, noticeably detached behaviour 'frozen fright'. Trapped in a life-threatening situation, the victim feels isolated and powerless. After denial of the situation, there is often a brief period of a delusion of imminent reprieve. Unrealistically, victims expect that authorities will rescue them within minutes or at least within a few hours. While such imaginings are usually not grounded in facts, this phase is generally thought to reflect a growing acceptance by the victim of his or her predicament. If unresolved, a period of adaptation sets in, which the literature invariably describes as 'coping'. It includes such activities as writing, reading, counting, handcrafts (if possible) or similar 'busy work', and for most victims, an embarking on a review and reflection upon one's past life. Strentz, after interviewing many former hostages of skyjacking events, notes that he has never interviewed anyone who did not take stock of his life, or vowed to change for the better, should he be given a second chance after the horrifying experience.[16]

If victims are not rescued during this period of initial adaptation—a period that can last from a few hours to one or two days—the pressures of the situation and terror combine to overwhelm most victims and produce a state of *traumatic psychological infantilism* in the majority of the victims.[17] Individuals in this condition lose their ability to function as adults and begin to respond instead with adaptive behaviour first learned in early childhood. Thus, behaviour exhibited under the phenomenon of traumatic psychological infantilism includes appeasement, compliance, submission and ingratiation. Even cooperative and wholly voluntary acts are often noted, which tend to confound rescuing authorities, the public and even the victims themselves. Persons experiencing this syndrome will empathise and sympathise with their victimiser. They may even come to his aid and contravene the efforts of their rescuers. If the situation is not resolved within a relatively short period of time and the terror continues unabated, the traumatised victim tends to attribute his continuing survival to the good will of the offender. At this point, many victims experience profound and lasting attitudinal as well as behavioural changes. Symonds calls this latest development *pathological transference.*[18] It tends to occur when a victim's life has initially been threatened by someone who later decides (perhaps only temporarily) not to kill. Given these conditions, victims no longer focus on the actual death threat but begin to feel that they have been given their very lives by the offender. These changes in victim perceptions are particularly acute and re-inforced in criminal or political terrorist hostage takings, where their instrumentality is obvious to all concerned. Victims will quickly delude themselves that their captors will not harm them, if only the intended victim—the one who has the power to meet the demands of the terrorists—acceded to their demands. It should be noted that the fact that police guns and other weapons are trained on terrorists and victims alike, is not lost on the latter. It further re-inforces their delusions that if the terrorists got what they wanted, and the police retreated, the matter would be resolved with no one being hurt. Pathological transference is said to be complete when the victims begin to perceive their release as being contingent upon the offender's realisation of his goals. This perceptual merging of the victim's hopes for freedom with the purposes of the terrorists has led some to speculate that we may be dealing with a variant of yet another psychological phenomenon, the *identification of the victim with the aggressor.*[19] It is a psychoanalytic concept and refers to the well-known socialisation processes of early childhood, during which children learn to identify with their parental role models. In normal childhood situations, this process describes a positive development. If, on the other hand, the parent-figure is excessively punitive and inconsistent, the child may incorporate the parent's punitive and aggressive traits, in an effort to adapt to highly stressful and often intolerable situations. The concept of identification with the aggressor is related to the notion of conversion and has been useful in explaining instances where prisoners of concentration or similar death camps assume the character of their keepers and begin to torture fellow prisoners, in an unconscious, last ditch effort to save themselves. The chief motivational factors in these instances are hate (not love) for their enemy and the primordial desire to survive.[20] As helpful as this concept has been in explaining the otherwise unexplainable, it is of doubtful theoretical value in illuminating the psychodynamics of most terroristic episodes. The literature records no recent event during which victims of terrorism either abused or tortured their fellow victims. The few instances where at least some elements of conversion may apply, are those where a victim, after being subjected to traumatic stress, joins the cause of the captors and actively participates in subsequent terrorist operations. A highly dramatic case in the recent past fitting this category involves the kidnapping of Patricia Hearst in 1974. Donald 'Cinque' DeFreeze, self-proclaimed leader of the 'Symbionese Liberation Army (SLA)', a small pseudo-revolutionary band of former prisoners and radicalised youths from the University of California at Berkeley, had been an inmate at the California Medical Facility at Vacaville from 1968 to 1972.[21] At Vacaville, DeFreeze underwent chemotherapy, aversive conditioning and similar experimental treatment techniques designed to rehabilitate or 'convert' seriously disturbed criminal offenders. If appears that DeFreeze subjected Patricia Hearst to a mixture of violence and drugs, as well as to variations of the same conversion techniques that had been applied to him. The rest is history. Patty joined the gang, denounced her parents, posed in a fetching battle dress complete with submachine gun in front of the seven-headed Cobra symbol of the SLA, assisted in a bank robbery in San Francisco, robbed a store and went on the lam. Until her capture in September 1975, she managed to lead the nation's law-enforcement apparatus on an embarrassingly fruitless chase. When the government finally did catch up with her and tried her, she took the Fifth Amendment to the Constitution to avoid self-incrimination no less than forty-two times.[22] Field, analysing the case, likens Hearst's experience to those of adolescents in Northern Ireland, who, when subjected to traumatic stress, are less able than adults to withstand assaults on their ego and notes:

> She was terrorized, and she converted to terrorism. Had she been less isolated from the support systems of the larger society, and had she experienced a shorter captivity, it is probable that she would never have assumed the role of a fugitive bank robber. The case of Patty Hearst epitomizes the dynamic relationship between victim and terrorist because of its singularity in combining the features evident in other cases: i.e. psychological and psychotechnological forces operating in a social context that exacerbates stress through denial of institutional supports, prolonged threat to life, identity, and bodily integrity, occurring in a circumstance of powerlessness, helplessness, and unpredictability.[23]

While the Hearst kidnapping appears to be a classic example of the phenomena of identification with the aggressor and conversion, we must look elsewhere to explain what has fittingly been described as an 'unholy alliance between terrorist and captive, involving fear, distrust or anger toward the authorities on the outside'.[24] As will be seen, the theoretical formulations describing the *Stockholm Syndrome* provides a better fit.

The Stockholm Syndrome. Traumatic psychological infantilism and pathological transference are two critical components of what has come to be recognised as the Stockholm Syndrome.[25] It is named for the unexpected positive feelings developed by captives for their captors, during a prolonged hostage taking at the Sveriges Kreditbank in Stockholm, Sweden, in 1973.[26] During the incident, four bank employees were held hostage in the bank's vault for one hundred and thirty-one hours by an escaped prisoner. The group was later joined by another convict and former cellmate of the would-be bank robber, who had demanded his release from prison. Once the Syndrome is manifest, it tends to last for the duration of the crisis and beyond. In fact, it may continue for years. Strenz reports that positive or negative bonds tend to develop between captors and captives with the passage of time.[27] In essence, if perpetrators do not abuse their victims, that is, if there is no serious physical abuse, assault, battery or rape, a positive bond (the Stockholm Syndrome) is likely to develop between them. However, if victims are seriously and persistently abused, the Syndrome is not likely to develop. But even in situations of abuse, exceptions are noted, as when victims, injured or assaulted during the initial rush of capture, come to identify with the offender and his cause during subsequent phases of their captivity. In these cases, victims rationalise initial abuse and/or injury as having been necessary for the offenders to gain control, and more often than not, blame themselves for their victimisation. Only when victims closely identify with their government, or when there has been at least some training or preparation for the ordeal of captivity, does the Stockholm Syndrome not tend to develop. The annals of terrorism reflect some outstanding examples of such instances. In the 1970s, British Ambassador to Uruguay Geoffry Jackson was captured and held hostage by Tupamaro terrorists for two hundred and forty-four days.[28] Maintaining his distance and dignity under the most difficult of circumstances, he won the grudging admiration of his captors without ever succumbing to the Stockholm Syndrome. The same applies to American agronomist Claude Fly, also held by the Tupamaros for two hundred and eight days. Similarly, military records bear witness to many instances where American prisoners of war in Korea and Viet Nam survived unspeakable horrors of captivity without ever approaching an alliance or identification with the captors.

While the Stockholm Syndrome is a relatively new phenomenon for law enforcement and the public, the fields of psychology, psychophysiology and psychosomatic medicine have long recognised its basic element of 'regression' as one of several defence mechanisms available to victims of inordinate psychosocial stress. Next to regression, the remaining defence mechanisms include the previously discussed conversion syndrome, repression, rationalisation and sublimation. Even though these concepts are well-accepted by researchers and theorists of stress disorders, they leave us with many unanswered questions.[29] For example, we know little about the processes involved in selecting and elaborating a particular defence mechanism. Also, what is the nature of interaction between unconscious cognitive activity of victims and their conscious awareness of the situation? What internal factors are at work that enable the unconscious to accept the success or failure of a particular defence strategy? In the absence of answers and unifying concepts in this area (and pending future research), we must be content with the conjecture that the processes of regression and the Stockholm Syndrome are probably functional for most victims of terrorist attacks. Given the trauma of sudden life-threatening events that characterise most incidents, the alternative ego defence mechanisms would hardly do. Thus, the victim's return to the adaptive patterns of infancy has substantial surface validity, since it provides him with behavioural modes that have worked before, when he was totally dependent upon a caring adult in terms of sustenance and life. As such, this adaptation speaks volumes not just about the horror of the terroristic victimisation but also about the apparent terror inherent in the ordinary childhood experience.

It is important to note that the Stockholm Syndrome goes beyond victim identification with and sympathy for the offender, which may last far beyond the actual period of captivity. It also involves the development of the captive's negative feelings and distrust towards police in particular and governmental authorities in general. These feelings are exacerbated the longer captivity and/or negotiations last. After all, the victim wants to survive. And survival is tied to release. Therefore, anything that delays his release will be interpreted as a rejection of the captive's needs, as cold-blooded indifference to his plight and as an outright expression of hostility towards the hostage who is facing a life-threatening situation.

The final component of the Stockholm Syndrome often involves the development of reciprocal positive feelings on the part of the terrorists towards their captives. It is this aspect of the Syndrome that is of major significance to law enforcement, since it can aid immeasurably in the successful resolution of the situation. Beyond these basic elements of the Stockholm Syndrome, it is best understood as an automatic, at least partly unconscious adaptation mechanism for the survival of exceedingly traumatic and highly lethal situations. Factors which seem to promote the Syndrome are (a) the quality and intensity of the victimisation experience, (b) the passage of time, (c) the degree of dependence of the captive on the captor for survival and (d) the psychological distance of the captive from his or her government.[30] It seems that no particular age group is exempt from the Syndrome. Males and females succumb to it equally. As noted before, this remarkable phenomenon does not develop immediately upon seizure but requires time to evolve. But if it takes hold at all, it will be well-established by the third day.[31]

The Stockholm Syndrome occurs with sufficient frequency during kidnappings, hostage takings and similar victimisation that the highly organised terrorist groups have begun to apply tactics to prevent its occurrence. For example, hostages may be kept in total isolation. They may have hoods placed over their heads to prevent any contact whatsoever with their captors. They may be bound and forced to lie face down to prevent eye contact with anyone. They may be permitted to have only one spokesman and guards may be changed frequently during prolonged captivity to interdict the development of any relationships between hostages and terrorists. Any such development, if known to law enforcement, adds special urgency to rescue efforts because of the added risks to the lives of the hostages.

Given the obvious advantages to the hostages of a fully developed Stockholm Syndrome, law-enforcement agents should foster its growth to the degree that it may be possible. As a result, any activity which may require captor and captives to work together for the common good should be encouraged. For example, food preparation, distribution of blankets or clothing etc., are ways in which joint activity and cooperation can be engendered.

Finally, given any extended exposure of captives to hostage takers, law enforcement should never count on the assistance of the victims, when they communicate and deal with them during rescue efforts. Otherwise, police may find, much to their dismay, some of the victims counteracting their rescue efforts. Similarly, prosecutors should expect considerable difficulty in gaining victim cooperation during subsequent prosecution of the offenders. The star witness for the prosecution too frequently turns into the star witness for the defence. And governmental authorities should prepare to hear bitter complaints from released hostages who tend to judge official responses to their plight as inadequate, bungling and grossly inept.

Up to this point, this analysis of the sequelae of victim responses to terrorism has been limited to the psychodynamics of the acute victim response. As important as these responses are to our understanding of the victim experience, the picture remains incomplete. The terroristic experience includes physiological and psychosomatic damage as well. Its impact reaches far beyond the actual event and is the subject of the section below.

The Physiology of Experiencing Terrorism. The physiological response of victims to highly threatening situations is best understood by examining stress and stress reactions. Stress, in the words of its foremost researcher Hans Selye is the 'non-specific response of the body to any demand made upon it'.[32] Of importance is that stress is not the 'precipitating incident', but rather the condition of the human organism as it responds to the event. Recent researchers have modified Selye's definition by emphasising that stress results from three interrelated elements: (a) stimulus, (b) response and (c) a combination of stimulus–response reactions.[33] Thus, stress is seen as disrupting a person's psychological and physiological condition such that he or she is forced to deviate from normal functioning.[34]

Even though the timing of the stress response varies considerably from person to person, the response does involve three distinct stages: the initial stage involves alarm, followed by resistance. If stress continues unabated, the body's resources become exhausted and the victim's defence mechanisms will break down. Selye labelled this adaptation pattern GAS or *General Adaptation Syndrome*. The alarm stage consists of two phases: during the 'shock' phase the body's resistance is lowered, while physiological defences are mobilised during the 'countershock' phase. Surging adrenaline triggers the release of glycogen from the liver, increases the rate of respiration and heart and shifts the blood flow away from the skin and digestive tract towards the muscles and brain. All this leads to the resistance stage, during which the body will show maximum adaptation to stress. An individual faced with a terrifying situation will now be able to perform at peak output, and, if possible, will either fight or engage in flight. If stress continues, the body's reserves will be depleted. The third stage involving exhaustion will last until the body's resources have been replenished.

Unalleviated stress is increasingly tied to symptoms of physical and mental illness. As such, stress will interact with the individual to disrupt psychophysiological homeostasis and may lead to psychosomatic disorders.[35]

Recent research findings in such diverse disciplines as psychoneuroendocrinology and psychoneuroimmunology on the subject of stress add special poignancy to victimisation by terror. It is not the stress itself that is dangerous to individuals but rather their inability to cope with it that is significant. Whether a person eventually succumbs to physical or mental illness, and whether that illness will be serious or fatal, seems to revolve around the individual's ability to do something about the situation and proactively change his or her predicament. And since the essence of terrorisation involves the negation of the victim's capacity for willing his behaviour, it must be seen as one of the most damaging stressors that can be inflicted on humans.

It is now known that prolonged stress affects at least five basic response systems: (a) the skeletal–muscular system, leading to muscular pain and tension headaches; (b) the parasympathetic nervous system, leading to gastro-intestinal distress, such as ulcerative colitis or ulcers; (c) the sympathetic nervous system, leading to hypertension, arrhythmia, palpitation, sodium and fluid retention; (d) the endocrine system, responsible for the overall integration of skeletal–muscular, parasympathetic and sympathetic nervous systems; and (e) the immune system, responsible for the body's complex infection-fighting mechanisms.[36]

Current research has begun to tease out the exact processes of stress responses. Upon perception of a serious threat, neurons in the brain tissue stimulate the hypothalamus which regulates all essential life-support systems. The hypothalamus then stimulates the pituitary gland of the endocrine system and triggers the sympathetic branch of the autonomic nervous system. The pituitary gland, in turn, releases a series of hormones: Beta-endorphin and adrenocorticotropin (ACTH), the most important and best-known hormones in the stress response. The ACTH travels to the adrenal glands (located near the anterior medial border of the kidney), which in turn release corticosteroids. The latter chemicals exert positive as well as negative effects on the body. While corticosteroids function to reduce inflammation in the body, they can also depress the body's immune system, when stress continues unresolved. The adrenal glands also secrete epinephrine and norepinephrine (better known as adrenaline and noradrenaline), which are substances designed to serve the goal of preparing the organism to meet threatening situations involving fear, rage or pain.[37]

In sum, epidemiological research on stress has come to recognise that hormonal secretions accompanying the stress response not only assist the body in coping with stress, but also can cause direct and indirect damage. Direct damage can occur during the alarm stage of the General Adaptation Syndrome through ulceration of the gastrointestinal tract,[38] and indirect damage can occur through the shrinkage of the thymus gland and the reduction in the number of lymphocytes in the blood. The latter phenomenon weakens the immune system's capacity to resist infection, and thereby increases the likelihood of illness.[39]

These findings, coupled with a growing body of research analysing the long-term effects of highly stressful situations on humans (and animals), all point to far-reaching consequences for the victim's state of health. As a result, the psychological shocks and trauma of the terroristic incident pall when compared with the long-range damage inflicted on victims.

A final aspect of the stress response to be discussed here has major significance for law enforcement. Judging from the results of physiological and psychological measurements of stress reactions, mind and body are not activated simultaneously as has previously been thought.[40] Rather, a victim's ability to think and act is not only modified under stress, but mind and body are also activated separately. First, the relationship between activation and performance under stress is best described by an inverted 'U', where performance is optimal for many activities at an intermediate level of activation, and where either too much or too little activation produces a decrease in performance. Second, mind and body are activated independently of each other. Under the concept of *dissociation of arousal*, a victim's (or terrorist's) ability to think clearly and rationally may be at maximum output, while the autonomic system may be on low, or vice versa. The relevance of these findings for hostage management situations is clear. A highly aroused victim may bungle a rescue operation, if complex tasks are expected of him. Nor is it prudent or productive to withhold food and/or water (or otherwise manipulate such stressors as heat or cold and lack of sleep), if the result is a reduction of the terrorist's or hostage's capacity to think rationally, while disinhibiting their visceral and autonomic nervous systems. The result of such action could easily be a 'finely tuned animal, unfettered by reason [and] dangerously coiled and ready to spring'.[41]

EXPERIENCING TERRORISM: THE DELAYED VICTIM RESPONSE

As noted earlier, there is considerable and growing evidence from long-range case studies and laboratory research that victims of terrorism suffer serious and long-lasting damage to their physical, mental and emotional health. Even brief events can produce major problems, years after they have occurred.[42] In this respect, these victims are not very different from any other victims of trauma and violence. Unfortunately, these findings have yet to enter the public's mind. Nor are they reflected in the criminal justice system in terms of compensatory and punitive damages awarded to victims. The same is applicable to sentencing practices because punishment, in most instances, is not commensurate with the harm done to victims.

The last two phases of victim responses to terror tend to occur long after the horrific incident has passed.[43] Phase three consists of an array of psychophysiological reactions. Phase four involves victim adaptation and formulation of new resolve. Both are the subject of the ensuing discussion.

Post-traumatic psychological reactions tend to involve the following response patterns.[44] Closely following an incident, victims tend to exhibit a wide variety of anxiety syndromes, ranging from intense anxiety to free-floating anxiety, to phobias. Victims will report insomnia, startle reactions, nightmares and nightsweats, inability to concentrate, memory lapses, sexual problems and interpersonal difficulties with spouses or significant others. Obsessive reviews of the terroristic incident lead to much self-recrimination, self-blame and circular spells of anger, apathy, depression, hostility, rage, reclusiveness, resentment and resignation. The motivation for these alternating responses is based on the absolutely devastating effects of depersonalisation, helplessness, powerlessness and humiliation that victims experience during the incidents. Depression, a mental state characterised by feelings of dejection, lack of hope and alienation, may last long after the traumatic event. Less frequent reactions include feelings of paranoia, with victims exhibiting abnormal sensitivity, suspicion, brooding, excessive self-consciousness and fixed ideas that may include systematised delusions of persecution.[45]

A reinforcing circle between psychological and physiological effects of terror emerges when insomnia, dietary changes and self-imposed restrictions affect the victim's gastrointestinal and circulatory systems which in turn can lead to further mental and physical impairments.

Still longer after the incident, physical and psychophysiological damage can bring about significant pathological changes in victims.[46] Hypertension, for example, has consistently been identified as a major contributing factor in the development of cerebral vascular accidents, the genesis of congestive heart failure, coronary thrombosis, atherosclerosis and kidney failure.[47] The previously discussed suppression of the body's immune system may lead to a plethora of illness, including cancer.

Differential Victim Responses. Even though victim response patterns reflect remarkable similarity, it should be clear that stress responses do not produce identical psychophysiological reactions in everyone. Roth identifies at least five sources of variability in stress responses:[48] (a) *stimulus–response specificity*, referring to specific kinds of stressors eliciting specific kinds of physiological responses; (b) *response specificity*, reflecting idiosyncratic differences in patterns of reactivity based on genetic and learned response differences; (c) *personality specificity*, attributable to differences in personality characteristics leading to differences in response patterns; (d) *emotional specificity*, assignable to differences in victim reactions to stressors; and (e) *conflict specificity*, traceable to differences in intrapsychic impedimenta victims bring into a stress situation.

Assessing delayed victim responses, differences emerge among a number of variables. Availability of treatment to the victim and his or her family appears to be a major factor affecting the extent of trauma and damage. System response can greatly ameliorate or aggravate the victim's feelings.[49] In addition, after-effects of traumatic experiences are inversely related to (a) previous experiences of a similar nature, (b) the age of the victim (maturity and a well-developed sense of identity lessen the traumatic effect); (c) the degree of humiliation and ego threat experienced by the victim; and (d) the degree of psychological and social isolation experienced by the victim.[50]

Delayed Victim Response—Final Phase. During the final phase of the victim response, a resolution of sorts is worked out, which integrates the victim's experiences into a new set of behavioural patterns. This involves regaining some feelings of control over his or her life, shoring up of self-respect and the development of new patterns of alertness and defence mechanisms. Those looking for encouraging evidence of victims returning to a state of normalcy will not find it in the literature. Even though there are many degrees of adjustment, the accumulated evidence suggests that the scarring of the experience of terror is so damaging to mind and body that victims will never be as they were before.[51] With time, most arrive at a modus vivendi, characterised by revised values and attitudes towards life, government, faith, criminal justice, people and material possessions. In sum, the trauma sustained by victims of terrorism appears to be of such magnitude that it is not an exaggeration to analogise the experience to an interstellar catastrophe during which planets are forever forced off their trajectory.

The foregoing sections have analysed the victim experience using a multidisciplinary perspective. The remaining and final sections of this chapter present a synopsis of adaptation or 'coping' mechanisms that have previously been proven to be helpful in withstanding traumatic experiences,[52] and some suggestions for improving society's response to victims of terrorism.

SUCCESSFUL ADAPTATION STRATEGIES TO THE TERRORIST EXPERIENCE

The analysis of a wide variety of victim experiences of stressful situations reveals a number of coping strategies,[53] all of them geared towards (a) bringing the crisis situation to a quick resolution with a minimum of loss in terms of life and limb; (b) keeping one's anxiety level within tolerable limits to remain alert and functional; (c) maintaining one's self-esteem in spite of frequently de-humanising and degrading experiences; (d) preservation of one's relationships with fellow victims; and (e) establishing some linkage with the terrorists (to the degree that is may be possible) without ingratiation. Once caught up in the crisis situation, the following repertoire of coping mechanisms appears to produce positive results:[54] (a) assuming a familiar role, if possible, by engaging in such varied activities as writing, handcraft, counting etc.; (b) adjusting one's expectations to the reality of the situation; (c) learning from successful coping behaviour of fellow victims; and (d) accepting constructive criticism without losing one's sense of self-worth and self-esteem.

IMPROVING INSTITUTIONAL SUPPORT SYSTEMS FOR THE VICTIMS OF TERRORISM

Given the documented deleterious effects of terrorism on its victims and the fact that the United States is now at a greater risk of terrorism than ever before, it is critically important to develop effective strategies for counteracting acts of terrorism and for assisting its victims. There is an urgent need to develop a thoroughly coordinated national policy to fight terrorism. Given the peculiar and inefficient structure of law enforcement in this country, most terrorist incidents come under the control of local law-enforcement agencies, with national organisations standing by or offering assistance. The net result is a veritable maze of too many agencies with little or no coordination between them. If terrorism is to be effectively controlled, we will have to have a totally integrated command, control, communications and intelligence system.

Looking at institutional support systems for victims, there is an equally critical need to develop an integrated and comprehensive system response. Embassy personnel, members of the military, airline staff, business executives (including mid-level managers) abroad and at home are fast becoming attractive potential victims. As a result, comprehensive security measures, defensive strategies and tactics, as well as training for seizure and captivity are urgently required. While some hostage training has been undertaken for embassy staff since the Iranian Embassy debacle, such efforts need to be systematised and extended to all persons at risk. At a minimum, business executives of US multinatinal firms overseas should be provided such training.

In addition, the scores of private firms offering an array of protection services, which have mushroomed in the face of rising anti-American terrorism the world over, should be scrutinised by government agencies to protect the consumers. The uncontrolled growth of these businesses cries out for objective evaluation of services and the development of at least some guiding principles and regulations.

On the individual level, law enforcement agencies and emergency personnel responding to victims of terrorism need to make sure they do not inflict secondary damage to the victims. Given their experience of de-humanisation and feelings of helplessness, care needs to be taken to act in a nurturing and patient manner. Symonds writes of the victims' 'silent expectations' that rescuers will help restore their self-esteem and injured pride.[55] If victims are met with indifference, detachment, emotional insulation so characteristic of professionals, their silent expectations will go unmet. Their feelings of helplessness and rejection will be reinforced and a 'second injury' will have been inflicted by the system. In sum, victims of terrorism require much re-assurance, comfort, a willingness to listen and much support, not only from law enforcement and emergency personnel, but from the entire criminal justice system, friends, family, the community and society as a whole. In this respect, current system responses are wholly inadequate. And yet, the necessary remedies are the easiest to procure. Other nations are doing a much better job in responding to their hostages:[56] Israel looks at victims of terrorism as heroes. England includes former hostages in training seminars for police negotiators and most Western nations provide compensatory damages and treatment for their victims. Is it not time to do justice to American victims?

NOTES

1 *Disorders and Terrorism*, Report of the Task Force on Disorders and Terrorism, Washington, DC: US Government Printing Office, 1976, pp. 3–6.

2 *Ibid.*, pp. 7–8; Brian M Jenkins, 'Statements about Terrorism', *The Annals*, Vol. 463, September 1982, pp. 11–23.
3 *Terrorism*, National Institute of Justice, Selected Library in Microfiche, 1982 edition.
4 Jenkins, p. 18.
5 Irving Louis Horowitz, 'Can Democracy Cope with Terrorism?', *The Civil Liberties Review*, May–June 1977, pp. 29–37.
6 Rona M Fields, 'Victims of Terrorism: The Effects of Prolonged Stress', *Evaluation and Change*, Special Issue, 1980, pp. 76–83.
7 Calvin J Frederick, 'Effects of Natural vs. Human-induced Violence Upon Victims', *Evaluation and Change*, Special Issue, 1980, pp. 71–75.
8 Robert J Lifton, *Thought Reform and the Psychology of Totalism*, New York: WW Norton, 1961.
9 Leo Eitinger and Axel Strom, *Mortality and Morbidity after Excessive Stress*, New York: Humanities Press, 1973.
10 Brian M Jenkins, *Hostage Survival: Some Preliminary Observations*, Rand Paper Series, Santa Monica, California: The Rand Corporation, April 1975, P-3627; Eleanor S Wainstein, *The Cross and Laporte Kidnappings, Montreal, October 1970*, Rand Paper, Santa Monica, California: The Rand Corporation, February 1977, R-1986/1-DOS/ARPA; *Mobilization I: The Iranian Crisis*, The Task Force on Families of Catastrophe, The Family Research Institute, West Lafayette, Indiana: Purdue University, February 1980, Final Report.
11 Paul Weiss, 'Idiocide', *Evaluation and Change*, Special Issue, 1980, p. 3.
11a *Ibid.*
12 Susan Salasin, 'Evaluation as a Tool for Restoring the Mental Health of Victims: An Interview with Frank Ochberg', *Evaluation and Change*, Special Issue, 1980, p. 21.
13 Morton Bard and Dawn Sangrey, 'Things Fall Apart: Victims in Crisis', *Evaluation and Change*, Special Issue, 1980, pp. 28–35; Gerald Caplan, *Principles of Preventive Psychiatry*, New York: Basic Books, 1964, p. 39; Leo Eitinger, 'The Stress in Captivity', Ronald D Crelinsten (ed.), *Dimensions of Victimization in the Context of Terroristic Acts*, Centre International de Criminologie Comparée, Université de Montréal, Montreal, September 1977.
14 Martin Symonds, 'The "Second Injury" to Victims', and 'Acute Responses of Victims to Terror', *Evaluation and Change*, Special Issue, 1980, pp. 36–41.
15 *Ibid.*, p. 36.
16 Thomas Strentz, 'Law Enforcement Policy and Ego Defenses of the Hostage', *FBI Law Enforcement Bulletin*, April 1979, p. 8.
17 Symonds, p. 36.
18 *Ibid.*
19 Strentz, p. 4.
20 Calvin S Hall, *A Primer of Freudian Psychology*, New York: The World Publishing Co., 1954, p. 78.
21 Albert Parry, *Terrorism from Robespierre to Arafat*, New York: The Vanguard Press, 1976, pp. 342–364.
22 *Ibid.*
23 Field, p. 80.
24 Frank Ochberg, 'The Victim of Terrorism: Psychiatric Considerations', *Terrorism*, Vol. 1, No. 2, 1978, pp. 147–168.
25 *Ibid.*, pp. 160–162.
26 An exact account of the bank robbery incident is given by Strentz, p. 2.

27 *Ibid.*, pp. 6–10.
28 Geoffrey Jackson, *Surviving the Long Night*, New York: Vanguard, 1973.
29 Barbara B Brown, 'Perspectives on Social Stress', Hans Selye (ed.), *Selye's Guide to Stress Research*, Vol. 1, New York: Van Nostrand Co., 1980, pp. 21–45.
30 Ochberg, pp. 160–162.
31 *Ibid.*
32 Hans Selye, *The Stress of Life*, New York: McGraw-Hill, 1956.
33 RS Lazarus, *Psychological Stress and the Coping Process*, New York: McGraw-Hill, 1966; JE McGrath, 'Stress and Behavior in Organizations', MD Dunnette (ed.), *Handbook of Industrial and Organizational Psychology*, Chicago: Rand-McNally, 1976; and CN Coffer and MH Appley, *Motivation: Theory and Research*, New York: John Wiley, 1964.
34 TA Beehr and JE Newman 'Job Stress, Employee Health, and Organizational Effectiveness: A Facet Analysis, Model and Literature Review', *Personnel Psychology*, Vol. 31, 1978.
35 *Ibid.*
36 Joseph P Buckley, 'Present Status of Stress Research Related to the Development of Cardiovascular Diseases', Hans Selye (ed.), *Selye's Guide to Stress Research*, Vol. 2, New York: Van Nostrand Reinhold Co., Inc., 1983, pp. 363–374; Sally K Severino 'Renal Failure and Stress', Hans Selye (ed.), *Selye's Guide to Stress Research*, Vol. 3, New York: Van Nostrand Reinhold Co., Inc., 1983, pp. 128–135; and Kathleen C Light, John P Koepke, Paul A Obrist and Park W Willis, IV, 'Psychological Stress Induces Sodium and Fluid Retention in Men at High Risk for Hypertension', *Science*, 22 April 1983, pp. 429–431.
37 Marianne Frankenaeuser, 'Psychoneuroendocrine Approaches to the Study of Stressful Person–Environment Transactions', Hans Selye (ed.), *Selye's Guide to Stress Research*, Vol. 1, New York: Van Nostrand Reinhold Co., Inc., 1980, pp. 46–70.
38 Hans Selye, *The Stress of Life*, New York: McGraw-Hill, 1956, Revised edn., 1976.
39 J Cassel, 'The Contribution of the Social Environment to Host Resistance', *American Journal of Epidemiology*, Vol. 104, 1976, pp. 107–123.
40 W Roth, 'Psychosomatic Implications of Confinement by Terrorists', Ronald D Crelinsten (ed.), *Dimensions of Victimization in the Context of Terrorist Acts*, Centre International de Criminologie Comparée, Université de Montréal, Montreal: Canada, September 1977.
41 Ochberg, p. 156.
42 Symonds, p. 39; Stan G Sommers, 'Ex-hostages & POWS: Serious Emotional Problems Develop-later', *Behavior Today*, Vol. 11, No. 43, 3 November 1980.
43 Symonds, pp. 36–38.
44 Ochberg, Roth, Fields, *op. cit.*
45 Ochberg, pp. 162–164.
46 AM Ostfeld, 'The Interaction of Biological and Social Variables in Cardiovascular Disease', *Milbank Memorial Fund Quarterly*, 45, 1967, pp. 13–18.
47 Joseph P Buckley, 'Present Status of Stress Research Related to the Development of Cardiovascular Diseases', Hans Selye (ed.), *Selye's Guide to Stress Research*, Vol. 2, New York: Van Nostrand Reinhold Co., Inc., 1983, p. 372.
48 Roth, *op. cit.*
49 Symonds, *op. cit.*
50 Fields, *op. cit.*
51 Mortimer Appley and Richard Trumbull (eds.), *Psychological Stress*, New York:

Appleton-Crofts, 1967; Alan Monat and Richard S Lazarus (eds.), *Stress and Coping: An Anthology*, New York: Columbia University Press, 1977; Fields, *op. cit.*

52 Ochberg, *op. cit.*, Monat and Lazarus, *op. cit.*

53 Ochberg, *op. cit.*; Jared R Tinklenberg, Peggy Murphy and Patricia Murphy, 'Adaptive Behaviour of Victims of Terrorism', *in* Ronald D Crelinsten (ed.), *Dimensions of Victimization in the Context of Terroristic Acts*, Centre International de Crimologie Comparée, Université de Montréal, Montreal: Canada, September 1977.

54 Ochberg, Tinklenberg, *et al.*, *op. cit.*

55 Symonds, pp. 36–38.

56 Ochberg, p. 160.

A Conceptual Framework in Victimology: The Adult and Child Hostage Experience

C Hatcher

Hostage-taking is not a new phenomenon. While one of the first documented cases can be seen in Helen of Troy, it was not until Munich, Attica and the airline hijackings of the early 1970s that hostage-taking assumed a contemporary importance. In a relatively short period of time, both the frequency and the number of people affected rose dramatically. Appropriately, the initial efforts of psychologists and government were aimed at incident resolution, primarily in the development of hostage negotiation techniques.[1,2] Part of this effort was directed towards studying, primarily, hostage behaviour within the incident, and, secondarily, after-incident behaviour by the ex-hostage. The study of within-incident behaviour produced information which has contributed significantly to the successful resolution of many subsequent hostage-takings. The study of after-incident behaviour began to show that even relatively brief hostage periods produced a range of short- and long-term reactions in a large percentage of the victims and their families.

Only recently, however, have psychologists and other prefossionals begun to assist in the re-adjustment process of the ex-hostage. In order to do this effectively, one must ask: (a) Is there a typical hostage behaviour pattern, and what is the range of that hostage behaviour? (b) Is hostage behaviour the same as other victim reactions or does it have some unique aspects? (c) Do individuals of different background react differently? If the answers to these questions point towards a typical pattern, with a limited range and with great similarity to other patterns of violent victimisation, then a psychologist or psychiatrist may more easily draw upon his broader experience in working with victims of rape, victims of violent crime, Vietnam war veterans etc. If the answers to these questions point towards a typical pattern, with substantial range variations and some marked differences from other victim patterns, then the psychologist or psychiatrist must proceed more cautiously, and with an awareness of the experimental nature of his work. The process

Table 1. Effects Upon Victims of Natural Violence, General Human-induced Violene, Adult Hostage Cases and Child Hostage Cases

Natural Violence/Major Disasters	General Human-induced Violence
Stages: 1. Initial impact (panic, movement, immobilisation) 2. Heroic 3. Phoenix Period 4. Disillusionment 5. Reorganisation	Stages: 1. Initial impact (freeze, flee, fight) 2. Acceptance/respect for perpetrators 3. Interaction between victims and perpetrators (develop simple survival strategy) 4. Disintegration or termination of perpetrators' control 5. Re-establishment of security
Psychological and Physical Reactions: Anxiety; insomnia; depression; anorexia; psychophysiological reactions; phobias about the event; little guilt about plight of other victims; hostility; resentment; paranoid reactions towards government officials and persons with fewer losses	Psychological and Physical Reactions: Anxiety; insomnia; depression; anorexia; psychophysiological reactions; phobias about the event, guilt about plight of other victims; mild to moderate annoyance and dissatisfaction with actions of government officials
No guilt about not preventing event	Guilt about not preventing event
No identification with aggressor Desire for reprisal Aberrant characterological acts, e.g., looting, deviance, alcoholism	Identification with aggressor Reluctant desire for reprisal No aberrant characterological acts
Wish to return to scene of event 'Burn-out' among workers and victims Feeling of loss	Reluctance to return to scene of event No customary 'burn-out' among workers and victims Feeling of loss
Social Reactions: Acceptance by other persons No humiliation No doubt by others about genuineness of complaints No belief by others that the event was victim-precipitated	Social Reactions: Rejection by other persons, mild to marked Humiliation Doubt by others about genuineness of complaints Belief by others that the event was at least partly victim-precipitated
Short-term cohesive feeling among group victims	Long-term cohesive feeling among group victims

of looking for these answers is complicated by one's general cognitive approach to problems, the so-called 'sharpening–levelling' dimension. Sharpeners tend to emphasise differences, whereas levellers tend to emphasise similarities. One's place on this dimension can be particularly important when an area of investigation is new and the data are preliminary.

As is frequently true in other areas, the viewpoints of the generalists and the specialists, and the 'levellers' and the 'sharpeners', have merit, but require a conceptual framework for examination and debate. The following is designed as a step towards such a framework, modifying initial work by Frederick[3] and expanding into the analysis of adult and child hostage victims. Table 1 provides a comparative look at the effects upon victims of natural violence/major disaster, general human-induced violence, adult hostage cases and child hostage cases. Phases of the event, psychological/physical reactions, and social reactions are presented for each victim group. The reactions and processes described are based upon the present author's experience as a hostage negotiator for eight years, as an interviewer and therapist of over seventy-five hostages from both US and foreign locations and in state/federal disaster response.

Table 1—*continued*

Adult Hostages	Child Hostages
Stages: 1. Initial impact (freeze, protect self, protect others) 2. Acceptance/respect for captors (frozen fright vs heroic action plans) 3. Increased interaction between victims and captors (develop survival strategy, often complex) Increased interaction among victims (develop self vs group survival strategy) 4. Disintegration or termination of captors' control (fear of change in stable situation) 5. Re-establish security (dramatic tension relief, verbal expression focused on one or two aspects of situation)	Stages: 1. Initial impact (freeze, panic with crying and screaming, make jokes) 2. Acceptance/respect for captors (frozen fright vs heroic action thoughts) 3. Increased interaction between victims and captors (develop survival strategy, usually simple fear, fail to utilise opportunities for escape) Increased interaction among victims (develop self vs group survival strategy, sub-group clustering by age and aggressiveness) 4. Disintegration or tormentation of captors' control (less fear of change in stable situation) 5. Re-establish security (greater verbal expressiveness with authorities than parents)
Psychological and Physical Reactions: Anxiety; sleep and eating disturbances; frequent gastrointestinal problems; inability to concentrate; intrusive images; dreams; guilt about others and own behaviour; occasional extreme reaction towards government actions; startle reactions; sharp shifts in mood; later reactions against authority; surfacing of prejudices; alternatively dealing with event or denying it	Psychological and Physical Reactions: Anxiety; sleep disturbances more than eating disturbances; less gastrointestinal problems; inability to concentrate; less intrusive images; dreams; guilt about others and own behaviour; startle reactions; pre-occupation with death; pre-occupation with loss of parent; increased play involving death and violence; irritability; distortions of the event itself; conduct problems
Guilt about not having acted as a 'stronger' individual; John Wayne Syndrome	Child-like survivor guilt
Identification with aggressor (Stockholm Syndrome), includes actual behaviour Desire for revenge is initially reluctant, then moderate Aberrant characterological acts Delayed return; three days to several weeks waiting period common Delayed 'burn-out' (alternatively dealing with event and then denying it) Smooth function alternates with immobilisation Feeling of loss	Identification with the aggressor, more in thought or fantasy than in behaviour Desire for revenge conflicts with moderate to strong fear of captors General regression to more infantile behaviour Usually no return 'Burn-out' less delayed than with adult hostages Feeling of loss (frequently expressed as fear of loss of current parent)
Social Processes: Rejection by others, mild to marked; Symonds' the 'second injury' Humiliation Doubt by others about genuineness of complaints Belief by others that victim could have done more Frequent short-term anger and rejection followed by long-term unspoken cohesion among victims	Social Process: Jealousy of attention by other adults and children Little humiliation Doubt by others about genuineness of complaints Little belief by others that victim could have done more; fantasy by victim of having done more Less cohesive overall; cohesive feeling by age group or by captive activity in group

NATURAL VIOLENCE/MAJOR DISASTER STAGES

Natural violence/major disasters are exemplified by fires, earthquakes, floods etc. Although one may later argue that design improvements or adequate maintenance may have prevented a building fire, such an event would be generally classed as natural violence. However, a major fire planned and deliberately started by an arsonist would not be included in this group even though the fact of arson may not be discovered until after the fire has been contained, as the victims are then aware of the wilful nature of the act.

The states during natural violence/major disaster have been well chronicled elsewhere[4,5,6] and will be only briefly highlighted here. The initial impact is usually characterised by simple appropriate movement, panic or physical immmobilisation. Mass initial hysteria is relatively rare in natural disasters. If a simple, direct movement will permit an escape, most victims will appropriately use it. If such a movement does not permit an escape, panic or immobilisation responses appear rapidly in the victim group. Panic is an often illogical attempt to flee the area: pushing, shoving, fighting through various exits or jumping from heights at which the possibilties of surviving are small. Physical immobilisation is later described by survivors as: 'I don't know what happened, I just froze', or 'I wanted to move, I tried to move, but my body just wouldn't respond'. Attempts by others to physically move the person are frequently rejected. The presence of a firm, directive authority figure has been shown to have a significant impact in many cases upon the extent of such reactions. In fact, most disaster planning is based upon providing simple, direct information about what to do initially.

The heroic stage does not occur for all, but many individuals, usually without a previous history of such behaviour, will place themselves at great risk to help other unknown victims. For some, the situation is so far out of their ordinary life that they are able to play out a fantasy role. For others, it is a way to keep reality out for a short period of time. In a major disaster over a large area, police and fire personnel will often state that they do not wish to know of their own family's condition until the disaster situation has been stabilised.

The next state is characterised by a great deal of community spirit, sharing of experience and influx of public aid. The idealistic theme is that like the mythical phoenix bird rising from its own ashes, 'We will rebuild it better than it was before'. Disillusionment follows as the extent of effort needed to rebuild becomes apparent, government assistance becomes slow and bureaucratic and individual problems become dominant. Re-organisation is the most lengthy phase, but must appear in a tangible way relatively soon, or the community will linger in the disillusionment state.

GENERAL HUMAN-INDUCED VIOLENCE STAGES

Stages of response to human-induced violence have also been well studied.[7,8]

The initial impact is marked by a thought that this is not real, it cannot be happening to me. This is quickly followed by selecting one of the freeze, flee or fight alternatives. The freeze response is by far the most common. Acceptance or respect for the dominance of the perpetrators is quickly established: 'I didn't want them to get nervous or have an excuse to shoot me. I just wanted to get through it.' In the third stage, interaction between victim and perpetrator begins to take place, as the victim develops a survival strategy. The survival strategies are almost always relatively straightforward, ranging from a simple, proposed bargain ('I'll do anyting you want, just don't hurt me', or 'You haven't done anything wrong yet, why don't you just leave') to an attempted diversion ('My husband is coming back soon', or 'Just give me a minute, I'm hurrying as fast as I can') to letting the fear response dominate ('Maybe if he sees how truly frightened I am, he won't hurt me'). Disintegration or termination of perpetrator's control is usually by the perpetrator himself or by other external factors, seldom by the victim alone. The last stage may occur simultaneously with the rescue, or if the victim is left at the scene of the crime may wait until security is re-established at a police station, friend's residence etc. As this security is re-established, a second wave of fear and anxiety over the risk just experienced frequently occurs, accompanied by expressions of embarrassment over this behaviour ('I don't know why I'm acting this way now, it's all over', or 'I'm sorry, I just can't stop shaking'). Although phyical security has been re-established, emotional security is still obviously absent. The continued fear and feeling of vulnerability is accentuated by what Symonds[9] has labelled the 'second injury'. The recent victim wants emergency personnel and family members to feel a part of their pain and help them emotionally. However, to survive themselves, emergency personnel have often learned to distance themselves from victims. Family members, unless they have been a previous victim themselves, simply do not have an experience base with which to relate to the victim. The extent of the second injury can be a major factor in the psychological and physical reactions that later follow.

ADULT HOSTAGE STATES

As the adult hostage is first captured, he reports two parallel processes. His thought and emotional processes begin in a similar way to those of the general human-induced violence victim. The hostage does not believe this is happening, but the anxiety and fear is rising within him despite this belief. At the same time, behaviourally, he seems to select from one of three response patterns: freeze, protect self or protect others. The hostage freeze response appears to be quite similar to the freeze response of the general victim. The protect self response is characterised by quick attempts to hide under cover or run from the scene. In contrast to natural disaster victims, there is very little panic movement. The protect self response constitutes a high risk–high gain action. Although it is not widely known to the public sector, such attempts have been successful in a number of incidents. However, if serious injuries or deaths are to occur, they are most likely to occur in the initial moments when the captors may see any action as a challenge to their control. Civilian hostages very rarely protect themselves through an initial aggressive act towards the captors. In the protect others response, the hostage will stand in front of someone else to shield them, stand in front of a doorway to try and block someone else's entrance into the situation, talk loudly ('don't shoot') in the hope of alerting someone or directly request protection of another hostage of high vulnerability ('Just don't hurt or scare the children'). Interestingly, the initial responses are reported as semi-automatic, without deliberation or extended conscious thought. In a recent bank hostage case, a young Black woman immediately grabbed unknown Caucasian children and fell to the floor, protecting them with her body. In an interview with this author the same day, she stated: 'I didn't think, I just responded, but I knew what I was doing as I did it.'

The second state is labelled as acceptance/respect for the captors. The dominance and control of the situation by the captors has been firmly established. The hostage responds with 'frozen fright'[10] versus heroic action plans. Frozen fright, also present in victims of other terrorism, is manifested by outwardly cooperative and compliant behaviour while inwardly the fright is terrifying the individual. Such a hostage does as he is told while his mind races with the various possibilities of his death. Other hostages are less fearful. Instead, the situation offers a potential opportunity for heroic action: 'It was just like a real life movie. I started looking for ways that I could get the gun away.' The key phrase here is potential opportunity. The thoughts and fantasies represent a frequent defence mechanism, but the thoughts are almost never translated into action. Time and time again, ex-hostages will connect this part of the experience to a television programme or a movie, and experience a sense of excitement about that. It would appear that the visual media has not only influenced captors, but has also touched a vicarious responsive cord in the general public as well.

As the situation continues to stabilise, the third stage of increased interaction between victims and captors begins. The initial rush of commands and threats has slowed. The captors have become less concerned with internal security and more concerned with external security, plus the process of negotiating itself. Sitting or lying down, the hostage has nothing to do except think. His mind turns to the development of a survival strategy. Some strategies are simple, but others are often very complex and closely adhered to. William Niehous,[11] kidnapped from his Caracas, Venezuela, home on 27 February 1976, and escaped on 29 June 1979, described his strategy in five points: (a) be human (b) communicate, (c) set individual goals, (d) eat and exercise and (e) have faith. Niehous' points parallel those of other successful ex-hostages, as well as POWs and other captivity survivors. Being human means communicating to establish yourself as an individual, with distinguishing and interesting characteristics. If killing does take place, captors have demonstrated a strong preference for troublesome, annoying hostages, or dehumanised 'objects', mere symbols instead of lives with families, likes, dislikes etc. Further, an object can be manipulated according to desire; a human being will resist sometimes on some issues. Selective resistance on small issues has been quite important in many hostage survivors. Setting individual goals, plus eating and exercising, become a part of the strategy only when the situation extends beyond several days. Niehous would set a goal of living until next Wednesday, then the next, then the next. He thereby made daily survival a source of some self-esteem. Eating and exercising provided some structure to the long days and kept him healthy. Niehous states that he was not a religious zealot before his captivity, but that the experience increased his faith 'a Hell of a lot'. The primary component appears to be faith in a positive outcome, a focus upon positive aspects of one's past life.

Such previous experience or association can have a fatalistic impact on the hostage as well. In Hanafi, in the Muslim takeover of the B'nai B'rith headquarters in Washington, DC, in 1977, some of the Jewish hostages made strong, immediate connections to the German concentration camps: 'Our bodies were piled one on top of the other like at Auschwitz. When I first saw that room, I thought these people might already be dead.'[12]

A third recurrent, complex strategy is to go along with the captors, while attempting to make fools of them to the outside world or other captors. Some Vietnam POWs allowed pictures, but made small obscene gestures, or allowed filmed interviews, but blinked messages in morse code. The mass media has widely educated a large portion of the general public about these strategies. The general public, in turn, has responded favourably, accepting the need of the captive to cooperate, as long as it is only partial cooperation. Frequently, however, the hostage creates strategies that are so obscure or complex that others cannot read them during the incident, and, after the incident, even this hostage finds it difficult to point out the coded resistance. At least one soldier in the American–Iranian hostage crisis found himself in this position.

Another recurrent, complex strategy is to attempt to assume a known role. Gerard Vaders, a newspaper editor held for thirteen days by Moluccan terrorists in a Dutch train in December 1975, almost immediately began taking notes for future writing. On the same train, another hostage who was not a doctor but knew something of medical care, assumed the role of doctor. In the Japanese Red Army hijacking of a JAL aircraft to Bangladesh in 1975, a US movie starlet used her acting skills to fake a nervous breakdown and gain her escape. The most frequent role assumption, however, is that of kind parent, employing warmth plus mild guilt and disapproval over the captor's behaviour. Sometimes a hostage's previous behaviour appears to heavily influence his strategy development. Vaders reported guilt for not having taken more risks to help the Jews in the Second World War. A state probation officer always held a strong belief that by not physically abusing others, he would not be severely physically abused himself. When he was held hostage by one of his probationers, he consistently referred back to this belief as part of his strategy, recalling his captor's words: 'I like you. You're a good guy. You've treated me fairly. I don't want to see you dead.'

Overall, then, the hostage who develops a strategy often creates a complex one based on partial cooperation with his captors. However, these strategies can become so complex as to be obscure, and are only partially employed. It is the process of a 'good' (e.g., complex and crafty) plan that is important to the hostage. This seems to renew his determination and self-esteem, even if the plan exists only in his mind.

The third stage also includes increased interaction among victims. The survival strategy discussed previously must make a practical decision about self versus group survival. The most common early decision is that no one must act to make the captors angry. Strong group pressure is exerted on anyone who acts out of turn or draws attention to himself. Gradually, however, the hostage selects one of four basic strategies: (a) protect self first, (b) construct plan of action with others, (c) support fellow hostages or (d) assume a protector/primary care-giver role to others.

In the first strategy, the hostage has a range of behaviour. He may attempt to isolate himself from interaction with others, or to willingly assist his captors in hopes they will favour him. Or he may become involved in the well-known Stockholm Syndrome. As defined by Ochberg,[13] three conditions characterise this syndrome. First, positive feelings are felt by the hostage towards the hostage taker. Second, negative feelings are felt by the hostage towards the authorities responsible for rescue. Third, positive feelings are reciprocated by the hostage-taker. Thus, in Ochberg's formulation, the genesis of the positive feelings on the part of the hostage is not identification with the aggressor, nor is it a conscious attempt to gain mercy. It is, rather, a result of infantilisation, denial of the fact that the hostage-taker is responsible for terror and confinement, and a primitive gratitude similar to the feeling of a one-year-old towards a parent.

The second group strategy usually begins with one hostage sharing an observation with another: 'I've been noticing the right door isn't guarded well', or 'The younger terrorist doesn't seem very bright'. If the other hostage is responsive, more conversation takes place, and plans of potential action are reviewed. The original planners are quite cautious about new members in their sub-group, making strong value judgements about trustworthiness and courage of the others. As is true in the individual survival strategy, the process of making the plans seems to be more important than their actual implementation. Relatively few of these plans are successfully carried out. An exception to this is noted in the experience of the People's Republic of China. In their only two recorded incidents (one bus and one aircraft hijacking occurring in 1982), Chinese passengers and employees overpowered the hijackers with exceptional physical force. Interestingly, the bus was filled mostly with Western tourists who remained quietly in their seats. This certainly raises interesting issues about the cultural conditioning of hostage behaviour.

The decision to support fellow hostages is the most frequently selected option in a group situation. This may take the form of assurances, holding hands or doing small things to make another more comfortable. This fits well into the individual strategy of assuming a known role, taking care of others without assuming group leadership. For others, it has a more child-like quality of drawing together into a protective group. This sub-group's need to see themselves as equal and the same is very intense. Again, from the Hanafi Muslim takeover, one hostage states: 'We identified with the people we were lying on the floor with, whether black or white, Christian or Jewish.'

Any individual member of this sub-group who asks for more food, or appears to be selfish in some other behaviour is sharply censured.

The fourth group strategy is to assume a protector/primary care-giver role to others. This is more than offering support to others, but involves trying to become known to captors and fellow hostages alike as a primary figure, who utilises active mediation rather than confrontation. This is the doctor-like or priest-like role, and is almost universally allowed by captors. The motivation for such a strategy may vary, of course, from assuming a known role such as parent, to avoidance of survivor guilt. Baders, held by Moluccan terrorists, wished himself, rather than another, to be taken out and shot. Once again we see a blurring between actual behaviour and the way a hostage wants to perceive himself.

If the incident is lengthy and hostage strategies have been relatively unsuccessful, many hostages will experience periods of wanting an assault or acting defiantly, even if it means the risk of their death. After the long American–Iranian hostage crisis, several ex-hostages publicly discussed times 'when we wanted to hear the planes', and know that the assault was beginning. Feelings of anger towards captors, frustrating boredom and increasing difficulty in tolerating anxiety all contribute to these periods of strong feelings. These feelings are often discussed among sub-groups, with a concurrent increase in small expressions of defiance towards the captors. Retaliation by captors for these small expressions ranges from non-existent to minimal. The recorded incidence of highly provocative behaviour resulting from these feelings is extremely low.

The fourth stage is labelled disintegration or termination of captors' control. The relationship between captors, hostages and negotiators has reached a kind of balance. There exists a pattern of give and take. Basic needs of the hostages have been attended to. As termination becomes a possibility, many hostages experience extreme fear and anxiety. They have become accustomed to the stability, and fear 'something would go wrong in the surrender. The police would start shooting. It was too quick. I was very frightened'. Thus, the attitude is partially attributed to a desire to maintain stability and partially to a lack of trust in the police response. Even in the United States where police hostage negotiation has been dramatically successful, citizens are still highly ambivalent towards the police officer. As one ex-hostage put it: 'I've seen too many SWAT TV shows. I didn't know if they wanted to save me or get the criminals.'

In the last stage, the adult hostage is freed or rescued. Tension relief is dramatic, both verbally and non-verbally. Non-verbally, handshakes, hugs and arms around the shoulder are exchanged between hostages and police officers. The previous ambivalent attitude is sharply reversed: 'I was worried, but they really came through for me.' Verbally, the focus is upon one or two aspects of risk in the situation. The freed hostage, using short comments, will go over and over these points of risk: 'I didn't know if I was going to make it when. . . .' These comments are made repetitively to everybody. As in the general violence pattern, apologies are also made for continuing to shake or show other outward signs of anxiety.

After this cathartic expression, the freed hostage will begin to ask about relatives or family, presenting the possibility of Symond's[14] second injury. This first contact between family and freed hostage can be quite significant. One recent bank hostage case, involving high risk, went on for several hours before successful resolution with no injuries. After the preliminary debriefings by local police and the FBI, one young female bank teller telephoned her mother. Excitedly, she explained that the bank had been robbed, a hostage situation had taken place, but she was unhurt. The mother's response was 'Oh really, dear?' The teller became quite angry, but did not express it until the telephone call was over. She turned to another teller, related the mother's response and exclaimed: 'I could have just killed her for that.' Later that evening, the mother saw the report on television news, and suddenly the event was now real. But the alienation and loss of support had already occurred.

In another similar incident, an adult male hostage called home and received the following immediate response from his family: 'We've all been so worried. We've all been sitting around the television set for hours. We're so relieved.' Again, the freed hostage did not express his feelings. Only later did he reveal that he felt he was the hostage, not them, and they should have had more concern for him. Relatives tend to express far greater anger towards the captors than do freed hostages. This discrepancy increases emotional distance, isolating the ex-hostage from his primary support systems. The discrepancy narrows after a short period, but does not seem to disappear. One hostage relates: 'After a time I just came to accept that she couldn't totally understand why I didn't hate the guy.'

In summary, in looking at the stages of the adult hostage situation, several items stand out. The basic pattern is indeed similar to that produced by general human-induced violence. However, the development of both individual and group survival strategies is often more complex, with the individual strategy being created first. Further, the hostage appears to highly value his development of such strategies, whether or not he is able to implement them. Finally, he has become exposed to a range of very new feelings and behaviours in a short period of time, including wanting to die, wanting to support his captors, extended vulnerability, fear of the police etc. Both the hostage and his family are faced with a rare complexity of events to integrate.

CHILD HOSTAGE STAGES

In reviewing child (ages 5–11) hostage stages, an initial acknowledgement is made of the overall similarity with adult hostage stages. The focus, then, is upon differences. In addition, the number of documented adult hostage cases is quite large, with documented child hostage cases being quite small. Accordingly, one's conclusions must be more tentative.

During the first moments of the takeover, the child's reactions are, expectedly, more primitive. For most American children, the first association is with television or a recent movie: 'It was just like on TV or something.'

Behaviourally, the child hostage seems to select from one of three response patterns: freeze, panic with crying and screaming or making jokes. In contrast to the adult patterns, attempts to immediately flee or fight are rare. The freeze response is accompanied by internal fear, anxiety and thoughts of being hurt. Panic with crying and screaming is an especially high frequency choice if the child is physically seized, or if one child in the group begins crying. Some children will first attempt to make jokes. These children appear to be assuming a known role, the comedian. The comedian is one of the few roles the young child has learned will gain acceptance from most adults and peers.

In each of these response choices, the child's conception of what is about to happen is variable. He may see the captor(s) as 'bad', 'robbers' or 'bad people Mummy told me to stay away from'. He fears that something very bad is going to happen, but he is not very sure what that is going to be. One important exception should be noted. Police hostage negotiators are often faced with dealing with the parent or relative who has seized their own child. These adults express a wish to 'save' the child from other family members, or to save the child from the pain the adult has experienced in his life. If the child resembles or is the favourite of a hated family member, the adult relative captor has the potential to emotionally injure the hated family member through the child. These children tend to see the adult relative captor as 'crazy', or 'acting funny'. They know that the adult relative 'acts funny' only a small percentage of the time. Amidst the fear, their thoughts and wishes are for the adult to return to his normal behaviour pattern.

The child's later reporting of the sequence of events during the takeover is generally better than the adult's. However, some children display a tendency to add an event, or misidentify a captor. In the Chowchilla bus kidnapping of twenty-six children in 1976, six of the children either described a non-existent kidnapper or created characteristics: 'a man with one leg who used his shotgun as a cane', or 'a fat chubby man when they took our names'.[15] The kidnappers were subsequently captured and convicted. They did not have such characteristics. Police detectives have long known about the unreliable nature of suspect descriptions from children. Confabulation in child play and parent–child interaction is also well known. What we do not know is what part of the child's report comes from his misperception ('seeing') versus his desire to please a questioning adult.

In the second child stage of acceptance/respect for captors, the choice is similar to that of the adult hostage: frozen fright versus heroic action thoughts. The primary difference seems to be in heroic action plans for adults versus heroic action thoughts for children. The child, in wishing to be a hero, has brief thoughts or ideas of taking action. As one might anticipate, these are not formulated into a heroic action plan in the way that the adult does. As with the adults, action is rarely taken, but the fantasy of action shows up once again as an important defence mechanism.

The third child stage of increased interaction between victims and captors is characterised by the development of simple survival strategies, as opposed to the complex strategies of the adult. Both physically and mentally, the adult captor is able to exert such extensive control over the child that it is not surprising that the child's response is submissive and cooperative. While some children engage in searching behaviour for means of escape, the most striking observation is the failure to utilise opportunities for escape. Even after the incident is over, the child experiences difficulty in explaining why he did not use such opportunities or why he picked the opportunity that he did. Whether such a degree of control is induced by the adult captor, or is attributed to the adult captor by the child hostage is an issue worthy of further investigation.

Increased interaction among victims does occur during the third stage, but to a lesser degree than with adults. Obtaining food, water and privacy during body eliminations become priority items involving limited group interaction. Sub-groups form based on two principal characteristics: age and aggressiveness. Younger children and less aggressive children form one cluster, with older and more aggressive children in another cluster. Such sub-grouping is consistent with normal play patterns. The more aggressive children do internally experience doubts and fears, and have shown a willingness to reveal them after the incident is over. One does not see the highly differentiated role assumptions that occur in this same stage among adults.

As disintegration or termination of captor's control begins, the child does not tend to show the adult's fear of loss of stability. Fear of death or injury during surrender or police assault appears to be largely an adult attitude. As a child, admiration for or trust of the police officers remains relatively high. The captor's guilt is elevated at this point, and apologies/assurances to the child are frequent.

In the last stage, the rescue is accomplished. Supportive physical exchanges between the child hostage and police officers are even more pronounced than with adults. The number of police officers involved is more limited, with the verbal exchanges being lower in audio level. The child usually has a lot to say, and is quite willing to talk at length about the incident. A much greater willingness is demonstrated to talk openly and at length with unknown police officers than with parents. The reasons for this remain speculative, and centre around a child's fear that he has not lived up to parental expectations. Further, the re-uniting process involves a great deal of parental emotion. Some children assume responsibility for this parental emotion, feeling that the whole event is somehow their fault.

PSYCHOLOGICAL AND PHYSICAL REACTIONS: GENERAL VICTIMS

To provide a framework for examining specific reactions of adult and child hostages, the general psychological, physical and social reactions of victims will be briefly overviewed. In referring to Table 1, a number of reactions can be seen to appear under all four types of violence categories; anxiety, sleep and eating disturbances, depression, psychophysiological reactions, phobias, hostility, dreams, intrusive waking images[13] and the inability to concentrate occur routinely in victims of many types. In most victims, the reactions are transitory, alternate with performing everyday tasks in a routine manner and decline over time. If the victim isolates himself, or is rejected by his social support systems, the probability of successful functioning is greatly reduced. In addition to the commonly shared reactions, the disaster victim shows little guilt about the problems of other victims and little guilt about not having prevented the event. It was a natural disaster, an act of God, so the victim feels legitimately excused from responsibility. At the same time, he resents those who suffered fewer losses, and does not feel the government is responsive and sensitive enough. The desire for reprisal is expressed in anger against God or Fate: 'Why me, why me?' The disaster has so disrupted established social control rules, that he will often loot, vandalise or act aggressively in a manner that he would not ordinarily do. There is a strong desire to return to the scene, to salvage items from the rubble, to compare recollections with others on the scene. The amount of energy expended in salvaging and planning for re-building cannot last, and 'burn-out' occurs rapidly.

The victim of general human-induced violence experiences considerable guilt over several aspects of the incident: 'I should have been hurt, not the other person', or 'If I had only taken a different way home, this would not have happened'. Themes of self-responsibility predominate. Whether out of fear of retaliation, sympathy for the aggressor or a desire to forget/encapsulate the incident, the desire for revenge is considerably less. Acts are rarely performed that are out of character. There is a great reluctance to return to the scene of the event. Further, since the injury is usually physical, monetary or emotional, little constructive effort can be directed towards salvaging or re-building. This precludes a 'burn-out' phase.

In brief, the adult victim of natural violence/major disaster has his status accepted by both his community and the larger society. There is little humiliation as the event is seen as an act of God or Fate. The victim did not cause or precipitate the disaster. Because of this and the graphic nature of a major disaster, others tend to accept the genuineness of victim complaints.

In contrast, the victim of human-induced violence is frequently seen as having done something to cause or precipitate the event. This rejection and censure is frequently accompanied by doubts by others of the genuineness of victim complaints. If these social processes are pronounced, even the individual with exceptional ego strength will begin to feel humiliated and isolated. Empathy and long-term cohesive feelings often exist among these victims. They share an intimacy of personal experience not shared by victims of major disasters.

SPECIFIC PSYCHOLOGICAL AND PHYSICAL REACTIONS: ADULT EX-HOSTAGES

The adult ex-hostage experiences considerable guilt and feelings of responsibility about his behaviour. Part of this is survivor guilt, but a major part is guilt for not having acted as a 'stronger individual', the John Wayne Syndrome. The ex-hostage feels better that he at least planned some heroic actions, but wishes that he could have at least resisted his captors more. In his dreams, the event may be frequently repeated with a heroic action added. If the Stockholm Syndrome or identification with the aggressor manifested itself in behaviour during the incident, the ex-hostage will experience difficulty rationalising his actions. This often leads to unsuccessful attempts to explain the captors' cause to others. Both Western and Eastern cultures strongly sanction loyalty to values and non-submissive behaviour under stress. There are few internal rationales available for the ex-hostage who failed to exhibit such behaviour under stress.

The return to work is a critical point. Almost all adult hostages report 'startle reactions', and watching for signs of another takeover to occur. This lasts from several days to several months. Embarrassed apologies are offered for such behaviour. Attitudes towards work authority and governmental authority can be quite resentful. A typical scenario involves the ex-hostage experiencing concentration difficulties in doing routine paperwork. The supervisor expresses the need to get back to work as usual. The hostage reacts angrily at the perceived insensitivity of the supervisor. Part of the reaction may indeed be due to a supervisor's insensitivity, but part is due to the ex-hostage's remaining resentment of the way he was dominated by his captors.

Intrusive waking images[16] are undesired mental pictures of the hostage event. Adult hostages rate this as a major problem, and will use it as an index of their overall re-adjustment. The frequency of the images declines with time; some continue to appear irregularly over a period of many years.

Among the psychophysiological reactions of adult hostage victims, gastrointestinal problems are the most commonly reported. Research has yet to be conducted to determine whether this can be explained by the possible internalisation versus externalisation of anger, or predisposing factors in the hostage population, or some other variable.

The desire for revenge is initially reluctant, then moderate to occasionally severe in strength. This may be attributed to the process of identification with the aggressor which lessens upon return to the usual social relationships. While the desire for revenge is expressed as moderate, most ex-hostages express a sense of relief and closure when the convictions or deaths of captors occur.

Adult ex-hostages commonly state an interest in returning to the scene, provided they are given a waiting period of several days to several weeks. The initial return to scene is emotional. Stories are re-told. Small items become stimuli to images and memories. Considerable relief is expressed afterwards: 'I knew I needed to do it. I'm glad I did it.' Once again, primary value is placed upon the 'strong' response to stress.

'Burn-out' does indeed occur, but in a delayed pattern. After several months, the ex-hostage wants to move on from the experience. He wants the return of his ability to concentrate and work, unhampered by intrusive images and thoughts. A great deal of effort is made to suppress these. This, of course, works for a period of several weeks to several months, then fails. Often feeling tired and defeated, the ex-hostage begins to accept the periodic coming and going of the images and thoughts.

In both work and personal obligations, smooth functioning alternates with immobilisation. Employers will report that the ex-hostage's work is back at his usual high level of quality. Then days will begin to appear where his productivity is extremely low. This frustrates employers and friends more than continuous difficulty in getting up to a productive level again. Angry, authoritarian exchanges are common, accompanied by isolation and depression.

SPECIFIC SOCIAL PROCESSES: ADULT EX-HOSTAGES

Rejection by others can take a number of forms, in addition to the previously described Symonds' 'second injury'. The most common form described by ex-hostages is the rejection of their need to re-tell the story. After the first couple of times, family and friends do not want to hear it again. It is old news. However, for the ex-hostage, the re-telling is an important way of ordering the experience and regaining a sense of mastery over it: 'I needed to go over and over it, but I felt I was boring people. I stopped talking and the feelings got worse.' Immediately after an incident, this author routinely tells ex-hostages to tell the story as frequently as *they* want to *when* they want to. They are further told that if no one wants to listen: 'Call me and I'll listen, even if it's the exact same story!' Ex-hostages find this amusing at the time, but later report that this very early permission giving was very meaningful to them.

If newspaper and television coverage is quite extensive, a special type of situation is created for some hostage victims.[17] In effect, this mass, detailed coverage 'steals the victim's story', so that the victim is often not the most complete source on the incident. This reduces the opportunities to master the experience through re-telling. The victim as well as his story soon become yesterday's news, and he is left with a feeling of incompleteness and depression.

Envy is another form of rejection. Attention is so valued by so many that envy can occur even when the attention is the result of tragedy or life risk. After the Hanafi Muslim takeover incident, a B'nai B'rith employee joked that his tombstone would be engraved: 'Here lies Sol Goldberg, who was not there. He had a stomach ache that day.'[18] On the one hand it was a joke. On the other hand it was a profound insight into the behaviour going on around him. Family members can be the object of envy also. During the American–Iranian hostage crisis, the family of one hostage soldier received a great deal of press attention. The family lived in an economically less advantaged area. When one small sister began to receive rides to school in a television network's 'limousine', the neighbourhood reaction was clearly critical and envious.

Often the curiosity of others takes the form of the Monday morning quarterback: 'Why didn't you try this' or, I would have tried to jump him when . . .'. These comments feed into the ex-hostage's internal John Wayne Syndrome, triggering feelings of humiliation and inadequacy. Others continue to enhance the John Wayne Syndrome by doubting the genuineness of complaints: 'She is just being a baby. She should quit trying for so much attention.'

Following the rescue, short-term anger and rejection occur among the ex-hostages. Anyone who did not seem to behave in the manner favoured by the group becomes the target of the anger. When the American ex-hostages were moved from Tehran to Wiesbaden, several were actively shunned by the others for several days. When ex-President Carter first met with them in Wiesbaden, a few ex-hostages angrily lashed out at him. A split developed later between those with remaining anger and those who did not feel this was the time or place to deal with it. As time passes, such differences seem to lessen with the profound nature of the event providing long-term felt cohesion, felt cohesion because group contact is relatively rare and usually brief when it does occur. The news of the death or serious injury to a fellow ex-hostage does have significant impact, resulting in depression or renewed feelings of vulnerability.

SPECIFIC PSYCHOLOGICAL AND PHYSICAL REACTIONS: CHILD EX-HOSTAGES

Among the reactions referenced in Table 1, several items are especially interesting. Both sleeping and eating disturbances occur, but sleep disturbances are more frequently reported. This may be attributed to the fact that both child and parent are reporting sources, or to the known vulnerability of child sleep patterns to trauma in general. Dreams are frequent, and more varied than with adults. In the child's dreams, he seems to actively deal with themes of vulnerability and mastery. Vulnerability themes involve re-playing the event with the child's death or someone else's taking place. This provides a relatively 'safe' and symbolic exploration of what was a very high risk experience. Mastery themes involve replaying the event with changes that give the child a more heroic role, but not necessarily the main heroic role. An ethic of doing better predominates over an ethic of doing best. Along with dreams involving mastery is a conscious concern with prediction. Retrospectively, child ex-hostages will state that they knew something bad was going to happen. This may be attributed to a feeling or to an event prior to the capture. In othe words, the child seems to say to himself, 'If I can't control the event, I can at least predict it'.

Along with the mastery dreams comes an allied effort at mastery with increased play involving death and violence. The incident and variations of it are acted out in play with the child alternately assuming hostage and captor roles. Parents are sometimes surprised or concerned by the degree of aggression that may be evident in such play. The mechanism of identification with the aggressor is certainly evident, but more in thought, play or fantasy. Assisting the captor during the incident or assuming a primary aggressor role after the incident is very rare.

Terr,[19] in her study of the Chowchilla school bus kidnapping, noted that the children seemed to have no intrusive, waking images. The children stated that they thought about the event as they wanted, although the occurrence of their dreams was not under similar control. It may be that this is the result of a semantic or interpretative difference over the intrusive phenomena. If not, it may represent a major clue as to how children process trauma.

Survivor guilt shows up in a special child-like manner. In a well-known Israeli terrorist incident, a booby-trapped refrigerator exploded on a crowded street killing several people. The surviving ten-year-old daughter of one of the victims developed very strong guilt feelings. These were based upon a fight she had with her father in which she wished he would die. Although this example is a terrorist, not hostage, incident, it illustrates well the combination of anger and magical thinking that induces what is labelled child-like survivor guilt. Even older children who rationally know that such thoughts did not cause an incident may still hold emotionally to this special type of guilt.

The child is logically far more vulnerable than the adult. Accordingly, wishes to see the captors punished conflict with fears of reprisal. These fears, that the original captors or friends of theirs will return, are quite consistent across different victims. An adult has the ability to move away, invest faith in the police or rationalise away a possible second incident. The child has limited access to such sophisticated defences, being primarily dependent upon adults for assurances, adults who 'failed' to protect him from the first incident. Both the feelings of loss related to the incident and fear of future loss are attached to adults/parents. This shows up in anxiety if a parent is late coming home or is away on a long trip.

Most child ex-hostages display little interest in returning to the scene. Even given the fact that parents are routinely reluctant for the child to return, the child does not seem to carry an imperative to return for incident mastery in the way the adult does. 'Burn-out' is considerably less delayed than with adult ex-hostages. After a few days, the child wants to return to normal play and activities: 'I don't want to talk about it any more. I want things to go back to the way they were.'

SPECIFIC SOCIAL PROCESSES: CHILD EX-HOSTAGES

Jealousy is a very real social process for the child as well as the adult, with the child often wishing to conceal the event to avoid such attention. David, age eleven, and Eric age nine, saw both their parents killed when Arab terrorists took over a passenger bus in Israel in 1978. David escaped during the attack and Eric escaped later after witnessing his mother being shot in the chest. A few moments later, the bus blew up with both parents inside. Within the range of reactions one might anticipate from such a tragedy, both boys developed strong feelings about wanting to be treated like others, not in a special way. Conversely, this envy may extend into doubt in some of those who do express complaints. The child can be labelled as an attention seeker, or manipulator.

In contrast to adults, there is little humiliation by others or belief that the victim could have done more. The John Wayne Syndrome is evident, though, in the child's wish to have done more or to have done 'better' if he were older. The reasonable acceptance and support by adults following this incident does not outweigh previous competitive, achievement-oriented learning by the child.

Finally, there is considerably less cohesion among child ex-hostages than with adults. Certainly one can establish a number of rationales here. Adult interpersonal behaviours are more complex in the hostage situation, and group affiliative patterns more established, for example. Cohesive feeling is by age group or activity when held captive. This exists in the child's re-telling of the story and the survival sub-group of which he became a part.

SUMMARY

Although not a new phenomenon, hostage-taking has only recently become so widespread. Consequently, more clinicians are being called upon to assist ex-hostages and their families in their post-incident adjustment. Unfortunately, information on the hostage experience has been limited. To assist those clinicians and researchers working in this area, a framework has been offered for viewing the place of the hostage experience within the general field of victimology. This sub-set of hostage victims is shown to have many common, and some highly unique, characteristics when compared to victims in general. Further, significant differences are evident between the adult and the child hostage experience.

One ex-hostage sought assistance after the Hanafi Muslim takeover. He later described the psychotherapist as 'very smart, but he doesn't know what we hostages have gone through'.[20] This chapter has been an attempt to bridge part of the gap between hostage victim and therapist. The other bridging must come from the sensitive attention to individual experience which should characterise all clinical work.

NOTES

1 Chris Hatcher, 'The Hostage Dilema', *Los Angeles Times*, Sunday Edition, 5 June 1977.

2 Chris Hatcher, 'Models for Mediation with Violent and Potentially Violent Groups', Paper presented at the Inter-american Congress of Forensic Sciences. 5 November 1982, Sacramento, California.
3 Calvin Frederick, 'Effects of Natural vs. Human-induced Violence Upon Victims', *Evaluation and Change*, Special Issue, 1980. Program Evaluation Resource Center, 619 South Fifth Street, Minneapolis, MN 55415.
4 LH Stephens and SJ Green, *Disaster Assistance: Appraisal, Reform and New Approaches*, New York: New York University Press, 1979.
5 E Stern, *The Buffalo Creek Disaster*, New York: Random House, 1976.
6 Morton Bard and Dawn Sangrey, *The Crime Victim's Book*, New York: Basic Books, 1979.
7 *Ibid.*
8 A Burgess and L Holmstrom, 'Coping Behavior of the Rape Victim', *American Journal of Psychiatry*, 13(4), 1976, pp. 413–417.
9 Martin Symonds, 'The "Second Injury" to Victims', *Evaluation and Change*, Special Issue, 1980. Program Evaluation Resource Center, 619 South Fifth Street, Minneapolis, MN 55415.
10 *Ibid.*
11 William Niehous, 'Hostage Survival—A First Hand Look', *Security Management*, 1980.
12 M Belz, EZ Parker, LI Sank, C Shaffer, J Shapiro and L Shriber, 'Is There a Treatment for Terror?', *Psychology Today*, October 1977, pp. 54–56, 108–112.
13 Frank Ochberg, Personal Communication, 3 May 1982.
14 Martin Symonds, *op. cit.*
15 Lenore C Terr, 'Children of Chowchilla: A Study of Psychic Trauma', *The Psychoanalytic Study of the Child*, 1979, 34, pp. 547–623.
16 M Horowitz, *Stress Response Syndrome*, New York: Aronson, 1976.
17 Frank Ochberg, *op. cit.*
18 Charles Fenyvesi, 'Six Months Later: Living With a Fearful Memory', *Psychology Today*, Vol. II, No. 5, October 1977.
19 Lenore C Terr, *op. cit.*
20 Charles Fenyvesi, *op. cit.*

Economic Methods and the Study of Terrorism

T Sandler *et al.**

the term *rational* is never applied to an agent's ends, but only to his means ... the economic definition refers solely to a man who moves toward his goals in a way which, to the best of his knowledge, uses the least possible input of scarce resources per unit of valued output.[1]

In recent years, terrorism has come increasingly to the public's attention; hardly a week goes by without the news media reporting an aerial hijacking, a dramatic hostage incident or a spectacular bombing. Current trends in terrorism are especially disturbing since they indicate that terrorist incidents are becoming less discriminate and more costly in terms of fatalities and injuries.[2] The last half of 1985 underscores these trends with the armed attack in the Rome and Vienna airports, the bloody rescue attempt of a hijacked Egyptian airliner and the massive car bombings in Lebanon. These latest trends are especially discouraging after the numerous successes in combatting terrorism achieved by governments during 1982 and 1983. Notable successes included the capture of the operational heads of the Red Army Faction in West Germany, the apprehension of members of the Red Brigades in Italy and the arrest of eleven members of FALN in Illinois.[3] The West's counterattack against specific acts of terrorism has been effective only temporarily, with terrorists either devising countermeasures or else substituting other kinds of incidents. The substituted event sometimes leads to far greater destruction and loss of life than the type of incident countered by the authorities. For instance, actions taken by the US State Department after the November 1979 takeover of its embassy in Iran have transformed US embassies in sensitive regions into formidable fortresses. Terrorists have countered these fortifications in at least two ways: (a) increased assassinations and kidnappings of embassy officials when they leave the compound, and (b) the use of massive car bombs when officials are in the embassy. These responses have frustrated

* Scott E Atkinson, Jon Cauley, Eric Ik Soon Im, John Scott and John Tschirhart.

policy makers, charged with the task to curb terrorism; however, the terrorist response clearly follows the standard predictions, derived from a choice-theoretic framework of economics.

The purpose here is to report on the use of economic methods in understanding terrorism and in determining the best means of thwarting it. In doing so, we will draw results and techniques from our published work and our work in progress. We believe that the use of economic methodology can provide valuable insights for the following issues: (a) how best to deter terrorism when terrorists are apt to substitute their operational modes, (b) how to form international agreements designed to eliminate safe havens, (c) how to manage an incident involving hostages held for ransom, (d) how to assess the net benefits associated with a countermeasure and (e) how to assign resources to thwarting terrorism in the face of limited budgets.

At the outset, we should indicate the limitations of the economic method. We operate under no illusion concerning the applicability of economics to the study of terrorism. In particular, we do not claim that economics is the only technique or the preferred one for understanding terrorism; instead, we would argue that economics has something to add to the study of terrorism, especially when used in conjunction with the insights gained from political science, international relations, criminology, sociology and diplomacy. No economic theory is meant to explain all forms of terrorism or to apply to all incidents drawn from the same class (e.g., barricade and hostage-taking). Since an economic theory is an abstraction based upon simplifying assumptions, it applies only to those cases which fulfil the essential assumptions upon which the generalisations have been made. Rigorous empirical testing is essential to see whether the facts are not inconsistent with the theory's predictions. The more involved the theory, the less likely that clear-cut predictions can be derived owing to complex interactions. Empirical testing may be then the sole means to ascertain the strength of opposing influences.

The body of the chapter contains six sections. In the first section, we characterise the so-called economic method and then review briefly the economics of crime literature. The second section provides a sketch of the choice-theoretic problem of the terrorist. The following section indicates how economic bargaining theory can be applied to hostage incidents, where negotiations are permitted. We also report some empirical findings of Atkinson, Sandler and Tschirhart.[4] In the fourth section, we display some choice-theoretic problems faced by government. The remaining two sections contain a plea for data and concluding remarks.

ECONOMICS, CRIME AND TERROR

Economics is concerned with optimisation in the face of constraints. In particular, economists study the allocation of scarce resources among alternative ends. Thus, the consumer is depicted as maximising utility subject to a budget constraint and a time constraint; the firm is characterised as maximising profits subject to the technology constraint or production function; and the production manager is seen as minimising costs subject to technology constraints. Since the start of classical economic thought in the eighteenth century, 'economic man' has been depicted as a rational being who maximises beneficial returns and minimises costs, while responding to constraints. Changes in these constraints, as might arise when prices or success probabilities are deliberately altered by authorities, are hypothesised to produce predictable behavioural responses, in which individuals substitute out of relatively more expensive activities into relatively less expensive ones. An economist judges rationality in terms of an individual's response to changes in his constraints, not in terms of the goals or tastes possessed. Thus, a terrorist group, which bombs military barracks and which kidnaps foreign military personnel in the hopes of removing foreign troops from its home soil, is viewed as rational, provided that it responds appropriately to constraints and that its actions might serve to further the members' goal.

Many people object to our depicting of terrorists as rational; these people argue that terrorists are irrational or mad, a view often fostered by the news media. Stohl[5] has contended that the madman depiction is a myth, because many terrorist groups have particular goals that are sought as part of an ongoing political struggle. Gurr[6], Mickolus[7] and the US Central Intelligence Agency[8] have shown that political terrorist groups rank the tactics that they adopt with respect to such factors as risk, time and the likelihood of confrontation with authorities. High-risk activities like hijacking, barricade and hostage-taking have the smallest incidence; low-risk tactics like bombings and assassinations have the highest.[9] Data on terrorist groups depict these groups as engaging in a variety of different activities, some with low risks and low payoffs and some with high risks and high payoffs. One cannot help but be struck by the similarity between the terrorist group's diversification response and that of the investor, who seeks to limit his risks. As economists have shown many times, diversification pays (i.e., it is a rational response) when making portfolio choices among risky activities.

After the demise of the Baader–Meinhof Gang in West Germany, the Revolutionary Cells organised themselves into autonomous groups consisting of a few individuals, each of whom know one another by assumed names.[10] Such an organisational structure is an optimal response to past successes displayed by government infiltrators and within-group informants. A cellular structure minimises the likelihood of large-scale infiltration by de-coupling the probability of success or failure between a group's component parts. The Irish Republican Army (IRA) has also adopted a cellular structure after the British Government's successful use of informants. Once again, terrorists have responded in a rational manner to changes in their constraints. Moreover, Mickolus[11] noted, as did the US CIA[12] report, that measures taken to raise the costs of certain types of terrorist activities (e.g., metal detectors at airports, more guards at embassies) have immediately induced terrorists to choose other types of tactics whose costs have not risen. In his study of US aircraft hijackings during 1961–1976, Landes[13] indicated with econometric techniques that the use of sky marshals and metal detectors had had a significant positive effect on the probability of apprehension and a significant negative influence on the number of offences committed. The data indicate a precipitous drop in skyjackings after these security measures became operational in January 1973. In the US, there were twenty-seven incidents of skyjackings in 1972 and only one in 1973.[14] Such a response again implies terrorist rationality.

A terrorist's willingness to assume a risk of death does not necessarily mean that he is irrational. Policemen and firefighters, to name but two groups, are willing to face an increased probability of death, provided that their remuneration compensates them for the added risks that employment entails.[15] Since the attacks on the Rome and Vienna airports, the perceived probability of death to foreign air travellers has increased somewhat; nevertheless, many people still travel and even attend conferences on terrorism. More risk-averse Americans have changed vacation plans from Europe to the US, where such indiscriminate attacks are perceived as less likely.

Gary Becker[16] was the first to apply rational-actor modelling to the study of criminal behaviour.[17] In the economic model of crime, a criminal is viewed as choosing between legal activities with a certain return and illegal activities with uncertain returns so as to maximise expected utility. In other words, a criminal is depicted as allocating his/her time and resources among various legal and illegal activities in the hope of maximising his/her expected return.

As Ehrlich[18] has shown, the expected return to illegal activities can be made to account for the probability of apprehension, the probability of sentencing when apprehended and the severity of of the sentence through the use of conditional probabilities. The use of these models has led to many interesting theoretical predictions, which are not inconsistent with the evidence. For instance, Ehrlich's[19] empirical analysis of the deterrent effects of capital punishment suggests that 'on average the trade-off between the execution of an offender and the lives of potential victims it might have saved was of the order of magnitude of 1 for 8 for the period 1933–1967 in the United States'. Ehrlich[20] and Becker[21] have shown that the deterrent effects of a one per cent increase in the penalty per offence is greater than those of a one per cent increase in the probability of apprehension when criminals are risk averse—i.e., they oppose an actuarially fair bet.[22] Knowledge gained from these studies can assist law-enforcement agencies in allocating their own scarce resources among alternative thwarting activities. Risk attitudes were also shown to determine whether a criminal will specialise in illegal activities to the exclusion of legal activities.

The economics of crime literature has helped analyse recidivism by applying career-choice models to the study of criminal choices. For these career-choice models, an individual is hypothesised as comparing alternative expected income streams when deciding to switch out of one career into another. Empirical estimates of offence functions, which relate the number of offences to deterrent actions of the police and to self-protecting actions of the criminals, have the potential to assist law-enforcement agencies to ascertain the efficacy of their methods. Many other empirical estimates have been derived from economic models of crime.

Once one realises that terrorism is a choice-theoretical sub-set of criminal activity, it is easy to conclude that the paradigms of the economics of crime might be fruitfully modified and applied to terrorism. Like the criminal, the terrorist confronts decision making under uncertainty. In modelling terrorist behaviour, the researcher must be careful to endow the model with its own unique assumptions so as to capture the environment of the terrorist. We turn to this exercise next.

THE TERRORIST CHOICE-THEORETICAL FRAMEWORK

We intend to sketch the typical choice-theoretical model of the terrorist, used by economists to predict terrorist behaviour. Since we provide only a brief outline, the interested reader is advised to read our other papers for details.[23] A terrorist group is viewed as allocating scarce resources, R, between legal activities (e.g., the distribution of pamphlets, running for office) with a certain gain g^1, and illegal terrorist activities (e.g., bombings, kidnappings) with an uncertain gain, g^t. A terrorist incident may end in at least two states: success where the incident is completed as planned, and failure. Failure is a random variable whose probability is π. If only two states of the world are permitted, then $(1-\pi)$ denotes the probability of success. A terrorist group's expected utility is

$$E(U) = \pi U(\hat{W}) + (1-\pi)U(W), \tag{1}$$

where $U(W)$ is the von Neumann–Morgenstern utility function. Arguments W and $\hat{W}$ are the net wealth equivalent measures over the two states and are defined as

$$W = \bar{w} + g^1(R^1) + g^t(R^t, e_1) \tag{2}$$

$$\hat{W} = \bar{w} + g^1(R^1) - f(R^t, e_2). \tag{3}$$

The net wealth after a successful terrorist incident includes the group's current assets net of current earnings, $\bar{w}$, the monetary equivalent net gains from the incident and the monetary equivalent net gains from the legal activities. R^1 represents the resources assigned to legal actions, and R^t denotes the resources assigned to a terrorist act. In either state of the world, monetary gains depend directly on the resources (including time) allocated by the terrorist to the activity and are assumed to display diminishing returns; i.e., $g^t_R > 0$, $g^1_R > 0$, $g^t_{RR} < 0$ and $g^1_{RR} < 0$, where subscripts on the respective gain functions indicate first- and second-order partial derivatives. In equation (3), the net wealth for a terrorist failure includes the group's current assets plus their net gains from legal activities minus the monetary value of the fine or penalty,

f. If the group fails but escapes, then this penalty includes the wasted resources expended on the unsuccessful event. When, however, they are captured, the fine refers to the wasted resources, the opportunity costs of incarceration and any monetary penalties assessed. In equation (2), e_1 represents the environmental factor that also helps determine gains; in equation (3), e_2 denotes the environmental factor that influences the loss. Each of these e's denotes so-called shift parameters that can be altered by the actions of the authorities. The terrorist group's resource constraint,

$$R = R^t + R^1, \tag{4}$$

closes the model and indicates that the group's total resources, R, are divided between legal and illegal activities. Cooperation between terrorist groups can lead to increases in total resources.

Expected utility can be re-written in terms of the choice variables (R^1, R^t) and the exogenous parameters by substituting equations (2)–(4) into (1). Both the optimal levels for R^1 and R^t are then determined by maximising the resulting expression for expected utility. The likely effects of government policy decisions resulting from changes in π, e_1 and e_2, are found through comparative static analysis, where the assumptions of the model are used to determine the influence that changes in these policy parameters have on the optimal choice of R^1 and R^t. Often, additional assumptions concerning the terrorist group's risk attitudes can help sign these comparative static impacts. Empirical analysis of the predicted relationship provides two pieces of information: (a) it tests the predicted sign of the comparative static change, and (b) it helps quantify the actual size of this change. This type of analysis can form the theoretical basis for an offence function, which relates the number of offences (i.e., incidents) committed by a group to the enforcement efforts of the government. These efforts determine the fines for unsuccessful acts, the probability of failure and the size of terrorist gains.

We have deliberately made the basic model simple for display purposes. A number of relevant extensions or refinements permit us to capture more accurately the terrorist choice problem. The first extension allows for more states of the world. For example, in an intended hostage-taking event, we could define Θ as the proportion of the desired demands fulfilled. In this extension, the terrorist group's expected utility becomes

$$E(U) = \int_0^1 U[W(R^t, R^1, \Theta, e_1)]\, dH(\Theta, e_3), \tag{5}$$

where Θ is a continuous random variable defined on the support [0, 1] with density $dH(\Theta, e_3)$.

A second extension would permit the terrorist group to assign resources to influence its own probability of failure or success; that is, resources can be assigned to affect π and $1-\pi$. When the group attempts to influence its probabilities, we say that the group engages in self-protection.[24] The notion of self-protection must be distinguished from self-insurance, whereby the terrorist group assigns resources to limit its losses in those instances when it fails. A terrorist group that provides itself with an escape plan is engaging in self-insurance, whereas a group that attempts to counter security measures is exercising self-protection. By making the probability distribution more compressed or peaked, self-insurance reduces the variance of the distribution and is desired by risk-averse groups. In contrast, self-protection shifts the distribution towards greater success probabilities, but may increase or decrease the variance; hence, without further assumptions, we cannot conclude whether risk-averse groups would favour self-protection. The introduction of self-protection means that the probability of success (or failure) can be partly controlled by conscious choices of the government and/or the terrorists. Thus, the success probability can be related to terrorist and government actions; an empirical analysis of this probability function can quantify the impact of different actions on the part of both sides. Logit and/or probit econometric techniques can be used to estimate the probability function. Currently, Scott and Sandler are attempting to estimate the logit relationship associated with hostage-taking events. Their initial results identify the following variables as being significant at the 0.05 level: the number of terrorists in the attack force, the number of nationalities of the terrorists, whether sequential release or substitution of hostages were allowed, the length of the incident, the type of the incident (i.e., was it a kidnapping) and whether negotiations occurred on more than one dimension (i.e., did the terrorist demand two or more things).

A third extension would permit the terrorist group to assign resources to different acts, each with its own probabilities of success and failure as well as its own gains and losses. A dynamic choice could then be posed which would permit the terrorists to allocate resources between events over a number of discrete time periods, much as an investor decides his portfolio over time. If we were to pursue this extension in detail, we would have to use the modelling technique of stochastic dynamic programming.[25] The use of conditional probability would also be appropriate to model the terrorist problem in an intertemporal framework.

The above extensions are *representative* of the kind of additional detail that we could impose on the model. Each added detail comes at a cost, since our ability to predict the impact of policy changes on the terrorist choices decreases as the model becomes more complex.

INCIDENTS INVOLVING BARGAINING

Although hostage seizures make up only a small percentage of terrorist incidents, these seizures represent some of the most publicised and influential events. From 1968 through 1982, of the approximate eight thousand reported terrorist events, seven per cent (five hundred and forty events) constituted hostage-taking acts involving three thousand, one hundred and sixty-two hostages.[26] The bulk of these acts have been directed at industrialised democracies, particularly the US and some Western European countries.[27] Even though governments are dealing more effectively with these incidents, terrorists have been very successful: (a) in kidnappings, terrorists successfully capture their hostage(s) in eighty per cent of the acts and receive their ransom demands in seventy per cent of the incidents; (b) in barricade and hostage incidents, the terrorists achieve at least a portion of demands in seventy-five per cent of the cases.[28]

Atkinson, Sandler and Tschirhart[29] have modified the bargaining model of John Cross[30,31] in order to analyse hostage negotiations. Unlike other bargaining models, the Cross model accounts explicitly for the length of the negotiations. In each period of the bargaining process, the terrorists (government officials) are viewed as maximising the difference between their time discounted utility, which is a function of their demands (concessions) and the time discounted costs of bargaining. These costs are incurred in each period of negotiations. Each side perceives that the duration of the incident equals the difference between current demands and concessions divided by the concession rate of the opponent. Thus, in deciding demands (concessions) in each period, the terrorists (government officials) can trade off large (small) values of demands (concessions) at the expense of a longer incident with its concomitant greater waiting costs. The incident ends in a settlement when demands equal concessions. If either side is unsatisfied with the progress of the negotiations, refuses to negotiate or views the final outcome as a stalemate, then the incident can end in violence.

Atkinson, Sandler and Tschirhart[32] test three hypotheses derived from the Cross model: (a) Increases (decreases) in bargaining costs to the terrorists induce them to decrease (increase) their demands. Similarly, increases (decreases) in bargaining costs to the government cause it to raise (reduce) concessions. (b) Increases (decreases) in bargaining costs to either side will shorten (lengthen) the duration of the incident. (c) Bluffing will diminish a terrorist group's payoff.

Empirical analysis of these hypotheses used the data from ITERATE 2, which contains the attributes of international terrorist events from 1968–1977.[33] In most instances, our proxies for bargaining costs had the predicted effects on terrorist demands as indicated by equations (1) and (3). To test the second hypothesis, Atkinson, Sandler and Tschirhart[34] used a time-to-failure regression technique, in which the incident's duration was regressed against bargaining costs proxies (e.g., the number of hostages held, type of hostage, sequential release of prisoners). Most costs proxies were significant with the predicted sign. These researchers also tested for the underlying distribution for the length of negotiated incidents. Their results indicated that incidents have a memory: as the incident drags on, the instantaneous probability of the incident ending continually declines. Roughly, the longer an incident goes on, the more difficult it is to end in the ensuing period. Even though the cumulative probability of ending the incident rises with time, the falling instantaneous probability means that the cumulative probability is rising at a declining rate. Thus, the marginal effects, associated with government actions to end an incident, appear to decline as the incident drags on. Atkinson and Sandler are currently examining different econometric specifications in the hope of analysing the efficacy of 'waiting out' the terrorists. The falling marginal impact *might* lead to some negative aspects of the waiting game not previously realised.

THE GOVERNMENT CHOICES

Government officials charged with the onerous task of combating terrorism also face an economic problem: how best to allocate limited resources among alternative terrorist-thwarting activities. This is an especially difficult choice involving uncertainty, long-term versus short-term tradeoffs and a dynamic environment. Uncertainty is germane to this allocation problem, since the future number of any type of event is not known with certainty; hence, the benefits derived from thwarting a particular kind of event cannot be known with certainty. Landes[35] experienced this difficulty when he tried to calculate the net benefits from using metal detectors. Whereas he had no problem in estimating the production and operation costs of these metal detectors, he had greater difficulty in calculating their benefits. These difficulties arose when Landes tried to estimate the number of events thwarted by these measures. To accomplish this task, he used past trends in the number of events. As Landes recognised, his proxy was quite imperfect and neither accounted for terrorists' substitution into other kinds of events nor for skyjackings that were temporarily put off until security countermeasures were derived. Hence, uncertainty also arises because raising the risks or costs to a terrorist group for engaging in one type of act will induce them to substitute into other kinds of acts, which have become relatively less costly.

Long-term versus short-term tradeoffs are involved in the government's choice-theoretical problem because large short-run benefits may come at the expense of significant long-run costs. For example, a negotiated end to a hostage crisis may yield large short-run benefits; but, by demonstrating to other potential hostage-takers that gains can be achieved, the negotiations may have greater long-run costs in terms of additional incidents. The environment surrounding the thwarting of terrorism is changeable owing to the instability of terrorist groups, the rapidly changing technology to counter terrorist actions and alterations in the division of responsibility between different parts of government.

Economic modelling and econometric techniques (i.e., statistical methods applied to economic models) can be used to quantify the substitution phenomenon and to suggest the most efficacious assignment of resources between terrorist-thwarting activities. Currently, Im, Cauley and Sandler are working on three empirical research projects, pertinent to the government choice-theoretical problem. Mickolus[36] has conjectured that there may be cyclical patterns in terrorist activities. The purpose of Im, Cauley and Sandler's first empirical study is to search for cycles or hidden periodicities in time series data on terrorist events. Spectral analysis is an ideal statistical technique to test for any regular or periodic variations in the data.[37] Spectral analytic tests can provide additional evidence of the rational-actor hypothesis (e.g., the complex attack–counterattack phenomenon) and may serve as a basis for government forecasting of terrorist activity.

Spectral analysis has been applied to residuals obtained from estimated trend regressions for the following time series: (a) skyjacking (SJ), (b) barricade and hostage-taking (BH), (c) kidnapping (KN), (d) others (OT) and (e) total (TL). The analysis shows that total terrorist activity (TL) has a twenty-eight-month periodicity (significant at the 0.05 level), which is somewhat longer than Mickolus'[38] hypothesised twenty-four-month cycle. This longer cycle might indicate that the attack–counterattack phenomenon is more complex than initially thought. Three of the four remaining de-trended time series have statistically significant cycles greater than twenty-four months; the sole exception is OT whose cycle is approximately twenty-four months. Skyjacking has the shortest cycle—five and a half months.

Cross-spectral analysis is utilised to provide evidence of the substitution phenomenon. In essence, cross-spectral methods can indicate the degree of association between two times series at individual frequencies. The precise measure of association is signified by the coherency reading, which, when squared, is analogous to the coefficient of determination in regression analysis. A coherency reading to one indicates that two time series are exactly associated in terms of amplitude at each frequency. The phase difference estimate ($|\Delta Ph|$) indicates angular displacement between two series. For a sinusoidal function that repeats every four years, 360° would corresond to the completion of a four-year cycle. A phase difference estimate of π would indicate that two series were completely out of phase (i.e., the two series are 180° out of phase so that as one series is increasing, the other is decreasing). For two types of terrorist activities, a phase difference equal to π would suggest that the activities are perfect substitutes. In short, the empirical issue of whether two terrorist activities with the same periodicity are substitutes boils down to testing the null hypothesis, Ho: $|\Delta Ph| = \pi$. Failure to reject this hypothesis is suggestive of a substitution effect. Our preliminary results indicate substitution between activities. The periodicities for which substitution is significant range from 2.3 to 7.8 months. Hence, substitution appears only for short-run cycles.

Im, Cauley and Sandler's second project involves the use of interrupted time series. This technique allows the investigator to examine the effectiveness of governmental policies designed to thwart particular kinds of terrorist activities (e.g., the installation of metal detectors in 1973, increased embassy security in 1975 and again in 1980). Our results are too preliminary to report at this time.

Finally, Im, Cauley and Sandler will employ STATESPACE modelling (i.e., the estimation of simultaneous, multivariate ARIMA equations) to provide for the most comprehensive test of interdependence between series. This statistical procedure is analogous to the estimation of ordinary econometric simultaneous equation systems. A system of ARIMA equations, where the different types of terrorism are specified to be endogenous, will be identified and estimated. The STATESPACE procedure allows for an investigation of the dynamic feedback effects between or among different types of terrorism, given an exogenous environmental change (e.g., a change in government policy). The STATESPACE model will be estimated for pre-intervention and complete data sets to test for structural changes in the coefficients.

In applying economic theory to the government's resource allocation issue, some observations can be offered with respect to different thwarting activities. We distinguish between a thwarting activity aimed at a single type of event and one aimed at multiple types of events. For example, metal detectors to screen airport passengers are only deployed against one kind of event, while the development of commando forces can be effective against a whole range of events. Similarly, embassy security measures protect solely against takeovers, whereas the development of communication and information networks between autonomous police forces for the purpose of curbing terrorism protects against a wide range of incidents. Clearly, multi-event thwarting actions should be more effective in countering the substitution phenomenon, inasmuch as fewer relative cost differentials are likely to change when a measure applies to a large number of events.

Some multi-event thwarting activities, such as developing information networks between governments and the elimination of safe havens, require international cooperation. Thus, the formation of transnational cooperative agreements is of importance when investigating how best to allocate governmental resources. Economists have begun to study such agreements using a transaction costs approach in which both costs and benefits associated with an agreement are delineated.[39] Furthermore, researchers distinguish between fixed costs, associated with the initial formation of an agreement, and variable costs, expended as the agreement is used to handle specific problems. Once all expected costs and benefits are distinguished, an agreement must provide positive *net* expected transaction benefits to all parties if it is to be viable. Agreements among a large number of governments are, in general, less likely to be viable since the set of agreements that provides each and every participant with positive net transaction benefits may be empty. On a related issue, Sandler, Tschirhart and Cauley[40] have employed the theory of clubs to examine the feasibility of sharing commando forces between nations. Such a sharing arrangement may be a more efficient use of resources than each country providing itself with its own commando forces, a practice common in the world today.

THE NEED FOR DATA

If economic modelling is to make a contribution to our understanding of terrorism and how to curb its spread, theories must be repeatedly tested against data drawn from terrorist incidents. Empirical estimation is required to test hypotheses against the evidence, to quantify the hypothesised relationship and to determine the effectiveness of a policy recommendation. To date, few data banks have been made readily available to academics. It is our hope that more government agencies that have compiled data banks will make the unclassified portions available.

As theoretic models become more complex, the need for additional variables on each event will be required. When collecting time series data, compilers must remember certain practices. A variable's definition must be decided early and all observations must fit the definition. Time series based upon varying definitions pose significant problems for statistical analysis. In most time series methods, the duration of the time series matters greatly to the success of the estimates—i.e., longer series are preferred to shorter series. Hence, time series collectors should try to avoid gaps in the continuity of the data. Finally, fine distinction between variables may assist the researcher when deciding the variables to include.

CONCLUDING REMARKS

No economic theory will ever enlighten us about the behaviour of a terrorist who drives a truckload of dynamite into an embassy compound. When a choice involves certain death, a change in relative costs is going to have little or no effect. Clearly, suicidal terrorist acts cannot be understood or explained by examining tradeoffs at the margin. Furthermore, terrorist acts perpetrated by truly mad or irrational individuals, whose behaviour adheres to no pattern of predictability, are also outside the scope of economic analysis. If, however, the bulk of terrorist incidents were suicidal or committed by mad individuals, then economic analysis would add little to our understanding of terrorism. The facts, however, present a different picture. Although the means used by terrorists to achieve their goals are morally offensive, most terrorist groups appear to display rational behaviour. They react quickly to changes in the costs and benefits associated with various modes of operation by substituting into less costly acts. In addition, they account for risks and diversify their 'portfolios' of acts to limit risks. Even though terrorists are willing to risk their lives, the efforts put into escape plans suggest that life is still important to them.

Without trying to claim too much, we feel that the application of economic analysis to the study of terrorism can augment our understanding. In particular, economic analysis can help explain the substitution phenomenon of terrorists and can suggest ways of countering it. Econometrics can quantify terrorist responses to costs and benefits by estimating offence functions and the terrorist's likelihood of success functions. The application of bargaining theory to incidents involving hostages can help analyse the dynamics and efficacy of negotiations. For example, this application when combined with time-to-failure regression techniques can illustrate the relevant tradeoffs associated with negotiation strategies, such as 'waiting out the terrorists'. We also believe that economics can enlighten us on the deterrent effects of various terrorist-thwarting activities. Finally, economics can assist us to fathom the kinds of agreements that sovereign governments might reach with one another when attempting to curb terrorism.

NOTES

1 Anthony Downs, *An Economic Theory of Democracy*, New York: Harper and Row, 1957.
2 Bonnie Cordes *et al.*, *Trends in International Terrorism, 1982 and 1983*, Santa Monica, California: Rand, 1984.
3 *Ibid.*
4 Scott E Atkinson, Todd Sandler and John Tschirhart, 'On Terrorism: Theoretical and Empirical Aspects', Unpublished manuscript, 1984.
5 M Stohl, 'Introduction: Myths and Realities of Political Terrorism', *in* M Stohl (ed.), *The Politics of Terrorism*, New York: Marcel Dekker, 1979.
6 TR Gurr, 'Some Characteristics of Political Terrorism in the 1960s', *in* M Stohl (ed.), *The Politics of Terrorism*, New York: Marcel Dekker, 1979.
7 Edward F Mickolus, *Transnational Terrorism: A Chronology of Events, 1968–1979*, Westport, Connecticut: Greenwood Press, 1980, pp. xix, xxv.
8 US Central Intelligence Agency, *Patterns of International Terrorism: 1980*, Springfield, Virginia: National Technical Information Service, 1981, p. 11.
9 Edward F Mickolus, *op. cit.*, pp. xii–xxx.
10 Brian M Jenkins, *Terrorism and Beyond: An International Conference on Terrorism and Low-level Conflict*, Santa Monica, California: Rand, 1982.
11 Edward F Mickolus, *op. cit.*, p. xxv.
12 US Central Intelligence Agency, *op. cit.*
13 William M Landes, 'An Economic Study of US Aircraft Hijackings, 1961–1976', *Journal of Law and Economics*, Vol. 21, April 1978, pp. 1–31.
14 *Ibid.*, p. 3.
15 R Thaler and S Rosen, 'The Value of Saving a Life: Evidence from the Labor Market', *in* NE Terleckji (ed.), *Household Production and Function*, New York: Columbia University Press for National Bureau of Economic Research, 1976.
16 Gary S Becker, 'Crime and Punishment: An Economic Approach', *Journal of Political Economy*, Vol. 78, March/April 1968, pp. 169–217.
17 The following articles represent some of the more important ones in the economics of crime literature:
Gary S Becker, *op. cit.*; MK Block and JM Heineke, 'A Labor Theoretic Analysis of the Criminal Choice', *American Economic Review*, Vol. 65, June 1975, pp. 314–325; Isaac Ehrlich, 'Participation in Illegitimate Activities: A Theoretical and Empirical Investigation', *Journal of Political Economy*, Vol. 81, May/June 1973, pp. 521–565; Isaac Ehrlich, 'The Deterrent Effect of Capital Punishment: A Question of Life and Death', *American Economic Review*, Vol. 65, June 1975, pp. 397–417; Isaac Ehrlich and Gary S Becker, 'Market Insurance, Self-insurance, and Self-protection', *Journal of Political Economy*, Vol. 80, July/August 1972, pp. 623–648; JM Heineke, 'Economic Models of Criminal Behavior:

An Overview', *in* JM Heineke (ed.), *Economic Models of Criminal Behavior*, Amsterdam: North Holland, 1978; The Heineke (1978) article provides an especially nice summary of the various models.

18 Isaac Ehrlich, 1975, *op. cit.*

19 *Ibid.*

20 Isaac Ehrlich, 1973, *op. cit.*

21 Gary S Becker, *op. cit.*

22 That is, a risk-averse agent would not pay 50 cents for the chance to win dollar by correctly calling the toss of an unbiased coin.

23 See Todd Sandler, John Tschirhart and Jon Cauley, 'A Theoretical Analysis of Transnational Terrorism', *American Political Science Review*, Vol. 77, March 1983, pp. 36–53; Scott E Atkinson, Todd Sandler and John Tschirhart, 1984, *op. cit.*; Scott E Atkinson, Todd Sandler and John Tschirhart, 'Terrorism in a Bargaining Framework', Unpublished manuscript, 1986.

24 On self-protection and self-insurance, see Ehrlich and Becker, 1972, *op. cit.* and Yang-Ming Chang and Isaac Ehrlich, 'Insurance Protection from Risk and Risk-bearing', *Canadian Journal of Economics*, Vol. 18, August 1985, pp. 574–586.

25 For intertemporal models, a terrorist group's preferences would be an important parameter when trying to predict how it will react to countermeasures imposed by government. A group's rate of time preference refers to their willingness to trade off rewards today for rewards tomorrow. Groups with a high rate of time preference need to receive large compensation to forego present returns for future returns. Such groups will engage in a campaign of terror with large immediate returns.

26 US Department of State, *International Terrorism: Hostage Seizures*, Washington, DC: Office for Combatting Terrorism,. 1983.

27 US Central Intelligence Agency, 1981, *op. cit.*

28 US Department of State, 1983, *op. cit.*

29 Scott E Atkinson, Todd Sandler and John Tschirhart, 1986, *op. cit.*

30 John G Cross, *The Economics of Bargaining*, New York: Basic Books, 1969.

31 John G Cross, 'Negotiation as a Learning Process', *Journal of Conflict Resolution*, Vol. 21, December 1977, pp. 581–606.

32 Scott E Atkinson, Todd Sandler and John Tschirhart, 1986, *op. cit.*

33 These data are described in Edward F Mickolus, *International Terrorism: Attributes of Terrorist Events, 1968-1977* (ITERATE 2), Ann Arbor, Michigan: Inter-university Consortium for Political and Social Research, 1982.

34 Scott E Atkinson, Todd Sandler and John Tschirhart, 1986, *op. cit.*

35 William M Landes, 1978, *op. cit.*

36 Edward F Mickolus, 1982, *op, cit.*, pp. xviii–xix.

37 John M Gottman, *Time-series Analysis: A Comprehensive Introduction for Social Scientists*, Cambridge: Cambridge University Press, 1981.

38 Edward F Mickolus, 1982, *op. cit.*, p. xviii.

39 See, for example, Todd Sandler and Jon Cauley, 'The Design of Supranational Structures', *International Studies Quarterly*, Vol. 21, June 1977, pp. 251–276; Todd Sandler, Jon Cauley and John Tschirhart, 'Toward a Unified Theory of Non market Institutional Structures', *Australian Economic Papers*, Vol. 42, June 1983, pp. 233–254 and the references cited in these two articles.

40 Todd Sandler, John Tschirhart and Jon Cauley, 'A Theoretical Analysis of Transnational Terrorism', *American Political Science Review*, Vol. 77, March 1983, pp. 36–53.

Kidnap and Ransom

Paul Wilkinson

It is of course true that ransom payments are a major source of income for the murderous terrorist groups which plague the innocent. They enable the gangs to buy more weapons, ammunition, safe houses, get-away vehicles, and all the other requisites of a terrorist campaign, and to mount further kidnappings.

In the period 1968–80 kidnapping was the third most popular action by international terrorists after explosive and incendiary bombings and threats. This figure excludes the high levels of domestic terrorist kidnapping in Latin American countries, in parts of the Middle East, and Italy. Moreover international legal measures against kidnapping are woefully inadequate. The long-debated International Convention Against the Taking of Hostages, framed at the UN, lacks adequate enforcement provisions—and specifically exempts vaguely-defined 'national liberation movements' from its key provisions.

There has also been a worrying increase recently in criminal gangs and terrorists using the ransom method to raise funds in countries formerly largely free of kidnappings.

These cases raises some important questions of policy which *all* Western governments and business firms must confront.

First, is it always wrong in principle to pay cash ransom demands?

It is important to recognise the distinction between kidnappings for purely criminal gain (the kind notoriously practised by the Mafia in Italy and the USA) and the political kidnapping generally mounted to secure both cash and political demands for a political cause. *Over 95 per cent of the kidnappings that occur in the world are of the former type.*

Most Western governments have taken the view that cash ransom payments are permissible in cases of purely criminal kidnapping in order to secure the safe release of hostages. A valuable consequence of this approach is that a skilled police force can use the clues yielded by the process of negotiating with the kidnappers in order to track down and convict the criminals after the safe release of the hostage. For example, in the 647 cases of kidnapping in the USA between 1934 and 1974, over 90 per cent of the kidnappers were captured, largely as a result of this policy.

Political kidnappers, however, raise much more intractable problems. These groups almost invariably pose political demands, the most popular being the release of fellow terrorists from jail. Thus they involve the government *directly* in the negotiations—and openly challenge its authority.

Government has a duty to protect all its citizens and to uphold the law. It has to balance the individual's interest in securing safe release against the public interest, which may be seriously harmed by the encouragement of further attacks.

Moreover, democratic governments are in several ways particularly vulnerable in the face of political terrorism. First, unlike private companies, they are accountable to their electorates, and will be held responsible for any worsening threat to the life, liberty and property of citizens. Democratic governments also have far more cumbersome decision-making processes in which all interested parties and agencies will expect to have their say, thus prolonging and complicating any crisis negotiations. But their more serious handicap is the sheer scale of their responsibilities. It is simply impracticable for a Western government to guarantee full protection against terrorism to all its citizens, officials and employees at home and abroad.

It is easy to argue that it is wrong in principle to pay ransom to any political group. It almost certainly encourages other groups to adopt the kidnap weapon; political and cash demands also tend to escalate rapidly, thus putting more innocent lives at risk, and the credibility and authority of government and the legal system are further weakened. The terrorist group stands not only to gain valuable resources for obtaining further arms and supplies, but dramatic publicity and encouragement that it will ultimately achieve victory.

This amounts to a powerful case for a strict no-ransom policy.

Nevertheless, there are circumstances when a private company or family should be permitted to negotiate a straight cash ransom deal for the release of an employee or relative. This is only possible if the terrorist group drops its political demands.

Western governments are right to pursue a strict policy of no ransom deals. It is certain that hundreds of their employees and citizens living and working abroad are more secure against kidnapping attempts as a direct result of this policy. Terrorist groups are less likely to mount complex and costly kidnap operations, with the attendant risks to their own safety, if they know in advance that their victims' employers will not make any concessions.

Much as one would like to see Western internationally based companies adopting a similarly tough approach, I believe it is unrealistic to expect them to do so. The ethics of business life do not encompass the willingness to die for one's company! Employees and their families expect their firms to look after them financially in high-risk employment. What commercial concern could survive for long it its executives and professional employees were told their lives were considered expendable? Moreover, there are now numerous instances of companies paying ransom, and the widespread practice of kidnap and ransom insurance has strengthened this expectation.

A very important point for potential targets to bear in mind is that they should keep as low a profile and be as unpredictable in their movements as is compatible with their efficiency. They should take the best available advice on security and swiftly remedy any weaknesses or gaps in the physical security of their homes, business premises, garages and vehicles.

It is worth remembering that in nearly 90 per cent of cases the kidnappers carry out the snatch while the victim is en route between home and place of work. It is therefore wise to vary your route to and from work, as well as your mode of transport, as much as possible. Drive yourself if possible and avoid using ostentatious or easily recognisable cars. If you are driven to work, sit at the front with the driver and ensure that you are both wearing casual clothes—a chauffeur's uniform is an obvious give-away.

Those who drive regularly in high-risk zones should be given special driving courses (there are many good ones now on the market) to teach them to drive themselves out of ambush attempts, attempts to block intersections, fraudulent 'police checks' and similar terrorist tricks of the trade.

Some of the most daring kidnappings have involved skilful impersonation or subterfuge by members of the gang, so it is particularly important to ensure that you know the identity or bona fides of all those who seek access of premises where they could seize a potential target. Card-key systems, lapel identity tags and similar systems all have loopholes, but if administered thoroughly they do constitute a deterrent.

If preventive measures fail, the safe recovery of the victim is very much in the hands of the police, the victim's family, friends and business associates, and may also depend on the goodwill and cooperation of the media and members of the public.

Even so, there are ways in which the hostage can help his or her own survival even under the most gruelling conditions of incarceration, and physical and mental torture. First, they should concentrate of keeping physically and mentally alert, using mental and physical exercises whenever possible. This will help them to endure their experience with less long-term damage to their physical and psychological well-being. It also helps them to be fit and ready to take any opportunity to escape, or to protect their own safety, in the event of a rescue attempt by police.

The effects of a kidnapping, even on a large company, can be extremely damaging: normal trade and productive activity is disrupted; staff are in danger of becoming demoralised and isolated. The financial costs to companies, in terms of ransom payments and other related extortion threats, can also be huge, and the public image of the firm may be gravely damaged if the crisis is mishandled.

If you or your company are potential targets in a high risk area you should get expert advice *now*. The costs of neglect are potentially enormous.

The Financing of Terror

J Adams

Both the British Government and the terrorists appear to have unwittingly joined forces to perpetuate the myth of NORAID's significance in the IRA scheme of things. The British Government, anxious to undercut any potential political interference from the United States, and in particular from Congress, have played on the guilt of the American people by constantly trading off the influence of NORAID—portrayed as the main supplier of guns and money to the IRA—and that of the terrorist bombing in the province. This has successfully defused any coherent and effective US political support for the campaign to get Britain out of Northern Ireland.

For their part the IRA have been only too happy to have the United States portrayed as their main supporter. It gives them much-needed credibility.

The assassination of Lord Mountbatten on 27 August 1979 appears to have marked a watershed in NORAID's affairs. Until that time the US Government had been very reluctant to take any steps to curb the activities of the IRA supporters in the United States, and there had been a relatively free flow of both arms and cash to the terrorists in Belfast. However, after the Mountbatten killing, where several members of his family died, and the assassination on the same day of eighteen British soldiers at Warrenpoint there seems to have been a change of heart in the United States. A number of FBI investigations were instigated that resulted in a series of trials of suspected IRA financiers and gun smugglers. By the middle of 1983 the organisation was forced to establish a fund for the various defendants who were coming before the courts. However, even that fund has not been sufficient to counter the drain on the IRA's resources that the prosecutions by US courts has caused. The shortage of cash has also hit NORAID's ability to supply guns and amunition to the IRA. Of those guns that have been recovered by the security forces in Northern Ireland, less than one-quarter have originated in the United States. So there again the influence of NORAID is less than popularly imagined.

In the early 1970s, shortly after the latest outbreak of violence began, the IRA was a very amateur organisation living hand-to-mouth on donations and handouts from sympathisers. To that extent they fit into the pattern of most terrorist organisations in their infancy. However, the organisation swiftly changed its nature so it was able to develop a more coherent financial structure. It is always the case that any terrorist organisation to survive needs to develop a more sophisticated financial apparatus than the common image, which is that of the gunman robbing a bank or kidnapping an individual to raise cash for the next supply of guns, to pay for the next robbery.

In the case of the IRA, they began by an extensive campaign of intimidation to raise protection money. They would normally sell protection to local shop owners, publicans and industrialists. Typically this would involve small concerns which had the advantage for the terrorists of being low risk and a regular source of income. As the terrorist business expanded, however, the type of protection it offers and the cost has expanded as well. Today, while the corner pub might still be contributing around £50 per week to a particular terrorist group, in the meantime every major business in the province has been sucked into the protection racket.

Ten years ago protection would be demanded in a quite straight-forward manner. The gang, typically three or four strong, would march into the premises, brandish a weapon and demand money; if the owner did not pay up they might break a few windows or beat him up. Today, the whole operation has become more sophisticated and gentlemanly. Any contractor or business new to an area controlled by one of the paramilitary organisations is approached by representatives of the group concerned, but now the approach is generally made by an apparently legitimate security company that has been established by a terrorist group to provide a legitimate veneer for what remains a simple racket.

These new and apparently legitimate sources of funds have been increasingly popular among the terrorists. The Belfast Yellow Pages in 1970 listed only seven security firms for the city but today there are more than sixty. Of course, the legitimate security firms have had extraordinary difficulties competing with terrorist-supported ones. Although they may be able to match the price, they do not benefit from the concealed threat of a beating or shooting to back up a profit bid.

This is only one of a number of operations that the IRA run which have gained semi-legitimacy in the extraordinary climate of Northern Ireland. The most public of those operations are the black cabs run by the IRA. Early thinking behind the black cab operation was that the IRA needed a method of circulating the illegal funds they were generating and a cash business like cabs seemed an easy answer. This was the equivalent of Al Capone's venture into the laundry business (hence the laundering of money). Once the IRA made the decision to move into the protection business in 1972 the High Command made a very sound business decision in taking the competition on to remove it from the field. A sustained campaign was launched against the city-run bus system and buses were systematically stoned and fire bombed. The media portrayed this as the repressed Catholics of Belfast expressing their frustrations through aggressive actions. In fact it was the IRA clearing the way for their own transport operation. City Bus, which operates the transport system in Belfast, had more than three hundred buses destroyed at a cost of nearly £10 million so that the IRA could get a monopoly on transport in the Catholic areas. In June 1972 the IRA's first consignment of five second-hand black cabs arrived from London. Within three months six hundred cabs were operating and the buses have been driven off the road. The IRA's taxi network consists of two cab companies operating as fronts for the organisation. They employ eighteen full-time workers, own two garages and an interest in a tyre company: all-told the companies claim assets in excess of £1 million.

The IRA's taxi companies, Falls Taxis and Peoples Taxis, together have around three hundred and fifty cabs and employ eight hundred drivers. Each driver pays £35 per week to be a member of the Taxi Drivers' Association and contributes £500 per year for group insurance which is organised centrally by the association. When the cabs first began to operate no attempt was made to license them or to comply with the law requiring insurance. However the Government introduced legislation that has forced the cabs to become more legitimate. They are now insured through their own company and have become re-insured through the legitimate market at Lloyds in London.

The IRA control all aspects of the taxi business. The cab drivers generally rent their cabs from provisional companies, have them repaired at a provo garage and buy their fuel from provo diesel companies. Such control over the city's transport is also useful to the provisionals for the movement of guns and assassins around the city.

With their eye on the main chance the Protestants quickly followed the provos' example and now, under the auspices of the North Belfast Mutual Association, the Ulster Volunteer Force (UVF) operates around ninety cabs in the Shankhill Road and Shore Road areas of Belfast. Officially, the cab drivers pay the association £1.50 per week to cover administration costs and if they buy their diesel from the Association they save an additional £150 per year in insurance premiums. However, it is generally believed that a person operating a black cab has to pay an unofficial initial fee of £90 and a weekly sum of £30. The taxis are also suspected of acting as a collection agency for people paying collection money to the UVF. Each driver is suspected of being charged with bringing in between £3500 and £4000 each week to the UVF coffers.

These sums are relatively insignificant when they are compared with those generated by other criminal activities such as frauds on building sites and the sale of legal and illegal drink in Northern Ireland's clubs.

In the early 1970s the official IRA began a series of frauds on building sites involving tax exemption certificates which enabled them to collect a thirty per cent income tax rather than handing it over to the Government. A major contractor who obtains a contract from a large organisation normally subcontracts work to smaller companies such as plasterers and electricians. If a subcontract is worth say, £800,000 per year, the major contractor would pay the subcontractor in twelve monthly payments of £66,000. The sub-contractor should then put aside around thirty per cent of his total wages bill to account for income tax from his employees.

However, because of the irregular nature of the business, subcontractors have been given special concessions by the the Inland Revenue which allow them to pay the tax in one sum at the end of the year. To enable the contractor to do this, the Inland Revenue issues a tax exemption certificate. Unfortunately, forged tax exemption certificates originally imported from England and selling for between £3000 and £13,500 have become widely available. This has enabled some subcontractors to claim that they, in turn, have passed work to other subcontractors and they can show tax exemption certificates to prove it. However, when the Inland Revenue attempts to trace the last buidling company in the chain, they find it does not exist and is often registered in the name of a dead man.

This particular type of fraud has become very popular among terrorist organisations.

When the authorities, and particularly the police, began to notice the fraud, they decided the whole matter was the responsibility of the Inland Revenue which has its own fraud investigation department. The Revenue decided that the fraud, judged purely in financial terms, was too small to bother about (at that time it generated less than £170,000 per year) and the investigation was halted. Ten years later the fraud has grown, according to police estimates—which the Northern Ireland office and others dispute—into a £40 million per year business from which the various paramilitary groups, both Protestant and Catholic, take a net annual profit of around £10 million.

The Protestant paramilitary organisation, the UDA, dabbled briefly in the building frauds business at the end of the 1970s but backed out after they discovered that the vast majority of the building work was taking place in the depressed Catholic areas. Instead of continuing to develop their particular end of the fraud in competition with the IRA, they did what any sensible businessman would do: they made a deal. Regular meetings are now held between the provisionals and the UDA resulting in Catholic workers under the control of the provos working at building sites in UDA-run sections of Belfast with the provisionals passing on an agreed percentage of the profits of the fraud to the UDA. (This is not the only area where the IRA and the Protestant paramilitary cooperate: they regularly meet to discuss where large robberies should take place. So, for example, one month the UDA may carry out a robbery in the Catholic area and then pass the goods to the IRA to fence and the next month it may be the other way around. This has the unfortunate consequence of crossing normal police lines of enquiry and makes life extremely difficult for those anxious to catch the robbers.)

Arguably the most successful of the terrorist business ventures, which perfectly combines the need to make money with social influence, was the development of the drinking clubs. As lawlessness began in Belfast in the beginning of the 1970s a large number of illegal drinking clubs—or shebeens as they are known locally—sprang up all over the city. This was due partly to the local demand for cheap liquor and partly to the terrorist need to re-circulate hot money while, at the same time, providing a social service. Most of the breweries paid the IRA for protection and were willing to supply drink at cut prices in return for protection for the pubs they control and for their distribution warehouses. The shebeens in Belfast and elsewhere in the province were, almost without exception, run by members of different terrorist organisations, either Protestant or Catholic.

Belfast rapidly took on the air of Chicago during prohibition, except that there was little attempt to conceal the existence of these new speakeasies from the authorities. Eventually, under pressure from the British Government, the police moved in and in a series of raids in 1977 shut down large numbers of shebeens (one was even found operating in an abandoned bus). The paramilitary groups began to work inside the law and some even applied for licences to operate publicly. The Government found this perfectly acceptable because legitimate front men were apparently used. In 1983 nearly six hundred members-only clubs were registered, with 254,270 members who bought over £27 million worth of drinks. The terrorist groups have operated the clubs within the law, although they often placed their own illegal slot machines along side those that may legitimately line the walls of the club. Along with the coercion that gets the machines into the pubs in the first place, comes an agreement from the club management that the provos or the UVF will receive all the proceeds from the machines. Since the police estimate that one machine can net £27,000 per year, this means that the terrorists make far more from slot machines than they ever did from NORAID.

This whole business has generated an enormous amount of money for the terrorist organisations. For example, the headquarters of Sinn Fein social life in Belfast is the Pound Lovey Bar, where £500,000 was spent on refurbishing the bar and building which includes a twelve-table snooker hall. The Pound Lovey is only one of twenty-two such bars in West Belfast that owe their allegiance to the IRA. The development of such a wide-ranging financial empire in Northern Ireland has enabled the IRA to become entrenched in the society. At the same time, the leadership of the IRA have been able to fund a two-tier campaign which has at its core terrorism but in a more public face has manifested itself in election campaigns, both local and national. In these campaigns, which are enormously expensive, the IRA have been fairly successful at getting a share of the vote that hovers around the thirteen per cent mark, although there are some indications that this may be falling.

The IRA have in part been able to succeed in this two-tier approach because the security forces, and indeed, the police, have concentrated their counterterrorist efforts in gaining good intelligence that predicts where the next terrorist attack may take place so they can stop it before it happens, or in sweeping up after a terrorist attack takes place, hopefully arresting the perpetrators of the act. The lot of investigating the finances of terrorist organisations has fallen largely on the police. However, they have in the past been ill-equipped to deal with this area as it falls outside their normal remit of simple criminal activity. It is only recently that the Royal Ulster Constabulary has established a squad that is specifically looking at terrorist funding. But the squad, known as C19, has only fifteen members and two supervisors, and although they have had limited success it is difficult to see how they will effectively combat a terrorist network which now permeates every level of Northern Ireland business. The IRA is the best European example of how a terrorist organisation can evolve from a rather low-level hand-to-mouth operation into a relatively sophisticated economic empire. However, we have to look to the Middle East and the Palestine Liberation Organisation (PLO) to fully understand the extent to which terrorist groups can change their nature.

Just off Sha Bandar Square in downtown Damascus is a three-storey building of light brown cement. It looks more like the office of a low-level government department, unpainted since the colonials departed, than the headquarters of one of the wealthiest multinational corporations in the world.

During the summer, the ground-floor rooms will be cooled by large, gently whirring fans that do little to counter the oppressive heat. Although the floors appear to have been swept, smudges and dirty fingerprints cover the light switches, and the general atmosphere is one of decay—all reminiscent of a scene from the film Casablanca.

The director's office is on the second floor. Outside the wooden door to his office is a telex machine with a list of international codes on a stand in front of it. The two secretaries who guard the entrance each have an IBM typewriter and a modern multibutton telephone sitting on their desks. Piles of economic digests and reports gather dust on the floor and against the wall.

The dark wood furnishings in the director's office are a cross between inferior mass-market 1930s art deco and 1940s utility. A large desk with two telephones, sofas and coffee tables covered in ageing coffee stains, full ashtrays, a few books and endless dust complete the decaying image.

Behind the desk is a locked heavy steel door leading from the fourth floor to the top storey. Behind this barrier lies a different world: a world of high-tech 1980s state-of-the-art computers; a world light-years away from the seedy old-fashioned appearance of the floors below, and even further removed from the popular image of the PLO terrorist.

In air-conditioned splendour, this whole floor, divided into two rooms, houses banks of Honeywell reel-to-reel computers. The machines are carefully tended by young white-coated Palestinians, most of whom have been trained in the United States, some at the Massachusetts Institute of Technology and Harvard.

These computers manage part of the PLO's worldwide financial empire. Some unofficial sources have estimated that the PLO has assets in excess of \$15 billion, but this is an exaggeration. However, it is generally agreed that, through the Palestine National Fund (PNF), the PLO has control of some \$2 billion in assets, and taking into account the assets of all the different groups that make up the PLO, as much as \$5 billion may be salted away. In 1983, approximately \$600 million in current-account income was generated for the PNF, and of this, less than \$100 million came in the form of donations from wealthy Palestinians or Arab nations: the balance was made up by investments all over the world. The total annual income of the various PLO factions runs to well in excess of \$1.25 billion. This sum, which is greater than the total budget of some Third World countries, makes the PLO the richest and most powerful terrorist group in the world.

The first head of the PNF was Abdul-Majeed Shoman. He is currently chairman of the Arab Bank which has assets in excess of $10 billion and branches all over the world. Quite accurately the Arab Bank is known as the PLO's banker as they handle many of the investments of the PLO in Wall Street, the City of London and elsewhere. Based in Amman, the bank has a reputation for integrity and conservatism which is quite justified. By 1983 the total assets of the bank had increased by $860 million and deposits by $840 million reaching respectively $10.4 billion and $9.9 billion. Shareholders' equity rose from $400 million in 1982 to $445 million in 1983. The Bank's conservatism has resulted in its retaining seventy per cent of its assets in cash and short-term bank deposits. Around one-third of the Bank's assets are in Europe, about one-quarter in Jordan. Of the remaining forty-two per cent, thirty per cent are in Saudi Arabia and the Gulf states and the rest in the Lebanon, Egypt and the United States.

The Bank has not only been useful in acting as an investment advisor and manager, but also in a more subtle way. For example, if a Middle East entrepreneur approaches the Arab Bank to perhaps develop an apartment block in one of the Gulf states, the local Arab Bank manger may tactfully suggest that the entrepreneur uses this or that company which may have close Palestinian links. In this way, the Palestinians have been able to prosper over the last twenty years. The traditional image of the PLO has it that they receive a vast majority of their income from sympathisers, either in the Gulf countries or from individual Palestinians spread around the world. This is in fact very wide of the mark. In 1983 the PLO received less than $100 million in state-sponsored donations, one-sixth of the total and in 1984 the figure was even less with only the Kuwaiti and Saudis continuing to give cash. Ten years ago, the PLO was almost entirely dependent on state donations for its existence. However, should all state funding be withdrawn today, it would undoubtedly be noticed, but the PLO would survive. This misunderstanding of the nature of the new PLO has led to fundamental miscalculations in the fight to counter the terrorist acts that are committed in their name. For example, when the Israeli's moved north into Lebanon in Operation Peace for Galilee in 1982, they believed that they would, if not wipe out, certainly severely damage the operations of the PLO. But this has not been the case. In the space of four days once Operation Peace for Galilee had begun, the PLO moved $400 million out of Lebanon and into banks in Switzerland. Although the war undoubtedly cost them several hundred million dollars in lost revenue from operations in Lebanon, most of their investments are located elsewhere and the organisation has been able to survive perfectly well without the income from the Lebanon. Even now, the PLO are beginning to move back into Lebanon and are once again posing a real threat to Israel's security.

The PLO's intelligent financial policy has left them with a wide-ranging portfolio that covers everything from banks to property, chicken farms, five huge estates in Africa, apartment blocks, factories and other semi-legitimate or conventional businesses. On the other hand, the PLO has not given up its attachment to the more illegitimate methods of raising money. For example, the Beka'a Valley in Lebanon is currently generating some $400 million per year in income entirely from the production and sale of drugs. These drugs are distributed widely through the Middle East and recently the PLO has spread its tentacles even further to include both Australia and Europe. In both cases police have discovered a disturbing similarity in the exchange of drugs for both cash and guns which has led to fears of a new threat which has been decribed as 'Narco-terrorism'.

As the PLO has become more financially sophisticated so it has become more ambitious in its financial enterprises. Two years ago it lent $12 million in soft loans to the fledgling government in Nicaragua. And again in that country it has done much to realise its ambitions of having a fully fledged national airline. The PLO donated a 727 airliner to Aeronica, the Nicaraguan national airline, at the end of 1979 and since then the PLO has donated several others to the airline, leading some forces to suggest that the organisation now owns twenty-five per cent of Aeronica although this has been impossible to confirm. What is known is that Carlos Zarouk, the Nicaraguan Minister of Transport, is of Palestinian origin and has links with the PLO, particularly through a gentleman called George Hallak, who, some sources say, is the key figure in the PLO attempt over the past ten years to purchase and run aircraft all over the world.

George Dibbs Hallak was born in Akka in the Lebanon (formerly Acre, Palestine) in 1940 and now lives in Athens where he has two houses. He first came to the attention of the authorities in 1968 when he was involved in various ticket frauds and he seems to have come to the attention of the PLO in the late 1970s when they turned his knowledge of the airline business to good advantage. Using Hallak's expertise and its own money, the PLO is now believed to have bought substantial shares in Maldive Airways and it also has some involvement with Sierra Leone Airways which has two Palestinians on its main board.

In 1984, Hallak went to both Austrialia and New Zealand to purchase two F28 Fokker Fellowship aircraft. Both were flown to Sanaa, the capital of North Yemen, from where one flew on to the Maldives and the other disappeared. Hallak is now the General Manager (Operations) of Aeronica, and there have been rumours that he may be appointed the Nicaraguan Ambassador to Greece. Such a powerful position for a man who is known to have links with the PLO will not be welcomed by the aircraft industry or counterterrorist forces.

Paying no tax and completely unrestricted by borders or government authority, the PLO has been able to invest in a wide portfolio in all the major Western centres. These investments have been handled well enough to give the PLO a return that would be the envy of many major multinational corporations.

Any discussion of the future of the PLO should concentrate on the organisation's evolution from a gang of hoodlums who hijacked planes in the 1960s into a sophisticated multinational corporation that uses terrorism and sound investment planning in equal measure to achieve its aims. In the same way as Israel would not disappear from any map of the Middle East, the PLO has grown to such a size and is so financially secure that it would be virtually impossible to remove.

As a serious, direct threat to modern society, terrorism in general has been remarkably unsuccessful. The roll call of famous terrorist organisations which arose in the 1960s and 1970s, briefly starred and then disappeared, is long and includes such famous names as Baader–Meinhof, the Japanese Red Army, the Weathermen and the Symbionese Liberation Army.

Other groups that began in those days, when it appeared to many that revolution was sweeping the world and democracies were all under threat, have done rather better. The reason is that they were better capitalists. To thrive, terrorism has had to compromise and adapt to changing circumstances. In every case, it has been an extraordinary metamorphosis.

Terrorism is generally perceived as being the pursuit of political ends through violent means and certainly, in the popular perception, involves such things as bank robberies and the kidnapping or killing of innocent civilians. In part, this remains true, but a high degree of sophistication has been added to this so that the terrorist is now more likely to conform to the image of a middle-ranking clerk than to a gun-toting hoodlum.

It seems that, to survive, terrorist groups need to cross an economic divide that separates those who live a hand-to-mouth existence from those who can actually plan ahead. All those groups which have come and gone in the last twenty years have failed to cross that divide. They have either been plagued by leaders who could not plan beyond the next bank robbery and therefore never had enough funds to expand their power base, or they had leaders who were seduced by the easy money and forgot their political principles among the fast cars and fancy apartments. The few who remain have cooler heads and have been able to see that good financial planning means having enough cash to buy and keep support, to pay for arms and to build a propaganda base among the people the organisation claims to represent.

However, while the terrorist has learned to survive and, in some cases, prosper in a hostile world, counterterrorism has remained largely static. This is partly because politicians who dictate the response to the terrorist threat always look for quick and easy solutions that will placate a fearful electorate. Therefore, the emphasis in counterterrorism is always on the arrest or killing of terrorists—in other words, a 'head count' of terrorists killed or captured is the yardstick by which success is measured.

This attitude is obviously inadequate given the hundreds of IRA prisoners currently in British jails, the hundreds of PLO supporters held by the Israelis and the thousands of Red Brigades members imprisoned by the Italians. In every case, the incarceration of large numbers of their members seems to have made little impact on the ability of a terrorist organisation to survive.

In response to the wishes of their political masters, counter-terrorist specialists tend to target the areas which they know will meet with approval; thus, all counterterrorism is aimed at dealing with the armed threat as and when it arrives. It is, of course, right that considerable effort should be put into active counterterrorism, with a high level of training and the best equipment being allocated to respond to the threat, but this is obviously not enough to counter those organisations which have managed to cross the economic divide and appear to prosper no matter what is done to reduce their numbers by conventional methods. While the way terrorism is popularly perceived has remained largely static, a number of myths have been created around the whole phenomenon. These have tended to confuse the issue and the judgements made concerning what should be done to counter the threat.

One major myth is that the Soviet Union and its allies have been largely responsible for the growth of international terrorism. This theory suggests that the Soviets and their friends are the architects of a grand conspiracy which is designed to undermine and eventually to overthrow the Western deomocracies, which will then automatically fall into the Soviet orbit.

Western journalists and authors have found it convenient to repeat the grand conspiracy theory without making any effort to check their facts. For those who come from the political right, it is obviously self-serving to paint the image of the Russian Bear as an all-embracing evil that is behind every wrinkle in what would otherwise be a smooth blanket covering the democratic world. Israel, too, finds it convenient to blame the USSR for the activities of the PLO. In the same way as some Americans can see a Cuban hand in much that goes on in Central America, so the Israelis, by pointing to Soviet support of the PLO, can rally the West to their position. They argue that, if the Palestinians are allowed to establish a state, it will, given the USSR's continued support for the organisation, merely be a Soviet client state.

However, the Soviets have never provided funding for the PLO, and the organisation's leaders talk in the most insulting terms about their alleged ally. Not only have the Soviets never contributed financially to the PLO cause, but they make the Palestinians pay in hard-earned foreign exchange for all arms delivered.

It is certainly the case that the Soviet Union and her allies have consistently supplied arms (almost invariably for hard cash) to a number of terrorist organisations, but this seems to be done on the basis that anything which undermines the West is to be encouraged. It is very difficult to discern an effective or coherent strategy behind all of this.

The conspiracists also make much of the point that terrorism is a uniquely Western phenomenon and that it therefore must be inspired by the Communists.

Terrorism has been able to flourish in the West because a free society is full of the blood on which a terrorist leech can feed: easy access to money supplies, good communications, a free press and a liberal judiciary. By contrast, the Eastern Bloc is invariably totally repressive and has scant regard for human rights, while any pretence at a judicial system is little more than a joke. Add to that the overwhelming might of the different police agencies that form such a pervasive part of Communist life and there is very little opportunity for terrorism to survive.

Of all those who have supported terrorism, the person who best illustrates the changing nature of that support, as well as the static perception of terrorism by the public, is Colonel Muammar al-Qaddafi, the leader of Libya. For many years, Qaddafi has been portrayed as the godfather of international terrorism, the man to whom all terrorists can go caps-in-hand to have their pockets filled with gold and as many Kalashnikovs as they might require to further a revolution. Astonishing as this may seem, particularly in the light of recent US government statements about Libya's support of terrorism, this image is hopelessly out of date and is nothing like an accurate reflection of Qaddafi or the nature of international terrorism today.

For the last five years, Qaddafi has supplied almost no money to terrorist groups. Even the PLO, which still receives the full brunt of supportive propaganda from the Libyan publicity machine, has received no money since 1982, much to the disgust of the PLO leadership, who have come to realise they cannot trust even the most extreme Arab leaders.

Qaddafi, of course, still has ambitions outside his own borders, but they have had to be contained within budgetary constraints. His agents still operate extensively in the countries of North Africa, and Qaddafi has proclaimed that he would like to see Libyan-style revolutions occur all over that region. However, this is a far cry from the early 1970s, when Qaddafi was supporting everybody from the Baader–Meinhof gang to the Japanese Red Army.

Qaddafi has also remained in the public eye because of his current habit of sending hit squads abroad to liquidate members of the Libyan opposition. However, the activities of these assassins have been confined to shooting their own people, and there is no evidence of a Qaddafi masterplan to send his hit squads around the world to attack world leaders and thus force revolution upon reluctant democracies.

While Qaddafi seems to have matured, the West continues to view him as if it were still 1969 and he still the young radical threatening to change the world. In particular, the United States maintains the myth that Qaddafi is the main architect behind the continued existence and growth of international terrorism as a threat to modern society, and has called for a total boycott of Libya and a trade embargo to try and force Qaddafi to mend his ways. There is, however, little enough evidence to support American allegations that Qaddafi is the prime mover behind world terrorism, and her allies have tended to dismiss such calls as mere rhetoric that shows a rather naive view of Qaddafi and a lack of understanding of the evolutionary process that has affected terrorism.

The PLO is the group that has most benefited from cash donations from governments, but even with this most famous and closely examined of terrorist organisations, there are serious misconceptions, including the widely held view that the PLO depends on Arab governments for its survival. This is another myth—it is no longer the case. Even if all Arab aid to the PLO were cut off tomorrow, the PLO would merely have to cut back its annual budget by one-sixth. It would still have $500 million to play with, and the organisation would undoubtedly survive.

Over the last twenty years, the PLO's income profile has completely reversed. In the early days, the organisation was entirely dependent on handouts from rich Arabs. Today, out of its $600 million annual income, more than $500 million comes from investments, with donations from Arab leaders making up the balance. If finances of all the different groups that fall under the PLO umbrella are taken into account, a total annual income of $1.25 billion and assets of around $5 billion are involved.

Following the example of the PLO, those terrorist groups that have survived the first flush of revolutionary fervour have quickly realised that they cannot count on outside aid for their survival. All too often, such aid depends on personal whim or has unacceptable conditions attached. It is hardly surprising, therefore, that successful terrorist groups have in recent times become largely self-financing. Certainly, outside aid is always a help, but today, for groups such as the IRA and the PLO, it is not crucial to survival.

In some respects, it could be argued that terrorism, once it has evolved sufficiently, actually performs a valuable social service. After all, the primary aim of the terrorist is to win over the broad mass of the people, and in the case of IRA, this has involved the introduction of an employment programme (albeit illegal) and various social benefits. These might be welcome in other circumstances, but nothing should be allowed to give the impression that terrorism pays. If it is allowed free rein to alter its direction and build a strong financial base, then it is able to advance politically. In crude terms, money buys votes and as the IRA have learned, the combination of the bullet and the ballot box is a very powerful one.

In 1981, 30,000 people voted for Bobby Sands, the imprisoned IRA leader who was on a hunger strike in the Maze Prison and who died four weeks later as MP for Fermanagh and South Tyrone. A year later 64,000 people voted for Sinn Fein, the political wing of the IRA, in the Northern Ireland Assembly elections. At the 1983 General Election the Sinn Fein vote rose to 103,000 and in the 1984 elections for the European Parliament, the Sinn Fein candidate, although beaten, received 13.3 per cent of the vote. This has been achieved by a terrorist organisation which, ten years ago, was dismissed, with some justification, as a bunch of hoodlums with machine guns. The IRA has moved on, but counterterrorism has remained stuck in the same rut.

Using the resources generated by their income and their power base among the working class, the IRA have been building a network of advice centres across the country that will, in effect, act as a counterpoint to the Government's own social service outlets. This, combined with their taxi service and other social pressure groups, will win the IRA many supporters.

So firm is the established image of terrorism in the minds of politicians and civil servants around the world that it is going to be exceptionally difficult to bring about a change in perception. What is required is a two-tier approach which stops the bombers while at the same time undercutting the economic base that feeds them.

Unfortunately, the changing nature of international terrorism has not yet been appreciated by those who dictate policy in the West. The current US administration has done much to raise the consciousness of the Western world regarding the threat that terrorism poses, and the United States has set itself up as the guardian of the free world and as the leading nation among the Western democracies, a role that it rightly assumes. The bombing of the American embassy and the Marine compound in Beirut in 1983 graphically and tragically brought home to the American Government and the world just how real the terrorist threat is today. These attacks gave added impetus to the US campaign against terrorism, but unfortunately even that impetus and subsequent policy appear to have been based on assumptions about terrorism that are at least ten years out of date.

It is time for Western governments to realise that there is no such quick and easy solution to the terrorist problem. Occasional short-term gains, while politically satisfying, will have to be sacrificed to achieve longer term benefits which will do more to undercut the economic power base of international terrorism. As much effort should be devoted to tracing the sources of money, the bank accounts and the investments of terrorist groups as is spent on countering the bomber and the assassin.

There is a natural reluctance among both the intelligence and the military communities to share information or to pass on responsibility for a role that has hitherto been their remit. Yet, it is time for their political masters to insist that the job of combating terrorism is broader than simple kill-counts.

V

Terrorism and the Media

Terrorism and Propaganda: Problem and Response

M Tugwell

Propaganda is defined by the North Atlantic Alliance as any information, ideas, doctrines or special appeals disseminated to influence the opinion, emotions, attitudes or behaviour of any specified group in order to benefit the sponsor either directly or indirectly.[1] Terrorism, in Grant Wardlaw's definition, is the use, or threat of use, of violence by an individual or a group, whether acting for or in opposition to established authority, when such action is designed to create extreme anxiety and/or fear-inducing effects in a target group larger than the immediate victims with the purpose of coercing that group into acceding to the political demands of he perpetrators.[2]

Propaganda and terrorism are identical insofar as they both seek to influence a mass audience in a way that is intended to benefit the sponsor. But while terror has a singular purpose—inducing fear and uncertainty—propaganda can and does serve every imaginable purpose from religion to politics to commerce. Terrorism is, as the nineteenth-century anarchists claimed, 'propaganda by deed'; in Brian Jenkins' more recent formulation, it is theatre.[3] Terrorism may be other things as well, but there is no doubting the very close links between these subjects. Indeed, terror might be seen as a sub-species of propaganda.

Yet terrorism is also a sub-species of revolution, which is a struggle for power. The key to that power is popular allegiance, whether given voluntarily or out of fear. Allegiance is transferred from regime to revolutionaries by shifts in the popular conception of relative credibility and legitimacy. Credibility rests on demonstrated ability to control events—being in command, running a government or an alternative power structure, winning small battles. Legitimacy is the public's conception of a right to rule based on whatever values the public may associate with that right. The legal definition of legitimacy, which sides with the incumbent regime, ceases to apply once the government's credibility is eroded. Consequently the fight for allegiance consists of myriad small battles over credibility and legitimacy, in which the two issues become inextricably mixed.

Clearly, in its revolutionary context, terrorism is very much more than a series of front-page stories. The direct and obvious link between terrorism and propaganda is merely the visible tip of an iceberg. Whether terrorism is part of a wider campaign of revolution or a free-standing conflict form, its political objectives can only be reached by a complex psychological–military process in which propaganda and violence are like a boxer's two fists. It is this operational propaganda that needs to be better understood and countered, because without it terrorism would fight with one had tied behind its back, and ought to be more easily defeated.

Revolution's three key ingredients are leadership, organisation and inspiration. Michael Elliott-Bateman calls the last ingredient the 'cultural–spiritual', and regards it as the foundation of the struggle.[4] Terrorism, as a sub-species of revolution or as a component, also relies on these essential ingredients: it too elevates the cultural–spiritual element to pride of place.

The cultural–spiritual inspiration goes far beyond normal political persuasion. The latter is concerned with concrete issues; it is the stuff of ballot boxes and activities *within* the existing political and social dispensation. Revolutionary inspiration transcends conventional politics and demands the overthrow of the existing order, existing laws, existing beliefs and ways of thinking, and their replacement by some higher truth. Of course concrete issues may feature in this vision of the future, but they are re-interpreted within the new cultural–spiritual value system.

Revolutionary inspiration may come from religion, nationalism, racism or political ideology, or from a mixture of these and other sources. Whatever the cause, the cultural–spiritual element must fire the imagination by revealing the beauty of the promised land; it must justify the resort to violence by depicting the incumbent regime as deaf to reason and incapable of reform; it must cast the regime and its institutions as the incarnation of evil, because they stand between the people and the promised land; and it must assure audiences that, with good on their side, they will surely overcome. These three themes of virtue, evil and inevitable victory dominate terrorist propaganda aimed at the convinced activists.

Because the regime and its institutions are evil, true believers are not bound by its laws, customs and moral codes, only by the higher truths and laws of the cause. This inspiration distinguishes the revolutionary, including the political terrorist, from the criminal. Whereas the profit-motivated activist may be amoral, and may commit crimes knowing them to be immoral, he or she expects to be judged by conventional standards. The true revolutionary, however, insists that violent crimes committed for the cause are just, and argues that he or she is answerable only to the revolutionary leadership, or to some higher authority such as God or history.

Revolutionary propaganda's first priority is to create such a circle of true believers. The objective is total, unquestioning loyalty. There is, therefore, a need for the totalitarian propaganda described by Jacques Ellul, which he insists can exist only within a tightly disciplined organisation:

> Without organization, psychological incitement leads to excesses and deviation of action in the very course of development. Through organization, the proselyte

> receives an overwhelming impulse that makes him act with the whole of his being. He is actually transformed into a religious man in the psychosociological sense of the term; justice enters into the action he performs because of the organization of which he is a part.[5]

Ellul explains how action makes propaganda's effect irreversible, how he who acts in obedience to propaganda can never go back. To justify his past action, the recruit must now *believe* the propaganda because he has broken old rules, values and friendships. The deeper his actions carry him into the world of reversed morality, the more dependent he becomes on propaganda to sustain him.[6]

Baruch Hazan suggests that propaganda must first attract an audience's attention by penetrating the 'absorption screen', a relatively easy task, and that, to be effective, it must then penetrate the 'personality screen'. During the latter process the beliefs, values, attitudes, concepts, expectations etc. of individuals in the audience relate to the propaganda message, simplify, classify and label it and produce an opinion. The individual acts because he has been influenced by the message and not because of his previous views. Eventually his personality is changed.[7] Families that have lost members to exotic religious cults will recognise this process. Clearly, Ellul's initiation of true believers, the terrorist's first priority, penetrates the personality screen. Without organisation, such penetration is presumably rare.

A second task of revolutionary propaganda is to influence the general public and even the international audience. Although terrorists regard the regime, its institutions and its agents as evil enemies to be destroyed without mercy, they look upon the general public as an audience whose allegiance is required. The purpose of all revolutionary activity is conversion. Elimination is reserved for symbolic or vengeance targets, those who threaten the movement and those who refuse conversion. The objectives for this wider audience are complex. Because the target is not yet incorporated within an organisation, complete allegiance is unlikely to be achieved, nor will the personality screen be penetrated. However, provided the absorption screen is pierced—and acts of terrorism are particularly effective in attracting attention—a climate of opinion can be created in which the cadre of true believers can increase in number and effectiveness, the government is restrained and hampered in its response and the public is made confused, ambivalent, fearful and vulnerable.

The concept of organisation may tend to conjure up an image of a physically compact group, isolated from society. This would be misleading. The group is psychologically compact but physically dispersed, infiltrating institutions, the media, even the armed forces and police. Some members may establish fronts, or re-direct existing ones. Only in the covert cells might a degree of isolation exist. Thus in the physical sense the two audiences are mixed. True believers dedicated to extreme objectives, who have secretly rejected the norms of society within the covert organisation, may be seen and heard by the public arguing within the existing norms for seemingly reasonable objectives. Their agenda is hidden behind tactical reasonableness.

Whether terrorism is a component of a wider revolutionary strategy or stands on its own, the themes aimed at the general public seem fairly constant. These are some of the most common.

Guilt Transfer. Terrorists blame the consequences of all violence on the regime they are opposing. Naturally, all that the police and military do is presented in the worst possible light, and casualties are made into innocent victims or martyrs, regardless of whether or not such terms are appropriate. Having associated the regime with violence and death, this theme then goes an important step further, blaming terrorist violence on the authorities too. This technique follows Napoleon Bonaparte, who, according to Clausewitz, insisted that his aggression was peaceful, war being the responsibility of victims who resisted.[8]

The El Salvadoran terrorists and rebels have been particularly successful in this theme: Western observers frequently attribute blame for the entire death toll to the regime, as if the FMLN had never hurt a fly.[9] Martin McGuinness, a senior Provisional IRA leader, explicitly blamed Britain for every death in Northern Ireland, including his own victims.[10]

Guilt transfer frequently involves the rejection of the term 'terrorist' by the violent groups and the transfer of the term to the regime. State sponsors of terrorism are particularly adept in this regard.

Invulnerability. Whereas true believers accept victory as inevitable as part of their ideological conditioning, the 'invulnerability' theme tries to rationalise the same message for the general public. It is said that liberal government is powerless in the face of clandestine attack, that the security forces are ill-equipped to deal effectively with terrorism, that time is on the side of the revolutionaries. The purpose of this theme is to demoralise the government and its supporters and to neutralise the mass. For no one wishes to back a loser.

The notion that time is on the terrorists' side dresses a terrorist campaign in the clothes of full-scale revolution. It argues that, for the regime to win, the authorities must eliminate every last terrorist and extinguish the cultural–spiritual inspiration—which is obviously impossible. So long as one terrorist survives, the struggle continues.

Eventually, protracted war will undermine the regime. Robert Taber wrote:

> Time works for the guerrilla both in the field—where it costs the enemy a daily fortune to pursue him—and in the politico-economic arena. . . . Protracted internal war threatens all of this [political and economic credibility], for no investor will wish to put his money where it is not safe and certain to produce a profit, no banks lend without guarantees, no ally wishes to treat with a government that is on the point of eviction.[11]

Latin American terrorists have often employed this technique.

The Provisional IRA exploited this theme in a novel way after their terrorists had bombed a Brighton hotel, narrowly missing the British Cabinet.

In their communiqué, the Provisionals boasted: 'Today we were unlucky. But remember, we have only to be lucky once. You will have to be lucky always.'[12]

The invulnerability theme, of course, depends for its credibility upon the armed actions of the terrorist group. Daring acts, appropriately publicised, make authority appear powerless and the terrorists invulnerable. The two fists must work together to accomplish desired psychological results.[13]

Spurious Justification. While the campaign as a whole endeavours to accumulate legitimacy for the organisation, at a lower, day-to-day tactical level spurious justifications are devised to protect terrorists from the full force of public wrath—wrath which might find expression in tougher anti-terrorism laws and procedures. Perhaps the commonest ploy is to justify murder by reference to alleged and sometimes real political or social injustices. The apparent intention is to confuse ends with means and to produce an ambivalent or even supportive public attitude.

After the Provisionals killed ten army bandsmen and cavalrymen in London in July 1982, their spokesman explained that 'Britain's interference' in Ireland's affairs 'makes bringing the war to Britain inevitable'.[14] Sheik Mohammad Hussein Fadlallah, a senior Iranian official, spoke of 'an open-ended war between the impoverished and deprived against the United States, Israel and all the enemies of Islam'.[15] FALN, a Puerto Rican group, justified a spate of bombings in December 1982 with a long communiqué speaking of 'fascist repressive actions of the FBI, US courts and police' and the use of Puerto Rico as 'a base of operations which will be used as a springboard to protect its interests in the Caribbean, Latin America . . .'.[16]

Sometimes the appeal is much more seductive. When young Canadian terrorists fire-bombed pornographic video stores in Vancouver, it would have been easy for this writer to have said: 'I cannot condone the violence, but I do understand why some people feel compelled to act.' But to have said this would have amounted to an attempt to profit from terrorism while evading moral responsibility. This is the reaction desired by terrorists, and confusion of ends and means arguably does more to keep terrorism alive than any other theme.

Television appearances by terrorist leaders and spokesmen also provide occasions for justification. On this medium, the 'presence' of the speaker influences audiences more than his or her words. By all accounts Josef Mengele was 'charming'. Had he been interviewed by the BBC in 1944, would he have persuaded some allied viewers that his actions were justified?

Another argument within this theme explains that violence by the terrorists is a reluctant but inevitable reaction to violence by the state. Costa Gravas's film *State of Siege* (1973) portrayed Tupamaro violence as a justified reaction to United States political and economic domination of Uruguay, a domination which, the film alleged, introduced torture to that country.[17] Reinhard Hauffs film *Stammheim—The Trial* (1986) reportedly grants legitimacy to Baader–Meinhof atrocities by portraying the suicides of convicted terrorists as 'state terrorism'. In both cases the justification theme merges with guilt transfer, because audiences are required to see authority in a worse light than the terrorists.

Disarming Themes. Here the aim is to discredit and destroy any method, individual, police or military unit, weapon or policy that, because of its potential effectiveness, threatens the terrorists' integrity and freedom of action. Unlike spurious justification, which usually advances from the upside-down morality of terrorist logic, disarming themes are often argued within the norms of conventional morality. Consequently fronts are extensively used, and they appear to advance their causes *pro bono publico*, to save the government from blundering into error. Consequently this is a very difficult area, because many pressure groups operating in this field will be devoid of sinister motive. Moreover, public input is valuable to government decision making. It would be extremely dangerous to label all appeals for restraint as terrorist propaganda. This difficulty is exploited by the terrorists by infiltrating innocent pressure groups and by burying demands of operational importance within a programme of reforms assembled in good faith by concerned citizens.

Northern Ireland in the early 1970s provided a host of examples where government security measures drew fire from loyal critics and terrorist fronts alike. Internment, deep interrogation, rubber bullets, the 'paras', army 'black propaganda', CS smoke, the Ulster Defence Regiment and many other real or imagined targets were made the subjects of investigations, exposés, legal actions and public agitation. Some were justified, many were understandable, some were parts of systematic disarming propaganda. It seems at least possible that a fearful anticipation of this type of propaganda deterred British governments from deploying units of the Special Air Service in Northern Ireland for about five years. In another setting but in the same period of time the United States 'Office of Public Safety' programme for Latin America was destroyed by this form of propaganda, of which Costa Gravas's film was a part.[18]

Terror. It is easy to overlook that terror is itself a theme of propaganda. To every member of its audience it says: 'oppose us, and you die!' The effect is hard to measure, because it is slow and unacknowledged. If someone begins to sympathise with the terrorist cause, he or she will seldom admit that fear is the reason. Many critics have alleged that Western reporting from Lebanon before and during the Israeli invasion was distorted by PLO intimidation tactics.[19] Journalists who decide to 'report from the other side' are almost inevitably going to slant their copy accordingly. Unless they are seeking martyrdom, how could they do otherwise? Terror can isolate the police and other security forces, because the judiciary, bureaucracy and general public fear to commit themselves to the fight. Frequently, police are singled out as targets, until they too cease to operate effectively.

Combined with a violent campaign, these themes can be instrumental in deflecting government responses until it is too late to reverse the shift of popular allegiance from regime to terrorist. That, at least, is the terrorist hope. Where terrorism is only a component of a wider revolutionary strategy, as in the de-colonisation campaigns of the 1940s, 1950s and early 1960s, rebel objectives have often been met. Success also crowned the efforts of Shia fundamentalists in Iran, Sandinistas in Nicaragua and other movements where terrorism was a subordinate means. Free-standing terrorist campaigns have, however, been much less successful. It it as though the strategic component of their propaganda—their spiritual–cultural core—was unable to fire sufficient imaginations. The true believers remained a small group and mass mobilisation never succeeded.

Yet many terrorist campaigns endure for decade after decade. A lack of strategic success does not seem to deter true believers whose commitment to the cause and the violent road cannot easily be rejected. Indeed, their whole reason for existing seems to be bound up in the struggle, which becomes an end in itself. Thus tactical success is sufficient reward and the game continues. Survival themes such as guilt transfer, spurious justification, disarming and terror are often brilliantly deployed and their success may be a key reason why so many ill-starred campaigns seem capable of indefinite prolongation.

If propaganda is half the terrorist's armoury, and perhaps the decisive half in terms of survival, there is surely a strong case for government counter-terrorist measures to contain a psychological component. The problem, of course, is public unease at any form of propaganda, and politicians' consequent unwillingness to touch the subject. This understandable squeamishness seems to have effectively deterred democracies from competing in the war of ideas and ideals on *any* front.

The question is too important, however, to be glossed over much longer. Western publics are also becoming squeamish about massacres in airport terminals. If the subject were handled intelligently, informed publics might agree that in a choice of evils, terrorism was worse than government publicity to help control it.

In place of repressive state terror which for centuries provided the standard government responses to challenges to its authority, and still does in some Third World and all Marxist–Leninist states, democratic countries have developed doctrines of counterinsurgency and counterterrorism. These doctrines confine government, police and military to lawful reactions. No one likes such processes, but they are not necessarily regarded as a threat to democracy and are accepted as a counterterrorism tool. What is needed, surely, is an acceptable doctrine of counterpropaganda to complement counterinsurgency.[20]

The controls suggested are that government counterpropaganda should operate within the accepted norms of publicity or public relations. It would reject 'black' and 'grey' operations, disinformation, deliberate untruth and all the manipulative characteristics associated with propaganda. Indeed, it would differ from publicity and public relations mainly in its operational aims and its close coordination with all other aspects of counterterrorism.

Much of this coordination would be connected with the collection and analysis of terrorist propaganda. Another function of the counterpropaganda

(CP) staff would be the provision of advice to all concerned with the planning and execution of counterterrorist operations on what might be called the 'public opinion factor'. The grist for the terrorists' propaganda mill is always provided by blunders of policy or execution, by poorly briefed soldiers or policemen and by nonsensical, aggravating procedures. Proper attention to the public opinion factor could minimise this source of raw material. Another task would be to ensure that the news media had access to all levels of responsibility, from the chief to the man on patrol, and that these individuals knew what they were doing, and why, and were therefore able (with training as necessary) to explain their functions convincingly to television, radio and newspaper audiences. If the media found the terrorists and their front spokesmen available, relaxed, articulate and seemingly well-motivated, and authority tight-lipped, tense, monosyllabic and seemingly paranoid, reporting would reflect the contrast. By no means should law-and-order people become excessively garrulous. Instead, they should be, and be seen to be, in command, quietly confident, and on the side on the angels.

Only when authority's house was in order would CP staffs address the outside world. Existing PR staffs handle this function already, if they are doing their jobs properly, providing accurate information and the government viewpoint. Counterpropaganda staffs would assist this process by their analysis of the terrorists psychological strategy, by recognising hostile themes and provocations as they emerged, so that they could be pre-empted or exposed, and by uncovering the topic of propaganda as a news story in its own right. Terrorist fronts could be challenged by being asked questions publicly over affiliations and motives. Of course, CP's liaison with the Intelligence staff would allow controlled release of hot material damaging to the cohesion and esteem of terrorist groups. The driving of wedges between hard-core terrorists and their circle of sympathisers and fronts is essential to success. Terrorist themes of guilt transfer, spurious justification and disarmament would command priority attention by CP staffs, since these are the notions which permit even the most discredited and hard-pressed groups to survive.

To a large extent, contact with the public would be through the media. Media coverage of terrorism is of course a subject for separate study, although closely linked to propaganda. CP's major challenge would be to persuade the media to recognise the role and importance of terrorist propaganda and the way that the media are often used as transmission belts.

Counterpropaganda could also go directly to the public by purchasing advertising space and time, through ministerial and other speeches, conferences, seminars, film production and other means. If saving fuel, driving safely, avoiding drugs and moderating sex are appropriate subjects for publicity of this kind so, one might think, is saving innocent life.

Remarkably, however, many may not agree. Opposition political parties are likely to object on the grounds that these measures are political and therefore improper topics for public funded advertising. In a democracy, counterterrorist measures of all kinds have as a rule to be introduced slowly, at times when public opinion and opposition parties will tolerate them. All that has been suggested about CP therefore relates to a certain stage in a terrorist campaign when public and media are disillusioned with the groups and sickened by their violence. At this stage, a bi-partisan publicity policy can possibly be agreed between ruling and opposition parties. Indeed, if a government attempts to move too fast in this field it may polarise public opinion, providing the terrorist with a ready-made constituency of sympathisers.

Above and beyond the minor tactics of countering terrorist propaganda, the West must endeavour to arm itself psychologically to defend democracy. This is not a non sequitur. Terrorism directed at the democracies is a direct attack on democracy itself, because by its very nature it proclaims that elected governments and their laws are subordinate to demands backed by violence or the threat of violence. Academics sensibly separate method from cause in their analysis of terrorism. In our endeavours to exclude value judgement, however, we ought not to overlook the method's inherently anti-democratic character, and this caution applies equally to politicians and opinion formers.

Jorge Nef recognised the West's moral dilemma in respect of terrorism as early as 1979, when he wrote:

> There is an alarming psycho-cultural aspect to contemporary terrorism. This is the growing acceptance of violence. ... In an echo of 'the war to end all wars,' we have even glorified violence as the solution to violence. It is this trend in our culture that makes the human tragedy of terrorism acceptable—tactically expedient in the short run, morally justifiable in the long run.[21]

The West's ambivalent attitude towards terrorism may be a manifestation of a wider spiritual–cultural malaise. Symptoms are the notions that nothing in the Western heritage is worth defending, that the use of force to defend democracy is illegitimate and that any amount of violence is justifiable in the hands of 'progressive' forces, because history is on their side, making victory inevitable. It is as though the totalitarian lurking inside each and every one of us is busy rationalising and compromising, hoping that the human half of our being will capitulate.

Henri Bergson argued that time spent refuting a rival philosophy was time wasted. Instead, the good philosophy was 'of itself able to displace the erroneous idea' becoming, 'without our having taken the trouble of refuting anyone, the best of refutations'.[22] At this cultural–spiritual level the battle against terrorism merges with the battle against totalitarianism. Political, spiritual and cultural leadership are in the end even more important than intelligence, response teams and firepower. Without surrendering objectivity and independence, scholars who value democracy may have a duty to help launch the ideas that will displace the erroneous philosophy.

NOTES

1 NATO, *Glossary of Military Terms*, pp. 2–205.
2 Grant Wardlaw, *Political Terrorism: Theory, Tactics, and Counter-measures*, Cambridge: Cambridge University Press, 1982, p. 16.

3 Concerning propaganda by deed, see Walter Laqueur, *Terrorism*, London: Weidenfeld and Nicolson, 1977, p. 67; concerning 'theatre', see Brian M Jenkins, *International Terrorism: A New Mode of Conflict*, Santa Monica, California: Rand Corporation P-5261, 1974, p. 4.
4 Michael Elliott-Bateman, 'The Battlefronts of People's War', *in* Elliot-Bateman, John Ellis and Tom Bowden (eds.), *Revolt to Revolution: Studies in the 19th and 20th Century European Experience*, Manchester: Manchester University Press, Rowman and Littlefield, 1974, pp. 314–315.
5 Jacques Ellul, *Propaganda: The Formation of Men's Attitudes*, New York: Knopf, 1965, Vintage edition, 1973, p. 29.
6 *Ibid.*
7 Baruch A Hazan, *Soviet Propaganda: A Case Study of the Middle East Conflict*, Jerusalem: Keter Publishing, 1976, pp. 19–25.
8 See Carl von Clausewitz, *On War* (ed. and transl. Michael Howard and Peter Paret), Princeton: Princeton University Press, 1976, p. 370; on guilt transfer generally, see Maurice Tugwell, 'Guilt Transfer', *in* David C Rapoport and Yonah Alexander (eds.), *The Morality of Terrorism: Religious and Secular Justifications*, New York: Pergamon, 1982, pp. 275–289.
9 In El Salvador the theme was given credibility by the brutal government and right-wing repression of the early 1980s. The notion that all deaths were attributable to the regime was therefore made easy to promulgate. See Liisa North, *Bitter Grounds: Roots of Revolt in El Salvador*, Kitchener, Ontario: Between the Lines, 1981, p. 108; Tommie Sue Montgomery, *Revolution in El Salvador: Origins and Evolution*, Boulder, Colorado: Westview, 1982, p. 191; Marcel Niedergang, 'Death Squads Back on the Rampage in El Salvador', *Washington Post*, 22 January 1985.
10 Stated explicitly by Martin McGuinness, Provisional IRA leader in an interview during BBC television documentary *Northern Ireland: At the Edge of the Union* (broadcast in UK in 1985 and in USA on Public Broadcast Service 18 February 1986).
11 Robert Taber, *The War of the Flea: Guerrilla Warfare Theory and Practice*, London: Paladin, 1970, pp. 29–30.
12 Quoted *Time*, 22 October 1984, p. 38.
13 For an example of violence supporting propaganda, see Maria McGuire, *To Take Arms*, London, 1973, p. 75.
14 Quoted *Globe and Mail* (Toronto), 23 July 1982.
15 Quoted *Philadelphia Inquirer*, 16 June 1985, p. 6.
16 Text of FALN communiqué, re-issued by the Praire Fire Organizing Committee (A Weather Underground front), 8 January 1983.
17 See Mark Falcoff, *Small Countries, Large Issues: Studies in US–Latin American Asymmetries*, Washington, DC: American Enterprise Institute, 1984, pp. 13–33.
18 *Globe and Mail* (Toronto), 14 March 1981, p. 10; Falcoff, *op. cit.; The National Reporter*, Winter 1986, pp. 18–21.
19 See Ze'ev Chafets, 'Beirut and the Great Media Cover-up', *Commentary*, September 1984, pp. 20–29.
20 This section is developed from Maurice Tugwell, 'Revolutionary Propaganda and Possible Counter-measures', Unpublished doctoral thesis, King's College, London, 1979, pp. 318–335.
21 Jorge Nef, 'Reign of Terror', *Weekend Magazine*, 5 May 1979.
22 Henri Bergson, quoted Will Durant, *The Story of Philosophy*, New York: Simon and Schuster, 1926—Washington Square edition, pp. 462–463.

Power and Meaning: Terrorism as a Struggle over Access to the Communication Structure

R D Crelinsten

TERRORISM, POLITICS AND THE MEDIA: A COMMUNICATION MODEL

Insurgent terrorism can be viewed as a form of political communication or a form of social protest in which the terrorist attempts to gain the attention of those in power or to promote some cause, via the combined use and threat of violence. The terrorist resorts to violence because he feels—rightly or wrongly—that he has been excluded from the political process.[1] In this view, terrorism functions as a form of 'propaganda of the deed' in which the terrorist sends messages to those in power, as well as to the general public. On a purely symbolic level, the message is equivalent to shouting 'look at me!' or 'listen to me!' If, by means of his initial act of violence, the terrorist can maintain the attention of a pertinent audience, he can then transmit more specific messages, such as a political manifesto, or particular demands. Within this perspective, the direct victims of the individual terrorist acts, such as hostages or bomb victims, are mere vehicles by which the terrorist gains the attention of those he wishes to address. Alex Schmid and Janny de Graaf refer to these direct victims as 'message generators' to highlight their purely functional role.[2] In this communication model of terrorism, the terrorist act constitutes a sign or a message within a wider political discourse. It is a claim for attention, for recognition as a player in political life and, ultimately, for legitimacy as a valid representative of a particular political cause. As such, the terrorist is a political actor who, by means of the threat and use of violence, is participating in a particular political discourse.

Viewing insurgent terrorism in this way leads directly to the larger question of which institutions are generally available for conducting political discourse, and how specific actors gain access to, are excluded from or monopolise such institutions. Clearly, there exists a whole range of avenues—legitimate or otherwise—that are open to individuals or groups for advocating, promoting and effecting social and political change. Whether one seeks change through electoral politics, collective action such as strikes or demonstrations, mass protest, agit-prop, clandestine terrorism, subversion or revolution depends to a large extent upon the access one has to the communication channels and institutions already available in a given society. If one has limited access or decides that available channels do not or cannot meet one's needs, then new channels can be sought and new institutions created. The formation of a new political party, a new organisation, a new newspaper, the creation of a new interest group or political lobby, can all serve to further some social or political cause.[3] Let us call the network of communication channels and institutions within which such political activity is usually conducted the 'communication structure' of a given society. This would include, for example, electoral fundraising, voter registration drives, mail and phone campaigns, political action committees and lobbying.

How does the mass media—newspapers, magazines, radio and television—fit into this communication structure? In an age where we have come to speak of our world as an electronic global village, the power of the mass media to affect political discourse on an ever-widening scale has become the object of increasing scientific attention.[4] One special focus has been the reporting of 'news' and the processes of selection, interpretation and presentation which mediate between events as they happen and events as they are reported to readers, listeners and viewers.[5] Two common findings have been that (a) the media tends to be attracted to violent incidents and, in reporting them, tends to ignore their historical antecedents and their social or political contexts,[6] and (b) the primary sources of information for reporting on political life tend to be those who represent authority or who belong to the existing power structure.[7] Stuart Hall and his colleagues distinguish between these 'primary definers', such as politicians, police spokesmen or government officials, and what they call 'secondary definers', such as political or social activists or reformers who remain outside the existing power structure.[8] Such secondary definers are used much less frequently by the media than are primary definers.

Given that the mass media plays an increasingly greater part in political life, by means of its role as a conduit and forum for political debate and its usefulness to political actors for attracting and attempting to influence public opinion, and given that, if one plays by the rules, access to the media is more readily available to those already within the power structure than those opposing it, an excellent way for someone, who feels excluded from the political process, to gain access to the communication structure is to disrupt the normal routine of political life by means of some reprehensible or fear-provoking act, thereby gaining the attention of the mass media. Harvey Molotch and Marilyn Lester refer to this as 'disruptive access' and distinguish it from what they call 'habitual access', which is available to those with power.[9] Press conferences, 'photo opportunities', such as a political leader visiting a hospital, public statements and official communiqués all serve as valuable sources of news for the media, thus providing the powerful with routine means for gaining media attention whensoever desired. By contrast, Molotch and Lester point out that:

> Those lacking habitual access to event-making who wish to contribute to the public experience, often come to rely on disruption. They must 'make news', by somehow crashing through the ongoing arrangements of newsmaking, generating surprise, shock, or some more violent form of 'trouble'. Thus, the relatively powerless disrupt the social world to disrupt the habitual forms of event-making.[10]

This is what much of modern insurgent terrorism is designed to do.[11] However, because the reporting of news tends to reinforce the official perspective of events via a selective emphasis on primary definers and an ahistorical, de-contextualised treatment of politically motivated violence, incidents of terrorism or political deviance which do attract media attention tend not to gain for their actors the legitimacy which they desire or seek.[12] Often, their treatment tends to be different from that accorded to primary definers, such as being placed in the inner pages of a newspaper rather than on the front page, or being depicted in pejorative or derogatory ways by reporters or announcers[13] or by unflattering photographs. The result is that, while modern insurgent terrorists can manipulate the media into devoting time and space to their activities and even to their political claims and demands, the media manipulates them in turn, by playing up the violent aspects at the expense of analysis, in order to attract consumers. This, in turn, tends to undermine the terrorist's claim to legitimacy by depicting him as merely violent, and not political.

Furthermore, precisely because the media tends to rely routinely on official sources of information and commentary, the image of the radical or violent political actor that is presented to the media consumer is usually shaped by the official perspective of those in positions of authority within the power structure. This is because, even if the secondary definer does gain access to the media, and his treatment is free of overt bias or distortion, his alternative perspective must address the agenda as already established by the primary definer. As a result, his view can be dismissed as irrelevant to the problem at hand as defined by official sources. In this manner, the way in which the media collects, interprets and presents information to the news-consuming public tends to reproduce the perspective of those in power and, thereby, to reinforce the legitimacy of the power structure itself.[14]

For this reason, whenever opposing discourses collide in the arena of political life, the media tends to favour the official discourse, which has easy, routinised access because it is legitimised by the power structure. Alternative discourses, and particularly radical or extremist ones, which are marginalised and discredited by the power structure, penetrate the media only with difficulty and, when they do, tend to be treated in ways which marginalise and discredit them further. In time of crisis, however, this process of reproduction and reinforcement of the existing order can be disrupted by the successful penetration of alternative discourses into the media to the extent that they hold their own with official attempts to discredit them. This is essentially what happened in Canada when Quebec separatist activists, acting under the name of *le Front de libération du Québec* (FLQ), kidnapped a British diplomat and a Quebec cabinet minister within the space of a week in October 1970.[15] In this chapter, I shall describe how the FLQ succeeded in penetrating the media in such a way that the traditional means of reporting political violence was undermined for a period, until the federal government adopted special emergency measures to control the crisis.

The chapter will focus on the pattern of public discourse as it was reflected in newspaper coverage during the acute phase of the crisis. This phase is defined as the fifteen-day period beginning on 5 October, when James Richard Cross was kidnapped by the Liberation Cell, and ending on 19 October, when the Canadian Parliament approved by a vote of one hundred and ninety to sixteen the invocation of the War Measures Act and the adoption of emergency measures.[16] The methodology upon which the analysis is based consisted of comparing coverage in seven newspapers—six Montreal dailies of which four were French and two English, and one French Quebec City daily.[17] The most important measures were the uniformity of reporting across newspapers as reflected by front-page headlines and articles, and the amount and accuracy of reports on the activities of government officials, police authorities and terrorists. While the data source for media coverage is comprised solely of newspapers, the ensuing discussion will make clear that the electronic media, and particularly the radio, played a central role in the development of the crisis. Two Montreal radio stations in particular, CKLM and CKAC, came to be known as the electronic 'mailboxes' for the two terrorist cells, each of which sent the majority of their communiqués to one of the two stations.

THE CROSS AFFAIR

PHASE ONE: THE STRUGGLE FOR ACCESS

On Monday morning, 5 October, James Richard Cross, British consul in Montreal, was kidnapped by four young men belonging to a group of seven people calling themselves the Liberation Cell of the FLQ. Within a matter of hours, one of them had deposited four copies of a first communiqué at a local university. This communiqué enumerated seven specific demands and was accompanied by a political manifesto of several pages.[18] The copies were addressed to four different recipients: two local radio stations, CKAC and CKLM, a pro-independence weekly, *Québec-Presse* and the authorities. Both CKAC and CKLM received phone calls alerting them to the existence of the communiqués, but the package was seized by the police. While the historical record is ambiguous, it is likely that CKLM called the police, while CKAC sent a reporter to collect the communiqué, but was pre-empted by the police.[19] The first reports, which appeared in the afternoon papers that same day, mentioned the kidnapping itself, the identity of the victim and the supposition that the kidnapping was the work of the FLQ.

The authorities immediately adopted a policy of silence on all details pertaining to the affair and, in particular, police activity. During a press conference on Monday afternoon, Quebec Minister of Justice, Jérôme Choquette, did not reveal the precise contents of the FLQ communiqué. He summarised six of the seven demands, without mentioning the very first one, which insisted that the police refrain from any searches or arrests designed to track the kidnappers down. As for the other principal demands, Choquette mentioned the publication of a manifesto, without revealing that the document in question was in police hands. He also mentioned the demand for the release of certain imprisoned FLQ activists, without specifying how many were listed or their names. The kidnappers imposed a forty-eight-hour deadline after the delivery of their communiqué for the authorities to meet their demands.

In large part due to the official policy of secrecy adopted by the authorities, press coverage during the first few days of the crisis was confused and full of speculation concerning the real demands of the Liberation Cell. Numerous errors and rumours concerning the intentions of the terrorists and the activities of the police were typical of the reporting of this period. The best example of a rumour arising from this policy of silence was that of an assassination threat against the three top political leaders: Prime Minister Pierre Trudeau, Quebec Premier Robert Bourassa and Montreal Mayor Jean Drapeau. In a sensationalistic front-page article published in *La Presse* on 6 October, reporter Marcel Dupré suggested that these three politicians' names headed a hit list for selective assassinations which was included in the document sent the preceding day by the Cross kidnappers to the authorities.[20] In fact, no such hit list existed and Dupré was interpreting the simple mention of political personalities in the accompanying manifesto as an indication that they were potential targets for selective assassination. On 6 October, however, this was unknown to the general public and the rumour was treated as fact in other newspapers the following day, 7 October.[21]

Two more communiqués were issued by the Liberation Cell during day two, 6 October. Communiqué no. 2, accompanied by a handwritten letter from James Cross to his wife, was sent directly to Mrs Cross, but was seized by the police and never published. Communiqué no. 3, accompanied by another letter from Cross to his wife, a copy of the second communiqué and a copy of the political manifesto, were delivered by taxi directly to the studios of radio station CKAC. In this third communiqué, the Liberation Cell appealed to the news media to break the wall of silence erected by the authorities. CKAC reporter, Louis Fournier, received the package and broadcast the two communiqués (nos. 2 and 3) that same evening, just about the same time that, in Ottawa, External Affairs Minister Mitchell Sharp was giving the Government's official reply to the kidnappers' demands. In a statement delivered to an almost empty House of Commons, Mitchell Sharp rejected 'this set of demands' as 'wholly unreasonable'. In doing so, the Minister revealed the complete set of seven demands for the first time.[22]

Out-manoeuvred by the kidnappers' strategy of sending copies of their communiqués directly to the media, Jérôme Choquette held a press conference the next morning, 7 October, less than one hour before the expiry of the kidnappers' deadline. The Quebec Justice Minister announced that Mrs Cross had received a letter from her husband the previous afternoon and he read the text of the Liberation Cell's second communiqué. The text differed slightly from that read by Louis Fournier the night before, suggesting that he was reading from the original which had been seized by the police. If Fournier had not broadcast the communiqués when he did, it is quite likely that Choquette would not have made the contents of communiqué no. 2 public. The kidnappers' tactic had forced his hand. It should be noted, however, that reporting on communiqués nos. 2 and 3 is full of errors and contradictions which are often reproduced in historical reconstructions.[23] This reflects the rapid evolution of events and the creation by the FLQ of parallel channels of information flow which produced sources of information that conflicted with and contradicted official declarations.

October 7 was the first day that the newspapers printed texts of the kidnappers' communiqués. The full text of communiqué no. 1 was published for the first time and two papers even published photos of the cover page, which carried a watermark drawing of a Quebec *patriote*, pipe in mouth, rifle in hand and sporting the classic tuque identified with the early French settlers. The words 'Front de libération du Québec', superimposed on a tri-colour letterhead of green, white and red (the colours of the 1837 rebellion), clearly identified the FLQ. With the reading of their communiqués on the radio and their appearance in the daily newspapers, the FLQ finally succeeded in penetrating the communication network. Their words and images became consumer products for mass consumption and began to shape the direction of ongoing political discourse. Yet it was only the following day, 8 October, with their fourth communiqué, that reporting on their communiqués became accurate and coherent.

This fourth communiqué, issued in the afternoon of 7 October, was the Liberation Cell's reply to Mitchell Sharp's rejection of their demands the previous night and to Jérôme Choquette's request, during his press conference, that the kidnappers establish direct contact, via telephone, with his office in Montreal. In this communiqué, which was delivered to radio station CKLM this time and addressed to reporter Pierre Pascau, the Liberation Cell extended their deadline by twenty-four hours and insisted on the broadcast of their manifesto by Radio-Canada, in prime time that same evening, and the cessation of all police activity, as indications of the governments' good faith. The communiqué was accompanied by two handwritten letters from James Cross, one to his wife and one addressed to 'the authorities'. In the latter, the British diplomat states that 'it will be faster and easier for everyone if all the FLQ communiqués are published in full'. It is highly likely that this letter was dictated by the kidnappers to their hostage as an additional tactic to counter the attempts by the authorities to suppress their communiqués. Knowing that a message from Mr Cross represented a valuable item for the media, they included this phrase to inform the public that their messages were the object of official censorship. The tactic worked. Pierre Pascau broadcast the fourth communiqué immediately upon its receipt and both the text and that of Cross's letter to the authorities appeared in all the newspapers the following day.

PHASE TWO: THE GOVERNMENT STALLS

The official reply to this second ultimatum was delivered by Mitchell Sharp on the evening of 7 October. His statement was broadcast in a special telecast by Radio-Canada. Ignoring completely the demand that police activity cease, the Minister for External Affairs noted that the kidnappers 'attach a particular importance to the broadcast... of a certain manifesto or communiqué'. Stating that the Government was prepared to make the necessary arrangements for such a broadcast, the Minister added that 'we do not know exactly what document is meant'. In fact, the authorities knew precisely which document was involved and Mr Sharp was simply pursuing a delay strategy which had been established on the very first day of the crisis, a strategy which relied on the police to resolve the affair before a concession had to be made.[24] In ending his declaration, the Minister suggested that an 'appropriate means of communication' be established with the kidnappers for the purpose of discussing what guarantees they could provide that they would indeed release their hostage if their demands were met. To this end, he requested that the kidnappers name someone with whom the authorities could pursue discussions 'in complete confidence'. Here, the Minister was clearly attempting to draw the dialogue between the Government and the kidnappers away from the public forum of media coverage into private talks between intermediaries, just as Jérôme Choquette had done in requesting direct contact by telephone. The greatest danger of the stalling strategy was that the longer the affair dragged on, the greater the opportunity for the terrorists to dominate media coverage.[25]

In the wake of this official reply to the FLQ concerning broadcast of their manifesto, Louis Fournier, with the permission of CKAC management, read the complete text of the manifesto live, on the air, making use of the copy that was sent to the station the previous evening. This was the very first time that the contents of the FLQ manifesto were revealed to the public. In addition, Fournier passed the text on to some Radio-Canada reporters, including Claude-Jean Devirieux, who has been suggested by the Liberation Cell in their fourth communiqué as the one who should read their manifesto when it was televised. Devirieux and his colleagues photocopied the manifesto and distributed copies to the print media.

By the next morning, 8 October, many of the Montreal French-language dailies were in possession of the full text. Nevertheless, no paper printed the manifesto that day. In fact, only two papers even mentioned the fact that Fournier had broadcast the text the night before. While morning papers, such as *Montréal-Matin*, published too early in the day to print the manifesto, *La Presse*, which published around noon, could well have done so. There is evidence to suggest that the publisher–owner of *La Presse* received a direct phone call from one of Prime Minister Trudeau's principal advisors, requesting that the manifesto not be published. It is clear that, beginning with Mitchell Sharp's declaration the night before, the Federal Government was doing everything in its power to block the FLQ from direct access to the media. It is one thing to be the object of dramatic reporting about kidnapping, hostages and police investigations; it is quite another to have one's own words reproduced in media reports.[27]

On 8 October, the fourth day of the crisis, almost all front-page headlines dealt with Mitchell Sharp's declaration of the previous evening and his invitation to the kidnappers to designate someone to speak in their name. The words used to depict such a person varied from paper to paper: some used 'mediator', others 'emissary', still others 'negotiator'. In fact, the status of these proposed discussions between the authorities and the kidnappers remained a burning issue of debate throughout the crisis. One editorial counselled the kidnappers to name a negotiator, since only private discussions would permit valid communication between the two parties. Press commentary during this period depicted negotiations as a secret process in which an emissary moved back and forth between the two contesting parties. The question of immunity from prosecution for such a go-between was even raised.[28]

While the media speculated about what kind of communication should be established between government and terrorist, the Liberation Cell issued their fifth communiqué, phoning radio station CKLM to indicate where it could be found. Pierre Pascau announced on the air that a new communiqué had been issued and sent two reporters to retrieve it. When they arrived with their booty, a Montreal police officer was waiting to take possession of it. However, he first allowed Pascau to open the envelope, which was addressed to him, and to read the contents. Pascau then announced on the air that the Liberation Cell had just extended their deadline another twelve hours, until midnight that night. He then gave the communiqué to a secretary, who went and photocopied it. Only then did he hand the original over to the officer, relating to him the full details of its discovery. Finally, about half an hour later, he broadcast the full text of the communiqué. It was late in the afternoon of 8 October.

Pascau's treatment of communiqué no. 5 set the pattern for the treatment of the majority of future communiqués until the War Measures Act was invoked. A police officer would allow the radio station in question to retrieve, broadcast and photocopy the communiqué and then take the original for verification and fingerprinting. In this way, as of 8 October, broadcast of each new communiqué, with few exceptions, was immediate, and photocopies were made available to the print media, which, in turn, reproduced them in full or, at the minimum, used them to type-set complete and accurate transcriptions or, in the case of the English papers, translations.

As for the contents of the fifth communiqué, the Liberation Cell refused Mitchell Sharp's request for an intermediary, insisting that they continue to establish communications in their own chosen way 'so as to avoid the traps set by the fascist police'. While the headline of *The Montreal Star*—the last paper to publish on the 8th—declared that 'Kidnappers refuse offer to negotiate', the Liberation Cell was really only refusing to communicate via a third person, who would be very likely to be tailed by the police. For them, communicating via the mass media was much more likely to give them the attention and recognition they desired. As for legitimacy, secret negotiations were useless. Only public negotiations could accord them the legitimising image of equal partners with government in a dialogue conducted in a public forum. To place even more pressure on the Government, the Liberation Cell also reduced their ultimate demand to a single one, the release of the political prisoners, and they demanded that the broadcast of their manifesto take place within the next twelve hours, during prime time of course.

Around 7.30 on the evening of 8 October, Radio-Canada announced that the political manifesto of the FLQ would be broadcast at 10.30 that night. Around the same time, the Quebec Government issued a communiqué requesting that the kidnappers of James Cross provide evidence that their hostage was still alive. To this end, the government requested that Mr Cross cite the 9 October headline of *Le Journal de Montréal* in a handwritten letter to the authorities. The decision to finally grant this minimum concession was taken after a second attempt by the Federal Government to block publication of the manifesto by the newspapers. The same advisor to Prime Minister Trudeau who had telephoned the publisher of *La Presse* spoke to the editor-in-chief of *Montréal-Matin*, which was planning to publish the manifesto in its 9 October edition. This time, the attempt failed and the editor-in-chief insisted that the plan to publish the manifesto would proceed. It is likely that the decision to broadcast the manifesto was taken when the authorities realised that they could no longer prevent its publication in the Friday papers.[29]

At 10.30 p.m., thus, at the tail-end of the 8 p.m. to 11 p.m. time-slot demanded by the FLQ, the manifesto was broadcast on Radio-Canada's television network. Read in a neutral monotone by announcer Gaétan Montreuil, the text took thirteen minutes to read and, throughout the broadcast, the words 'TEXTE DU MANIFESTE FLQ' (TEXT OF FLQ MANIFESTO) were superimposed on the bottom of the screen. In a pre-amble, the network advised its viewers that it was broadcasting the manifesto for humanitarian reasons. Arrangements has been made to treat the broadcast as a 'communication' rather than as a news item, and that it be read by an announcer rather than by a reporter or a commentator. Thus, the Government ignored the suggestion of the Liberation Cell that Claude-Jean Devirieux, who was well known for his aggressive reporting, read the text. Even in making its first concession, the Government tried to minimise as much as possible the full impact of the terrorists' message.

PHASE THREE: A LOST OPPORTUNITY

The broadcast of the FLQ manifesto by the State-run television network constitutes the turning point of the first week of the crisis. It represented the first official concession to the kidnappers and the successful penetration of the

FLQ perspective on Quebec political life into the communication structure. Its impact on the unfolding of the crisis during the following week should not be underestimated.[30] Its immediate impact was to dissipate the incredible tension which weighed on the minds of everyone and to provide some respite to the decision makers in government and within the Liberation Cell. In fact, the kidnappers' sixth communiqué was conciliatory: for the first time, no deadline was imposed and the death threat against Mr Cross was suspended. Furthermore, the communiqué was accompanied by a handwritten letter from their hostage, citing the 9 October headline of *Le Journal de Montréal*, as had been requested by the authorities. Unfortunately, this communiqué was never found[31] and Friday, 9 October, was a day of silence, waiting, rumours and tension.

Nevertheless, it was that Friday morning that the FLQ manifesto was published for the first time in the newspapers. Only one paper devoted its entire front page to the text, and several papers introduced the text with warnings to the reader about its contents and dissociating the paper from its message or justifying its publication as a humanitarian gesture aimed at saving the life of Mr Cross. Both *La Presse* and *Montréal-Matin*, who had been asked by the Federal Government not to publish the text the previous day, printed disclaimers of this sort along with the text. Most papers printed the text inside the first section of the paper, or on the first page of a later section. One paper printed a résumé of the text, sprinkled liberally with direct quotations, rather than the complete text itself. The two afternoon papers did not publish the manifesto at all. The treatment of the manifesto by the press was therefore a far cry from the original demand of the kidnappers that the full text be printed on the front pages of all major papers in the province. However, its penetration into the communication structure was sufficient to ensure that the Quebec public was well aware of its contents and its political message. In addition, the practice of publishing photocopies of communiqués continued, and the full text of the Liberation Cell's fifth communiqué appeared in all the papers.

Around 3 p.m., a spokeman for the Quebec Department of Justice asked CKLM to broadcast a message to the kidnappers requesting proof that he was still alive, since nothing had been heard from him since Wednesday, 7 October. As proof, the authorities requested a handwritten letter which included a specific phrase addressed to his wife which used the word 'darling'. At last, almost nineteen hours after the midnight deadline of the previous night, word finally arrived from the kidnappers. When it came, it was angry and frustrated. In communiqué no. 7, delivered by an unknown woman directly to CKLM, the kidnappers stated that they had sent an earlier communiqué, no. 6, addressed to Pierre Pascau, via a Mr Trudel who worked for the newspaper, *La Semaine*, and they gave the address where the communiqué had been left. They claimed that they had included a public letter from the hostage, citing the required headline to prove he was still alive. In retaliation for what they considered a deliberate attempt by the authorities to stall for time by blocking the publication of these documents, they declared that this was their final communiqué and set a last deadline of 6 p.m. the next day:

Saturday, 10 October. Attached to the communiqué were a letter from Mr Cross, citing the 'darling' phrase requested that afternoon by the authorities, and a copy of communiqué no. 6.

In their sixth communiqué, the kidnappers had set down their final demands: liberation of the consenting political prisoners and their transportation, along with their wives and children if these latter so desired, to Cuba or Algeria, plus an immediate stop to all police activity. The kidnappers also named Pierre Pascau, Louis Fournier and radical lawyer Robert Lemieux[32] as observers to assure that everything went smoothly. As their sole guarantee that Cross would be released following the fulfilment of these demands, the kidnappers gave their solemn pledge before the Quebec people that they would do so twenty-four hours after the return of the observers to Montreal. The Government response to the final communiqué from the kidnappers was prompt. Speaking through an external affairs spokesman, the Federal Government made it clear that the guarantee provided by the kidnappers in communiqué no. 6 was not enough. The only kind of guarantee that would be acceptable was a clear statement of the time and place of Mr Cross's release. Thus it was clear that the Government was still not ready to negotiate the last two conditions set by the Liberation Cell.

If Friday, 9 October, had constituted a day of silence, enforced or otherwise, on the part of terrorists and officials, it had not silenced the general public which, in conversations and, in particular, through telephone calls to radio station talk shows, expressed its opinions in the wake of broadcast of the FLQ's manifesto. In direct contrast to the prediction that its broadcast would do no harm, the public reaction to hearing the manifesto read on Radio-Canada was remarkably sympathetic. While most people condemned the FLQ *action*, the kidnapping itself, more than fifty per cent of the callers were in favour of the spirit of the manifesto.[33] For the Government, this wave of sympathy for the ideas of the FLQ was most unsettling and required a quick end to the charade played over the course of the preceding week.

PHASE FOUR: THE FINAL OFFER

The degree of support for the FLQ manifesto expressed by the French-speaking public in Quebec convinced Jérôme Choquette that the final response of the authorities should address this public sympathy. This led to the first serious disagreement between the Federal and Provincial levels of Government. Unknown to the public at large and completely invisible in press coverage, which merely speculated about the possibility of a negotiated settlement, Jérôme Choquette and Mitchell Sharp disagreed on the concessions that they were prepared to grant James Cross's kidnappers. Mr Choquette felt that the governments should act in good faith and that, without negotiating on the major points, they could make some concessions that would prove they were not inflexible on the ideological level, while still preserving the integrity of democratic institutions. These concessions included the creation of a ministry of social peace, to accommodate the widespread public sympathy for the FLQ manifesto, and the release of five of the twenty-three prisoners, who were already eligible for parole, in exchange for the release of Mr Cross. Mr Sharp, who felt that they had no real guarantee that such an offer would secure Cross's release, was opposed to the idea and threatened to dissociate the Ottawa Government from the Quebec course of action. After a series of telexes and phone calls throughout the afternoon of 10 October, Sharp's view prevailed on the refusal to release any prisoners. However, it was decided that Choquette would deliver the final offer, instead of Prime Minister Trudeau, as had been announced previously on Radio-Canada.[34]

In delivering the final offer, televised live just several minutes before 6 p.m., Mr Choquette adopted a conciliatory tone. The first part of his text, which constituted two-thirds of the total, did seem to reflect something akin to a declaration of intent to reform Quebec social institutions by democratic processes. It was only in the latter third of the text, dealing with the specific demands and the issue of the political prisoners, that the Federal line came through most strongly. In the name of the Federal Government, Mr Choquette offered the kidnappers safe passage to a foreign country in exchange for the release of Mr Cross. However, no prisoners would be released. Speaking of the parole process and of the cases currently before the courts, the Quebec Justice Minister insisted that the former would be applied objectively and that the latter would be considered with clemency if the kidnappers released their hostage. In the name of his own government, he also promised leniency before the courts if the kidnappers released their hostage, yet refused safe passage. In an interview with James Cross after his release some two months later, the former hostage stated that, upon hearing Mr Choquette's address, his captors decided that they would hold him a few more days, just to taunt the police, and then they would release him.[35] An arrest warrant was already out for one of them and his photo had appeared in several papers, so the offer of safe passage meant that he could avoid prosecution. It is quite likely that, had a second kidnapping not occurred, the Cross affair would have been resolved within several days.

THE CROSS–LAPORTE AFFAIR

PHASE ONE: A SUDDEN ESCALATION

Pierre Laporte, Quebec Minister of Labour and Immigration and Deputy Premier, was kidnapped from his suburban home at 6.18 p.m. Saturday evening, 10 October, just minutes after Jérôme Choquette delivered his final offer to the Liberation Cell. Laporte's kidnappers called themselves the Chenier Cell, after one of the heroes of the 1837 rebellion. Radio-Canada announced the stunning news of the kidnapping at 6.30 p.m. and, within the space of an hour, almost a thousand people had descended upon the Laporte residence—police, reporters, friends, neighbours and curiosity seekers from all over the Montreal area. There was a general mobilisation of the electronic media and all news personnel were called on duty. All programming was postponed or re-scheduled, and ongoing programmes were either cut short or interrupted by special bulletins. Reporters scurried everywhere, hunting down stories, and they repeatedly crossed paths with police officers in search of the same leads. A continuous stream of phone calls—hot tips, bomb scares, pranks—inundated the switchboards of radio stations and police stations.

Because the day following the kidnapping was a Sunday, no daily papers published and the electronic media—radio and television—dominated completely. Even the next day, Monday, not all papers published as it was a national holiday, Thanksgiving. However, five of the seven papers used for this analysis did publish, four of them being special editions put out simply because of the suddent turn of events. The twenty-four-hour period following Laporte's kidnapping was very dramatic. The Chenier Cell issued three separate communiqués within the space of several hours during Sunday afternoon. Deposited in rubbish bins at different locations throughout the downtown area of Montreal, these communiqués were addressed to the radio station CKAC, which would receive an anonymous phone call giving the location of the next communiqué. A reporter would then race to the spot and retrieve the new message. The texts would them be read on the air, photocopied and handed over to the police, much as CKLM had done with the Liberation Cell's communiqués the previous week. The photocopies were then distributed to the print media, which reproduced them in their next editions.

In this spate of communiqués, the Chenier Cell returned to the full set of seven demands set by the Liberation Cell at the beginning, and they set a deadline of 10 p.m. that night for the Government to meet these demands or else their hostage would be 'executed'. In these communiqués, the Chenier Cell also tried vainly to elicit some sort of response from the Liberation Cell. Each new message made some reference to the fact that the Liberation Cell would shortly summarise the situation. But the Liberation Cell, which was as surprised as anyone by the turn of events, remained silent throughout this period. As for Robert Bourassa, the Quebec Premier, he was implicated in a dramatic and highly personal way when the third communiqué arrived, accompanied by a letter from Pierre Laporte addressed to 'My dear Robert'. In this letter, which received saturation coverage and was reproduced word for word or in photocopy in all the newspapers, the Quebec Minister pleaded with the Premier to save his live: 'You have the power to decide my fate. Decide . . . [sic] my life or my death.' The Minister also referred to an 'organised escalation' and the possibility of a 'blood bath' if the political prisoners (Mr Laporte used quotation marks) were not released: 'After me, there will be a 3rd, then a 4th and a 20th.'

This initial twenty-four-hour period ended with a radio address[36] which was delivered by the Quebec leader just five minutes before the 10 p.m. deadline. In this address, Mr Bourassa implied that real negotiations could be pursued if initial guarantees for the release of the hostages—what he called 'the preliminary question'—could be established. His tone was conciliatory;

he even used the term 'political prisoners' without qualifying it, as Jérôme Choquette had done the previous evening. And, in the small hours of the morning, the Liberation Cell sent a conciliatory reply to CKLM, naming Robert Lemieux as their intermediary.[37] They also reiterated the same two demands, release of the prisoners and cessation of police activity, thereby contradicting the Chenier Cell's insistence on the full set of demands. A handwritten letter from Mr Cross accompanied this eighth communiqué. It was the first sign of life from the British diplomat since the Laporte kidnapping. What remained invisible to the public and the media that Sunday was the fact that the police felt overwhelmed by the new turn of events and that the legal advisor of the city of Montreal had begun looking for a legal mechanism which would loosen the strict controls on detaining suspects and obtaining search warrants.

Monday morning, 12 October, the papers that published were full of FLQ communiqués and Pierre Laporte's letters to Robert Bourassa and to his wife. As for reporting on Premier Bourassa's radio address, the papers presented contradictory interpretations of his message. Some suggested that the Quebec leader had agreed to negotiate with the kidnappers, and one paper, in juxtaposing the text of his address with that of Jérôme Choquette's address, under suggestive headlines for each text, implied that Bourassa had performed an about-face. In one English paper, two different reporters contradicted each other, one suggesting a softening in the hard line adopted by Ottawa, the other stating that negotiations could not proceed without first settling the question of guarantees. The full text of the Premier's address was reproduced in four of the five papers publishing on 12 October; the fifth simply cited extracts in a brief résumé of his declaration.

Only two papers published late enough in the day to report the news of a fourth communiqué from the Chenier Cell, which was received by CKAC late Monday morning. In this communiqué, the Chenier Cell, in response to Premier Bourassa's speech, stuck to the full set of demands, but suspended the death threat to their hostage. They, too, named Robert Lemieux as their official spokesman, to negotiate implementation of their demands. A handwritten letter from Pierre Laporte to Robert Bourassa, suggesting ways in which various demands could be met expeditiously, accompanied the communiqué. The full text of this letter would appear in all papers the next day.

It is no coincidence that, among the articles dealing with the Federal reaction to the expanded crisis, two parliamentary correspondents reported that Ottawa was troubled by the lack of public outrage over the kidnapping and by the role of the media, which persisted in disseminating unfounded rumours and broadcasting and publishing FLQ documents before handing them over to the police. Government officials, according to these reports, were particularly angered over the role played by CKLM and CKAC, since this easy access to the radio stations constituted a source of free publicity for the kidnappers and impeded the establishment of direct contact between the Government and any mediator.[38] Here we see very clearly the real stakes in the struggle: access to the media, and, thereby, to the hearts and minds of the general public. In fact, it was becoming clear by Thanksgiving morning that public opinion in Quebec was not one hundred per cent against the FLQ.

One of the main vehicles by which the general public expressed their opinions on the situation was the radio hot lines where callers could phone in and talk to various radio personalities. One of these talk shows was moderated by Pierre Pascau of CKLM. The majority of the callers to his show on 12 October felt that the Government should accept the conditions imposed by the FLQ. While most callers disapproved of their methods, some were sympathetic to the FLQ's ideas.[39] In addition, radio hosts would occasionally conduct informal polls, asking their listeners to call in with their opinion. That same Monday, on his 12.30 p.m. show, André Payette of Radio-Canada asked his listeners to call in their views on negotiations with the FLQ. Of twenty callers, fourteen were totally in favour of negotiations, while six were opposed.[40] These small, improvised, random samplings of public opinion were very influential in generating official perceptions that Quebec public opinion was less than unanimously opposed to the FLQ.

Following the arrival of yet another communiqué from the Chenier Cell, delivered this time to CKLM, which attempted to resolve the apparent conflict between the two cells by insisting on the full set of demands only for Mr Laporte's release and promising Mr Cross's release if the political prisoners were permitted to leave the country, Premier Bourassa designated a negotiator, Robert Demers, to pursue discussions with Robert Lemieux, who was still in prison. Mr Demers' mandate would be the 'preliminary question' concerning guarantees. At the same time that the Quebec leader embarked on the path of negotiations, Prime Minister Trudeau called the Canadian Army into the Federal capital, Ottawa, to take over guard duty at embassies and Government buildings from the Royal Canadian Mounted Police (RCMP), so as to free the latter for the continuing police investigation. Thus, Monday evening, 12 October, marks the first visible sign of a divergence between the two levels of government: Quebec took the road of dialogue, while Ottawa distanced itself from these discussions and resorted to a display of military strength.

What remained unknown to the general public was that everything was then ready for a massive military intervention in Quebec. The necessary documents had already been prepared and merely awaited the official signatures whenever the Quebec Government decided the time had come to call for Federal assistance.[41] Furthermore, it was that same day that preparations began in earnest for a large-scale police operation of arrests and preventive detention aimed at quelling the rising wave of public sympathy for the FLQ.[42] Thus, the night of 12 October marked the emergence of two parallel lines of action—one rendered visible by the media, the other remaining hidden except to those directly involved in the management of the crisis. The visible line was subjected to intense public (and private) debate; this was the path of negotiations. The invisible line, hidden until the invocation of the War Measures Act three days later, was the preparation for the short-circuiting of normal criminal justice procedures via the creation of special powers for the police and the Quebec Attorney-General.

PHASE TWO: THE PERIOD OF NEGOTIATIONS

All the papers of 13 October focused their front-page coverage of the FLQ crisis on the beginning of negotiations between the Quebec Government and the kidnappers' representative, Robert Lemieux. Signs of contradictory interpretations of the significance of the negotiations persisted, but most papers treated the onset of talks between Lemieux and Robert Demers as a hopeful sign. Texts and photocopies of FLQ documents continued to appear in the Tuesday papers, including the letters from the two hostages from the previous day. The arrival of troops in Ottawa was also covered by all the papers and some printed photos of troops or army vehicles on their front pages.

While all attention in Montreal was focused on the negotiations, in Ottawa, Prime Minister Trudeau took advantage of Question Period in the House of Commons to attack the media for giving the FLQ the very publicity which it was seeking. He also expressed the view that it was a mistake 'to encourage the use of the term "political prisoners" for men who are bandits'.[43] Later that afternoon, during an impromptu interview on the steps of Parliament in which he hotly defended the presence of soldiers in the Federal capital and attacked those 'weak-kneed bleeding hearts' who disliked soldiers and guns, Mr Trudeau expanded upon his earlier remarks concerning the media. He explained that the FLQ was trying to gain 'a hell of a lot of publicity for the movement' and that, while the media was playing into their hands, he was not interested in giving them that kind of victory. When one reporter suggested that calling people who held two men's lives in their hands 'bandits' was like waving a red flag in their face, Trudeau retorted that he had been referring not to the kidnappers, but to the people in jail:

> They're not political prisoners, they're outlaws. They're criminal prisoners, they're not political prisoners, and they're bandits. That's why they are in jail.

On the day that almost everyone else was talking about negotiations, Trudeau's was the only voice that continued to preach the hard line publicly.

As for those negotions, almost from the very outset they were in stalemate over the question of guarantees. While Robert Demers went to confirm his mandate with the Quebec Cabinet, Robert Lemieux held a press conference which attracted hundreds of journalists and a boisterous crowd of cheering supporters. Lemieux virulently criticised the authorities, while other speakers expressed their support for the goals of the FLQ to the cheers and applause of the highly partisan crowd. Later that night, a second meeting between Lemieux and Demers also ended in an impasse over the same question of guarantees. Lemieux called a second press conference and announced that he was breaking off negotiations since his mandate dealt only with the implementation of the kidnappers' demands, not the issue of guarantees. Addressing himself directly to the microphones and cameras, he explained that he could not proceed without a new mandate.

Throughout 13 October, while declarations in favour of the FLQ multiplied and Robert Lemieux dominated public attention, preparations discreetly continued for the intervention of troops and the police operation which would begin once emergency powers were adopted. While police officers compiled lists of names of people to be arrested, reports of troop movements around Montreal and Quebec City became more and more frequent. Despite the persistence of rumours in the media that military intervention was imminent, an official Army spokesman continued to deny that these troop movements were in any way related to the FLQ kidnappings. Also unknown to the public was the fact that one of Laporte's kidnappers has been sighted and tailed by police throughout the day, but had been lost in the evening, whereupon he finally met with a member of the Liberation Cell for the first time. The two could not agree on a common approach and decided that, from then on, only the Liberation Cell would speak in both their names, and the Chenier Cell would retreat into absolute silence. It was the Liberation Cell that replied to Robert Lemieux's request for a new mandate, in the name of both cells, giving the lawyer carte blanche to pursue negotiations. Issued early in the morning of 14 October and broadcast by CKLM, the communiqué imposed no new deadline, but declared that a final one would be set in the next communiqué.

While all the morning headlines on 14 October trumpeted the news of the rupture in negotiations the night before, the afternoon papers carried the news of the Liberation Cell's ninth communiqué and of the resumption of talks between Robert Lemieux and Robert Demers. Yet correspondents in Ottawa and Quebec City began speaking openly of the possibility of emergency powers for the police, although such reports were not taken very seriously at the time. The question was raised by the Leader of the Opposition during Question Period that afternoon and Prime Minister Trudeau stated that, while such an option had indeed been considered, no decision had yet been taken. That same afternoon, in a private conversation with the editor-in-chief of the most influential paper in French intellectual circles, Premier Bourassa hinted explicitly that there would be a change in his Government's position in the direction of firmness, and this was reflected in his comments at a press conference later that evening. Again, no one realised this at the time, although, with hindsight, one commentator noted several days later that, as of Wednesday, 14 October, public statements by Quebec Government personalities began to resemble the hard line adopted by Ottawa.

Prime Minister Trudeau's remarks of the previous day, concerning the role of the media, received widespread coverage in the Wednesday papers and media handling of the crisis became a newsworthy item in and of itself. One newspaper commentator pointed out that the radio stations, particularly the 'FLQ mailboxes' CKLM and CKAC, had become involuntary participants in the affair and that journalism had become an active agent of the news instead of its passive purveyor.[44] Certain editors took positions on one side or the other. One editor defended the media's right to provide all the news down to the last detail,[45] while another attacked the notion that radio announcers could become the equals of statesmen.[46] Yet another commentator reported that the radio stations were cooperating with the police in helping 'to preserve the tenuous line of communication with the FLQ upon which hung the lives of two men'.[47]

Parallel with these developments in the media and in official circles, public support for the FLQ cause continued to grow, as statements supporting the FLQ or the idea of negotiations proliferated, while a seemingly unending series of bomb threats and purported FLQ communiqués taxed police resources immeasurably and contributed to a sense of contagion or a kind of bandwagon effect in terrorist threats. Talks between Robert Lemieux and Robert Demers stalled once again and, in another press conference, Lemieux invited the kidnappers to set a new deadline, given the slow pace of negotiations. After criticising Prime Minister Trudeau's remarks about the FLQ as pure demagoguery, the lawyer ended his conference by appealing to all Québécois to take a public stand. The political and social climate began to heat up rapidly as more and more people joined the public debate.

The Premier of Ontario, Quebec's most powerful provincial neighbour, which represented the English-speaking financial elite, declared that 'total war' had broken out in Quebec. A group of sixteen influential Quebec personalities, representing labour, intellectual, nationalist and financial elites, issued a statement insisting that the crisis was a Quebec problem and could only be resolved in Quebec, by Québécois. Known as the 'declaration of the sixteen', it attacked the Ontario Premier and the Federal Government for interference in Quebec affairs and backed Premier Bourassa's initiative in negotiating with the kidnappers. The 'sixteen' called on all those who shared their point of view to make their support known as soon as possible. In a separate development, hundreds of university students attended a rally to hear fiery speeches by leading Quebec radicals, including Robert Lemieux, who invited the students to strike in order to pressure the Government to negotiate the release of the political prisoners. After the rally, the students began preparing thousands of pamphlets exhorting the student population of Quebec to hold study sessions in support of the FLQ.

The declaration of the sixteen and the mobilisation of the university students by radical activists consituted the climax of the visible line: the public debate surrounding negotiations. By Wednesday evening, the fate of the hostages and even that of the kidnappers and their specific demands had taken second place to the larger issue of the legitimacy of Quebec's political aspirations and the right of the Quebec Government to pursue an independent course from Ottawa. In fact, during the several days when this public debate was most intense, all mention of the hostages virtually disappeared from the newspapers. Pictures of them and their families were swept from the front pages, as dramatic shots of soldiers, politicians and the two negotiators dominated in their stead.[48] As for the invisible line, it was also on the evening of 14 October that the compilation of suspects' names was completed by the police. Furthermore, the politicisation of public debate over the issue of negotiations had convinced even the most hesitant decision makers that emergency measures were required. The fate of the hostages had been supplanted by the need to re-affirm the authority of the State.

PHASE THREE: THE TURNING POINT

Thursday, 5 October, marked the day on which the secret preparations carried on by the authorities throughout the week finally came to fruition. Documents which had been ready and waiting were signed, orders-in-council were drafted and formal intergovernmental communications were delivered. The army was called into Quebec, troops took up their assigned positions, police were freed for the coming search-and-arrest operation and negotiations between the Quebec Government and the kidnappers were abruptly terminated with a final offer. Quebec's formal request to Ottawa for emergency powers was readied for delivery in the middle of the night if, as was fully expected, the kidnappers failed to respond within the six-hour period following the final offer. In parallel with these official actions, the student protest strike spread, public expressions of support for the 'declaration of the sixteen' and for a negotiated settlement multiplied and a real sense of confrontation was only dissipated at the end of the day, when negotiations suddenly ended and Robert Lemieux stormed out of his final press conference in a rage.

The press coverage for that day, and especially the transition from morning to afternoon reporting, reflects the rapid change in the course of events. The morning papers continued to discuss the negotiations and the mood was one of cautious optimism. Press treatment of the negotiations between Robert Lemieux and Robert Demers suggested that most people believed that face-to-face talks between the two lawyers would resume that morning. All the morning papers printed the full text of the Liberation Cell's ninth communiqué which had given Robert Lemieux a new mandate the previous morning. However, as of noon, papers no longer reproduced this text, as word of the arrival of troops began to spread. On the front page of one paper, an article on troop movements, which contained the now-familiar denial that they had anything to do with the kidnapping crisis, was flagrantly contradicted by a brief bulletin announcing that Quebec had called in the Army to help deal with the crisis. The banner headline of the last paper to publish that day screamed: 'Troops called out by Bourassa.'

In addition, all the papers that day gave a high profile to the declaration of the sixteen and to the student rally and the ensuing protest strikes. Ontario Premier Robarts' remark on 'total war' also received considerable coverage. By contrast, only one paper mentioned the hostages at all. In this way, the press coverage mirrored the transition in public debate from the fate of the hostages towards the broader issues surrounding the negotiations. Yet, by the end of the afternoon, this focus on negotiations was, in turn, supplanted by the burgeoning official response.

On Friday, 16 October, what had been invisible before became visible. Whereas much of the Governments' decision making and preparations had been shrouded in secrecy before that day, once the War Measures Act was invoked in the early hours of the morning and the massive arrest-and-search operation had begun, everything was out in the open and official statements filled the air. By contrast, what had been by and large visible suddenly became invisible. Whereas before Friday, FLQ communiqués and declarations of support for FLQ goals and/or demands were everywhere to be heard or to be read, once the War Measures Act was invoked and special legislation outlawing the FLQ and forbidding all statements or communications in their favour was passed into law, nothing more was said by or for the FLQ. If anyone spoke of the terrorist organisation, it was to denounce it or to minimise its importance in light of the Government response. As far as the public was concerned, the actions and decisions of the kidnappers became as enshrouded in mystery and silence as were Government decisions and actions before. And, once again, public debate and media coverage became the forum for the visibility of the one and the invisibility of the other.

As was the case on the preceding day, press coverage on 16 October reflected the rapid pace of events by the fact that stories and commentary in the early morning papers differed markedly from those in papers published later in the day. The official announcement that the War Measures Act had been invoked was issued at 5.17 a.m. and rumours that a massive police operation was being mounted occurred only about an hour before that. As a result, while residents of Montreal and other cities woke up Friday morning to radio broadcasts announcing that the country was now under the authority of the War Measures Act, certain morning papers made no mention of this latest middle-of-night development, since they had gone to press before the news had broken. While the earliest papers featured the Quebec Government's final offer of the night before and the arrival of troops in Montreal, later ones featured the War Measures Act and the wave of police arrests, but only the afternoon papers featured the outlawing of the FLQ and the emergency provisions passed into law by virtue of the War Measures Act, since this legislation was only tabled in the House of Commons late in the morning. No reports or headlines dealt with the negotiations and only one story dealt in a peripheral way with the hostages: a rumour, which turned out to be completely false, that the police knew where one of them was being kept. A single headline mentioned Robert Lemieux by his name and only in a subtitle: the main headline referred to him as the 'FLQ lawyer'. Just as rumour and speculation had predominated in reporting on official activity beforehand, so it now predominated in reporting on the kidnappers and their hostages.

PHASE FOUR: THE DÉNOUEMENT

The major event of the ensuing days leading up to Parliament's approval of the Government action has to be the untimely death of Pierre Laporte on Saturday, 17 October. Yet this tragic event did not really alter in any significant way the course the crisis had taken. Even before he was killed by his captors, the hearts and minds of the general public had been captured by the stream of official discourse which arose in the wake of the invocation of the War Measures Act. The Government decision to invoke the Act and to outlaw the FLQ had the effect of drawing all attention away from the terrorist organisation and towards the Government in power. Supporter and critic alike, friend and foe, all eyes turned to the Government, and the Government action dominated public discourse at the expense of the FLQ. Even when voices were raised against the Government action, the pattern remained the same. No critic really challenged the Government's authority to take such action and many did not even question the legitimacy of the action itself. Any direct mention of the FLQ took the form of criticism, often as harsh as that directed against the Government. Furthermore, in their attempt to depict the Government action as one of panic or of overreaction, certain critics minimised and demeaned the strength of the FLQ, depicting it as a marginal and inconsequential force in Quebec political life.

Press coverage on 17 October reflects this lopsided pattern of public discourse, with official versions of events dominating over all others. While the papers had previously been filled with FLQ communiqués and reports on Robert Lemieux's press conferences, the texts which appeared in the papers of 17 October all came from Government leaders or from the law itself. Ten different texts emanating from a diverse range of authorities filled the pages of the papers. Together, they constituted a litany of official declarations reasserting the authority of Government: three legal texts, three official letters requesting emergency powers to quell a 'state of apprehended insurrection',[49] two Government communiqués and two addresses by the Prine Minister of Canada, one to Parliament and one televised to the nation. In addition, there were numerous reports on the flurry of parliamentary speeches or press conferences by Federal and Provincial ministers.[50]

By contrast, all those most likely to profit from the Cross–Laporte affair, to promote their own political cause or to act or to speak in favour of the FLQ, were reduced to silence. Robert Lemieux and the radical leaders who had spoken so loudly and freely, just days before, disappeared in the first wave of arrests. The emergency legislation prohibited all communications in favour of or in the name of the FLQ, including words, recordings, gestures, signs. Meetings in favour of the FLQ were outlawed and property owners allowing them to take place on their premises were subject to imprisonment. The student strikes fizzled out for fear of arrest or prosecution. Reporters became very circumspect in their reporting about FLQ communiqués. CKLM even refused to retrieve a tenth communiqué from the Liberation Cell on the morning of the 17th, but called the police instead when it received a call informing them of its location. The communiqué was never broadcast or published.

CKAC hesitated a long time before taking the persistent phone calls of one of the Chenier Cell seriously, when he phoned repeatedly to inform them where Pierre Laporte's body could be found.[51] When a reporter was finally sent to check out the story, and the Minister's body was indeed found, the station waited several hours before broadcasting the news, until police verified the identity of the corpse. Only because CKAC broke the news of Laporte's death and because speculation was rife that James Cross had also been killed did CKLM dare to retrieve a letter from the British diplomat that was delivered on the day following Laporte's death. Even then, the contents of the letter were broadcast only once, before the police moved in and seized it.[52] While the text was reproduced in Monday's papers, no photocopy appeared. Clearly, the media had suddenly become very cautious, and the issue of censorship became a focus of intense discussion in the ensuing weeks. But, by then, the acute sense of crisis was over.

POWER AND MEANING

> The Front de libération du Québec is not a movement of aggression, but the response to an aggression organized by high finance via the puppet governments in Ottawa and Quebec. (FLQ manifesto, October 1970)

> I appeal to all Canadians not to become so obsessed by what the government has done today in response to terrorism that they forget the opening play in this vicious game. That play was taken by the revolutionaries: they chose to use bombing, murder and kidnapping. (Prime Minister Trudeau, 16 October 1970)

Both terrorists and governments view their actions as legitimate responses to intolerable behaviour by the other side. In normal times, several factors tend to obscure the essential symmetry of the two positions.[53] In insurgent terrorism, or terrorism 'from below', the overtly violent nature of the actions taken or threatened by the terrorists allows governments to deny the legitimacy of their opponents and to use their criminal law and criminal justice systems to counter the terrorist claim. Second, the nature of the terrorist grievance is usually directed at a much broader social or political condition than a single government action or policy. As a result, the terrorist's claim of government violence or aggression is not as easy to justify as the government's claim of terrorist violence. The 'violence' of the system is usually either covert or such that the word 'violence', with its act-oriented connotation, is difficult to apply. It is much easier to speak of 'violence' when a clear victim can be identified. Finally, the State possesses a monopoly on the use of violence, as embodied in its military and policing institutions. As such, the legitimacy and power of the State tend to cloak any overt forms of violence in different guises, such as arrest instead of abduction, preventive detention instead of sequestration, bail instead of extortion, deterrence instead of terrorism, imprisonment instead of hostage-taking, execution instead of murder.

Insurgent terrorism can be characterised as an attempt to challenge this asymmetry in meaning and to equalise the power differential which sustains it. If we strip the adversaries, 'terrorist' and 'government', of their inherent power differential, and treat each side as an equal partner in a struggle for power, the strategies and tactics used by each side to marshall public opinion in support of their respective claims, and to discredit each other's claims, assume a new significance. Just as a symmetry in meaning can be rendered asymmetric by the imposition of a power differential upon two sides in a political contest, so an asymmetry in meaning that is sustained by a power differential can be rendered symmetric by a sudden display of power by the weaker side. Because of the nature of the terrorist strategy, the normal balance of power or, rather, the normal imbalance of power, can be upset or equalised as long as the terrorists can maintain the attention of the government and the public at large.

In the October Crisis, the symmetry between the positions of terrorist and government only became obvious once the terrorists succeeded in gaining access to the communication structure within which political discourse was conducted. The vehicle for this access was the mass media which, attracted by the terrorist's threat and use of violence, then played a central role in transmitting and interpreting the political message of the terrorists. In normal times, the power differential between terrorist and government means that the terrorist has limited, if any, access to the communication structure, while the government has easy, even monopolistic access. Nor is the media the only institution available to the government for disseminating its point of view and influencing political discourse. Only when the terrorist has succeeded in engaging the government in some form of communication which confers upon him some degree of legitimacy is it possible to discern a symmetrical relationship between their two positions. This usually takes the form of mediated communication via widespread coverage in the press, on radio and on television. Truly direct communication between terrorist and government, without media coverage, would not benefit the terrorist unless his threat were such that the government was prepared to negotiate seriously in secret.[54]

Throughout the roughly two weeks that communication was waged between terrorist and government, plus their publics, the symmetry between the two sides became more and more apparent as each side tried to force compliance from the other and to discredit their opponent in the eyes of the public. Premier Bourassa's decision to initiate talks between Robert Demers and Robert Lemieux exacerbated the trend set in the first week, before Pierre Laporte's kidnapping. Due to intensive media coverage, the FLQ was depicted as an equal partner in a political dialogue between symmetrically powerful adversaries. This image of equality was further accentuated by the privatisation of Premier Bourassa which was created by widespread publicity of Mr Laporte's 'My Dear Robert' letters, coupled with the elevation of Robert Lemieux into an official emissary for the negotiating FLQ. This levelling effect contributed to the concerted and increasingly coordinated pressure on the Quebec leader to negotiate a release of the FLQ prisoners. Despite Prime Minister Trudeau's attempt to counter the image of the FLQ as legitimate political actors by emphasising their violent tactics and labelling them 'bandits', media coverage continued to depict the terrorists as legitimate partners in a continuing dialogue with the Quebec Government.

It was during the three days leading up to the 'declaration of the sixteen' that the FLQ made their most spectacular propaganda gains. Newspaper editors tried to reason with the terrorists in their columns, reporters speculated publicly about jurisdictional issues which had been papered over in the first week, tensions increased between Ottawa and Quebec as their paths diverted, wild rumours of impending FLQ strikes multiplied, businessmen fled the province, a broad coalition of groups took up the cause of the terrorists and debated it endlessly in the pages of the newspapers and on the radio talk shows. The crisis became an international story, with journalists from all over the world camped out at CKAC studios, waiting breathlessly for word from the FLQ. By Wednesday, 14 October, the fate of the hostages had become secondary to the broader issue of the legitimacy of Government and the Federal system itself.

The appearance of the Army in Quebec, the abrupt cutting off of negotiations with a final offer and the imposition of the War Measures Act in the middle of the night all shared one common message: The State and only the State has the power to determine the political agenda of Quebec. Extraordinary powers were invoked as if a state of war existed—in this case, the mildest form set out in the War Measures Act, i.e., apprehended insurrection. Two legal mechanisms were used to highlight the violent nature of the FLQ enterprise. Military aid to civil power brought the military in as a legal arm of the police. This civilianisation of the military brought home the fact that the FLQ was considered a real threat to national security. The fact that many saw it as the militarisation of civilian authority (martial law) merely accentuated this perception. Second, by outlawing the FLQ, and any support for its objectives, the emergency legislation ensured that the FLQ's violent means would once again predominate over its political ends in the eyes of the public.

We have seen that the immediate impact of this combined action was to silence the public debate about the FLQ's demands, its political goals and the legitimacy of its grievances. In its stead, we saw emerge an official stream of discourse characterised by an inflation of the FLQ threat and a minimising of the dangers of the War Measures Act. Opposition to the Government took the complementary form of minimising the threat of the FLQ and inflating the dangers of the War Measures Act. The net result was a switch in the focus of public debate from the legitimacy of the terrorists to that of the governments. In doing so, the war model adopted by the authorities led to the re-marginalisation of the FLQ and the destruction of its newly acquired legitimacy. As soon as the overwhelmingly superior power of the State reasserted itself, the power differential between terrorist and government was restored. The meaning of the relationship between adversaries was, once again, defined solely by the official discourse. Because of this, what had been briefly recognised as an essential symmetry in meaning was reduced to an illusion, a brief aberration, an exception which proved the rule. The brief vision of symmetry was merely appearance after all, rendered visible by the transient power of the terrorist that was inherent in his action.

Those with power can define meaning. For a brief period, because of a certain skill in manipulating public opinion via media coverage, and because of the audacity of its action, the FLQ in 1970 was able to define the political agenda of Quebec. As one of Pierre Laporte's kidnappers put it, their action gave them the power to speak and to be heard.[55] The criminal justice system is usually an effective tool for stripping violent acts of their potential meaning, reducing them to idiosyncratic actions of isolated individuals, labelled as common criminals. For a brief period, this tool of social control was rendered ineffective. In its stead, the two governments were forced to resort to a combination of military occupation and political policing.[56] The War Measures Act encased the latter in a legal wrapping, rendering the police operation legal by legally suspending due process. The National Defence Act's provision for military aid to civil authoritity ensured that the former was not a military operation, but merely an adjunct to civil power. Where the criminal justice model failed to define the FLQ as criminals or bandits, the war model succeeded in turning them into enemies. In both cases, the message to the public was clear. The State was more powerful than the FLQ and therefore had sole authority to define the meaning of their two positions, as well as the relationship between the two. For the Government, that relationship was not a symmetrical one based on equality, but an asymmetrical, complementary one based on difference. The basis of that difference was power. Both control models were, in essence, re-asserting the asymmetric relationship between terrorist and government which existed before the crisis began.

CONCLUSION: A DISTINCTIVE PATTERN OF DISCOURSE

Access to the communication structure is intimately related to power. An examination of the patterns of communication before and after the imposition of the War Measures Act on 16 October demonstrates this relationship convincingly. If we take as a measure of public discourse the media coverage of 12–19 October, as analysed in this chapter, a flip-flop pattern emerges. Figure 1 depicts this pattern.

As long as negotiations went on between terrorists and governments, the terrorists dominated discussion. Proponents and opponents alike debated the merits of their case, and pressure on the Government to recognise the legitimacy of their political claim was intense. What enabled the terrorists to maintain a hold on public discourse was the power derived from their use and threat of violence. During this entire period, the preparations for military intervention and the massive police operation of searches and arrests were largely invisible to the public. While visible troop movements fuelled rumours of impending military intervention, these rumours were persistently denied. Only aspects of the police investigation connected with the search for the kidnappers and their hostages were visible, and the illegal nature of many of the searches and arrests only lent greater legitimacy to the terrorists and fuelled the mounting attacks on the legitimacy of the Government position. Thus, the criminal justice model failed to prevent the terrorists' domination of public discourse. With the switch to the war model and the end of negotiations, the pattern reversed completely. All public attention was focused upon the official stream of discourse justifying the actions taken. Opponent

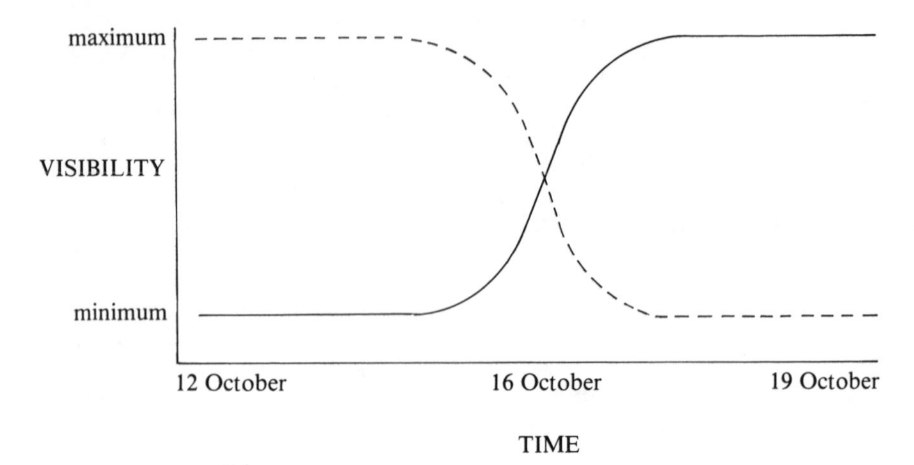

Figure 1. The pattern of public discourse before and after the War Measures Act. The upper part of the diagram represents what was visible and known to the public, as manifested by extensive newspaper coverage. As such, it represents information that has penetrated and spread throughout the communication structure. The bottom part of the diagram represents what was invisible and unknown to the public, as manifested by the absence of newspaper coverage or by extensive speculation and rumour rather than reporting and analysis. As such, it represents information that has been confined to local pockets of the communication structure, such as power elites, bureaucracies, clandestine groups or underground networks, and has failed to spread to the wider net of the mass media, except as rumour. The solid line represents the government definition of the situation, while the dotted line represents the terrorist definition of the situation.

and proponent alike argued the merits of the Government case, and the terrorists' political claims were no longer the object of discussion. As for the terrorists themselves, their communiqués were suppressed, their organisation was outlawed, public support for their cause was forbidden, rallies in their favour were banned and all those who had vocally supported them in the preceding days were swept off the streets into preventive detention.

The terrorists had forced their way into the communication network by means of kidnapping and threat of murder. They had dominated public discourse for almost two weeks by manipulating media hunger for news and the competitive search for scoops. The broadcast of their manifesto had triggered widespread support for their cause and the second, spectacular kidnapping had provoked a massive agit-prop campaign in support of their demands. When the traditional criminal justice model was finally abandoned by the authorities, in recognition of the fact that it was no longer effective in denying political legitimacy to the terrorists and their political goals, the war model, with its display of military force and its structuring of the situation as if it were the revolution the terrorists claimed they wanted, achieved the desired goal. The terrorists were expelled from the communication network, the media became most reluctant to let them back in, public support was silenced and the focus of discussion was drawn away from the terrorists' political programme to that of the Government. As of 16 October, the governments dominated public discourse, both as subjects and as objects.

From the preceding analysis, it is clear that changing patterns in the prevailing interpretation of events in the political life of a given society reflect changing patterns in the exercise of power by opposing parties in that poltical life. Because of the increasingly important role played by the mass media in mediating and shaping political discourse, these changing interpretations can be detected by analysing media coverage during political conflicts and crises. In the October Crisis, the superior power of the State to define the meaning of social and political events was sufficiently challenged by the terrorists' actions to be reflected in a temporary change in the focus and pattern of press coverage. When the State re-asserted its authority by a display of power, press coverage displayed a commensurate shift in the pattern of reporting that was consistent with the restoration of the balance of power to the State.

NOTES

1 RD Crelinsten, 'International Political Terrorism: A Challenge for Comparative Research', *International Journal of Comparative and Applied Criminal Justice*, Vol. 2, 1978, p. 111. Cf. also AP Schmid and J de Graaf, *Violence as Communication: Insurgent Terrorism and the Western News Media*, London and Beverly Hills: Sage, 1982.

2 Schmid and de Graaf, *op. cit.*, p. 29. Elsewhere, I suggest a distinction between secondary victim and primary victim respectively, to differentiate between the object of the terrorist's threat or violence and the object of his or her demand (RD Crelinsten and D Szabo, *Hostage-taking*, Part I, Lexington, Massachusetts: Lexington Books, 1979, p. 6; RD Crelinsten, 'Terrorist Victimization: The Interface between Research and Policy', *in* RD Crelinsten and D Szabo (eds.), *Hostage-taking*, Part III, 1979, p. 129). By labelling the hostage as secondary, I highlight the fact that he is merely a pawn in a communication game. Abraham Kaplan distinguishes between victim, target and audience (A Kaplan, 'The Psychodynamics of Terrorism', *Terrorism*, Vol. 1, 1978, pp. 234–254). These correspond to secondary victim, primary victim and that audience, such as the general public, which is not the object of specific demands, but is expected to be 'impressed' by the action. Alex Schmid (*Political Terrorism: A Research Guide to Concepts, Theories, Data Bases and Literature*, New Brunswick: Transaction Books, 1983, p. 111) differentiates the target of violence (secondary victim) and the target of terror (the class from which targets of violence are drawn) from the target of demands (primary victim) and the target of attention (e.g., public opinion).

3 William A Gamson's quantitative analysis of the strategies and organisational characteristics of a broad spectrum of successful and unsuccessful groups provides valuable insights into the factors which influence the success of a new

challenge. Cf. WA Gamson, *The Strategy of Social Protest*, Homewood, Illinois: Dorsey Press, 1975.

4 Cf. JT Klapper, *The Effects of Mass Communications*, Glencoe, Illinois: The Free Press, 1960, for a classic statement of what has come to be called the 'Limited Effects Model' (SJ Chaffee and JL Hochheimer, 'The Beginnings of Political Communication Research in the United States: Origins of the "Limited Effects" Model', *in* EM Rogers and F. Balle (eds.), *The Media Revolution in America and Western Europe*, Norwood, New Jersey: Ablex, 1982). For works which see a much greater effect of the mass media, cf., for example, C Seymour-Ure, *The Political Impact of the Media*, London: Constable, 1974; ER Black, *Politics and the News: The Political Functions of the Mass Media*, Toronto: Butterworths, 1982; T Gitlin, *The Whole World is Watching: Mass Media in the Making and Unmaking of the New Left*, Berkeley: University of California Press, 1980; A Siegel, *Politics and the Media in Canada*, Toronto: McGraw-Hill Ryerson, 1983. For discussion of the global dimensions of the 'world information order' debate, cf. A Schmid and J de Graaf, *op. cit.*, pp. 175–225; A Smith, *The Geopolitics of Information: How Western Culture Dominates the World*, London: Faber and Faber, 1980.

5 Cf., for example, G Tuchman, *Making News: A Study in the Construction of Reality*, New York: The Free Press, 1978; S Cohen and J Young (eds.), *The Manufacture of News: Deviance, Social Problems and the Mass Media*, Revised Edition, Beverly Hills: Sage, 1981; Glasgow University Media Group, *Bad News*, Vol. 1 and *More Bad News*, Vol. 2, London: Routledge and Kegan Paul, 1976, 1980.

6 Cf., for example, RJ Jackson, MJ Kelly and TH Mitchell, 'Collective Conflict, Violence, and the Media in Canada', *in* Ontario Royal Commission on Violence in the Communications Industry (eds.), *Report*, Volume 5: *Learning from the Media*, Toronto: Queen's Printer for Ontario, 1977, pp. 227–314; JD Halloran, 'Mass Communication: Symptom or Cause of Violence', *in* UNESCO, *Violence and Its Causes*, Paris: UNESCO, 1981, pp. 126–140.

7 S Hall, C Critcher, T Jefferson, J Clarke and B Roberts, *Policing the Crisis: Mugging, the State, and Law and Order*, London: Macmillan, 1978.

8 *Ibid.*, p. 57.

9 H Molotch and M Lester, 'News as Purposive Behaviour: On the Strategic Use of Routine Events, Accidents, and Scandals', reprinted in Cohen and Young, 1981, *op. cit.*, pp. 118–137. Originally published in *American Sociological Review*, Vol. 39, 1974.

10 *Ibid.*, 1981, p. 128.

11 Not all terrorism relies on the mediating and amplifying role of the mass media. As Schmid and de Graaf (1982, p. 2) point out, state terrorism tends to shun media coverage. This does not mean, however, that state terrorism does not communicate to a wider audience than its direct victims. The channels of fear generation are simply different—rumour and gossip probably play an important role, for instance via the families of tortured prisoners and the disappeared, into the larger community. It is also clear that terrorism preceded the development of mass media and that terror was not always aimed at a wider audience. In his study of the Thugs, David C Rapoport states that 'Thugs strove to avoid publicity, and although fear of Thugs was widespread, that was the unintended result of their acts' (DC Rapoport, 'Fear and Trembling: Terrorism in Three Religious Traditions', *American Political Science Review*, Vol. 78, 1984, p. 660). Cf. also DC Rapoport, 'Terror and the Messiah: An Ancient Experience and

Some Modern Parallels', *in* DC Rapoport and Y Alexander (eds.), *The Morality of Terrorism: Religious and Secular Justifications*. New York: Pergamon Press, 1982, pp. 13–42. Certain modern insurgent terrorists, such as the Sendero Luminoso of Peru, do not always rely on the media to achieve their terror effects. Again, rumour and gossip are probably major channels of fear propagation although, in the past year, spectacular attacks in urban centres, which automatically attract media attention, have become a more popular tactic in Peru.

12 Cf. MJ Kelly and TH Mitchell, 'Transnational Terrorism and the Western Elite Press', *Political Communication and Persuasion*, Vol. 1, 1981, pp. 269–296. For related case studies, cf. S Hall *et al.*, 1978, *op. cit.*; P Schlesinger, G Murdock and P Elliott, *Televising 'Terrorism': Political Violence in Popular Culture*, London: Comedia, 1983; L Curtis, *Ireland: The Propaganda War—The British Media and the 'Battle for Hearts and Minds'*, London: Pluto Press, 1984; G Murdock, 'Political Deviance: The Press Presentation of a Militant Mass Demonstration', *in* Cohen and Young, 1981, *op. cit.*, pp. 206–225.

13 The very word 'terrorist' is generally a pejorative used to describe insurgent actors who use violence against the State. 'Freedom fighter' or 'rebel' tend to be used for those insurgents whose cause is viewed favourably in the society in which the reporting is conducted. 'Criminal' is another pejorative commonly used by reporters to describe violent political actors. In this case, they are usually reproducing the image depicted by primary definers, such as the police.

14 Hall *et al.*, 1978, *op. cit.*, pp. 57–60.

15 For a detailed case study of the acute phase of this crisis, known as the 'October Crisis' or the 'FLQ Crisis' of 1970, cf. RD Crelinsten, 'Limits to Criminal Justice in the Control of Insurgent Political Violence: A Case Study of the October Crisis of 1970', Unpublished doctoral dissertation, Université de Montréal, 1985.

16 The key dates and events during this phase are as follows:

5 October (Monday): Liberation Cell kidnaps JR Cross;
10 October (Saturday): final Government offer to Liberation Cell and kidnapping of Pierre Laporte by Chenier Cell;
12 October (Monday): Prime Minister Trudeau calls troops into Ottawa and Quebec Premier Bourassa appoints a negotiator to pursue discussions with FLQ negotiator, radical lawyer Robert Lemieux;
14 October (Wednesday): sixteen Quebec intellectuals and labour leaders issue statement in favour of negotiations by Quebec (*la déclaration des 16*) and university students announce strike in favour of the FLQ;
15 October (Thursday): Army called into Montreal and Quebec City and Robert Lemieux rejects Quebec's final offer to the FLQ;
16 October (Friday): War Measures Act invoked by Ottawa at the request of Quebec and massive operation of arrests and searches begins; Parliamentary debate on Government action begins;
17 October (Saturday): Pierre Laporte is killed and Parliamentary debate ends;
19 October (Monday): Parliament approves Government action.

17 The papers are, in approximate order of time of publication: *Le Devoir, The Gazette, Montréal-Matin, Le Journal de Montréal, La Presse, Le Soleil* and *The Montreal Star*. *Le Soleil* is the Quebec City paper and, along with *The Montreal Star*, published in the afternoon. *La Presse* published around noon and the others are morning papers. *Montréal-Matin* and *Le Journal de Montréal* are tabloids, carrying only headlines and photos on their front pages.

18 The seven demands were:

(a) that the police refrain from all investigations, searches and arrests designed to find the kidnappers or their hostage;
(b) that the political manifesto be published on the front pages of all major Quebec newspapers and that it be read in its entirety and discussed by the released political prisoners (cf. demand no. 3) during a thirty-minute broadcast in prime time on the State-run television network (Radio-Canada, which is the French-language equivalent of the Canadian Broadcasting Corporation, CBC);
(c) that twenty FLQ activists currently serving jail sentences for terrorist activity and three currently out on bail be released and offered the opportunity to leave the country;
(d) that a plane be put at the disposal of these 'patriotic political prisoners' and that they be allowed to fly to Cuba or to Algeria, accompanied by their lawyers and at least two political reporters from the principal French-language dailies;
(e) that a union of postal-truck drivers—the Lapalme drivers—be reinstated by the Federal Government, after having been replaced by another company several months before, triggering a bitter labour dispute;
(f) that a 'voluntary tax' of 500,000 dollars in gold ingots be provided to the political prisoners upon their release and placed on their plane (cf. demand no. 4);
(g) that the name and photo of a presumed informer be made public.

19 Crelinsten, 1985, *op. cit.*, pp. 36–39.
20 The two-line banner headline reads: 'Bourassa, Trudeau and Drapeau are on list of persons targetted by the FLQ' (translation).
21 Crelinsten, 1985, *op. cit.*, pp. 263–264, 512.
22 Canada, *Debates of the House of Commons*, 2nd Session, 28th Parliament, 1970, Vol. VIII, p. 8836.
23 Crelinsten, 1985, *op. cit.*, pp. 65–67.
24 *Ibid.*, pp. 48, 505.
25 That same evening, Gérard Pelletier, Secretary of State and person in charge of Radio-Canada, declared to reporters that he was not opposed in principle to the broadcast of the manifesto, if this gesture would result in the release of Mr Cross. He expressed the opinion that the FLQ's programme was so unaceptable to the Canadian public that the manifesto's publication could do no harm. The Minister was compelled to retract his remark the next day, when no broadcast of the manifesto materialised. It is clear that his Cabinet colleagues in charge of crisis management were unwilling to risk that the Secretary of State was right.
26 Crelinsten, 1985, *op. cit.*, p. 120.
27 Cf. RD Crelinsten, 'Couverture de presse et légitimation de la violence politique', in preparation.
28 Crelinsten, 1985, *op. cit.*, pp. 74–75.
29 *Ibid.*, pp. 96–97.
30 *Ibid.*, pp. 511–512. The first week of the crisis, when only one hostage existed, is usually eclipsed in historical reconstructions by the dramatic events of the second week, when two hostages existed. Accounts of this first week are generally telescoped into a condensed version which suggests that the Liberation Cell gained instant access to the media when they kidnapped James Cross. Yet the first week, though it certainly lacked the sense of crisis characteristic of the second week, involved much more than that. As we have seen, the kidnappers had to struggle to achieve the gains that they did.

31 The communiqué was left under the hall-mat in the entrance of an apartment building, the address of which was given to a reporter at a small newspaper, *La Semaine*, by means of a telephone call. The young reporter who took the call thought that this was yet another of the stream of crank calls that had been going on throughout the week, and ignored it.

32 Robert Lemieux, who shared the independence goals espoused by the FLQ, had defended several of the FLQ activists already in prison or currently facing charges. Since the kidnapping of James Cross, he had been holding a series of daily press conferences each evening just in time for the evening news, in which he would speculate on the intentions of the kidnappers and vehemently criticise the authorities for stalling. He also took it upon himself to visit each of the imprisoned men named by the Liberation Cell, to obtain their written consent to be released if and when the Government granted the kidnappers' demands. Mr Lemieux's press conferences attracted more and more attention from the media during the course of the week and this growing attention, coupled with the increasing readiness of the media to give him a public forum, set the stage for his role as official negotiator for the FLQ in the second week of the crisis.

33 M Raboy, *Libérer la communication : Médias et mouvements sociaux au Québec : 1960–1980,* Montréal: Editions Nouvelle Optique, 1983, p. 62. Translated as *Movements and Messages: Media and Radical Politics in Quebec*, Toronto: Between the Lines, 1984.

34 Crelinsten, 1985, *op. cit.*, pp. 98–100. Cf. also R Gwyn, *The Northern Magus: Pierre Trudeau and Canadians*. Markham, Ontario: Paper Jacks, 1981, pp. 114–115. Originally published in 1980 by McCelland and Stewart.

35 R Haggart and AE Golden, *Rumours of War*, 2nd edition, Toronto: Lorimer, 1979, p. 232.

36 The Quebec leader decided not to appear live on television.

37 Mr Lemieux had been arrested for obstruction of justice on Sunday morning, 11 October, and would only be released on Tuesday morning, 13 October.

38 Crelinsten, 1985, *op. cit.*, p. 153.

39 J-M Piotte, 'Jour après jour', *in* J-M Piotte (ed.), *Québec occupé*, Montréal: Editions Parti Pris, 1971, p. 19.

40 J Provencher, *La grande peur d'octobre '70*, Montréal: L'Aurore, 1974, p. 39.

41 Crelinsten, 1985, *op,. cit.*, pp. 155–156.

42 *Ibid.*, pp. 155, 167, 169.

43 Canada, *Debates of the House of Commons*, 3rd Session, 28th Parliament, 1970, Vol. I, p. 52.

44 G Constantineau, 'A McLuhan par le FLQ . . .', *Le Devoir* (Montreal), 14 October 1970, p. 2.

45 P Gros d'Aillon, 'Les "maux" de la presse', *Montréal-Matin*, 14 October 1970, p. 8.

46 G Boyer, 'L'information et le terrorisme', *Le Soleil* (Quebec City), 14 October 1979, p. 4.

47 J Irwin, 'CKLM Broadcasts Followed Police Instructions', *The Montreal Star*, 14 October 1970, p. 66.

48 Crelinsten, *op. cit.*, in preparation.

49 Apprehended insurrection was the minimal condition necessary, according to law, before the War Measures Act could be invoked. The phrase therefore appears in all three official letters requesting emergency powers: from the Director of the Montreal police to the Mayor of Montreal; from the Mayor to Prime Minister Trudeau; and from Premier Bourassa to Prime Minister Trudeau.

50 For a detailed analysis of all these texts and speeches, cf. Crelinsten, 1985, *op. cit.*, chapters 18, 19 and 21.

51 For details, cf. *ibid.*, pp. 453, 460–465, 472.

52 For details, cf. *ibid.*, pp. 469–472.

53 In the ensuing analysis, I am referring to a symmetry in the *meaning* of the two positions, not the *accuracy* of these positions with regard to some objective assessment of the actual state of affairs in Quebec at the time. Both governments and terrorists were trying to put a particular point across and part of these opposing positions was that the other side was not to be trusted. One way to discredit an opponent's assessment of political reality is to discredit him as a legitimate actor in such an endeavour. Again, I am not interested in the accuracy of these assessments of each other's legitimacy, but in the meaning of these labels. Whether or not the kidnappers were *really* criminal or the authorities were *really* fascist oppressors, the symmetry in the *meaning* of the labels 'criminal' and 'fascist oppressor' is that both labels discredit the other side.

54 Robert Kupperman suggests that this latter situation could exist in cases of political extortion based on threats of mass destruction, in which public knowledge of the threat could create widespread panic (RH Kupperman, *Facing Tomorrow's Terrorist Incident Today*, Washington, DC: Law Enforcement Assistance Administration, US Department of Justice, 1977, pp. 11–13). As Schmid and de Graaf (1982, *op. cit.*) point out, however, modern insurgent terrorism generally relies on the mass media for its effectiveness. Cf. also B Jenkins, 'International Terrorism: A New Mode of Conflict', Paper presented at the fifth course of the International School of Disarmament and Research on Conflicts, Urbino, Italy, 1974, p. 4. Certainly the FLQ in 1970 was not interested in secret negotiations.

55 F Simard, *Pour en finir avec octobre*, Montréal: Stanké, 1982, p. 28.

56 For a discussion of political policing, cf. AT Turk, *Political Criminality: the Defiance and Defence of Authority*, Beverly Hills: Sage, 1982; J-P Brodeur, 'High Policing and Low Policing: Remarks about the Policing of Political Activities', *Social Problems*, Vol. 30, 1983, pp. 507–520.

VI

National and International Responses

Pathways Out of Terrorism for Democratic Societies

P Wilkinson

Terrorism is not a synonym for violence and insurgency in general. It is a special kind of violence, a weapons system that can be used on its own or as part of a whole repertoire of unconventional warfare. In Central America, for example, terrorism is typically used in conjunction with rural guerrilla warfare and with economic and political warfare in all-out bids to topple government. But in Western Europe, which experiences about forty per cent of all international terrorist incidents annually, terrorism is usually unaccompanied by any wider insurgency. It is extreme, often indiscriminate violence directed at innocent people, but it is at the pre-insurgency phase.

Terrorism can be briefly defined as coercive intimidation, or more fully as the systematic use of murder, injury and destruction, or threat of same, to create a climate of terror, to publicise a cause and to coerce a wider target into submitting to the terrorist's aims. International terrorism is terrorism exported across international frontiers or used against foreign targets in the terrorists' country of origin. There is no case of purely domestic terrorism, but there are, of course, many campaigns in which the political violence is concentrated in a single national territory or region (e.g., the Irish Republican Army (IRA), and the Basque and Corsican terrorists).

A major characteristic of political terror is its indiscriminate nature. This is not to deny that terrorists generally have a specific human 'target', whether individual or collective, which they intend shall be the victim of the most direct physical harm. Quite apart from the physical danger of persons who are not pre-selected targets being hurt, there is the unavoidable side-effect of widespread fear that others might be harmed. As Raymond Aron remarks in one of his most percipient observations on terror: 'An action of violence is labelled "terrorist" when its psychological effects are out of proportion to its purely physical result. In this sense, the so-called indiscriminate acts of revolutionaries are terrorist, as were the Anglo–American zone bombings. The lack of discrimination helps to spread fear, for if no one in particular is a target, no one can be safe.'[1] Terrorists are frequently prepared to engage in the indiscriminate murder of civilians. All men, women and children, regardless of their role or position in society, may be regarded as potential victims for the sake of the 'cause'. As a policy the waging of terror necessarily involves disregarding the rules and conventions of war: non-combatants, hostages, prisoners-of-war and neutrals have no inviolable rights in their eyes.

It is also characteristic of acts of terror that they appear entirely unpredictable and arbitrary to the society which suffers them. One writer has expressed this point very clearly: '... no observance of commands, no matter how punctilious, on the part of the prospective victims can ensure their safety.'[2] There are of course many instances of the individual victims of terroristic assassination or mass murder being given preliminary warning that they are to die. The point is that such acts are only 'selective' and 'predictable' according to the rationalisations of the terrorists. As Malraux writes 'le terroriste décidât seul exécutât seul',[3] and it is in this sense true to describe terrorism as a peculiar kind of tyranny in which the potential victim is unable to do anything to avoid his destruction because the terrorist is operating and judging on the basis of his own idiosyncratic code of norms and values. Do these characteristics of unpredictability and arbitrariness also apply in the case of the repressive terror of the State? There are two major reasons why they are common also to State terror. First, leaders and agencies of force in the State, who have acquired the preponderance of coercive power, may disregard the underlying values and norms of the existing law with impunity within their domain. Secondly, tyrannical dictators or totalitarian governments tend in the process of consolidating their power to subvert and manipulate the legal structure in order to forge it into a weapon of oppression of their internal opponents. Under such conditions, instead of the sovereignty of the State and the rule of law being used solely to apply punishment for clearly defined crimes or offences, judicial acts may become what Hobbes termed acts of hostility. For Hobbes a hostile act 'falls not under the name of Punishment'[4] because it is an act against one who is not politically obedient to the legal authority (i.e., the State). Punishment, argues Hobbes, is reserved for those citizens of a State who have broken the law. It is 'an Evil inflicted by publique authority ... to the end that the will of men may thereby better be disposed to obedience.'[5] But in response to an act of hostility, he claimed 'all infliction of evil is lawful,[6] that is, there are no limits to the violence that can be committed. It is clear that many tyrannies and terrorisms have sought to confuse this important distinction by lending their actions a quasi-legal rationale. They resort to defining any action they choose as an act of political disobedience, thus claiming that by their hostile acts they are in reality punishing political crimes.

Political terror can also be differentiated from other forms of violence, agitation, intimidation and coercion by virtue of its extreme and ruthlessly destructive methods. These may range from genocide, massacre and political murder and torture at one end of the scale of violence, to physical beatings, harassment and defamation campaigns at the other. For any large-scale campaign of repressive or of revolutionary terror, the terrorists find it necessary to arm themselves adequately to check any possible resistance. Whereas spears and machetes were once adequate weapons in African tribal regimes of terror, and the famous sect of the Assassins in the eleventh and twelfth centuries used the dagger, modern terrorists must depend upon a minimal supply of guns and explosives. The factor of dependence upon weaponry, combined with the reliance of many terrorist movements and agencies upon a military organisational structure and style, underlines the close relationship between terrorism and war. Indeed, many American and French scholars have been so impressed by this affinity that they have tended to study terror exclusively in the context of 'internal war' and problems of 'counter-insurgency'.

It is in practice extremely difficult to draw clear boundaries between war and terror. EV Walter, in his pioneering sociological analysis of the regime of terror, argues that, unlike civil terror, military terror aims ultimately at exterminating the enemy. Civil terror, he asserts, is always an instrument of power aimed at the control and not destruction of the population: 'When violence is employed in the service of power, the limit of force is the destruction of the thing that is forced.'[7] But there are two serious confusions in Walter's argument. Firstly, we cannot assume that all wars are wars of extermination: even in modern wars distinctions are sometimes made between the civilian population and the armed forces of protagonists, and one of the normal strategic objectives is still the acquisition and control of enemy territories and their inhabitants. Secondly, and more important, internal revolutionary and State terror can both be directed at the deliberate destruction of whole social groups who have been designated as enemies. Terrorists may believe such a policy of liquidation to be necessary in order to capture or sustain their political control, or it may be dictated by ideological reasons, or it may derive from motives of hatred, vengeance or even sadism or mass hysteria, or a combination of these factors. The point to be made is that, historically, acts of civil terror have not, unfortunately, always stopped short at the subjugation of certain real or imagined opponents. Totalitarian regimes of terror have committed crimes against humanity on a vast scale. We have no right to assume that the perpetrators of civil terror will arrive by some rational calculation at a notional limit to violence, and that they will always rule out extermination. As for the implications for political control, mass murders will intensify rather than extinguish the general terror: everyone in the population will be terrified lest they be caught in the next wave of terror. Thus, although this chapter does not attempt a detailed analysis of war terror (i.e., terroristic usages in military conflict), our discussion must necessarily include consideration of the many kinds of destruction against the civil population which can be understood as what Hobbes called 'hostile acts', or acts of war against the population.

What fundamentally distinguishes terrorism from other forms of organised violence is not simply its severity, but its features of amorality and antinomianism. Terrorists either profess indifference to existing moral codes or else claim exemption from all such obligations. Political terror, if it is waged consciously and deliberately, is implicitly prepared to sacrifice all moral and humanitarian consideration for the sake of some political end. Ideologies of terrorism assume that the death and suffering of those who are innocent of any crime are means entirely justified by their political ends. In their most explicit and candidly amoral form such terrorist rationalisations amount to a Nietzschean doctrine of the Will to Power. Might is right; terror can always be justified as the expediency of the strong; and such Judaeo–Christian notions as mercy, compassion and conscience must go with the weak to the wall of history. Political terror is not always justified in such explicit terms. Some utopian or messianic sects and movements that have resorted to terror have attempted a teleological justification, generally involving the rejection of all existing ethical principles and codes on the grounds that morality is manipulated in the interests of the rulers. In some cases it is argued that the acts of terror are necessary sacrifices to be made on the journey towards introducing a new revolutionary order which will introduce a New Man and a New Order and, of course, a Revolutionary Morality. But, of course, the first task is that the existing order and morality should be destroyed.

We have thus identified some of the key characteristics common to all forms of political terror: indiscriminateness, unpredictability, arbitrariness, ruthless destructiveness and the implicitly amoral and antinomian nature of a terrorist's challenge. There remains the important distinction between political terror and political terrorism. Clearly political terror may occur in isolated acts and also in the form of extreme, indiscriminate and arbitrary mass violence, the kind of insurrectionary outburst that characterised the lynchings and sackings at the height of the popular terror in parts of revolutionary France. Such terror is not systematic; it is unorganised and is often impossible to control. 'Therefore neither one isolated act, nor a series of random acts is terrorism.'[8] Political terrorism, properly speaking, is a sustained policy involving the waging of organised terror either on the part of the State, a movement or faction, or by a small group of individuals. Systematic terrorism invariably entails some organisational structure, however rudimentary, and some kind of theory or ideology of terror.

CAN THE END JUSTIFY THE MEANS?

Much confusion occurs in the debate on the morality of terrorism because of a failure to distinguish between ends and means. Terrorism is a *method* which can be used for an infinite variety of goals. The cliché that one man's terrorist is another man's freedom fighter simply reflects the paradox that many groups use terror in pursuit of a cause that most liberal democrats in principle regard as just, the goal of self-determination or national liberation.

Yet even in cases where we have firm grounds for believing that a group has a legitimate grievance or sense of grave injustice, this does not mean that we should refrain from posing the question 'Does a just cause justify the use of terrorism by its supporters?' Terrorism is inherently and inevitably a means of struggle involving indiscriminate and arbitrary violence against the innocent. It is almost universally agreed among the citizens of liberal democracies that the method of terrorism is morally indefensible in a free society in which, by definition, there are always other ways of campaigning for a cause, methods which do not involve a fundamental attack on the human rights of fellow citizens.

The writer takes an even more determined moral position against the use of terrorism, whether by States or factions. It is frequently claimed by the terrorists that actions such as bombings, hostage-taking and assassinations are the only means they have for removing a tyrannical or oppressive authoritarian regime. This claim does not bear serious examination. There are *always* some other means, including moral resistance, civil disobedience and well-planned and concerted economic and political action, which either alone or in combination may prove extremely effective in removing an unpleasant regime with the minimum of violence. There is no case of terrorism removing an autocracy, but there are many inspiring examples of the relatively bloodless removal of dictatorships, including Portugal and Spain in the mid-1970s, and Haiti and the Philippines in early 1986.

Thus, I would argue, we should question the received wisdom of the radical left which constantly asserts that terrorism is permissible, even desirable, as a weapon against non-democratic systems. From the humanitarian point of view there is a stench of double standards about such a policy. Should we be less concerned about the rights of the innocent in non-democratic societies? What right have we, sitting in the comfort of our free political systems, to condone a method of 'freedom fighting' which robs innocent civilians of life, maims many others and destroys their property? And how can we ignore the historical evidence that those who use such methods become corrupted and criminalised by the savagery of the infliction of terrorism. Moreover, the idea that terrorism is a precise, highly controlled, almost surgical, strategy is a cruel illusion. Once a society becomes launched on a spiral of terror and counterterror, there may be no way of stopping the carnage. Terrorism will become interwoven with the criminal sub-culture: for many it will become a way of life. The violence of the Internal Macedonian Revolutionary Organisation (IMRO) in the Balkans in the early twentieth century, and parts of Latin America and the Lebanon today are gruesome examples of the corrupting effects of habitual terrorism.

AN ALTERNATIVE TO WAR? OR A THREAT TO PEACE?

There can be no doubt that terrorism, despite its savage inhumanity to civilians, is a lesser evil than modern war. Even in a relatively short-lived civil war in a small country the level of violence will be vastly more lethal and destructive. For example, more people died in the Lebanese civil war, 1974–

1976, than were killed in the entire decade of international terrorism, 1975–1985.

Terrorism is sometimes described as a form of 'surrogate warfare'. In the sense that it is often adopted as a low-cost/low-risk/potentially high-yield instrument of foreign policy by pro-terrorist states, this is a useful concept. But it would be a dangerous error to assume that it therefore follows that the international community can face the growth of terrorism with equanimity. For just as severe internal terrorism often leads to a full-scale bloody civil war, so international terrorism has sometimes triggered international war, with all its accompanying wider dangers to international peace. Let us not forget that it was the assassination at Sarajevo in 1914 which was the catalyst for the First World War. More recently, the attempt on the life of Ambassador Argov in 1982 helped to spark the Israeli invasion of Lebanon, with all its inevitable dangers of escalation to a general war in the Middle East.

Democracies are clearly vulnerable to terrorist attacks because of the openness of their societies and the ease of movement across and within frontiers. It is always easy for extremists to exploit democratic freedoms with the aim of destroying democracy. But a well-established democratic political system also has enormous inner strengths. By definition, the majority of the population see the government as legitimate and accountable. They willingly cooperate in the upholding of the law, and they rally to defend democracy against the petty tyrants who try to substitute the gun and the bomb for the ballot box. There is no case in the modern history of terrorism in which a European democracy has been destroyed by a terrorist group and replaced by a pro-terrorist regime.

Even so, it is clear that prolonged and intensive terrorism can be very damaging to the democratic governments and societies that experience it.

For example, in Northern Ireland and Spain, terrorism not only fundamentally attacks innocent life and rights, it aims to undermine the democratic values, institutions, processes and rule of law. By scaring away investment and disrupting industry and commerce, terrorism can gravely weaken the economy. At its most intensive, terrorist violence serves to incite hatred, promote and provoke intercommunal conflict and violence and destroy the middle ground of normal politics. If unchecked, terrorism can easily escalate to a civil war situation, which the terrorist may seek to exploit in order to establish a terrorist-style dictatorship.

In the long run, the threat to human freedom from the spread of terrorism in Third World areas is far more serious. For terrorism in these often highly unstable areas is much more likely to lead to the undermining of fragile democratic governments and is widely used as part of the repertoire of revolutionary movements to bring about Marxist takeovers of Third World states. These wider revolutionary conflicts clearly alter the regional balance of power in Third World areas. They also threaten general economic interests, such as access to oil and raw materials, and this threatens general lines of maritime communication at strategic chokepoints.

Internationally, terrorism is far more than a challenge to the rule of law and a clear threat to individual life and safety. It has the potential to become far more than a minor problem of law and order. For the United States, the major target of international terrorism all over the world, terrorism can be a major national security problem. For example, the handling of the seizure of the entire United States diplomatic mission in Tehran in 1979 became a colossal burden to the Carter Administration, crippling other activities and weakening US morale and prestige internationally, particularly in the Middle East. More recently, the tragic bombings of US marines in Lebanon not only took large numbers of lives, but also severely curtailed President Reagan's military options in the Middle East and made it impossible for him to maintain a US presence in Lebanon, either through the multinational force or independently. The suicide bombers' atrocity reached US opinion, Congress and the media, as it was clearly designed to do.

WHY HAS THE COLLECTIVE RESPONSE OF THE DEMOCRACIES BEEN SO INEFFECTIVE?

In a world of sovereign states, it is inherently difficult to secure effective international cooperation. Despite the fact that Western states cooperate in such organisations as the Organisation for Economic Co-operation and Development (OECD) and the North Atlantic Treaty Organisation (NATO), it is extremely hard for them to cooperate in the sensitive area of internal security and law and order. On such matters, they have traditionally taken the view that the national government has total sovereign control. Western politicians and judiciaries are as chauvinistic in this respect as other states, despite the many moral and legal values they have in common with fellow Western governments.

A major political difficulty in cooperation against terrorism is the lack of a clear single forum for Western democratic cooperation. The European Community does not include all the major Western states, and in any case it is primarily concerned with economic matters. NATO, though it has a larger membership, is by no means comprehensive and essentially remains an intergovernmental organisation in which member states jealously guard their national sovereignty. It has been left to the Council of Europe to mount the most serious effort at West European legal cooperation against terrorism, the European Convention for the Suppression of Terrorism, but the Council lacks political weight and influence and its convention remains unratified by key states such as France and is unenforceable.

Some Western democracies have little or no direct experience of terrorism, and thus cannot see the importance of the problem. Enthusiasm for action often dissipates rapidly once shock at a specific outrage has died away. Some Western governments are unwilling to sacrifice or endanger commercial outlets, possible markets, trade links or sources of oil or raw materials by taking really tough action against pro-terrorist states like Libya. Some states are also afraid of attracting revenge attacks from terrorist states; they hope to buy security by appeasement. Some have a double standard; they insist on regarding some terrorists as 'freedom fighters' who need not be condemned (e.g., Irish–American attitudes to the IRA, French attitude to Armenian terrorists, Greek attitude to the Palestine Liberation Organisation).

Worst of all is the widespread defeatist illusion, assiduously cultivated by the propaganda of the terrorist movements, that democracies can do nothing to defeat terrorism. This is dangerous rubbish; look at the success of countries like Canada against the FLQ and Italy against the Red Bridgades. We do have experience and knowledge showing us how to defeat even severe campaigns of terrorism. It is basically up to each democratic government to learn and apply these lessons, and to improve its cooperation with fellow democracies.

PATHWAYS OUT OF TERRORISM

The experience of modern terrorism in democratic societies has shown that there are no simple solutions. There are many pathways out of terrorism: some lead in opposite directions, while others provide alternative routes to strengthening democracy and reducing violence. Let us briefly identify six main possible pathways out of terrorism.

(a) The terrorists solve the problem on *their* terms: they achieve their goals and abandon the violence as it is no longer seen as necessary. This has only happened very rarely. In a number of colonial independence struggles in the 1950s and 1960s (Palestine, Algeria, Cyprus, Aden) something very close to this did occur. But the conditions of decaying colonialism provided exceptional opportunities for terrorists which no longer exist in the 1980s: for example, the colonial regimes lacked the will to maintain their control and were gravely economically and militarily weakened by the exertions of the Second World War. The terrorists in most cases had vast popular support from their own populations.

(b) The terrorists perceive the inevitable failure of their campaign, or in any case grow weary of it, and give up their violent struggle without having achieved their goals. An example of this was the abandonment of the struggle by the IRA in Northern Ireland in 1962.

(c) The terrorist campaign may be eradicted within the borders of the State by determined and efficient military action. For example, a draconian military campaign virtually wiped out the Tupamaros' campaign in Uruguay. But this was at the heavy cost of the virtual suspension of democratic government in Uruguay and its replacement by military rule. A frequent effect of this strategy is to drive the terrorist residue into exile. The campaign may thus be continued abroad, including attacks on the diplomats of the target State, with the terrorist hope of carrying their fight back to their homeland.

(d) A fourth scenario is a political solution on the State's terms which nevertheless makes sufficient concessions to genuine and deeply felt grievances of a particular group that in effect it dries up the water in which the terrorist 'fish' swim. There have been a few examples of remarkably successful use of this strategy. It was extremely effective in the case of the South Tirol (Alto Adige) where the autonomy measure passed by the Italian Senate in 1971 defused a violent campaign. But in most cases this method has only limited success because there are always 'maximalists' or 'irreconcilables' among the terrorists who refuse to abandon the struggle unless or until their absolute demands are met. Hence, despite the bold and imaginative measures taken by the French and Spanish governments respectively to introduce a real regional autonomy in Corsica and the Basque region, hard-line terrorist groups in each case have continued to wage violence.

(e) Many democratic states attempt to deal with internal terrorism as essentially a problem of law enforcement and judicial control, viewing terrorist actions as serious crimes and dealing with them firmly under the criminal code. There have been some remarkably successful applications of this approach, for example against the early generations of the Red Army Faction in West Germany and against the Red Brigades and other terrorist groups in Italy. In both these cases it is true that the laws and the judicial process had to be strengthened in order to cope with the ruthlessness and cunning of the terrorists. But it is manifestly the case that in both countries essential democratic values and institutions and the rule of law remain intact despite these long and bitter campaigns of terrorists to undermine the State and to provoke it into over-reaction. There are often serious residual problems with this approach, however. Some terrorists will inevitably succeed in escaping justice by fleeing abroad, as has been the case with many Red Brigades and Red Army Faction members who have fled to France, 'Terre d'Asile'. From their new bases abroad they may then continue to wage violence and attempt to re-build their networks within their home countries. Nor does the problem end when terrorists are successfully apprehended, tried and convicted. As our penal systems are ill-adapted and under-equipped to handle large numbers of imprisoned terrorists, it is all too easy for militant and determined terrorists, with considerable experience of covert activity outside gaol, to begin to re-establish their terrorist organisations within the prison system. In addition, using the aid of pro-terrorist lawyers and friends, they can even hope to establish a network outside prison which they can direct, or at least strongly influence, from inside gaol. Hence the law-enforcement solution by itself is inevitably incomplete. Without additional measures there is the strong likelihood of new terrorist movements recreating themselves from the ashes of the old.

(f) Finally there is the educative solution, in which the combination of educational effort by democratic political parties, the mass media, trade unions, churches, schools, colleges and other major social institutions, succeeds in persuading the terrorists, or a sufficient proportion of their supporters, that terrorism is both undesirable and counterproductive to the realisation of the terrorists' political ideals. This approach is, of course, fraught with enormous difficulties and requires many years of patient work before it yields results. It has rarely been tried on a major scale. However, small-scale experiments in the re-education and re-habilitation of former members of ETA–militar and the Red Brigades indicate that it can be extraordinarily successful in certain cases.

Democratic pathways out of terrorism (d), (e) and (f), are obviously not mutually exclusive. Undoubtedly the most effective policy will be multi-pronged, involving skilfully coordinated elements of each. However, with the exception of models (a) and (b), in which the terrorist group itself takes the decision to abandon its violence, there is no sound basis for assuming that the *total* eradication of terrorist violence from democratic society is feasible. It is part of the price we must pay for our democratic freedoms that some may choose to abuse these freedoms for the purposes of destroying democracy, or some other goal.

It follows that an essential part of democratic effort must be to provide effective pathways out of terrorism for the individual. By so doing we will constantly be aiming to minimise the threat of residual or irreconcilable terrorism which may otherwise slowly re-group and re-gain sufficient support and strength to launch fresh campaigns of violence. In this constant moral and psychological battle of attrition, democratic authorities must constantly seek more imaginative and effective ways of enabling individual members of terrorist organisations to make a complete break with their comrades and leaders who, for their part, strive to keep their members under an iron grip.

INDIVIDUAL PATHWAYS OUT OF TERRORISM

The first thing to understand about the problem is the colossal pressure which keeps the individual terrorist bonded to the terrorist group. He or she will have been intensively indoctrinated, literally brainwashed, into seeing the world through terrorist spectacles. They will have been taught to hate every-one associated with government and the legal system, especially the police, with a blind loathing. They will be schooled into suspecting the authorities' every move, habitually disbelieving their every statement, constantly vigilant for new traps or ruses set by the 'enemy'. Moreover, they will have it instilled into them that the only important thing in life is the furtherance of their cause. Every involvement in a terrorist action will further reinforce this and will be rationalised as the dedicated pursuit of justice. They are taught to see every bombing, each shooting, each fresh act of violence against the 'enemy' state, as a heroic act, as the living of the true revolutionary existence. Terrorist violence is thus transvalued in their minds to provide meaning and purpose to their hitherto 'wasted' lives. Once this process of indoctrination and mental bonding to the ideology of the group has reached a certain point it is extremely difficult to even bring the terrorists to *question* their fundamental ideological assumptions and beliefs, let alone abandon them.

A second major constraint is the individual terrorist's fear of his/her own group. Terror has always been the method used to ruthlessly control discipline within the conspiratorial world of the terrorist organisation. Kneecapping, shooting in the hand or foot and torture are punishments frequently meted out for relatively minor violations of the rules laid down by the leadership. Major infractions or repeated disodedience of the leaders' orders usually mean death. If the individual terrorist is tempted to 'disappear' or is suspected of having gone over to the side of the authorities, the terrorists will try to mete out vegeance on their closest family members. Faced with such deadly threats from their own group, it is little wonder that few of them find the courage to try to break with the past.

Thirdly, even it they can break these bonds, some individual terrorists will be deterred from breaking with their group because of the apparently insuperable difficulties of rehabilitating themselves in normal society. They will be in constant fear of being handed over to the authorities. In order to get a job, buy a car or obtain a home, they will need false identity papers, and will be in constant fear of their true identity being discovered by their employers and by the police. If he or she wishes to get married, register a birth or death, obtain a passport, open a bank account or acquire social security benefits, then these difficulties will be compounded. If the terrorist knows that the normal sentence for the crime(s) of which they have been guilty is severe, say at least ten years' imprisonment, they may calculate that the dangers of leaving the group's protective 'underground' cover and the added risk of arrest outweigh the disadvantages of continued terrorist membership.

Countries such as Italy and the United Kingdom already have some considerable experience of the ways in which these conflicting pressures tug at the emotions and divide the loyalties of those who are hesitating on the brink of turning state's evidence. The 'repentant terrorist' legislation in Italy (which has now been permitted to lapse) and the 'Supergrass' system in Northern Ireland, have both provided invaluable intelligence about the operations, membership and plans of their respective terrorist groups. It is notoriously difficult for the police to infiltrate the cell structures of modern terrorist organisations. Hence this type of 'inside information' from informers is often the sole means of securing the information to bring terrorists to trial and to convict them. This experience has also led to an intensification of the terrorist leaderships' attempts to punish and deter those who may seek to betray them, for they known that once such a process gets well under way it can rapidly demoralise and destroy their whole campaign. This underlines the absolute necessity of providing 'supergrasses' with new identities and secure new lives to protect them from assassination by their former comrades.

In spite of this important and fascinating experience, which incidentally has hardly begun to be subjected to any serious research by social scientists, it must be said that our democratic legal and penal systems remain extraordinarily ill-suited to the specialised tasks of winning over individual members of the terror organisations and setting about their long-term rehabilitation in normal society.

There are many who would deny the need to bother with such efforts. It is easy to pour cold water on theories and policies of rehabilitation which have proved of very limited value in application to conventional crime. Yet there is reason to believe that the terrorist who has been subjected to intensive political indoctrination and conditioned by the terrorist training and way of life is potentially susceptible to determined, skilful and well-planned re-education and rehabilitation techniques, if only we could make these available within our penal systems.

It is of course a very important consideration in any rule of law system that there should be no special privileges or discrimination in favour of those who plead political motives for their crimes of violence. According terrorists special status only serves to legitimise and perpetuate their own self-perception as 'freedom fighters' and 'heroes', and simultaneously undermines the general public's confidence in the impartiality and consistency of the judicial system. But why should we not be more innovative and sophisticated in our *application* of penal policy? The prisons already have the broad tasks of education and rehabilitation, though few have the resources to do these jobs well. There is already considerable flexibility in reviewing sentences and in the parole system. There is no reason whatever, in principle, why we should not make a more serious effort within the prisons to re-educate and rehabilitate, and to inject the expertise and relatively modest resources necessary to cope with the special problems of terrorist offenders, in just the same way that we make special provision for trying to wean drug addicts away from their addictions. In the long term such measures would make a substantial contribution by significantly reducing the danger of terrorist cells reconstituting within the prison systems and of terrorists returning to their careers of violence when ultimately released. Currently in most penal systems little or nothing is being done to open up these individual pathways out of terrorism. Intense efforts in this field will be required if they are to have any effect, and we should be under no illusion that it will be easy to win back the committed terrorist.

All these major elements of an effective policy to deal with terrorism ultimately depend on the moral strength and political will of democratic society. The best general defence of a democracy against the alienation and violence of extremism is the sensitivity and effectiveness of the system of government in attending to the basic needs of the people. In a famous passage in *Vivian Grey* that brilliant British statesman, Disraeli, reminds us:

> that all power is a trust—that we are accountable for its exercise—that, from the people, and for the people, all springs, and all must exist.[9]

A democratic government that loses touch with this central principle risks not only losing the trust of its citizens, but utlimately its legitimacy. And it is only when there is a genuine crisis of democratic legitimacy that extremists have a chance of seizing power.[10]

NOTES

1 Raymond Aron, *Peace and War*, London: 1966, p. 170.
2 S Andreski, 'Terror', *in* Julius Gould and William L Kolb (eds.), *A Dictionary of the Social Sciences*, Glencoe: 1964.
3 André Malraux, *La Condition Humaine*, Paris: 1946, p. 189.
4 Thomas Hobbes, *Leviathan*, London: OUP, 1947, p. 241.
5 *Ibid.*, p. 238.
6 *Ibid.*, p. 241.
7 Eugene V Walter, *Terror and Resistance*, New York, 1969, p. 14.
8 Martha Crenshaw Hutchison, 'The Concept of Revolutionary Terrorism', *The Journal of Conflict Resolution*, Vol. 16, September 1972, p. 3.
9 *Vivian Grey*, book vi, chapter 7.
10 For a full analysis of the implications of terrorism for liberal democracy and the problems of response see the author's *Terrorism and the Liberal State*, second edition, London: Macmillan, 1986.

International Humanitarian Law and Terrorism

M Sassoli*

INTRODUCTION

Terrorist acts[1] and systematic resort to terrorist acts, i.e., terrorism, are problems of increasing concern not only to the general public and political leaders at national level, but also to the international community. Unlike other crimes, terrorism and terrorist acts are not only a challenge but also a twofold threat to the law of a State:

(a) a direct threat, in that they jeopardise the life and physical integrity of individuals, most of whom—whether in truth or merely in the eyes of the terrorists—represent the State and its polity, but who sometimes are ordinary citizens implicated merely by accident;
(b) an indirect threat, in that in combating terrorist acts, the aggressed State runs the risk of departing from the law—possibly under the influence of public opinion.

Thus, terrorists may themselves create the conditions which to their mind justify their deeds.[2]

However, terrorism threatens not only the law of each individual State, but also the law of the international community, that is, international law. Some States commit terrorist acts or support terrorism to attain their political objectives, some accuse their adversaries of supporting terrorism, while others deem it permissible to contravene international law in their drive against terrorism, and yet others justify alien occupation, racial segregation and violations of the most basic human rights by advocacy of the need to fight terrorism. All this is a threat to the peaceful coexistence of States and their cooperation in solving the world's problems, and consequently, to international law.

---

* The views expressed in this chapter are those of the author and are not binding on the International Committee of the Red Cross.

International law must therefore deal with the phenomenon of terrorism. It is not surprising that many people expect International Humanitarian Law to provide an answer to terrorism. Terrorists consider that any means are justified to realise their ends, their acts are often indiscriminate in their efects and are always directed against innocent people. And International Humanitarian Law precisely protects the innocent, outlaws indiscriminate attacks even in wartime and is based on the principle that not all means are justified by their ends—even in wartime. But many people observe that International Humanitarian Law is entirely inappropriate to constrain terrorism[3] and some even contend that Protocol I of 1977, a part of International Humanitarian Law, is a charter for terrorism, a 'pro-terrorist treaty masquerading as humanitarian law'.[4]

In the present contribution, I would like first to show that International Humanitarian Law *cannot* provide a direct answer to most questions raised by terrorism, simply because it is not applicable outside armed conflicts. Then we shall demonstrate that within its scope of application, i.e., in armed conflicts, International Humanitarian Law has an answer to terrorism, in that it unconditionally prohibits terrorist acts and provides for their repression.

TERRORISM—A PHENOMENON ARISING MAINLY OUTSIDE THE SCOPE OF INTERNATIONAL HUMANITARIAN LAW

INTERNATIONAL HUMANITARIAN LAW IS APPLICABLE IN ARMED CONFLICTS

The term 'International Humanitarian Law' applies to those rules of international law which aim to protect the victims of armed conflicts.

International Humanitarian Law is basically codified in the Hague Convention no. IV of 1907,[5] the Geneva Conventions of 1949[6] and the 1977 Protocols additional to the Geneva Conventions.[7] As International Humanitarian Law protects victims of armed conflicts, it necessarily applies only to armed conflicts. Conversely, terrorism is a phenomenon which raises the biggest problems outside armed conflicts.

Armed conflicts fall into two categories: armed conflicts of an international character, and armed conflicts not of an international character.

International Armed Conflicts. The major part of International Humanitarian Law is applicable only to armed conflicts of an international character, the majority of which are, in common parlance, wars between States. Consequently, terrorist acts are practically only covered by that part of International Humanitarian Law if they are committed in an armed conflict between two States. And we shall show that the law of international armed conflicts is characterised by an elaborate set of prohibitions of terrorist acts.

In addition, according to Art. 1 (4) of Protocol I, armed conflicts of an international character include national liberation wars, i.e., 'armed conflicts in which peoples are fighting against colonial domination and alien occupation and against racist regimes in the exercise of their right of self-determination, as enshrined in the Charter of the United Nations and the Declaration on Principles of International Law concerning Friendly Relations and Co-operation among States in accordance with the Charter of the United Nations'.

Some people contend that this provision makes terrorists into lawful combatants and gives legal clearance to terrorism.[8] From a legal viewpoint, though, that contention is untenable. Firstly, the provision itself specifies that it relates to situations of armed conflict. It is therefore not enough for somebody merely to consider himself engaged in a national liberation war: his activities must take place within the framework of organised hostilities of a certain intensity. Secondly, the national liberation war must take place in the exercise of *the people's* right of self-determination. In this respect, the term 'people' is used in an extremely restrictive sense in contemporary international law, especially by Third World countries. In particular the right to self-determination is not vested in entities which do not qualify as 'peoples', e.g., minorities or groups of political opponents. Furthermore, the right to self-determination is acknowledged only in exceptional cases—if at all—for peoples already living in a national community. The Declaration on Friendly Relations, to which Art. 1 (4) explicitly refers, emphasises that the right of self-determination is generally no justification for breaking up an existing sovereign state.

Finally, should a terrorist ever happen to take part in a genuine national liberation war, the import of Art. 1 (4) is that he must carry his arms openly and comply with the rules of International Humanitarian Law[9] which, as we shall see later on, strictly prohibits any terrorist act whatsoever.

Non-international Armed Conflicts. Armed conflicts not of an international character are covered by Art. 3 common to the four Geneva Conventions of 1949 and by Protocol II. To qualify for the designation of conflicts not of an international character as understood in Art. 3 common to the four Geneva Conventions, there have to be *armed forces* on either side engaged in *hostilities*; there has to be a conflict, in short, which is 'in many respects similar to an international war, but takes place within the confines of a single country'.[10] The definition of armed conflicts not of an international character is even more restricted under Protocol II. It covers only armed conflicts 'which take place in the territory of a High Contracting Party between its armed forces and dissident armed forces or other organized armed groups which, under responsible command, exercise such control over a part of its territory as to enable them to carry out sustained and concerted military operations and to implement this Protocol'.[11]

It is therefore obvious that this part of International Humanitarian Law, too, does not apply to terrorist acts in situations of internal disturbances, tensions or riots, and even less so to those terrorist acts which we fear most, i.e., those directed at random at members of the general public in peaceful countries. 'Sporadic acts of violence [...] not being armed conflicts',[12] terrorist acts alone are not enough for any provision of International Humanitarian Law to become applicable.

However, terrorist acts committed in a genuine armed conflict not of an international character are prohibited, as we shall show, both by Art. 3 common to the four Geneva Conventions and by Protocol II.

USEFULNESS OF CERTAIN NOTIONS OF INTERNATIONAL HUMANITARIAN LAW IN DEALING WITH TERRORISM IN PEACETIME

We have seen that International Humanitarian Law is not applicable outside armed conflicts. In peacetime, terrorist acts must and can generally be dealt with under the domestic laws of States. Only one set of problems must be solved by international law: the problems of international judicial cooperation in dealing with terrorism. One of these problems concerns the question of the exemption from extradition of those claiming a political motivation for their terrorist acts.[13]

The exemption from extradition in favour of political offenders is a traditional principle recognised in many municipal legal systems and in extradition treaties. But the concept of 'political crime' is not easy to define. There are 'absolute political offences', 'complex political offences', 'connex political offences' and 'relative political offences'.[14] Furthermore, there is no consensus as to whether all these categories or only some of them fall under the exemption. However, there should be a broad consensus that perpetrators of terrorist acts should not be allowed to plead that exemption.[15]

But the controversial question is how to define the terrorist acts which should not be covered by the exemption. It is precisely in this connection that consideration, by analogy, of a notion of International Humanitarian Law could be useful: the notion of grave breaches of International Humanitarian Law, commonly referred to as war crimes.[16] War crimes include all grave violations of the laws of war committed by the agents of a belligerent State against citizens or property of the enemy.[17] Terrorists attack civilians, launch indiscriminate attacks and take hostages. If committed in wartime by combatants, these acts would be war crimes—we shall deal with this further on. Consequently, one could define a terrorist act as an act that would be qualified as a war crime if committed in wartime by combatants.[18]

Admittedly, such a definition restricts the meaning of the term terrorist. It does of course not imply that private citizens may, in peacetime, commit acts which would have been justified had they been committed in wartime by combatants. Such acts, of course, are crimes which may and must be punished. But insofar as people have committed such crimes with a political motivation, they may fall under the exemption from extradition for political offenders (which of course does not mean that they must not be punished).

Conversely, terrorist acts as defined above should never be acknowledged as political offences granting exemption from extradition. The legal foundation for this statement is the fact that in the Geneva Conventions and in Protocol I, States have formally undertaken either to prosecute or to extradite war criminals.[19] Consequently, how could they refuse to prosecute or to extradite persons who, as private individuals, committed such acts in peacetime?

Politically and morally, such an exception to the exemption from extradition for political offenders should be justified even in the eyes of States which consider that the objectives pursued by the terrorists are to some extent legitimate. Indeed, one hundred and sixty-two States have acknowledged by being party to the Geneva Conventions that not even a soldier's perfectly legitimate objective to defend his country can possibly justify war crimes, and they even accepted the obligation to punish their own soldiers for their war crimes.[20]

Even from the terrorist's point of view, it should be perfectly justified that he, claiming to be engaged in a just war, is expected at least to comply with the laws of war, failing which he cannot expect any lenience because of his objectives.

INTERNATIONAL HUMANITARIAN LAW AND TERRORISM IN ARMED CONFLICTS

Within its field of application, International Humanitarian Law provides an answer to terrorism, and even a very clear one: terrorist acts are forbidden. To those who do not observe this prohibition, International Humanitarian Law grants a minimum of humane treatment, but at the same time allows and in most cases even obliges States to punish them for their acts.

PROHIBITION OF TERRORIST ACTS IN INTERNATIONAL HUMANITARIAN LAW

In International Armed Conflicts. In armed conflicts of an international character—including, by virtue of Art. 1 (4) of Protocol I, national liberation wars—terrorist acts are strictly forbidden.

Most victims of terrorist acts are *civilians*, who are protected against the effects of hostilities by the following provision: 'The civilian population as such, as well as individual civilians, shall not be the object of attack. Acts or threats of violence the primary purpose of which is to spread terror among the civilian population are prohibited'.[22] Attacks against civilians by way of reprisals are prohibited too.[23]

Once in the power of the enemy, civilians are protected by the Fourth Geneva Convention and its Art. 33 which explicitly stipulates that 'all measures of intimidation or of terrorism are prohibited'.

For the benefit of *combatants*, i.e., members of armed forces, International

Humanitarian Law also imposes certain restrictions on the terrorist acts which the enemy may direct at them.

First of all, the right of the Parties to the conflict to choose methods and means of warfare is not unlimited.[24] Then in more concrete terms, there are the prohibition of perfidy[25] and the prohibition of the refusal to give quarter.[26] Once in the power of the enemy or otherwise 'hors de combat', combatants are entitled to overall protection and respect: by virtue of the First Convention if they are wounded or sick in the field; by virtue of the Second Convention if they are wounded, sick or shipwrecked at sea and by virtue of the Third Convention if they fall into the power of the enemy.

In Non-international Armed Conflicts. The provisions of International Humanitarian Law applicable in internal armed conflicts are far less detailed than those applicable in international conflicts. They nonetheless unconditionally prohibit not only States but also insurgent parties from committing terrorist acts of any kind.

Art. 3 common to the four Geneva Conventions obliges each Party to treat humanely, persons not or no longer taking an active part in the hostilities and explicitly prohibits, inter alia, 'violence to life and person, in particular murder of all kinds, mutilation, cruel treatment and torture' and the 'taking of hostages'. Art. 4 of Protocol II re-affirms the aforementioned prohibitions and expressly bans 'acts of terrorism'. What is new in Protocol II compared with Art. 3 common to the four Conventions is the inclusion of a number of articles designed to increase the protection of civilians by influencing the very conduct of the hostilities.[27] These articles implicitly forbid terrorist acts in the conduct of the hostilities.

TREATMENT PRESCRIBED BY INTERNATIONAL HUMANITARIAN LAW FOR PERSONS WHO COMMITTED TERRORIST ACTS

Both in and outside armed conflicts, humane treatment of imprisoned terrorists is an important factor in combating terrorism. The International Committee of the Red Cross (ICRC) itself observes time and again in the activities it carries out in situations of internal strife and tension, in particular during its visits to persons detained in connection with such situations, that torture or summary and arbitrary executions of real or pretended terrorists never put an end to terrorism. On the contrary, they provide terrorist groups, after the event, with a justification for their crimes—primarily in their own eyes, but very often in the eyes of the general public too. Indeed, the non-respect of human rights by a government is sometimes what actually initiates the creation of terrorist groups.

In *internal armed conflicts* captured terrorists, be they civilians or military agents, benefit from the same fundamental guarantees (provided for in Art. 3 common to the Conventions and in Protocol II) as all other persons who do not or no longer take a direct part in the hostilities. Of course, they may and must be punished in accordance with municipal law for their terrorist acts, but only after trial by a court offering the essential guarantees of independence and impartiality.[28]

In *international armed conflicts*, we have to distinguish between terrorists who belong to the armed forces of a State and those who are civilians.

If a member of the armed forces commits terrorist acts, and if these constitute war crimes, he may and must be punished for his war crimes by the Power on which he depends.[29] If he has fallen into the power of the enemy, he has prisoner-of-war status but may and must be punished by the Detaining Power for his war crimes.[30]

However, if in addition, he even failed to comply properly with his fundamental obligation to distinguish himself from the civilian population while engaged in an attack or in a military operation preparatory to an attack, he forfeits his right to be a prisoner of war, but must nevertheless be granted equivalent treatment.[31] This means that he may be punished not only for his war crimes, but also for his mere participation in the hostilities.

If the armed forces of one party to the conflict systematically commit terrorist acts, one could even maintain that they do not qualify as armed forces[32] and that consequently, their members are not in any way entitled to prisoner-of-war status.

Finally, if the persons who have committed terrorist acts are civilians, their own party may and must punish them for their participation in the hostilities and for their terrorist acts. If they have fallen into the power of the enemy, they are protected civilians, but they may nevertheless be punished for their participation in the hostilities and for their terrorist acts, though only after a fair trial. If they are agents of a State, their acts can even be considered as war crimes.

In conclusion, we must remember that terrorist acts, insofar as they are grave breaches of the Conventions or of Protocol I, become universal crimes under the jurisdiction of all parties to these instruments. Each party is under an obligation to enact the necessary legislation to extend its criminal jurisdiction to any person who has committed a grave breach, regardless of the nationality of the perpetrator, the victim or the scene of the crime. If a party has custody of a person alleged to have committed grave breaches, it is obliged either to bring that person before its own courts for prosecution, or to extradite the person to another party which has made out a *prima facie* case.[33] But in this case, too, the accused person must in all circumstances be granted a fair trial.[34]

NOTES

1 I beware of trying to give a definition of terrorist acts. This difficult task is left to other contributions concerned with conceptual problems. For the purpose of this chapter, it is enough to call to mind some typical aspects of terrorist acts:

(a) terrorist acts are crimes under municipal law;

(b) terrorist acts consist of the use or threatened use of violence for political ends;
(c) terrorist acts are inherently indiscriminate in their effects and often directed at outsiders;
(d) terrorist acts aim at creating an atmosphere of terror directly or indirectly conducive to achievement of a political end;
(e) in the opinion of those who commit terrorist acts, no one has the right to be neutral.

2 Thus it is not surprising that terrorists are, quite consciously, natural allies of people in favour of capital punishment.
3 Paul Wilkinson, 'The Laws of War and Terrorism', *in* David C Rapoport and Yonah Alexander (ed.), *The Morality of Terrorism, Religious and Secular Justifications*, New York, 1982: pp. 308–324.
4 Douglas J Feith, 'Law in the Service of Terror', *The National Interest*, No. 1, 1985, p. 47 (Douglas J Feith is US Deputy Assistant Secretary of Defense for negotiations policy).
5 Hague Convention No. IV and Annexed Regulations respecting the Laws and Customs of War on Land, of 18 October 1907, *American Journal of International Law*, Vol. 2, 1908, Suppl., pp. 90–117.
6 Geneva Convention for the Amelioration of the Condition of the Wounded and Sick in Armed Forces in the Field of 12 August 1949 (First Convention) 75 UNTS 31–83; Geneva Convention for the Amelioration of the Condition of the Wounded, Sick and Shipwrecked Members of Armed Forces at Sea of 12 August 1949 (Second Convention) 75 UNTS 85–133; Geneva Convention relative to the Treatment of Prisoners of War of 12 August 1949 (Third Convention) 75 UNTS 135–285; Geneva Convention relative to the Protection of Civilian Persons in Time of War of 12 August 1949 (Fourth Convention) 75 UNTS 287–417.
7 Protocol Additional to the Geneva Conventions of 12 August 1949, and relating to the Protection of Victims of International Armed Conflicts (Protocol I), of 8 June 1977 and Protocol Additional to the Geneva Conventions of 12 August 1949, and relating to the Protection of Victims of Non-international Armed Conflicts (Protocol II), of 8 June 1977, *International Legal Materials*, Vol. 16, 1391, 1442 (1977).
8 Cf. for instance Feith, *op. cit.*, pp. 37–42.
9 Cf. Art. 44 (2) and (3) of Protocol I.
10 Jean Pictet (ed.), *The Geneva Conventions of 12 August 1949, Commentary*, Vol. III, Geneva Convention Relative to the Treatment of Prisoners of War, ICRC, Geneva, 1960, p. 37.
11 Art. 1 (1) *in fine*, of Protocol II.
12 Thus explicitly Art. 1 (2) of Protocol II.
13 On the possible interpretations of this exemption see: Geoffrey S. Gilbert, 'Terrorism and the Political Offence Exemption Reappraised', *International and Comparative Law Quarterly*, Vol. 34 (4), 1985, pp. 695–723.
14 See Hans Schultz, 'The Classic Law of Extradition and Temporary Needs', *in* Bassiouni (ed.), *A Treatise on International Criminal Law*, Vol. II, Springfield: 1973, pp. 314–317.
15 On 25 June 1985, the US and UK signed a Supplementary Treaty concerning the Extradition Treaty concluded between the US and UK, in order to avoid that (mainly IRA) terrorists should fall under the political offence exception to extradition (cf. International Legal Materials, 1985, pp. 1104–1109). But the ratification of this treaty seems to be meeting with difficulties in the Senate.

Likewise, the resolution on 'Measures to prevent international terrorism', (A/RES/40/61) adopted by consensus by the UN General Assembly on 9 December 1985 'urges all States not to allow any circumstances to obstruct the application of appropriate law enforcement measures provided for in the relevant conventions to which they are party to persons who commit acts of terrorism covered by those conventions'. See also Resolution 23 adopted by the Seventh United Nations Congress on Prevention of Crime and the Treatment of Offenders, held in Milan, Italy, 26 August to 6 September 1985 in: UN Doc. A/Conf. 121/22 of 26 September 1985.

16 All grave breaches of the Geneva Conventions and of Protocol I are war crimes [cf. Art. 85 (5) of Protocol I], but the concept of war crimes includes other crimes too.

17 Hans-Heinrich Jescheck, 'War Crimes', *Encyclopedia of Public International Law*, Instalment 4, Amsterdam, 1982, p. 294.

18 This idea can be found, for instance, in the 'Report of the Committee on International Terrorism at the 1984 Paris Conference of the International Law Association', *The International Law Association, Report of the Sixty-first Conference*, Paris, 1984, pp. 313–324 at 317.

19 Art. 49 (2) of the First Convention; Art. 50 (2) of the Second Convention; Art. 129 (2) of the Third Convention; Art. 146 (2) of the Fourth Convention, Art. 85 (1) of Protocol I.

20 Art. 49 (1) of the First Convention; Art. 50 (1) of the Second Convention; Art. 129 (1) of the Third Convention; Art. 146 (1) of the Fourth Convention; Art 85 (1) of Protocol I.

21 For a detailed study on the prohibition of terrorist acts in International Humanitarian Law cf. Hans-Peter Gasser, 'Prohibition of Terrorist Acts in International Humanitarian Law', to be published in *International Review of the Red Cross*, July/August 1986.

22 Cf. Art. 51 (2) of Protocol I.

23 Cf. Art. 51 (6) of Protocol I.

24 This principle is codified, for instance, in Art. 22 of the Hague Convention No. IV of 1907.

25 Cf. Art. 37 of Protocol I.

26 Cf. Art. 40 of Protocol I.

27 Cf. Art. 13 to 15 of Protocol II.

28 For the fundamental guarantees in penal prosecution, see Art. 3 (1) (1) (d) common to the Four Geneva Conventions and Art. 6 of Protocol II.

29 Cf. the provisions mentioned in note 20.

30 Cf. Art. 85 of the Third Convention and Art. 42 (2) of Protocol I.

31 Cf. Art. 44 (3) and (4) of Protocol I. By virtue of these provisions, a combatant may fulfil his obligation to distinguish himself from the civilian population—in certain specific situations—merely by carrying his arms openly.

32 Cf. Art. 43 (1) of Protocol I.

33 As stipulated by the provisions mentioned in note 19.

34 Art. 49 (4) of the First Convention; Art. 50 (4) of the Second Convention; Art. 105 ff and 129 (4) of the Third Convention and Art. 146 (4) of the Fourth Convention.

Extradition Law and Practice in the Crucible of Ulster, Ireland and Great Britain: A Metamorphosis?

B W Warner

The names Gerard Tuite, Dominic McGlinchey, Seamus Shannon and, potentially, Evelyn Glenholmes, are milestones as regards Anglo–Irish relations in the difficult area of extradition between Eire and the two constitutuent parts of the United Kingdom—Ulster and Great Britain. Some would say they represent a notable step forward in the application of the principle aut dedere, aut judicare to Republican 'terrorists', while others would insist that these same cases contain an odious reversal of Ireland's historic policy of asylum granted to Irish 'patriots'.

To understand and fully appreciate the significance of these decisions, it is initially necessary to briefly outline the Irish and British positions on the extradition of fugitive political offenders. From this the chapter moves to a consideration of the practical application of these positions following the renewal of civil conflict post-1969. The effect of the 'flanking movement' contained in the extra-territorial legislation of 1976 is detailed. Other suggested solutions to the extradition problem such as an all-Ireland Court are mentioned in passing. Finally the period post-1981 is studied and an examination is made of the aforementioned cases. Conclusions drawn from these and Ireland's recent signing of the European Convention for the Suppression of Terrorism provide some signposts as to the future direction of extradition among the three parties.

The Irish Republic occupies a peculiar place in British political culture as does Ulster in its relationship to Eire. Ireland is a sovereign republic, yet its citizens have the British franchise. Ulster, according to Art. 2 of the Irish Constitution, is an integral part of Eire, but this is without practical effect due to partition. This situation is characterised by the number of citizens of each state resident in the other. According to 1979 figures approximately 34,000 Irish citizens were usually resident in Ulster,[1] and calculations based upon the 1971 census indicate 26,183 Ulstermen and 84,038 persons born in

Great Britain were resident in Eire.[2] This interpermeability of populations suggests the historical ties in the triangular relationship better than any historical review.

The peculiarity of the relationship is also manifest in the rendition of fugitive offenders among the three. To speak of extradition as it occurs between other sovereign, foreign states is somewhat misleading since the return of fugitives between Eire and the UK occurred under a system of 'backing of warrants'. This operated not by treaty but under reciprocal legislation and validated warrants endorsed in Ireland as capable of enforcement in the UK and vice versa.[3] Although initiated when Ireland was a British colony the practice was maintained post-1921 after the Anglo–Irish Treaty. It lasted until 1964 between Eire and Great Britain but broke down as early as 1929 between Eire and Ulster due to a decision of the Dublin High Court that there was no authority for such a practice.[4] Authorities in Northern Ireland reciprocated by refusing to endorse Irish warrants and from 1930–1965 there was no formal rendition between the parts of Ireland.[5] The relationship between Eire and Great Britain worked more smoothly as shown by the fact that in 1957 some one hundred and nine Irish warrants were executed in Great Britain and eighty-nine British warrants in Eire.[6] However in 1964 the entire edifice crumbled with decisions in the House of Lords[7] which stopped endorsement of Irish warrants in Britain, and an Irish Supreme Court ruling[8] that the process of backing of warrants was repugnant to the Constitution. The situation stood in 1964 with all three jurisdictions as potential havens.

Even while the original system was in place it contained a number of departures from normal extradition procedures. There was no judicial control and therefore none of the safeguards normally open to the accused. Of primary significance to this chapter was the absence of the political offence exception. However, this did not prove a major barrier to the operation of the system and two reasons may be advanced. In the first instance the system within Ireland itself ceased operation within a decade of the founding of the Free State. Secondly the British authorities proved circumspect in advancing warrants with political overtones as seen in a 1923 Home Office circular urging restraint in using the system.[9] This demonstrates an acute awareness on the part of the British that rendition of fugitive political offenders, while feasible, could prove problematic. Just how much of a problem will become apparent, but first it is necessary to sketch out the British and Irish positions on the extradition of the fugitive political offender.

British extradition law is codified in the Extradition Act 1870, and the definition of the political offence has developed from case law dating back to 1890. In the case of Castioni the Court ruled that to benefit from the exception to extradition the offence must not only be incidental to and part of political disturbances, but must also be in furtherance of same.[10] Added to this in the case of Meunier was the requirement that there be two parties vying for control of the State.[11] These two cases form the basis of the British approach which is labelled the political incidence theory.[12] It concentrates on the offence and its context rather than on the motive of the offender. This concentration is evident in the famous opinion of Viscount Radcliffe in the case of Schtraks, and is worth quoting at length.

> In my opinion the idea that lies behind the phrase 'offence of a political character' is that the fugitive is at odds with the State that applies for his extradition on some issue connected with the political control or government of the country. . . . There may, for instance, be all sorts of contending political organizations or forces in a country and members of them may commit all sorts of infractions of the criminal law in the belief that by so doing they will further their political ends: but if the central government stands apart and is concerned only to enforce the criminal law that has been violated by these contestants, I see no reason why fugitives should be protected by this country from its jurisdiction on the ground that they are political offenders.[13]

This is the point at which British law stood in the mid-1960s when the Irish Republic formulated its own Extradition Act.

Faced with the breakdown of the old system the authorities on both sides of the Irish Sea worked out a new arrangement embodied in the UK by the Backing of Warrants (Republic of Ireland) Act 1965, and in Eire by Part III of the Extradition Act 1965. The terms of the Irish legislation were heavily influenced by the 1957 Council of Europe Multilateral Extradition Convention.[14] It differs significantly from British law in such matters as lack of the requirement of a prima facie case which the British use in dealing with other states. O'Higgins suggests that Irish insistence on dropping such items was due to their desire to harmonise Anglo–Irish practice with their extradition relations with other states.[15]

More significant, for our purposes, is the discrepancy as regards the statement of the political offence exception in the two pieces of legislation. The British law refers to denial of surrender for an 'offence of a political character'[16] while the Irish Act refers to 'a political offence or an offence connected with a political offence'.[17] Therefore there were two pieces of legislation intended to impose identical and reciprocal obligations which, by their wording, may not. It is clear that that two phrases are not necessarily the same thing[18] and in 1965 it was unclear whether the Irish courts would turn to the British case law defining political offences or the European examples given the central role of the 1957 Convention.[19] In his commentary written the year after the 1965 Act came into being O'Higgins opined 'the Irish courts in interpreting this provision will not be able to rely upon Anglo–American decision. . . . They will have nothing to guide them as to the meaning of "political offence"'.[20]

The wider interpretation given by the Irish courts in their developing case law from 1965 until the early 1970s and the onset of 'the Troubles' is best seen in two cases. *Bourke* vs *Attorney-General*,[21] and *The State* (*Magee*) vs *O'Rourke*[22] were both Supreme Court decisions and both contained a noteworthy dissent by Mr Justice Fitzgerald who later held the post of Chief Justice in 1973–1974. In the former the defendant assisted the escape and sheltering of a Soviet spy jailed in England. The Supreme Court ruled this as an offence connected with a political offence, and stated that the 'connected offence' itself didn't have to be political in character. Chief Justice O'Dālaigh believed the connection must be 'spelt out by the courts in the widest possible manner'.[23] In his dissent Fitzgerald J noted it was the spy's original offence which was political and not his offence of escape, therefore Bourke's offence of assisting the escape couldn't be connected with a political offence.[24] In the latter case extradition was requested for blatantly non-political crimes, but the appellant claimed he might be charged with political offences if returned. In support he produced affidavits concerning his role in a 1963 IRA raid on a British barracks in Ulster, which he had been questioned about by the RUC. The Chief Justice gave the court's opinion that due to his virtual admission of complicity in the political offence of the raid Magee had brought himself within S.50 (2) (b) of the Irish Act.[25] This limited application of the speciality rule in Anglo–Irish law disallows extradition if there are 'substantial grounds' for belief that, once returned, a fugitive will be tried for a connected offence or a political offence. This proves that in the early 1970s the Irish Supreme Court was willing to impute bad faith to the prosecuting authorities of Ulster. This is explicit in Fitzgerald J's dissent with which Teevan J was in concord. They felt that Magee failed to produce the necessary 'substantial grounds' and were unwilling to speculate that the Ulster authorities would not adhere to the limited speciality rule.[26]

Thus while the British position regarding the political offence exception pre-1970 can be characterised as the political incidence theory, the Irish position is less easily defined. Clearly their courts do not apply the British approach, but, as various commentators note, there were too few published cases to determine absolutely what the Irish position was beyond its tendency to the Continental.[27]

While the Irish Supreme Court was working towards this position the conflict in Ulster was coming to a head in 1969–1970. At the same time the British courts maintained their adherence to the stated position when faced with Irish requests for two Irish gunmen in the cases of Dwyer and then Keane. Patrick Dwyer was held in England after jumping bail on a charge of shooting at the Garda. The shots were allegedly fired from a car transporting arms in an attempt to evade arrest. Dwyer claimed membership of a group splintered from the IRA. In his decision granting extradition Lord Parker stated he was not satisfied that shooting at policemen was a political offence.[28] It is probable, given the decisions in Bourke and Magee, that an Irish court would have decided otherwise given the circumstances of the case.

Of equal import is the case of Patrick F Keane[29] accused of two bank robberies in Eire and the murder of a Garda during one. He claimed membership of Saor Eire which had claimed several such actions with the purpose of providing arms for Ulster.[30] He'd been a member of the IRA until 1964, served time for an attack on the governing Fianna Fail office in 1967 and was often questioned by the Garda. This was the background to his application to the High Court for a writ of habeas corpus claiming he feared that if returned for a non-political offence he would be detained or tried for a political offence under S.2 (2) (b).[31] Again Chief Justice Lord Parker refused the application, ruling Keane had failed to prove 'substantial grounds' for his claim.[32] This was upheld unanimously by the Law Lords whom Keane had been given leave to appeal to as a point of law of general public import was involved. In giving their decision Lord Pearson noted two affidavits from the Irish Attorney-General stating Keane would only be tried on the offences cited in the warrant. He stated,

> assurances such as are contained in these two affidavits are properly admissible and can properly be taken into account under S.2 (2) (b) of the Act, although, in view of the uncertainty of future developments and the possibility of new political situations and exigencies arising, they should not be regarded as conclusive.[33]

The importance of the Keane decision lies in the fact that it was the complete reversal of the highest Irish court's decision in the Magee case. The Irish Supreme Court was willing to impute bad faith to the courts in Ulster while the highest British court was unwilling to do so in regard to the Irish courts. A clearer division cannot be found.

The first British military fatality came in February 1971 and was followed by internment in August. In this period the RUC began to request the return of those from Eire who'd committed offences in the context of the spreading conflict in Ulster. It is almost impossible to give an exact figure for the number of returns sought by the Northern authorities in these early years. This is due to the lack of a central collection of such statistics and the inevitable discrepancy between various information sources. In November 1972 Joint Minister of State for Northern Ireland David Howell claimed that extradition was sought from Eire in thirty-one cases in 1971.[34] Another source claims the same figure of thirty-one warrants for 'subversive activities'.[35] However, a third, and by far the most well-documented source, claims only fifteen and lists the individuals by name and date the warrant was forwarded to Eire.[36] It must also be pointed out that there are cases of more than one request for individuals. This should be taken into account in any claim concerning the number of unsuccessful applications made by the RUC. A further point to note is the number of fugitives who, after a warrant if forwarded to Eire, are subsequently apprehended back in Ulster. A more detailed examination of these statistics will occur in the final section.

The two latter considerations are evident in the cases of two groups of IRA fugitives who escaped custody in Ulster in late 1971. Of seven individuals who broke out of Crumlin Road jail on 16 November 1971 and whose extradition was requested, five were eventually re-captured in the North.[37] A further three who escaped on 2 December 1971 and whose return was requested on 15 December 1971 illustrate both points.[38] Martin Meehan was re-captured in Belfast in August 1972, and there was a second request for Anthony 'Dutch' Docherty in January 1972.

Other problems encountered as the number of requests multiplied due to the violence in Ulster are illustrated by two of the first applications before the Irish courts in 1971. Edward MacDonald, Thomas McNulty and Edward Hamill were before Monaghan District Court in September. The extradition warrant listed a charge of possession of explosives in County Tyrone in early 1971. The district justice held that there was insufficient evidence before the court to identify the three as those named in the warrant and they were discharged.[39] A similar breakdown in the process occurred with the request for Sean Gallagher. He was held in October on a warrant alleging murder of an RUC constable but released by Killybegs District Court on the 20th. The court claimed inconclusive identification evidence again.[40] However, in answer to a parliamentary question, a government minister noted that a photograph, full description, details of tattoo marks, fingerprints and a witness were available.[41] The Minister of State for the Foreign and Commonwealth Office outlined the British position on such decisions.

> the Executive has no power to interfere in the actions of the judiciary. For this reason, it would serve no useful purpose to raise officially with the Government of the Irish Republic decisions made by the courts of that country. On certain occasions, however, there have been puzzling features about such decisions in extradition cases, for example, refusal to accept apparently conclusive identification evidence, and we have asked the authorities of the Irish Republic to explain them.[42]

Through 1972 the situation remained static. While British Ministers claimed there were approximately one hundred and fifty-five persons known to be in Eire and wanted by the RUC for questioning,[43] according to figures released in Parliament, only sixteen requests for extradition were made to Eire throughout 1972.[44] In Eire itself the government clampdown on the IRA was strengthened in May with the formation of the non-jury Special Criminal Court (SCC). It was to try 'scheduled offences' under the Offences Against the State Act 1939 and various arms and explosives offences. In October 1972 Irish Justice Minister O'Malley noted that the bulk of those convicted before the SCC were from Ulster.[45] Noteworthy as well was the apparent tightening of the Irish Government attitude towards extradition. Several of those released by the district courts in 1971 were re-arrested in 1972, often at the instigation of the Irish authorities. And in many of these cases the District Courts now granted the requests from Ulster and those affected appealed to the High Court.

This apparent tightening of attitude on the part of the Irish authorities, as distinct from the judiciary, may be attributable in part to the increase in violence in Eire directly linked to the conflict in Ulster. Furthermore the Republic itself in 1972–1973 was beginning to request the return of fugitives involved in the worsening situation. In October 1972 seven men detained in Curragh Camp escaped from custody. Four of the group were from Ulster and on 11 November 1972 one, Thomas Corrigan, was re-captured there. He was extradited to Eire two days later by a court in Armagh and raised no objection to his return.[46]

In another case Robert Taylor was accused by Irish police of the murder of a couple in County Donegal on 1 January 1973. Ordered extradited from Ulster, he appealed. He claimed the benefit of the political offence exception alleging that the male member of the couple was a member of the PIRA. This was not accepted in the Queen's Bench Divisional Court and a writ of habeas corpus was denied. The only evidence offered in support of the claim was the appellant's personal assertion and an affidavit. This stated that they'd received information that one of the victims belonged to the Provisionals. In dismissing the application Lowry LCJ found the evidence 'totally imprecise and lacking in detail' and added that he found it

> impossible to find any other judicial pronouncements which would support a definition of the phrase 'an offence of a political character' wide enough to assist the present applicant.[47]

Taylor was extradited to Eire in June. This occurred in an atmosphere of widespread Loyalist demonstrations orchestrated by the UDA and threats of disruption and worse if Taylor were returned.[48] Ironically the SCC acquitted the defendant ruling there were irregularities in the only major piece of evidence against him which was his own confession.[49]

During this period the appeal procedure in the Republic was proving extremely lengthy. Three applications were before the courts in December 1972 rising to ten by July 1973.[50] However, the Irish Government pressed the rules committee of the High Court to devise a speedier procedure so cases were heard by the High Court within three months of a lower court decision.[51] By November 1973 a total of eleven persons were appealing extradition orders[52] and the first High Court decision came in December. Anthony Francis Shields was charged with possessing ammunition in Belfast in 1971 and fled south while on bail. He admitted membership of an illegal organisation and claimed the RUC had threatened him with charges over the attempted murder of British soldiers. In quashing the extradition order Butler J based his finding on Shield's evidence of IRA membership. He noted it hadn't been challenged and said he

> could come to no other conclusion but that the offence charged in this case was a political offence and that if the plaintiff did have possession of the ammunition, it was to be used in furtherance of IRA activities.[53]

This decision accepted that activities engaged in by the IRA would be considered political by the second highest Irish court. The Shields ruling was soon buttressed by two more concerning much more serious charges. In both, the High Court's opinion was given by the later-to-be Chief Justice, Mr Justice Finlay. Sean Gallagher was detained on the second warrant for his return. The offence was deemed political based on previous cases and Finlay J stated that if an offence was committed by someone seeking to change by force the government then that crime was political.[54] It is also worth noting the comments of Finlay J in the case of James 'Seamus' O'Neill. He was accused of an RUC station bombing which killed two passers-by and had been ordered extradited for the murder of one. On appeal the murder was ruled political. In so ruling Mr Justice Finlay stated,

> I am not entitled to have any regard to the fact that the admitted activities of the present application seemed to breach any concept of humanity or any civilised form of conduct.[55]

These two cases reinforced the position of the Irish courts that however serious the offence and whatever its effects on the victims, so long as the applicants could develop a connection with the activities of the IRA their crimes would be ruled political offences. This was taken even further in the ruling in the case of Roisin McLaughlin. The crimed alleged was the murder of three unarmed, off-duty British soldiers lured into an ambush of which the plaintiff was a part.[56] Following the District Court decision to allow extradition there were rallies in Eire as occurred in Ulster regarding the Taylor case. Provisional Sinn Fein Vice-President Maire Drumm claimed at one rally that if McLaughlin were returned the conflict in Ulster could spread into the south.[57] Her appeal was heard in December 1974 and was remarkable for the fact that, unlike previous appeals, the appellant neither gave evidence nor admitted or denied commission of the offence. This removed the usual statement of motive before the court and a political link had to be built through others' evidence. McLaughlin's husband claimed the RUC had told him they believed she was involved in the ambush in her role as a PIRA Intelligence Officer. Mr Justice Finlay ruled out any likelihood of a personal motive of revenge or robbery due to the numbers of people involved, the degree of organisation and the obvious intent to kill all the soldiers involved. Echoing his previous findings he wrote,

> There could be no doubt that even murder, and even such a dastardly murder as that described ... in this case, if carried out by an organisation which, by such method, sought to overthrow the government of a country by force, was a political offence.[58]

The fullest expression of the Irish position concerning fugitive political offenders at that stage came in the case of a Catholic priest accused of handling explosives in Scotland. Michael Farrell characterises the decision as remaining 'for almost a decade as the key pronouncement on the political offence exception in relation to the IRA and the Northern Troubles'.[59]

In the case of Father Bartholemew Burns, as in the others, there was no doubt concerning his involvement in the offence charged. Two Irishmen convicted in Glasgow of the same explosives offences implicated the priest[60] and he himself admitted the offence in his appeal. Along with the appeal Father Burns was also reported to be attempting to challenge the constitutionality of the Extradition Act.[61] It is necessary to quote directly certain segments of Mr Justice Finlay's upholding of the appeal for two reasons: the reinforcement of points made in previous rulings, and a comparison later with his decisions in 1985 as Chief Justice.

He noted that the only issue necessary for his determination was whether or not the safekeeping of explosives for the PIRA, which was engaged in the attempt to 'overthrow and change the political structures of country by the use of violence' was a connected political offence or a political offence.[62] Referring to the Castioni decision and the political incidence theory of the UK he stated,

> It seems again to me impossible to categorize the existing situation in Northern Ireland and Britain ... as being otherwise than a political disturbance part of and incidental to which is the keeping of explosives for the organisation known as the IRA.[63]

This was the sole question on which he was required to rule by his own admission and he pronounced himself satisfied that the offence was political. However he went further and stated his belief also that the same conclusion would be reached by a commonsense appraisal of what constituted a political offence.[64]

Other requests from Great Britain for a number of individuals accused of involvement in bombings in England fared equally poorly. The first concerned Patrick Joseph Gilhooley, accused of planting a bomb at Aldershot station. He was detained on an extradition warrant on leaving Portlaoise Prison on 1 December 1975 having served a term for IRA membership.[65] Extradition was granted and appealed to the High Court.

In the interim the case of Margaret McKearney occasioned a series of confused moves in London and Dublin, but never reached the actual stage of forwarding a warrant to Eire. She was the subject of an April 1975 arrest warrant in Hampshire and in September became the centre of fevered media speculation. The Commander of the Bomb Squad claimed that an extradition application was likely, and the police issued an unusually detailed account of her alleged activities as a courier of arms and explosives and her involvement in several shootings. One report stated that there had been no political consultations prior to the decision 'to give her activities deliberate and wide publicity'.[66] Police sources were quoted as believing there was little chance of a successful extradition and the premise was that such widespread publicity would neutralise her usefulness. However on 29 November she was detained by the Irish Special Branch under the 1939 Act but released within forty-eight hours due to lack of evidence. Scotland Yard was then reported to have officially requested her detention pending the forwarding of an extradition warrant which was said to be with the DPP. But the application was never sent to Dublin and this same report speculated that the British were awaiting the outcome of the Gilhooley appeal just made to the High Court.[67] This reticence, especially following British police claims in September, caused not a little uncertainty and anger in Dublin. The result was a report that 'there is now widespread feeling in the Irish coalition Cabinet that the police in Britain do not possess enough evidence to support the charges they made against Miss McKearney in two press conferences'.[68]

Whether or not this was the case if the major reason for holding back was to await the outcome of Gilhooley's appeal the British were to be disappointed. In line with previous decisions the High Court found the offence political, however disagreeable were the facts of the offence according to Mr

Justice McMahon. Gilhooley's statement in court claiming IRA membership indicates why a court would have little difficulty in finding his crimes political. He stated,

> The IRA is an organisation, one of the aims and objectives of which is, by the use of armed force if necessary, to secure radical change in the continued government of that part of Ireland not yet reintegrated with the remainder.[69]

Finally there was the case of Brendan Swords, linked to an IRA arsenal in London in April 1976.[70] In February 1977 he was arrested in Eire on IRA membership charges but acquitted in March. Soon after, Scotland Yard applied for his extradition charging involvement in a series of bombings. On appeal to the High Court his offences were, as usual, ruled political and he was rendered immune from extradition. The timing of the offences proved crucial. When a Bomb Squad officer appeared before the District Court in July 1977 he stated the warrant was for conspiracy to cause explosions and they were investigating a series of sixteen incidents 'obviously committed by the same team'.[71] This same offence was the only one under the new Criminal Law (Jurisdiction) Act [CL(J)A] which, if committed in Great Britain, could be tried in Eire. Unfortunately for the British police the extra-territorial legislation was not retrospective and the offences were committed prior to the CL(J)A coming into force. Swords joined Gilhooley, McKearney and others as beneficiaries of the asylum Eire was granting to bombers and gunmen through the actions of her courts.

In complete contrast the British courts continued to return to Eire fugitives accused of offences there which were part of the Irish conflict. Space does not permit a detailed consideration. However, two, distinctive for similar reasons, can be examined.

In the celebrated case of the Littlejohn brothers, wanted for armed robbery in Ireland, they claimed the political offence exception stating they'd been working in Eire for British Intelligence as agents provocateurs. The MoD admitted contact but dismissed claims that offences committed in Ireland were at their behest. Following extradition proceedings held in camera the two were returned in March 1973 and subsequently convicted by the SCC. One year later they escaped and Kenneth made it to England. He was re-arrested there in December 1974 and during extradition proceedings the details of the secret 1973 proceedings were revealed.[72] In the earlier court case the applicants claimed that the robbery was a political crime within S.2 (2) of the 1965 Act due to their links with the IRA. This connection was not doubted by the court, nor was it disputed that the raid was to obtain funding for the IRA. However in 1973 Lord Widgery CJ referred to Viscount Radcliffe's dictum of 1962 regarding the court standing apart from the political issues. In summary he wrote,

> Thus one reaches the stage now on the weight of authority ... that an offence may be of a political character, either because the wrongdoer had some direct ulterior motive of a political kind when he committed the offence, or because the requesting

> state is anxious to obtain possession of the wrongdoer's person in order to punish him for his politics rather than for the simple criminal offence referred to in the extradition proceedings.[73]

Neither of these pertained in 1973 so the brothers were extradited. The only new element injected into the proceedings in 1975 was Kenneth Littlejohn's claim that trial by the SCC indicated their crime was a political offence under S.2 (2) (b). Lord Widgery examined the establishment of the SCC under the 1939 Act and could find no acknowledgement that trial before this non-jury court meant the offence in question was necessarily political. Extradition was granted.[74] Had the brothers carried out their robbery in Ulster on behalf of the IRA it is likely that an Irish court would have refused their extradition to Ulster on the same facts. The key difference is that in this reverse situation it could be argued that the suspects were at odds with the Government in Ulster and were engaged in an attempt to change it by obtaining funds for the IRA. By no means could the brothers be conceived of as attempting to overthrow the Irish Government despite their acknowledged links to British Intelligence.

The second case also involved an alleged link to British Intelligence and is distinctive for being characteristic of a couple of suspected abduction attempts in Eire. William Poacher failed in an attempt before the High Court in Great Britain in December 1973 to stop his extradition to Eire. He claimed to fear for his life due to involvement in the suspected abduction of senior PIRA member Sean Collins from Eire. Lord Widgery stated that it was apparent the appellant had infiltrated the PIRA to act as an informant at the behest of the British security forces. However the fact that he feared for his life as a result was not grounds on which the court could act.[75] The abduction to which Poacher alluded occurred in January 1972 in Dundalk and also allegedly involved Kenneth Littlejohn. Maze detainee Sean Collins' solicitor claimed that a man resembling Littlejohn abducted his client at gunpoint in the Republic on 13 January 1972 and drove him into Ulster where he was handed over to the British Army.[76]

If these claims are valid this case marked a descent into illegality by elements of the security forces in Ulster and can be traced to their frustration at the lack of success in extradition from Eire. Other incidents have emerged recently which suggest the alleged Collins kidnap was not an isolated case.[77]

In summary several points emerge from an examination of Anglo–Irish extradition practice in the period up to the mid-1970s and the enactment of the aforementioned extra-territorial legislation. The most compelling is the difference between the interpretations of the political offence exception in Irish and British courts. Those in the UK maintain a strict adherence to the political incidence theory and the related idea that the fugitive must be at odds with the requesting State over some issue connected with the governance of the country. While the Irish courts have followed a broader interpretation it is clear that the cases studied in some instances could also be defined as political under the British interpretation. Recalling Mr Justice Finlay's words, they could also be considered political under any 'commonsense' interpretation of the term. Furthermore, as several Irish judges maintained, this was the only issue before them. They had no authority to comment upon the morality, or lack thereof, of what were, in numerous cases, heinous crimes of murder and mutilation often involving innocent civilian bystanders.

A related point is that, while the courts limited their attention to strictly legal determinations, it can in no way be said that the Irish authorities were 'soft' on the IRA. It was a proscribed organisation in Eire well before being designated so in Ulster. Also, under the amended 1939 Act, all that was required for a conviction of IRA membership was the unsupported assertion by a police officer that he believed the defendant to be a member. These are not the acts of a government lax in its concern with the IRA. Perhaps the position of the Irish coalition Government in power in the mid–1970s is best summarised in the following statement of the Minister of Justice before the Dail in April 1975.

> I feel that there is well nigh universal embarrassment in this country at the predicament in which our judges find themselves, being constrained as they are in ... extradition applications to release persons accused of most serious crimes. The widespread embarrassment is compounded by the knowledge that the release of these fugitives is a matter of grave scandal in Northern Ireland where our fellow Irishmen have suffered so much in their persons and properties at the hands of these people.[78]

EXTRA-TERRITORIAL JURISDICTION—A FLANKING MOVEMENT

The deterioration in the security situation and the inability of the Ulster authorities to secure extradition of Republican gunmen occurred in the context of changes in the political situation in Ulster. In January 1972 'Bloody Sunday' crystallised anti-British feeling among large segments of the Nationalist minority hitherto unmoved by the situation. Two months later, in March, the Stormont Government was suspended and direct rule instituted. In Eire the Garda arrested Provisionals, seized arms and on 22 December 1971 had its first serious confrontation with the PIRA when the arrest of three members in County Donegal occasioned serious riots.[79] At the 'Ard Fheis' of Provisional Sinn Fein in October 1973 Vice-President David O'Connell reiterated the threat that Dublin could not remain immune in the event of extraditions of Republicans to Ulster.[80]

It was in this atmosphere that representatives from London, Dublin and Belfast met at the Sunningdale Conference in December 1973. The main aim was to structure a power-sharing executive but also discussed was the idea of a common law-enforcement area to bypass the problems of extradition. Irish ideas had been put to the Norther Ireland Secretary, William Whitelaw, in November by Foreign Minister Garrett Fitzgerald.[81] The conference led to the formation of an eight-man[82] legal commission to examine various alternatives. All parties at Sunningdale had agreed,

> that persons committing crimes of violence, however motivated, in any part of Ireland should be brought to trial irrespective of the part of Ireland in which they are located.[83]

The Commission examined four alternatives: an all-Ireland Court, extradition, extra-territorial jurisdiction and mixed courts. The first was dispensed with as being too involved to deal urgently with the problem as the Commission was ordered.[84] The idea of amending extradition by appending a list of scheduled offences for which the political offence exception could not be claimed was also discussed but discarded as the Commissioners could not agree on the legal validity of extraditing those who, at present, enjoyed immunity contingent on the exception.[85] A further innovation discussed was the concept of mixed courts containing judges from both jurisdictions, but, in the final analysis, this was thought to provide no legal or procedural advantage over purely domestic courts for the purposes of extra-territorial jurisdiction.[86]

The idea of extra-territorial jurisdiction was the method both parties were able to agree upon. Those opposed to extradition, the Irish jurists, favoured it above all, while the British jurists found it worthy of recommendation where extradition was unavailable.[87] This method also recommended itself due to the speed with which it might be instituted.

Two points were stressed by the Commissioners in regard to this method. The first was that its success depended upon measures designed to secure evidence and testimony and move it between jurisdictions. The second point was that it would only apply to a schedule of offences comprising crimes of violence, and such a list was appended to the report.[88] Even prior to the formation of the Commission some crimes had been made amenable to extra-territorial jurisdiction. On 20 December 1973 the Irish Government made an order reviving the dormant S.9 of the Offences Against the Person Act 1861.[89] This allowed the prosecution of an Irish citizen in Eire for the crime of murder committed in Ulster. It was followed by a sweep of IRA suspects in Eire and the first official meeting of RUC and Garda chiefs in years. However, the legislation was not retrospective and there were no cases known to be brought under its terms. An Irish Government official is reported to have noted,

> The fact that this exceptional legal provision has never been invoked shows clearly that there has been no evidence available against anyone resident in the Republic during the past two years ... that is not the impression given recently by some spokesmen in London and Belfast.[90]

Nonetheless the Irish courts dealt promptly with Republicans guilty of crimes within Eire. From the May 1972 introduction of the SCC to February 1974 a total of three hundred and thirty-eight persons were convicted of 'IRA offences', primarily related to arms and explosives.[91]

On the political front the collapse of the power-sharing executive left the only matter of substance to survive from Sunningdale as the agreement on extra-territorial jurisdiction. The two parliaments drafted implementing legislation. The only addition was the offence of causing explosions in Great Britain. This was due to the mainland bombing campaigns and was achieved by amending the Explosive Substances Act 1883.[92]

Legislation passed smoothly through Westminster but not so in the Dail. The opposition Fianna Fail fought it as unconstitutional,[93] and preferred the all-Ireland court solution. Passed with a small majority in March 1976 the Criminal Law (Jurisdiction) Act 1976 became law on 1 June 1976 at the same time as the British Criminal Jurisdiction Act 1975. Former Chief Justice, now President, O'Dālaigh had referred it to the Supreme Court for a ruling on its constitutionality and it had been pronounced legal and valid.[94] Following its enactment the PIRA announced a threat against any 'Free State civil servant, court official, solicitor, counsel, judge or police officer'[95] administering the law. This demonstrated the extent to which they viewed it as a threat and broke precedent with the decision of the old IRA, dating back to 1963, not to consider members of the Irish security forces as legitimate targets. During the election campaign of 1977 Fianna Fail leader Jack Lynch hinted they would scrap the law if elected.

> I have already said that I regard it as unworkable. We will look at it again. Our preference is for all-Ireland courts operating on both sides of the border.[96]

The proof of a pudding being in the eating it must be said that the legislation has proved of limited use. There have been a handful of cases in Eire and a couple in Ulster as far as can be ascertained. This is undoubtedly due, in part, to the problems of obtaining evidence and witnesses as the Commission had warned. As has been repeatedly noted, some ninety per cent of terrorist-type convictions in Ulster are the result of suspects incriminating themselves during interrogation which can last up to seven days.[97] The RUC cannot interrogate suspects in Eire or even be present at their questioning by the Garda. Due to the insuffiency of forensic evidence in such cases confessions are the key to conviction. It is understandable that there is a wariness concerning police methods of interrogation in that in Eire, Amnesty International, and in Ulster, both Amnesty and the European Commission on Human Rights have discovered evidence of maltreatment of suspects by the police.[98]

With this background it is perhaps surprising that there have been any prosecutions under the legislation and it is worth examining them in closer detail to ascertain their special features. Despite media speculation soon after the enactment of the CL(J)A that a charge was likely against a gunman recovering in Dundalk after a border gunbattle,[99] the first prosecution occurred in Ulster. Five men were charged with kidnapping army intelligence officer Captain R Nairac in Ulster and murdering him across the border in Eire in May 1977. On 15 December 1978 they were sentenced to terms ranging from three years to life on a variety of counts including kidnap, murder, manslaughter and firearms charges.[100]

The case was noteworthy in that a Garda officer gave evidence in Belfast on the murder which was the only extra-territorial crime.[101] Yet both sides initially displayed some reticence. A sixth person, Liam Townson, was charged in Eire with the murder, convicted on 8 November 1977 and given life. While a British officer gave evidence in Dublin, Townson's defence team were denied statements taken by the RUC in Ulster.[102] And when the Ulster trial began in February 1978 it had to be temporarily adjourned as the Irish would not release certain exhibits from the Townson trial for evidence. Their claim was that they would be needed at some unspecified future date for his appeal.[103] Despite these teething problems the authorities garnered convictions in both trials.

As far as can be determined there has only been one other prosecution in Ulster under the Criminal Jurisdiction Act 1975. Former Stormont Speaker Sir Norman Stronge and his son were murdered in Northern Ireland in 1981 and Owen McCartan Smyth was charged in Ulster. However, he was charged under the CJA with counselling and procuring the murder in Eire. Two notable features arose in the trial. At one point it was temporarily transferred to Dublin to enable Mr Justice Hatton to hear evidence, and Smyth was also taken there under guard. He was then returned to Ulster despite a separate hearing in Dublin's High Court where Smyth claimed a right to stay in Eire. He also claimed he had not been offered the opportunity of trial in Eire, but Hamilton J ruled this not to be the case and ordered his return to Ulster.[104] The second feature worthy of comment caused the abandonment of the charges. Under S.6 (3) of the Act the initiation of extra-territorial proceedings must have the consent of the Attorney-General. The court ruled that since this technicality had been overlooked the charges were therefore null and void.[105] This would seem to indicate a fairly basic ineptitude on the part of the prosecutors which can only be partially excused by their lack of familiarity due to the infrequency of cases brought under the CJA.

The situation south of the border presents more evidence from which tentative conclusions may be drawn concerning the efficacy of the extra-territorial laws. Press speculation mounted in 1979 that Desmond O'Hare was to be tried under the CL(J)A but nothing came of it, perhaps because he was jailed for nine years under the 1939 Act on 29 November 1979.[106] The first actual prosecution came in 1980 and concerned the murder of a former UDR officer in Ulster. Three men were charged and with the absence of confessions the case hinged upon forensic evidence. It took the SCC just thirty minutes to decide to acquit and Mr Justice Hamilton gave the court's reasons. He noted the purely circumstantial character of the forensic evidence. Mud and hay on the defendants' clothing, while matching the crime scene, didn't prove beyond a reasonable doubt that it couldn't have come from another place. As well, firearms discharge residue on their clothes connected them to the firing of a gun, but not necessarily with the murder in question.[107] The court had no option but to acquit.

The next case produced a conviction, but this was overturned on appeal.

The crime was again the murder of a former UDR officer and occurred this time in Eire, but the accused's guilt hinged upon his gathering of information about the victim in Ulster. The basis for conviction was a confession in an unsigned statement. The Court of Criminal Appeal quashed the conviction on 28 July 1981. It ruled that while there was no breach of fair procedure while the statement was taken, the defendant had been held for twenty-two hours of almost continuous interrogation by that point. Mr Justice Griffin gave the court's opinion that this went beyond the bounds of fairness. The statement shouldn't have been admitted in evidence and without it there was insufficient evidence to convict.[108]

During the same period the Irish authorities lost another case under the CL(J)A. An RUC reservist was kidnapped in Eire and murdered in Ulster in an exact reversal of the Nairac case. The defendant's lawyer, Sean McBride, noted that his client had not been given the option of trial in the jurisdiction containing the locus of the crime. Hamilton J agreed that this was the case, the court had failed to meet its statutory obligation and must disavow jurisdiction and dismiss the case. The defendant, Seamus Soroghan, didn't escape justice altogether for he was later convicted for firearms offences and received five years.[109] It is worth noting that the option Soroghan was not offered amounts, in effect, to an invitation to extradition and is unlikely to be taken up by many of those charged under the CL(J)A. The error on the part of the authorities indicates that unfamiliarity with the provisions of the legislation did not exist only in Northern Ireland.

Following on from these cases were two involving individuals from the same group who escaped from Crumlin Road jail in June 1981. Michael Ryan had been awaiting trial for a 1979 murder and Robert Campbell was on trial. He was sentenced in absentia to life for murder on 12 June 1981. A total of twleve RUC personnel gave evidence in the Irish trial concerning the escape and ensuing gunbattle. The two pleaded not guilty to a charge of escaping lawful custody, attempted murder and firearms possession.[110] Acquitted of the attempted murder charge they were convicted of escape and sentenced in December to ten years.[111] In that month and in January 1982 a number of their fellows were apprehended. A total of four went on trial on similar charges and were convicted and sentenced on 25 February 1982.[112]

These later cases illustrate the efficiency of the extra-territorial laws when faced with trials requiring no civilian witnesses and offences which are easily proved. Somewhat more complex, and the first CL(J)A case to concern offences in Great Britain, was that of Gerard Tuite. He'd been picked up in England but escaped Brixton Prison while on remand. He was charged with offences in relation to bombings in Great Britain in 1978–1979. British police flew to Dublin to give evidence.[113]

In the first trial Tuite was found guilty in July 1982 of possessing explosives in England. Mr Justice Hamilton also proclaimed himself satisfied that Tuite had hired autos used in two London car bombs. A second trial for conspiracy to cause explosions in Great Britain was deferred while the first conviction was appealed.[114] This failed and he was refused leave to go before the Supreme Court. There were seven grounds for appeal including a claim that the SCC lacked jurisdiction to try extra-territorial cases. Irish legal commentators proclaimed the decision

> as an effective tightening up of the . . . legislation that could pave the way to greater utilisation of the law aimed at stopping fugitives gaining a safe haven from United Kingdom justice in the Irish Republic.[115]

The Tuite case indicated that the CL(J)A could and would be used to cover scheduled offences committed in Great Britain. The Appeal Court ruling reinforced the legal standing of the legislation. Nonetheless the extra-territorial laws were not designed as a total replacement for extradition of fugitive political offenders. As the Law Enforcement Commission had said, it was an interim measure. Developments were to take place in the 1980s increasing the likelihood that fugitive political offenders would face justice either through the extra-territorial laws or via extradition.

THE NEW ERA

By no means was all the terrorism in one direction. Various Protestant Loyalist paramilitary groups (UDA, UVF, UFF) claimed responsibility for a series of bombings in Eire through the mid-1970s. Some of these bombers appeared before the Irish courts but the majority avoided detection. This led to an intriguing irony. For example, on 29 November 1975 a bomb at Dublin Airport claimed by the UDA killed one and injured several others. The Irish Foreign Ministry lodged an official complaint with the British Embassy claiming the North was being used as a sanctuary for Loyalist terrorists.[116] The irony was undoubtedly intended given claims in Ulster concerning the alleged immunity of PIRA gunmen in Eire. However, cases like the previously mentioned one involving Robert Taylor indicate that where the Irish were able to present valid warrants the courts in Northern Ireland were prepared to extradite.

What with the problems in the extra-territorial method the Ulster authorities continued to make extradition applications to the Republic. In the sixty-nine months from June 1976 to February 1982 there were a total of one hundred and forty-one warrants forwarded by the RUC and thirty-four of these related to terrorist-type offences.[117] Thus just under twenty-five per cent of the warrants sent south concerned terrorist actions. The success rate, as before 1 June 1976, was non-existent, but by 1982 there were changes occurring in both the judicial and political arena which would affect this situation. Before moving to this a brief look at public attitudes to the problem in both Ulster and Eire will provide the context.

Using an ESRI Survey for Eire and the 1978 Northern Ireland Attitude Survey as the data base a couple of interesting facts emerge.[118] Two Likert items produced the following results.

		Ulster Catholic	Ulster Protestant	Republic
'The Irish Government should agree to extradition, that is, to agree to hand over to the authorities in Northern Ireland or Britain, people accused of politically motivated crimes there.'	AGREE	67%	98%	46%
'The Irish Government is not doing its best to ensure that the IRA is unable to operate from the Republic's side of the Border.'	AGREE	41%	91%	45%

While the strength of Ulster Protestant feeling is unsurprising, what is interesting is the fact that sixty-seven per cent of their fellow citizens of Catholic background, the traditional IRA constituency, believe the Irish authorities should extradite. It is also worth noting that forty-six per cent, or just under half, of the Irish respondents were also in favour of this point. However the Irish Government remained opposed with the most common argument being that a change in policy would conflict with the Constitution. This was based on Art. 29.3 which stated that Ireland accepted the generally recognised principles of international law as its rule of conduct in international relations and one of these was claimed to be non-extradition of political offenders. The position was re-affirmed when Eire refused to sign the European Convention on the Suppression of Terrorism (ECST). The Foreign Affairs Department legal adviser stated,

> We have no alternative but to refuse because the generally recognised principles of international law do not allow a country to extradite someone wanted by another country for a political crime. For us the matter is closed unless these should change in the next five or ten years.[119]

Less than a decade later Ireland had signed the ECST.

The first change came with Dublin's signing of the Agreement Concerning the Application of the ECST, henceforth the Dublin Agreement.[120] This was born of a meeting in December 1979 of the nine EEC Justice Ministers. It obligates non-signatories to the ECST or those who have made reservations under it to submit for prosecution under its own law those whom it refuses to extradite. Eire was already possessed of the necessary machinery in the form of the CL(J)A. The purpose of the Dublin Agreement was to act as an interim measure among the nine while awaiting the full ratification without reservation of the ECST by all twenty members of the Council of Europe.

There was also increasing bipartisan support in Eire for the concept of the all-Ireland Court so beloved of Fianna Fail. When they regained power in June 1977 it was given increased prominence. Foreign Minister O'Kennedy claimed,

An all-Ireland court is the most effective way, because you have a representative court supervising the activities of the police force and army on both sides, and the court is the guarantor that the army and police, on whatever side, will act within the terms of the law ... any citizen breaking the law is made amenable to the court, and any citizen has the right to go to the court in the event of infringement of the law by the institutions of the state.[121]

By 1981 the new Fine Gael–Labour coalition Government was also reported to be favouring the concept. The institutional arrangements would consist of three judges, one from each jurisdiction, and the third from the locus of the crime, and it would sit wherever the need arose. Interrogation would be covered by a set of common rules enforced by the court and prosecution conducted by an all-Ireland prosecutor.[122] In an interview in November 1981 Prime Minister Fitzgerald stated,

The fact is that the problem is an all-Ireland one. They step across the border; but far from being a problem of fugitive offenders down here who can't be got at, the more crucial problem is the no-go area in Northern Ireland, in South Armagh—from which criminals operate into the Republic, and through the Republic into Northern Ireland, coming in and out again.[123]

Fitzgerald went on to explain that there would have to be an institutional umbrella under which the court could function such as an Anglo–Irish Council. And it is this feature that causes Ulster Loyalists to be unremittingly opposed to such an arrangement for fear that it impinges on their sovereignty and will eventually lead to the absorption of the Six Counties by the twenty-six. These fears are summarised in a pamphlet by the late Edgar Graham.

By setting up all-Ireland courts the Irish Republic would be invoking Articles 2 and 3 of the Irish Constitution which assert the right of the Irish Parliament to legislate for Northern Ireland. Those articles have always been deeply offensive to Unionists in Northern Ireland. But worse than that—they have always given a legitimacy to the IRA who claim to be fulfilling the constitutional claim by fighting for re-unification.[124]

While such ideas were discussed in political circles, the Irish courts continued to refuse to extradite those they deemed political offenders. In some cases the connection between the political cause and the offence was tenuous at best. In July 1978 Francis Heron successfully resisted extradition on a warrant alleging he'd caused grievous bodily harm to a woman in County Tyrone. He claimed it was the result of a punishment beating ordered by the PIRA and the High Court refused to sanction extradition. Counsel for the State labelled it 'an unconventional form of political activity' but didn't appeal the decision.[125]

By no means were all the RUC requests during the 1970s turned down on the grounds of the political offence exception, nor did all those whose extradition was refused remain immune from justice. Keeping in mind the earlier strictures concerning statistics some intriguing facts emerge from a compilation of extradition requests for Republican fugitives in the period 1971–1980.[126] Some eighty requests are listed with four pending for a total of seventy-six requests. Of these a total of eleven were withdrawn by the RUC (14.5 per cent), and eighteen individuals were apprehended in the United Kingdom after their warrants had been sent to Eire (23.7 per cent). Some of those later detained in the UK may have been the beneficiaries of refusals by the Irish courts but the compilation does not reveal this. It does reveal that there were forty-five refusals (59.2 per cent). These break down into thirty-four refused on grounds of political offence (44.7 per cent), nine refused on grounds of no comparable offence in Eire (11.8 per cent) and two granted habeas corpus by the courts. This totals seventy-four cases. Of the two remaining, one was extradited and the other was in prison in Eire for offences committed there at the time of request. The most interesting figure to arise from this simple statistical analysis is that almost 25 per cent of those whose extradition was requested for terrorist-type offences were subsequently apprehended in the UK. This again weakens Loyalist assertions that all Republican bombers and gunmen were totally immune from prosecution due to the sanctuary they enjoyed in Eire.

In 1976 a lower Irish court had agreed to the only extradition of an alleged political offender on record until the 1980s. Patrick Damien McCloskey was returned to face arson charges in Ulster. But it was not until 1981 that the Supreme Court was again called upon to further delineate the Irish position. Ten years had passed since the last Supreme Court ruling on an IRA case in *Magee* vs *O'Rourke*, and the actual crime the court was ruling upon in 1981 also occurred in 1971. Maurice Hanlon was charged with handling stolen explosives in England, had been arrested there in January 1972 and then fled to Eire in March while on bail.[127] Such a hiatus between the granting of bail in January and flight three months later indicates that Hanlon was not a professional Provisional bomber. Detained in Eire and ordered extradited by a district court, Hanlon appealed to the High Court which reserved judgement in April 1975. This judgement was not delivered until October 1980 when it was held that the appellant should be denied relief on any and all of the three grounds he claimed: inordinate delay, no comparable offence and/or the offence was political or connected with a political offence. Hanlon then appealed to the Supreme Court.

By this point Ireland's highest court had changed character from that which had produced the liberal interpretations of the political offence in Bourke and then Magee. The Chief Justice at that time, Cearbhall O'Dālaigh, had moved in 1973 and been replaced by WO'B Fitzgerald in 1973–1974 who, in turn, was replaced by Thomas O'Higgins who held the post from 1974 until 1985. His family background, significantly, was strongly anti-IRA and the Chief Justice had lost both a grandfather and an uncle to IRA assassins in the 1920s.[128] However, the Supreme Court still had in its ranks in 1981 two judges, Walsh J and Henchy J, who'd put the Irish position against extradition while serving on the Law Enforcement Commission. The court's composition had changed, but not entirely.

In their decision on the Hanlon case in October 1981 the Supreme Court

Justices held that the High Court had been correct in its findings, Mr Justice Henchy declared his acceptance of their reasoning that,

> there is no acceptable evidence to satisfy ... that any of the proceeds of (the accused's) criminal activities was used for the purposes of the IRA in such a way as to lend political colour to the offences.[129]

However Mr Justice Henchy went an important step further, and with the concurrence of Chief Justice O'Higgins and Mr Justice Griffin stated,

> even if it had been found as a fact that the explosive material mentioned in the charge ... had been intended for transmission to the IRA, it would not necessarily follow that the accused would be exempt from extradition on the ground that the offence charged is a political offence, or an offence connected with a political offence. There has been no decision of this court on such a point. It must be left open for an appropriate case.[130]

Henchy J also criticised the loophole provided by the idea of corresponding offences and called for the negotiation of new extradition arrangements on the basis of specifying a list of offences for which extradition would be granted.[131] This is worth noting in light of the statistical analysis mentioned previously.

What was signalled in the Hanlon decision and 'left open for an appropriate case' was the changing nature of the political offence. Such a case came before the Supreme Court in late 1982 in the person of Dominic McGlinchey. During that year the climate of opinion towards the bombers and gunmen had grown increasingly hostile. In March the annual meeting of the Association of Sergeants and Inspectors of the Garda Siochana gave indication of this mood. Their General Secretary called for joint questioning of suspects to bolster the extra-territorial laws. He also supported the view of former Attorney-General Lord Robinson that the definition of a political offence should be re-considered and added that the Irish Government should initiate an international debate aimed at a more precise definition.[132]

> Nowadays, so called political crimes very often involve murder or injury to completely innocent people. . . . How long can we allow the most vile criminals to live freely and openly in this country when we know, and in some cases they have publicly admitted, that they have committed all forms of crime including the murder of our colleagues in the North, the destruction of property and the killing and maiming of innocent civilians.[133]

Dominic McGlinchey seemed to fit perfectly such a characterisation. Interned in the early 1970s he also served time for arms possession in Ulster and formed part of an ASU which terrorised south Londonderry through the mid-1970s. Arrested in Eire in September 1977 following a mail van robbery he received four years.[134] While in jail a warrant was forwarded for his extradition. The offence charged was the murder of an elderly woman killed on 28 March 1977 when several gunmen sprayed her house with automatic weapon fire. Her only connection with the security forces was a son who was an RUC reservist who was wounded in the incident, and a daughter in the RUC.

Released from the Irish sentence in January 1982 McGlinchey was re-arrested on the extradition warrant and ordered returned by a District Court. He claimed the offence was political in an application for a writ of habeas corpus to the High Court. This was dismissed in May 1982 with Mr Justice Gannon holding there was nothing in the appeal to connect the murder with a political offence.[135] He then appealed to the Supreme Court. In this McGlinchey dropped the claim under S.50 (2) (a) that the crime was a political offence although it was claimed by the PIRA and he'd claimed to have been on active service for them at the time. Instead he stated that, as he was wanted for other offences by the RUC he came under S.50 (2) (b) and would be prosecuted or detained for a political offence if returned for the non-political offence named in the warrant.[136]

McGlinchey faced the same Supreme Court judges who'd decided in Hanlon that a re-definition of the political offence awaited an appropriate case and this was it. Because the appellant had withdrawn his claim under S.50 (2) (a) the court was not required to rule on whether the offence in question itself was political. Nevertheless Chief Justice O'Higgins, with the concurrence of the others, laid out what was obviously a departure from previous determinations concerning political offences. Stressing the fact that the victim was a civilian, the Chief Justice went on to state that even if she hadn't been and was killed or injured it would not necessarily follow that the offence could be categorised as political. He added,

> The judicial authorities on the scope of such offences have in many respects been rendered obsolete by the fact that modern terrorist violence . . . is often the antithesis of what could reasonably be regarded as political, either in itself or in its connections.[137]

In discussing McGlinchey's claim under S.50 (2) (b) Chief Justice O'Higgins developed the Irish position further. He used phrases such as 'what could reasonably be regarded as political' and 'the ordinary scope of political activity'[39] thus alluding to a 'reasonable man' test of the political offence. He also spoke of the suffering caused by 'self-ordained arbiters' and claimed that the excusing of such offenders under the exception 'is the very antithesis of the ordinances of Christianity and civilisation and of the basic requirement of political activity'.[139]

The executive was absolved of the necessity to make an immediate decision on whether or not to return McGlinchey as he'd jumped bail prior to the Supreme Court decision. Legal commentators characterised the ruling as a landmark decision, but also noted that further case law would be required to confirm its status.[140] This was not long in coming but wasn't quite as straightforward as the authorities in the UK might have wished. Indeed developments from 1983–1986 were strewn with basic technical errors, misjudgements and frequent recrimination on both sides of the border and the Irish Sea.

In May 1983 there were reports that Scotland Yard had identified John

Downey as one of the Hyde Park and Regent's Park bombers of 1982. He denied this and there was no attempt then to extradite him, perhaps due to insufficient evidence,[141] which is reminiscent of the McKearney incident mentioned previously. In August the High Court granted a request for Philip McMahon which was then appealed. He was one of a group which escaped custody in Ulster in March 1975. He'd been jailed in Eire for one year in October 1975 and the Ulster authorities were thus aware of his whereabouts, but they didn't issue a request until 1983 after the McGlinchey ruling.[142] The reasons for this became apparent in the Supreme Court appeal the following summer. In the interim the High Court ordered the extradition of Seamus Shannon in January 1984. Attorney-General Peter Sutherland based the State's argument on the McGlinchey ruling and the High Court judges agreed that the murders named in the warrant were too 'heinous' to be reasonably described as political.[143] Both Shannon and McMahon came before the Supreme Court in the summer of 1984.

Prior to this McGlinchey was re-captured in March 1984. His lawyers obtained an injunction to delay any handover so they could challenge the validity of the original order but the Supreme Court overturned this in an unprecedented Bank Holiday evening sitting.[144] The panel was identical to that which granted the original order and the fugitive was placed in RUC custody on 18 March 1984. In response to critics of the decision, Taoiseach Fitzgerald said,

> It is a sad kind of nationalism that thinks that people against whom there are charges of murder, would not be proceeded against by the normal processes of the law and that murder could be a political offence.[145]

In the cases of McMahon and Shannon the Supreme Court produced decisions with contradictory results. The order for McMahon's return was quashed in June, but there were special circumstances in this first post-McGlinchey decision. Four of McMahon's fellow escapers had been apprehended in Eire in 1975 and their extradition had been refused on the grounds of the political offence exception. McMahon also argued that his escape was a political act to enable him to continue the struggle. In a unanimous decision the Supreme Court quashed the High Court order[146] basing the decision on the four previous rulings. Chief Justice O'Higgins explained that extradition,

> would mean that contradictory declarations in relation to the same incident would have issued from our courts. If such occurred, respect for the administration of justice in our courts would surely suffer and the courts' process would certainly have been abused.[147]

Irish Supreme Court decisions in this period seem to be a case of two steps forward and one step back and the McMahon decision was a retreat. However, in the Shannon case the following month the judges circumscribed the political offence further. In following the McGlinchey ruling and expanding it the judges were in total agreement on extradition but divided upon the reasoning. Three were of like mind including the Chief Justice.[148] He concentrated on the objective circumstances of the offence stating,

> the Provisional IRA have abjured normal political activity in favour of violence and terrorism, [and] the circumstances disclosed as to the murders in question here were so brutal, cowardly and callous that it would be a distortion of language if they were to be accorded the status of political offences or offences connected with political offences.[149]

It must be pointed out that while this opinion concentrated on the 'objective' circumstances rather than the 'subjective' motivation of the offender it went beyond the English political incidence theory which avoided commentary on the morality of actions carried out incident to, or in furtherance of, a political disturbance. Mr Justice Anthony Hederman, a former Fianna Fail Attorney-General, and defence counsel in the McLaughlin appeal previously mentioned, explicitly rejected the McGlinchey test of the 'reasonable man' believing it 'could only create uncertainty' given that many things usually considered political activity such as rebellion, assassination and other violent acts might be considered by many people as unreasonable.[150] He noted the PIRA was engaged in just such a political struggle and that acts done in furtherance of this could be seen as relative political offences. However he made the fine distinction in the instant case that as the offences charged to Shannon were claimed as 'reprisals' by the Provisionals they could not be considered part of the armed struggle to remove the British authorities. More significantly the judge stated that 'the decisive criterion ... is whether the perpetrator acted with a political motive or for a political purpose'.[151] Since Shannon denied involvement in the offence his motive could not be determined and he was eligible for extradition. This 'subjective' test creates its own problems, as Farrell notes. It could cause self-incrimination which would operate against the person if extradited anyway, and put innocent persons at a decided disadvantage since they could not give evidence of motive for something they didn't do.[152] Mr Justice McCarthy rejected Hederman's approach and produced his own criterion for determining the political offence combining both 'objective' and 'subjective' features. These were motivation, circumstances of the offence, identity of the victims and central to all these was the proximity of each factor to the alleged political aim which was objectively determinable.[153] In Shannon's case McCarthy felt the distance between the offence and the political purpose was sufficient to allow extradition. This approach is reminiscent of the Swiss proportionality or predominance theory,[154] and seems to combine the best features of both approaches; one outlined in McGlinchey and supported by Chief Justice O'Higgins, and the other supported by Mr Justice McCarthy.

Shannon had also challenged the constitutionality of Part III of the Extradition Act but this was rejected by the court and he was returned in July 1984. The Supreme Court gave its reasons for this rejection on 16 November 1984. In the meantime the Dublin High Court seemed to be taking another step back from the Supreme Court mood, but only through negligence.

Founder member of the Scottish Republic Socialist Party, David Dinsmore, had been arrested in Eire in December 1983. He'd fled Scotland while on bail on a letter-bomb charge. An Irish district court granted extradition and he appealed as expected. Incredibly, given the circumstances of his flight from Scotland, he was granted bail while awaiting his appeal in Eire and promptly decamped to Spain which had no extradition treaty with the UK.[155] Such laxity did not encourage the British authorities' belief in the willingness of the Irish courts to return political terrorists. Nonetheless in early September 1984 at a conference in London the DPP, Attorney-General and the head of the Anti-terrorist Squad agreed to prepare papers for a series of extradition attempts.[156] The mistake in the Dinsmore case could not be taken as a deflection of the trend apparent in McGlinchey and Shannon.

In the challenge to the constitutionality of the 1965 Act in November 1984 Shannon's lawyers had raised three substantive issues as well as technical points. The three concerned the lack of necessity for a prima facie case under the backing of warrants system, the lack of a clause prohibiting return where a fugitive might be prejudiced due to race, religion, nationality or political opinion and the fact that interrogation, detention and trial of terrorist suspects in Ulster fell short of the minimum requirements of fair procedure in Eire.[157] In May 1984 High Court President, Mr Justice Finlay had rejected all three claims,[158] and the Supreme Court held the same opinion. Both courts were, in effect, giving the Northern Ireland legal system what amounted to an explicit endorsement.

During the same period of this decision the British authorities attempted to secure the extradition of suspected PIRA bomber Evelyn Glenholmes at the beginning of a seventeen-month catalogue of technical errors and misjudgements leavened with recrimination. In late October 1984 a Lambeth magistrate issued warrants on the basis of information sworn under oath by an official of the DPP. They were taken to Dublin by an Inspector of the ATS, found to be faulty and returned to London and withdrawn. The errors were revealed by the DPP through a written reply in the House of Lords in March 1986 and were mainly incomplete addresses of the criminal incidents named in the warrants.[159] On 6 November 1984 the same Lambeth magistrate issued new warrants but these were again technically faulty as was subsequently revealed. In the meantime the suspect vanished, on 8 November, and reports which broke in the British media on 11 November caused a storm of criticism.[160] In this first phase the British authorities took pains to ensure that no criticism would be directed towards the Irish authorities and the Attorney-General issued a statement clearing them of either negligence or bureaucratic foot-dragging.[161]

During the sixteen months before Glenholmes was arrested the Supreme Court continued its tightening of the political offence exception under new leadership but the High Court seemed more hesitant. In January 1985 Chief Justice O'Higgins moved to the European Court and was replaced by former High Court President, Mr Justice Finlay. In his first six months of office he and his fellow judges were faced with two more cases where the political offence exception was claimed in relation to alleged Republican activities.

John Patrick Quinn was wanted in England for passing stolen travellers' cheques and had been ordered extradited. In appeal to the High Court he submitted an affidavit that admitted the crime but claimed it was an attempt to raise funds for the INLA and thus a political offence.[162] The High Court rejected this stating that Quinn hadn't established sufficient connection between the crime and a political offence.[163] He appealed to the Supreme Court which dismissed the appeal and ordered extradition in February 1985. In his judgement the new Chief Justice went beyond the McGlinchey and even Shannon decisions to what could be described with validity as a 'new frontier' of the political offence. He noted that Quinn's affidavit said that the INLA, of which he claimed membership, aimed to create a thirty-two-county workers' Republic through armed conflict in Ulster, Great Britain and elsewhere. He further stated that it must be assumed that the Dail did not intend the Extradition Act to be interpreted in a manner which would offend against the Constitution, but achievement of the INLA objective would require the destruction of that Constitution by prohibited means. Therefore a member of the INLA could not escape extradition through the political offence exception.[164] The Chief Justice was supported by Justices Henchy and Griffin in this statement, and also Justices Hederman and McCarthy in separate judgements. The import of his decision seems to be that INLA members were completely removed from the scope of the political offence as inherently opposed to the Irish Government. This approaches the idea advanced almost one hundred years previously by British courts in the Meunier case that anarchists could not avail themselves of the exception as they were the enemies of all governments. The decision is also interesting for demonstrating the change in thinking by Chief Justice Finlay. In 1974 in the case of Father Bartholemew Burns, mentioned earlier, Finlay had said the crime of keeping explosives 'for an organisation attempting to overthrow the state by violence is ... an offence of a political character'.[165] The Quinn decision seems an almost complete reversal of this position almost exactly eleven years later.

In June 1985 the High Court refused to order extradition of Clareman Gerard Maguire to England for a robbery he claimed to have undertaken on behalf of the PIRA. Mr Justice Egan, in obvious reference to the Quinn decision, said he found nothing in Maguire's affidavit concerning the overthrowal of the Constitution. Therefore he was not prepared to hold PIRA offences couldn't be considered political 'until the Supreme Court tells me specifically'.[166] The Supreme Court overturned this decision and ordered extradition in July 1985 but on the basis that there was not sufficient evidence to establish robbery as an act of the PIRA. Mr Justice Walsh did not comment on the question of whether or not IRA offences would no longer be considered political and thus avoided Egan's request for a specific ruling.[167]

The aftermath of the Quinn extradition had produced some tension between Dublin and London due to errors on the part of the British prosecuting authorities which led to his release. Following mistakes by both Scotland Yard and the DPP there were rumours that the British would abandon the charge and pursue another offence. This caused the Irish Attorney-General John Rogers to phone his British counterpart and indicate that the Irish authorities would condemn unreservedly any such move, and after the collapse of the case Ireland lodged complaints with London.[168] This demonstrates the sensitivity in Eire where political risks were being taken by the Executive in sanctioning such decisions by the Supreme Court only to see their efforts overturned by rudimentary mistakes on the part of the British.

Such mistakes were again apparent in early 1986 in the Glenholmes case. Prior to this in December 1985 the Dublin High Court had again demonstrated the two steps forward, one step back tendency of the Irish courts. A District court had ordered the extradition of Brendan Burns who was wanted in connection with the murder of five British soldiers in 1981 in a landmine explosion. In December 1985 the High Court upheld his appeal and quashed the extradition order. It ruled he'd been held illegally and that the warrants were faulty. Apparently an RUC Inspector hadn't been on oath when the warrants were issued and thus they were null and void.[169] As in Quinn, basic errors on the part of the requesting authorities had allowed the fugitive to gain his freedom.

Incredibly a similar mistake was involved in the Glenholmes fiasco. She was arrested in Dublin on 12 March 1986 on the basis of the nine warrants issued in November 1984. However, during the proceedings on the 21st the ATS Inspector who'd delivered the warrants in both cases was forced to admit that when they'd been re-done in 1984 the evidence contained hadn't been re-sworn in front of the magistrate. Immediately the defence counsel claimed this made them invalid pointing out that such warrants state they are issued as a result of information sworn before the magistrate 'on this day'.[170] The authorities were only able to gain a twenty-four-hour adjournment and were unable to produce any further clarification in this time and so the fugitive was released.[171] A new, corrected, warrant was issued by Bow Street magistrates on the day she was released but a second district justice would not accept that a telephone call informing Irish authorities of its existence was sufficient reason to detain Glenholmes.[172] This new warrant arrived in Dublin on the 24th, two days after the release whereupon the fugitive had gone underground.

The catalogue of errors in both phases of the Glenholmes incident caused renewed criticism in Ireland. Irish Justice Minister, Alan Dukes, said that 'furious' was an accurate description of governmental reaction.[173] Again the British Government was pushed into the position of explaining and rationalising while trying to defuse Dublin's anger. Northern Ireland Secretary, Douglas Hurd, maintained there was 'no criticism of the cooperation we received from the Irish authorities', but added, 'choosing my words with care, it would have been possible for the court to take a different decision'.[174] Even such muted and implicit a criticism of the Irish courts is unhelpful in a situation which can only be characterised by terms such as delicate. The court in this instance was maintaining the letter of the law if perhaps not the spirit which has been demonstrated in the Supreme Court. After the errors in the cases of Burns and Quinn and the initial mistakes in the first Glenholmes warrants it is nothing short of amazing that the second set wouldn't have been checked more scrupulously for technical errors. In fact one source reports that in November 1985 the Irish Attorney-General's office had requested just such a thing.[175] Following the Glenholmes failure the British Attorney-General, Sir Michael Havers, has now instructed the DPP for both Great Britain and Northern Ireland to,

> ensure personally that all outstanding warrants in respect of terrorist offences are checked at once for accuracy and sufficiency.[176]

The old cliché about the barn door and the horse bears some relevance.

That the current Irish Government has demonstrated the political will to try and extradite Republican terrorists to the UK is clear. Indeed in February 1986 Dublin finally signed the ECST removing the political offence from a list of offences and legislation is expected soon to place this on the Irish statutes. This, coupled with the changes in the political offence exception delineated by the Supreme Court and outlined above, and the extra-territorial legislation, means the bomber and the gunman in Ireland face a tightening net. The difference between 1975 and 1985 is striking.

Complacency on the part of observers would be ill-advised. There is still much controversy in Eire surrounding the recent decisions of the higher courts. Furthermore it cannot be assumed that the political will to ensure extradition will always exist in Dublin. Following the Glenholmes incident, the Opposition Leader, Charles Haughey, criticised both Dublin and London and stated his opposition to what he saw as a 'catastrophic change' in Irish extradition practices. He believed Glenholmes shouldn't be returned if re-arrested and added,

> In view of the serious doubts I have about the fairness of the trial they would get in British courts, anybody accused of these crimes should be dealt with before our courts so that we know at least they would get a scrupulously fair trial.[177]

Haughey's doubts may be relieved by the fact that both McGlinchey, on appeal, and Shannon were acquitted by Northern Ireland courts following their extradition.[178] As well, Northern Ireland Secretary Hurd has noted that of those who plead not guilty before the courts in Ulster, 50 per cent are acquitted in jury trials, and a higher proportion, 53 per cent, are acquitted by the non-jury Diplock courts.[179] However it is unlikely that Fianna Fail will drop its opposition to extradition.

This makes it all the more necessary for the British authorities in both London and Belfast to encourage the recent shifts in opinion in Dublin. There must be a more careful attitude towards requests for extradition and the absolute assurance that human error is minimised in the issuing of the requests and any prosecutions which may result. Success in this field will hopefully improve the acceptance by Unionists in Ulster of the Anglo–Irish accord agreed last year as it must be remembered that advances such as this on the political front are much more likely to destroy the basis for terrorism than any movements in the criminal justice arena.

NOTES

1 *Hansard*, 6th Series, Vol. 6, col. 28, 8 June 1981.
2 *Hansard*, 6th Series, Vol. 52, col. 232, 18 January 1984.
3 Paul O'Higgins, 'The Irish Extradition Act, 1965', *International and Comparative Law Quarterly*, Vol. 15, No. 2, April 1966, p. 370—Lists all statutory provisions for backing of warrants between England, Irleand, Scotland, Isle of Man and the Channel Islands.
Warrants issued in the UK were endorsed by the Inspector-General of the RIC or his deputy and vice versa.
4 *O'Boyle and Rodgers* vs *Attorney-General O'Duffy* (1929) *Irish Reports*, p. 558. Counsel had argued that since Northern Ireland didn't exist when the Petty Sessions (Ireland) Act 1851 came into effect there was no authority to extend it to the north and Meredith J concurred. As has been since noted this was bad law as the Irish Government had made an order in 1924 which provided inter alia that provisions for execution of all UK warrants should also apply to warrants from Ulster. Cf. Michael Farrell, *Sheltering the Fugitive? The Extradition of Irish Political Offenders*, Cork and Dublin: The Mercier Press, 1985, p. 30, and Margaret McGrath, 'Extradition: Another Irish Problem', *Northern Ireland Legal Quarterly*, Vol. 34, No. 4, Winter 1983, p. 295.
5 Informally the RUC and the Garda engaged in what amounted to abduction until this was declared a 'contempt of court' in *The State* (*Quinn*) vs *Ryan* (1965) *Irish Reports*, p. 70. Cf. Farrell, *op. cit*., pp. 34–36, 39; O'Higgins, *I & CLQ*, p. 370, fn. 15; Paul O'Higgins, 'Irish Extradition Law and Practice', *British Yearbook of International Law*, Vol. 34, 1958, p. 294; Seamus Breathnach, *The Irish Police from Earliest Times to the Present Day*, Dublin: Anvil Books, 1974, p. 171; and Alexander McCall-Smith and Philip Magee, 'The Anglo–Irish Law Enforcement Report in Historical and Political Context', *Criminal Law Review*, 1975, p. 205.
6 O'Higgins, *BYIL*, p. 305.
7 *Metropolitan Police Commissioner* vs *Hammond* (1964) 2 *All England Reports*, p. 772.
8 *The State* (*Quinn*) vs *Ryan* (1965) *Irish Reports*, p. 70.
9 Farrell, *op. cit*., p. 29.
10 In re Castioni (1891) 1 *Queen's Bench*, p. 149.
11 In re Meunier (1894) 2 *Queen's Bench*, p. 415.
12 Christine Van den Wijngaert, *The Political Offence Exception to Extradition*, Deventer, Boston, Antwerp, London, Frankfurt: Kluwer, 1980, p. 111.
13 *Schtraks* vs *The Government of Israel* (1962) 3 *All England Reports*, p. 540.
14 *European Treaty Series*, No. 24.
15 O'Higgins, *I & CLQ*, pp. 391–392.
16 S.2 (2) Backing of Warrants (Republic of Irleand) Act 1965, identical phrase is employed in the Extradition Act 1870.
17 S.44 (2) and S.50 (2) Irish Extradition Act 1965.
18 O'Higgins, *I & CLQ*, pp. 382, 392.
19 McGrath, *NILQ*, p. 299.
20 O'Higgins, *I & CLQ*, p. 382.
21 *Bourke* vs *Attorney-General* (1972) *Irish Reports*, p. 36.
22 *The State* (*Magee*) vs *O'Rourke* (1971) *Irish Reports*, p. 205.
23 (1972) *IR*, pp. 36–38.

24 McCall-Smith and Magee, *CLR*, p. 207.
25 (1971) *IR*, p. 211.
26 *Ibid.*, p. 216.
27 Wijngaert, *op. cit.*, pp. 119–120, and McGrath, *NILQ*, p. 303.
28 Re Dwyer (1970) April 13 (unreported) DC, as cited in Ivor Stanbrook and Clive Stanbrook, *The Law and Practice of Extradition*, Chichester and London: Barry Rose Publishers, 1980, p. 111. Cf. *Guardian*, 6 November 1979, p. 5 and *Irish Press*, 14 April 1970, p. 3.
29 *R* vs *Governor of Brixton Prison and another, ex parte Keane* (1970) 3 *All England Reports*, p. 741.
30 *New York Times*, 6 December 1970, p. 8.
31 (1970) 3 *All ER*, pp. 741, 744.
32 *Ibid.*, p. 745.
33 *Keane* vs *Governor of Brixton Prison* (1971) 1 *All England Reports*, p. 1168.
34 *Hansard*, 5th Series, Vol. 847, col. 109, 28 November 1972. Of these nine warrants were executed, eight more were refused, nine were outstanding and five referred to persons who couldn't be found in Eire or were subsequently arrested in Northern Ireland.
35 Farrell, *op. cit.*, p. 57.
36 Cleaver, Fulton and Rankin (Solicitors), *Submission on Admissibility—Council of Europe, European Commission of Human Rights—Application No. 9360/81, Edith Elliot and others Against Ireland*, Belfast, February 1982, Appendix 3.
37 *Ibid.*, p. 67. Those recaptured were: Thomas Maguire, Thomas Kane, Peter Hennessey, James Storey and Terence Clarke.
38 *Ibid.*
39 Farrell, *op. cit.*, p. 57. Just over a year later they were arrested again and the District Court granted extradition but on appeal to the Dublin High Court the offences were ruled political and extradition refused.
40 *Times*, 6 December 1972, p. 16.
41 *Hansard*, 5th Series, Vol. 829, col. 957, 24 January 1972.
42 *Hansard*, 5th Series, Vol. 846, cols. 240–241, 17 November 1972.
43 *Hansard*, 5th Series, Vol. 836, col. 179, 4 May 1972, statement of David Howell, Joint Minister of State for Northern Ireland.
44 *Hansard*, 5th Series, Vol. 848, col. 597, 14 December 1972.
45 *Times*, 16 October 1972, p. 12. From 1973–1976 a total of 25% of those convicted in the Special Criminal Court were from Ulster. Cf. M Robinson, 'The Special Criminal Court: Almost 10 Years On', *Fortnight*, No. 175, March 1980.
46 Farrell, *op. cit.*, p. 58 and *Times*, 18 November 1972, p. 14. In a much larger escape nineteen men fled from Portlaoise Prison on 18 August 1974 and at least two were re-captured in the UK. Martin McAllister seized in Ulster on 13 September 1974 and Sean Kinsella in Liverpool on 10 July 1975.
47 In re Taylor (1973) *Northern Ireland Law Reports*, p. 164.
48 Richard Deutsch and Vivien Magowan, *Northern Ireland 1968–73, A Chronology of Events*, Vol. II, Belfast: Blackstaff Press, 1974, pp. 294–296, and *Sunday Times*, 29 April 1973, p. 1.
49 *Times*, 21 September 1973, p. 2.
50 *Hansard*, 5th Series, Vol. 851, col. 40, 19 February 1973 and Vol. 860, col. 1600, 25 July 1973.
51 *Times*, 16 July 1973, p. 2.
52 *Sunday Times*, 30 September 1973, p. 8. The eleven and the decisions on requests

for them are as follows: Roisin McLaughlin—refused on grounds of political offence; James 'Seamus' O'Neill—refused on grounds of political offence; Marguerite 'Rita' O'Hare—refused on grounds of political offence; Anthony 'Dutch' Docherty—refused on grounds of political offence; Bernard Elliman—refused, granted habeas corpus; Thomas Fox—refused, granted habeas corpus; Peter Hennessey—arrested in Ulster; Edward McDonald—refused on grounds of political offence; Thomas McNulty—refused on grounds of political offence; Michael Willis—refused on grounds of no comparable offence; Anthony Shields—refused on grounds of political offence. Details from Cleaver, Fulton and Rankin, *op. cit.*, pp. 67–69.

53 *Irish Press*, 5 December 1973 as cited in Farrell, *op. cit.*, pp. 59–60.

54 Edgar Graham, *Ireland and Extradition, a Protection for Terrorists*, Belfast: European Human Rights Unit, Ulster Unionist Party, September 1982, p. 3.

55 *Times*, 30 July 1974, p. 2.

56 *Times*, 18 May 1973, p. 2.

57 *Economist*, 16 June 1973, p. 34.

58 *Irish Press*, 21 December 1974 as cited in Farrell, *op. cit.*, p. 63.

59 Farrell, *op. cit.*, p. 60.

60 *Times*, 5 May 1973, p. 2.

61 *Economist*, 16 June 1973, p. 34.

62 *Bartholemew Burns* vs *Attorney-General*, 4 February 1974 (unreported) as cited in Farrell, *op. cit.*, p. 60.

63 Farrell, *op. cit.*, p. 61.

64 *Ibid.*, pp. 61–62.

65 *Times*, 3 December 1975, p. 2.

66 *Times*, 9 September 1975, p. 2.

67 *Times*, 5 December 1975, p. 2.

68 *Times*, 16 December 1975, p. 2.

69 *Times*, 4 June 1976, p. 5.

70 *Times*, 23 April 1976, p. 1. Swords was arrested alongside eight others in Dublin in April 1983 but the SCC acquitted all of IRA membership. *Keesing's Contemporary Archives*, 33482A.

71 *Times*, 12 July 1977, p. 2.

72 *R* vs *Governor of Winson Green Prison, Birmingham, ex parte Littlejohn* (1975) 3 *All England Reports*, p. 209.

73 *Ibid.*, pp. 211–212.

74 *Ibid.*, pp. 213–215.

75 *Times*, 22 December 1973, p. 3.

76 *Times*, 8 October 1973, p. 2.

77 In 1976 Sean McKenna was allegedly abducted from Dundalk although an official Army Press statement says he 'stumbled across' the border into a patrol. Even more conclusive is evidence surrounding kidnap attempt on 29 March 1974 on PIRA suspects Patrick McLoughlin and Seamus Grew. Grew's extradition had been requested in August 1973 on an attempted murder charge and refused. Three Ulster Protestants were arrested by the Garda on 29 March 1974 in possession of maps, details of Grew's movements and a plan indicating where to dump their victims in Ulster. The three initially pleaded not guilty to kidnap charges, but changed their plea on the lesser charge of conspiracy to assault. All got five years at the SCC. It has since been claimed that the plot was organised by Army Intelligence in Lurgan and one of the three has admitted this while refusing to identify the officers involved. Cf. *New Statesman*, 11 May

1984, p. 12 and *Times*, 15 June 1974, p. 2. The DPP was considering allegations on two kidnaps by intelligence officers in late 1984. *Observer*, 18 November 1984, p. 6.

78 Dail Debates, cols. 450–451, 24 April 1975 as cited in McGrath, *NILQ*, p. 303.

79 *Keesing's Contemporary Archives*, 25108A.

80 *Times*, 22 October 1973, p. 1.

81 *Times*, 9 November 1973, p. 4.

82 Members were: Supreme Court judge, Mr Justice Walsh; Supreme Court judge, Mr Justice Henchy; TA Doyle, Esq SC; D Quigley, Esq; Lord Chief Justice for Northern Ireland, Sir Robert Lowry; Lord Justice Scarman; Sir Kenneth Jones, Home Office Legal Adviser; JBE Hutton, Esq QC, Senior Crown Counsel, Northern Ireland.

83 *Report of the Law Enforcement Commission* (*Cmnd. 5627*), London: HMSO, 1974.

84 *Ibid.*, p. 3. 'If time had been a less important factor, the all-Ireland court method would call for a more careful and detailed examination.'

85 *Ibid.*, p. 6.

86 *Ibid.*, p. 13.

87 *Ibid.*, p. 41.

88 *Ibid.*, p. 42. The scheduled offences are listed below along with comparable sentencing details in Ulster and Eire.

Offence	*Maximum term* *Ulster*	*Eire*
Capital murder (Eire retained death penalty for certain cateogires of murder into 1980s)	Not applicable	Death
Murder	Life	Life
Arson	Life	Life
Kidnap and false imprisonment	Life	Life
Offences against the person		
(a) wounding with intent to cause GBH	Life	Life
(b) causing GBH	5 yrs	5 yrs
Explosives		
(a) causing explosion likely to endanger life or property	Life	Life
(b) attempting to cause an explosion likely to endanger life or property or possessing explosives with intent to do so	20 yrs	20 yrs
(c) making or possessing explosives in suspicious circumstances	14 yrs	14 yrs
Robbery and burglary		
(a) robbery	Life	Life
(b) aggravated burglary	Life	Life
Firearms		
(a) possession with intent to endanger life or seriously damage property	Life	20 yrs
(b) possession in suspicious circumstances	10 yrs	5 yrs
(c) carrying with criminal intent	14 yrs	10 yrs
Hijacking of vehicles	15 yrs	15 yrs
Membership of		
(a) illegal organisations	5 yrs	7 yrs
(b) inciting or inviting people to join	5 yrs	10 yrs

Taken from *Hansard*, 5th Series, Vol. 918, cols. 473–474, 1 November 1976.

89 *Times*, 7 March 1975, p. 9 and 3 January 1974, p. 1.
90 *Times*, 6 December 1975, p. 2.
91 *Economist*, 9 March 1974, p. 47.
92 *Times*, 9 December 1974, p. 2 and Michael Hirst, 'The Criminal Law Abroad', *Criminal Law Review*, 1982, pp. 503–504.
93 FHA Micklewright, 'Irish Criminal Law (Jurisdiction) Act', *New Law Journal*, 26 August 1976, p. 856.
94 In the matter of Article 26 of the Constitution and in the matter of the Criminal Law (Jurisdiction) Bill, 1975 (1977) *Irish Reports*, p. 129.
95 *Times*, 2 June 1976, p. 2.
96 *Times*, 27 May 1977, p. 2.
97 *Times*, 8 February 1981, p. 6 and *Daily Telegraph*, 13 July 1979, p. 8.
98 Farrell, *op. cit.*, pp. 75, 77.
99 *Times*, 30 June 1976, p. 2.
100 *Daily Telegraph*, 16 December 1978, p. 3.
101 *Daily Telegraph*, 13 July 1979, p. 8.
102 *Times*, 11 October 1977, p. 4 and 12 October 1977, p. 4. Cf. *New Statesman*, 21 October 1977, p. 535.
103 *Times*, 8 March 1978, p. 2.
104 *Times*, 18 May 1982, p. 2.
105 McGrath, *NILQ*, p. 308 citing *R* vs *McCartan Smyth* (1982) November. *Regina* vs *Smyth* (1982) *Northern Ireland Law Reports*, p. 271.
106 *Daily Telegraph*, 12 November 1979, p. 2 and *Guardian*, 30 November 1979, p. 28.
107 *Times*, 10 October 1980, p. 6 and Graham, *op. cit.*, p. 11.
108 *Irish Times*, 29 July 1981 as cited in Cleaver, Fulton and Rankin, *op. cit.*, p. 77.
109 *Guardian*, 21 July 1981, p. 1.
110 *Times*, 15 December 1981, p. 2.
111 *Times*, 24 December 1981, p. 2.
112 *Keesing's Contemporary Archives*, 31577A.
113 *Times*, 8 March 1982, p. 2; 2 July 1982, p. 3; 7 July 1982, p. 2.
114 *Times*, 14 July 1982, p. 2.
115 *Guardian*, 3 May 1983, p. 2.
116 *Times*, 4 December 1975, p. 1.
117 *Hansard*, 6th Series, Vol. 19, col. 296, 8 March 1982.
118 Cited in E Moxon-Browne, 'The Water and the Fish: Public Opinion and the Provisional IRA in Northern Ireland', *Terrorism*, Vol. 5, Nos. 1 and 2 (1981), p. 61.
119 *Times*, 26 January 1977, p. 2. The UK signed and ratified the ECST and implemented it by enacting the Suppression of Terrorism Act 1978.
120 *Bulletin of the European Communities*, Vol. 12, No. 12 (1979), pp. 90–91.
121 Interviewed by BBC Northern Ireland Political Correspondent for Radio Ulster and interview printed in *The Listener*, 15 September 1977, p. 327.
122 *Sunday Times*, 15 November 1981, p. 6.
123 *Sunday Times*, 1 November 1981, p. 16.
124 Graham, *op. cit.*, p. 13. He was former Chairman of the Ulster Young Unionist Council, Honorary Secretary of the Ulster Unionist Council, and was himself assassinated by the PIRA in December 1983.
125 Farrell, *op. cit.*, p. 93.
126 Cleaver, Fulton and Rankin, *op. cit.*, Appendix 3.

127 *Hanlon* vs *Fleming* (1981) *Irish Reports*, p. 493.
128 Farrell, *op. cit.*, p. 94.
129 (1981) *IR*, p. 495.
130 *Ibid.*
131 *Ibid.*, p. 500.
132 *Times*, 1 April 1982, p. 2 and 3 April 1982, p. 7.
133 *Times*, 1 April 1982, p. 2.
134 Details drawn from the following: *Times*, 13 April 1977, p. 2; *Observer*, 17 July1983, p. 2; *Sunday Times*, 16 October 1983, p. 5; *Guardian*, 12 March 1986, p. 5 and Farrell, *op. cit.*, p. 96.
135 Farrell, *op. cit.*, p. 97 and McGrath, *NILQ*, p. 312 citing unreported decision of High Court.
136 *McGlinchey* vs *Wren* (1982) *Irish Reports*, p. 154.
137 *Ibid.*, p. 159.
138 *Ibid.*, p. 160.
139 *Ibid.*
140 McGrath, *NILQ*, p. 314.
141 *Times*, 27 May 1983, p. 1; 28 May 1983, pp. 1 and 4; and 31 May 1983, p. 1.
142 Farrell, *op. cit.*, p. 100.
143 *Guardian*, 28 January 1984, p. 2. Owen McCartan Smyth had already been tried under CJA for offences connected with this incident.
144 Farrell, *op. cit.*, p. 100.
145 *Times*, 19 March 1984, p. 30.
146 *Guardian*, 27 June 1984, p. 4.
147 *McMahon* vs *Governor of Mountjoy Prison and David Leahy*, 26 June 1984 (unreported), cited in Farrell, *op. cit.*, p. 101.
148 Extradition cases can be heard by a three-man court as in McGlinchey but all subsequent decisions were heard by five Supreme Court Justices.
149 *Shannon* vs *Fanning*, 31 July 1984 (unreported) as cited in Farrell, *op. cit.*, p. 102.
150 *Ibid.*
151 *Ibid.*
152 Farrell, *op. cit.*, pp. 104–105.
153 *Shannon* vs *Fanning*, as cited in Farrell, *op. cit.*, p. 105.
154 For further explanation see Wijngaert, *op. cit.*, pp. 126–132.
155 *Observer*, 18 November 1984, p. 6.
156 *Observer*, 18 November 1984, p. 6.
157 *Shannon* vs *Ireland and the Attorney-General*, SC, 16 November 1984 (unreported) as cited in Farrell, *op. cit.*, p. 111.
158 *Shannon* vs *Ireland and the Attorney-General*, HC, 11 May 1984 (unreported) as cited in Farrell, *op. cit.*, p. 112.
159 Lord Glenarthur in House of Lords, written reply, *Guardian*, 27 March 1986, p. 2.
160 For details of events and their chronological order see: *Sunday Times*, 11 November 1984, p. 1; *Times*, 12 November 1984, p. 1; *Guardian*, 12 November 1984, pp. 1 and 28; *Times*, 13 November 1984, p. 2; *Guardian*, 13 November 1984, p. 4; *Guardian*, 21 November 1984, p. 3; and *Sunday Times*, 25 November 1984, p. 4.
161 *Guardian*, 12 November 1984, pp. 1 and 28.
162 *Observer*, 4 August 1985, p. 3.
163 Farrell, *op. cit.*, p. 117.

164 *Guardian*, 1 March 1985, p. 2 and Farrell, *op. cit.*, p. 118 citing *Quinn* vs *Wren*, SC, 28 February 1985 (unreported).
165 *Bartholemew Burns* vs *Attorney-General*, 4 February 1974 (unreported) as cited in Farrell, *op. cit.*, p. 119.
166 Farrell, *op. cit.*, p. 120.
167 Farrell, *op. cit.*, p. 137 citing *Maguire* vs *Keane*, SC, 31 July 1985 (unreported).
168 *Guardian*, 4 August 1985, p. 3.
169 *Guardian*, 16 February 1984, p. 1; *Observer*, 25 March 1984, p. 2; *Guardian*, 14 December 1985, p. 28; and *Guardian*, 25 March 1986, p. 3.
170 *Guardian*, 24 March 1986, p. 3.
171 *Guardian*, 24 March 1986, pp. 1 and 32.
172 *Guardian*, 25 March 1986, p. 7.
173 *Guardian*, 24 March 1986, p. 1.
174 *Guardian*, 25 March 1986, p. 7.
175 *Observer*, 30 March 1986, p. 12.
176 *Guardian*, 25 March 1986, p. 7.
177 *Guardian*, 25 March 1986, p. 1.
178 *Guardian*, 21 February 1986, p. 4 and 14 December 1985, p. 28. Following acquittal McGlinchey was returned to Eire, tried on arms charges connected with his apprehension in Eire prior to extradition and jailed for ten years. See *Guardian*, 12 March 1986, p. 5.
179 *Hansard*, 6th Series, Vol. 80, col. 1001, 13 June 1985.

The Supergrass System in Northern Ireland

S C Greer

INTRODUCTION

On 21 November 1981 Christopher Black, from the Ardoyne area of Belfast, was arrested in the north of the city after having participated in an IRA road block staged for publicity purposes. After two days of silence in police custody he began to make the first of a large number of statements implicating himself and others in a catalogue of IRA-related offences. On 24 November he was granted immunity from prosecution and subsequently, in a trial which began in December 1982 and ended in August 1983, he gave evidence against thirty-eight accused, thirty-five of whom were convicted.

Although there were at least four paramilitary supergrasses in Northern Ireland in the ten-year period before Black's arrest,[1] his appearance is generally taken as the beginning of the 'supergrass system' because it was so rapidly followed by a flood of similar cases. Although complete accuracy concerning numbers is precluded by the fact that a number of these supergrasses retracted their evidence before their names became public it is possible to state that between November 1981 and November 1983 at least seven Loyalist and eighteen Republican supergrasses were responsible for over five hundred and ninety[2] people being arrested and charged with offences connected with paramilitary activities in Northern Ireland. Several of these defendants were implicated by one supergrass after another, either as a result of having been acquitted in one case or the evidence against them having been retracted. Three of the accused in the Kirkpatrick trial, for example, were implicated by five successive supergrasses and spent nearly four years in custody before being found guilty of any offence. This state of affairs has inspired the accusation that the supergrass system facilitates a form of 'internment by remand'.[3] Fifteen supergrasses retracted their evidence either before the trials in which they were involved began or before they could be concluded, and in another case involving IRA informer James Williamson, charges were withdrawn against all but two accused who had made confessions.[4] In the ten trials to have reached judgement so far, one hundred and twenty out of the two hundred and seventeen defendants (55 per cent) tried at first instance,[5] were convicted or pleaded guilty but fourteen of these convictions were subsequently quashed on appeal.[6] Taking this appeal decision into account, the overall conviction rate now stands.

The appearance of key members of illegal organisations as prosecution witnesses in the trials of their erstwhile associates is not unique to Northern Ireland. The nickname 'grass' for informer seems to derive largely from the Cockney rhyming slang 'grasshopper-copper' but it may also owe something to the popular song *Whispering Grass* and the term 'snake in the grass'. The word 'supergrass' was originally coined by journalists for a succession of London bank robbers who, in the early 1970s, not only informed on a large number of suspects but took the next step and entered the witness box to testify against them. 'Supergrasses' from terrorist organisations have also recently been used by the authorities in Italy.[7]

Apart from the number of defendants involved in supergrass cases, three main features distinguish the supergrass as a type of witness from run-of-the-mill accomplices who decide to give evidence for the prosecution. First, almost without exception, supergrasses in the UK have been the products of deliberate law-enforcement initiatives directed specifically at organised acquisitive crime mostly in the south of England or paramilitary activity in Northern Ireland. Second, they have been deeply involved in these serious, violent crimes rather than any other type of offence. Third, in almost every case they have been motivated by a highly developed sense of self-interest. Other accomplices turning Queen's evidence, on the other hand, may emerge anywhere in the UK, may have committed any offence involving more than one participant and may take this step at the impetus of any one or more of a variety of motives including genuine contrition, the desire for revenge or the hope of obtaining some personal advantage, e.g., leniency in punishment, immunity from prosecution or a financial or other material reward.

The prosecuting authorities in Northern Ireland maintain that the closed and secretive nature of paramilitary organisations precludes recourse to normal investigative policing and that if those who have been active in such organisations are prepared to testify it would be wrong for charges not to be preferred on their evidence.[8] Officially the initiative in each case comes from a suspect who voluntarily decides, usually after having been arrested, to testify for the Crown. Because the law-enforcement process is deemed to be greatly facilitated by such decisions, certain rewards, e.g., police protection from potentially vengeful ex-comrades, immunity from prosecution[9] or help in securing a reduced sentence and, in some cases, new identities and new lives elsewhere,[10] are considered appropriate. These, it is said, are agreed on a case to case basis and the allegation that the use of supergrasses has ever amounted to a prosecution 'strategy' or 'system' has been vigorously denied. The available evidence throws considerable doubt on this view. The fact that so many supergrasses have appeared over a comparatively short period of time in Northern Ireland suggests that a deliberate shift in prosecution policy has occurred. The key elements facilitating this change appear to be (a) alterations in interrogation priorities involving greater prominence for inducements and threats at the expense of questions with a neutral fact-finding purpose and (b) advance manpower and financial planning authorised at a high level for the sort of deals which have been made. Moreover, evidence from supergrasses who have retracted their statements gives some support to the view that the prospect of turning Queen's evidence is usually first mooted by the police rather than the suspect.[11]

In attempting to understand Northern Ireland's supergrass phenomenon it is important to answer a number of central questions. How have the judges in these cases applied the relevant law? How has the system emerged and developed? What contrasts and comparisons can be drawn between it and the comparable experience in England? In what direction is it heading and what contribution has it made to the control of politically motivated violence?

THE LAW ON ACCOMPLICE EVIDENCE

There is no law on supergrass trials as such. Since the first English supergrass case was heard on appeal in 1975[12] it has been clear that the standard law on accomplice evidence applies. This has three principal facets. The 'accomplice evidence rule' obliges judges to warn juries of the dangers of convicting an accused on uncorroborated accomplice evidence in any case where an accomplice testifies for the prosecution.[13] If the warning is omitted any convictions secured are likely to be quashed on appeal unless no substantial miscarriage of justice is deemed to have occurred.[14] Second, a number of rules deal with the credibility required of accomplice evidence in order for convictions to be justified. Third, other rules govern what constitutes corroboration. The judgements delivered in several of Northern Ireland's supergrass cases and in another Diplock trial involving the evidence of an accomplice, *R* vs *McCormick*,[15] have contributed to the development of each of these areas.

THE ACCOMPLICE EVIDENCE RULE

The accomplice evidence rule is based upon the premise that accomplices as a class of witness are inherently untrustworthy and that their evidence, in consequence, must be presumed to be unreliable: hence the emphasis on corroboration. The following dangers have traditionally been cited.[16] First, an accomplice–witness is, by definition a criminal, and therefore a person of bad character whose evidence is 'not entitled to the same consideration as the evidence of a clean man, free from infamy'.[17] Second, he or she may fabricate chunks of his or her 'evidence'. Third, the accomplice may tell the truth about the incidents in question but substitute the names of innocent people, or suspects whom the police are especially anxious to see convicted, for those who actually took part. Fourth, the accomplice–witness may tell the truth about the offences and implicate those who were genuinely involved but change the roles to cast him or herself in the most favourable light and the others in the worst. Fifth, spurious plausibility could be accorded false accomplice evidence by virtue of the accomplice's familiarity with the details of the crime or crimes.

All these dangers are particularly acute with respect to supergrasses. Each has been involved in serious and mostly violent crime and is, therefore, of unusually bad character even compared with other possible accomplice–witnesses. The pressure to tell a story sufficiently appealing to the prosecuting authorities to attract the various rewards on offer is also likely to be more intense than with most other accomplices turning Queen's evidence. There is, in addition, ample time and opportunity during the many months spent in police 'protective custody' for false evidence to be rehearsed in preparation for a convincing courtroom appearance.

The mandatory nature of the accomplice evidence warning has led to a bizarre practice in Northern Ireland, where since 1973 a list of offences contained in a schedule to the Northern Ireland (Emergency Provisions) Act 1973 and usually associated with the activities of paramilitary organisations ('scheduled ofences') have been tried by the non-jury 'Diplock' courts. Since the judges in these trials are required to discharge the functions of 'tribunal of fact' and 'tribunal of law', the judiciary in Northern Ireland have assumed that the accomplice evidence rule obliges the judge trying a scheduled offence case to issue the danger warning to himself.[18] However, since the accomplice evidence rule is based upon the assumption that there is a jury, and upon the separation of identities and functions which this implies, it is not at all clear that this is a legitimate interpretation. Amongst other things, the jury brings to every criminal trial in which it is involved, a collective decision about guilt or innocence rather than the decision of a single person. This is particularly important where the outcome of a trial hinges upon the uncorroborated evidence of an accomplice because where this is the case reasonable people are likely to disagree about whether or not it represents the truth. Indeed it could even be argued that the accomplice evidence rule is designed to put pressure on juries not to convict in such circumstances by strengthening the doubts of those who would have been reluctant to convict in the first place, or at least, that it is intended to provoke an intense discussion about the justice of convicting without corroboration. In fact the available evidence shows that juries tend to acquit when the only evidence against an accused is the uncorroborated testimony of a supergrass.[19] It would seem that disagreement amongst jurors as to whether the supergrass's evidence should be trusted or not indicates that reasonable doubt persists and, therefore, that guilt has not been proved to the requisite standard.

In Northern Ireland's first three supergrass trials, *R* vs *Graham*[20] (the Bennett case), *R* vs *Donnelly*[21] (the Black case) and *R* vs *Gibney*[22] (the McGrady case) sixty-one per cent of those convicted were found guilty on the uncorroborated evidence of the accomplice–witnesses concerned. It is generally agreed that in discharging their function of tribunal of fact judges in Northern Ireland's Diplock courts must act as a 'reasonable jury'.[23] But if this concept is to bear any relation to the behaviour of actual juries then, on this issue, the trial judges in these three cases fell far short of the appropriate standard.

This shortcoming could have been avoided if the judiciary in Northern Ireland had interpreted the accomplice evidence rule more restrictively. It can be plausibly argued that the logic of the principles underpinning the rule requires judges, in the absence of a jury, not to convict upon uncorroborated accomplice evidence at all in trials on indictment since this is the only appropriate alternative safeguard to a jury's evaluation. In *R* vs *Graham*,[24] the first supergrass case in Northern Ireland to be heard on appeal, the Northern Ireland Court of Appeal dismissed this argument. Although quashing all fourteen convictions because of the manner in which the trial judge had assessed the credibility of the accomplice evidence, Lord Lowry stated:

> the evidence of a largely uncorroborated accomplice of bad character who has a lot to gain by giving evidence can still be accepted.[25]

THE CREDIBILITY REQUIREMENT

In any criminal trial the vital question which the tribunal of fact (normally the jury, but in a Diplock trial, the judge) must answer is—does the totality of the evidence establish the guilt of the accused beyond reasonable doubt? It is generally the case that, where it is called, the evidence of an accomplice will constitute the principal evidence for the prosecution. Consequently, the verdict in such cases will normally hinge upon whether the tribunal of fact believes it or not. In such circumstances the only line of defence open to the accused is to attempt to discredit the accomplice–witness. It is at this point that the inherent weaknesses of a supergrass's evidence should enter the equation. The independent evidence in any given trial on the evidence of an accomplice e.g., a confession,[26] may, nonetheless, be taken as proving guilt beyond reasonable doubt by itself, and, therefore, justifying a conviction, even where the accomplice evidence is deemed untrustworthy.[27] But where it is an issue the credibility of the accomplice's testimony must be considered in the light of all the evidence in the case[28] including his or her personal credibility and character,[29] his or her demeanour in the witness box and the circumstances which led him or her to become a prosecution witness.[30]

In *R* vs *Graham*[31] the Northern Ireland Court of Appeal held that the trial judge, Mr Justice Murray, had overestimated the degree to which items of independent evidence which either implicated none of the defendants or only a few, were capable of enhancing the general credibility of the accomplice evidence. The court also declared that the judge had placed unwarranted significance on the failure of the defendants to testify on their own behalf. In the view of the Court of Appeal when the credibility of a 'suspect witness'[32] is called into question by the defence, as in this case, his or her evidence will rarely if ever be so compelling as to require the defendants to testify or suffer adverse consequences if they do not.

The decision in the Bennett appeal, while valid and welcome in other respects, contributes little towards redressing the imbalance in non-jury supergrass trials currently tipped against the accused. The elaborate discussion about the degree to which the general credibility of the accomplice evidence can be enhanced by independent evidence which at most only implicates some defendants, merely means that if they want their decisions to stand on appeal, Diplock judges should not state in their judgements that they regard such evidence as 'crucially' supporting the accomplice evidence or a 'best test' of its credibility. They could, of course, continue to take this view whilst refraining from admitting to it. Similarly, in affirming that defendants will rarely, if ever, be penalised for failing to testify on their own behalf in an accomplice evidence case, the Northern Ireland Court of Appeal has eliminated one of the factors which judges can explicitly bring to bear upon their decisions. But because it does not appear in the written judgement does not necessarily mean that it has not entered into the decision.

CORROBORATION

The leading case on what constitutes corroboration of accomplice evidence is *R* vs *Baskerville*. The then Lord Chief Justice, Lord Reading, stated:

> We hold that the evidence in corroboration must be independent testimony which affects the accused by connecting or tending to connect him with the crime. In other words it must be evidence which implicates him, that is, which confirms in some material particular not only the evidence that the crime has been committed, but also that the prisoner committed it ...[33]

His Lordship also approved *R* vs *Noakes*[34] which decided that the evidence of one accomplice cannot corroborate another but in *R* vs *Kilbourne*[35] and *R* vs *Boardman*[36] the House of Lords rejected this view and held that accomplices can corroborate one another providing they give independent evidence of separate incidents and the circumstances exclude the danger of a jointly fabricated story.

The most significant component of the *Baskerville* test is the requirement that corroborative evidence must *implicate* the accused in the offence with which he or she is charged by confirming in a material particular that he or she committed it. Lord Reading understood this to include circumstantial evidence. As he remarked;

> The corroboration need not be direct evidence that the accused committed the crime; it is sufficient if it is merely circumstantial evidence of his connection with the crime.[37]

By and large, since *Baskerville* the courts have applied Lord Reading's interpretation of the 'implicates' requirement. For example in the McGrady case Lord Lowry said:

> Corroboration is independent testimony which affects the accused by connecting or tending to connect him with the crime. . . . It can include an admissible oral and or written statement made by that accused. Independent evidence which tends to confirm the truth of the suspect witness's evidence in a material respect may help the tribunal of fact to assess the giver of the evidence but it is not corroboration unless it satisfies the test defined above.[38]

Other evidence which tends to verify the truth of those parts of the accomplice evidence which do not implicate the accused is termed 'supportive evidence'.

In *R* vs *McCormick*[39] the Northern Ireland Court of Appeal departed from Lord Reading's broad approach by adding a further distinction to that already widely recognised between 'corroborating' and 'supporting' evidence. Delivering the judgement of the court the Lord Chief Justice, Lord Lowry, held that evidence which may be corroborative in the *Baskerville* sense may still not justify a conviction if the tribunal of fact considers the credibility of the accomplice evidence to be such that a higher than usual calibre of corroboration is required.

A detective-sergeant in the Special Branch of the RUC was charged with a number of scheduled offences ranging from armed robbery to the murder of an RUC sergeant. The Crown case was based upon the testimony of Antony O'Doherty, a paid police informer, then serving an eighteen-year prison sentence for his part in some of the offences with which the defendant was charged. The judge, Mr Justice Murray, held that,

> It would be highly dangerous and wrong to convict the accused on any of the crimes charged against him on the evidence of O'Doherty unless that evidence is supported by clear and compelling corroboration.[40]

Mr Justice Murray inferred that discrepancies between the defendant's evidence and that of other witnesses indicated that the accused was lying and that taken together these things amounted to corroboration of the necessary standard. The defendant had found himself in a worsening financial situation at the time of the robbery. He made a statement admitting buying a van and claiming that O'Doherty, the accomplice–witness, gave him 'Nan's money', some £600–700 to purchase it while Mrs McLaughlin ('Nan') denied in evidence that she had parted with such a sum. He denied possessing a hand-grenade but his landlady found one in his room and a detective-sergeant gave evidence that he had taken one from a police security cabinet. O'Doherty alleged that a hand-grenade was used in a robbery which he claimed he and the accused committed. An entry in the defendant's official diary referred to his having met O'Doherty on the day the robbery for which McCormick was eventually convicted was carried out.

The Northern Ireland Court of Appeal overturned the conviction on the grounds that in the circumstances the discrepancies between McCormick's evidence and that of other witnesses did not justify the inference that he had lied to conceal his guilt and though the meeting between O'Doherty and McCormick recorded in the appellant's official diary could give rise to suspicion, and suspicion could in certain circumstances afford corroboration, it also admitted an innocent interpretation. Since O'Doherty was a paid police informer and McCormick was his 'handler', the two had a legitimate reason for being together. The judge, therefore, 'lacked the cogent and compelling corroboration which he declared to be indispensible to a finding of guilty'.[41]

Since the Northern Ireland Court of Appeal accepted the trial judge's conclusion that O'Doherty's evidence required 'clear and compelling corroboration', the decision would appear to amount to no more than a disagreement with Mr Justice Murray concerning whether these criteria had been fulfilled.[42] But there is more to it than that. By endorsing the trial judge's assessment that a high standard of corroboration was required in this case the Northern Ireland Court of Appeal has affirmed that the credibility of accomplice evidence and the 'implicates' requirement can stand in inverse relation. It would appear that in some cases the lower the credibility of the former, the stricter the corroboration test. At a certain point on this continuum, to be determined by the view the tribunal of the fact takes of the credibility of the accomplice evidence, circumstantial evidence of the sort which was presented against McCormick will not be considered corroborative. Unfortunately Lord Lowry did not make clear whether the Court of Appeal's decision rested solely upon the trial judge's view that the evidence of the *particular* accomplice in question required especially compelling corroboration or whether there is, or should be, a rebuttable presumption that the evidence of *certain classes of accomplice*, for example those whose cooperation clearly stems from inducement rather than remorse, cannot be sufficient to sustain a conviction without independent evidence which is corroborative in the higher sense.

The McCormick case also raises a further query. In terms of character, motivation and performance in the witness box (with the possible exception of Christopher Black and Jackie Grimley at opposite ends of the spectrum) there was very little to distinguish O'Doherty from any of the supergrasses. Yet, far from requiring 'clear and compelling corroboration', the judges in the Bennett, Black and McGrady cases based sixty-one per cent of the convictions on the uncorroborated testimony of these witnesses. Two of these judges were none other than Mr Justice Murray and Lord Lowry.

THE ORIGINS OF THE SUPERGRASS SYSTEM

The use of accomplice evidence as a method of controlling violent political unrest is not a new departure in Ireland. In both the United Irishmen and Fenian uprisings in the eighteenth and nineteenth centuries respectively, the authorities relied heavily for convictions on those prepared to betray their comrades in arms.[43] But the use of supergrasses in the 1980s as a routine method of dealing with large numbers of terrorist suspects developed out of the unique succession of counterinsurgency initiatives introduced since the early 1970s to control the violence of Loyalist and particularly Republican paramilitary organisations.

The intervention of the British Army in August 1969 failed to quell the sectarian disturbances which had erupted in Northern Ireland in the previous year.[44] In August 1971 with the agreement of the Westminster cabinet the Unionist Government introduced internment without trial as authorised by the Civil Authorities (Special Powers) Act (NI) 1922. This resulted in a dramatic escalation in the intensity of the conflict. By March 1972 it was clear that the Unionist regime had lost control of public order so the British Government suspended the Stormont Parliament and executive and undertook direct responsibility for the affairs of Northern Ireland.

A Commission of Inquiry chaired by Lord Diplock was appointed in October 1972 to examine

> whether changes should be made in the administration of justice in order to deal more effectively with terrorism without using internment under the Special Powers Act.[45]

A package of measures was proposed, the bulk of which were enacted in the Northern Ireland (Emergency Provisions) Act 1973 (the 'EPA'). Police and army powers to stop and question, search and seize and arrest and detain were extended, the law was altered in order to facilitate convictions on confessions extracted in special anti-terrorist centres and jury trial was suspended for a list of mostly violent offences contained in a schedule to the Act ('scheduled offences').

Following the enactment of the EPA the use of internment was greatly reduced in favour of imprisonment by the courts rather than by executive decision.[46] The police, therefore, came under increased pressure to show a satisfactory conviction rate[47] especially when internment was finally discontinued in 1975.[48] Until the advent of the supergrass strategy the critical point in the Diplock process was whether a suspect confessed or not. Only thirty-two confessions out of nearly four thousand were declared inadmissible by the courts between 1976 and 1980[49] and 75–80 per cent of the 93 per cent conviction rate in scheduled offence cases in the first six months of 1978, a not untypical period, rested on confessions alone.[50] The drive for confessions occasioned a flood of complaints about the physical abuse of suspects in interrogation centres.[51] In 1978 Amnesty International confirmed that many of these allegations were justified[52] and in 1979 the report of the Bennett Inquiry outlined several ways in which the opportunities for physical ill-treatment could be curtailed e.g., that the right of access to a solicitor should be absolute after forty-eight hours without prejudice to prior access, that medical checks should be carried out at least every twenty-four hours, that a closed circuit television system should be installed in interrogation centres to monitor interviews, that each suspect should be provided with a printed notice of his or her rights on arrival at the police station and that a formal code of conduct for interviewing officers should be incorporated into the

RUC Code.[53] The number of complaints from suspects concerning physical abuse dropped dramatically shortly after the publication of Bennett's conclusions and recommendations.[54]

The Bennett Report appears to have made the extraction of confessions much more difficult and consequently the policy of securing convictions on confession alone became no longer viable. This seems to have prompted the prosecuting authorities to concentrate their efforts into enlisting the services of informers.[55] While the quest for informers has been an integral part of law enforcement the world over since time immemorial, and a particularly favoured method of countering politically motivated violence in Ireland,[56] the objective in Northern Ireland in the early 1980s seems to have been not only to garner low-grade intelligence but also to cultivate a batch of high-powered accomplice–witnesses who would be prepared to testify in court against those suspected of being the big fish in the Republican and Loyalist paramilitary organisations. It seems inconceivable that the financial and manpower resources which this has required[57] were not authorised at the executive level in advance rather than, as the authorities maintain, agreed on a case to case basis as each 'converted terrorist' came forward. For this reason the term 'supergrass system' is not inappropriate.

THE SUPERGRASS SYSTEM IN THE ASCENDANCY—THE BENNETT, BLACK AND McGRADY CASES

The first three supergrass cases established several important benchmarks which seemed to bode well for the future promotion of the supergrass system but which, in retrospect, seem to have contained the seeds of its subsequent decline (see Table 1).

First, and of greatest importance, eighty-eight per cent of the sixty-four accused in these three trials were found guilty. This seemed to indicate that the courts were prepared to cooperate with the supergrass strategy more or less as it stood,[58] thereby making it a highly efficient method of obtaining convictions. Second, the fact that sixty-one per cent of these convictions were secured on the uncorroborated evidence of the supergrasses suggested that at least some judges would not require much independent evidence in order to arrive at guilty verdicts. This was particularly encouraging from the point of view of the prosecuting authorities since it tended to vindicate the decision to concentrate resources into the cultivation of supergrass evidence at the expense of the accumulation of evidence from the normal range of sources. Third, the Bennett, Black and McGrady cases showed that judges were prepared to trust the supergrass's uncorroborated evidence despite the fact that both it and other aspects of the prosecution case in each trial contained serious

Table 1. Supergrass Trials in Northern Ireland

Supergrass (in order of completion of trials)	*Position regarding own offences*	*Year of trial*	*Nos. prosecuted*	*Nos. tried*	*Nos. convicted at supergrass trial*	*Nos. convicted on uncorroborated accomplice evidence*	*Type of corroboration where present*
Joseph Bennett (UVF)	Immunity	1983	16	16	14 (all set aside on appeal)	11	2 confessions 1 forensic
Christopher Black (IRA)	Immunity	1983	38	38	35	20	15 confessions
Kevin McGrady (IRA)	Serving life for murder and other offences	1983	10	10	7	3	4 confessions
Jackie Grimley (INLA)	Immunity	1983	22	21 (1 did not answer bail)	14 (inc. 3 plead guilty)	0	11 confessions
John Morgan (IRA)	Immunity	1984	5	5	0	0	0
Robert Quigley (IRA)	Immunity	1984	16	11 (4 sent for re-trial. 1 no case to answer)	10	8	2 confessions
Raymond Gilmour (IRA)	Immunity	1984	35	35	0	0	0
James Crockard (UVF)	Serving life for murder and other offences	1985	29	29	8	0	8 confessions
William 'Budgie' Allen (UVF)	Serving 14-year prison sentence for various offences	1985	25	25	5	0	5 confessions
Harry Kirkpatrick	3 life sentences	1985	27	27	27	26	1 confession
Totals:			223	217	120 (106)*	68 (57)*	48 (46)* confessions 1 (0)* forensic

* Convictions quashed in Bennett appeal.

specific flaws, in addition to those generally associated with the evidence of supergrasses.

THE BENNETT CASE

The arrest of Christopher Black is generally taken as signalling the start of the supergrass system. But before the trial of those charged on his testimony was finished fourteen of the sixteen defendants prosecuted on the evidence of UVF supergrass Joseph Bennett were convicted.

Bennett had a significant criminal record even before he became involved in the activities of the proscribed Ulster Volunteer Force in 1972. In August of that year he was arrested and charged with possession of guns, ammunition and explosives but was released on compassionate bail in December on the grounds that his wife was terminally ill with cancer. Following her death in April 1973 he absconded and was re-arrested in March 1974. The house in which he was then living was found to contain a considerable quantity of firearms and explosives. He was sentenced to twelve years' imprisonment but under the standard remission arrangements[59] he only served six, during the last year and a half of which he acted as the UVF Commander of Compound 21 in the Maze Prison. Following his release in 1980 he became a UVF Company Commander in the Sandy Row area of Belfast but was subsequently sentenced to death in his absence by a UVF Court Martial for stealing money from his employer. In May 1982 he was arrested following the armed robbery of a post office in Killinchy, County Down, during which the elderly post-mistress was brutally murdered. Bennett denied having inflicted the fatal knife wounds but admitted having been armed with a loaded gun.

While in custody he realised his dilemma. As he later told the court;

> I was inside for life or sentence of death outside. . . . The future was bleak. The police offered a third alternative. . . . My life depended on impressing the police and on my first day in custody I mentioned immunity. . . . There was a strong incentive to cooperate. . . . At the end of the day my usefulness to the police would be measured in the number of men I put away.[60]

Despite his involvement in the Killinchy murder and seven other serious crimes before the court Bennett was guaranteed complete immunity for his own offences in return for his testimony. The trial judge Mr Justice Murray declared that he was:

> A ruthless, resourceful criminal whose criminal acts extended to the use of his dead father's police uniform to carry out daring armed robberies from which considerable sums of money were stolen and divided amongst himself and his accomplices.[61]

The judge also concluded that Bennett's dominant motive in giving evidence was to avoid a second long prison sentence.[62]

It is possible to identify other flaws in Mr Justice Murray's assessment of

Bennett's credibility apart from those upon which the Northern Ireland Court of Appeal based its decision. Most seriously he accepted that Bennett had committed perjury during the course of the trial yet felt this did not sufficiently damage his credibility to warrant acquitting the twelve who were convicted on the uncorroborated accomplice evidence. A cheque for £200 bearing Bennett's signature was produced in court which Bennett had previously denied having endorsed. Mr Justice Murray stated:

> I have to say, and say clearly, that Mr Boal has convinced me that Bennett told a lie about it. I think that must be so but it seems to me to be clear that it was an extraneous matter entirely as the evidence emerged.[63]

But is it possible to be sure of guilt beyond reasonable doubt where the evidence of such a witness is completely uncorroborated?

THE BLACK CASE

Christopher Black had joined the IRA in 1975 but was arrested in December of the same year and convicted of attempted robbery. Having served the customary fifty per cent of his ten-year prison sentence he was released in December 1980 and immediately rejoined the IRA. According to Mr Justice Kelly, the judge at the trial of those charged on his evidence, he was 'up to his neck in terrorist activity throughout 1981'[64] playing a major role in a catalogue of violent incidents. The judge also stated that his over-riding motive in deciding to give evidence was, as with Bennett, the desire to evade a second term of imprisonment.

The scale of the Black trial was staggering. Thirty-eight defendants were seated in rows around three sides of the courtroom guarded by a score of prison officers and police some of whom were heavily armed. The indictment contained one hundred and eighty-four charges based on forty-five separate incidents and the trial lasted from December 1982 to August 1983 occupying one hundred and twenty court sitting days. The committal proceedings or the 'preliminary inquiry' had been avoided by the DPP obtaining a Bill of Indictment from the High Court, a controversial and rarely used procedure[65] which spared Black the ordeal of having to give his evidence twice.[66]

Although Black was, by all accounts, an impressive witness with a phenomenal memory, serious questions remain about the truth of many of his allegations. Particularly acute doubts persist with respect to two defendants. Tobias McMahon was convicted on Black's uncorroborated evidence for his part in a conspiracy to murder and sentenced to fifteen years' imprisonment, yet Black did not name him until after having spent nine months in protective custody, and he admitted in court that he and McMahon had a strong personal antipathy towards one another.[67] Joseph Kelly was convicted of membership of the IRA purely on Black's testimony even though the evidence against him was extremely confused.[68] Black claimed Kelly had been with him at a training camp in Donegal in the Irish Republic in the pre-Easter period, March/April 1981. However, the indictment charged Kelly with having been at the camp between 1 June–15 July 1981. Kelly had signed a confession admitting being at an IRA camp in Donegal in August 1981 but the admissibility and weight of this statement was contested at the trial and forty alibi witnesses were produced to show that the defendant had been in Belfast throughout August and the pre-Easter periods in the year in question. Mr Justice Kelly allowed the Crown to change the dates on the indictment to 1 March–31 August 1981. This contrasts sharply with the approach taken by the English Court of Appeal in *R* vs *Throne*[69] where a similar request was refused, and in *Thorne* the desired change was only a matter of a few days. The alibis were dismissed as being supplied by 'hardly disinterested witnesses'[70] and Kelly's account as revealing 'a massive lack of credibility'.[71] Although membership of an organisation proscribed by the EPA normally attracts a custodial sentence of five years or more, Kelly received a two-year suspended sentence, perhaps an admission by the judge that he was not convinced beyond reasonable doubt about his guilt after all. As Gifford states:

> The problem was that if Black was shown to be embroidering his evidence or inserting wrong names or simply unreliable, about any one defendant, his unshakeable credibility, which was the sheet anchor of the judge's decision would be undermined.[72]

THE McGRADY CASE

Kevin McGrady joined the IRA in 1975 and had already participated in a number of serious incidents before his arrest for murder in December. The charge was dropped when a key witness withdrew his evidence but McGrady served a three-month prison sentence for having assaulted a police officer in the course of his interrogation. Following his release he went to London and then on to Amsterdam where he joined an evangelical Christian sect claiming that he had had a religious conversion.

Unique among the supergrasses in England and Northern Ireland, McGrady gave himself up voluntarily to the police in Belfast in January 1982 maintaining that some men, including his brother Sean, had been wrongfully convicted of offences for which he had been responsible himself. He also told the court at the trial of those charged on his evidence that he felt he had to expiate his misdeeds in order to make progress in the religious sect he had joined. Following his confession McGrady was interviewed at length by the police during the course of which he made a number of written statements. On 26 June 1982 he pleaded guilty to twenty-seven charges including three murders and was sentenced to life imprisonment.

The most remarkable feature of the McGrady supergrass trial was that despite the fact that, on a number of charges, the evidence which he gave was completely disbelieved by the presiding judge, Lord Lowry, three defendants were convicted without corroboration. Those parts of McGrady's testimony which were believed had 'the ring of authenticity'[73] the judge stated.

Referring to those offences with respect to which McGrady's testimony was rejected, Lord Lowry said:

> to have convicted on any of the counts in these groups of charges would have been a perversion of justice according to law, so contradictory, bizarre and in some respects incredible was McGrady's evidence and so devious and deliberately evasive was his manner of giving it.[74]

In one such case the person originally implicated by McGrady in an attempted murder, Eugene Pinkey, turned out to have been in prison at the relevant time so McGrady substituted his brother, the defendant Thomas Pinkey.[75] Perhaps even more so than with Bennett and Black the question can be asked—is it possible to be sure of guilt beyond reasonable doubt where the evidence of a witness such as McGrady is entirely uncorroborated as it was for three of the seven defendants who were convicted? If it is, why were three others acquitted?

A subsequent decision of the Northern Ireland Court of Appeal supports the view that McGrady was an unreliable witness whose testimony deserved not to be trusted. Dismissing Sean McGrady's appeal against conviction for murder Lords Justice Gibson and Murray declared that the 'new evidence' supplied by Kevin was 'quite unimpressive and indeed incredible' and irreconcilable with 'other evidence which is unshakeable and flatly contradictory'.[76]

THE SUPERGRASS SYSTEM IN DECLINE

Since the McGrady case another seven supergrass trials featuring, in chronological order, the accomplice–witnesses Jackie Grimley, John Morgan, Robert Quigley, Raymond Gilmour, James Crockard, William 'Budgie' Allen and Harry Kirkpatrick have reached a verdict. In only two, the Quigley and Kirkpatrick trials, were convictions secured purely on the evidence of the supergrass. In the Quigley case, ten of the eleven defendants were found guilty, eight of these on uncorroborated accomplice evidence, and in the Kirkpatrick trial twenty-six of the twenty-seven accused, all of whom were convicted, were found guilty without the supergrass's testimony being corroborated.

The conviction rate for the seven trials in this second phase of the supergrass system was 42 per cent, 53 per cent of these convictions being based on uncorroborated accomplice evidence and the others resting on confessions or alleged admissions plus three guilty pleas. Much of the 42 per cent and the 53 per cent figures are due to the Kirkpatrick verdicts. The conviction rate in the six trials prior to Kirkpatrick had dropped to 29 per cent, only 22 per cent of which involved uncorroborated accomplice evidence.

The overall conviction rate for all ten supergrass trials in Northern Ireland stands at 49 per cent. Fifty-four per cent of these convictions were secured on uncorroborated accomplice evidence while the remainder were based on confessions and alleged admissions. The supergrass conviction rate is, therefore, considerably lower than the approximately 80 per cent conviction rate when confessions were the preferred source of prosecution evidence in scheduled offence cases. Since the Court of Appeal based its decision in *Graham* upon a specific failure of the trial judge to assess the credibility of the accomplice evidence properly, it would be foolish to state that every conviction in every supergrass case is now in jeopardy. However, at the very least, the decision in *Graham* shows that the convictions in any of the cases where the evidence of the supergrass was trusted are not watertight. All the outstanding convictions on the supergrass's evidence concern alleged members of Republican paramilitary organisations.

There has been much debate about the significance of these developments for the future of the supergrass system. Two things are, however, beyond dispute. First, the pattern of convictions falls into two distinct phases, the first covering the first three trials and the second covering the subsequent seven plus the Bennett appeal. Secondly, only a handful of suspects have been arrested on the evidence of the supergrasses Collins and Whoriskey since November 1983 and many of these were released shortly afterwards when Collins withdrew his cooperation. This contrasts sharply with the previous two-year period when proceedings were initiated against the two hundred and seventeen defendants who were eventually tried on the evidence of the ten supergrasses.

The orthodox interpretation of these developments would run something like this. Since all trials are decided on their individual merits in accordance with the law, the judges in the Grimley, Morgan, Gilmour, Crockard and Allen cases simply found the particular witness before them unworthy of belief. On the other hand the judges who presided over the other cases had sufficient confidence in the testimonies of Bennett, Black, McGrady, Quigley and Kirkpatrick respectively to justify convictions. The comparatively low conviction rate over the seven most recent cases is merely a coincidence which indicates nothing about the 'general attitude' of the courts to the evidence of supergrasses since no such attitude exists beyond that permitted by the law i.e., that accomplice evidence can provide a basis for convictions whether corroborated or not provided the tribunal of fact, having been properly warned, is convinced that the sum total of the evidence in the particular cases in question proves guilt beyond reasonable doubt. The recent dearth of supergrasses would be attributed by advocates of this view to the failure of any other accomplices to turn Queen's evidence since November 1983. According to this line of reasoning, therefore, nothing can be predicted about either the appearance of new supergrasses or the behaviour of the courts in any such future trials.

The official view is difficult to accept for two principal reasons. First, the difference between phases one and two of the conviction pattern is too significant to justify such dismissive treatment. With the possible exception of Jackie Grimley and Raymond Gilmour who appear to have been police agents[77] the character and background of the supergrasses in phase two were much the same as that of those in phase one. John Morgan had been convicted of the manslaughter of his brother-in-law before becoming an active member of both the INLA and IRA. Robert Quigley, also an IRA activist, claimed at the trial of those charged on his evidence that he had no feelings of remorse for the widows or families of IRA victims, that he had lied on oath and that he had turned Queen's evidence purely to save his own skin. Ulster Volunteer Force supergrasses John Gibson and James Crockard had each been convicted of murder and William 'Budgie' Allen had also been an active member of this paramilitary group. According to barristers appearing for the defence in many of the trials in both phases one and two there was little to distinguish the court room performances of any of the supergrasses except for Black who was outstandingly impressive and Grimley who was outstandingly bad.

If follows, therefore, that either the judges who presided over the supergrass trials have adopted an extremely inconsistent attitude to supergrass evidence, and that this inexplicably falls into two successive phases, or else a change in judicial attitude occurred around November 1983 which resulted in the sharply reduced conviction rate in phase two. Second, it stretches credibility to argue that at least twenty-five supergrasses simply and inexplicably volunteered to turn Queen's evidence between November 1981 and November 1983 without some corresponding, and in all probability prior, change in attitude on the part of the prosecuting authorities, while in the previous twelve years only a handful surfaced and over the past two years only two have made an appearance, and one of these only briefly.

A second view, diametrically opposed to the first, takes the form of a conspiracy theory.[78] The judiciary in Northern Ireland, particularly in scheduled offence cases, it has been argued, are essentially an integral part of the anti-Republican counterinsurgency effort thinly disguised by the cloak of legal impartiality and independence. Adherents to this view tend to regard the promotion of Loyalist supergrasses as a ploy by the authorities to give this exercise a veneer of even handedness. Within this perspective two interpretations of the history of the supergrass system can be distinguished. On the one hand it could be argued that the two-phase conviction pattern was arranged by the executive, judiciary and law-enforcement agencies at the outset or, on the other, that it ought to be seen as a sophisticated and autonomous attempt by the judiciary to deflect the criticism that the supergrass system is a conviction conveyor belt. The intention, it is alleged, is to show that the judges are willing to acquit many whom the prosecuting authorities would like to see behind bars. This, it is said, far from undermining or weakening the supergrass system will enhance its credibility and increase the chances of its survival.

The second of these two versions of the conspiracy theory is the more usually canvassed but neither is particularly plausible. There is simply no evidence that the conviction pattern was pre-arranged. Moreover, it is difficult to accept that it could have been even if the will to do so had existed, given the unpredictable nature of important features of supergrass trials, e.g., whether or not any given supergrass will retract his or her evidence. Furthermore, the anticipated result of the second version, the strengthening of the supergrass system, has clearly not occurred. Whether there are any paramilitary supergrass cases in Northern Ireland in future or not, it can be stated with confidence that the use of accomplice evidence as a routine method of convicting large numbers of suspects is not nearly as viable now as it was in the autumn and winter months of 1983. Moreover, while there can be little doubt that the authorities see the operation of Republican paramilitary organisations as the main threat to stability and established interests in Northern Ireland, the activities of Loyalist paramilitary groups are also regarded as prejudicial to the delicate status quo. The use of Loyalist supergrasses ought, therefore, to be regarded not as a balancing act but as a genuine attempt to deal with troublesome elements.

There is a third more credible explanation. Regarding the attitude of the courts it would seem that following the McGrady trial in November 1983 judges trying supergrass cases in Northern Ireland deliberately became more critical of this type of evidence than the judges in the first three trials had been. It is impossible to identify precisely the factors which have produced this result. It could be argued that Northern Ireland's judges, drawn largely from Unionist backgrounds,[79] recognised the dangers inherent in the disenchantment of large sections of the Loyalist community with the legal system and Government policy which the supergrass system has inspired. Alternatively, and more convincingly, it could be argued that the decisions in the Bennett, Black and McGrady cases were open to criticism on purely legal grounds, as Lord Gifford QC demonstrated in his cogently reasoned report which was published in January 1984, and that the judiciary realised that they would have to adjust their behaviour in order to maintain plausibility for the view that their role in such trials is to apply a set of politically neutral legal rules to certain proven facts.

The evidence suggests that the prosecuting authorities were very satisfied with the results in the Bennett, Black and McGrady cases and initially saw the supergrass system as an efficient device for obtaining convictions.[80] It would seem, therefore, that they would have preferred to promote as many supergrass cases as possible. It seems inconceivable that the supply of satisfactory recruits simply and inexplicably dried up around November 1983 when, arpart from the recent appearances of Eamon Collins and Angela Whoriskey the last supergrass, James Crockard, surfaced. It is much more likely that the collapse of the Grimley trial, the first to end with the discrediting of a supergrass in court, coinciding as it did with the peak of the unusually broadly based public campaign against the supergrass system[81] and the effective beginning of Lord Gifford's inquiry, persuaded the prosecuting authorities that the costs of the supergrass policy in propaganda, financial and manpower terms outweighed its counterinsurgency benefits and justified the quest for an alternative strategy. The justification for this view appears to have been strengthened by the subsequent developments in the courts. It is not beyond the bounds of possibility that new supergrasses will appear in future, since it is clear that the RUC find them useful as a psychological weapon with which to sow mistrust in the tightly knit communities which sustain the paramilitary organisations. But as a routine method of securing convictions the supergrass system is clearly at an end, at least for some time.

SUPERGRASSES IN ENGLAND AND NORTHERN IRELAND —CONTRASTS AND COMPARISONS

The supergrass phenomenon in Northern Ireland shares two major features in common with its English counterpart[82] apart from those implied by the term 'supergrass'.

First, the utilitarian justification for using supergrass evidence has been accepted by the courts in both places. This was expressed by Lord Justice Lawton in *R* vs *Turner* and endorsed by the courts in succeeding supergrass trials. His Lordship stated:

> It is in the interests of the public that criminals be brought to justice; and the more serious the crimes the greater is the need for justice to be done. Employing Queen's evidence to accomplish this end is distasteful and has been distasteful for at least 300 years to judges, lawyers and members of the public.[83]

Second, the law on accomplice evidence in each jurisdiction is substantially the same.[84] However, there are also six major differences:

(a) In England, following the Smalls case, the practice of granting immunity from prosecution to supergrasses was abandoned in 1972 in favour of having them tried and sentenced before allowing their appearance as prosecution witnesses in other trials. In Northern Ireland, on the other hand, at least thirteen supergrasses[85] were offered an immunity deal between 1981 and 1983 and it is not clear that the prosecuting authorities in this jurisdiction have now rejected this option.

(b) In England and Wales the prosecution of defendants on the uncorroborated evidence of a supergrass was apparently discontinued on the DPP's instructions in 1977[86] while in Northern Ireland it has persisted up to and including the most recent cases.

(c) According to Gifford, as far as the English experience is concerned, 'From the information available, there is no case in which it is clear that a person has been convicted on the evidence of a single supergrass, without corroboration from any other testimony'.[87]

This contrasts sharply with the fact that 54 per cent of those convicted in the ten supergrass cases in Northern Ireland were found guilty of entirely uncorroborated accomplice evidence.

(d) Several supergrass trials in Northern Ireland have been considerably larger than any seen in England despite the English Court of Appeal's advice that:

> No more accused should be indicted together than is necessary for the proper presentation of the prosecution's case against the principal accused. Necessity not convenience should be the guiding factor. Our experience warns us ... that in cases

involving a number of accused, there is a danger that those on the fringes will be dragged down by those at the centre.[88]

(e) The supergrass system in Northern Ireland emerged from a background of political instability, political violence, emergency laws, non-jury courts and a unique succession of counterinsurgency initiatives whereas in England it was developed as a response to a regional, though nonetheless serious, professional crime problem.

(f) Public concern about the English supergrass trials diminished as the prosecuting authorities, responding to the guidelines set by the courts, eliminated its most controversial features, immunity from prosecution and prosecutions on uncorroborated accomplice evidence. This allowed a string of subsequent supergrass cases to be processed relatively smoothly through the criminal justice system.[89] In Northern Ireland, on the other hand, public disquiet was intensified by the initial rubber-stamping attitude of the judiciary which in its turn apparently forced the courts to take a more critical approach. This appears to have rendered the supergrass policy no longer viable.

CONCLUSION

Northern Ireland's supergrass system is the latest in a series of controversial law-enforcement initiatives introduced in the attempt to deal with the violence of Loyalist and particularly Republican paramilitary organisations. The same objective, conviction maximisation, has been the dominant theme in nearly all of these strategies, although the supergrass policy has had other spin-off advantages from the authorities' point of view, e.g., holding suspects on remand for long periods and sowing fear and mistrust in Loyalist and Republican communities. In the Bennett, Black and McGrady cases the presiding judges were prepared to facilitate a high conviction rate by, on the one hand, interpreting the law on accomplice evidence narrowly, thus making the danger warning a largely empty ritual and on the other applying the credibility rules broadly. This resulted in a conviction rate of 88 per cent, 61 per cent of which were on the accomplice's uncorroborated testimony. It would seem, according to the available evidence, that this is unlikely to have happened had these cases been tried by jury. The constraints upon the readiness to convict provided by the jury system could have been more effectively reproduced for the Diplock courts had the judiciary refused to convict upon accomplice evidence without corroboration. It would also be easier to regard the decision of the Northern Ireland Court of Appeal in *McCormick* as a valid development of the corroboration rules if the courts had applied it generally to accomplice–witnesses of O'Doherty's calibre. This would clearly have included all the supergrasses.

In promoting the supergrass system conviction maximisation has been relentlessly pursued by the prosecuting authorities. There has been little attempt to follow the English policy of trying and sentencing supergrasses before permitting them to appear as prosecution witnesses rather than granting them immunity from prosecution. No attempt whatever has been made to follow the English practice of prosecuting only where the evidence of a supergrass is corroborated. The English Court of Appeal's advice about limiting the size of trials has also been completely ignored.

This blatant and somewhat crude attempt to convict virtually everyone whom the supergrasses implicated has clearly come unstuck. The judiciary seem to have realised that the response of the judges in the Bennett, Black and McGrady cases to the evidence of these informers seriously undermined the claim that the role of the courts is to apply a body of politically neutral rules to proven facts in complete independence from the executive. This change of heart can be attributed, at least in part, to the criticisms of the supergrass system voiced from many diverse quarters. The result has been a radically reduced conviction rate, 42 per cent, over the seven cases following McGrady which in its turn seems to have deterred the prosecuting authorities from initiating as many prosecutions on the evidence of a supergrass since November 1983 as they did in the previous two-year period. Neither courts nor prosecuting authorities have taken any steps, however, which would make it impossible to revive the supergrass policy at some future date. But this would not be easy and it is, therefore, unlikely to happen.

What then has the supergrass system achieved? At its inception many claimed that it was saving lives because the 'godfathers of terrorism' were at last being taken into custody and prosecuted.[90] Some even went so far as to predict that the supergrass trials heralded the end of paramilitary activity in Northern Ireland altogether. Subsequent events have cast considerable doubt on the first claim and have completely discredited the second.

With respect to the saving of lives it is possible that some of those arrested and charged on the evidence of one or more of the supergrasses might have participated in acts of violence had they not been in custody. But this is not the end of the matter. The supergrasses' contribution to the evolving pattern of political violence in Northern Ireland must also be assessed. This leads on to the second point.

The nature of the conflict in Nothern Ireland has altered significantly over the past sixteen years as the result of a complex interplay between anti-terrorist policies and self-initiated changes on the part of the various paramilitary organisations. In 1977, for example, the Republican movement, which embraces both the IRA and Sinn Féin, decided to embark upon the 'ballot-armalite' strategy[91] which required increasing emphasis on political activity accompanied by a shift in paramilitary operations away from random bombings etc. to carefully targeted killings.

In fact the number of violent incidents has been in steady decline since 1976 following a dramatic decrease from 12,010 in 1972 to 2202 in 1975. The number of violent deaths has also been dropping since 1976 except for a small rise in 1981, the year of the hunger strike by Republican prisoners demanding political status. However, the number of deaths per violent incident has been increasing since 1972. Deaths which occurred as a result of assassinations at the homes or places of work or leisure of the victims have been rising as a proportion of total violent deaths from 25 per cent in the 1969–1973 period to 40 per cent in 1980–1984 and 50 per cent in 1983 and 1984 while deaths arising from riots, explosions, gun battles, cross-fire and sniper activity have been declining both in proportionate and absolute terms. While the IRA has maintained a constant level of killings since 1977 the number of fatalities caused by Loyalist and other Republican paramilitary organisations has been declining.[92]

In other words peace and stability are not being restored to Northern Ireland. Rather the conflict is increasingly being channelled into much more focused killings both by security force personnel and the IRA.[93] It is impossible to measure precisely the contribution the supergrass system has made, or will make, to this developing pattern. It is clear, however, that it has not succeeded in eliminating terrorism from Northern Ireland. Indeed in overall terms it would seem that it is more likely to have increased rather than decreased the likelihood of further violence. Paramilitary organisations thrive upon bitterness and a sense of grievance and injustice particularly when this is directed against authority. The supergrass system has apparently nourished such attitudes particularly amongst the Nationalist community. In a recent poll[94] 72 per cent of Catholic respondents either disapproved or strongly disapproved of the supergrass policy whereas only 21 per cent of Protestant respondents fell into this category. In another poll[95] 57 per cent of Catholics expressed the view that the legal system in Nothern Ireland dispenses justice unfairly or very unfairly. Only 9 per cent of Protestant respondents took this view. Although the statistics do not establish clear causal links between disenchantment with the supergrass strategy and support for paramilitary activities it seems reasonable to suppose that such links exist. A parallel can be drawn with internment. In the early 1970s detention without trial was seen by those who advocated it as a potential panacea for the mounting disorder. It is now widely recognised, however, that this security initiative resulted in the incarceration of innocent men, thus further estranging large sections of the Nationalist community from the legal process, and that this in its turn dramatically increased the flow of recruits to the IRA and added fuel to an already bitter civil conflict. The supergrass system has perhaps sown the seeds for a similar harvest.

NOTES

1 See Workers Research Unit, *Belfast Bulletin*, No. 11: *Supergrasses*, Belfast: Workers Research Unit, 1984.

2 The figure 593 for 1982–1985 was given in a Commons written reply by Mr Nicholas Scott, Northern Ireland Junior Minister (HC Debs., Vol. 73, col. 100).

3 See S Greer, 'Internment with a Judge's Stamp', *Fortnight*, April 1984; DPJ Walsh, *The Use and Abuse of Emergency Legislation in Northern Ireland*, The Cobden Trust, 1983, chapter 5.

4 T Gifford, *Supergrasses—The Use of Accomplice Evidence in Northern Ireland*, The Cobden Trust, 1984, p. 10 as up-dated by author's own research.
5 These figures are based on the author's own research. On 2 April 1985 the Attorney General told the House of Commons that 68 defendants in the four scheduled offence trials being held on the evidence of an accomplice in 1983 pleaded guilty or were either acquitted or convicted (HC Debs., Vol. 77, col. 317). However, in a letter from the Attorney General's Office to the author dated 23 August 1985 the number of defendants tried in the four supergrass trials in 1983 was stated to be 87. My own figure is 86.
6 *R* vs *Graham* (1984) 16 *NIJB* (CA).
7 See P Hillyard and J Percy-Smith, 'Converting Terrorists—The Use of Supergrasses in Northern Ireland', *Journal of Law and Society*, Vol. 335, 1984; *Sunday Times Colour Supplement*, 8 April 1984.
8 Gifford, *op. cit.*, para. 29.
9 At least 12 of the 25 supergrasses identified by Lord Gifford, QC were granted immunity from prosecution (Gifford, *op. cit.*, p. 10). For an account of the law and policy relating to the granting of immunity from prosecution see ATM Smith, 'Immunity from Prosecution', *CLJ*, Vol. 299, 1983.
10 The claim that several of Northern Ireland's supergrasses have found new homes in South Africa has been denied by the South African ambassador to the UK (*Irish News*, 13 April 1985).
11 See Gifford, *op. cit.*
12 *R* vs *Turner* (1975) 61 Cr. App. R. 67.
13 *Davies* vs *DPP* [1954] A.C. 378.
14 S.9 (1) Criminal Appeal (NI) Act 1968; *R* vs *Turner* (1978) 66 Cr. App. R.6, 16.
15 (1984) 1 *NIJB* (CA).
16 See e.g. JD Heydon, 'The Corroboration of Accomplices', 1973, Crim. L.R. 264; T Gifford, *op. cit.*, paras. 29 and 67.
17 *People* vs *Coffey* 39 *LRANS* 704, 706 (1911).
18 See e.g. *R* vs *Graham* (1983) 7 *NIJB*, p. 55.
19 Gifford, *op. cit.*, paras. 12–20.
20 (1983) 7 *NIJB*.
21 (1983) (unreported).
22 (1983) (unreported).
23 See JD Jackson, *Northern Ireland Supplement to Cross on Evidence*, 5th edition, SLS, 1983, p. 16.
24 (1984) 16 *NIJB* (CA).
25 *Ibid.*, p. 23.
26 In the Grimley supergrass trial 11 of the 22 defendants were convicted on this basis even though the accomplice evidence was rejected.
27 *Boardman* vs *DPP* (1975) 60 Cr. App. R. 165, 183.
28 *R* vs *Turner* (1975) 61 Cr. App. R. 67, 84; *R* vs *Graham* (1983) 7 *NIJB*, p. 68; *Cross on Evidence*, 5th edition, London: Butterworths, 1979, p. 208. In *R* vs *Gibney* (1983) (unreported), Lord Lowry held that the 'great anxiety' displayed by Gibney on having been confronted with McGrady while in police custody strengthened McGrady's credibility (p. 21).
29 *R* vs *McCormick* (1984) 1 *NIJB* (CA) p. 13.
30 *R* vs *Graham* (1983) 7 *NIJB*, p. 56.
31 (1984) 16 *NIJB* (CA).
32 *Ibid.*, pp. 6–7.
33 [1916] 2 K.B. 658, 667.

34 (1832) 5 C. & P. 326.
35 (1973) 57 Cr. App. R. 381.
36 (1975) 60 Cr. App. R. 165.
37 [1916] 2 K.B. 658, 667.
38 (1983) (unreported), p. 5.
39 (1984) 1 *NIJB* (CA).
40 (1982) 3 *NIJB*, p. 8.
41 (1984) 1 *NIJB* (CA) p. 12.
42 *Ibid.*
43 See e.g. A Boyd, *The Informers—A Chilling Account of the Supergrasses in Northern Ireland*, Mercier Press, 1984, chapter 1; Hillyard and Percy-Smith, *op. cit.*
44 For a good account of the disturbances of the late 1960s and early 1970s see The Sunday Times Insight Team, *Ulster*, Harmondsworth: Penguin, 1972. See also A Boyd, *Holy War in Belfast*, Grove Press, 1969; M Farrell, *The Orange State*, 2nd edition, Pluto Press, 1980; P Buckland, *A History of Northern Ireland*, Gill and MacMillan, 1981.
45 Mr William Whitelaw, Secretary of State for Northern Ireland, HC Debs., Vol. 855, col. 276.
46 K Boyle, T Hadden and P Hillyard, *Ten Years on in Northern Ireland—The Legal Control of Political Violence*, The Cobden Trust, 1980, p. 1.
47 *Ibid.*, p. 40.
48 For further details see *Review of the Operation of the Northern Ireland (Emergency Provisions) Act 1978* (The Baker Report), Cmnd. 9222, London: HMSO, 1984, para. 225.
49 See DS Greer, 'The Admissibility of Confessions under the Northern Ireland (Emergency Provisions) Act' (1980) 31 *NILQ*, pp. 205, 233.
50 *Report of the Committee of Inquiry into Police Interrogation Procedures in Northern Ireland* (The Bennett Report), Cmnd. 7497, London: HMSO, 1979, para. 30.
51 Boyle, Hadden and Hillyard, *op. cit.*, p. 39. See also *Ireland* vs *UK* (1976) *Yearbook of European Convention on Human Rights*, p. 512.
52 Report of an Amnesty International Mission to Northern Ireland (28 November–6 December 1977).
53 The Bennett Report, para. 404.
54 Boyle, Hadden and Hillyard, *op. cit.*, p. 40.
55 In his survey of 60 individuals arrested and detained under the EPA between September 1980 and June 1981 but released without charge after a period of interrogation, Walsh found that 35% claimed they had been pressurised by the police to become informers (Walsh, *op. cit.*, p. 68).
56 See p. 517 above.
57 In a written reply on 22 February 1985, the Secretary of State for Northern Ireland, Douglas Hurd, disclosed that providing protection for people who had given evidence against former accomplices in terrorist organisations had cost the taxpayer £1.3 million over the last seven years (HC Deb., Vol. 74 col. 126).
58 In the Bennett case the judge, Mr Justice Murray, criticised the prosecution for not spelling out the details of Bennett's immunity deal [*R* vs *Graham* (1983) 7 *NIJB*, p. 23].
59 See The Baker Report, paras. 455–459.
60 *R* vs *Graham* (1983) 7 *NIJB*, pp. 25–26.
61 *Ibid.*, p. 22.

62 *Ibid.*, pp. 23–26.
63 *Ibid.*, p. 87. In his report Lord Gifford appears to confuse this with a sum for £600 which Bennett alleged he was given by the defendants Hewitt and Houston acting as officers for the UVF (Gifford, *op. cit.*, para. 39). Nevertheless Gifford's conclusion that this proven lie undermined Bennett's credibility remains valid as a general point.
64 *R* vs *Donnelly* (1983) (unreported) Day 1, p. 71.
65 The only other supergrass cases in which it was used were those featuring Patrick McGurk who retracted his evidence the day the trial of those he had implicated was due to start, and Harry Kirkpatrick.
66 For a discussion of the voluntary Bill of Indictment procedure see Walsh, *op. cit.*, pp. 88–90.
67 (1983) (unreported) Day 1 pp. 157–159.
68 (1983) (unreported) Day 2 pp. 9–50.
69 (1978) 66 Cr. App. R. 6.
70 (1983) (unreported) Day 2 p. 27.
71 *Ibid.*, p. 37.
72 Gifford, *op. cit.*, para. 52.
73 (1983) (unreported) p. 21.
74 *Ibid.*, pp. 11–12.
75 *Ibid.*, p. 29.
76 *R* vs *Sean P McGrady* (1984) (unreported), p. 16.
77 Strictly speaking agents provocateurs and police agents should not be treated as accomplices at the trials of those charged on their evidence (*Cross on Evidence*, p. 198). Since the evidence supplied by Grimley and Gilmour was entirely discredited in court their precise status as witnesses was not established by the respective judges.
78 See e.g. E McDonagh, 'Are the Judges another Arm of British Policy?' *Fortnight*, 18 March 1985.
79 See e.g., the thumb-nail sketches in Workers Research Unit, *Belfast Bulletin*, No. 10: *Rough Justice*, Spring 1982.
80 The Chief Constable of the RUC, Sir John Hermon, stated in his annual report for 1982: 'It is clearly beyond question that the community as a whole has benefited immeasurably from this development. . . . The outcome is crucial to the well-being of Northern Ireland . . .' (pp. xi–xii).
81 Concern about the supergrass system has been expressed by prominent Protestant and Catholic clergymen (*Irish News*, 9 September 1983), trade unionists (*Irish News*, 26 October 1983), civil liberties groups (*The Guardian*, 5 November 1983), Canadian and American legal observers (*Irish News*, 8 October 1983 and 23 June 1984), the British Liberal Party (*Irish News*, 28 November 1983), the British Labour Party (*Belfast Telegraph*, 15 January 1984), Amnesty International (*Irish News*, 24 February 1984), the Irish Government (*Irish News*, 18 May 1984), Loyalist and Nationalist politicians (*Irish News*, 4 April 1984) and local lawyers (*Irish News*, 3 November 1983) to name but some.
82 For an account of the English supergrass phenomenon see D Seymour, 'What Good have Supergrasses done for Anyone but Themselves?' *LAG Bulletin*, December 1982. This appears to be the only available study.
83 (1975) 61 Cr. App. R. 67, 79.
84 It would be exactly the same were it not for the Northern Ireland Court of Appeal decisions in *R* vs *McCormick* (1984) 1 *NIJB* and *R* vs *Graham* (1984) 16 *NIJB*, the implications of which for the law in England and Wales are not clear.

85 Gifford, *op. cit.*, p. 10. The police have maintained that immunity is never granted to anyone who has been directly responsible for murder (Gifford, *op. cit.*, para. 27).
86 *The Guardian*, 29 and 30 May 1977.
87 Gifford, *op. cit.*, para. 182.
88 *R* vs *Thorne* (1978) 66 Cr. App. R. 6, 12–14. The Black trial involved 38 defendants, the Gilmour trial 35 and the Crockard case 29.
89 Seymour, *op. cit.*
90 See e.g. E Graham, 'A Vital Weapon in the Anti-terrorist Arsenal', *Fortnight*, October 1983. See also note 66.
91 See *Fortnight*, July–August 1982, p. 4.
92 These figures are taken from D Roche, 'Patterns of Political Violence in Northern Ireland in 1984', *Fortnight*, 29 April 1985.
93 *Ibid.*
94 *Fortnight*, November 1984.
95 *Belfast Telegraph*, 6 February 1985.

The Police Response to Terrorism: A Critical Overview

D Th Schiller

Other definitional problems apart, the perpetration of terrorist acts has been and always will be considered first and foremost within the context of criminal law. Whether we are dealing with a transnationally or internationally operating group of perpetrators or with small-scale 'home-grown' terrorists, countering the effects and dealing with the offenders falls within the framework of internal security and is therefore a job for the department of justice and the police forces. This is more than legal semantics: the question of how a State or a society counters terrorism touches the foundations of democracy. We have ample evidence of the fate of those governments[1] which decided to drop legal restrictions, to step outside the borders set by the democratic system and deal with terrorism at its own level, fighting fire with fire, employing the military to the full extent. It also means playing into the hands of the terrorists, helping them to dismantle the existing order, meeting them on their chosen battleground and thereby granting them the status of combatants. If we use military units against terrorists in our streets, are we going to apply military law and are we going to recognise them as prisoners-of-war, as nearly every modern terrorist group (from the IRA to the Baader–Meinhof gang) has demanded?

There is the obverse side to this coin. How useful are military units in maintaining internal security? How well are even elite formations like paratroopers or marine commandos suited to fight an enemy, whose tactics include the use of disguises, hidden weapons, time-bombs, and the absence of uniforms and bases, defended positions and the like? After the spate of airport attacks around Christmas 1985, the public was again treated to the spectacle of British Army formations moving in to protect the London airports. Admittedly, the Army had the manpower reserves available to cordon off such large areas, but besides the dubious deterrent value of the highly visible checkpoints with their armoured vehicles, their Scorpion tanks and machine guns, the effect of these security measures remains doubtful. Furthermore, they are only a step-gap, short-term response. Europe's peacetime armies simply cannot afford to detail year-round internal security units without training and overall defensive capabilities beginning to suffer.

This is not to say that the current police efforts to counter terrorism have been so overwhelmingly successful. In fact, the overall results appear mediocre at best. The German example is a case in point, a set-piece model which has its parallels in other European countries. As other nations, the Federal Republic of Germany needed a dramatic shock to jar her authorities out of the slumber of complacency in which police and government officials have so long indulged. The massacre by Black September/Fatah terrorists perpetrated during the Olympic Games in 1972 in Munich brought the German police face to face with its own ineptitude. Even the strongly doctored 'after-action report' submitted by the Munich Police Chief Dr Martin Schreiber could not cover up or lessen the fiasco at the Fürstenfeldbrück airport. Everything was lacking—a plan with a chance of success, trained personnel, functioning command and control procedures, an authority figure willing to take responsibility and to react according to the rapidly changing situation. Intelligence efforts to safeguard the Games were insufficient from the start.

Not that Germany—or other European nations—should have been too surprised by what happened during those tragic September days; the writing had been on the wall long enough. Terrorism had made its debut years before the Munich massacre. Jewish and Israeli installations had been the target of bombings since 1968. With the frustration of PLO insurgency efforts on the Israeli-occupied Westbank in 1968, various Palestinian groups had turned to Europe to conduct a campaign with fewer risks and larger propaganda effects. By 1970 hijackings had become commonplace; in Munich and Zurich PLO activists attacked airplanes and passengers at airports, using modes of operation not dissimilar to those recently encountered in Rome and Vienna. The 1968 student revolt gave birth to local radical groups[2] which quickly transformed themselves into transnationally operating terrorist teams as was the case with the Baader–Meinhof 'Red Army Faction' and their PLO connection. In addition to that, Germany had experienced the rivalries of conflicting radical exiles, as was the case in the continuous post-war feud between Croatian extremists and Yugoslavian hit-teams or Iranian pro- and anti-Shah factions.

Unlike the Anglo–American community-orientated police, the German police force (as well as those of most other European countries) was historically a government-orientated structure which emerged from the military. This is not only evident in such terms as 'gendarmerie' which dates back to a military rural unit of the eighteenth century, but also in uniforms, armament and training. For centuries and also after the Second World War, police officers were discharged army veterans and this left its mark on the tactical and structural development of the police force. Garrisoned riot police formations were trained in dealing with strikes and armed uprisings, a relic of the nineteenth century and the 1920s, when the post-war Weimar Republic was embroiled in a violent civil war between left- and right-wing radicals. While police formations equipped with machine guns, mortars and armoured cars trained (and one might add, still train) in remote country sites to encircle and attack similarly equipped insurgents, regular policemen found themselves unable to deal with bank robberies which turned into hostage/barricade situations. Simply firing a hail of bullets, as was done in 1971 in Munich when a single hostage-taker held off the police, could surely not be the sole solution. In retrospect, this incident where the criminal and a hostage died in the hail of more than two hundred rounds fired by the officers at the scene, should have been enough to warn police officials that their existing *instrumentarium* was not adequate.

Police response to terrorism follows two lines. It has to be dealt with at the tactical level and it demands an investigative/intelligence aproach. At both levels—that is, on the patrol level and in the criminal investigation department, hierarchical bureaucracies exist which have (as all existing systems of this kind) an inbred reluctance to accept change and reforms. The police apparatus is more often than not a cumbersome, top-heavy closed circuit, seldom responsive to outside criticism or advice. This is even more true in Germany, where the existing civil service regulations (Beamtenrecht) provide strong hierarchical boundaries within the system as well as preventing outside expertise being funnelled into the command levels. The results are outmoded training, a strong conventionalism in all measures taken and a solid distrust of innovative thinking. The net effect of these circumstances is a tendency not unlike that found in some army circles: instead of preparing for future wars, one trains for yesterday's battles. Any progress only comes slowly and runs the danger of being already outmoded by the time it is implemented.

THE TACTICAL LEVEL

The year 1972 provided a healthy shock to this system, a failure which could not be argued away in front of the whole world, a world which was able to watch the drama unfold on their TV screens. At Federal and State level the authorities began to react along the tactical and intelligence line: the 'Grenzschutzgruppe 9', better known by its abbreviation GSG 9, was founded within the framework of the border police force, as a special, now close to three hundred-strong, unit to deal with any form of terrorist threat. The GSG 9's development became an example and pacesetter for the implementation of special task forces in Germany and abroad. For anyone familiar with the post-war German bureaucracy and its resulting inefficiency it remains unbelievable how the long-serving commanding officer of the unit, Ulrich K Wegener, succeeded in overcoming the numerous obstacles thrown in his way, how this unit was set up and equipped in the most modern way, how ideas were openly accepted from such foreign sources as the SAS, the FBI or the Israeli Army and how regulations were ignored whenever they conflicted with the efficiency of the unit. Much of the privilege and freedom enjoyed by the GSG 9 today is a direct result of Wegener's personal efforts, which he undertook without regard to the possible detrimental effects on his career.

At the State or local level, reaction teams were set up by the patrol divisions, named 'Spezialeinsatzkommandos' (SEK), which were to deal with terrorists of all kinds as long as the case remained under the jurisdiction of the State or city government. Similarly trained and equipped as the GSG 9, the SEKs with their attached countersniper groups (PSK) are the mainstay of tactical police operations. These units (on average forty to sixty members strong), are not limited to dealing with cases of political terrorism—they also deal with other criminals, conduct arrests and are sometimes used as a shock force in riot situations.

Still, it was a long time before the new units were accepted. For years the reaction of the liberal press ranged from joking about them as 'expensive toys of the Ministries of the Interior' to slandering them as 'killer teams', which had the 'licence to kill', thereby 'opening the backdoor to capital punishment'. Not a few police chiefs remained unconvinced, and a number of politicians had similar doubts about the political drawbacks of giving the go ahead to such units. When the GSG 9 asked to be integrated into the search units of the Länder, one minister reportedly remarked that this would result 'in a stretch of scorched earth from the Alps to the Northern Sea'. It took five years of waiting before the GSG 9 was deployed on an actual mission, and the Mogadishu hostage rescue had all the makings of an extraordinary case. Even to date, the GSG 9 has only been called out on a handful of missions in its twelve years of existence, while the Länder units have found greater acceptance and seen their share of activity. The tendency remains to keep the Federal unit out of the case and solve the problem within the framework of Länder authority in police matters.

At this point, some basic facts should be mentioned to explain the character of specialised tactical police response teams.[3]

(a) First and foremost these men are police officers, with training and prior experience as officers of the law. They come from regular patrol or investigative work and will most probably return to similar duty after their service in the specialised teams. Though they might have to dress and act as military commando soldiers, their background and outlook is that of a police officer.

(b) Their missions, their use of force, their employment of firearms fall basically into the same legal categories as normal police actions. There are no, and there should not be any, special legal loopholes for these units. They are part and parcel of the overall police network and should be understood just as another tool at the disposal of Government and police leaders.

What then is the difference between a tactical response team and the average squad of police officers from any patrol division, aside from the weaponry, the equipment and the training? The difference lies in their approach to a problem. The average police officer is trained to encounter and handle any situation as an individually responsible agent from a one-man standpoint; that is, he will act to the best of his ability and judgement as a single unit, or in conjunction with his partner. His reaction is to rush forward if the situation calls for him to do so. The approach is one of immediate, on the spot reaction.

By contrast, the team of trained specialists will always use a team approach, where tasks and responsibilities are divided, making it much easier for a member of that team to fulfil his appointed task, to concentrate on his part—knowing full well that every other member in his team can be relied upon to do his part. It is through constant training together and experiencing this team approach that confidence is generated in the team in their ability to handle even the most complicated assignments. Every officer in the unit knows his part and what all the other members will do (which comes from 'proper prior planning') and so it becomes that much easier to use intricate schemes of action and to switch plans when resistance or difficulties are encountered. Speed—not haste—which is essential to any counterterrorist operation, results from this team approach. Instead of a group of individual officers rushing to the rescue, the ideal team is trained to operate like the fingers of a hand, as one multi-handed, multi-eyed and multi-armed body. Thus an arrest involving an armed, violent felon which would probably end in a deadly shootout if normal patrol officers were called to the scene, often ends without the use of lethal force by the SWAT or SEK team. Unlike the regular street police officer, the team alerted knows that it is about to enter a dangerous situation, it is prepared and has a chance to pre-plan its moves. It will always look for the chance to use the element of surprise, employ distraction schemes, irritants and other means to overwhelm the opponent. The key to success is a system of mutual 'overwatch', by which every team member is covered by one or two of his partners, so that a real need to use one's guns seldom arises from a self-defence situation. Many incidents over the years have proven that even hard-core criminals and terrorists are likely to give up when faced by a swift-moving police response team barring all exits. Experience has shown that the use of such teams has actually lowered a department's use of deadly force in arrest situations, thereby exposing the often-encountered pejorative term 'killer teams' as sheer nonsense.

An example is provided by the West Berlin SEK, which in its twelve years of existence has arrested 1295 people, among these thirty-five terrorists and numerous other armed criminals. Some three hundred guns were confiscated in these raids along with hand-grenades and explosives. Fourteen non-terrorist hostage incidents were solved. To date nobody has been shot by the SEK and firearms were only used in two or three incidents to fire warning shots. The Berlin SEK would be the first to admit that a lot of luck was on their side, but these statistics, which are paralleled to some degree by other departments, are underlined by the 'after-action' reports. The prime motive in a tactical police response to a terrorist threat such as a hostage-taking can be labelled as 'damage limitation'. The first move is to contain the situation and then to save lives, those of the wounded, if there are any, then to liberate the hostages. 'Getting the bad guys' takes second priority to saving lives.

Ideally the tactical personnel, assault and sniper teams should belong to the same unit set-up as the negotiators (as is the case in Berlin and some other places). Both are part of the same effort and have to cooperate closely. There is no room for competition here, and friction will result in dangerous situations. Cross-training will enhance this necessary cooperation and further understanding between these two levels of the tactical response.

THE INVESTIGATIVE/INTELLIGENCE LEVEL

Considerable progress had been made in this area since the late 1960s. In West Germany, 1971 provided a turning point in the history of criminal investigation. The Bundeskriminalamt, the Federal Investigative Office (BKA), was remodelled to become a central agency to guide, control and coordinate the work of the various Länder investigative offices, the 'Länderkriminalämter'. Regarding equipment and personel, long-needed investments were made. Since 1968 the BKA has increased these investments tenfold and it became an innovative agency under the directorship of Dr Horst Herold,[4] who pioneered the use of computerised files and search concepts. Directed by the Federal Prosecutor's Office in Karlsruhe, the BKA either heads the investigation with its own team of agents or supports the local criminal investigation department by putting its resources at that agency's disposal. The BKA also increased the exchange of information with intelligence agencies such as the 'Office for the Protection of the Constitution (*Verfassungsschutzamt*)' and the *Bundesnachrichtendienst*, Germany's intelligence agency for foreign affairs. It quickly became obvious that an effective counterterrorism campaign cannot be run without a centralised intelligence-gathering and evaluation network. Any build-up of such a network will be in direct conflict with the constitutional restrictions, which are part and parcel of a democratic society. This is especially evident in Germany, where any scheme suggestive of a 'superpolice' raises the fear of the return of a centralised police apparatus as Himmler had built up in the 'Reichssicherheithauptamt'. Germany's post-war constitution had especially designed safeguards against the recurrence of such a power instrument. A lot of criticism was levelled against Herold's computer search systems. By 1979—when a ministerial enquiry was ordered by the new Minister of Interior, Gerhard Baum—the BKA had amassed a total of thirty-seven data banks or file systems, containing some 4.7 million names, 3100 organisations, 2.1 million fingerprints and 1.9 million photos of people. These computerised search procedures came into their own in 1975, when PIOS and BEFA were implemented in regard to terrorist acts and persons connected to suspects:

(a) PIOS (the abbreviation stands for 'persons, institutions, objects and things) listed more than 135,000 people, 5500 institutions, 115,000 objects and things such as lost passports, guns, cars etc.

(b) BEFA (the abbreviation stands for 'beobachtende Fahndung', observations and search) list more than 6000 persons who were in one way or other connected to known terrorists, and this helped to plot travel routes, border crossings, time schedules, meetings and contacts within the circles supporting the Baader-Meinhof group.

Police departments all over the country could be hooked into these data banks; information was available at short notice; comparisons could be made; and something of the intricate network of the terrorist underground movement was slowly revealed. When certain patterns of operation and underground living were analysed, computer search programmes were designed to identify safehouses and strategies. By 1978, when the second generation of German terrorist groups went on a rampage to free their imprisoned cadres, the BKA was ready and tried to counter the attacks by masterminding the search procedures, using the full network of intelligence-gathering capabilities when Hanns-Martin Schleyer was abducted.

There were some initial successes in those years and statistics of 1978 showed that some three hundred and fifty terrorists had been arrested since the early 1970s. But these numbers were misleading, as only sixty of these were real hardcore members—the rest were fringe supporters. Of the sixty arrests, twenty were made by foreign police, and some thirty were caught due to their own mistakes or because they were recognised by members of the public. Today it is evident that the terrorists are very fast in analysing their own errors and changing their mode of operation accordingly, so that computer 'dragnet' models are often more quickly outmoded than they are implemented. This is not to say that data banks and computerised concepts are not very helpful in countering terrorist acts, but we are prone to fall victim to technical fascination when it comes to responding to terrorism.

Furthermore, there is a tendency to neglect more conventional detective work in favour of the highly technicalised systems, which in the end very often do not completely fulfil expectations. Computer terminals are an invaluable asset, but they are only as fail-safe as the people who handle them. Certain cases[5] in Germany demonstrate that the mere collecting of data does not help much if the data are not filtered and utilised correctly or properly analysed. Very often, we do not lack information, but we are swamped with material and unable to exploit it. The police effort will remain reactive as long as it mainly focuses on building court cases, sifting through the evidence, while trying to link certain acts to certain individual perpetrators, instead of concentrating on the terrorist 'mind-set'. Practical fieldwork is often neglected within the investigative branch of the police; reality is perceived only through the formalistic set-up of data procedures. Some of the worst failures of the BKA and related agencies have resulted from the inability to function in normal police procedures (such as routine observation), or to use commonsense approaches.

PREVENTION AND REACTION—A RETURN TO OLD MISTAKES?

If we assess material found in safehouses and depots, if we scrutinise those statements we have from ex-terrorists, imprisoned members of the gangs or from 'retired' individuals such as Hans-Joachim Klein,[6] we get an interesting insight into the daily planning and scheming of terrorist groups: amazingly little energy and time goes into the actual terrorist act; ex-members confessed that most of daily routine was needed for providing the simple logistics of safehouses, food, living accommodation. Then many hours were invested in reading newspapers, journals and magazines to gain intelligence on what 'the other side is up to'. Targets are chosen and discussed with great attention to details and to their symbolic value. Again and again this author gets the impression that few victims are chosen at random, and that the protection of targets, the 'hardening', is of relatively minor concern for the terrorists. Schleyer and Moro were kidnapped even though both were guarded by a detail of policemen; the terrorists took possible resistance into account and used more firepower. The same holds true for the 'stand-off' attacks directed against the American Generals Haig and Kroesen. Throughout recent years, airport security has considerably increased, but this does not deter attackers willing to pay the price.

On the other hand, the industrialist Zimmermann, who was shot in his home at the height of the recent hungerstrike campaign by RAF members, was a soft target—consequently some authorities argued that he was chosen because of that fact, and they thought that added police protection has frightened off the terrorists from other, more prominent figures. Of course, Ernst Zimmermann was not selected because of the absence of bodyguards, but because of his involvement in French–German military–industrial cooperation. He was the civilian equivalent to General Audran, who only days before died in Paris at the hands of Action Directe murderers. It is doubtful whether deterrence really works against terrorists. Special units do have a deterrent effect to some degree and I am convinced that most of the currently existing groups worldwide have a healthy respect for such units as the GSG 9, the SAS, Delta Force, the Israeli Jamam or the French GIGN—but they also understand that these teams cannot guard every airport, every embassy or every politician. The terrorists recognise the reactive character of the tactical response units and plan accordingly—to create the damage before the police can rush in their specialised counterterrorist teams.

On the other hand millions of manhours are wasted every year in highly visible 'deterrent' guard duties and similar conservative police jobs. Most of us are familiar with the armed uniformed policemen at airports, in front of official buildings or at similar guardposts. Did those guards ever deter a planned terrorist act? When Zimmermann was killed last January, the whole routine of police activities was set into motion and given prime TV time: one might add, extra police details were rushed to the airports to frisk passengers and dig into luggage (as if the RAF hit team would be leaving Munich by plane, with revolver and sub machine gun carried along in suitcases). Roadblocks were set up throughout southern Germany for days on end, mostly around the major highways—as if the murderers would be spending their time driving around Germany after the killing. More energy and time was wasted on similar efforts. It goes without saying that all these measures produced no results; even the police officers involved in these roadblocks, searches and guard jobs did not believe in the prospects of success of their assignments. In recent years, similar dragnet attempts had followed earlier assassinations and bombings and had never brought results.

It has long been obvious that these and similar conservative police reactions to terrorist acts are nothing else but alibi operations, designed to pretend adequate reaction, but in truth only protecting police officials and government politicians from reproaches. They are more meant to impress the public than the criminals. These pseudo responses to terrorism should have been exposed long ago as wasteful and mindless, being a pure excuse for failure to take any real counteraction. They take away needed manpower, spread frustration among the lower ranks and in the long run openly demonstrate the authorities' inability to adapt their methods to terrorist tactics. But these assessments are seldom made and even less frequently expressed. When it happens, the authorities have shown themselves unable to deal with constructive criticism. In a recent example, a high-ranking police official explained in one police magazine why the currently used system of roadblocks and cordon search patterns was not working, except in the case of very dumb perpetrators. His objections were waived aside, and he was threatened with disciplinary action for allegedly publishing secret facts.

Two years after the Schleyer kidnapping a training exercise by local and Federal police agencies was held, which turned into a shambles as similar failures were surfacing during the scenario as had happened in the real incident in 1977. Loss of cohesion between agencies, inability to deal with the amount of incoming information, mismanagement of the available police personnel. Though a parliamentary inquiry (the 'Höcherl' Report) had analysed the mistakes made during the Schleyer case, the higher police administration appeared to be unable to correct their operative patterns accordingly. A year later, in 1980, another anti-terrorist exercise was run in the same area, which attempted to avoid the earlier mistakes. The exercise, following a 157-page-long script involved various agencies at the same time: BKA, Border Police, Customs, Riverine police units, the police departments of the Länder and the administrative staffs of three neighbouring Länder, along with various delegated SWAT teams.

This time everything went well, the terrorists were caught, the incoming intelligence was filtered and used correctly, the existing units employed to their full capability. There was only one catch to the whole affair. The whole script prescribed an outcome of the terrorist attack, and the resulting moves were highly simplistic. The perpetrators were playing into the hands of the law-enforcement agencies and at the right time one of the captured gang members turned into a 'supergrass' and divulged all the details of the gang's plan. The whole exercise was designed to make the police look good.

In planning and training for counterterrorism, this syndrome will surface again and again. As nobody wants to be made a fool of, the scenarios will remain at a specific level, designed in such a way as to involve everybody and to make everybody look good. In order to stay simplistic, the terrorist attacks on which these exercises centre are those of a well-known, well-practised kind. The worst disaster envisioned these days in Germany is either a kidnapping or a hijacking of an airplane. As targets, terrorists, counterterrorists, planners and umpires belong to the same agency and are all policemen, nobody will actively try to foil the counterterrorist scheme beyond a certain degree. Last but not least—all think like police officers. Even if some are trying to slip into the role of the perpetrators, they will still stay inside certain boundaries. In the end, even the evaluation is done by members of the same profession.[7] Having been a witness to more than one of these training exercises and programmes, I have seen the negative drawbacks of this closed-circuit system and the inability of all concerned to draw lessons out of these simulation exercises.

The law-enforcement agencies have come a long way in their efforts to counter terrorism since the 1960s. Drastic changes have occurred. With the build-up of special units, the introduction of high-tech tools, computer systems and the like a step has been taken in the right direction. Still, we are far from effectively countering terrorism at the police level, and a dangerous complacency has now set in not unlike that which existed prior to 1972. It was best expressed in a recent statement by Germany's Minister of Interior, Dr Friedrich Zimmermann, following the attacks against the airports in Rome and Vienna. Referring to police measures and security precautions taken in the Federal Republic, Dr Zimmermann impressed the cabinet with the announcement that internal security was now at a level where it could not be improved anymore. Naturally, he had statistics about guard details and manhours employed to underline that 'everything possible is always done'.

RESPONDING INTERNATIONALLY

One of the major characteristics of modern terrorism is its transnational aspect, the disregard even 'homegrown' terrorists like the RAF or IRA have shown for national boundaries. International terrorism has demonstrated repeatedly that there is no neutral ground anywhere and that in the long run, no country is spared from becoming the battleground for one group or another. Amazingly little has been done in effective international cooperation between the democratic nations apart from political, legal or international declarations, which are just that: words. A few individuals in the international law-enforcement community have attempted to create something like a 'buddy-system' to circumvent political and national restrictions when it comes to gaining information or exchanging tips. The tactical response groups have been in the forefront of such an informal cooperation, but they are also restricted by certain directives of their respective agencies and governments. Still, a start is made here and a network does exist which can and should be enlarged. Regular contacts and integrated cooperation between national police agencies are still a thing of the future. Interpol has been reluctant to accept the role of the central exchange in regard to politically motivated crime. It has neither the personnel nor the computer systems to really function as a supranational counterterrorist agency. Furthermore, Interpol is greatly restricted by definitional problems in regard to terrorism, and a number[8] of member states will be quick to point to Article 3 of the organisation's statutes, which forbids any activities in regard to 'political, military, religious or racist' cases. But Interpol can and has furthered the exchange of information referring to stolen material, i.e., guns, documents, vehicles, licence plates, explosives and other ordnance, which belong to the 'life support system' of terrorist groups.

Currently most progress can be made if international police cooperation is limited to the victimised democratic states in Europe, Northern America and the Middle East on a mutual level between the individual states. Even in Europe, we are far from establishing an effective network to that degree. Though 'Euroterrorism' has made headlines in 1985 and has led to numerous declarations and consultations between European heads of state, the net result of all this political activity is mediocre. Judging soberly and taking the recent *Achille Lauro* case as a guideline, we have to realise that most countries are not willing to endanger their economic relations with certain terrorist-supporting states, even if that spells out increased danger to their own citizens—the reaction to President Reagan's request to isolate Libya is symptomatic of the ongoing toleration of 'crazy states'.

Any progress in this sector is going to be a slow and halting process, as the police response is definitely limited by a political ceiling, which is dominated by different interests. As a first step to bypass these restrictions, the international exchange of information should be deepened and something of a pool has to be founded among the aforementioned democratic states, centring first on material information to ease the prevention of terrorist acts and the free travelling of perpetrators. Step by step this intelligence pool can be enlarged, later to become a vehicle for information seminars and for real cooperation. To avoid legal complications, the first steps would refer only to materials:

(a) data on stolen guns and other lethal ordnance, which disappeared from civilian, military or police depots, or which have been found;
(b) data on identity papers, passports and similar documents (as above);
(c) information on terrorist methods, bomb construction and relevant manuals found in safehouses;
(d) licence plates, forged money and other written material or objects used;
(e) fingerprints, photos, wanted lists etc.

Of course, the inclusion of personal identity facts in such an intelligence pool would already touch very sensitive legal ground and can only be admitted at a later stage. Some of the above-mentioned intel bits are already being exchanged between concerned countries, albeit incompletely.

What would be needed most at this stage would be an operational agreement between the states concerned to regulate the proceedings of dealing with international terrorist attacks such as the hijacking of planes, ships, trains etc. Currently the sole reponsibility lies with the 'host country', even though citizens of other nations might be involved, too. It is unthinkable for the future that something like the Landshut incident can be repeated—where Italian authorities permitted the hijackers of the German plane to have the plane refuelled and leave the Rome airport, just to avoid a 'bloodbath on Italian soil'—the German Government had urgently requested the Italian authorities to ground the plane in Rome. A further level of that operational agreement would be the cooperation of tactical forces in concerted efforts to free hostages. For that, the various national units should finally be permitted to train together in annual, multinational exercises. A precedent for such international cooperation does exist already and has proven itself beyond expectations: NATO has within its framework of deterrent forces the 'Allied Command Europe Mobile Force (AMF)', a multinational brigade which would be airlifted into a conflict zone in the event of the Warsaw Pact threatening one country of the Alliance. Such a multinational anti-terrorist force would have at least a deterrent value against internationally operating terrorist groups, who now play on the dissent between victim states whenever they strike a multinational target such as a plane or liner. In short, it is about time that the Western democracies presented a united front against the terrorist threat. The tactical level could be a suitable trial ground for such cooperation, and would be less politically sensitive than economical or political sanctions.

NOTES

1 A list of examples would be long and would range from Latin America to British Palestine, the latter of which is well researched by Rand's Bruce Hoffmann's Oxford doctoral thesis on Britain's ill-fated counterinsurgency campaign against the urban terrorists of the Jewish Underground.

2 An incomplete compilation of the Bundeskriminalamt named more than 90 shootings and bombings by German left-wing terrorists from summer 1967 to autumn 1977, see Manfred Funke (ed.), *Terrorismus, Untersuchungen zur Struktur und Strategie revolutionärer Gewaltpolitik*, Bonn-Düsseldorf: 1977, pp. 331–365.

3 Various different terms are used in the USA for these task forces: SWAT for 'Special Weapons And Tactics', CIRT = 'Critical Incident Response Team' etc. France has the Groupe d'Intervention Gendarmerie National, GIGN; Austria the 'Cobra'; Spain the 'GEO' after the example set by the GSG 9.

4 Herold, born in 1923, became DA in 1953 in Nürnberg and in 1967 chief of police in that town. He headed the BKA from September 1971 to March 1981. His

successor is Dr Heinrich Boge, formerly from the Ministry of Interior, Bonn, where he headed the police administration department.

5 In the Schleyer case a valuable 'bit' of information, pointing to the hide-out of the kidnappers and their victim was lost for crucial days due to demarcation problems between special commissions working at State and city level. More so, other hints in advance of the attack were not exploited when a short computer failure hindered a patrol car in the checking of a terrorist vehicle.

6 Certain books should become mandatory reading for police officers: for example, H-J Klein *Rückkehr in die Menschlichkeit* (*Return to Humanity*), Hamburg: 1979; Bommi Baumann, *Wie alles anfing*, Munich: 1975, translated as *How It all Began*, Vancouver; 1977, and *Terror or Love?* London: 1979; or even the recent book on the RAF, Stefan Aust, *Der Baader–Meinhof Komplex*, Hamburg: 1985. They all deal extensively with police measures and how they were perceived and outwitted by the terorrists.

7 Stephen Sloan, 'Simulating Terrorism', Oklahoma City: University of Oklahoma Press, 1981, has analysed this problem in depth and given examples of how to avoid these pitfalls by (a) using outside planners to design, run and control the training programme and exercise scenario; (b) employ outside personnel to act as perpetrators and victims; (c) use long-term evaluation methods to draw the correct lessons out of the resulting proceedings. It should be underlined that a training exercise is not a performance, but a test of the respective agencies' capabilities to handle the threat.

8 Though the organisation has grown rapidly in the post-war years (there are now more than 125 member states), it remains doubtful which of the more than 70 members from Asian and African countries would actively support counter-terrorist intelligence work as soon as the Middle East groups became involved.

Intelligence Terrorism and Civil Liberties

K G Robertson

INTRODUCTION

It has become commonplace in the literature on terrorism that intelligence is indispensable to successful counterterrorism[1] but despite some useful efforts[2] several key issues remain to be explored. This chapter will focus on four questions: How different in nature is terrorism from the other threats faced by democratic states? What is intelligence? How can intelligence help in responding to terrorism? And finally, what are the tensions between the role of intelligence in countering terrorism and civil liberties in democratic states?

THE NATURE OF TERRORISM

Terrorism can be treated as a form of criminal behaviour which requires no more than 'normal policing'. This view is particularly stressed[3] by those who argue that civil liberties are at grave risk from governments using the 'menace' of terrorism as an 'excuse' for altering the balance of power between the citizen and the State. Frank Donner of the American Civil Liberties Union has argued that terrorists have become the scapegoats for the reactivation of 'political surveillance'. He argues that the FBI and a 'highly conservative economic and social order' have an interest in utilising public fears of 'unseen foes' to justify demands for an increase in domestic intelligence and to making links in the public mind between legitimate opposition movements and 'terrorists' in order to discredit the former. Donner sees terrorism as the new 'conspiracy theory' which enables conservatives to block reform, justify surveillance and to 'chill' opposition. His 'solution' to the problem is to argue that the terrorist threat be put in perspective and so avoid the danger of a moral panic and to place restrictions on the surveillance activities of government by limiting investigations to only those allowed when dealing with 'normal' crime.[4]

It is clear that some writers are of the opinion that the greatest menace facing democracy is not terrorism but the reaction to it. The characteristics which lead to such differing views on the nature of the terrorist threat are: its secrecy or clandestine nature, the risk of death, its ideological motivation, its 'indiscriminate' nature, its popularity, its use of publicity, its collective nature and its political aims. Without an agreed conceptualisation of terrorism it is impossible to state precisely how terrorism differs from other forms of crime. Furthermore, as in the case of crime, there are different approaches to the problem of definition, ranging from the legalistic to broad concepts of 'liberation'. Finally, it is made difficult because of the variety of 'theories' as to its origins and dynamics.

Most concepts of terrorism include at least some of the following characteristics:[5]

(a) Violence.
(b) Political motive.
(c) Objective is to instil fear, to terrorise.
(d) Threat is unpredictable, no one can feel secure.
(e) Targets are symbolic, *any* representative of a 'hated' category is a legitimate target.
(f) The methods used are unusually brutal (e.g., knee-capping) and are not constrained by the rules of war.
(g) Compliance with demands does *not* guarantee a reduction in the level of violence.
(h) Publicity is a part of the coercive strategy.
(i) It is planned and executed in secret.
(j) It is a collective act.
(k) It can involve weapons of unusual sophistication.

However, some of these characteristics are shared in common with other forms of 'harmful' and illegal behaviour; secrecy, violence, collective action and fear. Others are more obviously unique; the political motive, the desire for publicity and its indiscriminate nature. In this chapter terrorism will be treated as a unique phenomenon because it is the only form of illegal or harmful act which is politically motivated, makes demands which are only indirectly connected with the immediate crime, has the objective of instilling fear but not in relation to the achievement of immediate goals, uses methods which are unusual such as sophisticated weapons, bombings, and knee-cappings and finally it may involve the participation of states.

These elements make terrorism different from that behaviour labelled 'criminal' and requires a different response from the State. Each one of the above factors however, needs to be examined in more detail.

The fact that terrorism is politically motivated brings it within the debate over the nature and distinctive features of political crime. Traditionally, the political criminal is one who commits a crime against the State such as treason, espionage or an assault on the person of the ruler. The motive for the action is political, it involves the achievement of a political aim, and is contrasted with those crimes motivated by personal gain such as robbery. However, motive is often difficult to establish, whether in a court of law or by social scientists, and many criminal acts involving the State may have more than one motive. To get round this problem some commentators have defined political crime as being whatever the State so defines it to be.[6] According to this definition the motive of the actor is irrelevant; it is the perception of the State which is all important. For example, a strike can be 'political' depending not only upon the 'real' motive but the consequences as perceived by the government. Other writers come close to abandoning the concept altogether on the grounds that all crimes are 'political', involve a challenge to the established order.[7] This view argues that the difference between mugging and terrorism is simply one of degree and is a product of the perceived threat posed by such crimes to the existing structure of property and power. Schafer expresses this view as follows:

> However, in view of the political–ideological cradle of all crimes, it might be more appropriate to see the common or ordinary offences as relative political crimes, as opposed to the absolute political crimes where the target of the law-breaking is the ruling power's value system as a whole, rather than a part or an issue of it.[8]

There are few authors who would argue that certain crimes have specific qualities which belong to a unique set which can be labelled 'political'. The two most common conceptualisations are (a) to examine the *conflicts* which give rise to certain types of collective action such as protest, demonstration, terrorism and (b) to examine the reasons why states identify some crimes/threats as requiring a different *response*. The first seeks to explain all forms of crime/harm in relation to certain social characteristics and focuses on collective experiences to explain collective behaviour whilst the second explains the application of the label 'political' to certain crimes/harme in terms of the interests of the established order. These approaches are not necessarily exclusive, indeed, it is often a matter of pragmatism whether a writer operates with one more than the other but they do give rise to different problems.

The first approach focuses upon the need to examine the origins of certain actions by the public and to stress the tensions which exist in societies. This often leads to the conclusion that the solution to such acts is to alter the structure of society so as to reduce the tensions. It also leads to the conclusion that State action to 'repress' such behaviour is bound to be ineffective and immoral. The second approach examines the historical circumstances in which states apply the label political crime to particular actions. This often leads to the conclusion that the threat which it perceives itself as facing is 'unreal', a form of 'moral panic'. It also leads to the conclusion that democracy is ineffective and that politicians, intelligence officers, civil servants and the military are engaged in a conspiracy to protect their own, rather than the general, interest. That interest being the holding on to power and the privileges which go with it. The 'solution' to this is said to lie in more effective 'democratic' controls over the State.

However, both of these approaches are flawed by the fact that they assume that there are no 'real' threats to public order, the State or the social fabric. They either assume that terrorism and mugging are the product of 'moral panics' or that terrorism and mugging require the same response because they are the product of the same cause, social tensions.

A major difference between ordinary crime and terrorism lies in the demands which are made. This is so irrespective of whether the demands are legitimate or otherwise. To demand an alteration in sovereignty or territorial domination cannot be seen in the same light as ordinary crime whatever the nature of the regime. One obvious such difference is that a change in sovereignty has implications for other states. It may be seen as furthering or threatening their interests. A change in sovereignty may be desired by a foreign power and it may therefore act to encourage terrorism. The use of sophisticated weapons and the indiscriminate nature of terrorism make it difficult for normal police methods to achieve results. Community policing is not the answer to terrorism! The nature of the terrorist threat may be exaggerated but it is hardly credible to deny that it poses particular problems for the State. Indeed the mere possibility of such a threat leads states to take action. A challenge to the sovereignty of a State is not going to be treated in the same way as mugging irrespective of the causes or the fear which they both create.

WHAT IS INTELLIGENCE?

Most authors don't define intelligence, they list its elements. An example is the conception of intelligence offered by Roger Hillsman.[9] A definition should identify those features of the set to which a phenomenon belongs and identify those characteristics which distinguish it from other sets and this is not done by most authors. For example, Roger Hillsman lists three activities associated with 'intelligence'; the collection of facts, the making of judgements and finally the presentation of these to policy makers.[10] However this list is flawed by the fact that such elements are common to all decision making whether by business corporations or the social services. In practice, he 'defines' intelligence not by reference to its activities, but the type of information which is collected; military, political and strategic. A more satisfactory definition is offered by Roy Godson of the Consortium for the Study of Intelligence in *What is Intelligence?*[11] He defines intelligence as:

> the effort by a government, or of a private individual or body, devoted to: the collection, analysis, production, dissemination and use of information which relates to any other government, political group, party, military force, movement or other association which is believed to relate to the group's or government's security.[12]

However, the problem with this definition lies in the concept of 'security'. A businessman may feel insecure because of falling demand or a wife feel insecure because of lipstick on the collar! It is true that these have something in common with intelligence but what they have in common is so general and everyday that it fails to differentiate a unique phenomenon.

A satisfactory definition of intelligence ought to include the following features; threat, states, secrecy, collection, analysis and purpose. The most important of these being the concept of threat since, without threats, there would be no need for intelligence services. It is the existence of threats, or the possibility of such, which gives rise to the requirement that governments collect secret information and plan to counter threats, in secret. A threat is not simply an unknown factor which may effect one's interests but is something capable of causing serious harm or injury. The seriousness of the threat depends on the degree of harm which may arise and the likelihood of the threat being carried out. Governments need to be supplied with a great deal of information about the environment but it is the information related to threats which is the province of intelligence services. Furthermore although the gathering of information from open sources is a vital and significant part of all intelligence activity it is not its distinguishing feature. Its unique characteristic is the secret collection of others' secrets. A threat may be reduced or even eliminated by the acquisition of knowledge. For example, to have knowledge of the intentions of a hostile power may give one a feeling of security which extra guns or ships could not. It is the acquisition of knowledge of intentions which remains one of the key functions of the traditional spy, human intelligence (HUMINT).[13] The agent in place is likely to be the only collection mechanism which can tell whether the Generals in Country X are actually about to stage a coup and not simply that the capacity to stage such a coup exists.

The intelligence service must, however, turn information into knowledge, that is, assess its significance, context, pattern, meaning, relationship to other information, history, reliability and value to the purposes of other members of the executive branch. The process of analysis is fraught with hazards but it is one from which there is no escape. It must be performed whether by the collection agency, the user or by some intermediate body. If raw data are given to a General on the battlefield, he must still analyse it in terms of the previous knowledge he possesses and the other current information which he has as to the nature of the enemy he is facing.

Finally, the user of intelligence plays a key role by specifying his needs. Intelligence collection of information for which no one has a need or purpose is wasteful, inefficient, ineffective and creates unnecessary risks. The problem is that very often users don't know what information they would like to have and yet they will blame the collectors if they are caught by surprise. Indeed, users can deliberately create uncertainty concerning their priorities and the information they wish to have in order to avoid responsibility for any shortfalls or surprises which may arise.[14] Users can very easily blame the collectors for not collecting enough information, or the right kind of information and avoid responsibility for the fact that no intelligence service in the world can collect all possibly useful information on any subject. Decisions must be taken on priorities. This involves risks to the users of information since they are trying to guess their requirements and make difficult judgements of the seriousness of various threats. This problem is compounded by the fact that collectors have an interest in this uncertainty on the grounds that it gives them more 'flexibility' and room for manoeuvre. The defining of collection requirements can be the least formalised and coherent part of the intelligence process because of the incentive each party, collector or user, has to avoid any blame for any gaps which may exist. However, to make the goal of collection the acquisition of all 'useful' information about all possible threats is to create a bureaucratic monster in which much employment but little value is created. This is one of the strong arguments in favour of a decentralised intelligence service with specialised divisions capable of developing a close relationship between collectors and users.

To conclude, an intelligence service is an organisation devoted to collecting, by clandestine means, the secrets of those who have the capacity and intention to inflict harm on the interests, goals and values of a nation state.

Intelligence services in democratic countries are of two main types—those concerned with domestic intelligence and those with foreign. This division reflects the fear in democracies that a single secret service would lead to a concentration of power and because of a democratic reluctance to treat aliens and citizens in the same manner.

A security service collects information on those threats which exist within the territory under the sovereignty of a State by clandestine means. The means used to collect information are similar to those used by intelligence services although there are differences of emphasis due to the differences in the nature of the threat and the threatened. The interception of communications, the placing of 'bugging devices' and the use of human agents are common to both services. However, spy satellites and the collection of intelligence from radar signals are unlikely to be useful in collecting information on terrorists. Infiltration, the planting of agents, is common to both although in the case of foreign intelligence services this is seen as a largely legitimate activity which is given the honourable description of 'placing agents' or having a 'human source'. In the case of internal security such activities are 'dishonourable' and are described by terms such as 'informers', 'stool-pigeons' and 'agents provocateurs'. This difference in terminology does not reflect any difference in method but rather in the attitude towards the legitimacy of using such methods against one's own citizens. However, HUMINT does appear to be a more important method to security services than to intelligence services.[15] The use of human agents is easier and less risky in the case of domestic operations than in the case of foreign operations. For example, it is likely to be easier to mount a support operation and therefore easier to rescue an agent if an operation goes wrong. Also, recruitment is likely to be more straightforward since to find someone who is able to pass as a member of a domestic group is likely to be easier than in the case of a foreign group.

Historically, the missing dimension of security services has been analysis.

Neither Britain nor the United States has any permanent committee equivalent to either the Joint Intelligence Committee or the National Security Council who task, coordinate or analyse the information concerning domestic threats.[16] This, I will argue, is due to the association of internal security with law enforcement which links the collection of information to prosecution rather than to evaluating trends and the long-term planning of resources and responses. Furthermore, given the fact that domestic threats are less likely to involve the military, the diplomatic corps, the specialist coding and cryptography departments, this reduces the need for interagency cooperation and therefore produces less of an incentive to form specialist analysis bodies. However, this is not a good reason for the neglect of analysis within domestic intelligence. As I shall show later this neglect has unfortunate consequences for both the quality of intelligence and civil liberties.

INTELLIGENCE AND TERRORISM

Intelligence can be useful against terrorism in the following ways:[17]

(a) It can identify those involved, whatever the level of their involvement.
(b) It can build a database which can be used to establish patterns of demands, methods etc. which can improve decision making in times of crisis.
(c) It can identify those most at risk and the property most at risk. It can, therefore, help to save lives.
(d) It can be used to mount clandestine counterattacks (covert action).
(e) It can establish the supply routes, safe-houses and sources of recruits, weapons and finances.
(f) It can assist in the development of a counterpropaganda effort targeted either at the support population or those immediately involved.
(g) It can be used to spread black propaganda.
(h) The fear of an intelligence effort directed against a group can disrupt the solidarity of those involved.
(i) It can warn of impending attack and be used to disrupt such attacks.
(j) It can influence the placement of resources such as police, military and hardware.
(k) It can disrupt the communications network of those involved through interception or the fear of interception.
(l) Information can be selectively released to win allies or dissuade hostile powers.
(m) Information can guide decisions concerning the political reforms which may isolate or discourage the terrorist.
(n) Information can be exchanged with other services in order to increase the pool available.
(o) It can assist in the management of crisis situations, the equivalent of battlefield as opposed to strategic intelligence.

For all the above reasons, and there may well be others, intelligence is considered to be at the heart of an effective counterterrorism strategy. Although none of the above are without risk, all have been practised by democratic states at one time or another.

However, intelligence is only able to perform the above tasks if it has the capacity, authority, organisation, skills and resources necessary. Intelligence will produce few results if little or no use is made of it. Intelligence can only be effective if it has a clear sense of its objectives, the purposes for which it is being collected. Intelligence cannot produce results if it is subject to continual interference whether from political leaders, legislatures or other bureaucratic agencies. Good intelligence requires clear tasks, agreed methods, common perceptions and a degree of autonomy. These requirements are rarely met in full. All too often intelligence services are given very general remits, none at all or they are given impossible remits such as 'stop terrorism' or 'collect all information about terrorism'. Such 'remits' fail to give guidance as to the priorities for collection or the perception of the political leadership of the threat posed by different types of terrorist/terrorism. Another common problem is that democracies, for reasons outlined above, have feared the concentration of intelligence capacity in a single agency. This may reassure the public that no 'spy' system is being created but it creates problems of coordination, bureaucratic in-fighting, exchanging information, allocating responsibility and public monitoring. Intelligence implies the bringing together of all pieces of information and perspectives in order to analyse the data. If there are several agencies involved it is likely that they will see information as a scarce resource to be 'bartered' with politicians and other members of the 'national security' community. Competition between different agencies, or even divisions within them, may produce 'over-zealous' officials who use unethical methods to achieve a 'scoop'. It can be argued that centralisation is necessary for effective monitoring of adherence to laws and guide-lines.[18] More on this later. It can also be argued that without clear policies and a unitary structure to carry them out, responsibility is difficult to allocate and easy to evade.

It is clear that knowing what intelligence can do in the fight against terrorism is not to say that intelligence has the capacity to carry out the fight. One of the key factors affecting this has been the concept of civil liberties. However, in order to understand the civil liberties issues one must understand the differences which exist between intelligence work and law enforcement.

INTELLIGENCE, LAW ENFORCEMENT AND TERRORISM

The key to understanding the fears which domestic intelligence has generated is the confusion between intelligence as a preliminary to prosecution and intelligence as an aid to policy making. Information gathered about domestic threats may be used to support or initiate prosecutions and trials but, in intelligence work, a trial is often a symptom of failure—failure to turn the uncovering of an agent against the enemy or to manipulate the information going to a hostile group. The goal of counterintelligence work is to utilise the enemy's agents and other methods of collection against him rather than to destroy or punish those involved. This is much less acceptable when those caught in such activities are one's own citizens. This is partly a product of moral outrage, the need to punish the 'guilty' and the need to preserve the principle that those found breaking the law must be treated equally—there is often moral indignation when traitors are treated differently from ordinary criminals even though this may be in the best interest of the nation. Such a policy runs counter to the egalitarian ideal of one law for all and not one law for the rich and one for the poor or one for spies and one for shop-lifters. The relationship between law enforcement and intelligence is a major cause of problems for the proper understanding of the nature of security services. In theory, domestic intelligence would be a worthwhile operation even though no one was ever tried or convicted for any offence in a court of law. However, this will only be acceptable to the public where there is a high degree of consensus on the nature of the threat being faced. Only when such agreement exists would security services be allowed to operate in 'secret' without the need for the occasional 'show-trial' to air the threat and what is being done in public. Given consensus, one can envision a situation in which the government is entitled to examine the extent of, intensity of and the effective methods to counter threats without this involving prosecution.

A key question is whether such a consensus exists over terrorism. In time of war there has been a tradition within democracies that civil liberties can be eroded in the interest of victory but it is doubtful whether terrorism is perceived in such a way except after some 'spectacular' incident. Without such agreement people will see intelligence as an adjunct to the process of arrest and prosecution which necessarily leads to certain policies being adopted on the allocation and management of scarce resources. For example, it may not be seen as legitimate to use the full battery of collection techniques or secret operations against terrorists. The latter could involve spreading false rumours amongst the group, disrupting their routine by switching on and off visible surveillance, or by informing their friends, employers or relatives that they are 'unreliable'. It is undoubtedly the case that such methods have been used against domestic targets but the legitimacy of such actions depends upon two related issues. The first of these concerns the extent to which the State's right of surveillance depends upon an immediate and direct threat of injury or illegal action. The second issue is whether the State's response to a threat must be confined to responses which lead to punishment and trial. The issue is the legitimacy of what, in other contexts, is known as 'preventive policing', that is, actions designed to deter, prevent or reduce the probability of actions harmful to the State other than the deterrent effect of conviction.

The following quotations all object to 'intrusions' by domestic intelligence agencies on the grounds that such activities are harmful to civil liberties. They also object on the grounds that the secrecy associated with them means that citizens are unable to object to or control such activities. It is the latter which seems to be the main focus of anger and yet without secrecy intelligence is impossible. However, little or nothing is said about many of the activities of security services which do not involve intrusions or which do not involve technology. Much intelligence gathering involves the collection of the public statements of individuals or groups, the clipping of items from newspapers, the sending of agents to attend public meetings, the use of informers and finally the deliberate planting of such agents inside the group itself. None of these involves any act which is unlawful and only the latter two imply any breach of privacy and yet the literature is largely bereft of comment on these practices. They are less dramatic but no less important and their absence leaves open the question of who is experiencing the moral panic.

> The emphasis in investigation has changed from evidence gathering after the commission of crime to intelligence gathering in advance of any particular crime being committed. In this 'pre-emptive' view, any citizen, certainly any socially uncharacteristic citizen, is a target for suspicion and observation. This quite explicit development in police planning has virtually put the whole of society under surveillance.[19]

> What is clear is that democracy has been diminished and individual freedom curtailed without the nation's knowing what was happening. Even the victims of FBI harassment seldom suspected that the government was behind their difficulties.[20]

> Whereas an arrest should be based on reasonable suspicion that the suspect has committed an offence, the surveillance involved in information-gathering starts several stages before reasonable suspicion can exist—so that someone innocent of criminal involvement, or against whom no evidence exists, may become the target of special enquiries, phone-tapping or mail interception as a result of mixing with the 'wrong' people.[21]

> Less obvious intrusion by technology is now possible through the use of various photographic and listening devices. The very unobtrusiveness of such intrusions makes it quite possible for them to be unknown to the individual whose privacy is invaded . . .[22]

All of the above quotations imply that all such secret activities are harmful. It is true that some of the practices of intelligence services are harmful but not all are so clear cut. One such clearly harmful practice involves the sending of a poison pen letter by the security service to a wife suggesting her husband is having an affair in order to harass him and this behaviour should not be tolerated, but is sending an agent to a public meeting necessarily harmful? Is recording the public statements of a member of a group on the radio or television necessarily harmful? I would argue that these latter activities are only possibly harmful if they come to the attention of those concerned or to the public at large. Ironically, if these 'intrusions' remain secret they cause no harm.

Most people would be willing to concede that if one could show that a particular response by the State was harmless to civil liberties, the State should be allowed wide discretion in its use. More debatable are the circumstances under which the State should be allowed to use intelligence techniques which are harmful to civil liberties or which are illegal such as sending a letter as above. A second example concerns the use of the law on taxation to carry out an investigation on an individual suspected of links with hostile intelligence services. A third example would be to use the law relating to the road-worthiness of motor vehicles to punish someone believed to have broken into a laboratory carrying out animal experiments.[23] Such activities are clearly harmful and should not be used against citizens except in a situation of virtual war. Once again, we are back to the key question of whether the public see the terrorist threat as equivalent to war—or to be more precise, whether the public see certain terrorist groups as being involved in a virtual war.

Finally, there is the problem of the proper relationship between law enforcement and security activities. The three key issues are firstly, the relationship between the institutions of policing and that of the security service, secondly the extent to which prosecution and trial are the main objects of the security service and thirdly, the admissibility of evidence obtained by clandestine means. The first issue is crucial since Britain and the United States have adopted differing formulae. Although the CIA has no law-enforcement or internal security functions, the FBI is both a security service and law-enforcement agency whilst in Britain the Security Service has no law-enforcement powers and must rely on the police to carry out this function. The advantage of the British approach is that the methods and goals of intelligence gathering are kept clearly distinct from those associated with law enforcement—the latter are less likely to contaminate the former. In the United States one of the problems has been that the methods appropriate to dealing with hostile intelligence services and terrorists have spread to areas where they are inappropriate such as dealing with student demonstrations or even riots. The objectives of intelligence gathering are often long term and precautionary and these should not be allowed to contaminate the much more precise goal of arresting and punishing law-breakers. Although prevention is admirable, whether performed by the police or the security service, preventive policing is not and should not be seen as a justification for the massive and indiscriminate collection, infiltration and surveillance of criminal acts however 'political' they may appear to be to 'conservative' policemen.

Intelligence gathering must be based on a clear conception of threat and it must be a perception of threat which can command a high degree of public support. 'Tasking' is a matter for political judgement and not one for the police. The police in a democratic society are directly accountable to the law; they are the servants of the law, and not of political masters, whilst in the case of the security service the exact opposite is the case. They are amassing information in response to political decisions concerning threats to the State. Such decisions are inescapably political and involve the need to weigh public support for the definition of threat, the methods used to collect information and the response made. There is no sense in which it would be desirable to keep the security service free from 'political interference' in the way that this has been seen as desirable for the police.

The second problem is that the methods which are used in intelligence gathering are not necessarily legitimate when applied to crime fighting. The bugging of telephones, interception of communications, the planting of informers and the development of a database based on rumour and gossip are more acceptable when one is dealing with hostile intelligence services or terrorists than when one is dealing with bank robberies. This is not to say that such methods are not on occasion legitimate against such criminals but it *is* to state that the dangers of abuse of civil liberties and the infringement of the rights of a defendant are greater when punishment is involved. Most civil liberties have emerged as a protection against the State's ability to inflict harm on the individual, whether through seizure of goods, imprisonment or loss of privilege.[24] When punishment is not involved or is not the main objective then the individual has less need for protection and the security services need be under fewer constraints. This will undoubtedly be a controversial proposition but as a statement of historical fact it is incontrovertible. Arguments about whether greater constraints on security or intelligence services are necessary today will be dealt with in the later section on Civil Liberties.

A major protection against the abuse of security service methods has been the willingness of courts to strike out evidence obtained unlawfully. This protection is not so great in Britain as in the United States although British judges do have the power to strike out such evidence. In Britain the situation is described by Hartley and Griffiths as follows:

> The fact that an article or document has been illegally obtained by the police does not prevent its being used in evidence in criminal proceedings.[23]

The power of the courts to strike out evidence unlawfully obtained or which is deemed 'inadmissible' is a key protection against 'transference'—the utilisation of methods appropriate for one form of activity to another. In many instances this form of protection is the most crucial of all since it is very dangerous if information, gathered for one purpose using means which are justified *because* they do not relate to punishment, should then be used in a prosecution and trial. The conclusion is that both civil liberties and intelligence work can be maintained and be effective if the distinction between intelligence methods and law-enforcement techniques is clearly preserved and if the courts actively maintain the distinction between that evidence which is admissible and that which is inadmissible within the criminal justice system of trial and prosecution.

INTELLIGENCE AND CIVIL LIBERTIES

In Britain it is more common to speak of liberties rather than rights since there is no Bill of Rights or written constitution which establishes positive legal rights to perform certain actions or hold certain beliefs. When lawyers speak of 'liberties' they are talking of those freedoms which we possess on the basis that they are not prohibited by law. We have the freedom to do that which is not unlawful and the State is constrained from interfering with actions which are not unlawful. These differences in the concept of 'basic freedoms' can lead to misunderstandings between nations, particularly between the US and Britain. In the United States, commentators on these matters see rights as being positive possessions and as therefore implying duties. Most commentators agree that liberties do not imply a corresponding duty whereas rights do. To say that one has the liberty to work means that no impediment in law exists to one seeking or accepting employment. To say that there is a right to work would imply not only that persons have the right to seek work but that others have the duty to employ those seeking work, all other circumstances being equal.[26] Another difference between the US and Britain is that in the UK the citizen owes obligations (duties) to the Crown and not to an abstract concept such as the republic, constitution or Bill of Rights. Of course, many would argue that Britain ought to have a Bill of Rights which would bestow legal rights and corresponding duties to uphold such rights but at present this situation does not exist.[27] However, a problem would remain as to whether such a Bill of Rights would remove the traditional power of Parliament to remove, modify or otherwise alter existing liberties. Traditionally there have been no limits on the authority of Parliament to legislate on *any* matter.

The following discussion will use the concepts which are most appropriate to a particular national legal/political context and will be differentiated as above, i.e., 'liberties' imply that one has the freedom to do what is not unlawful and 'rights' imply a positive legal privilege.

A major anxiety in all of the literature which discusses the problem of the democratic response to terrorism is that democracy can be damaged or even abolished by governments 'over-reacting'. One fear of such over-reaction is a fear of increased State surveillance of citizens. Such surveillance is said to 'chill' citizen willingness to express opinions or to participate in social movements, to damage personal privacy, lead to the denial of State employment, concentrate power, erode normal police and court procedures and lead to the use of 'dirty tricks'. This catalogue of fears would certainly seem sufficient to give rise to the need for eternal vigilance if nothing else but these fears are *not* sufficient, in and by themselves, to justify restricting the intelligence activities of a State in responding to terrorism. The reason for this is the simple one that the erosion of civil liberties must be examined in relation to the fundamental liberty of self-preservation and the preservation of a political system within which these other liberties have meaning. This implies that the relationship between terrorism, intelligence and civil liberties is one of balance. This has been often stated but without some basis by which to make judgements between alternatives it is a bland and not very helpful statement. Questions remain such as: What level of terrorist threat is sufficient to justify what level of State surveillance even when this involves the erosion of civil liberties? What is the actual consequence of particular intelligence activities on civil liberties? Are such responses effective in reducing or containing terrorism? The answer to such questions requires empirical knowledge as well as philosophical considerations.

I offer several criteria by which to make this balancing judgement. The obvious starting point for any democracy considering what intelligence it requires and the value of clandestine measures is to examine the threat which it faces. However, this is not as simple as it appears. Firstly, a good intelligence service must be in place in order to be able to make such an assessment: one which is capable of analysing existing information and coming to an objective assessment of the threat posed by terrorism at a very early stage of activity. This is inherently difficult since, at an early stage, there will be few patterns or trends to assess. It will be difficult to assess whether the first targets hit or the early methods used are indicative of the future. It is even more difficult to assess the level of support such activities may have either within the general population or within a particular sector of it. This difficulty is compounded by the fact that little may be known of the perpetrators, their motives, goals, finances, organisation, links to other groups or states, or their personal backgrounds. And yet, despite this lack of information, decisions have to be taken as to whether to mount a major investigation using the full range of intelligence techniques or whether to see the terrorism as nothing more than isolated criminal activity which is no more dangerous to the State or general public than drunken drivers. The key issue is what level of activity is sufficient to justify labelling a group as terrorist and what degree of terrorist threat is sufficient to trigger an all-out response? The temptation is to reply by saying 'wait and see' and so avoid making an assessment until 'further information is available'. This is particularly understandable given the dilemma that it is precisely in the early stages that an effective response may be mounted and yet it may also be in the early stages that the accusation of over-reaction is most likely to be made against the State. Death is the normal criterion referred to when justifying making a group an object of intelligence activity. As soon as dead bodies are claimed as the outcome of a politically motivated action, group intelligence interest is virtually automatic. However, there is still the problem of justifying the degree of intelligence effort. Intelligence, like any other State bureaucracy, does not possess unlimited manpower and resources. Tailing people, intercepting communications and planting informers are all expensive of time and money. A decision still needs to be made about priorities and how this new threat is to be ranked against existing intelligence priorities.

In order to make such a decision, several criteria need to be borne in mind. Firstly, the extent to which intelligence activity is likely to be the only method by which to counter the threat. To tap telephones or place people under surveillance is justified if it is the only method likely to produce results. In essence, this is the claim that the response must be the minimum necessary in order to gather information. The danger is that politicians or the intelligence community will exaggerate the threat in order to achieve other goals such as harassment or expansion. The use of intelligence to harass has certainly occurred in the USA. This was partly due to the lack of political will to control intelligence and partly due to the ambitions of the FBI to become the principle agency for countering 'subversion'.[28] Intelligence agencies are not immune from such sins as pride and avarice. In the literature there are two favourite approaches to this problem. The first is to construct a set of rules or guidelines which attempt to constrain or limit intelligence services. The second is to construct an effective system of accountability involving the legislature and/or the executive. It is of course possible to develop a joint approach in which both tactics are used. However, each has its problems. A set of rules may not be capable of allowing sufficient flexibility in an area where judgements of degree of risk are inherently uncertain. The danger may be reversed so that intelligence services hesitate to trigger surveillance when it is justified in order to avoid 'scandal'. This, it has been argued was the result of the guidelines produced by Attorney General Levi following upon the Church Committee investigations.[29] The Levi guidelines adopted a step-by-step approach to investigations. This involved setting triggers which would allow an investigation to be opened and then a higher level of trigger in order for more intrusive techniques to be used. It was a requirement of the guidelines that the threat of force, an actual criminal act be alleged, before *any* investigation could take place. Statements by groups that they intended to use force or saw force as justified were not sufficient to trigger an investigation. It was argued that many groups make statements which are not preparatory to action but are mere rhetoric and that it is unreasonable to use such rhetoric as a basis for opening a file. The classic illustration of this is the unreasonableness of opening an investigation into a group of old bolsheviks sitting in a New York café planning the overthrow of the Government when each has been a law-abiding citizen of the country since they emigrated in 1910! These rules led to the FBI reducing its activities including the collection of publicly available material.[30] It has been argued that the mere collection of publicly available material by an agency such as the FBI indicates that the group is somehow unlawful or subversive. The debate centres on the issue of the 'criminal standard' as the trigger of investigation. However, although this may be appropriate for a law-enforcement agency it is not appropriate for an intelligence agency. The reason for this being that effective intelligence work requires the build-up of a picture of a group before the bombs go off and it has gone fully underground. Furthermore, good intelligence work requires information beyond the criminal activities of a group such as information concerning its ideology, support groups, front organisations, those willing to give more active support but not plant bombs, the links with foreign powers or overseas groups and the sources of finance and recruits. Much of this may involve 'legal' activity and yet information about such activities is essential for successful intelligence work.

The second approach is to monitor intelligence activities via legislative committees or by an internal system of authority and accountability which places key decisions in the hads of a restricted number of identifiable people. It can be argued that some intelligence abuses were a product of decisions being taken by those in a low position in the hierarchy who attempted to produce results using whatever techniques they had command of. It is argued that if operational decisions must be cleared with a figure such as the Attorney

General or a court judge then this temptation is removed. The problem is that this may make intelligence officers over-cautious.[31] To ask permission to use a technique or open a file may place an officer in the position of being seen as over-zealous, a 'cowboy' who wishes to wield a weapon when inaction and being 'cool' is preferable. One must not ask one's lower officers to be too courageous in calling for an investigation when they only have limited information, for example a mere piece of gossip, and yet this is the very kind of information which may greatly assist in constructing a picture. In this climate they are likely to keep this information to themselves and to ask for an investigation only when they have good hard evidence. By then it may be too late to act.

None of the above is an adequate solution for each creates problems for the intelligence professional and risks rendering intelligence ineffective. A more satisfactory solution is not to construct rigid standards for the collection of information in terms of some trigger but in terms of the purpose for which it is being collected. There are two distinct though related purposes that underlie intelligence work against terrorism. The first is to apprehend, arrest and try those suspected of committing a criminal offence. This purpose is one which ought to be constrained as to the type of information which can be used to convict in a court of law. In Britain, this requires a modification to the Judge's Rules so that information collected for intelligence purposes cannot be allowed in a court of law as legitimate evidence. The principle underlying this approach is that civil liberties are vital when the State intends to punish a citizen. If the citizen is not carrying out an unlawful act there ought to be special rules governing the use of State power to 'punish'. For example there ought to be very tight rules governing the use of information to harass a citizen. It is clear that apart from the due process of law there are many other ways of punishing a citizen and that this is the key area where the focus on civil liberties ought to be concentrated and not on collection or 'surveillance'. It is the *use* of information which poses the greatest threat to the liberties of the citizen.

The other essential requirement of 'democratic' intelligence is that information should be collected for an identifiable purpose, a threat which the State can identify. Furthermore, it is essential that political leaders be convinced that the threat identification is one which can be justified to the public and so gain or maintain public support for the policy. This is both helpful to the collection agency *and* to civil liberties. The setting of priorities and the tasking of intelligence agencies by politicians are both essential for effective intelligence. All too often problems of intelligence abuse have arisen because of a lack of control by politicians who are the only ones capable of making the judgements involved in deciding what is, and what is not, a threat to the body politic. This means the creation of bodies capable of setting priorities and reviewing achievements. This is a serious gap in both US and British Intelligence. Neither society has created an agency such as the National Security Council or the Joint Intelligence Committee to monitor and task domestic intelligence. This function is one which has its own special problems and characteristics and should not be considered in the same committee as foreign intelligence. This is not a problem of operational coordination, which underlies bodies such as the Cobra Committee, but is concerned with long-term intelligence planning and analysis.[32]

Finally, it is essential that questions of effectiveness and efficiency be taken into account when assessing intelligence. There is little point in eroding civil liberties if by doing so there are no appreciable results. One must have reassurance that someone is continuously examining the extent to which collection, operations and analysis are producing results in order to allow the State to justify such practices by reference to the threats which it faces. Countermeasures can only be justified by the existence of a threat when such measures reduce the threat.

CONCLUSION

This chapter has attempted to take a new approach to the problem of terrorism, intelligence and civil liberties. The argument has been that secret intelligence collection about terrorism poses fewer problems for civil liberties than has traditionally been claimed. Many anxieties will be reduced if the public have assurance that information is being collected for a clearly identifiable purpose and is being properly analysed. Improvements in this area will benefit both civil liberties and intelligence work. Many of the abuses which have occurred and the fears which they have generated have arisen as a result of a lack of clarity over the nature of the threat which society faces, the purposes for which information is being collected and the uses to which it is being put. The responsibility for this situation lies with legislators and the executive who have failed to give proper guidance in these key areas. An effective intelligence service is less dangerous to civil liberties since it is less likely to collect information which is not related to a clear goal and for which there is no clear purpose. The main such purpose is to aid policy making. Intelligence is not simply or mainly about prosecution but about aiding decision makers to make better decisions. The decisions concern such matters as the extent, seriousness, resources, organisation, foreign connections and implications of a terrorist group and the options available to respond to the terrorist threat. To have an effective intelligence service capable of performing these functions requires the creation of a consensus on the threat being faced, tasking of intelligence by decision makers and the analysis of information collected to make it useful to policy makers in the taking of decisions.

This task is not impossible provided the public are convinced, and have explained to them, that terrorism is not merely a form of criminal activity. Although the 'menace' of terrorism should not be exaggerated it is vital that its unique qualities are understood. Terrorism involves a challenge to a democratic society which is qualitatively different from crime. It poses a challenge to the democratic principle of rule by the people and to the State to cope with the problems which generate terrorism without having policies determined by the terrorist. If terrorism is to be properly assessed and responses are to be effective and proportionate it is essential that intelligence services collect information on terrorism. Without adequate intelligence one may see panic on the part of police forces, intelligence operatives and politicians which is likely to endanger civil liberties. It is also essential to maintain the distinction between collecting information for the purpose of prosecution and collecting information for the purpose of aiding policy making however difficult this may be in practice. The argument of this chapter has been that many of the fears and anxieties concerning domestic intelligence activity can be reduced if such a distinction is made. Putting this principle into practice will not be easy but it is no more difficult than living with rigid rules of intelligence gathering or monitoring the separation of powers between Congress and the Executive. All distinctions involve grey areas and difficult judgements but to re-direct the efforts of academics and policy makers towards consideration of how to implement this policy would be more fruitful than the continuing debate between the civil libertarians and the 'get the terrorist' advocates. It is inadequate to focus on the constraints which civil liberties impose on intelligence without recognising that many such constraints arise because of the fear of punishment. It is also inadequate to believe that 'more effort' is all that is required to 'defeat' terrorism. The public must be convinced that intelligence is well-directed towards ends which have been determined by policy makers after the most careful scrutiny. If the public can be assured that intelligence has aiding policy making as its main purpose then the fears that civil liberties are likely to be eroded ought to be substantially reduced.

This will be even more persuasive if three criteria are used to guide intelligence work against terrorism. Firstly, that intelligence is collected for a clear and identifiable purpose which has been set at the highest level, that is, by the politicians responsible. Secondly, that the intelligence collected and the operations it performs are continuously reviewed by a specialist committee similar in status and role to the National Security Council or the Joint Intelligence Committee. Thirdly, that intelligence activity is effective and produces results. This requires the monitoring of intelligence with a view to assessing performance as well as civil liberty issues.

If these requirements are met the public can have a degree of confidence that 'abuses' will be less likely than they have been in the past and this can be done without reducing the overall significance of intelligence in the struggle against terrorism.

NOTES

1 For example J Bowyer Bell, *A Time of Terror*, New York; Basic Books, 1978: 'Nearly all of the threatened or their experts agree that the key to an effective response to terrorism is good intelligence' p. 134.

2 Such efforts include: G Wardlaw, *Political Terrorism*, Cambridge: CUP, 1982, chapter 12; JB Wolff, *Fear of Fear*, New York: Plenum Press, 1981 esp. Part 2

and various articles; W Kerstetter, 'Terrorism and Intelligence', *Terrorism*, Vol. 3 part 1–2, 1979; S Gazit and M Handel, 'Insurgency, Terrorism and Intelligence', *in* R Godson (ed), *Counter-intelligence*, New Brunswick: Transaction Books, 1980; HHA Cooper, 'Terrorism and the Intelligence Function', *in* MH Livingston *et al.* (eds.), *International Terrorism in the Contemporary World*, Westport Connecticut: Greenwood Press, 1978.

3 F Donner, 'The Terrorist as Scapegoat', *The Nation*, 20 May 1978.

4 This is the theme of the 'Epilogue' to Donner's *The Age of Surveillance*, New York: Vintage Books, 1981, esp. pp. 455–463.

5 This section owes a debt to the excellent survey in AP Schmidt, *Political Terrorism*, Leiden: COMT, 1983.

6 'A crime is not a "political crime" simply by virtue of the act's natural and direct tendency to disturb the political order of the State. Instead, *the "political" nature of the crime depends on the kind of legal response the act evokes from those in authority*' (author's emphasis) pp. 18–19, BL Ingraham, *Political Crime in Europe*, Berkeley: University of California Press, 1979.

7 For example, Stephen Schafer, *The Political Criminal*, New York: Free Press, 1974.

8 *Ibid.*, p. 29.

9 Roger Hillsman, 'Intelligence through the Eyes of the Policy Maker', *in* RH Blum (ed.), *Surveillance and Espionage in a Free Society*, New York: Irvington Press, 1973, pp. 163–177.

10 *Ibid.*, p. 163. See also Hillsman's *Strategic Intelligence and National Decisions*, Glenco Illinois: Free Press, 1956.

11 Roy Godson, 'What is Intelligence?', *in* KG Roberston (ed.), *British and American Approaches to Intelligence*, London: Macmillan Press, 1986.

12 *Ibid.*, p. 4.

13 Although fiction has devoted an overwhelming amount of space to the human agent, the spy, there has been very little serious work done in this area. J Masterman, *The Double Cross System*, London: Sphere Books, 1973 and William Hood, *Mole*, New York: Ballantine Books, 1983, are two of the few books devoted to 'agent handling'. Secrecy alone cannot explain this since the interception of communications and code breaking was, and is, a highly significant source of intelligence and yet we know a great deal about Ultra for example.

14 There is a large literature on 'surprise' but see: R Wohlstetter, *Pearl Harbor, Warning and Decision*, Stanford: Stanford University Press, 1976; R Betts, *Surprise Attack*, Washington DC: The Brookings Institution, 1982; M Handel, 'Avoiding Political and Technological Surprise', *in* R Godson (ed.), *Analysis and Estimates*, New Brunswick: Transaction Books, 1980; K Knorr and P Morgan, *Strategic Military Surprise*, New Brunswick: Transaction Books, 1983; ER May (ed.), *Knowing One's Enemies*, Princeton: Princeton University Press, 1984; GW Hopple *et al.* (eds.), *National Security Crisis, Forecasting and Management*, Bowker, Essex: Westview Press, 1984.

15 For an interesting insight into the debate within CIA on the relative importance of HUMINT and SIGINT see chapters 4 and 5 of R Godson (ed.), *Clandestine Collection*, New Brunswick: Transaction Books, 1982.

16 The JIC is responsible for making assessments for Ministers and Officials. These assessments are first prepared by the Current Intelligence Groups. These Groups can be tasked by a Minister, Department of State or the JIC itself. The JIC also has a coordinating role which includes the Security Service and the Secret

Intelligence Service (SIS). However, given the structure of the JIC, its involvement in security matters is largely concerned with countering hostile intelligence services and not with domestic threats. It has been said of the NSC that 'there is no NSC-level mechanism for coordinating, reviewing or approving counterintelligence activities in the United States, even those directed at US citizens ...' p. 428, Vol. 1, Final Report of the Select Committee to Study Governmental Operations with respect to Intelligence Activities (Church Committee), Washington DC: US Government, 1976.

17 For other efforts along somewhat similar lines see note 2 above.

18 For arguments on these lines see, National Advisory Committee on Criminal Justice Standards and Goals, *Disorders and Terrorism*, Washington DC: US Government, 1976, sections 7.1 and 7.2.

19 Duncan Campbell, 'Society under Surveillance', *in* Peter Hain (ed.), *Policing the Police*, Vol. 2, London: John Calder, 1980, p. 65.

20 David Wise, *The American Police State*, New York: Vintage Books, 1978, p. 405.

21 P Hewitt, *Privacy—The Information Gatherers*, London: NCCL, 1980, p. 65.

22 James Michael, 'Privacy', *in* M Wallington, (ed.), *Civil Liberties 1984*, Oxford: Martin Robertson, 1984, p. 143.

23 Such tactics are recounted in Nelson Blackstock, *Cointelpro—The FBI's Secret War on Political Freedom*, New York: Vintage Books, 1976; M Halperin *et al.*, *The Lawless State—The Crimes of the US Intelligence Agencies*, New York: Penguin Books, 1976; A Theoharis, *Spying on Americans*, Philadelphia: Temple University Press, 1978; D Martin, 'Investigating the FBI', *Policy Review*, Vol. 18, Fall 1981; Wise, *op. cit.*; Donner, *op. cit.*, 1981.

24 See PL Murphy, *WW1 and the Origins of Civil Liberties*, New York: WW Norton, 1979; David Fellman, *The Defendant's Rights*, New York: Rinehart and Co., 1958 for excellent historical perspectives.

25 TC Hartley and JAG Griffiths, *Government and Law*, London: Weidenfeld and Nicolson, 1975, p. 151.

26 Paul O'Higgins, *Cases and Materials on Civil Liberties*, London: Sweet and Maxwell, 1980; DM Walker, *The Oxford Companion to Law*, Oxford: Clarendon Press, 1980.

27 The situation is somewhat complicated by the fact that Britain is a signatory to the European Convention on Human Rights but it has not, so far, been incorporated into British domestic law.

28 A Theoharis, 'The Stretching of Presidential Directives', *Political Science Quarterly*, Vol. 91(4), 1976–1977; F Donner, 'How J Edgar Hoover Created his Intelligence Powers', *Civil Liberties Review*, Vol. 3(6), 1977.

29 For an excellent account of the 'rise and fall' of domestic intelligence see Richard Morgan, *Domestic Intelligence*, Austin: University of Texas Press, 1980. See also JT Eliff, *The Reform of FBI Intelligence Operations*, Princeton; Princeton University Press, 1979.

30 For example, the number of FBI domestic intelligence operations were reduced by 95% between 1974–1977. The FBI had less than 20 domestic intelligence investigation operations by 1977. Source: Tony Poveda, 'The Rise and Fall of FBI Domestic Intelligence Operations', *Contemporary Crisis*, Vol. 6, 1982 and his 'The FBI and Domestic Intelligence', *Crime and Delinquency*, Vol. 28, April 1982.

31 Largely based on interviews with professional staff members of the US Congress, House and Senate Select Committees on Intelligence, and with representatives

of the FBI. Not all of the FBI bureaucracy shared this view, some saw the new rules as creating greater efficiency.

32 Cobra, an emergency committee of the Cabinet which, for example, supervised the handling of the Libyan Bureau murder and 'siege' in April 1984.

Vulnerable America

R H Kupperman

It may seem inconceivable that we will one day look back upon the Cold War era as a time of relative peace and stability—a time when the only major global threat was that the two largest powers would annihilate each other. But in fact that bipolar order has even now deteriorated into a much less certain, much more fluid international environment. As power and influence have become increasingly diffuse, the traditional mechanisms of international political restraint have become decreasingly effective. It is far less clear who can do what to whom, why and with what effect.

The mysteries of atomic weaponry are neither as secret nor as difficult to master as we had once hoped. The number of near-nuclear and nuclear powers is expected to grow significantly by the end of the century. As a result, we face the very real danger of a nuclear holocaust triggered by the aggression of rogue states or by catalytic conflict in the Third World. Chemical and biological weapons—less expensive and easier to fabricate—may yet become the poor man's bomb, a means by which radical subnational and national groups can attain the extortion potential of a nuclear device.

The tools and techniques for mass destruction have so proliferated as to force our planners to think about the unthinkable. The proposals before the nation span the spectrum between unilateral disarmament and unabated nuclear arms competition. More and better of everything is clearly not the answer but neither is it axiomatic that less is always more secure. In fact, reduced nuclear arsenals in conjunction with the proliferation of small nuclear forces present a very real danger that minor errors in verification or marginal cheating by the other side can propagate overwhelming strategic advantages. Clearly, we need to re-think the options for stable and substantial arms reductions and possibly contemplate some kind of buffering mechanism—such as a limited ballistic missile defence—that could eliminate the first incoming warheads in the event our faith in bilateral agreements or our own verification capabilities prove misplaced.

The spectre of nuclear holocaust, however, tends to be almost a hypnotic pre-occupation. Lost in the national security debate is the fact that the United

States faces very real—and much more imminent—threats at the other end of the conflict spectrum in low-intensity warfare.

Our crisis managers devote themselves to planning for big disasters—fantasising about the nation's capacity to cope with nuclear carnage. The sad truth is that the US is not prepared to respond to most kinds of emergencies—from natural disasters to industrial accidents—much less an induced and strategic disruption or organised response to a carefully selected, technologically sophisticated attack on our industrial base. No up-to-date inventory exists of medical, logistical, civil engineering, food, temporary shelter or trained manpower resources—all of which are essential to deal, for example, with the terrorist-induced blackout of a major city lasting for weeks. Our capabilities to mobilise industry and re-direct the flow of materials from a civilian economy to a national defence footing are virtually non-existent. The fact is that despite a massive nuclear and conventional arsenal—among the largest in the world—we are dangerously vulnerable to attack.

In today's changing global environment, the vulnerability of our industrial and service infrastructure to disruption represents a slowly developing (hence ignored) crisis. Although the facts are in plain view, the will and precautions necessary to counter the threat lag behind.

THE LOW-INTENSITY THREAT: TERRORISM

The most likely danger confronting us may not, after all, be the threat of nuclear holocaust. In fact, it is difficult to conceive why any nation would risk certain retribution (and probable escalation) for an overt act of war when unconventional forms of attack offer such unique advantages. Employing limited firepower, they can be profound in leverage and just as disruptive. The initial uncertainty about the origin of attack—or even whether an attack has occurred—often limits the range of diplomatic and military responses. With the collapse of the traditional networks of intra- and international relations, the temptation to rely on unconventional action mechanisms may become irresistible. For the relatively weaker countries, the high-leverage/low-cost element of low-intensity warfare is essential because they cannot afford to compete economically or militarily. For the more powerful, the high-leverage/low-risk factor is decisive because the costs of large-scale conventional or nuclear confrontations are unacceptable. Hence, the 'action' we may expect to see over the next two decades will be at the margins, below the level of war but with the power to cripple governments or topple nations.

The techniques of unconventional warfare are hardly a new dimension of international rivalry. Disinformation, overt or covert thefts of high technology, export of undesirables as refugees or support of movements of national liberation have long formed part of the spectrum of low-intensity conflict. What is new, however, is an international climate that offers a strategic rationale for such tactics.

An increasingly important tool of conflict at the low end of the spectrum is terrorism. Hardly a day passes without a terrorist incident occurring somewhere in the world; it permeates the fabric of contemporary civilisation. And the significance of the terror act has been raised exponentially by several different but interrelated factors. First, the tools available for destruction are much more lethal and much more frightening than ever before. Second, the media attention focused on terrorism is immediate, global and usually undisciplined. Third, motives for terrorist attack today span a spectrum that includes, at the extremes, personal grudges and superpower ambitions of global hegemony—and there is little certainty as to which underlying motive may really be at play in any particular case. Finally the United States (unlike others in the Western Alliance) has no internal consensus on how to respond either to acts of supercriminal violence or to coercive political threats. It has no common philosophical basis for accepting the high costs (in lives, materials, pride and power) of occasional failure in dealing with terrorism and it has no internationally recognised commitment for firm, retributive deterrence of such violence.

Although the United States has not so far been a primary target of attack, recent events prove that we are far from immune. The 1979 seizure of the American embassy in Teheran demonstrated that the US is not only a visible target but a vulnerable one as well. America failed diplomatically and militarily to deal with the terrorist tactics of a rogue nation and a national disaster was the result. Threats from a Libyan death squad against the President represented a direct attack on the foundations of our democratic society. In the end, it was irrelevant whether or not a Libyan 'hit' team actually existed; the threat itself forced the President to retreat into a 'steel cocoon' and appeared to paralyse the American Government. The attempted assassination of General Kroesen in Germany and the kidnapping of General Dozier in Italy represented an attack on a cornerstone of US foreign policy: the NATO alliance and the decision on theatre force modernisation. Using the media as a springboard, the terrorists attempted a 'cushion shot' to capitalise on the political stresses in the Alliance and the growing worldwide anti-nuclear movement.

The full extent of our vulnerability was made most dramatically evident when an anonymous killer in Chicago contaminated a few bottles of Tylenol with a small amount of commercially available cyanide. That single act not only cost a number of individuals their lives and the pharmaceutical industry $100 million; it also generated widespread anxiety in the general population and outright terror in a small portion. That individual gave the United States a profound lesson in the disruptive potential of the strategically vectored terrorist attack.

Terrorist assaults, like a martial art, can turn our chief strengths—our democratic tradition of fairness and restraint, the openness of our news media—against us. They can also directly attack, with potentially devastating results, our technological and economic infrastructure.

THE MODERN VULNERABILITY

The greatest strength of modern Western society, its strong technological base, is also its Achilles' heel. In a remarkably short span, Western man has translated his observations of the natural world into forms of control over energy and materials, and has exercised that control for his own benefit and comfort. The rate of change of knowledge—and the technologies that flow from it—has been dramatic, making possible conurbation on an unprecedented scale. In effect, we have reached a point of no return; we no longer can go back to a pre-industrial, agrarian society without severe cultural disruption.

Urban man has become wholly reliant on the technological infrastructure for the continuity of goods and services necessary to his survival. But at least in the United States, that infrastructure is the product of accretion, patched together with little continuous planning and with no provisions for survivability against attack. The design and placement of individual systems, such as electric generation and distribution, water reservoirs, oil and gas refineries, pumping stations and pipelines reflect the priorities of a past era. The efficiency of these systems lies in their size (large and few) and centralisation. Today, their lack of redundancy, duplication and dispersion creates appealing and leverageable nodes of attack.

Taken together, the systems form an intricate, interdependent and extremely fragile infrastructural web. The ad hoc process of growth has resulted in critical 'choke-points' where major utilities come together; hence, the failure of any one system can mean the disruption of many others. For the embracing systems, like electrical power, there are no available damage control options, no way to halt the feedback (the asynergies) into the other networks. A major power failure—perhaps the most extreme case—could paralyse the sanitary and water systems, the food supply chains, computerised networks (e.g., banking and insurance), the manufacturing sector, transportation; in short, nearly every vital service of the affected area.

The broad problem, cutting across all industries, arises from the fact that the costs of protecting against every natural or accidental disaster are prohibitively high: in any technologically based, democratic society, some degree of risk must always be accepted. As Louisianans discovered, their levees are designed to contain the yearly flood waters, not the once-in-a-century flood. Californians protect their schools and hospitals against the intermediate earthquake, not the massive one. In general, we rely on the statistical conclusion that the effects of most kinds of disasters can be isolated, and are temporary and reversible.

The special danger today, however, stems from induced as well as natural disasters of a vastly different magnitude. The vulnerability of the society's life-supporting physical networks invites focused sabotage and low-intensity warfare attacks, which, if successful, could conceivably exceed the self-healing limits of the society at large.

These kinds of attacks have already begun. Since 1970, there have been over two hundred attacks worldwide directed against electric utilities from California to Puerto Rico, from France to the Philippines. In the US, the New World Liberation Front has targeted Pacific Gas and Electric some seventy times, albeit with minimal damage. Nuclear power stations in France, Spain, Germany and the US have been unsuccessfully attacked. A raid on an FALN safehouse prior to the 1980 Democratic National Convention turned up detailed plans of the power system of Madison Square Garden, possibly signalling a plot to black out the facility and disrupt the electoral process. To date these terrorist attacks have been largely ineffective, but they raise the prospect of very large disruptive impacts caused by few human and material resources.

Without providing a blueprint for destruction, one can describe a number of areas of extreme vulnerability. The nation's energy system, especially the electric power system, is the most vulnerable target. Beyond that, even critical components in the US defence production system itself are vulnerable to attacks of quite elementary sabotage. For example, this country maintains only two very large extrusion presses on which the titanium-based aircraft industry depends and only one facility where all of the gun tubes for both the army and navy are produced. The United States maintains a large reserve of critical strategic materials—invaluable in the event we need to re-fight the Second World War. However, it stockpiles none of the critically important intermediate goods, such as heavy transformers or natural gas pumping stations, that are essential in countering current threats against our infrastructure.

The only utility system that possesses the necessary redundancy and decentralisation to be truly survivable is the national telecommunications network—which is currently being dismantled by judicial edict. An indispensable element of secure telecommunications is the ability to maintain local contact in time of disaster by re-routing connections through the nationwide network. It is questionable whether this flexibility can be maintained in a patchwork regional system. This case presents a classic example of potential conflict between socially desirable goals and national security. In pursuit of anti-monopoly policy, the courts have required an integrated telecommunications system to decentralise both in facilities and in management. Unless the new regional telecommunications systems are carefully modernised for interoperability and for survival, the US thus may lose in the national security arena more than it gains from the social benefits of de-regulation. For example, if each regional telephone system ignored state-of-the-art advances or rejected commonality of connections, US civil telecommunications capabilities could be Balkanised, encouraging the military services to develop their own integrated systems for non-emergency use.

These problems of vulnerability, combined with those in our energy systems, endanger more than our standard of living or industrial productivity; they also have long-range national security implications for military preparedness and mobilisation capability. The military, like the civilian sector, operates on the assumption that a reliable technological infrastructure is guaranteed. Given the strategic vulnerability of that infrastructure, one may appreciate how fragile our actual military capability might be.

The problem is aggravated by growing evidence that terrorist organisations are developing and refining training for attacks on our energy and industrial infrastructure. Some governments may have the necessary contingency response plans, trained personnel and dedicated equipment to guarantee the continuity of goods and services in their societies; the United States does not.

PREPAREDNESS LIMITATIONS

The emergency preparedness/civil defence apparatus in the United States is designed to cope with either the unimaginable or the unimportant. No preparation is made for superdisasters because they are perceived to be beyond human managerial skills or credible planning. It is true of devastating earthquakes, the hundred-year rain over Lake Pontchartrain or even the terrorist detonation of a nuclear weapon in a major American city. Since no government would be blamed for failing to organise, say, the aftermath of a nuclear holocaust, our government officials can freely exhibit bravado when faced with theoretical carnage. At the opposite end of the spectrum, little disasters present no substantial problems. Whether they are managed efficiently or poorly, little disasters usually go away on their own and, in any case, fade quickly from the public eye.

The real danger is posed by the intermediate disaster. This country is completely unprepared—physically or politically—to deal with the reconstructive phases of disasters with widespread geographical or technological effects.

The problem of inadequate emergency preparations is not limited to malevolent acts against the United States. Our technological infrastructure is not only vulnerable; it is also ageing and rapidly deteriorating. We face the prospect of condemned bridges, impassable roads, grid-locked electrical systems and unreliable networks to distribute food, water and energy. The market economy offers few incentives to make the investment required for a complete systematic overhaul; and in the current climate of public budget constraints, the political temptation to defer maintenance of capital infrastructure is overwhelming. With so much money tied up in debt service on existing capital investments, only minor and minimal adjustments are made to upgrade these systems.

Where are the national strategies and meaningful contingency plans to cope with the decay of our industrial infrastructure and ultimately of our mobilisation base? It is unfortunate that while the image of civil emergency preparedness has been maintained as a political necessity, the capability for planning and execution is largely illusory. Civil defence, in its classic sense, is clearly a worthwhile notion, but in the absence of any real capacity to deal with the lesser disasters, the concept has little meaning. We are victims of denial—and not only for disasters on a massive scale.

In fact, there is no embracing plan for crisis management, no national means of command and control linking the myriad of state and local agencies charged with meeting disaster and civil defence responsibilities. The first line of response in any disaster is the local police and fire officials who are largely cut off from the Federal bureaucracies. Indeed, much of the nation's emergency management apparatus is an assortment of ageing programmes built on twenty-year-old technology.

The Federal Emergency Management Agency (FEMA) is assigned overall responsibility for disaster management and relief. The legislative intent behind FEMA and its predecessor agencies is to build a 'bridge' between national security concerns and domestic emergency management.

FEMA is therefore charged with responsibilities ranging from disaster relief to crisis management, from continuity of government to industrial mobilisation for conventional war and civil defence against nuclear attack. It is asked not only to fulfil critical national security and civil emergency functions, but to cope with the administration of social programmes such as flood insurance. All are important, but administrative duties distract the agency from its first order of business: civil emergency preparedness. And it is a sad truism that FEMA, like its predecessors, has an over-abundance of responsibility and a corresponding dearth of authority and resources.

Another classic example of a Federal bureaucratic structure poorly positioned to handle emergent crises is in the field of counterterrorism. The Justice Department is the lead agency for incidents of domestic terrorism, while the State Department has jurisdiction over terrorist acts against US interests abroad. Although this may appear to be a rational division of responsibility, it proceeds from the assumption that our primary goal is to apprehend the culprits. If the electricity goes out along the Eastern seaboard, we may be able to count on the FBI to handcuff the perpetrators—a satisfying prospect that does not, however, redress the main problem. In effect, the tendency towards political denial that a problem exists is rooted in—and perpetuated by—the mismatch between the responsibilities of Federal agencies and their problem-solving capabilities. The agencies thus typically take the path of least resistance in coping with a crisis; bureaucratic niceties become substitutes for careful planning and thoughtful crisis management.

As we being to recognise the enormously complex and threatening nature of modern crises, it becomes clear that we can no longer rely on ad hoc processes of automatic reaction. *Crisis management* should become inseparable from *crisis preparedness*. Politicians may become emotionally devastated by disaster; the crisis manager must not.

A ROLE FOR PROFESSIONALISM

One of our most serious problems is that at present we have no clearly defined authority structure to set priorities, determine the command, control and jurisdictional parameters of effective management and allocate available resources among competing needs. The typical crisis manager is usually another kind of victim: he is often pulled away from his normal duties after emergencies already exist, given few guidelines, limited resources and poor information. Without having participated in any of the prior planning stages—if indeed there were any—he is the relief pitcher called in to bring order out of chaos. Not surprisingly, the result is that frenetic activity and an obsession with minutiae substitute for strategy. Under present conditions crisis managers appear busy and react to the flow of events, but they have no embracing concept of how to deal with disaster.

We need a professional cadre of disaster managers who do not change hats on non-emergency days and who are intimately familiar with both the planning and execution phases of disaster response. Ideally, when a real crisis hits, no difference should exist, either operationally or emotionally, between the current reality and the previous training simulations. The same people who planned for and managed the last crisis should be prepared to handle the next.

The Executive Office of the President is the only logical organisational placement for these professional crisis managers. Under the present structure, the emergency management apparatus is at the independent agency level, with power only parallel or subordinate to that available to many other Federal institutions involved in various aspects of crisis management. Only from the White House can action authority and management responsibility be readily and visibly delegated. Such a group should maintain perhaps 1100 professionals at a national command centre and some two hundred liaison, logistics and organisational experts in the field, and would have responsibility for coordinating between the White House and the relevant state and local agencies.

One major function of such a group would be to provide continuous and realistic contingency planning to prepare for the variety of accidents and incidents that can occur, a basic requisite of any effective crisis management. Such planning is designed not to prepare in detail for every potential crisis, but to develop modes of operation and analytical models to cope with crisis, to gain an awareness of available resources and to arrange the logistics involved in using them. Gaming exercises, computer simulations and adversary 'Red Team' attacks would all provide training and testing at many levels of threat.

TECHNOLOGY AND INTERACTIVE DECISION MAKING

The use of intelligent, interactive computer systems[1] has not been adequately explored as a means of developing planning, training and operational bases for crisis modelling and management. The distinctive feature of computer conferencing systems is ease of use, breadth of applicability and great flexibility. Rather than requiring knowledge of a computer language, they actively present the user with a 'menu' of things that he can do, allowing him to select the appropriate items. Working with liaison agents in the field, he can redefine choices and correct mistakes. In this way the nature of the choices presented to users and the form and content of resulting information can be changed relatively rapidly to suit a specific crisis and the preferences of the decision makers managing it.

The significant feature of these systems is their underlying concept of dynamic modelling. To keep the process vital, both the designers of the interactive models and the decision makers must stay in close contact to understand each other's requirements and limitations. This places a new demand on the available talent pool—one that is just coming to be recognised as our schools move towards computer awareness and utilisation curricula. Computer-based interactive techniques will be able to clarify problems of collective judgement as well as the communications and resource-allocation problems that occur when making policy operational. Moreover, the hardware systems in use here will allow the more routine but equally important functions of efficient teleconferencing, model building and testing and training.

But all such sophisticated management and communications systems will be for naught unless senior government officials at least become familiar with the kinds of decisions they may have to make. Without leadership interest, new institutions and machines can make few contributions to the problems confronting top-level policy makers at times of crisis.

PROPOSALS FOR REFORM

The civil and military infrastructure on which the US depends for its survival is a highly visible and systematically vulnerable target for low-intensity warfare. As the increasingly fluid global environment multiplies opportunities for such warfare, that vulnerability is increasing. At the present time, the United States has few defences against this kind of focused attack. Our strategic planners have tended to be shortsighted, measuring the strength of our defence simply in terms of weapons systems or troops. Our logistical base in fact, if not in prevailing policy, is only as strong as our domestic technological infrastructure. If that network is disrupted by sabotage or neglect,the United States will hardly be able to mobilise, let alone effectively conduct, the canonical extended NATO conflict.

The following is a reform agenda to correct this serious vulnerability:

Re-organise the Federal Emergency Planning Agency. As an independent agency, FEMA at present lacks the authority to perform essential tasks of planning for and coping with the effects of natural disasters, industrial accidents, or highly disruptive acts of terrorism.

The first, most important reform, therefore, must be to relocate FEMA in the White House, reporting to either the vice-president or the national security advisor. The agency should be re-organised as an elite group, reducing its current staff to two hundred professionals drawn on a rotating basis (for, say, four-year interleafed tours) from various agencies involved in responding to crises. Half of this reduced staff would remain in the White House to do elite planning and crisis management; the other half would operate in the field, working with industry, local, state and Federal officials in the reconstructive phases of disaster.

The balance of FEMA's current staff of 2400 should be re-assigned to the constituent agencies responsible for various disaster functions: people involved in Federal insurance and in natural disaster relief should be re-assigned to the Department of Housing and Urban Development; those involved in liaison with fire departments should be moved to the Department of Commerce; Civil Defence planning professionals should be re-located to the Department of the Army; and so on.

This would leave an elite staff that would perform only essential functions, operating under the imprimatur of the White House with bureaucratic authority to perform essential tasks. Among other responsibilities, this re-constituted FEMA should be intimately familiar with the set of contingency plans to cope with disaster, knowing what the nodes of vulnerability are and understanding the resources needed to manage the crisis and the logistical difficulties involved in using them.

There is no question that information technology plays a particularly important role in improving both our emergency preparedness and our ability to cope effectively with crisis. The professional crisis manager must have a modernised 'situation room' from which to handle the various problems of resource allocations and command, control and communications during times of crisis. Modern digital equipment for more reliable communications, computer conferencing capabilities to allow multiple inputs without physical proximity and interactive use of computers for problem analysis are largely un-utilised tools in disaster management.

Develop a programme of command post and field training exercises. An effective crisis management structure requires joint planning to iron out jurisdictional issues between the agencies involved. For crisis planning and management these include most agencies in the Government in various ways, from the Internal Revenue Service (for tax relief) to the Defense Department (for relief functions and maintenance of civic order). Joint 'gaming' exercises and computer simulations, both at the FEMA command centre and in the field, are essential to developing smooth working routines in crisis conditions. These simulations should provide training and testing opportunities at many levels of threat.

Develop analytical models to explore the vulnerable and critical nodes of the technological infrastructure. Current efforts at system modelling are conducted in a number of agencies, including FEMA, the Department of

Energy and the Department of Transportation, among others. Current efforts, however, do not take into account the asynergies resulting from mutual interaction between systems. An electric power failure implies automatically the failure of many other systems. Indeed, any major failure would have ripple effects across the infrastructure spectrum. It is thus critical that we clearly understand the nature of these interactions. Without such understanding, we have no effective way to isolate the incident or contain the damage.

Re-think implications of infrastructure vulnerability for national defence capability. While the US has made some provisions for redundancy, it tends to prepare for the wrong crises. The estimated $15 billion worth of materials stored in the Critical Strategic Materials Stockpile might be useful if we had to re-fight the Second World War, but it is not tailored to deal with the range of crises we currently face.

FEMA should take immediate planning steps under the Defense Production Act to re-configure the stockpile with a view towards protecting ourselves from technological disruption. This might include, for example, stockpiling semi-finished and finished goods instead of raw materials or critical components, such as very large custom-made electrical transformers—the procurement of which takes several years and without which widespread economic and social disruptions would occur.

NOTE

1 An analogue to robotics, interactive computer systems offer a man–machine relationship that, properly constructed, may actually create an interactive learning process. Interactive computer systems combine human inputs with highly sophisticated processing centres to sort data, perform statistical analyses and set forth decision trees. By employing sophisticated models of warfare, environmental matters or flows of people and resources, for example, it becomes possible to process data in ways that maximise the information content of both the human and computational actors.

The Future Course of International Terrorism

B M Jenkins

International terrorism emerged as a problem in the late 1960s and despite increased governmental efforts to combat it, terrorism remains a serious problem in the 1980s. *Will terrorism continue?* Yes.

Political violence in one form or another has existed for centuries. Earlier waves of terrorist violence at the beginning of the century and again in the 1920s and 1930s were eclipsed only by world wars.

Terrorist activity accompanied post-war de-colonisation, which continued through the 1960s. Some of the colonial liberation movements, most notably the Algerian FLN, provided a model for later terrorist groups.

Modern theories of guerrilla war—which, of course, is not synonymous with terrorism but did contribute doctrinally to the use of terrorist tactics—developed during this same period, from the late 1940s to the early 1960s. The Second World War represented the culmination of State-organised violence. Since then, there has been a long-range trend towards the 'privatisation' of violence.

All of these facts argue for the continuation of some kind of political violence outside of conventional warfare, but will international terrorism persist in its present form? I think it will, for a number of reasons.

International terrorism as we know it today had its origins in the political circumstances that prevailed at the end of the 1960s: the frustration of the Palestinian Arabs after Israel's crushing defeat of the Arab armies in 1967; the failure of Latin America's guerrillas to duplicate the success of Castro's revolution in Cuba and their increasing attention to the struggle in the cities, which led to the increasing use of terrorist tactics; the war in Vietnam, which galvanised a generation of youth in America, Western Europe and Japan to protest in the streets, and resulted in a few at the extremist fringe carrying on the protest with guns and bombs.

But, contemporary international terrorism also reflects some recent technological developments which enhanced the use of terrorist tactics:

(a) Modern air travel provided unprecedented worldwide mobility.

(b) Radio, television and communications satellites provided almost instantaneous access to a worldwide audience.
(c) Weapons and explosives became increasingly available to anybody with the money to buy them.
(d) Modern society offered new vulnerabilities, in particular, airplanes.

Political circumstances may change but these technological developments have permanently altered the environment.

The first generation of modern terrorists has provided a model of behaviour. Terrorist tactics have become a routine way of focusing attention on a dispute, of bringing pressure on a government. New causes and new groups have emerged—Armenian terrorists, Sikh terrorists, issue-oriented groups opposed to nuclear power, abortion, technology, pollution, animal vivisection. There certainly will be no lack of causes.

There are economic incentives to use terrorist tactics. Kidnapping and extortion based upon threats of violence have become routine means of financing revolutionary movements.

A semi-permanent infrastructure of support has emerged. Beneath the terrorist groups, and supporting them often without regard to ideology or cause, is an ephemeral but resilient network of connections, alliances, safe houses, arms suppliers, and provisioners of counterfeit documents and other services. This network resembles the infrastructure that supports organised crime.

States have recognised in terrorism a useful weapon and are exploiting it for their own purposes. To a certain extent, international terrorism has become institutionalised.

And, increasingly, terrorism is expected and 'tolerated'.

All these reasons suggest that terrorism as we know it now is likely to persist as a mode of political expression for various groups, and as a means of warfare among states. It probably will continue, but at what level? *Will we see more or less terrorism?*

Measured by the number of incidents, terrorism has increased in volume over the last seventeen years. It is a ragged increase, with peaks and valleys, but the overall trajectory is clearly upward. There were, for example, four times as many incidents of international terrorism in 1984 as there were in 1972, the year of the Munich attack. Insofar as we can tell, the increase is genuine—it is not due merely to better reporting. The increase in the late 1970s and the early 1980s was quite dramatic. Terrorist activity, according to our figures, levelled off in 1984, but based upon the figures from the first five months of this year, it looks as if 1985 will surpass all previous years in the volume of activity.

Overall, the annual growth rate in the volume of terrorist activity has been in the area of twelve to fifteen per cent. If that rate of increase continues, we could see something between 800 and 900 incidents a year by the end of the decade, which is not inconceivable given the other factors I have mentioned.

There are several other factors which suggest the likelihood of continued growth:

1. The increase in the volume of terrorist activity has been matched by its geographic spread—a slow, long-term trend. The number of countries experiencing some sort of terrorist activity each year has gradually increased.
2. Although a handful of nations—the United States, France, Israel, the United Kingdom, and Turkey—remain the favourite targets of terrorists and account for approximately half of all the victims, the number of nations targeted by terrorists has also increased. Last year, we saw terrorist attacks directed against the nationals of 60 countries.
3. Although it is difficult to monitor with any precision the appearance and disappearance of the many hundreds of groups that claim credit for terrorist actions—some of them are only fictitious banners—the level of international terrorist activity no longer appears to depend on a handful of groups. Despite the virtual destruction of some terrorist groups and the decline in operations by others, the total volume of terrorist activity grows.
4. As international communications spread, as populations move or are pushed about—two features of the 1980s—I suspect we may see more local conflicts manifesting themselves at the international level through terrorist tactics.

Will terrorists escalate? Simply killing a lot of people has seldom been a terrorist objective. As I have said on numerous occasions, terrorists want a lot of people *watching*, not a lot of people *dead*. Terrorists operate on the principle of the minimum force necessary. They find it unnecessary to kill many, as long as killing a few suffices for their purposes.

Statistics bear this out. Only fifteen to twenty per cent of all terrorist incidents involve fatalities; and of those, two-thirds involve only one death. Less than one per cent of the thousands of terrorist incidents that have occurred in the last two decades involve 10 or more fatalities, and incidents of mass murder are truly rare.

Arbitrarily taking 100 deaths as the criterion, only a handful of incidents of this scale have occurred since the beginning of the century. Lowering the criterion to 50 deaths produces a dozen or more additional incidents. To get even a meaningful sample, the criterion has to be lowered to 25. This in itself suggests that it is either very hard to kill large numbers of persons, or it is very rarely tried.

Unfortunately, as we have seen in recent years, things are changing. Terrorist activity over the last 20 years has escalated in volume and in bloodshed. At the beginning of the 1970s, terrorists concentrated their attacks on property. In the 1980s, according to US government statistics, half of all terrorist attacks have been directed against people. The number of incidents with fatalities and multiple fatalities has increased. A more alarming trend in the 1980s has been the growing number of incidents of large-scale indiscriminate violence: huge car bombs detonated on city streets, bombs planted aboard trains and airliners, in airline terminals, railroad stations, and hotel lobbies, all calculated to kill in quantity. Ten major international terrorist incidents have resulted in a total of more than 1000 deaths in the last 15 years, but more than two-thirds of these have occurred in the last two years.

There are several explanations for the escalation:

1. Like soldiers in a war, terrorists who have been in the field for many years have been brutalised by the long struggle; killing becomes easier.
2. As terrorism has become more commonplace, the public has become to a degree desensitised. Terrorists can no longer obtain the same amount of publicity using the same tactics they used 10 years ago, and they may feel compelled to escalate their violence in order to keep public attention or to recover coercive power lost as governments have become more resistant to their demands.
3. Terrorists have become technically more proficient, enabling them to operate on a higher level of violence.
4. The composition of some terrorist groups has changed as the fainthearted who have no stomach for indiscriminate killing drop out or are shoved aside by more ruthless elements.
5. The religious aspect of current conflicts in the Middle East pushes towards mass murder. As we have seen throughout history, the presumed approval of God for the killing of pagans, heathens or infidels can permit acts of great destruction and self-destruction.
6. And finally, state sponsorship has provided terrorists with the resources and technical know-how to operate at a higher, more lethal level of violence.

At the same time, several factors work against escalation. There are self-imposed constraints, which I will address later, and there are technical ceilings. Without resorting to more exotic weapons, terrorists are approaching limits to their violence. The deadliest terrorist incidents—huge bombs detonated in buildings, the bomb presumably detonated aboard the Air India jumbo jet, a deliberately set fire in a crowded Teheran theatre—each of which produced several hundred deaths, roughly equal the worst accidental disasters: hotel fires, explosions, airline crashes. Death on a larger scale is seen only in the slaughter of great battles or in natural disasters like earthquakes and floods. The most plausible scenarios involving chemical or biological weapons in a contained environment—a hotel, a convention, a banquet—would produce deaths in the hundreds. To get above that, terrorists would have to possess large quantities of deadly substances and solve problems of dispersal, or they would have to resort to nuclear weapons. But this raises questions of technical capacity and intentions, which I will deal with momentarily.

A third limiting factor is security. Protective measures taken in the wake of the huge car and truck bombings in the Middle East are reducing the vulnerability of the most obvious targets to this type of attack. More stringent security measures may be applied on a permanent basis to prevent a repeat of the Air India bombing. Of course, terrorists can obviate these by shifting their sights to other, still vulnerable targets, but security measures force them to become even less discriminate.

On balance, it appears that incidents involving significant fatalities probably will become more common, with incidents resulting in hundreds of deaths remaining for the foreseeable future the outer limit of terrorist violence.

What changes will we see in terrorist tactics? I don't think we will see much tactical innovation. Terrorists operate with a fairly limited repertoire. Six basic tactics have accounted for ninety-five per cent of all terrorist incidents: bombings, assassinations, armed assaults, kidnappings, hijackings and barricade and hostage incidents. Looking at it another way, terrorists blow up things, kill people or seize hostages. Every terrorist incident is merely a variation on these three activities.

There have been few changes in tactics over the years. Indeed, the relative percentage of the various tactics has remained stable for a number of years, except for a decline in barricade and hostage incidents. Seizing embassies was a popular tactic in the 1970s. It declined as security measures made embassy takeovers more difficult, and as governments became more resistant to the demands of terrorists holding hostages and more willing to use force to end such episodes, thus increasing the hostage-takers' risk of death or capture.

This is indicative of the kind of innovation we are likely to see. Terrorists innovate in an incremental way to solve specific problems created by security measures. If one tactic ceases to work, they abandon it in favour of another one or merely shift their sights to another target. Since terrorists have virtually unlimited targets, they have little need for tactical innovation.

For example, how might terrorists respond to the new security measures aimed at protecting embassies against car bombs? Conceivably, they might resort to aerial suicide attacks, which are technically and physically more demanding. Or they might resort to standoff attacks, the traditional response to strong defences. Or they might simply detonate large bombs at other, still vulnerable targets. This brings me to the next question.

What changes will we see in terrorist targets? The greatest advantage that terrorists have and will continue to have is a virtually unlimited range of targets. Terrorists can attack anything, anywhere, anytime, limited only by operational considerations. Terrorists do not attack defended targets; they seek soft targets. If one target or set of targets is well protected, terrorists merely shift their sights to other targets that are not so well protected.

Over the years, the range of targets attacked by terrorists has expanded enormously. They now include embassies, airlines, airline terminals, ticket offices, trains, railroad stations, subways, buses, power lines, electrical transformers, mailboxes, mosques, hotels, restaurants, schools, libraries, churches, temples, newspapers, journalists, diplomats, businessmen, military officials, missionaries, priests, nuns, the Pope, men, women, adults and children.

There are a few things terrorists have not done. With the exception of a couple of minor episodes, they have not attacked nuclear reactors. For the most part, terrorists have not operated at sea. There have been no attempts to take over offshore platforms. Prior to the recent hijack of the *Achille Lauro*, there had been a number of bombs planted aboard ships or mines planted on their hulls. There had been several ship hijackings and attempted hijackings suggesting that the idea of taking over a large vessel had crossed the terrorists' mind. Whether the recent hijackings will inspire imitation or other actions in the maritime environment remains to be seen. Terrorists have blown up computers and set fires in data processing centres, but they have not tried to penetrate computers in any sophisticated fashion to disrupt or destroy data.

What will be the future targets of terrorism? Pretty much the same ones they prefer today:

(a) Representatives of governments and symbols of nations—notably, diplomats and airlines.
(b) Representatives of economic systems—corporations and corporate executives.
(c) Symbols of policies and presence—military officials.
(d) Political leaders (in the past fifteen years, terrorists have killed, tried to kill or have been reported on their way to kill Carrero Blanco, Aldo Moro, Lord Mountbatten, Anwar Sadat, the Pope, Ronald Reagan, Indira Gandhi and Margaret Thatcher).

Will terrorists attack high-technology targets such as refineries, offshore platforms or nuclear reactors? They already have, although in technically undemanding ways. Terrorists have blown up pylons and transformers, sometimes causing widespread blackouts. Guerrillas in Latin America have frequently attacked electrical power grids as a means of waging economic warfare against governments. Less concerned with economic warfare, urban terrorists have attacked electrical energy systems to get attention, to protest government or corporate policies or to indirectly disable nuclear power plants. Terrorist saboteurs have also attacked pipelines, oil tank farms and refineries, again with the objective of attracting publicity or protesting specific policies. These targets will remain attractive to some groups. However, apparently not all terrorists see value in attacking energy systems. There is no discernible trend towards more frequent attacks. Moreover, to seriously disrupt energy systems requires either a sustained campaign or larger scale action at certain critical nodes. Targets such as nuclear reactors or offshore platforms are technically demanding and require certain knowledge and skills.

Overall, attacks on high-technology targets must be anticipated as a feature of guerrilla warfare, but they are likely to remain only an occasional event in the realm of terrorism. State sponsorship, however, may alter targeting preferences.

Will we see a more sophisticated 'white collar' terrorism, that is, attacks on telecommunications, data processing systems or other targets where the terrorists' objective is not crude destruction but widespread disruption? Disruptive 'terrorism' of this type may be more appealing to armchair terrorists than to those who are active in today's terrorist groups. We may occasionally see terrorist incidents of this type, but probably not many. Such operations are technically demanding, and they produce no *immediate visible effects*. There is no drama. No lives hang in the balance. There is no bang, no blood. They do not satisfy the hostility of the terrorists.

What weapons will terrorists use in the future? Terrorists now use what is readily available in the gunshops and arsenals or on the black market. They seek powerful, rapid-fire, concealable weapons. They use commercial explosives, military stuff when they can get it. These suffice for current operations. Since terrorists generally do not attack defended targets, they have no need for more advanced arms. They now match the firepower of the authorities. They have no need for sophisticated weapons. Terrorists probably will use more sophisticated explosives, in larger quantities, although there is no great need to increase quantity. Terrorists in the Middle East have on several occasions built bombs containing more than a thousand pounds of explosives. Car bombs with two hundred or more pounds of explosives are not uncommon. Fifteen to twenty pounds of Frangex planted inside a large building will take its front off.

We will probably see increased use of standoff weapons—mortars, rocket launchers, rocket-propelled grenades—to overcome security measures. Finally, there remains a potential for the use of portable precision-guided munitions, which terrorists already have employed on several occasions.

Will terrorists resort to weapons of mass destruction? Will they employ chemical or biological warfare? Will terrorists go nuclear? Many people believe that nuclear terrorism of some sort is likely and may be inevitable. Reflecting the results of a poll conducted among 1346 opinion leaders in the United States, George Gallup Jr, in his recent book, *Forecast 2000*, wrote that 'while a war between the superpowers, the US and the Soviet Union, is a real cause for concern, [a disastrous nuclear incident involving terrorists in this country] seems to be the most imminent danger'.

I happen to think nuclear terrorism is neither imminent nor inevitable—if by nuclear terrorism we mean terrorists employing stolen nuclear weapons or a clandestinely fabricated nuclear explosive device to kill or threaten to kill large numbers of people. Lesser terrorist acts in the nuclear domain are possible—the seizure or attempted sabotage of a nuclear reactor, the dispersal of radioactive material, an alarming nuclear hoax that may cause panic.

The question of nuclear terrorism involves an assessment of both capabilities and motivations. It is conceivable that someone outside of government who is familiar with the principles of nuclear weapons could design an atomic bomb. However, the ease with which someone outside of government can build one, assuming he or she had somehow acquired the necessary nuclear material, has been greatly exaggerated. But let's for a moment say they can. Would they want to? Terrorism has certainly escalated, but it is still a quantum jump from the kinds of things that terrorists do today to the realms of nuclear destruction. Why would terrorists take that jump?

As I said before, simply killing as lot of people is not an objective of terrorism. Terrorists could do more now, yet they don't. Why? Beyond the technical constraints, there may be self-imposed constraints that derive from moral considerations or political calculations. Some terrorists may view indiscriminate violence as immoral. The terrorists' enemy is the government, not the people. Also, terrorists pretend to be governments, and wanton murder might imperil this image.

There are political considerations as well. Terrorists fear alienating their perceived constituents. They fear provoking public revulsion. They fear unleashing government crackdowns that their groups might not survive. Certainly, in the face of a nuclear threat, the rules that now limit police authorities in most democracies would change.

Terrorists must maintain group cohesion. Attitudes towards violence vary not only from group to group but also within a group. Inevitably, there would be disagreements over mass murder, which could expose the operation and the group to betrayal.

Obviously not all groups share the same operation code, and as we have seen, certain conditions or circumstances might erode these self-imposed constraints.

What about chemical or biological weapons, which are technically less demanding? Although there have been isolated incidents, neither chemical nor biological warfare seems to fit the pattern of most terrorist attacks. These attacks are generally intended to produce immediate dramatic effects.

Terrorist incidents have a finite quality—an assassination, a bombing, a handful of deaths, and that is the end of the episode.

Finally, the terrorists retain control. That is quite different from initiating an event that offers no explosion but instead produces indiscriminate deaths and lingering illness, an event over which the terrorists who set it in motion would have little control. For the near-term future—say, the next five years—we are more likely to see threats of chemical or biological contamination made by authentic lunatics or criminal extortionists. There will be moments of alarm. Over the long term—the next ten to fifteen years—my concern is that chemical weaponry will be acquired by unstable, dangerous countries like Iraq, Iran or Syria, and will increasingly be used in warfare. If chemical warfare becomes more commonplace, particularly in a region like the Middle East, we cannot dismiss its potential use by terrorists. The same is true of nuclear weapons, but probably over a longer time period.

Where will terrorism fit in the future of armed conflict? I think the current trend towards state sponsorship of terrorism will continue. As I have said before, limited conventional war, classic rural guerrilla and international terrorism will coexist and may appear simultaneously. The Iranian revolution and its spread to Lebanon, which has involved the effective use of international terrorism as an instrument of policy, may provide a model for other Third World revolutions and revolutionary states, just as the Cuban model inspired a generation of imitators in Latin America. If it does, we are in for a lot of trouble.

We also may see international terrorism emerge as a new kind of global guerrilla warfare in which terrorist groups sally forth from the political jungles of the Third World to carry out highly publicised hit-and-run attacks, militarily insignificant but politically of great consequence, avoiding confrontations where they might run into well-equipped, well-trained, specialised anti-terrorist forces.

Terrorists now avoid seizing embassies in Western capitals. They hijack airliners, keep them on the move to evade any rescue attempt, and retreat with their hostages to sanctuaries like Teheran or Beirut. Benefiting from the absence of government, as in Lebanon, or the presence of a hostile government, as in Iran, these sanctuaries lie beyond the reach of the world regime of treaty and law. If Iran defeats Iraq and the Gulf States fall, then the world's 'badlands' might be centred in the Middle East, a crescent reaching from the Mediterranean to Persia.

Finally, what developments will we see in security? We will see an increased diversion of resources to internal security.

The 'privatisation' of violence has been matched by the 'privatisation' of security, as illustrated by the tremendous growth of private sector security expenditures. In the United States, a total of $21 billion is now spent annually for security services and hardware (as compared with $14 billion spent annually on all police). The figure will reach $50 to $60 billion a year by the end of the century. Private security corporations will grow to meet the demand.

We will see the further proliferation of inner perimeters, the rings of security that now surround airline terminals, government buildings and, increasingly, corporate offices. From this last development, however, emerges a crude counterterrorist strategy. By protecting the most obvious symbols, terrorists' preferred targets, terrorists will be forced to become less discriminate in their attacks. That will create greater public outrage, which governments can exploit to obtain domestic support and international cooperation to crush the terrorists.

In sum:

(a) Terrorism certainly will persist.
(b) Probably it will increase.
(c) Large-scale incidents will become more common.
(d) At the same time, I don't think terrorism will enter the mind-boggling world of high technology or mass destruction.
(e) In terms of tactics, targets and weapons, terrorism will be for the foreseeable future a continuation of the past.
(f) States will continue to exploit terrorism—to use it for their own purposes. We may enter a protracted worldwide guerrilla war.
(g) And terrorists will create crises, forcing governments and corporations to divert more and more resources toward combating them.

Academics and Policy Makers

Jacques Léauté

The role of university research input to policy making in dealing with terrorism is, I believe, only one aspect of a broader problem, namely how universities and academics approach contemporary world problems. Consequently terrorism as a field of research is subject to rigorous scrutiny by wary policy makers dubious about its applicability. There is always an ancient Chinese tale to fit every Western contingency—even if we have to invent the tale. In this case one is reminded of two figures in an ancient tale! On the one hand there is the very old woman (who, of course, represents the university). She is very careful not to leave her garden, anxious to avoid any involvement with the outside world. By way of contrast there is the figure of the young man who is keen to be involved in action, dashing everywhere, rushing to make decisions, ambitious and fully immersed in the contemporary scene. These two figures, the university academic and the decision-maker, cannot come to an agreement because the gulf is a theoretical one. It is the difference between a theoretical approach and a practical approach. The result is that researchers are isolated although they are really trying to be useful to policy making decisions. It seems to me however that we are currently witnessing a change in the climate of opinion. There has been a general change of mind, mentality and attitude in the case of academics involved in research applied to social science and contemporary political problems.

It seems to me that we are confronted by two groups of changes. The first one is that, on the one hand, some of the policy makers, some of the police in charge of planning strategy against domestic terrorism, and some of the army headquarters staff involved in contingency planning to reply to acts of international terrorism, are now more ready to admit that some sort of research by academics may be of some use; and on the other hand academics themselves are perhaps beginning to re-think their approach to research and to its applicability to contemporary life.

One of the changes I detect is that both groups agree that thought and reflection cannot be isolated from action, even if there is a kind of division of labour. There is on the one hand the role of action, and on the other hand analysis of the issues, and evaluation of possible consequences, of various options.

Another change I detect is the progress from a merely analytical process, a step further to include research into achieving some sort of synthesis, some mixture or blend of analysis methods. Such a synthesis helps the decision makers by giving substance to the prescriptions suggested as applicable by academic research. A third change one may detect is the closer coordination of study of the past and study of the present in order to forecast the future. The roles of historians and politicians have tended to be restricted hitherto; with the historian relegated to the past, the politician confined to the present and utopian dreamers unleashed on the future. This demarcation of roles is tending to disappear. It is this blend of past, present and future—using experiences from the past and extrapolation of present decisions to forecast future trends—which gives university research its perspective and larger dimensions.

A fourth change is in sponsorship. Universities in the West (and you may be proud of the University of Aberdeen as being one of those belonging to the sphere of influence of Erasmus and the Humanism of the Northern Renaissance in Europe) in former times were characterised by the attitude of academics who felt that their dignity would not permit them to accept funding from private sources. Their belief was that they were obliged to maintain their independence in pursuing their own entirely personal work. To these early modern academics their independence, their objectivity crucially depended on their freedom from dependence on sponsorship from private budgets or private groups or rulers or governments. This earlier attitude is changing. In most countries of the Western world we now believe that it is possible to accept sponsorship while still retaining independence. We do not see these as antagonistic forces. This belief enables academics to carry out more practical research. Another major change for researchers is in their way of recording facts and collecting data. The use of the computer in social science has, I feel, led to a growth of objectivity and a corresponding diminution of subjectivity in the methodology and postulates of academic research. Formerly when the researcher was faced with a number of varying parameters he felt forced to select in advance three or four parameters as being the most important ones. This involved the subjective element of the researcher's decision to limit the selection to the small number of parameters or factors he felt confident he could manipulate and deal with using classical statistical methods. Due to computers, this restriction is no longer pressing.

Let me exemplify this need to be selective. If I were to limit my study to the audience I am addressing, you are all of you so different in so many areas that I would be forced to limit my study. Being a Frenchman I might try to limit my study to the feminine members of the audience, and try to classify them in order to construct a typology of the feminine presence at a seminar or international conference on terrorism. Let us suppose I were to take firstly colour of eyes and colour of hair as two parameters. If I wished to add colour of skin as a third parameter and examine whether there is a link between the colour of hair, the colour of eyes and the colour of the skin, then I would be forced to add a third dimension. (This might be done by using plastic boxes on the floor, for example.) However, if I wished to add a fourth parameter to our comparison, I would be unable to proceed. However, computers allow us to conduct research in more than three dimensions. One can include as many elements as one wishes. Computers allow us to include any number of parameters. We are not forced to make the subjective pre-selection we mentioned. It is possible through what we call an 'end dimension system' to carry out an exhaustive process and be sure that there is no elimination of any of the connections. Through computers we can be sure that none of any possibilities is excluded. One can also be absolutely sure that any other research using the same approach will reach the same conclusion. Electronic data gathering has opened up hitherto unsuspected distinctions in differentiating phenomena.

Computerisation has brought researchers and policy makers closer together. In the special case of research in the field of terrorism, there are a few caveats. There is currently a mutation in terrorism itself and research has to adapt quickly to be accurate in its comprehensive understanding of the new aspect of terrorism. Terrorism research has to adapt to study the new symptoms of what may be a different social disease and research and must find the new methods to cope with the changes in terrorism. Changes in the terrorists and changes in the victims are observable. The classical form of contemporary terrorism was not very different from the earlier nihilistic or anarchist terrorism of the nineteenth century. This 'classical' terrorism contained a blend of two things—the element of crime, murder, possibly theft and other acts punishable under the criminal laws of the country, and the second element the 'communication meaning'. The murders or bombings expressed a message from the terrorist to the rest of the country, or even the rest of the world. Terrorist acts were meaningful acts of violence expressing the strongly felt will of a group of people who could not express their will through normal channels of democracy. This is claimed to be the meaning of Corsican terrorism and may still be claimed for Irish terrorism and others too. Some traditional terrorism was mostly domestic and not transnational or international.

The new type of terrorism has escalated into warfare. We are witnessing a change from low level conflict into a new form of war between countries—or even between ideological blocs involving all mankind. This new dimension to terrorism can be demonstrated by examining changes in the triangle characteristics of hostage-taking. Hostage-taking in the field of normal crime is a bilateral relationship, as between thief and victim, murderer and victim. In the field of terrorism, hostage-taking has always been, not a bilateral, but a triangular relationship.

There has also been a change in the pattern of terrorist targeting. When, for example, the First World War was started by an act of terrorism, in that case the victim was an individual who had been selected and was elevated into a symbol. Nowadays the terrorist target is now as likely to be a collective one—a number of victims—not an individual. The indiscriminate random uncaring targeting of whoever happens to be in a particular train, plane, or street in Paris, at the time of the attack. This moves terrorism closer to warfare: and closer to genocide. An attack on a French Jewish restaurant, can be expected to kill Jews. An attack on a TWA plane can be expected to kill Americans. The triangular relationship consists of the terrorist making demands to a second party through hostage-taking and murder of innocent people. This is blackmail.

Future academic research must tackle this new concept of the move from internal domestic terrorism to transnational warfare. Research must also incorporate the dimension of the victims and take into account changes in this regard as well. Such terrorist attacks are trying to eliminate or stop the power of ethnic groups, or of national groups. They use the phraseology of guerrilla warfare, and military imagery. The new reactions conjured up in potential victims of this recent terrorism are general feelings of insecurity. We have witnessed the reluctance of American tourists to visit Europe. Incidentally, similar feelings of fear mirror the increase in criminal mugging which has led to the reluctance of older people to go out at night in cities of Europe. This raises more general philosophical questions about the goals of modern society. Modern society which had been ridding mankind of what we regarded as primitive medieval fears is being plunged back into these fears by the regression caused by this new aspect of collective targeting by terrorism. Such fear of course can lead to a reaction of revenge. We all know the close connection between fear and aggression. The Libyan/American confrontation has highlighted this interaction clearly. It exemplifies hope of attaining deterrence through retaliation. There is the danger that we are witnessing a move away from judicial reaction to events, a move from law and justice to warfare as a reaction. This is a move from justice to force as a guiding principle. Violence is justified as a legitimate way of avoiding escalation. It is debatable whether it can achieve this aim. Even if Libya is deterred, will those in Lebanon or Iran be deterred by the example of what happened in Tripoli?

We appear to be in a new field of war. Academics may choose to remain aloof. However, it is my contention that there is need for cooperation between policy makers, decision makers and academics—in particular, in two ways. Firstly, cooperation can take the form of research contracts with academics working in their universities on projects that may be useful to the government, to the defence forces etc. Secondly, however, cooperation can take the form of the academics belonging to a joint team of advisers and decision makers. The academic adviser might be helpful at various levels right to the top. This will vary from country to country. For example, where the system has a commissioner of police, the adviser might appropriately provide input at the level of the Chief Constable. In a centralised police system, the input would be more appropriate at ministerial level. The academic adviser should not be based in this ivory tower making occasional descents to impart wisdom to the decision maker. An academic should be bright and intelligent naturally, but I advise him not to be too sophisticated. His language should not be too esoteric. He has to give up the specialised language of his own discipline. He must translate the jargon of sociology, criminology, philosophy or other speciality into common parlance comprehensible to the decision maker. To achieve his aim of persuasion the academic adviser has to be prepared to phrase his advice clearly even if the nuances of definitions and concepts are not as subtle as in academic discourse.

The academic has to be prepared to make a clear recommendation. Academics habitually prefer to balance pros and cons, to examine all ramifications, complexities and implications, and to try to foresee all contingencies. Too many academic advisers have proved useless to decision makers because of their inability to present any clear conclusions. They require, they can always argue, more time to do further research. What is required is an adviser who is fair but clear in recommending choices. At the same time the adviser has to be modest, and prepared to remain in the background. He will have the quiet satisfaction of having contributed to the final decision made publicly by others.

The adviser nowadays is required to be equipped to cope with thorny ethical problems such as the implications for innocent victims of their decisions. The academic adviser should have deep ethical values. Academics are marked by an ethos which requires them to be not merely expert specialists but members of a university, a body in which ethical values are still guiding principles. One should not be too pompous about this, but the adviser can be faced by a real problem for his conscience of acceptable compromise and unwillingness to be tarnished by implication in practical affairs.

My final, not so serious advice for the adviser would be for the need to smile. The adviser's smile is important. It must not be a half smile. It must not be a reluctant smile. If you join the game, you must show that you believe in it, and smile without any reservation.

Contributors

James ADAMS is Assistant Editor and Defence Correspondent with *The Sunday Times*.

Nicholas O BERRY is Professor and Chair, Ursinus College, Pennsylvania.

Frederick Macadie CLIFFORD-VAUGHAN lectures in Political and Strategic Studies at the University of Natal, Durban, South Africa.

Bonnie CORDES is a Staff member of the Security and Subnational Conflict Research Program at the Rand Corporation, Santa Monica, California.

Ronald D CRELINSTEN is Assistant Professor in the Department of Criminology at the University of Ottawa, Canada.

Richard DRAKE is Associate Professor of History at the Univeristy of Montana.

Rachel EHRENFELD, PhD, is a Visiting Scholar at the Institute of War and Peace Studies at Columbia University.

Edith Elisabeth FLYNN is Professor of Criminal Justice, Northeastern University, Boston.

Marsha FREY is Professor of History, Kansas State University, Manhattan, Kansas.

Linda FREY is Professor of History at the University of Montana, Missoula, Montana.

Steven C GREER is lecturer in the Faculty of Law, University of Bristol.

Chris HATCHER, PhD, is at the University of California Langley Porter Institute, San Francisco.

Bruce HOFFMAN, PhD, is a staff member of the Security and Sub National Conflict Research Program at the Rand Corporation.

Dr Hans Josef HORCHEM, former head of the Office for the Protection of the Constitution in Hamburg, is currently an Industrial Consultant and Special Adviser to the Basque Government on police affairs.

Brian JENKINS Director of Rand Corporation's Research Program on Subnational Conflict and Political Violence. Prolific writer on various aspects of terrorism. Editor-in-chief of *TVI Report*, Quarterly Journal. Associate editor of journals: *Terrorism*, *Conflict*.

Michael KAHAN is Associate Professor of Political Science, Brooklyn College,

CUNY, and a Principal of Multinational Strategies, Inc, NY, research firm specialising in risk analysis.

Robert H KUPPERMAN is Senior Adviser at the Center for Strategic and International Studies, Georgetown University, Washington, DC.

Jacques LÉAUTÉ, former Directeur de l'Institut de Criminologie de Paris, Université d'Economie et de Sciences Sociales de Paris, currently in legal practice.

Richard C MARTIN Associate Professor, Chairman, Department of Religious Studies, Arizona State University, Tempe, Arizona.

Dr Michael McKINLEY lectures in International Relations and Strategic Studies, Department of Politics, University of Western Australia.

Dennis PLUCHINSKY is West European Analyst in the Threat Analysis Division, Bureau of Diplomatic Security in the US Department of State.

Jerrold M POST, MD, is Director, Political and Military Psychology, Defense Systems, Inc, and Associate Clinical Professor of Psychiatry and Behavioral Sciences, George Washington University.

David C RAPOPORT is Professor of Political Science at the University of California, Los Angeles.

Fernando REINARES, previously at the University of Madrid, currently holds a research position in the Department of Political and Social Sciences at the European University Institute, Florence.

Dr Ken G ROBERTSON lectures on Sociology and in the Graduate School of European and International Studies, University of Reading.

Todd SANDLER is Professor of Economics, University of South Carolina Co-authors of the contribution: Scott Atkinson and John Tschirhart (University of Wyoming); Jon Cauley and Eric Ik Soon Im (University of Hawaii-Hilo); John Scott (University of South Carolina).

Marco SASSOLI is a member of the Legal Division of the International Committee of the Red Cross in Geneva.

Dr D Th SCHILLER is a consultant for Rand, various security firms and police departments, and contributing editor to *TVI Report*.

Khachig TOLOLYAN is at Wesleyan University, Middletown, Connecticut.

Dr Robert W TAYLOR is with the Department of Criminal Justice, Northern Arizona University, Flagstaff, Arizona.

Dr Richard THACKRAH is at the Police Staff College, Bramshill, Hampshire.

Charles TOWNSHEND is Professor of Modern History at the University of Keele.

Dr Maurice A J TUGWELL Director of the Centre for Conflict Studies, University of New Brunswick (1980–1986).

Harry E VANDEN is at the Department of Political Science, Univeristy of South Florida, Tampa, Florida.

Bruce W WARNER is a Canadian doctoral candidate, studying in the Department of Politics, University of Exeter.

Paul WILKINSON is Professor of International Relations and Head of Department of Politics and International Relations, University of Aberdeen.

Selected English Language Bibliography

BOOKS

Adams, James, *The Financing of Terror* (London: New English Library, 1986)
Adeniran, Tunde, and Alexander, Yonah (eds) *International Violence* (New York: Praeger, 1983)
Alexander, Yonah (ed) *International Terrorism: National, Regional, and Global Perspectives*. 2nd edn (New York: Praeger, 1980)
Alexander, Yonah, and Finger, Seymour Maxwell (eds) *Terrorism: Interdisciplinary Perspectives* (New York: John Jay and McGraw-Hill, 1977)
Alexander, Yonah; Carlton, David; and Wilkinson, Paul (eds) *Terrorism: Theory and Practice* (Boulder: Westview Press, 1979)
Alexander, Yonah, and Friedlander, Robert A, *Self-Determination: National, Regional and Global Perspectives* (Boulder: Westview Press, 1980)
Alexander, Yonah, and Ebinger, Charles K (eds) *Political Terrorism and Energy: The Threat and Response* (New York: Praeger, 1982)
Alexander, Yonah, and Meyers, Kenneth (eds) *Terrorism in Europe* (London: Croom Helm, 1982)
Alexander, Yonah, and O'Day, Alan (eds) *Terrorism in Ireland* (London: Croom Helm, 1984)
Andrew, Christopher, and Dilks, David (eds) *The Missing Dimension: Governments and Intelligence Communities in the Twentieth Century* (London: Macmillan, 1984)
Andrew, Christopher, *Secret Services* (London: Heineman, 1985)
Antonius, George, *The Arab Awakening* (Beirut: Khayat, 1955)
Arendt, Hannah, *On Revolution* (New York: Viking Press, 1963)
—— *On Violence* (New York: Harcourt Brace Jovanovich, 1969)
—— *The Origins of Totalitarianism* (New York: Harcourt Brace Jovanovich, 1966)
Arey, James A, *The Sky Pirates* (New York: Scribner's Sons, 1972)
Ariel, Dan, *Explosion!* (Tel Aviv: Olive Books, 1972)
Aron, Raymond, *History and the Dialectic of Violence*: An Analysis of Sartre's 'Critique de la Raison Dialectique.' Translated by Garry Cooper (London: Blackwell, 1975)
Aron, Raymond, *Peace and War* (London: Weidenfeld and Nicolson, 1966)
Asprey, Robert B, *War in the Shadows*. 2 vols (New York: Doubleday and Co Inc, 1975)
Aston, Clive C, *A Contemporary Crisis: Political Hostage-Taking and the Experience of Western Europe* (London: Greenwood Press, 1982)

Avineri, Shlomo (ed) *Israel and the Palestinians: Reflections on the Clash of Two National Movements* (New York: St Martin's, 1971)
Avner [pseud.], *Memoirs of an Assassin* (New York: Yoseloff, 1959)
Avrich, Paul, *The Russian Anarchists* (Princeton, NJ: Princeton University Press, 1967)
Avriel, Ehud, *Open the Gates! The Dramatic Personal Story of 'Illegal' Immigration to Israel* (London: Weidenfeld & Nicolson, 1975)
Azad, Abul Kalam, *India Wins Freedom* (Calcutta: Orient Longmans, 1959)

Bagts, Alfred, *A History of Militarism, Civilian and Military* (London: Hollis and Carter, 1959)
Bain, Chester A, *Vietnam: The Roots of Conflict* (Englewood Cliffs, NJ: Prentice-Hall, 1967)
Bamford, James, *The Puzzle Palace* (New York: Penguin, 1983)
Bander, Edward J (ed) *Turmoil on the Campus* (New York: HW Wilson, 1970)
Bandura, Albert, *Aggression: A Social Learning Analysis* (Englewood Cliffs, NJ: Prentice-Hall, 1973)
Barber, Noel, *The War of the Running Dogs* (New York: Weybright and Talley, 1977)
Barnett, Correlli, *The Collapse of British Power* (New York: William Morrow & Co, 1972)
Barron, John, *KGB: The Secret Work of Soviet Secret Agents* (New York: Reader's Digest Press, 1974)
Barzilay, David, *The British Army in Ulster*. 3 vols (Belfast: Century Services Ltd, 1973, 1977, 1978)
Bassiouni, MC (ed) *International Terrorism and Political Crimes* (Springfield, Ill: Charles C Thomas, 1975)
—— *The Law of Dissent and Riots* (Springfield, Ill: Charles C Thomas, 1971)
Bassiouni, MC and Nanda, VP, *A Treatise on International Criminal Law, Jurisdiction, and Cooperation* (Springfield, Ill: Charles C Thomas, 1973)
Bauer, Yehuda, *From Diplomacy to Resistance: A History of Jewish Palestine, 1939–1945* (Philadelphia: Jewish Publication Society, 1970)
Baumann, Carol Edler, *The Diplomatic Kidnappings: A Revolutionary Tactic of Urban Terrorism* (The Hague: Martinius Nijhoff, 1973)
Bayo, Alberto, *150 Questions to a Guerrilla*. Translated by RI Madigan and Angel de Lumus Medina (Montgomery, Ala: Air University, nd)
Becker, Jillian, *Hitler's Children: The Story of the Baader–Meinhof Gang* (London: Michael Joseph, 1977: Granada Publishing, 1978)
Beckwith, Colonel, Charlier A, USA (Ret) and Knox, Donald, *Delta Force* (Glasgow: William Collins Sons & Co, 1985)
Begin, Menachem, *The Revolt* (New York: Henry Schuman, 1951)
Bell, J Bowyer, *On Revolt: Strategies of National Liberation* (Cambridge, Mass: Harvard University Press, 1976)
—— *The Secret Army: A History of the IRA* (Cambridge, Mass: MIT Press, 1974)
—— *The Secret Army: The IRA 1916–1979* (Dublin Academy Press rev. edn 1979: Cambridge, Mass: MIT Press, 1980)
—— *Terror Out of Zion: Irgun, Lehi, and the Palestine Underground, 1929–1949* (New York: St Martin's 1976)
—— *Transnational Terror* (Washington, DC: American Enterprise Institute for Public Policy Research, 1975)
—— *A Time of Terror: How Democratic Societies Respond to Revolutionary Violence* (New York: Basic Books, Inc, 1978)

Ben-Dak, Joseph D (ed) *The Future of Collective Violence: Societal and International Perspectives* (New York: Humanities, 1974)
Bennett, George, *The Concepts of Empire: Burke to Attlee, 1774–1947* (New York: Barnes & Noble Books, 1962)
Bennett, Richard Lawrence, *The Black and Tans* (Boston: Houghton Mifflin Co, 1959)
Benson, Mary, *South Africa: The Struggle for a Birthright* (London: Penguin, 1966)
Beqiraj, Mehmet, *Peasantry in Revolution* (Ithaca: Center for International Studies, Cornell University, 1966)
Beres, Louis Rene, *Terrorism and Global Security: The Nuclear Threat* (Boulder: Westview Press, 1979)
Berger, Peter L, and Richard J Heuhaus, *Movement and Revolution* (Garden City, NY: Doubleday & Co, 1970)
Berkman, Alexander, *Now and After: The ABC of Communist Anarchism* (New York: Vanguard Press, 1929)
Berkowitz, BJ, et al, *Superviolence: The Civil Threat of Mass Destruction Weapons* (Santa Barbara, Calif: Ascon Corporation, 1972)
Berkowitz, Leonard, *A Social Psychological Analysis* (New York: McGraw-Hill Book Co, 1962)
Bern, Major H von Dach, *Total Resistance* (Boulder, Colo: Panther, 1965)
Bettelheim, Bruno, *The Informed Heart* (New York: Free Press, 1960)
Bienen, Henry, *Violence and Social Change* (Chicago: University of Chicago Press, 1968)
Bingham, Jonathan B, and Alfred M Bingham, *Violence and Democracy* (New York: World, 1971)
Black, Cyril E, and Thompson P Thornton, *Communism and Revolution* (Princeton: Princeton University Press, 1964)
Blanchard, WH, *Rousseau and the Spirit of Revolt* (Ann Arbor: University of Michigan Press, 1967)
Blaufard, Douglas S, *The Counterinsurgency Era: US doctrine and performance* (London: The Free Press, Collier-Macmillan, 1977)
Bloomfield, Louis M, and Gerald F Fitzgerald, *Crimes Against Internationally Protected Persons: Prevention and Punishment* (New York: Praeger Publishers, 1975)
Bocca, Geoffrey, *The Secret Army* (Englewood Cliffs, NJ: Prentice-Hall 1968)
Boesel, David, and Peter H Rossi (eds) *Cities Under Siege: An Anatomy of the Ghetto Riots, 1964–1968* (New York: Basic Books, 1971)
Bond, James E, *The Rules of Riot* (New Jersey: Princeton University Press, 1974)
Bonner, David, *Emergency Powers in Peacetime* (London: Sweet & Maxwell, 1985)
Borisov, J, *Palestine Underground: The Story of Jewish Resistance* (New York: Judea Publishing, 1947)
Boston, Guy D, Marvin Marcus, and Robert J Wheaton, *Terrorism: A Selected Bibliography* (Washington, DC: National Criminal Reference Service, March 1976)
Boulton, David, *The Ulster Volunteer Force, 1966–1973* (Dublin: Gill and McMillan, 1973)
Bowden, Tom, *The Breakdown of Public Security* (London: Sage Publications, 1977)
—— *Beyond the Limits of the Law* (Harmondsworth: Penguin Books, 1978)
Bowen, D, and Masotti, LH, *Civil Violence: A Theoretical Overview* (Cleveland, Ohio: Case Western Reserve Civil Violence Research Center, 1968)
Boyle, Kevin, Hadden, Tom, and Hillyard, Paddy, *Ten Years on in Northern Ireland* (London: Cobden Trust, 1980)
Brennan, Ray, *Castro, Cuba, and Justice* (Garden City, NY: Doubleday & Co, 1959)

Brinton, Crane, *The Anatomy of a Revolution* (Englewood Cliffs, NJ: Prentice-Hall, 1965)
Brock, George, Lustig, R, Marks, L, Parker, R, and Seale, P, with McConville, M, *Siege* (London: Macmillan, 1980)
Brodie, FG, *Bombs and Bombings* (Springfield, Ill: Charles C Thomas, 1972)
Broehl, Wayne G, *The Molly Maguires* (Cambridge: Harvard University Press, 1964)
Brogan, Dennis W, *The Price of Revolution* (New York: Harper & Row, 1951)
Brown, Richard M, *Strain of Violence: Historical Studies of American Violence and Vigilantism* (London: Oxford University Press, 1975)
Browne, Jeffrey T, *International Terrorism: The American Response* School of International Service (Washington, DC: The American University, December 1973)
Browne, Malcolm W, *The New Face of War* (Indianapolis: Bobbs-Merrill Co, 1965)
Bunting, Brian, *The Rise of the South African Reich* (London: Penguin, 1964)
Burckhardt, Jacob, *Force and Freedom* (New York: Random House, 1943)
Burns, Alan, *In Defence of Colonies* (London: Allen and Unwin, 1957)
Burton, Anthony M, *Urban Terrorism* (New York: Macmillan, 1975; Free Press, 1975)
Burton, Anthony, *Revolutionary Violence* (New York: Crane, Russak & Co, 1978)
Burton, Frank, *The Politics of Legitimacy* (London: Routledge & Kegan Paul, 1978)

Campbell, Colin, *Governments Under Stress* (Toronto: University of Toronto Press, 1983)
Camus, Albert, *Neither Victims nor Executioners* (Chicago: World Without War, 1968)
Carlton, David, and Carlo Schaerf (eds) *International Terrorism and World Security* (New York: John Wiley & Sons, 1975; London: Croom Helm, 1975)
—— *Contemporary Terror* (London: The Macmillan Press, 1981)
Carr, EH, *Studies in Revolution* (New York: Grosset & Dunlap, 1964)
Carr, Gordon, *The Angry Brigade: A History of Britain's First Urban Guerrilla Group* (London: Housmans, 1970)
Carter, April, David Haggett, and Adam Roberts, *Non-Violent Action: A Selected Bibliography* (London: Housmans, 1970)
Chailand, Gerard, *The Palestinian Resistance* (Baltimore, Md: & London: Penguin, 1972)
Chakhotin, S, *The Rape of the Masses* (New York: Haskell, 1971)
Chalmers, DM, *Hooded Americanism* (New York: Quadrangle, 1968)
Chambard, Claude, *The Maquis: A History of the French Resistance Movement* (Indianapolis: Bobbs-Merrill Co, 1976)
Chorley, Katherine, *Armies and the Art of Revolution* (London: Faber & Faber, 1943)
Choucri, Nazli, and Robert C North, *Nations in Conflict* (San Francisco: WH Freeman and Co, 1945)
Christopher, Warren, *American Hostages in Iran: The Conduct of a Crisis* (New Haven: Yale University Press, 1985)
Clark, Dennis J, *Irish Blood: Northern Ireland and the American Conscience* (Fort Washington, NY: Kennikat, 1977)
Clark, Michael K, *Algeria in Turmoil* (New York: Praeger Publishers, 1959)
Cline, Ray S, and Alexander, Yonah, *Terrorism: The Soviet Connection* (New York: Crane, Russak, 1984)
Clutterbuck, Richard, *Living With Terrorism* (London: Faber & Faber, 1975)

Clutterbuck, Richard, *Protest and The Urban Guerrilla* (London: Cassell, 1973)
—— *The Long, Long War* (London: Cassell, 1966)
—— *Kidnap and Ransom: The Response* (London: Faber & Faber, 1978)
Clyne, Peter, *An Anatomy of Skyjacking* (London: Abelard-Schuman, 1973)
Coblentz, SA, *The Militant Dissenters* (South Brunswick, NJ: Barner, 1976)
Cohen, Geula, *Women of Violence: Memoirs of a Young Terrorist, 1943–1948* (London: Hart-Davis, 1966)
Collier, Richard, *The Great Indian Mutiny* (New York: EP Dutton & Co, 1964)
Conant, R, *The Prospects for Revolution: A Study of Riots, Civil Disobedience and Insurrection in Contemporary America* (New York: Harper's Magazine Press, 1971)
Confino, Michael (ed) *Daughter of a Revolutionary* (London: Alcove Press, 1974)
Connery, Robert H, ed., *Urban Riots: Violence and Social Change* (New York: Random House, 1969)
Conquest, Robert, *The Great Terror* (New York: Macmillan, 1968)
Coogan, Tim Patrick, *The IRA* (New York: Praeger Publishers, 1970; London: Pall Mall Press, 1970; rev edn London: Fontana, 1980)
Cooley, John K, *Green March, Black September: The Story of Palestinian Arabs* (London: Frank Cass, 1973)
Crelinsten, Ronald D, Danielle Laberge-Altmejd, and Denis Szabo, *Terrorism and Criminal Justice* (Lexington, Mass: Lexington Books, 1978)
Crelinsten, Ronald, Szabo, Denis (eds) *Hostage-taking* (Lexington: Lexington Books, 1978)
Crenshaw, Martha, *Revolutionary Terrorism* (Stanford: Hoover Institution Publication, 1978)
—— *Terrorism, Legitimacy, and Power* (Middletown: Wesleyan University Press, 1983)
Critchley, TA, *The Conquest of Violence* (London: Constable, 1970)
Crosby, John, *An Affair of Strangers* (Briarcliff Manor, NY: Stein & Day, 1975)
Cross, Colin, *The Fall of the Empire* (New York: Coward, McCann & Geoghenan, 1969)
Cross, James Eliot, *Conflict in the Shadows* (New York: Doubleday & Co, 1963)
Crotty, William J (ed) *Assassinations and the Political Order* (New York: Harper & Row, 1971)
Crozier, Brian, *The Rebels: A Study of Post-War Insurrections* (London: Chatto & Windus, 1960)
—— *South-East Asia in Turmoil* (Baltimore, Md: Penguin, 1965)
—— *A Theory of Conflict* (London: Hamish Hamilton, 1974)
Curtis, Lynn, A, *Violence, Race and Culture* (Lexington, Mass: Lexington Books, 1975)
Curtis, Michael, *et al.* (eds) *The Palestinians: People, History, Politics* (Edison, NJ: Transaction Books, 1975)

Da Cuncha, Eueides, *Rebellion in the Backlands* (Chicago: University of Chicago Press, 1944)
Daigon, Arthur, *Violence—USA* (New York: Bantam, 1975)
Dallin, Alexander, and George W Breslauer, *Political Terror in Communist Systems* (Stanford: Stanford University Press, 1970)
Davies, James C, (ed) *When Men revolt and Why* (New York: Free Press, 1971)
Davis, Angela, *An Autobiography* (New York: Random House, 1974)
Davis, M, *Jews Fight Too!* (New York: Jordan, 1945)
Davison, Phillips W, *International Political Communication* (New York: Praeger Publishers, 1985)

Debray, Régis, *Ché's Guerrilla War* (London: Penguin, 1975)
—— *Revolution on the Revolution* (New York: Monthly Review Press, 1967)
Dekel, Ephraim (Krasner), *Shai: Historical Exploits of Haganah Intelligence* (New York: Yoseloff, 1959)
Des Pres, Terrence, *An Anatomy of Life in the Death Camps* (New York: Oxford University Press, 1976)
Deutsch, Richard, and Magowan, Vivien, *Northern Ireland Chronology of Events*. 3 vols (Belfast: Blackstaff Press, 1973, 1974, 1975)
de Vault, Carole, with Johnston, William, *The Informer* (Toronto: Fleet Books, 1982)
Dewitt, Howard A, *Images of Ethnic and Radical Violence in California Politics, 1917–1930: A Survey* (San Francisco: R and E Research Associates, 1975)
Dillon, Martin, and Dennis Lehane, *Political Murder in Northern Ireland* (Baltimore, Md: Penguin, 1974)
Dionisopoulog, PA, *Rebellion, Racism and Representation* (DeKalb, Ill: Northern Illinois University Press, 1970)
Dixon, CA, and D Heilbrunn, *Communist Guerrilla Warfare* (New York: Praeger Publishers, 1954)
Dobson, Christopher, *Black September: Its Short, Violent History* (New York: Macmillan, 1974)
Dobson, Christopher, and Roland Payne, *The Carlos Complex* (London: Hodder & Stoughton, 1977)
—— *The Terrorists* (New York: Facts on File, 1979)
—— *Terror, The West Fights Back* (London: Macmillan, 1982)
—— *War Without End* (London: Harrap Ltd, 1986)
Donovan, Robert J, *The Assassins* (New York: Harper & Row, 1952)
Dortzbach, Karl and Debbie, *Kidnapped* (New York: Harper & Row, 1975)
Douglas, William O, *Points of Rebellion* (New York: Vintage, 1970)
Downton, JV, *Rebel Leadership* (New York: Vintage, 1970)
Draper, Theodore, *Castro's Revolution: Myths and Realities* (New York: Praeger Publishers, 1962)
Drapkin, Israel, and Emilio Viano (eds) *Victimology: A New Focus*: Pt. 2: 'Mass Violence and Genocide.' (Lexington, Mass: Lexington Books, DC Heath, 1975)
Dror, Yehezkel, *Crazy States: A Counterconventional Strategic Problem* (Tel Aviv: Department of Defense, 1973)
Duff, Ernest A, and John F McCamant, *Violence and Repression in Latin America: A Quantitative and Historical Analysis* (New York: Macmillan, 1976)
Duncan, Patrick, *South Africa's Rule of Violence* (London: Methuen, 1964)

Eayrs, James, *Diplomacy and Its Discontents* (Toronto: University of Toronto Press, 1971)
Eckstein, Harry, *Internal War* (Westport: Greenwood Press, 1964)
Eckstein, Harry (ed) *Internal War* (New York: Free Press, 1964)
Edwardes, Michael, *Red Years: The Indian Rebellion of 1957* (London: Hamish Hamilton, 1973)
Edwards, Lyford P, *The Natural History of Revolution* (New York: Free Press, 1963)
Eggers, William, *Terrorism: The Slaughter of Innocents* (Chatsworth, Calif: Sage Publications, 1971)
Einaudi, Luigi R (ed) *Beyond Cuba: Latin America Takes Charge of its Future* (New York: Crane, Russak, 1974)
Eliff, John T, *Crime, Dissent and the Attorney General* (Beverly Hills, Calif: Sage Publications, 1971)

Elliot-Bateman, Michael, Ellis, John, and Bowden, Tom (eds) *Revolt To Revolution* (Manchester: Manchester University Press, 1974)
Elliott, John D, and Gibson, Leslie K (eds) *Contemporary Terrorism* (Gaithersburg: International Association of Chiefs of Police, 1978)
Ellis, Albert, and John Gulls, *Murder and Assassination* (New York: Lyle Stuart, 1971)
El-Rayyes, Riad N, and Dunia Nahas (eds) *Guerrillas for Palestine: A Study of the Palestinian Commando Organization* (Beirut: An-Nahar Press Services, 1974)
Emerson, Rupert, *From Empire to Nation: The Rise to Self-Assertion of Asian and African Peoples* (Cambridge, Mass: Harvard University Press, 1960)
Evans, AE, and Murphy, JF (eds), *Legal Aspects of International Terrorism* (Lexington: Heath, 1978)
Evans, Ernest, *Calling a Truce to Terror* (Westport: Greenwood Press, 1979)
Evelegh, Robin, *Peace-keeping in a Democratic Society* (London: C Hurst & Co, 1978)

Fairbairn, Geoffrey, *Revolutionary Warfare and Communist Strategy* (London: Faber & Faber, 1958)
—— *Revolutionary Guerrilla Warfare* (Harmondsworth: Penguin, 1974)
Fall, Bernard B, *The Two Viet Nams* 2nd rev ed (New York: Frederick A Praeger, 1967)
Fanon, Frantz, *The Wretched of the Earth* (New York: Grove Press, 1965)
Fanon, Frantz, *Towards the African Revolution: Political Essays* Translated by Haakon Chevalier (New York: Grove Press, 1967)
Farrell, William Regis, *The US Government Responses to Terrorism* (Boulder: Westview Press, 1982)
Feierabend, Ivo K, RL Feierabend, and TR Gurr (eds) *Anger, Violence, and Politics: Theories and Research* (Englewood Cliffs, NJ: Prentice-Hall, 1972)
Felt, Edward, *Urban Revolt in South Africa, 1960–1964: A Case Study* (Evanston, Ill: Northwestern University Press, 1971)
Ferguson, J Halcro, *The revolution of Latin America* (London: Thames & Hudson, 1963)
Ferreira, JC, *Carlos Marighella* (Havana: Tricontinental, 1970)
Fisk, Robert, *The Point of no Return* (London: Andre Deutsch, 1975)
Fitzgerald, Charles P, *Revolution in China* (New York: Praeger Publishers, 1952)
Flackes, WD, *Northern Ireland: A Political Directory* (London: The British Broadcasting Corporation, 1983)
Flynn, Joe B, *The Design of Executive Protective Systems* Springfield: Charles C Thomas, 1979)
Forman, J, *The Making of Black Revolutionaries* (New York: Macmillan, 1972)
Fortas, Abe, *Concerning Dissent and Civil Disobedience* (New York: New American Library, 1968)
Franklin, WM, *Protection of Foreign Interests* (New York: Greenwood, 1969)
Franzius, Enno, *History of the Order of Assassins* (New York: Funk & Wagnalls Co, 1969)
Freedman, Robert Owen, *Soviet Policy Towards the Middle East Since Nasser* (New York: Praeger Publishers, 1975)
Freeman, Thomas [pseud], *The Crisis in Cuba* (Derby, Conn: Monarch Books, 1963)
Freedman, Lawrence Zelic, and Alexander, Yonah, (eds) *Perspectives On Terrorism* (Wilmington: Scholarly Resources, Inc, 1983)
Freedman, L, *Terrorism and International Order* [= Chatham House Special Paper]

Lawrence Freedman, Christopher Hill, Adam Roberts, RJ Vincent, Paul Wilkinson, & Philip Windsor (RIIA) (R & K Paul: London, 1986)

Friedlander, Robert A, *Terrorism, Documents of International and Local Control* (Dobbs Ferry, NY: Oceana, 1978)

Fournier, Louis, Translated by Edward Baxter, *FLQ The Anatomy of an Underground Movement* (Toronto: NC Press Limited, 1984)

Fromm, Erich, *The Anatomy of Human Destructiveness* (New York: Holt, Rinehart and Winston, 1973; London: Cape, 1974)

Gablonski, Edward, *Terror from the Sky: Air War* (Garden City, NY: Doubleday & Co, 1971)

Galula, David, *Counterinsurgency Warfare: Theory and Practice* (New York: Praeger Publishers, 1964)

Gann, LH, *Guerrillas in History* (Stanford: Hoover Institute, 1971)

Gaucher, Roland, *The Terrorists: From Tsarist Russia to the OAS* Translated by P Spurlin (London: Secker & Warburg, 1968)

Gellner, John, *Bayonets in the Streets: Urban Guerrilla at Home and Abroad* (Don Mills, Ont: Collier MacMillan of Canada, 1974)

Geraghty, Tony, *Who Dares Wins: The Story of the SAS, 1950–1980* (London: Arms and Armour Press, 1980)

Gerassi, John (ed) *Towards Revolution* (London: Weidenfeld and Nicolson, 1971)

Gerassi, F (ed) *Venceremos!* (New York: Simon & Schuster, 1968)

Giap, Vo-nguyen, *People's War, People's Army: The Viet-Cong Insurrection Manual for Underdeveloped Countries* (New York: Praeger Publishers, 1962)

—— *The Tupamaro Guerrillas* Translated by Anne Edmondston (New York: Saturday Review Press, 1972)

Goldberg, Yona, *Haganah or Terror* (New York: Hechalutz, 1947)

Goren, Roberta, *The Soviet Union and Terrorism* (London: Allen & Unwin, 1984)

Gott, Richard, *Guerrilla Movements in Latin America* (London: Thomas Nelson, 1970)

Graham, Hugh Davis, and Ted Robert Gurr (eds) *The History of Violence in America* (New York: Bantam, 1970)

Green, G, *The Hostage Heart* (Chicago: Playboy Press, 1976)

—— *Terrorism: Is it Revolutionary?* (New York: Outlook Publications, 1970)

Greene, Thomas H, *Comparative Revolutionary Movements* (Englewood Cliffs, NJ: Prentice-Hall, 1974)

Grivas, G, *Guerrilla Warfare and EOKA's Struggle* (London: Longmans, 1964)

Gross, Feliks, *The Seizure of Political Power* (New York: Philosophical Library 1958)

Groussard, Serge, *The Blood of Israel: The Massacre of the Israeli Athletes, The Olympics, 1972* (New York: William Morrow & Co, 1975)

Guevara, Che, *Guerrilla Warfare* (New York: Random, 1968)

Guillen, Abraham, *Philosophy of the Urban Guerrilla* Translated by DC Hodges (New York: William Morrow & Co, 1973)

Gurr, Ted R, *Why Men Rebel* (Princeton, NJ: Princeton University Press, 1971)

Gutteridge, William (ed) *The New Terrorism* (London: Mansell Publishing, 1986)

Hacker, Frederick, J, *Crusaders, Criminals, Crazies* (New York: WW Norton & Co, 1976)

Haddad, George M, *Revolution and Military Rule in the Middle East* (New York: Speller, 1965)

Hamill, Desmond, *Pig in the Middle* (London: Methuen, 1985)
Han, Henry Hyunwook (ed) *Terrorism, Political Violence, and World Order* (London: University Press of America, 1984)
Hansen, Emmanuel, *Frantz Fanon: Social and Political Thought* (Columbus: Ohio University Press, 1976)
Harkabi, Yehoshafat, *The Arabs' Position in Their Conflict with Israel* (Jerusalem: Israel Universities Press, 1972)
Havens, Murray C, Carl Leiden, and Karl M Schmitt, *The Politics of Assassination* (Englewood Cliffs, NJ: Prentice-Hall, 1970)
Haycock, Ronald, (ed) *Regular Armies and Insurgency* (London: Croom Helm, 1979)
Hayden, Tom, *Rebellion in Newark* (New York: Random House, 1967)
Herz, Martin F (ed) *Diplomats and Terrorists: What works, what doesn't* (Washington, DC: Institute for the Study of Diplomacy, Georgetown University, 1982)
Heskin, Ken, *Northern Ireland: A Psychological Analysis* (New York: Columbia Press, 1980)
Hewitt, Christopher, *The Effectiveness of Anti-Terrorist Policies* (New York: University Press of America, 1984)
Hodges, DC (ed) *Philosophy of Urban Guerrilla, the Revolutionary Writings of Abraham Guillen* (New York: William Morrow & Co, 1973)
Hofstadter, Richard, and Michael Wallace (eds) *American Violence: A Documentary History* (New York: Alfred A Knopf, 1970)
Horchem, Hans J, *Right Wing Extremism in Western Germany* (London: Institute for the Study of Conflict, 1975)
—— *West Germany's Red Army Anarchists* (London: Institute for the Study of Conflict, 1975)
Horowitz, Irving L (ed) *The Anarchists* (New York: Dell Publishing Co, 1964)
Horrell, Muriel, *Terrorism in South Africa* (Johannesburg: South African Institute on Race Relations, 1968)
Hubbard, David G, *The Skyjacker: His Flights of Fantasy* (New York: Macmillan, 1971)
Huberman, L, and PM, Sweezy (eds) *Regis Debray and the Latin American Revolution* (New York: Monthly Review, 1968)
Hull, Roger H, *The Irish Triangle* (Princeton: Princeton University Press, 1976)
Hunt, Sir David, *On the Spot* (London: Peter Davies, 1975)
Hussain, Mehmood, *The Palestine Liberation Organization: A Study in Ideology and Tactics* (New York: International Publications Service, 1975)
Hyams, Edward, *Terrorists and Terrorism* (New York: St Martin's Press, 1974; London: JM Dent, 1975)
Hyde, Douglas Arnold, *The Roots of Guerrilla Warfare* (Chester Springs, Pa: Dufour Editions 1968)

Israeli, Raphael (ed) *PLO in Lebanon: Selected Documents* (London: Weidenfeld and Nicolson, 1983)

Jackson, Sir Geoffrey, *Surviving the Long Nights—An Autobiographical Account of a Political Kidnapping* (New York: Vanguard Press, 1974)
Janke, Peter, *Guerrilla and Terrorist Organizations: A World Directory and Bibliography* (Brighton: The Harvester Press, 1983)
Jenkins, Brian, *International Terrorism: A New Mode of Conflict* (Los Angeles: Crescent Publications, 1975)
Johnson, Chalmers A, *Revolutionary Change* (Boston: Little, Brown and Co, 1966)
Johnson, Chalmers, *Revolutionary Change* 2dn ed (London: Longman, 1983)

Joyner, Nancy D, *Aerial Hijacking as an International Crime* Dobbs Ferry, NY: Oceana, 1974)

Kaplan, Morton A (ed) *Revolution in World Politics* (New York: Wiley, 1962)
Katz, Samuel, *Days of Fire* (Garden City, NY: Doubleday & Co, 1968)
Kautsky, Karl, *Terrorism and Communism: A Contribution to the National History of Revolution* Translated by WH Kerridge, (London: Allen & Unwin, 1920)
Kedward, HR, *Fascism in Western Europe, 1900–1945* (New York: New York University Press, 1971)
Khaled, Leila, *My People Shall Live* (New York: Bantam, 1974)
Kiernan, Thomas, *Arafat: The Man and the Myth* (New York: Norton & Co, 1976)
Kirkham, JF, and S Levy, *Assassination and Political Violence* National Commission on the Causes and Prevention of Violence (Washington, DC: US Government Printing Office, 1969)
Kirkham, James F, Sheldon G Levy, and William J Crotty, *Assassination and Political Violence: A Staff Report to the National Commission on the Causes and Prevention of Violence* (New York: Bantam, 1970)
Kitson, Frank, *Low Intensity Operations: Subversion, Insurgency, Peace-Keeping* (London: Faber, 1972)
—— *A Bunch of Five* (London: Faber & Faber, 1977)
Kobetz, Richard W, and Cooper, HHA, *Target Terrorism: Providing Protective Services* (Gaithersburg: International Association of Chiefs of Police, 1978)
Kuper, Leo, *Genocide* (New Haven: Yale UP, 1981)
Kupperman, Robert H, and Trent, Darrell M, *Terrorism: Threat, Reality, and Response* (Stanford: Hoover Institution Press, 1979)
Kohl, J, and J Litt, *Urban Guerrilla Warfare in Latin America* (Cambridge, Mass: MIT Press, 1974)

Labrousse, Alain, *The Tupamaros: Urban Guerillas in Uruguay* (Harmondsworth: Penguin, 1973)
Laffin, J, *Fedayeen: The Arab-Israeli Dilemma* (New York: Free Press, 1973)
Lakos, Amos, *International Terrorism: A Bibliography* (Boulder, Colorado: Westview Press; London: Mansell Pub Ltd, 1986)
Lambrick, HT, *The Terrorist* (London: Rowman, 1972)
Laqueur, Walter, *Guerrilla* (Boston: Little, Brown and Co, 1976)
—— *The Guerrilla Reader: A Historical Anthology* (New York: New American Library, 1977)
—— *The Terrorism Reader* (New York: The New American Library, Inc, 1978)
—— *The Age of Terrorism* (London: Weidenfeld and Nicolson, 1987)
Lasswell, Harold, and Daniel Lerner (eds) *World Revolutionary Elites: Studies in Coercive Ideological Movements* (Cambridge, Mass: MIT Press, 1965)
Laushey, David M, *Bengal Terrorism and the Marxist Left* (Calcutta: Firma KL Mukhopadhyay, 1975)
Leachman, Robert B, and Philip Althoff (eds) *Preventing Nuclear Theft: Guidelines for Industry and Government* (New York: Praeger Publishers, 1972)
Leiden, Carl, and Schmitt, Karl M, *The Politics of Violence* (Englewood Cliffs: Prentice-Hall, Inc, 1968)
Leites, Nathan, and Charles Wolf, Jr, *Rebellion and Authority: An Analytic Essay on Insurgent Conflicts* (Chicago: Markham, 1970)
Lineberry, William P (ed) *The Struggle Against Terrorism* (New York: HW Wilson, 1977)

Liston, Robert A, *Terrorism* (New York: Thomas Nelson, 1977)
Livingston, Marius H, with Kress, LB, and Wanek, Marie G (eds) *International Terrorism in the Contemporary World* (Westport: Greenwood Press, 1978)
Livingstone, Neil C, *The War Against Terrorism* (Lexington: DC Heath and Company, 1982)
Lodge, Juliet (ed) *Terrorism: A Challenge to the State* (Oxford: Martin Robertson, 1981)
Lowe, E Nobles, and Shargel, Harry D, *Legal and Other Aspects of Terrorism* (New York: Practicing Law Institute, 1979)

Macfarlane, Leslie, *Violence and the State* (London: Nelson and Sons, Ltd, 1974)
McGuire, Maria, *To Take Arms: My Years with the IRA Provisionals* (New York: Viking Press, 1973)
McKnight, Gerald, *The Mind of the Terrorist* (London: Michael Joseph, 1974)
McNee, Sir David, *McNee's Law* (London: Collins, 1983)
McWhinney, Edward, *The Illegal Diversion of Aircraft and International Law* (Leiden: Sijhoff, 1975)
McWhinney, Edward, and others, *Aerial Piracy and International Law* (Dobbs Ferry, NY: Oceana, 1971)
Magee, John, *Northern Ireland: Crisis and Conflict* (London: Routledge and Kegan Paul, 1974)
Mallin, Jay, *Strategy for Conquest* (Coral Gables: University of Miami Press, 1970)
Mallin, Jay (ed) *Terror and Urban Guerrillas: A Study of Tactics and Documents* (Coral Gables, Fla: University of Miami Press, 1971)
Malloy, James, *Bolivia: The Uncompleted Revolution* (Pittsburgh: University of Pittsburgh Press, 1970)
May, Rollo, *Power and Innocence: A Search for the Sources of Violence* (New York: WW Norton & Co, 1972)
Marighella, Carlos, *Minimanual of the Urban Guerrilla* (Boulder: Paladin Press, 1978)
Mickolus, Edward F, *The Literature of Terrorism: A Selectively Annotated Bibliography* (Westport: Greenwood Press, 1980)
—— *Transnational Terrorism* (London: Aldwych Press, 1980)
Miller, Abraham H, *Terrorism: The Media and The Law* (Dobbs Ferry, New York: Transnational Publishers, 1982)
Milner, Sheilagh Hodgins, and Henry Miller, *The Decolonization of Quebec: An Analysis of Left Wing Nationalism* (Toronto: McClelland and Stewart, 1973)
Miron, Murray S, and Arnold P Goldstein, *Hostage* (Kalamazoo, Mich: Behaviordelia, 1978)
Momboisse, RM, *Blueprint of Revolution: The Rebel, the Party, the Techniques of Revolt* (Springfield, Ill: Charles C Thomas, 1970)
—— *Riots, Revolts and Insurrections* (Springfield, Ill: Charles C Thomas, 1967)
Moore, Barrington M Jr, *Terror and Progress in the USSR* (Cambridge, Mass: Harvard University Press, 1954)
Morf, Gustave, *Terrorism in Quebec: Case Studies of the FLQ* (Toronto: Clark Irvin & Company, 1970)
Moss, Robert, *Counter Terrorism* (London: The Economist Brief Books, 1972)
—— *The War For the Cities* (New York: Coward, McCann & Geoghegan, 1972)
Murphy, John F, *The UN and the Control of International Violence* (Manchester: Manchester University Press, 1983)
—— *Punishing International Terrorists* (New Jersey: Rowman and Allenheld, 1985)

Naipaul, VS, *Guerrillas* (New York: Alfred A Knopf, 1975)
National Advisory Committee on Criminal Justice Standards and Goals, *Disorders and Terrorism* (Washington, DC: Report of the Task Force on Terrorism, 1976)
Netanyahu, Benjamin (ed) *International Terrorism: Challenge and Response* (Jerusalem: The Jonathan Institute, 1980)
—— *Terrorism: How The West Can Win* (London: Weidenfeld and Nicolson, 1986)
Neiburg, Harold L, *Political Violence: The Behavioral Process* (New York: St Martin's Press, 1969)
Niezing, Johan (ed) *Urban Guerrilla: Studies on the Theory, Strategy and Practice of Political Violence in Modern Societies* (Rotterdam: Rotterdam University Press, 1974)
Norton, Augustus R, and Greenberg, Martin H, *International Terrorism: An Annotated Bibliography and Research Guide* (Boulder: Westview Press, 1980)

O'Ballance, Edgar, *Terror In Ireland* (Novato, Calif: Presidio Press, 1981)
O'Brien, Conor C, *Herod: Reflections on Political Violence* (London: Hutchinson, 1978)
—— *States of Ireland* (London: Panther, 1974)
O'Sullivan, Noel (ed) *Terrorism, Ideology and Revolution: The Origins of Modern Political Violence* (Brighton: Wheatsheaf Books Ltd, 1986)
Oppenheimer, Martin, *The Urban Guerrilla* (Chicago: Quadrangle Books, 1969)

Paret, Peter, and John W Shy, *Guerrillas in the 1960's* (New York: Praeger Publishers, 1962)
Parritt, Brian AH (ed) *Violence at Sea* (Paris: ICC Publishing, 1986)
Parry, Albert, *Terrorism: From Robespierre to Arafat* (New York: Vanguard Press, 1976)
Pearsall, RB (ed) *Symbionese Liberation Army—Documents and Communications* (Amsterdam: Rodopi NV Keizergracht, 1974)
Pelletier, Gerard, *The October Crisis* (Toronto: McClelland and Stewart, 1971)
Phillips, David, *Skyjack: The Story of Air Piracy* (London: Harrap, 1973)
Pike, Douglas, *Viet Cong* (Cambridge: MIT Press, 1966)
—— *The Viet Cong Strategy of Terror* (Saigon: np, 1970)
Porzicanski, AC, *Uruguay's Tupamaros: The Urban Guerrilla* (New York: Praeger Publishers, 1973)
Pryce-Jones, David, *The Face of Defeat: Palestinian Refugees and Guerrillas* (London: Weidenfeld and Nicolson, 1972)
Pye, Lucien, W, *Guerrilla Communism in Malaya: Its Social and Political Meaning* (Princeton: Princeton University Press, 1956)

Ra'anan Uri *et al. Hydra of Carnage The International Linkages of Terrorism and Other Low Intensity Operations: The Witnesses Speak* (Toronto: Lexington, Massachusetts: Lexington Books DC Heath & Co, 1986)
Rapoport, David C, *Assassination and Terrorism* (Toronto: Canadian Broadcasting Corporation, 1971)
Rapoport, David C, and Alexander, Yonah, *The Morality of Terrorism* (New York: Pergamon Press, 1982)
Reid, Malcolm, *The Shouting Signpainters: A Literary and Political Account of Quebec Revolutionary Nationalism* (Toronto and London: McClelland and Stewart, 1972)

Richelson, Jeffrey T, *The US Intelligence Community* (Cambridge, Mass: Ballinger Publishing Company, 1985)
Riddell, Patrick, *Fire Over Ulster* (London: Hamish Hamilton, 1970)
Rojo, R, *My Friend Ché* (New York: Dial Press, 1969)
Rose, Richard, *Governing Without Consensus* (London: Faber and Faber, 1971)
—— *Northern Ireland: A Time of Choice* (London: Macmillan, 1976)

Sacks, A, *The Violence of Apartheid* (London: International Defense and Air Fund, 1970)
Sarkesian, Sam C (ed) *Revolutionary Guerrilla Warfare* (Chicago: Precedent Publishing, 1975)
Saywell, John T, *Quebec 70: A Documentary Narrative* (Toronto: University of Toronto Press, 1971)
Schiff, Zeev, and Raphael Rothstein, *Fedayeen: The Story of the Palestinian Guerrillas* (London: Vallentine, Mitchell and Co, 1972)
Schmid, Alex P, *Political Terrorism: A Research Guide to Concepts, Theories, Data Bases, and Literature* (Amsterdam: North-Holland Publishing Co, 1983)
Shaw, Jennifer, Gueritz, EF, Younger, AE, Gregory, F, and Palmer, J (eds) *Ten Years of Terrorism: Collected Views* (New York: Crane, Russak and Co, 1979; London, (RUSI), 1979)
Sick, Garry, *All Fall Down: America's Tragic Encounter with Iran* (New York: Random House, 1985)
Silj, Alessandro, *Never Again Without a Rifle* (New York: Karz Publishers, 1979)
Sloan, Steven, *Simulating Terrorism* (Norman, Okla: University of Oklahoma Press, 1981)
Smith, Colin, *Carlos, Portrait of a Terrorist* (London: Sphere Books, 1976)
Smith, Myron J Jr, *The Secret Wars: A Guide to Sources in English* 3 vols (Oxford: Clio Press, Ltd, 1980)
Sobel, Lester A (ed) *Political Terrorism* (New York: Facts on File, 1975)
—— *Political Terrorism* vol. 2, new ed (New York, 1978)
—— *Political Terrorism* 2 vols (Oxford: Clio Press, Ltd, 1975)
Solzhenitsyn, Alexander, *The Gulag Archipelago* (New York: Harper & Row, 1973)
Sorel, Georges, *Reflections on Violence* (New York: Collier, 1961)
Stohl, Michael (ed) *The Politics of Terrorism* (New York: Marcel Dekker, 1979)
Sterling, Claire, *The Terror Network* (London: Weidenfeld and Nicolson, 1981)
Stevenson, William, *90 Minutes at Entebbe* (New York: Bantam Books, 1976)
Storr, Anthony, *Human Destructiveness* (New York: Basic Books, 1972)
Styles, George, *Bombs Have no Pity: The War Against Terrorism* (London: William Luscombe, 1975)
Sun Tzu, Translated by Samuel B Griffith, *The Art of War* (London: Oxford University Press, 1963)

Tanham, George Kilpatrick, *Communist Revolutionary Warfare* (New York: Praeger Publishers, 1961)
Taylor, Peter, *Beating the Terrorists?* (Harmondsworth: Penguin, 1980)
Thackrah, JR (ed) *Contemporary Policing* (London: Sphere Reference, 1985)
Thompson, Sir Robert, *Defeating Communist Insurgency* (London: Chatto and Windus, 1974)
—— *Terrorism in India* (New Delhi: Deep Publications, 1974)
Tinnin, David, *Hit Team* (London: Weidenfeld and Nicolson, 1976)
Tophoven, Rolf, *GSG-9: Anti-Terrorist Unit* (Berlin: Wehr und Wissen, 1977)

Tophoven, Rolf, *GSG-9 : German Response to Terrorism* (Koblenz : Bernard & Graefe Verlag, 1984)

Townshend, Charles, *The British Campaign in Ireland, 1919–1921* (Oxford : Oxford University Press, 1975)

—— *Political Violence in Ireland* (Oxford : Clarendon Press, 1983)

—— *Britain's Civil Wars* (London : Faber and Faber, 1986)

Trelease, Allen W, *White Terror : The Ku Klux Klan Conspiracy and Southern Reconstruction* (New York : Harper & Row, 1971)

Trotsky, Leon, *The Defence of Terrorism* (London : George Allen and Unwin, 1921)

Truby, J David, *How Terrorists Kill* (Boulder : Paladin Press, 1978)

Turner, Stansfield, *Secrecy and Diplomacy* (London : Sidgwick and Jackson, 1986)

Utley, TE, *Lessons of Ulster* (London : JM Dent and Sons, 1975)

Van den Haag, Ernest, *Political Violence and Civil Disobedience* (New York : Harper & Row, 1972)

Van Voris, William H, *Violence in Ulster : An Oral Documentary* (Amherst : University of Massachusetts Press, 1975)

Vallieres, Pierre, *White Niggers of America : The Precocious Autobiography of a Quebec Terrorist* (New York : Monthly Review Press, 1971)

Venturi, Franco, *Roots of Revolution* (New York : Grosset & Dunlap, 1966)

Walter, EV, *Terror and Resistance : A Study of Political Violence* (New York : London, Oxford University Press, 1969)

Walter, Michael, *Just and Unjust Wars* (London : Allen Lane, 1978)

Walzer, Michael, *The Revolution of the Saints : A Study of the Origins of Radical Politics* (Cambridge, Mass : Harvard University Press, 1965)

Wardlaw, Grant, *Political Terrorism : Political Tactics and Counter Measures* (Cambridge : CUP, 1982)

Watson, Francis M, *Political Terrorism : The Threat and the Response* (Washington, DC : Robert B Luce, 1976)

Waugh, William L Jr, *International Terrorism* (Salisbury, NC : Documentary Publications, 1982)

Whelton, Charles, *Skyjack!* (New York : Tower Publications, 1970)

Wilkinson, Paul, *Political Terrorism* (London : The Macmillan Press, 1974)

—— *The New Fascists* rev edn (London : Pan Books, 1983)

—— *Terrorism and the Liberal State*, rev edn (London : The Macmillan Press, 1986)

Wilkinson, Paul (ed) *British Perspectives on Terrorism* (London : George Allen & Unwin, 1981)

Wilson, Colin, *Order of Assassins : The Psychology of Murder* (London : Rupert Hart-Davis, 1972)

Wilson, James Q, *The Investigators : Managing FBI and Narcotics Agents* (New York : Basic Books, 1978)

Wolf, John B, *Fear of Fear : A Survey of Terrorist Operations and Controls in Open Societies* (New York : Plenum Press, 1981)

Young, Oran R, *The Intermediaries : Third Parties in International Crises* (Princeton : Princeton University Press, 1967)

Zweibach, Burton, *Civility and Disobedience* (New York : Cambridge University Press, 1975)

ARTICLES, MONOGRAPHS, PAPERS, PROCEEDINGS

Aggarwala, Narinder, 'Political Aspects of Hijacking', *International Conciliation*, no 585 (1971), pp 7–27

Ahmad, Eqbal, 'The Theory and Fallacy of Counterinsurgency', *Nation*, vol 213 (1971), pp 70–85

—— 'Airport Security Searches and the Fourth Amendment', *Columbia Law Review*, vol 71 (1971), pp 1039–58

Akehurst, Michael, 'Arab-Israeli Conflict and International Law', *New Zealand University Law Review*, vol 5 (1973), p 231

Akers, ER and Fox V, 'The Detroit Rioters and Looters Committed to Prison', *Journal of Criminal Law, Criminology and Police Science*, vol 35 (1964), p 105

Alexander, Yonah, 'Communications Aspects of International Terrorism', *International Problems*, vol 16, nos 1–2 (Spring 1977), pp 55–60

—— 'The Legacy of Palestinian Terrorism', *International Problems*, vol 15 (Fall 1976), pp 57–64

—— 'Some Perspectives on International Terrorism', *International Problems*, vol 14 (1975), pp 24–9

—— 'Terrorism, the Media, and the Police', *Journal of International Affairs*, vol 32, no 1 (Spring–Summer 1978), pp 72–83

Alexander, Yonah and Levine, Herbert M, 'Prepare For the Next Entebbe', *Chitty's Law Journal*, vol 25 (1977), pp 240–2

Alsina, Geronimo, 'The War and the Tupamaros', *Bulletin Tricontinental*, (1972), pp 29–42

Alves, Márcio Moreira, 'Kidnapped Diplomats: Greek Tragedy on a Latin Stage', *Commonweal*, vol 92 (1970), pp 311–14

Anable, David, 'Terrorists in New York Threatened U.S.-Soviet Links', *Christian Science Monitor* (5 April 1976), p 4.

Anderson, Jack, 'Urban Guerrilla Operations Feared', *Washington Post* (23 April 1974)

'And Now, Mail-a-Death', *Time* (2 October 1972), 28ff

Annual of Power and Conflict. Institute for the Study of Conflict (1975–76; 1977–78; 1978–79; 1979–80; 1980–81; 1981–82)

'Anti-Soviet Zionist Terrorism in the U.S.', *Current Digest of the Soviet Press*, vol 23 (1971), pp 6–8

'Approaches to the Problem of International Terrorism—Symposium 10', *Journal of International Labour and Economics*, vol 10 (1976), p 483

'Arab Terrorism', *Jewish Frontier*, vol 36 (1969), pp 13–16

Arendt, Hannah, 'Reflections on Violence', *Journal of International Affairs*, vol 23, no 1 (1969), pp 1–35

'Argentina: Revolution within the Revolution', *Latin America*, vol 5, no 54 (1971), pp 337–8

Ashayb, Naim, 'To Overcome the Crisis of the Palestine Resistance', *World Marxist Review*, vol 15, no 5 (1972), pp 71–8

'As Violence Spreads, United States Goes on Guard', *U.S. News and World Report* (2 November 1970), p 15

Atwater, J, 'Time to Get Tough with Terrorists', *Reader's Digest*, vol 102 (April 1973), pp 89–93

Bants, Major Michael, 'The Army in Northern Ireland', *Brassey's Annual* (1973), pp 60–80

Barclay, Brigadier CN, 'British Forces and Internal Security', *Brassey's Annual* (1973), pp 81–95

Barner, Don, 'P.L.O. at U.N., What Now?', *New Outlook*, vol 17, no 9 (1974), pp 62–6

Barnett, RW, 'The U.S. Navy's Role in Countering Maritime Terrorism', *Terrorism, An International Journal*, vol 6 (1983), pp 469–80

Barrie, GN, 'Crimes Committed Aboard Aircraft', *South African Law Journal*, vol 83 (1968), pp 203–8

Bartos, M, 'International Terrorism', *Review of International Affairs*, vol 23 (20 April 1972), p 25

'Basques: Business and Bombs', *Time*, vol 103 (January 1974), pp 48–49

Bassiouni, M Cherif, 'Ideologically Motivated Offenses and the Political Offense Exceptions in Extradition: A Proposed Judicial Standard for an Unruly Problem', *DePaul Law Review*, vol 19 (1969), p 217

—— 'International Extradition: An American Experience and a Proposed Formula', *Revue Internationale de Droit Penal*, vol 39 (1968), p 3

—— 'Terrorism, Law Enforcement, and the Mass Media: Perspectives, Problems, Proposals', *Journal of Criminal Law and Criminology*, vol 72 (Spring 1981), pp 1–51

Bayer, Alan E and Astin, Alexander W, 'Violence and Disruption on the U.S. Campus, 1968–1969', *Educational Record*, vol 50 (1969), p 337

Beaton, L, 'Crisis in Quebec', *Round Table*, no 241 (1971), pp 147–52

Beckett, JC, 'Northern Ireland', *Journal of Contemporary History*, vol 6, no 1 (1971), pp 121–34

—— 'Behind the Terror Bombings', *U.S. News and World Report* (30 March 1970), p 15

Bell, J Bowyer, 'Assassination in International Politics: Lord Moyne, Count Bernadotte, and the Lehi', *International Studies Quarterly*, no 1 (1972), pp 59–82

—— 'Transnational Terror and World Order', *South Atlantic Quarterly*, vol 74, no 4 (Autumn 1975), pp 404–17

Bell, Robert G, 'The U.S. Response to Terrorism Against International Civil Aviation', *Orbis*, vol 19 (Winter 1976), pp 1326–43

Bennett, RK, 'Brotherhood of the Bomb', *Reader's Digest* (December 1970), pp 102–6

—— 'Terrorists Among Us: An Intelligence Report', *Reader's Digest* (October 1971), pp 115–20

Bennett, WT, Jr, 'U.S. Initiatives in the United Nations to Combat International Terrorism', *International Lawyer*, vol 7 (1973), p 752

Beres, Louis Rene, 'Guerrillas, Terrorists and Polarity: New Structural Models of World Politics', *Western Political Science Quarterly* (December 1974), pp 624–36

Besedin, Alexander, 'Against Air Piracy', *New Times* (2 November 1970), pp 24–25

'Biggest Blast', *Newsweek* (7 September 1970), p 33

Binder, David, 'U.S. Is Said to Plan a New Approach on Terrorism', *New York Times* (27 March 1976), p 3

'Black Men and Bombs', *Ebony*, vol 25 (May 1970), pp 49–50

'Blowing Up Bridges', *Newsweek* (7 February 1972), p 28

'Blown Up', *Economist* (16 January 1971), p 16

'Bomb at the Golden Arch', *Washington Star-News* (20 August 1975)

'Bombing Fallout', *Business Week* (22 November 1969), p 44
'Bombing Incidents—1972', *F.B.I. Law Enforcement Bulletin* (April 1973), p 21
'Bombing Jitters', *Newsweek* (30 March 1970), p 23
'Bombing Research Center', *New York Morning Telegraph* (8 December 1971)
'Bombing Threats', *Environment* (October 1974), p 21
'Bomb Plots: Warning on Terror War', *U.S. News and World Report* (26 October 1970), p 36
Bond, James, 'Application of the Law of War to International Conflicts', *Georgia Journal of International and Comparative Law*, vol 3 (1973), p 345
Bourne, Robin, 'Terrorist Incident Management and Jurisdictional Issues: A Canadian Perspective', *Terrorism, An International Journal*, vol 1, nos 3 and 4 (1978), pp 307–13
—— 'Terrorism Incident Management In A Federal State', Paper presented at Emergency Planning Research Conference, Arnprior, Ontario (January 1979)
Bowden, Tom, 'Guarding the State: The Police Response to Crisis Politics in Europe', *British Journal of Law and Society*, vol 5 (Summer 1978), pp 69–88
Boyle, Robert P, 'International Action to Combat Aircraft Hijacking', *Lawyer of the Americas*, vol 4 (1972), pp 460–73
Bozakis, Christos L, 'Terrorism and the Internationally Protected Persons in the Light of the I.L.C.'s Draft Articles', *International and Comparative Law Quarterly*, vol 23 (1974), p 32
Brach, Richard S, 'The Inter-American Convention on the Kidnapping of Diplomats', *Columbia Journal of Transnational Law*, vol 10, (1971), pp 392–412
Bradford, AL, 'Legal Ramifications of Hijacking Airplanes', *American Bar Association Journal*, vol 48 (1962), pp 1034–39
Brandon, Henry, 'Were We Masterful ...', *Foreign Policy*, no. 10 (1973), pp 158–70
Buckley, WF, 'Politics of Assassination', *Esquire*, vol 70 (October 1968)
Burki, SJ, 'Social and Economic Determinants of Political Violence: A Case Study of the Punjab', *Middle East Journal*, vol 25 (1971), pp 465–80
Burnham, J, 'Notes on Terrorism', *National Review* (13 October 1972), p 1116
Burns, Major Julian H, Jr, 'Tripoli to Tehran: Terrorism's Road Well-Travelled', *Joint Perspectives* (Fall 1981), pp 42–53

Callanan, Edward F, 'Terror in Venezuela', *Military Review*, vol 49 (1969), pp 49–56
Caloyanni, MA, 'The Proposal of M. Laval to the League of Nations for the Establishment of an International Permanent Tribunal in Criminal Matters', *Transactions of the Grotius Society*, vol 21 (1936), p 77
Calvert, Peter, 'The Diminishing Returns of Political Violence', *New Middle East*, vol 56 (May 1973), p 25
Charles, Russell, and Hildner, Robert E, 'Urban Insurgency in Latin America: Its Implications for the Future', *Air University Review*, vol 22 (September–October 1971), pp 561–4
Charters, David, 'Intelligence and Psychological Warfare Operations in Northern Ireland', *RUSI Journal*, 122 (September 1977), pp 22–7
—— 'Security Services in an Open Society', and 'The Changing Forms of Conflict in Northern Ireland', *Conflict Quarterly* I (Fall 1980), pp 8–14 and 32–8
—— 'Organization, Selection and Training of National Response Teams—A Canadian Perspective', *Conflict Quarterly*, vol I (Winter 1981), pp 26–30
Chaturvedi, SC, 'Hijacking and the Law', *Indian Journal of International Law*, vol 11 (1971), pp 89–105.

Clark, Dennis, 'Which Way the I.R.A.?' *Commonweal*, no 13 (1973), pp 294–7
Clark, Leone S, 'The Struggle to Cure Hijacking', *International Perspectives* (January–February 1973), pp 47–51
Clissold, Stephen, 'Croat Separatism: Nationalism, Dissidence, and Terrorism', *Conflict Studies*, vol 103 (1979)
Clutterbuck, Richard, 'Terrorist International', *Army Quarterly and Defence Journal*, vol 104 (January 1974), pp 154–9
—— 'Ireland's American Enemies', *The New Republic*, vol 181 (December 1979), pp 17–18
Cobo, Juan, 'The Roots of "Violencia"', *New Times* (5 August 1970), pp 25–7
Colebrook, Joan, 'Israel with Terrorists', *Commentary*, vol 58, no 1 (July 1974), p 30
Collins, L, 'Orgy of Killing: Algeria's European Secret Army Organization', *Newsweek*, vol 59 (29 January 1962), p 42
'Comment, Constitutional and Statutory Basis of Governor's Emergency Powers', *Michigan Law Review*, vol 64 (1965), p 1290
'The Convention for the Prevention and Punishment of Terrorism', *British Yearbook of International Law*, vol 19 (1983), p 214
'Convention to Prevent and Punish the Acts of Terrorism Taking the Form of Crimes against Persons and Related Extortions that are of International Significance, *Serie Sobre Tratados*, vol 37. Washington, D.C.: Pan American Union (2 February 1971)
Cooley, John K, 'China and the Palestinians', *Journal of Palestinian Studies*, vol 1, no 2 (1972), pp 19–34
Cooper, HHA, 'Terrorism and the Intelligence Function', *Chitty's Law Journal*, vol 73 (March 1976), p 24
—— 'Terrorism and the Media', *Chitty's Law Journal*, vol 24, no 7 (1976), pp 226–32
—— 'The Terrorist and His Victims', *Victimology*, vol 1, no 2 (June 1976)
Craig, Alexander, 'Urban Guerrillas in Latin America', *Survey*, vol 17, no 3 (1971), pp 112–28
Cranston, Maurice, 'Sartre and Violence', *Encounter* (July 1967)
'Curbing Terrorism', *Christian Science Monitor* (16 January 1976), p 32
Czerniejewski, HJ, 'Guidelines for the Coverage of Terrorism', *The Quill* (1977), pp 21–3

Dadrian, V, 'Factors of Anger and Aggression in Genocide', *Journal of Human Relations*, vol 19 (1971), pp 394–417
Davies, James C, 'The Circumstances and Causes of Revolution: A Review', *Journal of Conflict Resolution* (June 1967), p 11
—— 'Towards a Theory of Revolution', *American Sociological Review*, vol 27 (1962), pp 5–14
Davis, Donald M, 'Terrorism: Motives and Means', *Foreign Science Journal* (September 1962), p 14
Deakin, TJ, 'Legacy of Carlos Marighella', *F.B.I. Law Enforcement Bulletin*, vol 43, no 10 (October 1974), pp 19–25
'Death Penalty for Terrorists?', *Christian Century*, vol 9 (21 March 1973), p 333
Defense Nuclear Agency, *Proceedings of the 10th Annual Symposium on the Role of Behavioural Science in Physical Security*. Springfield, Va: np (April 1985)
de Gramont, Sanche, 'Moslem Terrorists in New Jobs', *New York Herald Tribune* (9 July 1962), pp 1–2
Denaro, JM, 'In-flight Crimes, the Tokyo Convention and Federal Jurisdiction', *Journal of Air Law and Commerce*, vol 35 (1969), pp 171–203

Derber, M, 'Terrorism and the Movement', *Monthly Review*, vol 22 (February 1971), p 36
Derrer, Lt Cdr Douglas S, USNR, 'Terrorism', *Proceedings*, Naval Review 1985 (May 1985), pp 190–203
Dugard, John, 'International Terrorism: Problems of Definition', *International Affairs*, vol 50 (January 1974), pp 67–81
Dershowitz, Alan M, 'Terrorism and Preventive Detention', *Commentary Report* (1970), pp 3–14
Dinstein, Yoram, 'Criminal Jurisdiction Over Aircraft Hijacking', *Israel Law Review*, vol 7 (1972), pp 195–206
—— 'Terrorism and Wars of Liberation Applied to the Arab-Israeli Conflict: An Israeli Perspective', *Israel Yearbook of Human Rights*, vol 3 (1973), p 78
'Dir Yassin', *West Asia Affairs* (Summer 1969), pp 27–30
'Document on Terror', *News from Behind the Iron Curtain*, vol 1 (1952), pp 44–57
'Draft Convention for the Prevention and Punishment of Certain Acts of International Terrorism', *Department of State Bulletin*, vol 67 (16 October 1972), p 431
Dugard, John, 'International Terrorism: Problems of a Definition', *International Affairs*, vol 50, no 1 (1974), pp 67–81
—— 'Towards a Definition of International Terrorism', *American Journal of International Law*, vol 67, no 5 (1973), pp 94–100

Eave, L, 'Political Terrorism: Hysteria on the Left', *New York Times Magazine* (12 April 1970), pp 25–7
Eckstein, Harry, 'On the Etiology of Internal War', *History and Theory*, vol 4 (1965), pp 133–63
Epstein, DG, 'Combating Campus Terrorism', *Police Chief*, vol 38, no 1 (January 1971), pp 46–7, 49
Erskine, Hazel, 'Fear of Violence and Crime', *Public Opinion Quarterly*, vol 38 (1974), p 131
Esson, DMR, 'The Secret Weapon—Terrorism', *Army Quarterly*, vol 78 (1959), p 167
Evans, Alona E, 'Aircraft Hijacking: What Is to Be Done?' *American Journal of International Law*, vol 66 (1972), pp 819–22
—— 'Its Cause and Cure', *American Journal of International Law*, vol 63 (1969), pp 695–710
—— 'Jurisdiction-Fugitive Offender-Forcible Abduction-Ker-Frisbie Rule-Treaties-Extradition', *American Journal of International Law*, vol 69 (1975), p 406
—— 'A Proposed Method of Control', *Journal of Air Law and Commerce*, vol 37 (1971), pp 171–81
—— 'Reflections Upon the Political Offenses in International Practice', *American Journal of International Law*, vol 57 (1963), p 1

Fadersori, Alberto S, 'What Is an Urban Guerrilla?', *Military Review*, vol 47 (1969), p 94
Falk, Richard A, 'Terror, Liberation Movements, and the Process of Social Change', *American Journal of International Law*, vol 63 (1969), pp 423–7
Fellaci, Oriana, 'A Leader of Fedayeen: "We Want a War Like the Vietnam War": Interview with George Habash', *Life* (12 June 1970), pp 32–4
Feller, SZ, 'Comment on Criminal Jurisdiction Over Aircraft Hijacking', *Israel Law Review*, vol 7 (1972), pp 207–14

Fenello, Michael J, 'Technical Prevention of Air Piracy', *International Coalition*, no 585 (1971), pp 28–41

Fenwick, CC, 'Piracy in the Caribbean', *American Journal of International Law*, vol 55 (1961), pp 426–8

Fenyvesi, C, 'Looking into the Muzzle of Terrorists', *The Quill* (1977), pp 16–18

Finegan, Jay, 'Terrorism', *Air Force Times Magazine* (October 1983), pp 13–14, 16, 18, 20

Firestone, Joseph M, 'Continuities in the Theory of Violence', *Journal of Conflict Resolution*, vol 18 (1974), p 117

Fitzgerald, GF, 'Development of International Rules Concerning Offenses and Certain Other Acts Committed on Board Aircraft', *Canadian Yearbook of International Law*, vol 1 (1963), pp 230–51

—— 'Towards Legal Suppression of Acts Against Civil Aviation', *International Conciliation*, no 505 (1971), pp 42–78

Fitzgibbon, Russell H, 'Revolution in Latin America: A Tentative Prognosis', *Virginia Quarterly Review* (Spring 1963), p 39

Flacks, R, 'The Liberated Generation: An Exploration of the Roots of Student Protest', *Journal of Social Issues*, vol 23 (1967), p 52

Franck, Thomas M and Lockwood, Bert B, 'Preliminary Thoughts Towards an International Convention on Terrorism', *American Journal of International Law*, vol 68 (1974), pp 4, 69–90

Franjeck, S, 'How Revolutionary Is the Palestinian Resistance: A Marxist Interpretation', *Journal of Palestine Studies*, vol 1, no 2 (1972), pp 52–60

Frank, Gerold, 'The Moyne Case: A Tragic History', *Commentary* (December 1945), pp 64–71

Friedlander, RA, 'Terrorism', *Barrister*, vol 2 (Summer 1975), p 10

Friedmann, W, 'Terrorists and Subversive Activities', *American Journal of International Law*, vol 50 (1956), p 475

Fromkin, David, 'The Strategy of Terrorism', *Foreign Affairs*, vol 53 (July 1975), p 683

Galyean, TE, 'Acts of Terrorism and Combat by Irregular Forces: An Insurance "War" Risk', *California Western International Law Journal*, vol 4 (1974), p 314

Garcia-Mora, Manuel R, 'Crimes against Humanity and the Principle of Non-extradition of Political Offenders', *Michigan Law Review*, vol 62 (1964), p 927

—— 'The Crimes Against Peace', *Fordham Law Review*, vol 34 (1965), p 1

—— 'Criminal Jurisdiction over Foreigners for Treason and Offenses against the Safety of the State Committed Upon Foreign Territory', *University of Pittsburgh Law Review*, vol 19 (1958), p 567

Gerassi, Marysa, 'Uruguay's Urban Guerrillas', *Nation*, vol 209, no 10 (1969), pp 306–10

'Getting Away with Murder', *Economist* (4 November 1972), pp 15–16

'The Girl Who Almost Killed Ford', *Time* (15 September 1975), p 8

Goldberg, Arthur J, 'The Murder in St. James's Square', *Encounter*, vol 63 (November 1984), pp 67–70

Gott, Richard, 'Latin American Guerrillas', *Listener*, vol 84 (1970), pp 437–40

'Greece Takes Tougher Stance Following Airport Terrorism', *Aviation Week*, vol 99 (13 August 1973), p 26

Green, LC, 'International Law and the Suppression of Terrorism', edited by GW Bartholomew, *Malaya Law Review Legal Essays* (1975).

—— 'International Terrorism and Its Legal Control', *Chitty's Law Journal*, vol 21 (1973), pp 289–301

Green, LC, 'Aspects of Terrorism', *Terrorism, An International Journal*, vol 5 (1982), pp 373–400

Gross, Leo, 'International Terrorism and International Criminal Jurisdiction', *American Journal of International Law*, vol 67 (July 1973), pp 508–11

Gunter, Michael M, 'The Armenian Terrorist Campaign Against Turkey', *Orbis*, vol 27 (Summer 1983), pp 447–77

Hardman, JBS, 'Terrorism', *The Encyclopedia of the Social Sciences*, vol XIV (1964)

Hassel, Conrad V, 'Terror: The Crime of the Privileged—An Examination and Prognosis', *Terrorism: An International Journal*, vol 1, no 1 (1977), pp 1–16

Hoffacker, Lewis, 'The U.S. Government Response to Terrorism: A Global Approach', *Department of State Bulletin* (18 March 1974), pp 274–8

Horchem, Hans Josef, 'The Urban Guerrilla in West Germany—Origins and Perspectives', unpubl paper presented to the *US Department of State Conference on Terrorism* held on 25–26 March 1976 at Washington DC. 40 pp

Horowitz, Irving L, 'Political Terrorism and State Power', *Journal of Political and Military Sociology*, vol 1 (Spring 1973), pp 147–57

Hoveyda, Fereydoun, 'The Problem of International Terrorism at the United Nations', *Terrorism: An International Journal*, vol 1, no 1 (1977), pp 71–84

Hutchinson, Martha C, 'The Concept of Revolutionary Terrorism', *Journal of Conflict Resolution*, vol 16 (September 1972), pp 383–96

Ingram, Timothy H, 'Nuclear Hijacking: Now Within Grasp of Any Bright Lunatic', *Washington Monthly* (December 1972), pp 26–8

Institute for the Study of Conflict, 'Northern Ireland: An Anglo-Irish Dilemma?', *Conflict Studies*, no 185 (1986)

Iviansky, Ze'ev, 'Individual Terror: Concept and Typology', *Journal of Contemporary History*, vol 12 (January 1977), pp 43–63

Janke, Peter, 'Ulster: A Decade of Violence', *Conflict Studies*, no 108 (1979)

Jenkins, Brian, 'International Terrorism: A Balance Sheet', *Survival*, vol 17 (July–August 1975), pp 158–64

—— 'Research Note: Rand's Research on Terrorism', *Terrorism: An International Journal*, vol 1, no 1 (1977), 85–96

—— 'The Study of Terrorism: Definitional Problems', *Rand Corporation Monograph*, P-656 (December 1980)

—— 'Terrorism in the 1980s', *Rand Corporation Monograph*, P-6564 (December 1980)

—— 'Testimony Before The Senate Governmental Affairs Committee, January 27, 1978', *Rand Corporation Monograph*, P-6586 (February 1981).

—— 'A Strategy For Combating Terrorism', *Rand Corporation Monograph*, P-6624 (May 1981).

—— 'Combating Terrorism: Some Policy Implications', *Rand Corporation Monograph*, P-6666 (August 1981).

—— 'Terrorism And Beyond', *Rand Corporation Report*, R-2714 (December 1982)

—— 'New Modes of Conflict', *Orbis*, no 28 (Spring 1984), pp 5–16

Karber, Philip A, 'Urban Terrorism: Baseline Data and a Conceptual Framework', *Social Science Quarterly*, vol 52 (December 1971), pp 521–33

Kellen, Konrad, 'On Terrorists And Terrorism', *Rand Corporation Report*, N-1942-RC (December 1982)

Krieger, David M, 'Terrorists and Nuclear Technology: The Danger is Great, the Question is not whether the Worst will Happen but Where and How', *Bulletin of the Atomic Scientists* (June 1975), pp 28–34

Kupperman, Robert H, 'Treating the Symptoms of Terrorism: Some Principles of Good Hygiene', *Terrorism: An International Journal*, vol 1, no 1 (1977), pp 35–50

Kuriyama, Y, 'Young Palestinian Commandos in Political Socialization Perspectives', *Middle East Journal*, vol 26 (Summer 1972), pp 325–50

Kutner, Luis, 'Constructive Notice: A Proposal to End International Terrorism', *New York Law Forum*, vol 19 (Fall 1973), pp 325–50

Langguth, Gerd, 'Origins and Aims of Terrorism in Europe', *Aussenpolitik*, vol 37, Quarterly Edition, no 2 (1986), pp 163–75

Laqueur, Walter, 'Can Terrorism Succeed?', *Skeptic*, no 11, pp 24–9

—— 'Coming to Terms with Terror', *Times Literary Supplement* (2 April 1976), p 362

—— 'The Continuing Failure of Terrorism', *Harper's* (November 1976), pp 69–74

—— 'The Futility of Terrorism', *Harper's* (March 1976), p 99

—— 'Guerrillas and Terrorists', *Commentary* (October 1974), pp 40–8

—— 'Interpretations of Terrorism: Fact, Fiction and Political Science', *Journal of Contemporary History*, vol 12 (January 1977), pp 1–42

Lasky, Melvin J, 'Ulrike and Andreas: The Bonnie and Clyde of West Germany's Radical Subculture may have failed to make a Revolution, but they have bruised the Body Politic', *New York Times Magazine* (11 May 1975), pp 14ff

—— 'Ulrike Meinhof and the Baader-Meinhof "Gang"', *Encounter*, vol 44: 6 (June 1975), pp 9–23

Lavin, Marvin M, 'Intelligence Constraints of the 1970s and Domestic Terrorism: A Survey of Legal, Legislative, and Administrative Constraints', *Rand Corporation Report*, N-1902-DOJ (December 1982).

Leiden, Carl, 'Assassination in the Middle East', *Trans-Action*, vol 6 (May 1969), pp 20–3

McDowell, Michael, 'The British Initiative In Ulster', *Conflict Quarterly*, vol I (Summer 1980), pp 35–9

McIlheney, Colin J, 'Arbiters of Ulster's Destiny? The Military Role of the Protestant Paramilitaries in Northern Ireland', *Conflict Quarterly*, vol V (Spring 1985), pp 33–9

Maechling, Charles, Jr, 'Containing Terrorism', *Foreign Service Journal* (July/August 1984), pp 33–7

Mallin, Jay, 'Terrorism as a Political Weapon', *Air University Review*, vol 22 (July–August 1971), pp 45–52

—— 'Terrorism in Revolutionary Warfare', *Strategic Review* (Fall 1974), pp 48–55

Mallison, WT, Jr and Mallison, SV, 'Concept of Public Purpose Terror in International Law', *Journal of Palestine Studies* (Winter 1975), pp 36–51; also in *Howard Law Journal*, vol 18 (1973), pp 12–28

Mans, Rowland, 'Canada's Constitutional Crisis. Separatism and Subversion', *Conflict Studies*, no 98 (1978)

Mazuri, Ali A, 'Thoughts On Assassination in Africa', *Political Science Quarterly*, vol 83 (March 1968), pp 40–58

Means, John, 'Political Kidnappings and Terrorism', *North American Review*, vol 4 (Winter 1970), pp 16–19

Mickolus, Edward, 'Negotiating for Hostages: A Policy Dilemma', *Orbis* (Winter 1976), pp 1251–69

Moss, Robert, 'International Terrorism and Western Societies', *International Journal*, vol 28 (Summer 1973), pp 418–30

Motley, Colonel James B, 'Terrorist Warfare: A Reassessment', *Military Review*, vol LXV (June 1985), pp 45–57

Murphy, John F, 'International Legal Control of International Terrorism: Performance and Prospects', *Illinois Bar Journal*, vol 63 (April 1975), p 444

Murray, Russell, 'Killings in Northern Ireland 1969–1981', *Terrorism, An International Journal*, vol 7 (1984), pp 1–50

Nelson, Sarah, 'From Soldiers to Politicians—and Back: Political Violence and the Protestant Paramilitaries of Northern Ireland', Collected Seminar Papers, no 30, *Political Violence*, University of London, Institute of Commonwealth Studies (1982), pp 46–54

O'Ballance, Edgar, 'Policing By Consent', *Contemporary Review*, vol 240 (April 1982), pp 188–92

Ofri, Arie, 'Intelligence and Counterterrorism', *Orbis*, vol 28 (Spring 1984), pp 41–52

'Organization of American States: Convention to Prevent and Punish Acts of Terrorism', *International Legal Materials*, vol 10 (March 1971), pp 255–8

Oseth, Lt Col John M, 'Intelligence and Low-Intensity Conflict', *Naval War College Review* (November–December 1984), pp 19–36

—— 'Combating Terrorism: The Dilemmas of a Decent Nation', *Parameters*, vol XV (1985), pp 65–76

Paust, J, 'An Approach to Decision with Regard to Terrorism', *Akron Law Review*, vol 7 (1974), pp 397–403

—— 'Some Thoughts on "Preliminary Thoughts" on Terrorism', *American Journal of International Law*, vol 68 (1974), pp 502–3

—— 'Survey of Possible Legal Responses to International Terrorism: Prevention, Punishment, and Cooperative Action', *Georgia Journal of International and Comparative Law*, vol 5 (1975), pp 431–69

—— 'Terrorism and the International Law of War', *Military Law Review*, vol 64 (1974), pp 1–36

Pierre, Andrew J, 'The Politics of International Terrorism', *Orbis*, vol 19 (Winter 1976), pp 1251–69

Pisano, VS, 'The Red Brigades: a Challenge to Italian Democracy', *Conflict Studies*, no 120 (1980).

—— 'A Survey of Terrorism of the Left in Italy, 1970–78', *Terrorism*, vol 2 (1979), pp 171–212

Prevention of Terrorism Bill 1983–4 (Bill 8). Reference Sheet 83/13. House of Commons Library Research Division

Price, H Edward, Jr, 'The Strategy and Tactics of Revolutionary Terrorism', *Comparative Studies in Society and History*, vol 19 (January 1977), pp 52–66

Quainton, Ambassador Anthony CE, 'Terrorism: Do Something! But What?' *Department of State Bulletin* (September 1979), pp 60–4

Reid, Edna F, 'An Analysis of Terrorism Literature: A Bibliometric and Content Analysis Study', PhD dissertation, University of Southern California, 1983
Romaniecki, Leon, 'The Soviet Union and International Terrorism', *Soviet Studies*, vol 26, no 3 (July 1974), pp 417–40
Roucek, JS, 'Sociological Element of a Theory of Terror and Violence', *American Journal of Economics and Sociology*, vol 21 (April 1962), pp 165–72
Rozakis, Christos L, 'Terrorism and the Internationally Protected Persons in the Light of the ILC Draft Articles', *International and Comparative Law Quarterly*, vol 23 (January 1974), pp 32–72
Russell, Charles A and Miller, Bowman H, 'Profile of a Terrorist', *Terrorism: An International Journal*, vol 1, no 1 (1977), pp 17–34

Schwarzenberger, G, 'Terrorists, Hijackers, Guerrilleros, and Mercenaries', *Current Legal Problems*, vol 24 (1971), pp 257–82
Segre, DV and Adler, JH, 'The Ecology of Terrorism', *Encounter*, vol 40 (February 1973), pp 17–24
Shapley, Deborah, 'Plutonium: Reactor Proliferation Threatens a Nuclear Black Market', *Science*, vol 172 (9 April 1971), pp 143–6
Shultz, George, 'Terrorism and the Modern World', *Department of State Bulletin* (December 1984), pp 12–17
Silverstein, Martin Elliot, 'Emergency Medical Preparedness', *Terrorism: An International Journal*, vol 1, no 1 (1977), pp 51–70
Sim, Joe and Thomas, Philip A, 'The Prevention of Terrorism Act: Normalizing the Politics of Repression', *Journal of Law and Society*, vol 10 (Summer 1983), pp 71–84
Smart, IMH, 'The Power of Terror', *International Journal*, vol 30 (Spring 1975), pp 225–37
Smith, G Davidson, 'The Military in Aid of the Civil Power: Limits in a Democratic Society', *Canadian Defence Quarterly*, vol 13 (Spring 1984), pp 27–33
—— 'A Positive Approach to Terrorism: The Case for an Elite Counter-Force in Canada', *RUSI Journal*, vol 129 (September 1984), pp 17–22
—— 'Political Violence In Animal Liberation', *Contemporary Review*, vol 247 (July 1985), pp 26–31
—— 'Issue Group Terrorism: Animal Rights Militancy in Britain', *Terrorism Violence Insurgency Journal*, vol 5 (Spring 1985), pp 44–7
Starnes, John, 'Canadian Internal Security. The Need for a New Approach, a New Organization', *Canadian Defence Quarterly* (Summer 1979), pp 21–6
Stern, Geoffrey, 'The Use of Terror as a Political Weapon', *Journal of International Studies*, vol 4 (Winter 1975–6), pp 263–7
Stevenson, John R, 'International Law and the Export of Terrorism', *The Record of the Association of the Bar of the City of New York*, vol 27 (December 1972), pp 716–29
Suvorov, Victor, 'Spetsnaz: The Soviet Union's Special Forces', *Military Review*, vol LXIV (March 1984), pp 30–46

Taylor, Robert W, 'Managing Terrorist Incidents', *The Bureaucrat* (Winter 1983–4), pp 53–8
Taylor, Theodore B, 'Nuclear Terrorism: A Threat of the Future', *Science Digest* (August 1974), pp 12–16
'Terrorism and the Liberal State: A Reasonable Response', *Police Studies*, vol 4 (Fall 1981), pp 34–51

'Terrorism: Why business is now a prime target', *International Management*, vol 40 (August 1985), pp 20–6

'The War Against Terrorism', *Harvard International Review*, vol VII (May/June 1985)

Thompson, W Scott, 'Political Violence and the "Correlation of Forces"', *Orbis*, vol 19 (Winter 1976), pp 1270–88

Walsh, Dermot PJ, 'Arrest and Interrogation: Northern Ireland 1981', *Journal of Law and Society*, vol 9 (Summer 1982), pp 37–59

Watkins, Admiral James D, 'Terrorism: An "Already Declared" War', *Wings of Gold* (Summer 1984), pp 19–21

Wildhorn, Sorrel, Jenkins, Brian Michael and Lavin, Marvin M, 'Intelligence Constraints of the 1970s and Domestic Terrorism: Effects on the Incidence, Investigation, and Prosecution of Terrorist Activity', *Rand Corporation Report*, N-1901-DOJ (December 1982).

Wilkinson, Paul, 'Terrorism versus Liberal Democracy—The Problem of Response', *Conflict Studies*, no 67 (1976)

—— 'Three Questions on Terrorism', *Government and Opposition*, vol 8, no 3 (1973), pp 290–312

—— 'Terrorism: The International Response', *The World Today* (January 1978), pp 5–13

—— 'Terrorism and the Media', *Journalism Studies Review* (Summer 1978), pp 1–6

—— 'Terrorism: International Dimensions. Answering the Challenge', *Conflict Studies*, no 113 (1979)

—— 'The Provisional IRA: in the Wake of the 1981 Hunger Strike', *Government and Opposition*, vol 17 (Spring 1982), pp 140–56

—— 'Armenian Terrorism', *The World Today* (September 1983), pp 344–50

—— 'How Do Democratic States Cope With Terrorism?', *Ditchley Conference Report*, no 5, 1984/85

—— 'State-sponsored international terrorism: the problems of response', *The World Today* (July 1984), pp 292–8

—— 'Northern Ireland: An Alternative To Terrorism', *Contemporary Affairs Briefing*, vol 2 (February 1986)

—— 'After Tehran', *Conflict Quarterly*, vol 1 Spring 1981), pp 5–14

—— 'Terrorism—Global Links', in *RUSI and Brassey's Defence Yearbook* (1984), pp 209–34

—— 'Navies in a Terrorist World', in *Jane's Naval Review* (1986), pp 166–76

Winn, GFT, 'Terrorism, alienation and German Society', in Y Alexander and J Gleason (eds), *Behavioural and Quantitative Perspectives on Terrorism* (New York: Pergamon Press, 1981), pp 256–82.

Wohlstetter, Roberta, 'Kidnapping to Win Friends and Influence People', *Survey*, vol 20, no 4 (Autumn 1974), pp 1–40

Wolf, John B, 'Controlling Political Terrorism in a Free Society', *Orbis*, vol 19 (Winter 1976), pp 1289–308

Wolfgang, Marvin E (ed), 'International Terrorism', *The Annals of the American Academy of Political and Social Science*, vol 463 (September 1982)

Wright, Major Jeffrey W, US Army, 'Terrorism: A mode of warfare', *Military Review*, vol LXIV (October 1984), pp 35–45

Yoder, Amos, 'United Nations Resolutions Against International Terrorism', *Terrorism, An International Journal*, vol 6 (1983), pp 503–17

Index

Index of Terrorist Movements and Groups